CHROMOSOMES TODAY

VOLUME FIVE

Leiden Chromosome Conference

ORGANIZED BY
The Department of Human Genetics of
The State University of Leiden and
The Boerhaave Committee for Postgraduate Education, Leiden.

UNDER THE AUSPICES OF
The State University of Leiden
The Boerhaave Committee for Postgraduate Education
The Dutch Human Genetics Society
The National Foundation March of Dimes

This was the fifth of the
International Chromosome Conferences
inaugurated by C. D. Darlington and K. R. Lewis,
held in Oxford in 1964, 1967, and 1970,
and in Jerusalem in 1972.
The proceedings of the conferences
appeared under the title
Chromosomes Today, volumes 1, 2, 3 and 4.

CHROMOSOMES TODAY

VOLUME FIVE

Proceedings of the Leiden Chromosome Conference,
July 15–17, 1974

Edited by

P. L. PEARSON and K. R. LEWIS

The State University of Leiden and the University of Oxford

A HALSTED PRESS BOOK

JOHN WILEY & SONS, New York • Toronto
ISRAEL UNIVERSITIES PRESS, Jerusalem

ISRAEL UNIVERSITIES PRESS
is a publishing division of
KETER PUBLISHING HOUSE JERUSALEM LTD.
P.O. Box 7145, Jerusalem, Israel

Published in the Western Hemisphere by
HALSTED PRESS, a division of
JOHN WILEY & SONS, INC., NEW YORK

Library of Congress Cataloging in Publication Data

Leiden Chromosome Conference, 5th, State University
of Leiden, 1974.
Chromosomes today.

"A Halsted Press book."
"Volume five."
Includes bibliographies and indexes.
1. Chromosomes—Congresses. I. Pearson, P.L.
II. Lewis, Kenneth Roderick. III. Title.
[DNLM: 1. Chromosomes—Congresses. W3 0156M v. 5
1974/QH600 L527p 1974]
QH600.L44 1974 575.2′1 75–43619
ISBN 0–470–14997–3

Distributors for the U.K., Europe, Africa and the Middle East
JOHN WILEY & SONS, LTD., CHICHESTER

Distributors for Japan, Southeast Asia and India
TOPPAN COMPANY, LTD., TOKYO AND SINGAPORE

Distributed in the rest of the world by
KETER PUBLISHING HOUSE JERUSALEM LTD.
IUP Cat. No. 26200 0
ISBN 0 7065 1529 3

Set, printed and bound by Keterpress Enterprises, Jerusalem
PRINTED IN ISRAEL

CONTENTS

ABSTRACTS OF ADDITIONAL PAPERS

CONFERENCE MEMBERS

AKSTEIN, EDNA, Cytogenetics Laboratory, Sheba Medical Center, Tel-Hashomer, Israel.

ANTICH, J., c/Balmes 341, B, 302a, Barcelona 6, Spain.

ARRIGHI, FRANCES E., Biology Department, M.D. Anderson Hospital, Houston, Texas 77025, U.S.A.

BACCAR, HÉDIA, Assistant Director, Mediterranean Marine Sorting Center, Khereddine, Tunisia

BARIGOZZI, CLAUDIO, Instituto di Genetica, Università di Milano, Via Celoria 10, 20133, Milano, Italy.

BARTSCH-SANDHOFF, M., 4 Düsseldorf 1, Mannesmannufer 7 III, Germany.

BAYLISS, MICHAEL WILLIAM, Department of Botany, Leicester University, Leicester LE1 7RH, U.K.

BEATTY, R. A., ARC Unit of Animal Genetics, Department of Genetics, King's Buildings, West Mains Rd, Edinburgh 9, U.K.

BERGSMA, D., National Foundation, March of Dimes, 1275 Mamaroneck Avenue, White Plains, New York 01605, U.S.A.

BIJLSMA, JAN BERNARDUS, Department of Human Genetics, University of Amsterdam, Sarphatistraat 217, Amsterdam, The Netherlands.

BOBROW, MARTIN, Genetics Laboratory, Department of Biochemistry, South Parks Rd, Oxford, U.K.

BOOTSMA, D., Afdeling Celbiologie, Medische Faculteit der Erasmus Universiteit, Postbus 1738, Rotterdam, The Netherlands.

BORGAONKAR, D. S., Division of Medical Genetics, Johns Hopkins University, School of Medicine, Baltimore, Md., 21205, U.S.A.

BOSMA, A. A., Vet. Anatomisch Instituut, Bekkerstraat 141, Utrecht, The Netherlands.

BOSMAN, F. T., Pathologisch Laboratorium, Rijks Universiteit, Leiden, The Netherlands.

BRANDHAM, PETER EDWARD, Jodrell Laboratory, Royal Botanic Gardens, Kew, Richmond, Surrey TW9 3DS, U.K.

BRESSON, J. J., Laboratoire Cytogénetique, CHU, 25000 Besancon, France.

BRØGGER, A., Norsk Hydro's Institute for Cancer Research, Montebello, Oslo 3, Norway.

BRUMMER-DINGER, C. H., Jac. van Maerlantlaan 24, Eindhoven, The Netherlands.

BRUTLAG, D., P.O. Box 1600, Csiro, Canberra A.C.T. 2601, Australia.

BUCKTON, KARIN ELIZABETH, MRC Clinical and Population Cytogenetics Unit, Western General Hospital, Edinburgh EH4 2XU, U.K.

BURGERHOUT, W., Afdeling Celbiologie, Medische Faculteit der Erasmus Universiteit, Postbus 1738, Rotterdam, The Netherlands.

CANN, H. M., Department of Pediatrics, Stanford University School of Medicine, Stanford, California 94305, U.S.A.

CAPANNA, E., Istituto Anatomia Comparata, Via Borelli 50, I-00161 Roma, Italy.

CARLON, Nicole, Laboratoire d'Histologie II, Faculté de Médicine, 27 Bd. J. Moulin, 13005 Marseille, France.

CASPERSSON, T., Institute for Medical Cell Research and Genetics, Karolinska Institutet, S 104 01 Stockholm 60, Sweden.

CASSEMAN, H., Centrum voor menselijke Erfelijkheid, Vesalius Instituut, Minderbroederstraat 12, Leuven, Belgium.

CASTLEMAN, K. R., 3655 Fiqueroa St., Glendale, California 91206, U.S.A.

CHAUDHURI, J. P., Max Planck Institut, Abt. Cytogenetik, 8 München 40, Kraepelinstr. 2, West Germany.

CHIARELLI, B., Instituto di Antropologia, Via Acc. Albertina 17, Torino, Italy.

COHEN, MAIMON M., Department of Human Genetics, Hadassah University Hospital, Jerusalem, Israel.

COMINGS, D. E., City of Hope Medical Center, Duarte, California, U.S.A.

COOKE, PATRICIA, Department of Biology, University of Southampton, Southampton, U.K.

DAKER, M. G., Paediatric Research Unit, Guy's Hospital, Medical School, London, S.E. 1, U.K.

DARLINGTON, CYRIL DEAN, Botany School, South Parks Road, Oxford OX1 3RA, U.K.

DE BOER, P., Afd. erfelijkheidsleer L.H., Gen. Foulkesweg 53, Wageningen, The Netherlands.

DE FRANCE, H. F., Dept. of Human Genetics, Sarphatistraat 217, Amsterdam C, The Netherlands.

DE LA CHAPELLE, Albert, Folkälsan Institute of Genetics, P.O. Box 819, SF-00101 Helsinki 10, Finland.

DE VRIES, GRETA FOKJE, National Institute of Public Health, P.O. Box 1, Bilthoven, The Netherlands.

DONS, J. J. M., Biochemisch Laboratorium, Leiden, The Netherlands.

DOUGLAS, L. T., Genetisch Laboratorium, Driehuiserweg 200, Nijmegen, The Netherlands.

DOVER, GABRIEL A., Department of Genetics, University of Cambridge, Milton Road, Cambridge CB4 1XH, U.K.

DUIJNDAM-VAN-DEN BERGHE, M., Psych. Ziekenhuis "Endegeest", Oegstgeest, The Netherlands.

DUIJNDAM, W. A. L., Histochem. Lab., Leiden, The Netherlands.

DUTRILLAUX, B., Institut de Prognèse, Rue de l'école de médecine, 75006 Paris, France.

EVANS, E. P., Sir William Dunn School of Pathology, South Parks Rd, Oxford, U.K.

FAED, MICHAEL JAMES WILLOUGHBY, Ninewells Medical School, The University, Dundee DD1 4HN, U.K.

FERGUSON-SMITH, MALCOLM ANDREW, Institute of Genetics, University of Glasgow, Glasgow G11 5JS, U.K.

FISCHER, PATRICIA, Krebsforschungs-Institut, Borschkegasse 1 a, Wien 1090, Austria.

FLAVELL, R., Plant Breeding Institute, Cambridge CB2 2IQ, U.K.

FORD, CHARLES EDMUND, Sir William Dunn School of Pathology, South Parks Rd, Oxford OX1 3RE, U.K.

FOX, D. P., Department of Genetics, University of Aberdeen, Aberdeen, U.K.

FRACCARO, M., Via Forlanini 14, 27100 Pavia, Italy.

FREDGA, K., Inst. of Genetics, Sölvegat 29, S-22362, Lund, Sweden.

GENEIX, AIMÉ, 8 Rue du Grand Champ, 63110 Beaumont, France.

GERAEDTS, J. P. M., Afdeling Anthropogenetica, Wassenaarseweg 62, Leiden, The Netherlands.

GERMAN, JAMES L., The New York Blood Center, 310 East 67th Street, New York City, New York 10021, U.S.A.

GIGLIANI, FRANCA, Instituto di Genetica, Universita Roma, Roma 00100, Italy.

GOUW, W. L. N., Department of Human Genetics, Antonius Deusinglaan 4, Groningen, The Netherlands.

GRANBERG, INGRED, Morfologiska Avelingen, Huddinge Hospital, Stockholm, Sweden.

GRANUM, E., Laboratoriet for Elektronik, Danmarks tekniske Højskole, Bygning 344, 2800 Lyngby, Denmark.

GREILHUBER, J., Botanisches Institut der Universität Wien, Rennweg 14, A-1030 Wien, Austria.

GROPP, A. Institut für Pathologie der Medizinischen Hochschule, 24 Lübeck, Kronsforder, West Germany.

GRZESCHIK, K. H., Institut für Humangenetik, 44 Münster, Vesaliusweg 12–14, West Germany.

HARTMANN-GOLDSTEIN, INGEBORG, Genetics Department, Sheffield University, Sheffield, U.K.

HAUSCHTECK-JUNGEN, ELISABETH, Strahlenbiologisches Institut, August Forelstrasse 7, 8008 Zürich, Switzerland.

HILWIG, INGEBORG, Farbwerke Hoechst AG, Gewebezüchtung H 811, 623 Frankfurt/Main-80, West Germany.

HUSTINX, TH. W. J., Anthropogenetica, Faculteit geneeskunde, Nijmegen, The Netherlands.

JACOBSON, P., Research in Mental Retardation, Cytogenetics Department, Brejning 7080, Börkop, Denmark.

JAFFRAY, J. Y., 12 Rue de la Pradelle, 6300 Clermont-Ferrand, France.

JAGIELLO, GEORGIANA, 630 West 168 Street, New York, N.Y. 10032, U.S.A.

JAUHAR, P., Cytology Department, Welsh Plant Breeding Station, Aberystwyth, Wales, U.K.

JONES, K. W., Institute of Animal Genetics, Edinburgh, U.K.

JONES, ROBERT NEIL, Department of Agricultural Botany, The University College of Wales, Penglais, Aberystwyth SY23 3DD, Wales, U.K.

JONGSMA, A., Afdeling Celbiologie, Medische Faculteit der Erasmus Universiteit, Postbus 1738, Rotterdam, The Netherlands.

KALISCH, W. E., Lehrstuhl für Genetik, Ruhr-Universität-Bochum, West Germany.

KHOSLA, P. K., Department of Botany, South Parks Rd., Oxford, OX1 3RA, U.K.

KIM, MY. A., Institut für Hamangenetik, 44 Münster, West Germany.

KLINGER, HAROLD P., Department of Genetics, Albert Einstein College of Medicine, 1300 Morris Park Avenue, Bronx, New York 10461, U.S.A.

LADIZINSKY, GIDEON, Faculty of Agriculture, The Hebrew University of Jerusalem, Rehovot, Israel.

LATT, S. A., Children's Hospital Medical Center, 300 Longwood Ave., Boston, Mass. 02115, U.S.A.

LAURENT, COLETTE, Institut Pasteur, 77 rue Pasteur, Lyon 69007, France.

LEIGH, B., Afd. Stralengenetica, Wassenaarseweg 62, Leiden, The Netherlands.

LESSARD, M., Laboratoire d'Hematologie, Centre Hospitalier Universitaire, 35011 Rennes, France.

LEWIS, F. J. W., Department Cytog. Department Pathology, Southmead Hospital, Bristol, U.K.

LEWIS, KENNETH RODERICK, Botany School, South Parks Road, Oxford OX1 3RA, U.K.

LIN, C. C., Divisions of Pediatrics and Medical Biochemistry, Faculty of Medicine, University of Calgary, Alberta T2N In4, Canada.

LUBS, HERBERT A., Department of Pediatrics, University of Colorado Medical Center, Denver, Colorado 80220, U.S.A.

LUCIANI, J. M., Laboratoire Histologie-Embryologie II, Faculté de Medecine, 27 Bd. J. Moulin, 13385 Marseille Cedex 4, France.

LUNDSTEEN, C., Kromosomlab, Rigshospitalet, DK 2100 Copenhagen, Denmark.

MACGREGOR, H. C., Zoology Dept., University of Leicester LE1 7RH, U.K.

MADAN, KAMLESH, Chromosome Unit, Department of Human Genetics, University of Liverpool, U.K.

MANDAHL, N., The Wallenberg Laboratory, Sölveg 33, S-223 62 Lund, Sweden.

MARKS, G. E., Joh. Innes Institute, Norwich, U.K.

MARTINEZ, A., Jodrell Laboratory, Kew Gardens, Surrey, U.K.

MARTINEZ, FRANCISCA BALLESTA, Plaza Tetuan 38, Barcelona 10, Spain.

MCDERMOTT, ALAN, Department of Human Genetics, Birmingham Maternity Hospital, Birmingham B15 2Tg, U.K.

MCKAY, R. D. G., MRC Mammalian Genome Unit, Department of Zoology, University of Edinburgh, W. Mains Rd., Edinburgh EH9 3JT, U.K.

MENDELSOHN, D., Afdeling Stralengenetica, Wassenaarseweg 62, Leiden, The Netherlands.

MIKKELSEN, MARGARETA, John F. Kennedy Institute, Gl. Landevej 7–9, DK2600 Glostrup, Denmark.

MILLER, O. J., 145 Pinewood Place, Teaneck, N.J. 07666, U.S.A.

MITTWOCH, URSULA, The Galton Laboratory, University College, London NW1, U.K.

MIZUNO, S., Zoology Department, University of Leicester, Leicester LE1 7RH, U.K.

MOENS, P., Department of Biology, York University, Downsview, Ontario, Canada.

MÜLLER, H. J., Department of Genetics, Albert Einstein College of Medicine, 1300 Morris Park, Bronx, N.Y. 10461, U.S.A.

NATARAJAN, A. T., Wallenberg Lab., Stockholm University, S-10405 Stockholm 50, Sweden.

NEZER, RAFAEL, Department of Genetics, The Hebrew University of Jerusalem, Israel.

OLMO, ETTORE, Institute of Histology and Embriology, Via Mezzocannone 8, 80134 Napoli, Italy.

OOSTERLINCK, A., Centrum voor menselijke Erfelijkheid, Vesalius Instituut, Minderbroederstraat 12, Leuven, Belgium.

OUD, J. L. Nat. Inst. Public Health, Sterrenbos 1, Utrecht, The Netherlands.

PANGALOS, C., 149, 7, Ioannon Drossopoulou St., Athens TT801, Greece.

PARKER, J. S., Dept. of Plant Biology, Queen Mary College, Mile End Rd., London E1 4NS, U.K.

PARRINGTON, JENIFER M., Galton Laboratory, Wolfson House, 4, Stephenson Way, London NW1 2HE, U.K.

PARSLOW, M., Department of Community Health, Medical School, Auckland, New Zealand.

PAWLOWITZKI, I. H., Institut für Humangenetik der Universität Münster, 44 Münster, Vesaliusweg 12/14, West Germany.

PEARSON, PETER L., Department of Human Genetics, State University of Leiden, Wassenaarseweg 62, Leiden, The Netherlands.

PERRY, P. E., M.R.C. Cytogenetics Unit, Western General Hospital, Crewe Rd., Edinburgh EH4 2XO, U.K.

PFEIFFER, R. A., D 24 Lübeck, Institut für Humangenetik, Ratzeburger Allee 160, West Germany.

PHILIP, J., Department of Obstetrics and Gynaecology, Rigshospitalet, Blegdamsvej 2100 DK, Denmark.

PIZA, SALVADOR DE TOLEDO, Escola Superior de Agricultura "Luiz de Queiroz", Piracicaba, São Paulo, Brazil.

PLOEM, J. S., Afdeling Pathologie, Wassenaarseweg 62, Leiden, The Netherlands.

QUACK, BERNADETTE, Laboratoire de Cytogénétique, Centre de Transfusion, Faubourg Maché 7300, Chambery, France.

RAICU, PETRE, Catedra de Genetică, University of Bucharest, Aleea Portocalilor 1–3, Bucharest, Romania.

RAMANNA, M. S., Institute of plant breeding, Lawickse Allee 166, Wageningen, The Netherlands.

RAO, S. R. V., Department of Zoology, University of Delhi, Delhi-7, India.

RAPOSA, T., 1088, Budapest, Szentkiralyi u. 46, Semmelweis Orv. Tud. Egy. II Belklinika, Hungary.

RIMPAU, J., Plant Breeding Institute, Cambridge CB2 2LQ, U.K.

ROCCHI, ANGELA, Istituto di Genetica, Universita, Roma 00100, Italy.

ROST, F. W. D., Histochemistry Department, Royal Postgraduate Medical School, London W12 OHS, U.K.

ROTHE, D. J., 435 East 70th Street, New York 10021, U.S.A.

RUDDLE, F. H., Yale University, Kline Biology Tower, New Haven/Connec. U.S.A.

RUTOVITZ, D., M.R.C. Clinical and Cytogenetics Unit, Western General Hospital, Edinburgh EH4 2XU, U.K.

RUTTEN, F. J., Plant Breeding Institute, Cambridge CB2 2LQ, U.K.

SACHSEE, W., Institut für Genetik, Universität Mainz, West Germany.

SANTESSON, BERTA, University Institute for Medical Genetics, V. Agatan 24, S-75220 Uppsala, Sweden.

SATYA PRAKASH, K. L., Department of Zoology, University of Mysore, Manasa Gangotri, Mysore 570006, India.

SAVAGE, JOHN RAYMOND KELYNACK, MRC Radiobiology Unit, Harwell, Didcot, Berkshire OX11 ORD, U.K.

SCHABERG, A., Pathologisch Lab., Wassenaarseweg 62, Leiden, The Netherlands.

SCHERES, J. M. J. C., Department of Human Genetics, University of Nijmegen, Nijmegen, The Netherlands.

SCHWARZACHER, H. G., Histologisches Institut, Schwarzspanierstr. 17, A-1090 Wien, Austria.

SCHWEIZER, D., MRC Radiobiology Unit, Harwell, Didcot, Oxfordshire, U.K.

SEABRIGHT, MARINA, Salisbury General Hospital, Salisbury, Wilts, U.K.

SENTEIN, P., Laboratoire d'Histologie, Faculté de Medecine, 27 Bd. J. Moulin, 13005 Marseille, France.

SERRA, A., Universita Cattoloca, Via dello Pineta Sacchetti, Roma 00158, Italy.

SETH, P. K., Cottage 7, Road 69, Punjabi Bagh, New Dehli 110026, India.

SHARAT CHANDRA, H., Microbiology and Pharmacology, Lab. Indian Institute of Science, Bangalore 560012, India.

SHARMA, A. K., Department of Botany, University of Calcutta, 35 Ballygunj Circular Road, Calcutta 700019, India.

SHARMA, T., Cytogenetics Laboratory, Department of Zoology, Benares Hindu University, Varanasi 221005, India.

SMITH, F. J., Genetisch Instituut van de Universiteit van Amsterdam, Amsterdam, The Netherlands.

SOKOLOFF, STEPHEN, Max-Planck-Institut für Biologie, D-7400 Tübingen, Spemannstrasse 34, West Germany.

SOLARI, A. J., Bernardo de Irigoyen 1524, Buenos Aires, Argentina.

SOSA-ROMERO, A., Seccion de Bioquimica de la Reproducción, Departemento de Investigación Científica I.M.S.S. Mexico 73, D.F., Mexico.

SPARVOLI, ELIO, Instituto di Scienze Botaniche dell'Università, Via Giuseppe Colombo 60, 21033 Milano, Italy.

SPERLING, K., Institut für Genetik der F.U. Berlin, Arminallee 5–7, Berlin, West Germany.

STAHL, A., Laboratoire d'Histologie et Embryologie II, Faculté de Medecine, Boulevard Jean Moulin, Marseille, France.

STENGEL-RUTHOWSKI, S., Genetisches Laboratorium der Universität München, 8 München 2, West Germany.

SUMNER, ADRIAN T., MRC Clinical and Cytogenetics Unit, Western General Hospital, Edinburgh EH4 2XU, U.K.

SYBENGA, J., Afdeling Erfelijkheidsleer, Gen. Foulkesweg 53, Wageningen, The Netherlands.

TAKENOUCHI, YASUSHI, Biology Laboratory, Sapporo College, Hokkaido University of Education, South 22, West 12, Sapporo, 060 Hokkaido, Japan.

TIMSON, JOHN, Department of Medical Genetics, University of Manchester, Stopford Building, The University, Manchester M13 9PL, U.K.

TING, YU-CHEN, Department of Biology, Boston College, Chestnut Hill, Massachusetts 02167, U.S.A.

TURC, CLAUDE, Laboratoire de Cytogénétique, Faculté de Médecine, 7 Boulevard Jeanne d'Arc, 21 033 Dijon-Cedex, France.

UTAKOJI, TADASHI, Pathology Department, Cancer Institute, Toshima-ku, Tokyo 170, Japan.

VAGNER-CAPODANO, A. M., Laboratoire d'Embryologie et Histologie II, Faculté de Médecine, 13385 Marseille Cedex 4, 27 Bd. Jean Moulin 13005, Marseille, France.

VAN BRINK, JANNY, Genetisch Instituut, Opaalweg 20, Utrecht, The Netherlands.

VAN DEN BERGHE, H., Centrum voor menselijke Erfelijkheid, Vesalius Instituut, Minderbroederstraat 12, Leuven, Belgium.

VAN DER LINDEN, A. G. J. M., Afd. Anthropogenetica, Wassenaarseweg 62, Leiden, The Netherlands.

VAN DER MEER-FIEGGEN, W., Guido Gezellestraat 2, Amsterdam (1009), The Netherlands.

VAN DER PLOEG, M., Afdeling Pathologie, Wassenaarseweg 62, Leiden, The Netherlands.

VAN DORP, A., Klompven 12, Oisterwijk (N-B), The Netherlands.

VAN DUIJN, Afdeling Pathologie, Wassenaarseweg 62, Leiden, The Netherlands.

VAN HEMEL, J. O., Genetisch Instituut, Opaalweg 20, Utrecht, The Netherlands.

VAN NIEKERK, W. A., Department of Obstetrics and Gynaecology, Tygerberg Hospital, Tiervlei, South Africa.

VERSCHRAEGEN-SPAE, MARIE-ROSE, Dienst Medische Genetica Blik A, Academisch Ziekenhuis, De Pintelaan 135, 9000 Gent, Belgium.

VLAD, M., Zoology Department, University of Leicester, Leicester LE1 7RH, U.K.

VOGEL, W., Humangenetisches Institut der Universität, D-78 Frieburg, Albertstr. 11, West Germany.

VOSA, CANIO GIUSEPPE, Botany School, South Parks Road, Oxford OX1 3RA, U.K.

WAHRMAN, JACOB, Department of Genetics, The Hebrew University of Jerusalem, Israel.

WALKER, M. H., Zoology Department, University of Leicester, Leicester LE1 7RH, U.K.

WALL, R. J., 1910 Crestshire DR, Glendale, California 91208, U.S.A.

WALLACE, C., Anatomy Department, Medical School, Hospital Street, Johannesburg, South Africa.

WARGENT, JUDITH MARY, Department of Genetics, University of Sheffield, Sheffield S10 2TN, U.K.

WILTON, EUGENE, Cytogenetic Unit, The South African Institute for Medical Research, P.O. Box 1038, Johannesburg, South Africa.

WITKOWSKI, REGINE, DDR 112, Berlin, Bitburger Strasse 24, Germany.

WOLF, BRUNO ERICH, Institut für Genetik der Freien Universität Berlin, 1 Berlin 33 (Dahlem), Arnimallee 5–7, West Germany.

WOLF, U., Institut für Humangenetik der Universität, Albertstrasse 11, 78 Freiburg, West Germany.

WOLFF, CHARLOTTE CLAIR, Laboratoire de Biologie Cellulaire C.E.N.G., B.P. 85, 38041 Grenoble Cedex, France.

WOLFF, S., MRC Clinical and Cytogenetics Unit, Western General Hospital, Crewe Rd., Edinburgh EH4, U.K.

WULF, H. CHR., Finseninstitutet, Strandboulevarden 49, Copenhagen, Denmark.

ZECH, LORE, Institute of Medical Cell Research and Genetics, Karolinska Institutet, S-10401 Stockholm 60, Sweden.

CHROMOSOMES, MEIOSIS AND MAN

C. D. DARLINGTON
Botany School, Oxford, U. K.

1. INTRODUCTION

In opening the Fifth Chromosome Conference I must thank those whose labours have happily brought it about and brought us together. I must also thank them for giving me the privilege of addressing you in Leiden, in this famous university and this environment so auspicious for those like us who live with and by and through the microscope.

As for the environment, the idea means a great deal to us for the environment of our chromosomes is the cytoplasm and their relations with this environment teach us, and might teach others, something useful. It is that when the cytoplasm influences the chromosomes it changes their behaviour; but when the chromosomes influence the cytoplasm they change its character: they are in effect creating their own environment. It is a genetic environment which serves them and their descendants. There is an analogy here with the affairs of men close enough to be worth bearing in mind, not less so because it is part of our business to bring human chromosomes into useful connection with human affairs.

As for useful connections we know, or think we know, well enough how useful, how necessary, are the connections between cells with their different cycles of mitosis and meiosis, between organisms with their different modes of development, between breeding groups with their different breeding systems extended in time and space, and between all forms of life available for evolutionary comparison. Between these various units of activity with their corresponding levels of thinking the chromosomes are the connections. But even to us, most of the time, they are out of sight. The very names that we use for our studies, like chemistry or genetics, cytology or molecular biology, have their effect: they emphasise separation and conceal connection. Those who try to expose the connections therefore (as I have found) need to explain themselves from many points of view, turning their problem inside out and back again, if they are to be understood.

2. MULTIPLICATION AND DIVISION

A word about our history will show you what I mean. We shall soon be celebrating the centenary of an event which opened the door to the world we work in. In 1880 Flemming illustrated the beautiful chromosomes in the endosperm of *Fritillaria.* He found they were exactly replicated and split in prophase to give what we call chromatids. The genetic significance of this replication or splitting was pointed out a little later. A hundred years later what are the consequences for us?

We have found that the processes of replication or division of the cell and the nucleus, the chromosomes, and the DNA threads are normally correlated; but abnormally the correlation can be broken. And when it is broken what do we get? We get polynemy, polyteny and polyploidy, endomitosis and polymitosis, misdivision of centromeres, isochromosomes and diplochromosomes, diminution and parthenogenesis, and perhaps other dire events. No wonder the visiting academician, faced with so many vicissitudes, asked me the Marxist question (it was in 1951): when the chromosomes reproduce, do they multiply or do they divide? I had not yet ventured to attack this dialectical problem. For some time, however, I had been asking myself an easier question: *when* do they multiply and *when* do they divide? For this had seemed to me to be what matters in the relations of mitosis and meiosis. I had suggested that these processes were relatively out of step for the nucleus and the cell in the two modes of propagation.

When I proposed this explanation of meiosis, the accepted wisdom of the day was a mystery. It still is a mystery. Was the pairing of the chromosomes perhaps necessary for consummating the sexual process? Or for vindicating the laws of Mendelian inheritance? Or was meiosis an Act of God, something ordained at Creation? Such views would be easier to understand than mine and, perhaps on this account, may be more widely held today.

In advancing my hypothesis I now ask myself whether I was perhaps picking up theoretical issues so outrageous (whether by their magnitude or their minuteness) that that generation, unable to face them, had to deny their existence.

First there was the *reductionist* issue: to replace vitalistic or teleological views of chromosome behaviour by utterly mechanical assumptions. People did not like that. A second issue was *evolutionary*: to put sexual reproduction in an evolutionary setting and sequence. I had to call attention to the universal character of meiosis which had been implied by Weismann but had now been safely buried with all his speculations. This universality implied a common origin at the first invention of meiosis and a maintenance and survival after 2,000 million years or 10^{10} or 10^{11} cell generations. This could be due only to its common genetic advantage of recombination feeding back by natural selection, selection not just of individuals but of populations and a system. People did not like that either.

A third issue had therefore to be genetic and experimental: to put the variant forms of meiosis in relation to one another, and to put their physiological causes into connection with their genetic and evolutionary consequences.

These genetic relations took shape in my terms as the prime variables of meiosis, the crude effects of differences in the timing and spatial arrangements of prophase pairing. In parallel, the special properties of the centromere brought to light another timing difference, i.e., its delayed cycle of replication or division relative to that of the other chromomeres or genes. Its independence was exposed at meiosis by its misdivision in univalents and also by its non-division in the production of diplochromosomes (Barber, 1940), and its influence on the reproduction and movement of the rest of the chromosomes was exposed by radiation experiments (Darlington, 1957).

These connections can themselves now often be connected by new techniques with precise molecular agents. We enter a new phase. In doing so we find our project at once simplified and complicated by the special character of meiosis. At mitosis, buried in the resting nucleus, we cannot normally separate replication and division. But at meiosis they are spread out on an extended time scale, partly separated but partly overlapping. Reaching forward into prophase they terminate together in processes of breakage, reunion, and repair, which together constitute crossing over (Hotta and Stern, 1971).

As to the sites of crossing over, electron microscopy has made it possible to recognise them, by the growth of special structures, the synaptinemal or (may we say?) *synaptic complexes.* These structures, according to Westergaard and von Wettstein, while varying between great systematic groups, have a certain universal character of their own. This character is shown in their molecular constitution and in the release of torsion through the generation within them of what will become visible chiasmata. It indicates an evolutionary origin close to that of meiosis itself.

3. SOME EXPERIMENTS

The new methods and new discoveries make it worthwhile to recall some experiments whose connections with our present problems are easily overlooked. There are four such types of experimental situation:

1. Mitosis with single chromatids, where the chromosomes have altogether failed to replicate or to divide (in *Zea* and *Tradescantia*).

2. A double track of meiosis arising through failure of differentiation in mother-cell tissues of sterile plant mutants (in *Scilla* and *Allium*).

3. A double track of meiosis arising through the evolution of alternative tracks of development in a fertile animal species (in *Scutigera*).

4. Mitotically out-of-step cell fusion aided by virus treatment (in man, mouse, or muntjac).

What these experimental situations have in common is that chromosomes are brought into prophase and even into metaphase of a nuclear division, which is expected to be either mitotic or meiotic, without having doubled their DNA content or split into chromatids. The four kinds of abnormality have arisen in four ways (fig. 1):

1. Single chromatid mitoses were found in genetically abnormal plants: Beadle's recessive segregates in *Zea* and Oestergren's X-ray mutants in *Tradescantia*; both are in pollen grains where (since they constitute both natural populations and terminal tissues) genetic abnormalities of mitosis so readily make themselves visible to us. In both examples, as we might expect, there is a suggestion of meiotic intra-haploid pairing between presumably repeated segments, at prophase in *Tradescantia*, at metaphase in *Zea*. In *Tradescantia* there is also, as could be expected, an unreadiness of the centromeres to divide, as indicated by misdivision, spindle weakness, and some chromosome breakage.

2. Two-track meioses appear in our *Allium* as abortions among sexual (premeiotic and meiotic) cells in the anthers. However, the abortive cells consist of central islands or enclaves of larger cells arising by an error of differentiation. Since larger cells have been connected experimentally with reduced chiasma frequency (cf. Henderson, 1970) we might well suppose that a barrier had arisen to the diffusion of a substance which should arrest the growth of the cell and set it on the path of meiotic prophase development, perhaps by a switch from aerobic to anaerobic respiration. Whatever

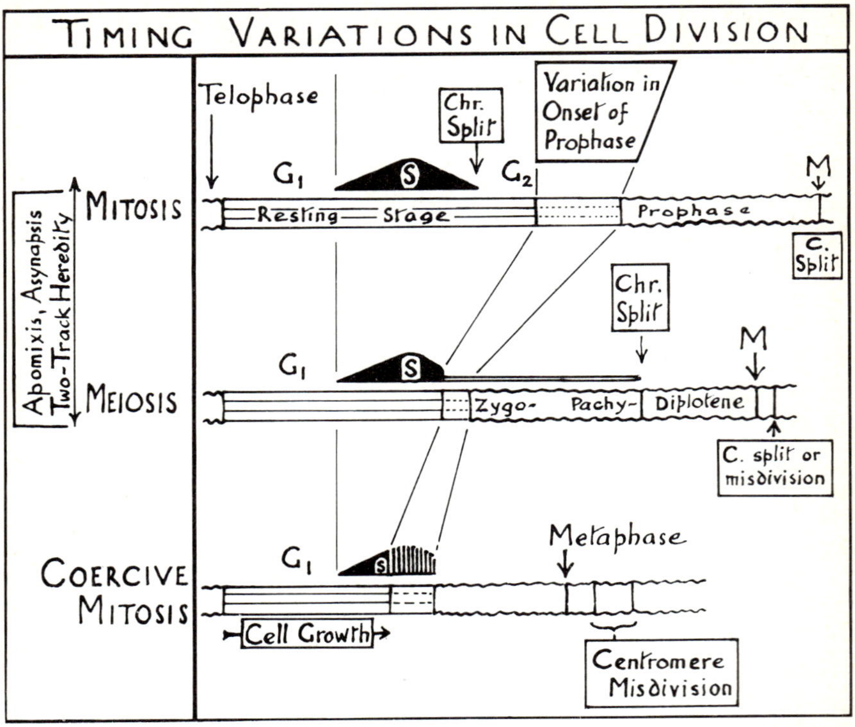

FIG. 1.—Diagram showing the effects of variation in the timing relations of onset of prophase and phase of chromosome reproduction in cell division. Top: onset in G_2 gives normal mitosis with reproduced and divided chromosomes. Middle: onset in late S gives meiosis with complete or incomplete pairing, localised chiasmata or asynapsis. Bottom: onset in early S gives breakage or pulverization as in *Allium* and virus induction. Omitted: onset in G_1 gives mitosis with undivided chromosomes and rudimentary meiotic pairing as in mutant *Tradescantia*, polymitotic maize and early virus induction (after Ansley, 1954; Darlington and Haque, 1955; Darlington, 1965; Oestergren and Oestergren, 1966; Hotta and Stern, 1971; Mazia, 1974; Röhme, 1974).

the cause, the diverted cells continue growing; their chromosomes duplicate, their chiasmata mostly fail, and their pairing lapses. Instead of forming chiasmata the chromosomes often break into fragments. This apparently happens at the time when they are duplicating, for these are chromosome breaks (B″) and most of the broken ends reunite by sister reunion. The result is mechanically equivalent to what we call sister-strand crossing over but with a U-turn instead of an X-twist.

3. With the alternative types of meiosis in the centipede *Scutigera* a similar mutant abnormality has in effect been controlled and exploited in differentiation to produce a mitotic meiosis by delaying the onset of prophase until after doubling of the DNA and the chromosomes (Ansley, 1954).

4. The last group of experiments produces both a contrast and an analogy. For if the enclave abortions arise through the formation of barriers to diffusion between cells, the cell-fusion experiments depend on the use of viruses for the removal of such barriers. In this way cells with nuclei at metaphase in the mouse can force the

resting nuclei of other cells in G_1 or S phase into mitosis, which they enter without their chromosomes having reproduced.

The analogy is a double one. The cell fusion in the mouse gives us single-chromatid mitoses with suggestions of pairing as in *Zea* and *Tradescantia*. It also gives us fragmented or pulverised chromosomes as in *Scilla* and *Allium* as well as in *Tradescantia*. Clearly later these observations will have a bearing on the interpretation not only of meiosis but also of other types of chromosome breakage, both spontaneous and induced. But already we see why there is a concentration of sensitivity to irradiation in the S phase of the resting nucleus (Darlington and La Cour, 1945).

Comparisons of this kind relate to certain general principles which, I hope, are not too obvious to be worth stating:

1. Time of onset of prophase in relation to the S phase is the simplest and most crucial variable affecting chromosome behaviour at mitosis and meiosis.

2. Its variations show that chromosome replication and nuclear prophase can be physiologically separated: prophase can be induced at G_1 (as it normally is in meiosis II), at early stages of S, as well as at late stages (as in meiosis I), and at G_2 as in ordinary mitosis.

3. Their mutual dependence in normal mitosis and meiosis, like the chromosome repair mechanism, is an original adaptation of nuclear or karyotic organisms.

4. In our experimental situations and in meiosis the centromere is out of step with the rest of the chromosome, its division and misdivision thus acting as an experimental control.

5. More obscure and also subordinate is the differentiation within chromosomes in timing of replication and spiralisation which I have referred to *allocycly*, differential reactivity, and a pachytene gradient, all of them related to heterochromatin, to repetitive segments, and to the field of banding studies.

6. The synchronisation of cells in mitosis and meiosis is evidence for the interactions of nucleus and cytoplasm, as shown in the evolution of barriers between pollen grains in the Orchidaceae, the effects of complementary balance in *Uvularia*, the cooperation of nuclei with and without nucleoli and heterochromatin in *Vicia*, and the function of nucleoli in meiosis (Barber, 1940, 1942*a*; McLeish, 1954; Williams et al., 1973).

These generalisations, especially as they concern the centromere, are not irrelevant to what are now the great practical problems of how the chromosomes work in man, in the development, heredity, and evolution of our own species.

4. X AND Y IN MAN

At our last conference I offered a model of the relations of the sex chromosomes in *Dropsophila*. It was a necessary model but (owing to the difficulty of mapping inactivity) after 60 years' study it was still a provisional one. The problem of the sex chromosomes in man is analogous in theory but in experimental practice it is quite a different one.

The first step would seem to be to relate the early models of sex chromosomes with the recent observations of the synaptic complex and the detailed consequences of the redundancy inactivation of the X chromosome as explained by Mary Lyon.

My original models of the sex chromosomes in plants and animals require, except where Y is disappearing, a separation of (i) two non-homologous *differential* segments, one in X and the other in Y, and (ii) two homologous *pairing* segments which are kept homologous owing to the sequence of pairing, crossing over and chiasma formation being responsible for the segregation of the whole XY bivalent (Darlington, 1934; Koller and Darlington, 1934). This segmental model has so far worked for all species of mammals, including marsupials, and in man it is confirmed by the recognition of the synaptic complex. The model, however, leaves two questions open for each species. The first is whether the centromeres of X and Y lie in the pairing segments, as in the rat and *Apodemus* (Fraccaro et al., 1969), or in the differential segments, as they evidently do in man (fig. 2).

What does this mean? In man the primary and perhaps multiple sex differentials seem to lie in parts of the differential segments, immediately next to the allelic pairing segments between them and the centromere. The evidence is that exceptional crossing over between X and Y gives comparable "XX" and "XY" individuals, perhaps in equal numbers with defective gonads (Ford, 1970). Such boundary crossing over I have suggested for the gene *bobbed* in *Drosophila* which also appears in both X and Y (Darlington, 1931, p. 88, n., and p. 91). The difference is that for *Drosophila* in nature, unlike man, the transfer is of no selective importance.

The second question concerns the differential segments of X and Y. It has two parts. First, we must ask, how does Y maintain the positive role of its differential

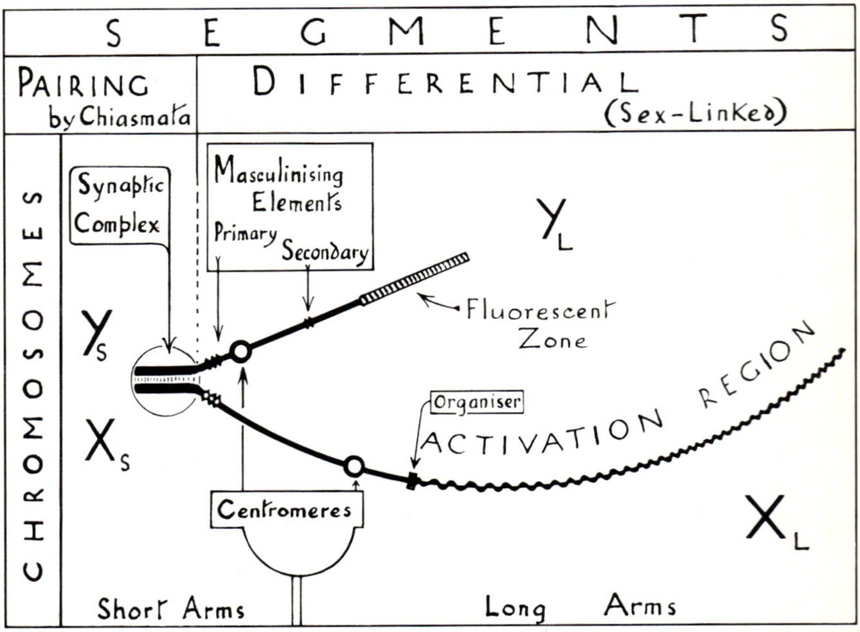

FIG. 2.—Diagram showing the provisional segmental relations of the sex chromosomes at pachytene in man in the light of individual variation due to random and centric chromosome rearrangements. The boundary between pairing and differential segments is assumed to be unstable as in *Drosophila*, giving recombination of some sex determinants (after Darlington, 1931, 1934; Lyon, 1968; Ford, 1970; Sarto et al., 1973; Pearson, 1973; Therman et al., 1974*a*, *b*; Langmaid and Laurence, 1974).

segment in sex determination, despite the exclusion of this segment from internal recombination by crossing over? Does it perhaps possess its own means of spontaneous variation connected with the properties of its otherwise inert fluorescent zone? Secondly in X, what are the causes and consequences of the Lyon effect, its redundant or competitive inactivation? What happens with deficiencies for which the two X's are heterozygous? We may agree that if defective X's usually appear to be the inactivated partners, it is because selection has eliminated cell lineages which have taken the alternative (active) option (Sarto et al., 1973). But how defective do they need to be? What would happen if the two X's were both defective but in different ways? And are these questions connected with the properties of repetitive DNA (Jones, 1973)?

5. CHROMOSOME EVOLUTION IN MAN

Having examined the chromosomes of a million human beings, we are now in a position (following Hamerton) to survey the results, to consider how the chromosomes in man have developed their present character. There are three main problems.

First, we have to compare what we see in man with our knowledge in other fields: notably in *Drosophila* with its radiation-induced breakage; in mammals, urodoles and Orthoptera with their systematic differences, in plant species and hybrids with large chromosomes whose range of variation and experimental treatments has taught us most of our principles. In all these fields we have to note the alternative, perhaps opposed, selective uses of chromosome variation. Is it splitting the species? Or is it creating balanced polymorphisms which will hold the species together (Darlington, 1965, 1971*a*)?

Secondly, we have to look at selection at different levels. For in all nuclear organisms selection may be (i) nuclear and mitotic, (ii) meiotic in relation either to heterozygotes for polymorphism or to homozygotes for race formation, (iii) individual or somatic in relation to balance, or (iv) generative in relation to fertility in a breeding population.

Thirdly, we have to take account of the breeding system. In man, the incest taboo operates more like incompatibility in plants than any other known animal system. It prevents the splitting of the species and hence favours polymorphism and inversions. It demands the fertility of heterozygotes and hence restricts the exploitation of interchanges.

6. CHROMOSOME BREAKAGE IN MAN

Our habit of preserving human life, however defective, and our success in doing so have brought us face to face in man with a hitherto unrealised contrast between the two modes of spontaneous chromosome rearrangement which had evaded experimentors with *Drosophila*, *Zea mays*, and elsewhere for 60 years. The contrast is between the results of random and centric breakage.

Random chromosome rearrangement depends on breakage at random in the chromosome usually followed by reunion. It is probably concentrated in the S phase of the resting nucleus and gives rise to inversions and interchanges. The structural heterozygotes it produces have frequent mispairing so that crossing-over, we believe, leads to secondary structural change, notably repetition (*Trillium*, fig. 8 in Darlington and Shaw, 1959; man, Ferguson-Smith, 1974), including a repetition of the centromere in dicentrics.

Centric rearrangements are fixed in position since they arise from misdivision or crosswise splitting, equal or unequal, of the centromere itself. This leads to breakage of a two-armed chromosome, usually into two telocentrics. It occurs not in the nucleus but on the spindle; it is a timing error, largely confined to chromosomes unpaired at meiosis. The telocentrics may be stable at mitosis (Darlington and La Cour, 1950) but they may unite to give interchanges (Morrison, 1953) or to give isochromosomes which can form part of the regular or irregular complement (Darlington and Janaki-Ammal, 1945).

Centric rearrangements have an extended prehistory. They were first inferred in Orthoptera by McClung in 1905 and by Robertson and others in 1915 (cf. Darlington, 1932, fig. 37, or 1965, fig. 46). Further I have suggested that in *Drosophila* attached X's, and in *Datura*, secondary and tertiary trisomics arose from misdivision. They would then be contrasted with ordinary random interchanges, natural or induced in diploids, whether in *Datura*, other plants, or animals or man.

In man we have already learned more than in any other organism about the contrast between these two modes of chromosome rearrangement. We notice that centric splitting of the kind discussed by Wahrman and Gourevitz in the gerbil and by Ford in the shrew and the mouse occurs also in man. But the telocentrics formed by misdivision of the unpaired X and Y are evidently eliminated (Langmaid and Laurence, 1974). So also probably and in the long run are the dicentrics formed by random breakage since we know them apart from man only in experimental situations (Darlington and Wylie, 1953; Hair, 1953; Koller, 1953).

The contrast between random and centric breakages thus reaches from the cellular to the evolutionary level. We have long seen the paradox that for genes small changes help genetic evolution, while big changes help genetic analysis. Now we see that for chromosomes, at least in man, random breakages are what have mattered in evolution. But centric breakages help in analysis: being fixed in position and surviving mitosis, although eliminated at meiosis, they are of crucial value in locating determinants and thus exposing the genetic structure of the chromosomes.

Elimination during development is the third sphere of selection and one in which man, through the frequencies of losses during pregnancy, already tells us far more than any other organism:

1. The abnormalities themselves, notably trisomics and monosomics, are eliminated; for example four-fiths of mongols are lost before birth.

2. The whole genotypes must therefore be heavily selected. Only individual mongols with genic combinations adapted to a trisomic condition as a whole will survive: hence all unbalanced types will show a variable *genotypic compensation* for their unbalance from which we may expect a distortion in their sex ratio.

3. Polyploid embryos are eliminated early, we may assume by failure not of the resting nucleus but rather of the mitotic spindle in the differentiation of particular tissues.

4. In mosaics a vast field of selection study has been opened to us in mammals by Tarkowski (1961) and in amphibia by Fankhauser (cf. Darlington, 1965).

We have long had evidence from intra-haploid pairing in plants, and also from the behaviour of centromeres, nucleolar organisers, and heterochromatin, that repetition of sequences occurs generally in the evolution of chromosomes. We can see how in man's heterogeneous populations the properties of repetitive DNA (Jones, 1973) will allow a survival of duplications and deficiencies in a variety foreshadowed by the *bar* locus in *Drosophila* but far beyond the assumptions of classical genetic theory.

Several factors, however, limit the use of structural change in the evolution of man's chromosomes:

1. Man allows himself liberties with his sex chromosomes but the low fertility of all primates reduces the scope for experiment by interchange and misdivision enjoyed by rodents.

2. The structure of man's chromosomes, particularly their centromeres, may have limited or excluded centromere change.

3. Taboo-enforced outbreeding, itself selected, holds a species together. It has favoured polymorphism and disfavoured the alternative use of variation in splitting the species. Hence also man's geographical as opposed to sympatric diversification of races.

7. THE CHROMOSOME VIEW OF GENETIC THEORY

The development of chromosome studies, chemical and microscopic, is now beginning to integrate our knowledge of heredity and variation and selection in a pattern which, being at a deeper analytical level, will supersede that derived purely from Mendelism. For we can no longer see Johannsen's genotype as the sum of its "genes". The classical framework used by Morgan and Muller, by Fisher, Haldane and Sewall Wright—even when sophisticated to include polygenes, major genes, and super-genes—can hardly accommodate the balances and interactions, the sequence effects and repetitions, euchromatic and heterochromatic, at all levels of size from the chromosome down to the nucleotide, revealed by chromosome work.

Misgivings and reservations have been evident in plant cytology for 40 years. They are now supported by the growing mass of human evidence. Human beings, like the pollen grains of our former studies, constitute natural populations with a spectrum of variation radically different from that of the experimental stocks of *Drosophila* and *Zea mays* which fostered the classical theory.

The levels of variation, action, and selection between the nucleotide and the population, between cell division and the genetic system, and in the centre the organisation of the chromosome itself, these are what we can now separate and what we shall also in due course have to connect. The ways in which we do this were hidden from our predecessors who chose to see only the Mendelian tip of the iceberg of variation. But our new resources are forced on our attention by the chromosomes themselves. Their visible variability underlies any integrated understanding of evolution as a whole.

In using human chromosomes equally for theoretical and for practical purposes the investigator has at his disposal the experience of nearly 100 years of research on plants and animals. Experiments with plant chromosomes have done most to reveal the causes of evolution. Comparisons among animal chromosomes have done most to reveal its consequences. But our surpassingly accurate knowledge of our own species and our concern for the well-being and survival of human individuals as well as of human races means that here we are likely to reach an understanding beyond what any other organism has allowed us to envisage. We are indeed (like Antony van Leeuwenhoek) stepping into a new world.

8. REFERENCES

ANSLEY, H. R. 1954. Alternative pathways of meiosis in the house centipede *(Scutigera)*. *Chromosoma (Berl.)*, *6*, 656–695.

BARBER, H. N. 1940. The suppression of meiosis and the origin of diplochromosomes. *Proc. Roy. Soc. Lond. Ser. B. Biol. Sci.*, *128*, 170–185.

BARBER, H. N. 1941. Chromosome behaviour in *Uvularia*. *J. Genet.*, *42*, 223–257.

BARBER, H. N. 1942*a*. The pollen grain division in the Orchidaceae. *J. Genet.*, *43*, 97–103.

BARBER, H. N. 1942*b*. The experimental control of chromosome pairing in *Fritillaria*. *J. Genet.*, *43*, 359–374.

BEADLE, G. W. 1931. A gene in maize for supernumerary cell divisions following meiosis. *Cornell U. Exp. Stn.* Mem. 129.

DARLINGTON, C. D. 1931. Meiosis in diploid and tetraploid *Primula sinensis*. *J. Genet.*, *24*, 65–96.

DARLINGTON, C. D. 1932. *Recent Advances in Cytology*. Churchill, London.

DARLINGTON, C. D. 1934. Anomalous chromosome pairing in the male *Drosophila pseudo-obscura*. *Genetics*, *19*, 95–118.

DARLINGTON, C. D. 1939. Misdivision and the genetics of the centromere *(Fritillaria)*. *J. Genet.*, *37*, 341–364.

DARLINGTON, C. D. 1952. The cell and heredity under ionisation. *Biological Hazards of Atomic Energy* (A. HADDOW, ed.), pp. 33–45. Oxford University Press.

DARLINGTON, C. D. 1957. Messages and movements in the cell. In *Conference on Chromosomes, Wageningen*. Willink Zwolle.

DARLINGTON, C. D. 1965. *Cytology*. Churchill, London.

DARLINGTON, C. D. 1969. Mosaics, twins and intersexes (Rev.). *Nature (Lond.)*, *223*, 328–329.

DARLINGTON, C. D. 1971*a*. The evolution of polymorphic systems. In *Ecological Genetics and Evolution* (R. CREED, ed.), pp. 1–9. Blackwell, Oxford.

DARLINGTON, C. D. 1971*b*. Axiom and process in genetics. *Nature (Lond.)*, *234*, 521–525.

DARLINGTON, C. D., and HAQUE, A. 1955. The timing of mitosis and meiosis in *Allium ascalonicum*. *Heredity*, *9*, 117–127.

DARLINGTON, C. D., and JANAKI-AMMAL, E. K. 1945. Adaptive isochromosomes in *Nicandra*. *Ann. Bot.*, *9*, 267–281.

DARLINGTON, C. D., and LA COUR, L. F. 1945. Chromosome breakage and the nucleic acid cycle. *J. Genet.*, *46*, 180–267.

DARLINGTON, C. D., and LA COUR, L. F. 1950. Hybridity selection in *Campanula*. *Heridity*, *4*, 217–248.

DARLINGTON, C. D., and SHAW, G. W. 1959. Parallel polymorphism in the heterochromatin of *Trillium*. *Heredity*, *13*, 89–121.

DARLINGTON, C. D., and WYLIE, A. P. 1953. A dicentric cycle in *Narcisus*. *Heredity*, *6*, (Suppl.), 197–213.

DEVICTOR-VUILLET, M. 1971. Anomalies de structure et rôle du chromosome Y chez l'Homme. *Path. Biol.*, *19*, 231–249.

FERGUSON-SMITH, M. A. 1974. Human autosomal polymorphism and non-random translocations. In *Chromosomes Today*, *4* (J. WAHRMAN and K. R. LEWIS, eds.), pp. 235–246. Israel Universities Press, Jerusalem, and John Wiley & Sons, New York.

FLEMMING, W. 1880. Cited by WILSON, E. B. *The Cell* (1900, fig. 54; 1925, fig. 51).

FORD, C. E. 1970. Cytogenetics and sex determination in man and mammals. *J. Biosoc. Sci.* (Suppl.), *2,* 7–20.

FORD, C. E., and EVANS, E. P. 1974. Robertsonian translocations in mice. In *Chromosomes Today, 4* (J. WAHRMAN and K. R. LEWIS, eds.), pp. 387–397. Israel Universities Press, Jerusalem, and John Wiley & Sons, New York.

FRACCARO, M., GUSTAVSSON, I., HULTEN, M., LINDSTEN, J., and TIEPOLD, L. 1969. The sex chromosomes in *Apodemus*. In *Chromosomes Today, 2* (C. D. DARLINGTON and K. R. LEWIS, eds.), pp. 154–157. Oliver and Boyd, Edinburgh and London.

HAIR, J. B. 1953. The origin of new chromosomes in *Agropyron. Heredity* (Suppl.) *6,* 215–233.

HAMERTON, J. L. 1971–3. *Human Cytogenetics* (2 vols.). Academic Press, New York and London.

HENDERSON, S. A. 1970. The time and place of meiotic crossing over. *Ann. Rev. Gen., 4,* 295–324.

HOTTA, Y., and STERN, H. 1971. Analysis of DNA synthesis during meiotic prophase in *Lilium. J. Mol. Biol., 55,* 337–355.

JONES, K. W. 1973. Annotation: satellite DNA. *J. Med. Gen., 10,* 273–281.

KOLLER, P. C. 1953. Dicentric chromosomes in a rat tumour induced by an aromatic nitrogen mustard. *Heredity* (Suppl.), *6,* 181–196.

KOLLER, P. C., and DARLINGTON, C. D. 1934. The genetical and mechanical properties of the sex chromosomes. I. *Rattus norvegicus. J. Genet., 29,* 159–173.

LA COUR, L. F., and WELLS, B. 1970. Chromocentres and the synaptinemal complex. *J. Cell Sci., 6,* 655–667.

LANGMAID, H., and LAURENCE, K. M. 1974. Deletion of the long arms of the Y chromosome with normal male development and intelligence. *J. Med. Genet., 11,* 208–211.

LYON, M. F. 1968. Chromosomal and subchromosomal inactivation. *Ann. Rev. Genet., 2,* 31–52.

MCCLUNG, C. E. 1905. The chromosome complex of orthopteran spermatocytes. *Biol. Bull., 9,* 304–320.

MCLEISH, J. 1954. The consequences of localised chromosome breakage. *Heredity, 8,* 385–407.

MAZIA, D. 1974. The Cell Cycle. *Sci. Am., 220 (1),* 55–63.

MORRISON, J. W. 1953. Chromosome interchange by misdivision in *Triticum. Can. J. Bot., 32,* 281–284.

NICHOLS, W. W. *et al.* 1965. Chromosome damage associated with the measles virus *in vitro. Hereditas, 54,* 101–118.

OESTERGREN, G., and OESTERGREN, K. 1966. Mitosis with undivided chromosomes. In *Chromosomes Today, 1* (C. D. DARLINGTON and K. R. LEWIS, eds.), pp. 128–130. Oliver and Boyd, Edinburgh and London.

PEARSON, P. L. 1973. The behaviour of chromosomes (fertility control). *Adv. Biosciences, 10,* 15–26.

REES, H. 1952. Asynapsis and spontaneous chromosome breakage in *Scilla. Heredity, 6,* 89–97.

ROBERTSON, W. R. B. 1915. Chromosome studies. I. *J. Morph., 26,* 109–141.

RÖHME, DAN. 1974. Prematurely condensed chromosomes of the Indian muntjac. *Hereditas, 76,* 251–258.

SANDBERG, A. A. *et al.* 1970. Definition and morphologic features of chromosome pulverisation. *J. Nat. Cancer Inst., 45,* 615–623.

SARTO, G. E., THERMAN, E., and PATAU, K. 1973. X inactivation in man: a woman with t(xq –; 12q +). *Am. J. Hum. Gen., 25,* 262–270.

STENMAN, S., and SAKSELA, E. 1971. The relationship of Sendai virus-induced chromosome pulverisation to cell cyclus in Hela cells. *Hereditas, 69,* 1–14.

STERN, C. 1968. *Genetic Mosaics and Other Essays.* Harvard University Press.

TARKOWSKI, A. K. 1961. Mouse chimaeras developed from fused eggs. *Nature (Lond.), 190,* 857–860.

THERMAN, E. *et al.* 1974*a*. Apparently isodicentric but functionally monocentric X chromosome in man. *Am. J. Hum. Gen., 26,* 83–92.

THERMAN, E. *et al.* 1974*b*. Center for Barr body condensation on the proximal part of the human Xq: a hypothesis. *Chromosoma (Berl.), 44,* 361–366.

WAHLSTRÖM, J. 1971. Variations in length of Y chromosome. *Hereditas, 69,* 125–128.

WAHRMAN, J., and GOUREVITZ, P. 1974. Extreme chromosome variability in a colonising rodent. In *Chromosomes Today, 4* (J. WAHRMAN AND K. R. LEWIS, eds.), pp. 399–424. Israel Universities Press, Jerusalem, and John Wiley & Sons, New York.

WESTERGAARD, M., and VON WETTSTEIN, D. 1972. The synaptinemal complex. *Ann. Rev. Gen., 6,* 71–110.

WILLIAMS, E., HESLOP-HARRISON, J., and DICKINSON, H. G. 1973. The activity of the nucleolus organising region and the origin of cytoplasmic nucleoloids in meiocytes of *Lilium. Protoplasma, 77,* 79–93.

WILSON, E. B. 1896. *The Cell.* Macmillan, New York.

CHROMOSOMES IN ELONGATE SPERM HEADS

MURIEL H. WALKER and HERBERT C. MACGREGOR

Department of Zoology, School of Biological Sciences,
University of Leicester, Leicester, U.K.

There is a comparatively large literature on the subject of the changes which occur in the spermatid during spermiogenesis. In the case of elongate sperm heads, these changes consist in an alteration in shape of the nucleus from spherical in the early spermatid to thin and elongated in the mature sperm head. The appearance of the nuclear contents also changes from the interphase-like early spermatid to the mature nucleus, which has densely packed nucleoprotein of homogeneous appearance, within which no fine structure can be determined.

The changes in the ultrastructure of the nucleus during spermiogenesis vary from species to species, but in elongate sperm heads there are three basic patterns which these changes follow (Walker, 1971). The first of these is a fibrous pattern. The nucleoprotein of the early spermatid aggretates into fibers or filaments. The fibers become thicker as spermiogenesis proceeds and eventually fuse in the mature sperm nucleus. The second pattern, the lamellar type, is seen in the desert locust, *Schistocera gregaria.* The early spermatid nucleus is spherical and has a diameter of about 8 μm. The nuclear contents appear granular with several dense patches localized randomly in the nucleoplasm (fig. 1). At a slightly later stage the nucleus is still rounded, but several indentations can be seen at various points around the perimeter. The nucleoprotein appears as thin threads randomly orientated among a background of dispersed granular material (fig. 2). As the nucleus elongates, the nucleoprotein threads aggregate into sheets or lamellae. When these first appear they show no definite pattern when viewed in transverse section, sometimes coiling back on themselves to form complete circles (fig. 3). These sheets are about 12 to 16 nm thick. The amount of granular material apparent in the nucleus is considerably reduced. Later spermatids have a smaller nuclear diameter and there is no longer any evidence of invaginations around the periphery. In transverse section the nucleoprotein appears as a meshwork of interconnecting polygons with walls of fairly uniform thickness, about 12 nm (fig. 4). Oblique longitudinal sections of nuclei at this stage demonstrate a parallel alignment of the nucleoprotein lamellae (fig. 5). Gradually the spaces between the lamellae become variable in shape (fig. 6). The mature nucleus is about 0.35 μm in diameter and about 100 μm in length. Its nucleoprotein appears as an electron-dense mass of homogeneous material (fig. 7).

Condensation patterns similar to that of *Schistocera* are found in other locusts and grasshoppers (Gibbons and Bradfield, 1957; Dass and Ris, 1958; Gall and Bjork, 1958).

The red-backed salamander, *Plethodon cinereus cinereus*, provides an example of the third pattern of condensation, the granular pattern (Macgregor and Walker, 1973). During spermiogenesis the spermatid nucleus gradually becomes longer and thinner. While the spermatid nucleus is elongating, its nucleoprotein has a fine granular appearance (fig. 8). After elongation is complete the nucleoprotein clumps

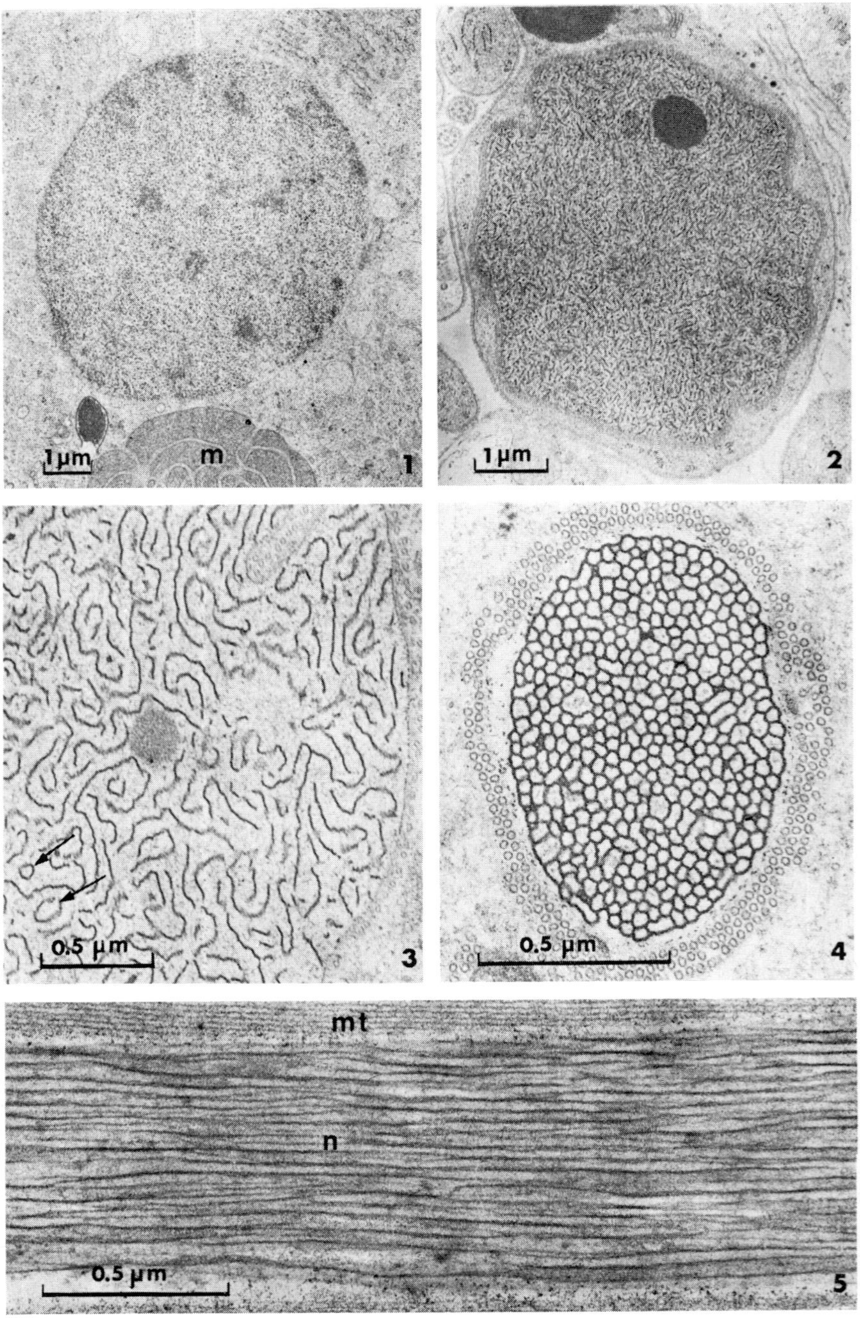

into a coarse granular form, the granules being 38 to 53 nm in diameter (fig. 9). At first there are relatively few granules scattered randomly throughout the nucleus. Later they become more numerous and are uniformly distributed. These coarse granules coalesce to form the compact nucleoprotein of the mature nucleus fig. 10). The dimensions of the mature nucleus are 72 × 1 μm.

These patterns of condensation have been observed in many different species; examples are given in table 1.

From ultrastructural studies, Gall and Bjork (1958) and Hsu (1968) have suggested that the fibers seen in early spermatids of the grasshoppers *Dissosteira* and *Melanoplus* and the ascidian *Boltenia villosa* represent uncoiled chromosomes. Gall and Bjork further suggested that in the grasshopper the chromosomes might be arranged in tandem. Hsu suggested that in *Boltenia* the chromosomes are possibly arranged in tandem, with each chromosome folded back and forth within a particular segment of the nucleus. We feel, however, that such deductions as to the possible arrangement of chromosomes in sperm heads made from thin sectioned material should be viewed most critically.

There is more conclusive evidence from several other workers which indicates that in elongate sperm heads the chromosomes are arranged in a tandem but possibly random order along the length of the sperm head. These data are summarized in table 2. From table 2 it is apparent that the condensation patterns seen in these species are either fibrous or lamellar.

We have used the technique of *in situ* hybridization (Gall and Pardue, 1969) to search for further information. *Plethodon cinereus cinereus* has 14 metacentric or submetacentric chromosomes, and it also has a high-density "satellite" DNA which has been shown to be cytologically localized around the centromeres on all 14 chromosomes of this animal (Macgregor and Kezer, 1971; Macgregor et al., 1973). ^{3}H-RNA complementary to this high-density satellite has been hybridized *in situ* to spermatids and sperm from *P. c. cinereus* and its site of binding has been determined by autoradiography (Macgregor and Walker, 1973). Labeling of round early spermatid nuclei is localized in a single patch. Elongate spermatid nuclei are labeled only over the rear quarter of the nucleus (fig. 11). In the mature sperm the label is localized in a region extending 10–20 μm forwards from the rear of the nucleus (fig. 12).

In *P. c. cinereus* the ribosomal genes are located near the centromere on the short arm of the seventh longest chromosome (Macgregor and Kezer, 1973). Ribosomal ^{3}H-RNA hybridizes to DNA in a short segment in the rear half of the elongated

---

FIG. 1.—Early spermatid nucleus from *Schistocera gregaria* (*m*—mitochondrial nebenkerne). × 5,700.

FIG. 2.—Spermatid nucleus from *Schistocera* showing the fine threads of nucleoprotein. × 10,100.

FIG. 3.—Transverse section of a later spermatid nucleus from *Schistocerca* showing the nucleoprotein aggregated into lamellae. Some of the lamellae are seen to coil back on themselves and form complete circles (arrowed). × 30,200.

FIG. 4.—Transverse section of an elongated spermatid nucleus from *Schistocera*. The nucleoprotein lamellae are arranged as a meshwork of interconnecting polygons. × 50,500.

FIG. 5.—Longitudinal section of an elongated spermatid nucleus from *Schistocera* showing the parallel alignment of the nucleoprotein lamellae (*n*—nucleus; *mt*—microtubules). × 49,100.

spermatid nucleus (fig. 13). In nearly mature spermatids, the length of the labeled segment is never more than 20 μm. We suggest that these results indicate that in *P. c. cinereus* each chromosome is arranged in a U formation, with its centromere at the base of the sperm nucleus and its arms extending forwards along the length of

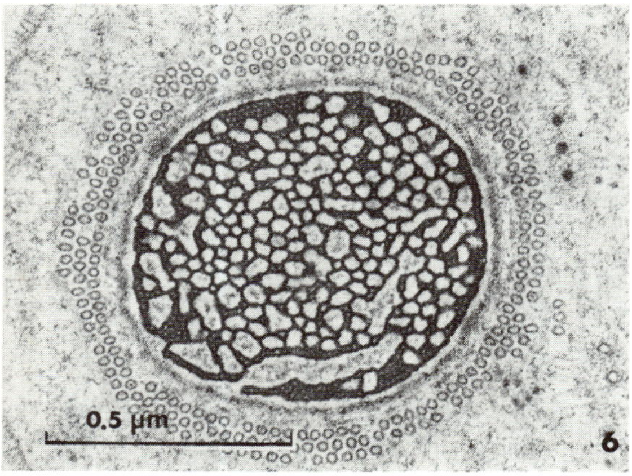

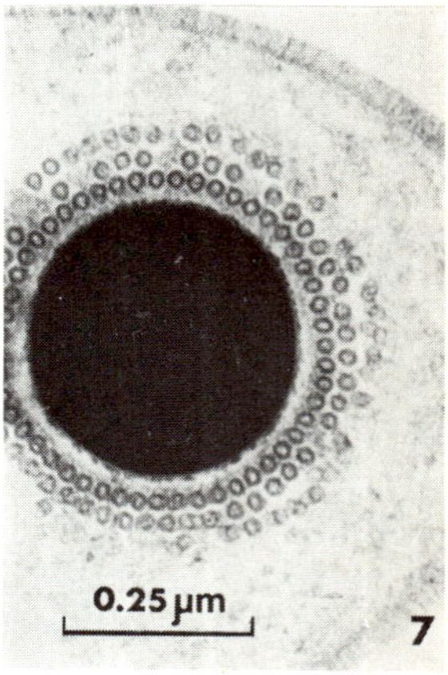

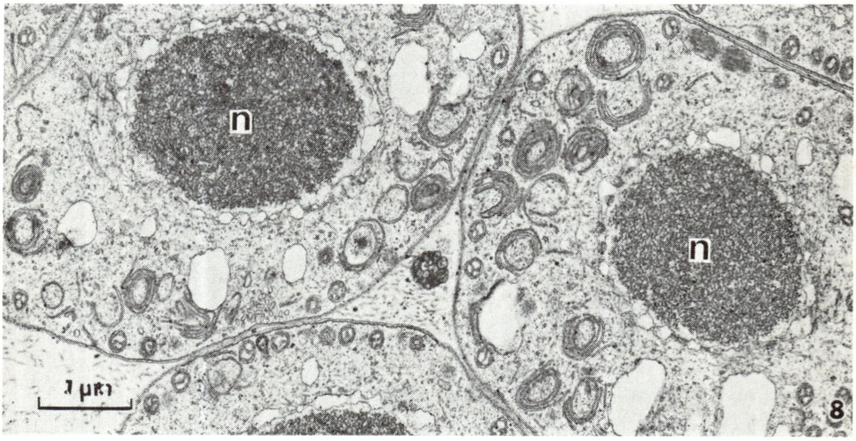

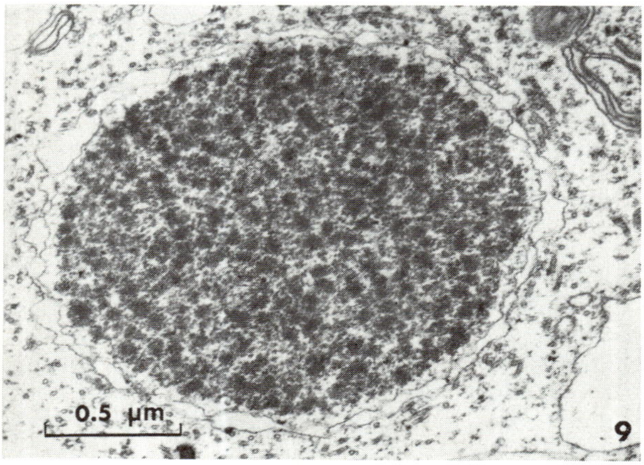

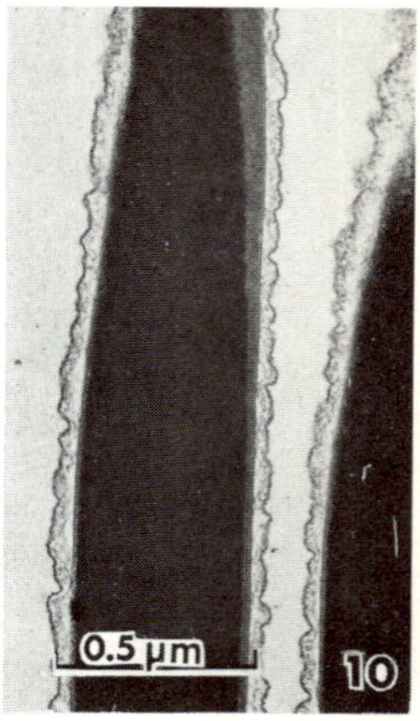

TABLE 1

	Fibrous	Lamellar	Granular
Annelida	*Spirorbis mörchi* (Potswald, 1967)	*Enchytraeus albidus* (Reger, 1967)	
Insecta	*Steatococcus tuberculatus* (Moses and Wilson, 1970) *Aeschna grandis* (Kessel, 1966) *Acheta domestica* (Kaye and McMaster-Kaye, 1966)	*Locusta migratoria* (Gibbons and Bradfield, 1957) *Chortophaga viridifasciata* *Chorthippus curtipennis* *Romalea microptera* (Dass and Ris, 1958) *Dissosteira carolina* *Melanoplus femur-rubrum* (Gall and Bjork, 1958) *Schistocera gregaria* (Dunn and Walker, unpubl.)	
Mollusca	*Cipangopaludina malleata* (Yasuzumi and Tanaka, (1958)	*Nucella lapillus* (Walker and Macgregor, 1968) *Viviparus contectoides* (Kaye, 1958) *Otala lactea* (Rebhun, 1957).	
Chordata			*Plethodon cinereus* (Macgregor and Walker, 1973) *Pleurodeles walthii* (Picheral, 1967) *Xenopus laevis* *Triturus cristatus cristatus* (Walker, unpublished) *Desmognathus fuscus fuscus* (Lommen, 1970) *Gallus domesticus* (McIntosh and Porter, 1967)

FIG. 6.—Transverse section of a late spermatid nucleus from *Schistocerca* showing the variation in the spaces between the nucleoprotein lamellae. × 57,700.

FIG. 7.—Transverse section of an almost mature sperm head from *Schistocerca*. The nucleoprotein appears homogeneous. × 63,800.

FIG. 8.—Transverse section of a spermatid nucleus (*n*) from *Plethodon cinereus cinereus* after elongation and before condensation. × 12,800.

FIG. 9.—Transverse section of a later spermatid from *P. c. cinereus* showing the nucleoprotein clumped into coarse granules 38 to 54 nm in diameter. × 33,250.

FIG. 10.—Oblique section of part of a mature sperm nucleus from *P. c. cinereus* showing the homogeneous appearance of the nucleoprotein. × 31,500.

the nucleus. Also in support of this suggestion is the observation that among plethodontid salamanders that have the same number of chromosomes, an increase in the "C" value (Macgregor and Horner, unpublished) and a corresponding increase in chromosome size is accompanied by an increase in length rather than width of the sperm nucleus (Macgregor and Walker, 1973).

What conclusions can be drawn from these results? The most striking conclusion

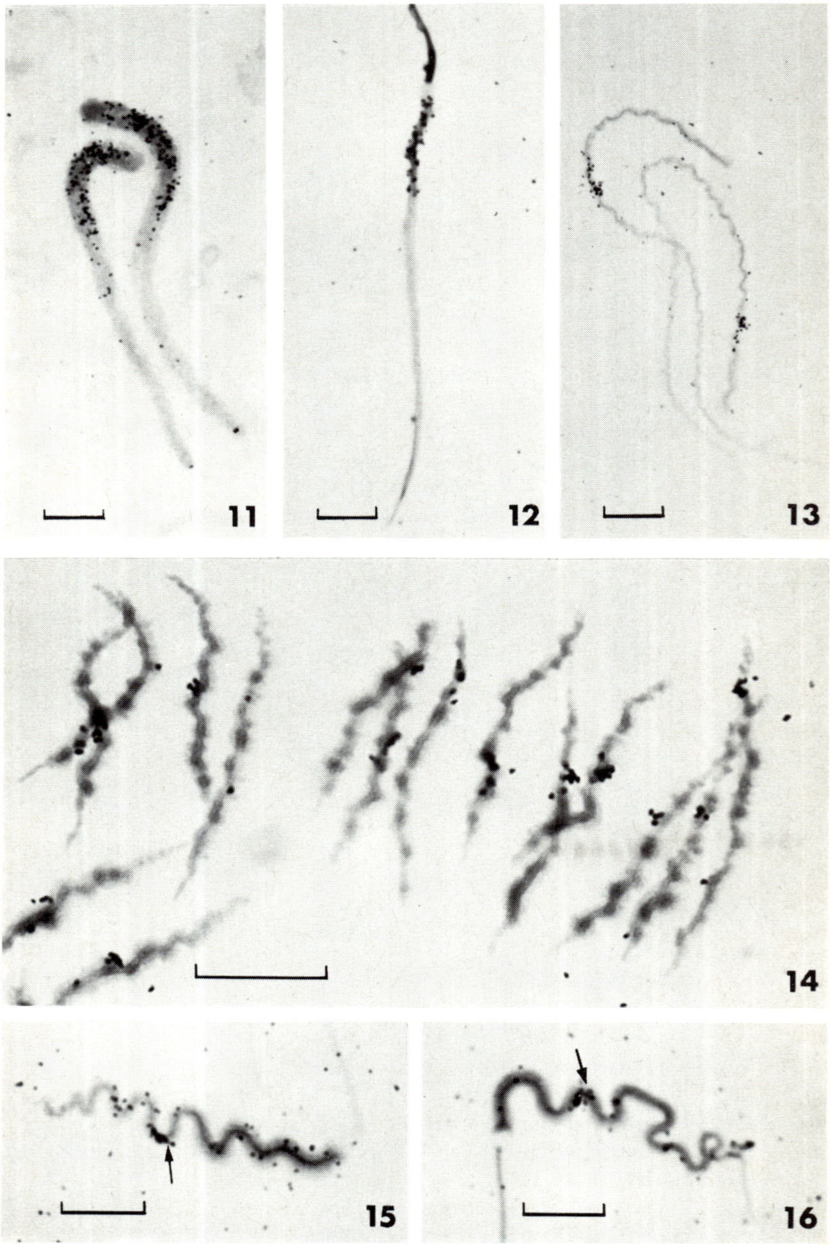

TABLE 2

Species	Haploid chromosome number	Condensation pattern	Chromosome arrangement	Reference
Steatococcus tuberculatus	2	Fibrous	Tandem, non-random	Hughes-Schrader (1946) Moses and Wilson (1970)
Romalea microptera	11(±X)	Lamellar	Tandem and random	Taylor (1964)
Ceuthophilus nigricans	18 and 19	Fibrous	Tanden, non-random	Inoué and Sato (1962, 1966)

is that in *P. c. cinereus* the arrangement of the chromosomes in the sperm head is quite different from that described in other species with elongate sperm heads. The second factor which is of probable significance is that in *P. c. cinereus* the nucleus condenses in a granular pattern, whereas in species which are known to have a tandem arrangement of chromosomes, the nuclei have been shown to condense in either a fibrous or lamellar pattern. We would suggest that the arrangement of chromosomes in elongate sperm heads is linked to the pattern of condensation seen during spermiogenesis. In sperm where the condensation pattern is fibrous or lamellar the chromosomes are arranged in tandem, and where the pattern is granular, as in *P. c. cinereus*, the chromosome arms lie alongside one another, the chromosomes being in a U formation.

Unfortunately the picture is not simple. Ribosomal ^{3}H-RNA hybridizes to a short segment in spermatid and sperm nuclei from *Xenopus* and *Triturus* (Macgregor and Walker, 1973). In these animals the position of the labeled segment varies from sperm to sperm (figs. 14, 15, and 16). In both the condensation pattern is granular (Walker, unpublished). In *Xenopus* the nucleolar organizer is located on the short arm of a submetacentric chromosome (Kahn, 1962). Also in *Xenopus*, Pardue et al. (1973) have shown by *in situ* hybridization that 5S ribosomal RNA is located at or

FIGS. 11–16.—Autoradiographs of squash preparations that have been processed for *in situ* hybridization and stained with Giemsa. In every case the scale indicated on the photograph represents 10 μm. FIG. 11.—*P. c. cinereus*. Elongate spermatid nuclei after *in situ* hybridization with ^{3}H-RNA complementary to high-density satellite DNA. Silver grains indicating bound RNA are confined to the rear quarter of the nucleus. × 810. FIG. 12.—*P. c. cinereus*. Mature sperm nucleus after *in situ* hybridization with ^{3}H-RNA complementary to high-density satellite DNA. Silver grains are present over the rear quarter of the nucleus only. × 810. FIG. 13.—*P. c. cinereus*. Nearly mature spermatid nuclei after *in situ* hybridization with ribosomal ^{3}H-RNA. The nucleolar organizer is marked by a cluster of silver grains, about 10 μm long, located in the rear half of the nucleus. × 810. FIG. 14.—*Xenopus laevis*. Late spermatid nuclei after *in situ* hybridization with ribosomal ^{3}H-RNA. The position of the nucleolar organizer is marked in most nuclei by a small cluster of silver grains, the position of which varies from nucleus to nucleus. × 1,700. FIGS. 15 and 16.—*Triturus cristatus cristatus*. Nuclei of mature sperm after *in situ* hybridization with ribosomal ^{3}H-RNA. The position of the nucleolar organizer is marked in each case by a compact cluster of silver grains (arrow). × 1,100.

near the telomere region of the long arm of many, if not all, chromosomes. They also hybridized 5S ^{3}H-RNA to *Xenopus* spermatids and found the label as a series of clusters along the length of the nucleus. The pattern of the clusters varied from sperm to sperm.

We would therefore suggest that where the nucleoprotein condenses in a granular pattern the chromosome arms lie side by side along the length of the sperm head. However, the position of the chromosomes within the sperm head will show variation according to the variations in the sizes and centromere position of chromosomes in different species. In *P. c. cinereus* where the chromosomes are large metacentric or submetacentric, the side-by-side arrangement of the chromosome arms is accommodated in the sperm head with the chromosomes in a U configuration.

We feel that, when suitable markers are available, the technique of *in situ* hybridization offers many possibilities for the study of chromosome arrangement in sperm heads. The markers must be localized regions of highly repetitive DNA the position of which can be cytologically demonstrated. So far ribosomal DNA, centromeric satellite DNA (Macgregor and Walker, 1973), and 5S DNA (Pardue et al., 1973) have been successfully used as markers. Many more cytological peculiarities, such as B chromosomes and heterochromatic chromosome ends, may be worth investigating in this regard. We are at present investigating a potentially useful situation in *Schistocera* which has early diplotene chromosomes with heterochromatic ends, a heterochromatic X chromosome, a small high-density satellite DNA that can be purified by preparative ultracentrifugation, and long filamentous sperm heads.

SUMMARY

1. Mature sperm nuclei from *Plethodon cinereus cinereus* measure 72 × 1 μm. The nucleoprotein of *P. c. cinereus* spermatids is at first finely granular. As the spermatids elongate it clumps into larger granules which then fuse to form the compact nucleoprotein of the mature sperm nucleus.

2. Plethodontid salamanders have n = 13 or 14 large metacentric or submetacentric chromosomes. ^{3}H-RNA complementary to high-density satellite DNA of centromeric heterochromatin in *P. c. cinereus* has been hybridized *in situ* to spermatids and mature sperm. Its site of binding to these cells has been examined by autoradiography. These results indicate that in *P. c. cinereus* each chromosome is arranged in a U formation with its centromere at the base of the sperm nucleus, and its arms extending forwards along the length of the nucleus. In *P. c. cinereus*, the arrangement of chromosomes differs from that described by other authors for other elongate sperm heads.

3. These observations will be discussed in the light of possible relationships between the pattern of condensation of the sperm nucleus during spermiogenesis and the arrangement of chromosomes in a sperm head.

Acknowledgement. We would like to express our thanks to Miss Marian Dunn who carried out the initial work on the ultrastructure of *Schistocerca*. The work was supported by S.R.C. Grant No. B/SR/4468, and M.R.C. Grant No. 971/55/B. Figures 8–16 are reproduced by permission of Springer-Verlag.

REFERENCES

DASS, C. M., and RIS, H. 1958. Submicroscopic organization of the nucleus during spermiogenesis in a grasshopper. *J. Biophys. Biochem. Cytol., 4,* 129–132.

GALL, J. G., and BJORK, L. B. 1958. The spermatid nucleus in two species of grasshopper. *J. Biophys. Biochem. Cytol., 4,* 479–484.

GALL, J. G., and PARDUE, M. L. 1969. Formation and detection of RNA–DNA hybrid molecules in cytological preparations. *Proc. Natl. Acad. Sci. U.S.A., 63,* 378–383.

GIBBONS, I. P., and BRADFIELD, J. R. G. 1957. The fine structure of nuclei during sperm maturation in the locust. *J. Biophys. Biochem. Cytol., 3,* 133–140.

HSU, W. S. 1968. Fine structure observations on the chromosomes in the spermatids of the ascidian, *Boltenia villosa. Chromosoma (Berl.), 24,* 288–299.

HUGHES-SCHRADER, S. 1946. A new type of spermiogenesis in iceryine coccids, with linear alignment of chromosomes in the sperm. *J. Morphol., 78,* 43–84.

INOUÉ, S., and SATO, H. 1962. Arrangement of DNA in living sperm: a biophysical analysis. *Science (Wash. D.C.), 136,* 1122–1124.

INOUÉ, S., and SATO, H. 1966. Deoxyribonucleic acid arrangement in living sperm. In *Molecular Architecture in Cell Physiology* (HAYASHI and SZENT-GYÖRGI, eds.). Prentice-Hall Inc, Englewood Cliffs, New Jersey.

KAHN, J. 1962. The nucleolar organizer in the mitotic chromosome complement of *Xenopus laevis. Q. J. Microsc. Sci., 103,* 407–409.

KAYE, J. S. 1958. Changes in the fine structure of nuclei during spermiogenesis. *J. Morphol., 103,* 311–329.

KAYE, J. S., and MCMASTER-KAYE, R. 1966. The fine structure and chemical composition of nuclei during spermiogenesis in the house cricket. I. Initial stages of differentiation and the loss of non-histone protein. *J. Cell Biol., 31,* 159–179.

KESSEL, R. G. 1966. The association between microtubules and nuclei during spermiogenesis in the dragonfly. *J. Ultrastruct. Res., 16,* 293–304.

LOMMEN, M. A. J. 1970. Development of the ring during spermiogenesis of a salamander. *J. Microsc. (Paris), 8,* 785–800.

MACGREGOR, H. C., and KEZER, J. 1971. The chromosomal localization of a heavy satellite DNA in the testis of *Plethodon c. cinereus. Chromosoma (Berl.), 33,* 167–182.

MACGREGOR, H. C., and KEZER. J. 1973. The nucleolar organizer of *Plethodon cinereus cinereus* (Green). I Location of the nucleolar organizer by *in situ* nucleic acid hybridization. *Chromosoma (Berl.), 42,* 415–426.

MACGREGOR, H. C., and WALKER, M. H. 1973. The arrangement of chromosomes in nuclei of sperm from plethodontid salamanders. *Chromosoma (Berl.), 40,* 243–262.

MACGREGOR, H. C., HORNER, H., OWEN, C. A., and PARKER, I. 1973. Observations on centromeric heterochromatin and satellite DNA in salamanders of the genus *Plethodon. Chromosoma (Berl.), 43,* 329–348.

MCINTOSH, J. R., and PORTER, K. R. 1967. Microtubules in the spermatids of the domestic fowl. *J. Cell Biol., 35,* 153–173.

MOSES, M. J., and WILSON, M. H. 1970. Spermiogenesis in an iceryine coccid, *Steatococcus tubercalatus,* Morrison. *Chromosoma (Berl.), 30,* 373–429.

PARDUE, M. L., BROWN, D. M., and BIRNSTIEL, M. L. 1973. Location of the genes for 5S ribosomal RNA in *Xenopus laevis. Chromosoma (Berl.), 42,* 191–203.

PICHERAL, B. 1967. Structure et organization du spermatozoide de *Pleurodeles waltlii* Michah (Amphibien Urodele). *Arch. Biol., 78,* 193–221.

POTSWALD, H. E. 1967. An electron microscope study of spermiogenesis in *Spirorbis (Laeospira) mörchi* Levinson (Polychaeta). *Z. Zellforsch. Mikrosk. Anat., 83,* 231–240.

REBHUN, L. J. 1957. Nuclear changes during spermiogenesis in a pulmonate snail. *J. Biophys. Biochem. Cytol., 3,* 509–524.

REGER, J. F. 1967. A study on the fine structure of developing spermatozoa from the oligochaete, *Enchytraeus albidus*. *Z. Zellforsch. Mikrosk. Anat.*, *82*, 257–264.

TAYLOR, J. H. 1964. The arrangement of chromosomes in the mature sperm of the grasshopper. *J. Cell Biol.*, *21*, 296–289.

WALKER, M. H. 1971. Studies on the arrangement of nucleoprotein in elongate sperm heads. *Chromosoma (Berl.)*, *34*, 340–354.

WALKER, M. H., and MACGREGOR, H. C. 1968. Spermatogenesis and the structure of the mature sperm in *Nucella lapillus* (L). *J. Cell Sci.*, *3*, 95–104.

YASUZUMI, G., and TANAKA, H. 1958. Spermatogenesis in animals revealed by electron microscopy. VI. Researches on the spermatozoon dimorphism in a pond snail, *Cipangopalundina malleata*. *J. Biophys. Biochem. Cytol.*, *4*, 621–632.

CHROMOSOMES IN HUMAN SPERMATOZOA

J. P. M. GERAEDTS and P. L. PEARSON

Instituut voor Anthropogenetica, Rijksuniversiteit, Leiden, The Netherlands

1. INTRODUCTION

Theoretically there are a number of ways one can study the chromosomal content of spermatozoa; some of these are applicable to man. If one chromosome is known to be late replicating, such as the Y chromosome in several rodent species (Bianchi and De Bianchi, 1969; Tiepolo et al., 1967), it is possible to demonstrate the asynchronously replicating chromosome by autoradiography. This method is of no use in human studies where it is almost impossible to obtain testis biopsy material combined with an administration of radioactive chemicals. A second approach is the *in situ* hybridization of satellite DNA complementary labeled RNA (Walker and Macgregor, this volume, p. 13). In man this probably can be done with satellites II and III which are known to be preferentially located on chromosomes 1 and 16 (Jones and Corneo, 1971) and chromosome 9, respectively (Saunders et al., 1972). A third theoretical possibility is the fusion of spermatozoa with somatic cells, which has been demonstrated for rabbit spermatozoa (Gledhill et al. 1972), followed by premature chromosome condensation. In this type of experiment it is not the fusion efficiency but the rate of premature chromosome condensation which seems to be the limiting factor (Johnson et al., 1970).

The development of differential chromosomal staining techniques has led to a new approach in the study of the chromosomal constitution of human male gametes. In dividing somatic and meiotic cells it is now possible to stain up specifically three human chromosomes, namely chromosomes 1, 9, and Y. These chromosomes can also be identified in interphase cells and spermatozoa. The distal part of the long arm of the Y chromosome was discovered to be brightly fluorescent after quinacrine mustard staining of human metaphase chromosomes (Zech, 1969), and shortly afterwards it was found that it could also be visualized by atebrine fluorescence in somatic interphase nuclei (Pearson et al., 1970), the meiotic series (Pearson and Bobrow, 1970), and human spermatozoa (Barlow and Vosa, 1970). The later development of specific staining techniques for human chromosomes 9 and 1 has shown that once a specific staining reaction is obtained on mitotic metaphases, one can attempt to identify the chromosomes in resting cells and in testis biopsy material,

The secondary constriction region of chromosome 9 can be differentiated by a Giemsa solution of pH 11.6 (Bobrow et al., 1972; Gagné and Laberge, 1972). After this so-called Giemsa-11 procedure has been applied to a sperm slide, some regions show completely blue cells and others completely red ones. In the area where these regions meet, blue spermatozoa show a red-staining secondary constriction region of chromosome 9.

The staining of chromosome 1 (Geraedts and Pearson, 1973*a*) is based on heat denaturation followed by incubation in 0.2 M CsCl at 65°C prior to Leishman staining. Chromosome 1 is then visible as a body which is similar to chromosome 9 in respect to its size but not to its color. It is only distinguishable from the nuclear background by its high stain density (fig 1). While studying a number of specimens with these techniques, it soon became clear that relatively many human spermatozoa contain two copies instead of one of each of the chromosomes under study. We have paid special attention to this aspect of spermatogenesis, namely meiotic non-disjunction, by looking at differentially stained spermatozoa.

"Human male meiosis, however, faithfully follows the norm of meiosis. There is nothing exceptional about the process," was stated by Ohno in 1970. Now, only four years later, we have evidence to doubt this opinion.

For exact staining recipes the reader is referred to the original articles.

2. Y CHROMOSOMES IN HUMAN SPERMATOZOA

The three studies represented in table 1 indicate that on average, about 55, 44, and 1% of all human gametes contain 0, 1, and 2 Y bodies, respectively. The criteria for scoring a cell as double Y body positive are that these bodies are identical in size and intensity and that they are far enough apart to distinguish them from a bifid structure. Giant forms are not included in the category containing the doubles, since they may be polyploid (Sumner, 1971). In fact, Pawlowitzki and Pearson (1972) showed that about one in every seven spermatozoa with two Y bodies is polyploid. Even under the most favorable microscopical circumstances, such as little or no background fluorescense, large Y bodies, and few morphologically abnormal sperm cells, the quinacrine staining technique does not permit one to observe the expected 50% Y body-positive cells.

3. AUTOSOMES IN HUMAN SPERMATOZOA

To date, the studies on the two autosomes 1 and 9 are less extensive than those reported for the Y chromosome. This is due to the greater technical difficulties in getting the staining reaction to work adequately on spermatozoa.

For chromosome 9, the frequency of disomics has been estimated to be on average 2.8 ± 1.0 % (Pearson et al., 1973).

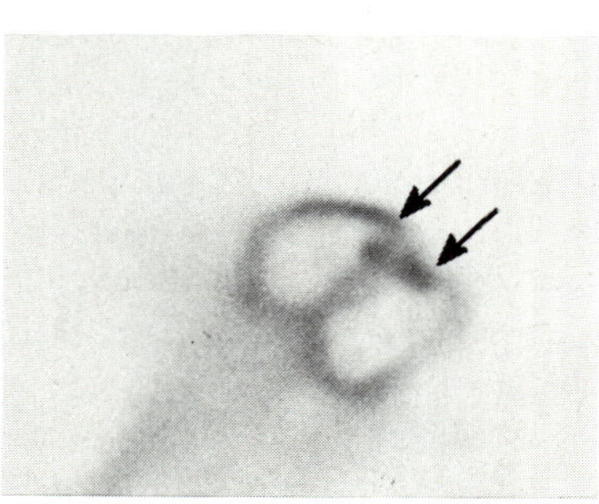

FIG. 1.—Each head of this bicephalic spermatozoan contains a chromosome 1 body. In respect of the positions of these bodies, the two daughter nuclei appear to be mirror images.

TABLE 1

Total no. of cells	O Y bodies	1 Y body	2 Y bodies	Specimens obtained from	Reference
1,420 spermatids	733 (51.62 %)	666 (46.90 %)	21 (1.48 %)	3 normal subjects	Pearson and Bobrow (1970)
5,000 spermatozoa	2,850 (56.94 %)	2,087 (41.80 %)	63 (1.26 ± 0.26 %)	1 normal subject + 3 ind. attend. inf. clinic	Sumner et al. (1971)
9,835 spermatozoa	5,379 (54.69 %)	4.333 (44.06 %)	123 (1.25 ± 0.45 %)	11 normal subjects	Pawlowitzki and Pearson (1972)
Total	8,962 (55.13 %)	7,086 (43.59 %)	207 (1.27 %)		

The data on chromosome 1 are also limited. However, at present we have found a non-disjunction rate which is slightly less than the one observed for chromosome 9. The sizes of both 1 and 9 bodies in sperm are similar to those observed in somatic interphase nuclei and they seem to remain constant during spermatogenesis.

One very plausible interpretation of the finding that the autosomal non-disjunction rates are higher than those observed for the Y chromosome is that these chromosomes have a greater chance of undergoing meiotic disjunction, namely possibilities for non-disjunction at both MI and MII as compared to only MII non-disjunction in the Y. The relative proportions of non-disjunction events occurring at each division can be calculated from bicephalic spermatozoa as described in the following section.

4. CHROMOSOMES IN HUMAN BICEPHALIC SPERMATOZOA

In one volunteer, 22 % of the spermatozoa were bicephalic. We believe that the two heads united together on the same tail contain the daughter nuclei of the second meiotic division. These double-headed cells gave us the opportunity to study the non-disjunction events during MI and MII separately. Spermatozoa with normal disjunction of chromosomes 1 and 9 will show one body in every head. After non-segregation during MI, there are two possible types of double-headed spermatozoa: either both with two (disomic) or with no (nullosomic) bodies. A second meiotic non-disjunction, on the other hand, will result in a pair of spermatozoa, one of which is disomic and the other nullosomic.

Theoretically, half the number of bicephalics are Y bearing and will therefore show a 1:1 distribution. The observed number of cells showing Y staining will be lowered by staining incompleteness as in normal spermatozoa. Since the Y chromosome is the only sex chromosome we can recognize, first meiotic metaphase non-disjunction will remain undiscovered in this system and only the 2:0 situation which originates at MII may be found. In table 2 the data are summarized.

The double nullosomics were left out, because it is impossible to make the distinction between true nullosomy and inadequate staining. For all other expected classes, spermatozoa were found to occur, which means that at both meiotic divisions

TABLE 2

Staining of chromosomes 1, 9, and Y in bicephalic spermatozoa from a single subject (*Pearson et al., 1973*)

Chromosomes	Distribution in each head					% positive
	1:1	1:0	2:0	2:2	2:1	non-disjunction
1	184	2	4	2	(1)	2.1
9	39	0	1	1	0	3.7
Y lab I	267	11	5	(1)	0	0.9
Y lab II	929	135	12	0	(4)	0.6

non-disjunctions occur for the autosomes. Furthermore, the non-disjunction frequencies observed in this experiment do not disagree with those found in morphologically normal spermatozoa.

Understaining occurs much more frequently among the cells stained for Y chromosomes than among those stained for chromosomes 1 and 9. This can be seen from the numbers of cells in the 0:1 category. The observations on the 2:2 and 2:0 distributions show that, although we are unable to identify nullosomic sperms in normal ejaculates, these cells probably occur at the same frequency as the doubles.

Therefore, the total frequency of aneuploid spermatozoa for the three chromosomes studied so far must be double the observed number. This means that only about 96% of all spermatozoa are normal for chromosomes 1, 9, or Y. If this figure is extrapolated to all chromosomal pairs, only 0.96^{23}, i.e., about 40% of human spermatozoa, will have the correct haploid chromosomal content. The result of this extrapolation depends not only on the limited estimates carried out so far, but also on the assumption that chromosomes without large blocks of heterochromatin (which cannot be differentially stained at present) undergo non-disjunction at similar rates as chromosomes 1, 9, and Y.

One way of getting information on this matter would be to investigate the DNA distribution in a population of spermatozoa which have undergone non-disjunction and to compare it with the distribution of DNA in a standard with little or no non-disjunction.

5. DNA AND AREA MEASUREMENTS

The production and measurement of DNA of spermatozoa were simulated in a digital computer. A random number generator was used to induce non-disjunction during meiosis; the frequency could be varied independently for each chromosomal pair. In addition, the Feulgen staining and Leitz MPV II measuring error could be varied. A typical result of this simulation was that, with a 2% non-disjunction and 4% measuring error, the mean DNA contents of two spermatozoa populations differing in their X and Y chromosome content were significantly different at the 0.01% level after measuring only 160 cells. Accordingly, we have measured the DNA content of a population of human X and Y spermatozoa by Feulgen photometry (Geraedts and Pearson, 1973*b*). After actually measuring 100 cells per population, the predicted difference between the two populations was observed; it was 3.9%, which is exactly the DNA content difference between the two sex chromosomes.

From the Monte Carlo experiments it could perhaps be concluded that the observed high standard deviations on the means (11% for Y-, 10% for X-bearing spermatozoa) has a biological basis over and above the variations induced by staining and measuring errors. A series of DNA measurements carried out by Sumner et al. (1971) gave the same result in respect to the DNA difference between X- and Y-bearing populations. However, these authors did not observe any surface area difference, while we observed a 7% difference between the two populations. Apart from technical measurement details, the two series of measurements differed in the way the cells were pretreated. Sumner et al. used fixed smears while the ejaculated spermatozoa in our experiments were washed prior to fixation and air-drying. At present we are conducting a new series of measurements to confirm the DNA and area differences in two other individuals and to define other parameters such as shape and dry mass.

6. THE POSITION OF CHROMOSOMES

When the Y body was observed for the first time in spermatozoa, Barlow and Vosa (1970) reported that it was seen to lie at the boundary between the dense and less dense regions of chromatin in more than 60% of the spermatozoa. The results of our observations on chromosome position are shown in fig. 2. Two hundred Giemsa-11-stained sperms were recorded on photographs and, after destaining in methanol, were stained with atebrine. Although many of the cells were swollen after the procedure

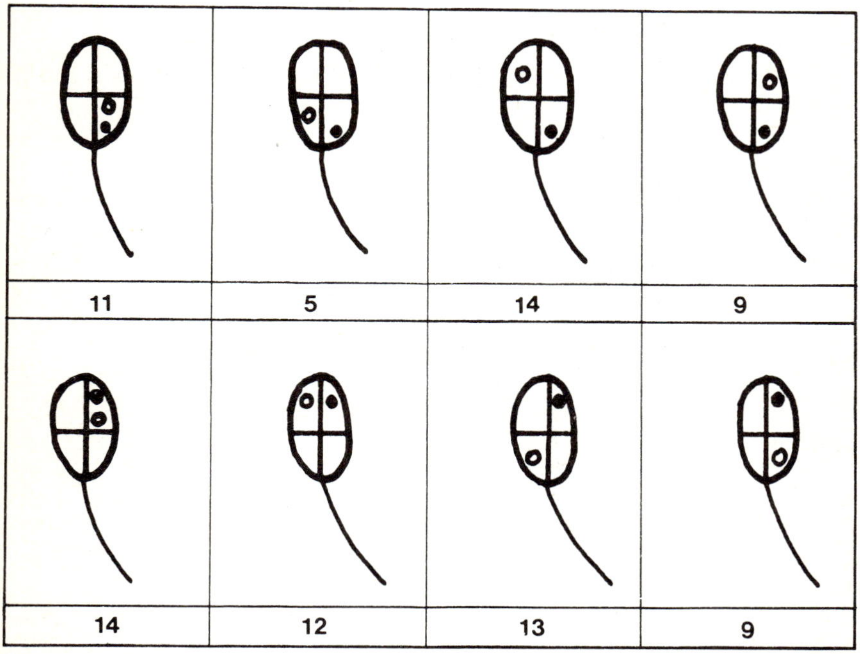

FIG. 2.—The positions of the Y chromosome (open circle) and chromosome 9 (closed circle) of the same cells. The sperm head was arbitrarily divided into four segments. The eight possible permutations were found to have an equal frequency.

(fig. 3), the position of the Y chromosome could be identified and localized in 87 of them (43.5%). The sperm head was arbitrarily divided into four parts with the tail as a fixed reference point, and chromosomes Y and 9 were drawn in one of these quarters. Excluding mirror images for either the two bottom or top segments, eight possible permutations can be expected. From this experiment two conclusions can be drawn: (a) there is no absolute preferential location of either chromosome 9 or Y; and (b) the positions of 9 and Y relative to each other seem random. However, this experiment cannot substantiate the second conclusion since we can only interpret the three-dimensional object as a two-dimensional image for this purpose. However, the observations on bicephalic spermatozoa support the idea that some ordering and non-randomness occurs, at least among daughter nuclei. In the cells with both a 1:1 and 2:2 distribution, the two heads were very often seen as mirror images. This finding indicates that the packing of the chromatin may be non-random as far as the daughter cells resulting from the same MII division are concerned.

7. X AND Y CHROMOSOMES IN GAMETES OF *MICROTUS OECONOMUS*

In respect to his apparently high non-disjunction frequencies, man may be a unique creature; he is certainly unique in his inaccessibility to experimentation. Therefore, development of a sperm staining system in experimental animals would

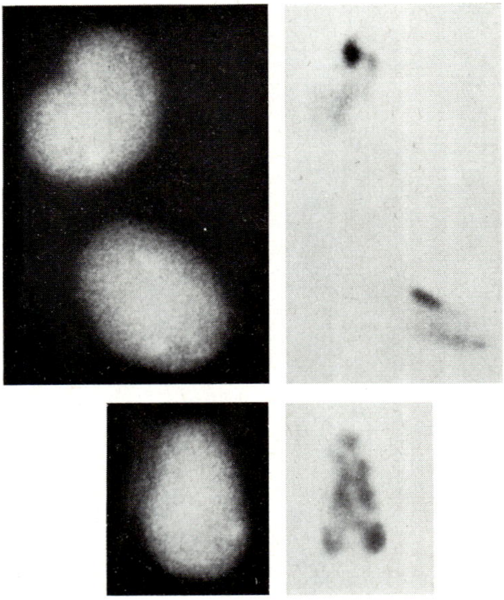

FIG. 3.—The same spermatozoa after atebrine (left) and Giemsa-11 (right) staining. In the two upper cells, chromosomes 9 and Y are diametrically opposite, whereas in the bottom cell the position of both chromosomes is identical. Note the swelling of spermatozoa after atebrine staining.

be useful. Firstly, it would give an insight into the spontaneous non-disjunction frequency in a species other than man. Secondly, the effect of environmental agents on non-disjunction induction could be investigated. In addition, the technique could serve as an indicator of the success with which X and Y spermatozoa can be separated, as in man (Ericsson et al., 1973), but with the advantage that the sex ratio could be compared with the one at birth after artificial insemination. *Microtus oeconomus* is an animal with a heterochromatic Y chromosome and no other large heterochromatic regions in its karyotype. By applying a normal C-banding procedure on meiotic chromosome preparations of two fertile males, it was shown that the Y chromosome was easily identified at diakinesis as an overall darkly stained chromosome (Tates et al., 1975). In early spermatids, the X- and Y-containing cells could be distinguished (fig. 4). We regard the darkly staining block in about half the number of spermatids as the Y chromosome. In the other cells, which lack a Y and therefore contain an X chromosome, a much more diffuse, lighter, and larger body than the

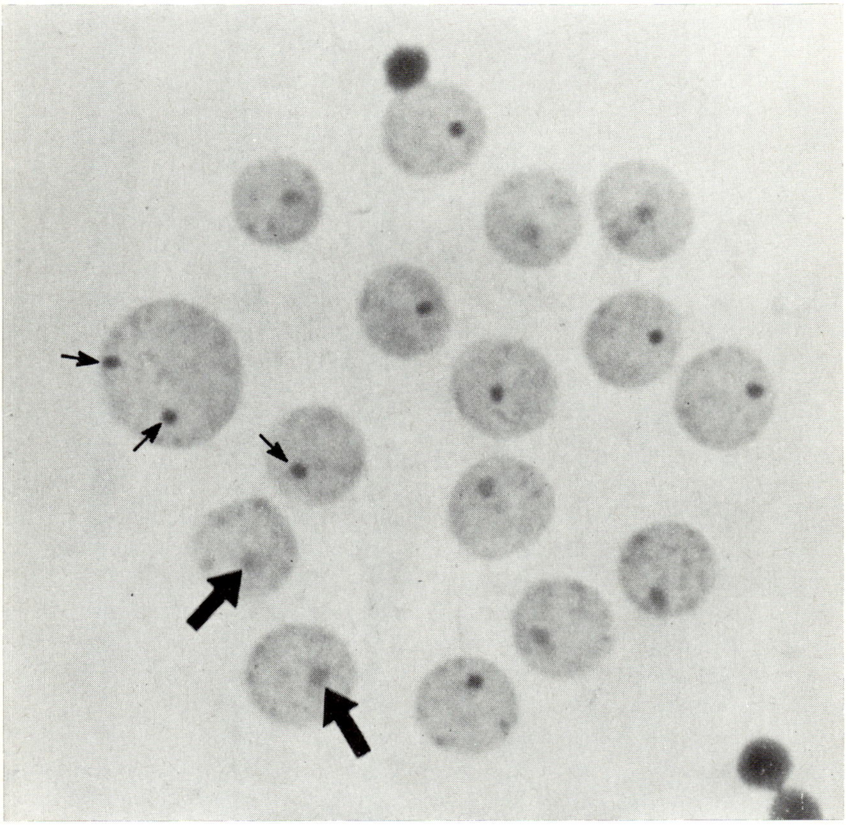

FIG. 4.—This group of spermatids of *Microtus oeconomus* shows a clear distinction between X- (large arrow) and Y-bearing cells (small arrow). There is also a diploid spermatid containing two Y chromosomes.

Y body was present. During late spermiogenesis the presumed X body disappears and about half the mature sperm cells show only the Y chromosomal heterochromatin.

Spermatids of *M. oeconomus* show 0.25% YY-bearing cells (table 3), which is about five times less than human spermatids (Pearson and Bobrow, 1970). Other sex chromosome non-disjunctions which can be positively identified also occur at a very low rate. Finally, table 3 demonstrates that the sex ratio at the beginning of spermiogenesis is not significantly different from 1. These findings indicate that *Microtus oeconomus* is a suitable animal for the experimental approach of non-disjunction studies in mammals.

TABLE 3

Frequencies of normal and non-disjunctional gametes in two male M. oeconomus (*Tates et al., 1975*)

Cell type	Animal 1	Animal 2
Y	388	401
X	350	382
YY	2	2
YX	1	1
XX	1	—

8. SUMMARY

1. This paper describes a way of studying the chromosomal content of spermatozoa, i.e., by using differential staining techniques specific for constitutive heterochromatin.

2. Types of C-banding were developed to demonstrate human chromosomes 1 and 9.

3. The identification of specific chromosomes in spermatozoa allowed us to derive a figure of at least 2% meiotic non-disjunction for all three chromosomes.

4. Almost one-half of all human spermatozoa must be chromosomally abnormal if the nondisjunction frequency is equally high and randomly distributed for every chromosomal pair. From DNA measurements and Monte Carlo experiments this theoretical extrapolation has so far not been invalidated.

5. The study of the position of the different chromosomes in spermatozoa is still a great problem since a microscopical object is a more or less two-dimensional representation of the spatial relationships and, furthermore, it is a problem to use two or three of these peculiar staining techniques on the same cells.

6. Finally, a differential staining technique is presented which distinguishes the Y chromosome in all cell types of *M. oeconomus* and the X chromosomes exclusively in spermatids and the sex vesicle. This technique makes it possible to look for effects which might contribute to the extremely high rate of non-disjunction in man.

Acknowledgements. We gratefully thank Dr. I. H. Pawlowitzki for his cooperation during the study on bicephalic spermatozoa, Dr. K. Fredga for providing *Microtus oeconomus*, and Dr. A. T. Tates for help during the development of the *Microtus* system.

9. REFERENCES

BARLOW, P., and VOSA, C. G. 1970. The Y chromosome in human spermatozoa. *Nature (Lond.)*, *226*, 961–962.

BIANCHI, N. O., and DE BIANCHI, M. S. 1969. Y chromosome replication and chromosome arrangement in germ line cells and sperms of the rat. *Chromosoma (Berl.)*, *28*, 370–378.

BOBROW, M., MADAN, K., and PEARSON, P. L. 1972. Staining of some specific regions of human chromosomes, particularly the secondary constriction of No. 9. *Nat. New Biol.*, *238*, 122–124.

ERICSSON, R. J., LANGEVIN, C. N., and NISHINO, M. 1973. Isolation of fractions rich in human Y sperm. *Nature (Lond.)*, *246*, 421–424.

GAGNÉ, R., and LABERGE, C. 1972. Specific cytological recognition of the heterochromatic segment of number 9 chromosomes in man. *Exp. Cell Res.*, *73*, 239–242.

GERAEDTS, J. P. M., and PEARSON, P. L. 1973*a*. Specific staining of the human No. 1 chromosome in spermatozoa. *Humangenetik*, *20*, 171–173.

GERAEDTS, J. P. M., and PEARSON, P. L. 1973*b*. Chromosomes Y, 1 and 9 in human spermatozoa. *Bull. Eur. Soc. Hum. Genet.*, *5*, 24–31.

GLEDHILL, B. L., SAWICKI, W., CROCE, C. M., and KOPROWSKI, H. 1972. DNA synthesis in rabbit spermatozoa after treatment with lysolecithin and fusion with somatic cells. *Exp. Cell Res.*, *73*, 33–40.

JOHNSON, R. T., RAO, P. N., and HUGHES, H. D. 1970. Mammalian cell fusion. III. A Hela cell inducer of premature chromosome condensation active in cells from a variety of animal species. *J. Cell. Physiol.*, *76*, 151–158.

JONES, K. W., and CORNEO, G. 1971. Location of satellite and homogeneous DNA sequences on human chromosomes. *Nat. New Biol.*, *233*, 268–271.

OHNO, S. 1970. Morphological aspects of meiosis and their general significance. In *The Human Testis* (E. ROSEMBERG and C. A. PAULSEN, eds.), pp. 115–125. Plenum Press, New York.

PAWLOWITZKI, I. H., and PEARSON, P. L. 1972. Chromosomal aneuploidy in human spermatozoa. *Humangenetik*, *16*, 119–122.

PEARSON, P. L., and BOBROW, M. 1970. Fluorescent staining of the Y chromosome in meiotic stages of the human male. *J. Reprod. Fertil.*, *22*, 177–179.

PEARSON, P. L., BOBROW, M., and VOSA, C. G. 1970. Technique for identifying Y chromosomes in human interphase nuclei. *Nature (Lond.)*, *226*, 78–80.

PEARSON, P. L., GERAEDTS, J. P. M., and PAWLOWITZKI, I. H. 1973. Chromosomal studies on human male gametes. In *Les accidents chromosomique de la reproduction* (A. BOUÉ and C. THIBAULT, eds.), pp. 219–229. INSERM, Paris.

SAUNDERS, G. F., HSU, T. C., GETZ, M. J., SIMES, E. L., and ARRIGHI, F. E. 1972. Locations of human satellite in human chromosomes. *Nat. New Biol.*, *236*, 244–246.

SUMNER, A. T. 1971. Frequency of polyploid spermatozoa in man. *Nature (Lond.)*, *231*, 49.

SUMNER, A. T. ROBINSON, J. A., and EVANS, H. J. 1971. Distinguishing between X, Y and YY-bearing human spermatozoa by fluorescence and DNA content. *Nat. New Biol.*, *229*, 231–233.

TATES, A. D., PEARSON, P. L., and GERAEDTS, J. P. M. 1975. Identification of X and Y spermatozoa in *Microtus oeconomus* (Northern vole). *J. Reprod. Fert.*, *42*, 195–198.

TIEPOLO, L., FRACCARO, M., HULTEN, M., LINDSTEN, J., MANNINI, A., and MING, P.-M. L. 1967. Timing of sex chromosome replication in somatic and germ-like cells of the mouse and the rat. *Cytogenetics (Basel)*, *6*, 51–66.

WALKER, M. H. and MACGREGOR, H. C. 1976. Chromosomes in elongate sperm heads. This volume, 13–22.

ZECH, L. 1969. Investigation of metaphase chromosomes with DNA-binding fluorochromes. *Exp. Cell Res.*, *58*, 463.

MEIOSIS IN THE HUMAN MALE

M. A. FERGUSON-SMITH
Department of Genetics, University of Glasgow, Glasgow, U.K.

1. INTRODUCTION

The study of meiosis in man has not received the attention it deserves, largely because opportunities to examine fresh testis material are comparatively rare. Post mortem material is unsuitable as germ cells are rapidly affected by autolysis. Samples of testis taken at operation for testicular biopsy or during orchidectomy for prostatic cancer are the most suitable provided they are processed immediately. Most of our material is obtained by testicular biopsy through the generous collaboration of the staff of the Male Infertility Clinic at the Western Infirmary, Glasgow. During the past seven years we have made meiotic preparations in 154 cases from the Infertility Clinic and approximately 20 others, including eight patients heterozygous for a chromosomal translocation. This paper describes two aspects of our work, namely steps towards the construction of a human pachytene map, and an account of the types of aberrations which we have found to be associated with male infertility. My principal collaborators in this work have been Drs. Colin Campbell, Brenda Page and Eilean Carlin.

2. NORMAL MEIOSIS AND PROBLEMS CONCERNING THE GENETIC MAP LENGTH

Most of our meiotic preparations are made by various modifications of the air-drying method, using different hypotonic treatments for pachytene and diakinesis (Ferguson-Smith, 1964; Hungerford, 1971). The slides are stained lightly in 2% aceto-orcein and are examined under phase contrast. The quinacrine fluorescence and C-banding techniques are valuable for the individual identification of bivalents, but these methods show less of the detailed structure than the time-honoured aceto-orcein technique.

Descriptions of the various stages of male meiosis are detailed elsewhere (Ferguson-Smith, 1973). Spermatogonial metaphase, leptotene, zygotene, pachytene, diakinesis, and second meiotic metaphase are readily distinguished. Diplotene is rarely seen. Estimations of the number of chiasmata, and thus the human map length, have been derived almost exclusively from cells in diakinesis. In our material the mean chiasma count is 51.1 $\pm$ 3.0. This is based on 849 cells in 23 males with normal spermatogenesis and a mean age of 39.5 years. Other estimates of the mean chiasma frequency in man have ranged from 44 to 56, indicating a map length of 22 to 28 morgans (Ford and Hamerton, 1956; Kjessler, 1966; Eberle, 1963; Hultén and Lindsten, 1970; Luciani, 1970). Each bivalent has at least one chiasma and chromosome 1 has on average four chiasmata (table 1). As univalents are almost never seen in normal male meiosis, it follows that each chromosome has one obligatory chiasma. Metacentrics almost invariably have at least one chiasma in each arm. Therefore chiasmata are not distributed randomly per unit length of chromosome. Other factors contribute to an uneven distribution of chiasmata along the chromosome. Hultén (1974) studied the position of chiasmata at diakinesis in bivalents identified by quinacrine fluorescence. She found that chiasmata tend to be clustered at the ends of the arms. When a bivalent arm has only one chiasma, its position is terminal; when there are two chiasmata per arm, one is more distal and the other is proximal.

There is much speculation about the significance of the clustering of chiasmata at the ends of the bivalents. If the positions of the chiasmata remain unchanged from early pachytene to diakinesis, crossing over must be more frequent at the ends of

TABLE 1

Mean chiasma count per bivalent. Control series of 297 cells from 21 patients with apparently normal spermatogenesis (mean age of 38.29 years, SD 10.44)

	Number of chiasmata	S.D.	Relative number of chiasmata
Bivalent 1	4.01	0.39	7.72
2	3.90	0.49	7.51
3	3.12	0.45	6.01
4	3.01	0.31	5.80
5	2.84	0.35	5.47
6	2.65	0.28	5.10
7	2.50	0.20	4.82
8	2.49	0.20	4.80
9	2.38	0.18	4.58
10	2.41	0.26	4.64
11	2.29	0.24	4.41
12	2.28	0.21	4.39
13	2.02	0.19	3.89
14	1.95	0.28	3.76
15	1.87	0.17	3.60
16	2.04	0.06	3.93
17	2.08	0.17	4.01
18	1.92	0.14	3.70
19	1.82	0.14	3.51
20	1.85	0.16	3.56
21	1.31	0.18	2.52
22	1.17	0.14	2.25
Mean number of chiasmata/cell	51.91		
Mean number of chiasmata/bivalent	2.36		

Data compiled by Brenda M. Page and M. A. Ferguson-Smith, Department of Genetics, University of Glasgow.

bivalents than elsewhere. It is difficult to obtain evidence of terminalisation of chiasmata in human meiosis because diplotene is so rare. We compared chiasma counts in 60 cells in early diakinesis with 60 cells in late diakinesis. The mean chiasma count fell from 53.3 ± 5.5 to 51.2 ± 5.0, which is not significant. Bivalents were not individually identified in this study, so we did not compare the distribution of chiasmata in the two samples; this would be well worth attempting.

Support for the view that recombination is more frequent at the ends of the chromosome arms now comes from those actively mapping human genes by chromosome segregation in somatic cell hybrids, by deletion mapping, and by family studies. This work suggests that current estimates of the genetic map length may be too small to accommodate the known linkage groups. In the case of chromosome 1, Cook showed that the genes assigned to the short arm can only be accommodated by extending the end of the arm a further 40 centimorgans (Cook et al., 1974).

Although it might be difficult to demonstrate, it would seem reasonable to expect crossing over at pachytene to occur in the inter-chromomere regions rather than at chromomeres. If this is correct, it would imply that crossing over is less frequent in heterochromatic regions because of the evidence that the large chromomere clusters correspond to positive G bands in mitosis (Ferguson-Smith and Page, 1973). A working hypothesis, based on current information, would be that recombination is non-random and occurs more frequently at the ends of chromosome arms and in negative G bands.

Diakinesis is the most useful stage of meiosis for the identification of chromosome rearrangements, and there are now many reports of ring and chain quadrivalents in males heterozygous for a reciprocal translocation. Trivalents have also been demonstrated in cases of trisomy and centric fusion translocation heterozygotes. More rarely, cases of insertional translocation (Therkelsen et al., 1973), isochromosomes (Hultén and Lindsten, 1970), and inversions (Van der Linden and Pearson, 1975) have been described. All these observations illustrate the value of meiotic analysis in the correct identification of chromosomal rearrangements, although the number which cannot be interpreted without meiotic studies has been reduced by the advent of banding methods.

In second meiotic metaphase most of the chromosomes are difficult to identify owing to the extreme coiling, irregular condensation, and separation of chromatids. Chromosome 9 can be identified by its secondary constriction and the sex chromosomes by their relative heteropyknosis. Up to the present, analysis of second metaphase has been unrewarding in cases of chromosomal rearrangement as so few can be scored unequivocally into balanced, unbalanced, and normal categories.

3. THE HUMAN PACHYTENE MAP

With human gene mapping now proceeding apace, it is of interest to study the behaviour of human bivalents at pachytene. An important preliminary is the identification of each bivalent in terms of the mitotic karyotype. This has been attempted in a number of different ways. It is possible to construct a rough karyotype based on length and centromere position in early pachytene and in well-spread cells. C-banding methods help to define the centromere. More specific identification depends on other factors. Apart from the XY bivalent which is easily identified by its precocious condensation, the first autosomal bivalents to be identified correctly in pachytene were the three large and two small nucleolar bivalents corresponding to the five pairs of satellited chromosomes (Ferguson-Smith, 1964). These were identified in preparations treated without hypotonic solutions, in which the terminal nucleoli were clearly visible. In many cells, the satellited chromosomes cooperate in forming common nucleoli—the meiotic equivalent of satellite association. The individual bivalents of the D and G groups can now often be recognised by their chromomere patterns which, in the main, correspond to the positive G bands in mitosis (figs. 1A and 1B). Hungerford also studied the nucleolar chromosomes at pachytene and showed in an adult male with mosaic Down's syndrome that the smallest of the nucleolar bivalents is the one trisomic in Down's syndrome (Hungerford et al., 1970).

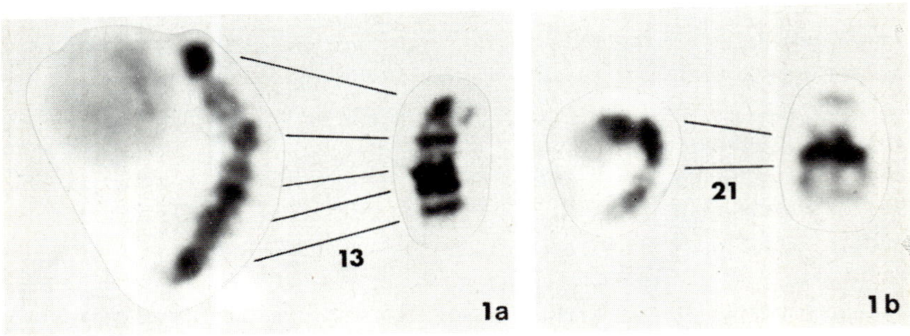

FIG. 1.—Nucleolar bivalent 13 (fig. 1A) and nucleolar bivalent 21 (fig. 1B) stained by 2% aceto-orcein, shown alongside their mitotic counterparts stained by the trypsin-Leishman technique. Note the similarity between the major chromomere patterns at pachytene and the G-banding patterns of the mitotic chromosomes.

The next group of chromosomes to be identified in pachytene are those that carry recognisable polymorphisms. These are the fluorescent centric polymorphisms of 3, 4, and 13 and the paracentric secondary constriction polymorphisms of 1, 9, and 16. Chromosome 16 was first identified in a male heterozygous for a gross enlargement of the centric heterochromatin (Ferguson-Smith, 1973). In the case of chromosome 9, the specific magenta staining reaction of Giemsa at pH 11 (Bobrow et al., 1972) makes its identification throughout meiosis relatively simple (Page, 1973). Geraedts and Pearson (1973) showed recently that chromosome 1 can also be identified by a specific staining reaction.

A promising approach to the correct identification of nonpolymorphic chromosomes is by the use of chromosomal translocations. In a case of a reciprocal 10/11 translocation it was possible to identify the quadrivalent at pachytene (Ferguson-Smith and Page, 1973). The translocation bivalents had such characteristic chromomere patterns that it proved possible to identify chromosomes 10 and 11 in pachytene cells from normal individuals. The relative positions of the major chromomere clusters correspond well with the positive G-bands in the mitotic karyotype. It is hoped that with these techniques it may soon be possible to construct an accurate pachytene map which incorporates the main characteristics of every bivalent.

4. CAUSES OF MALE INFERTILITY REVEALED BY MEIOTIC ANALYSIS

Twenty-one of our 154 consecutive cases undergoing testicular biopsy during the investigation of infertility showed abnormalities on either mitotic or meiotic analysis (table 2). The frequency of 7.3% is similar to that observed in other series (Kjessler, 1966; McIlree et al., 1966; Chandley, 1973). The abnormalities are associated with 3 classes of testicular histopathology, namely, partial or complete absence of germ cells (del Castillo syndrome), maturation arrest of spermatogenesis, and Klinefelter's syndrome. The association of infertility and Klinefelter's syndrome is so well known that the nine cases in this category deserve no further comment.

One patient with a pericentric inversion of chromosome 9 had normal spermatogenesis and the association with infertility was clearly fortuitous as he was later shown to have an obstructive lesion. The bivalent 9 was identified at pachytene and had an unusual appearance. The characteristic cluster of chromomeres usually seen on the long arm close to the centric heterochromatin (Page, 1973) was invariably displaced so that it appeared lateral to the centromere itself. This was the only suggestion of an inversion loop at pachytene. At diakinesis bivalent 9 appeared asymmetrical.

Of the four chromosomally abnormal cases in the del Castillo group, three had no meiotic cells and one had scanty meiotic cells. Two of the three cases without meiosis had 45, X/46, XY mosaicism, and the third had a minute Y chromosome in which the greater part of the long arm of the Y was deficient, including all the intensely fluorescent segment and some of the proximal less fluorescent region as well.

One case with partial absence of germ cells and four cases with maturation arrest showed X–Y asynapsis in a high proportion of cells in diakinesis. The presence of X and Y univalents in proportions of 50–90% is significantly higher than the frequency of $21.8 \pm 14\%$ in controls. The cause is unknown, but among the possibilities is a small aberration involving one of the pairing segments. Infertility in these cases could either result from the presence of univalents or from the underlying aberration, or from some quite unrelated cause.

5. PRESUMPTIVE Y DELETIONS

The four cases of 45, X/46, XY mosaicism (three with absence of germ cells and one with maturation arrest) are particularly interesting as in each case the Y chromosome was non-fluorescent despite the fact that the Y chromosome of the father of each patient had a normal fluorescent segment. In two of the patients, the effect of the 45, X cell line was evident in the associated short stature, abnormal genitalia and features of Turner's syndrome; one of the two had a rudimentary unicornuate uterus and a streak gonad. The other cases had no clinical abnormality except for the absence of germ cells. All four had markedly reduced Y-chromatin counts in buccal smears suggesting that this would be a useful method for screening for this disorder. A number of similar cases are now recorded in the literature (Caspersson et al., 1971) and it is assumed that most are the result of translocation between the Y and an unidentified autosome during paternal meiosis.

TABLE 2

Infertility series, 1967–73

	Number of cases	Mitotic analysis normal	Mitotic analysis abnormal	No meiotic cells	Meiotic analysis normal	Meiotic analysis abnormal	Abnormality
AGC (P or C)	42	39	3	33	8	1	XYq-, 2-XO/XY, X-Y asynapsis*
Maturation arrest	41	40	1	15	19	7	XO/XY, 2 OLIGO, 4 X-Y asynapsis*
PPTA	2	2	0	1	1	0	
Klinefelter	9	0	9	9	0	0	8-XXY, 1-XX
Hyposperm.	4	4	0	3	1	0	
Normal	49	48	1	8	41	0	9 INV
Inflam.	3	3	0	0	3	0	
Others	4	4	0	4	0	0	
Totals	154	140	14	73	73	8	21 (7.3%)

* X and Y present as univalents in 50, 57, 60, 66, and 87% of spermatocytes.

AGC (P or C) = Absence of germ cells (partial or complete)

PPTA = Post-pubertal testicular atrophy

Hyposperm. = Hypospermatogenesis

Inflam. = Chronic inflammation

6. OLIGOCHIASMATE MATURATION ARREST

In two of the 41 cases of maturation arrest, meiotic analysis revealed a marked deficiency of chiasmata. In the first case, the mean chiasma count at diakinesis was 21.5 ± 9.5 with a range from 5 to 40. In 88% of cells the X and Y were present as univalents. 15% of the pachytene cells were abnormal, with defective pairing and absent sex vesicle. Many degenerating spermatocytes were seen and this was also evident in the pathological sections.

The second case was much more severely affected with a mean chiasma count of 3.1 ± 2.8. There were no normal pachytenes and the sex vesicle was not identified. Under the electron microscope there were many degenerating spermatocytes and the most mature cells seen were zygotene-like cells but these were clearly abnormal. Only single axes corresponding to the lateral component of the synaptinemal complex were normally identified. Rarely, a short section of the complete complex was seen, but this occurred with a frequency of less than 1% of the normal. These findings suggest that the basic defect is failure of synapsis rather than precocious desynapsis. The rare complete synaptinemal complexes were not preferentially associated with the nuclear membrane and this argues against the nuclear membrane being the site of origin of the complex.

Unscheduled DNA synthesis was tested in the second case and found to be normal. Similarly, the amount of chromosome breakage in response to irradiation was normal. No cause for the defective synapsis was found, but it seems likely that the disorder is due to an autosomal recessive mutation. The parents of Case 1 are first cousins, and Case 2 comes from a small village in Turkey where his family have been for many generations. In addition, one of Case 2's two married brothers and one of his two married sisters are infertile.

Three cases of oligochiasmate maturation arrest are reported in the literature with mean chiasma counts of 9, 39, and 41 respectively (Pearson et al., 1970; Hultén et al., 1970) Parental consanguinity is known in one of these cases. It seems likely that a number of different mutations may cause defects in chiasma formation. Further studies of these cases may be rewarding and might help in our understanding of the mechanism of synapsis in man.

7. SUMMARY

1. Meiosis in the human male is most frequently studied by testicular biopsy. Chiasma counts made on individuals with normal spermatogenesis give a mean chiasma count of 51.1.

2. The chiasmata appear to be clustered at the ends of bivalents in diakinesis and there is some evidence that crossing over is more frequent in these regions also.

3. Progress towards the identification of each bivalent at pachytene is reviewed and it is suggested that the major chromomere patterns correspond to the main G bands in mitotic chromosomes.

4. Mitotic and meiotic analysis in a series of 154 infertile males revealed a significant chromosome abnormality in 7.3%. The abnormalities include Klinefelter's syndrome (9 cases), 45,X/46,XY mosaicism and non-fluorescent Y (3 cases), Y chromosome deletion (1 case), pericentric inversion of 9 (1 case), defective X–Y

synapsis (5 cases), and oligochiasmate maturation arrest (2 cases). The pericentric inversion (described in pachytene for the first time) is believed to be a fortuitous finding. Electron microscopy in one of the cases of oligochiasmate maturation arrest shows a striking deficiency (1 % of normal) of synaptinemal complexes.

8. REFERENCES

BOBROW, M., MADAN, K., and PEARSON, P. L. 1972. Staining of some specific regions of human chromosomes, particularly the secondary constriction of No. 9. *Nat. New Biol., 238,* 122–124.

CASPERSSON, T., HULTÉN, M., JOHANSSEN, J., LINDSTEN, J., THERKELSEN, A., and ZECH, L. 1971. Translocations causing non-fluorescent Y chromosomes in human XO/XY mosaics. *Hereditas, 68,* 317–324.

CHANDLEY, A. C. 1973. Karyotypes and phenotypes of infertility. *Bull. Europ. Soc. Hum. Genet., 6,* 4–20.

COOK, P. J. L., ROBSON, E. B., BUCKTON, K. E., JACOBS, P. A., and POLANI, P. E. 1974. Segregation of genetic markers in families with chromosomes polymorphisms and structural re-arrangements involving chromosome 1. *Ann. Hum. Genet., 37,* 24–274.

EBERLE, P. 1963. Meiotische Chromosomen des Mannes. *Klin. Wochenschr., 41,* 848.

FERGUSON-SMITH, M. A. 1964. The sites of nucleolus formation in human pachytene chromosomes. *Cytogenetics (Basel), 3,* 124–134.

FERGUSON-SMITH, M. A. 1973. Human chromosomes in meiosis. In *Human Genetics,* Proceedings of IVth International Congress of Human Genetics, Paris, 1971, (J. de GROUCHY, ed.), pp. 195–211.

FERGUSON-SMITH, M. A., and PAGE, B. M. 1973. Pachytene analysis in a human reciprocal (10;11) translocation. *J. Med. Genet., 10,* 282–287.

FORD, C. E., and HAMERTON, J. L. 1956. The chromosomes of man. *Nature (Lond.), 178,* 1020.

GERAEDTS, J., and PEARSON, P. 1973. Specific staining of the human No. 1 chromosome in spermatozoa. *Humangenetik, 20,* 171–173.

HULTÉN, M. 1974. Chiasma distribution at diakinesis in the normal human male. *Hereditas, 76,* 55–78.

HULTÉN, M., and LINDSTEN, J. 1970. The behaviour of structural aberrations at male meiosis. Information from man. In *Human Population Cytogenetics* (P. A. JACOBS, W. H. PRICE, and P. LAW, eds), pp. 24–61, Pfizer Medical Monographs, *5.* Edinburgh University Press, Edinburgh.

HULTÉN, M., ELIASSON, P., and TILLINGER, K. G. 1970. Low chiasma count and other meiotic irregularities in two infertile 46, XY men with spermatogenic arrest. *Hereditas, 65,* 285–290.

HUNGERFORD, D. A. 1971. Chromosome structure and function in man. I. Pachytene mapping in the male, improved methods and general discussion of initial results. *Cytogenetics (Basel), 10,* 23–32.

HUNGERFORD, D. A., MELLMAN, W. J., BACABAN, G. B., LABADIE, G. U., MESSATZZIA, C. R., and HALLER, G. 1970. Chromosome structure and function in man, III. Pachytene analysis and identification of the supernumerary chromosome in a case of Down's syndrome (Mongolism). *Proc. Natl. Acad. Sci. U.S.A., 67,* 221–224.

KJESSLER, B. 1966. Karyotype, meiosis and spermatogenesis in a sample of men attending an infertility clinic. S. Karger, Basel/New York.

LUCIANI, J. 1970. Les chromosomes méiotiques de l'homme II. Le nucléole les chiasmas. III. La stérilité masculine. *Ann. Gen., 13* (3), 169–182.

MCILREE, M. E., PRICE, W. H., COURT-BROWN, W. M., SELBY-TULLOCH, W., NEWSAM, J. E., and MACLEAN, N. 1966. Chromosome studies on testicular cells from 50 subfertile men. *Lancet, ii,* 60–71.

PAGE, B. 1973. Identification of chromosome 9 in human male meiosis. *Cytogenet. and Cell Genet., 12,* 254–263.

PEARSON, P. L., ELLIS, J. D., and EVANS, H. J. 1970. A gross reduction in chiasma formation during meiotic prophase and a defective DNA repair mechanism associated with a case of human male infertility. *Cytogenetics (Basel), 9,* 460–467.

THERKELSEN, A. J., HULTÉN, M., JONASSON, J., LINDSTEN, J., CHRISTENSEN, N. C., and IVERSEN, T. 1973. Presumptive direct insertion within chromosome 2 in man. *Ann. Hum. Genet., 36,* 367–373.

VAN DER LINDEN, A. G. J. M., and PEARSON, P. L. 1975. Cytological assessment of meiotic exchange in a human male with a pericentric inversion of chromosome No. 4. *Cytogenet. and Cell Genet., 14,* 126–139.

CYTOGENETIC OBSERVATIONS IN MAMMALIAN OOCYTES

GEORGIANA JAGIELLO, MERCEDES DUCAYEN, JYE-SIUNG FANG, and JOHN GRAFFEO

College of Physicians and Surgeons, Columbia University, New York, N. Y., U.S.A.

1. INTRODUCTION

Data on the meiotic characteristics of higher female mammals, particularly with reference to the frequency and location of chiasma and structural abnormalities at diakiness/first metaphase, as well as information on the disjunction, number, and structure of second metaphase chromosomes, are sparse. Some reports on female rodents exist (Henderson and Edwards, 1968; Polani, 1972) and somewhat more on male mammals (Ford and Hamerton, 1956; Hultén, 1974). It is the purpose of this paper to summarize the observations made over the past few years in our laboratories on these cytogenetic phenomena utilizing oocytes matured *in vitro* from guinea pig, ewe, cow, monkey, baboon, marmoset, and human.

2. MATERIALS AND METHODS

Oocytes were rapidly removed under sterile conditions from the ovaries of young adult dioestrous guinea pigs, mixed breed anoestrous ewes and cows, or at random times in the oestrous cycle from ovaries of female *Macaca mulatta* and *Nemestrina*, baboon, marmoset, and human as previously described (Jagiello, 1969; Jagiello et al., 1973, 1974). Of the latter group all save human were young adults. The oocytes were matured *in vitro* in a 5% CO_2/air atmosphere utilizing previously described complete media generally made up by a bicarbonate buffered base to a final pH of 7.2 and supplemented with appropriate serum. Harvests of oocytes were made at times appropriate for each species as seen in table 1; it can be noted that all the species studied yielded diakinesis MI cells after approximately 24 hours of culture. As noted by others (Klinger et al., 1970), two peaks of MII harvests occurred, the first at around 24 hours and a second larger peak at approximately 46 hours. In all species except the ewe where early atresia of the oocytes was noted, both harvest times yielded technically excellent preparations.

Cytologic preparations were made by a modification of the method of Tarkowski (1966) and stained with 2% toluidine blue in resin. Locations of centromeres (fig. 1) were subsequently determined utilizing a modification of the $Ba(OH)_2$ method of Chandley and Fletcher (1973). The mitotic complement for each species studied was determined from ovarian material cultured short term and compared with standard karyotypes.

Several constraints pertain to the scoring and interpretation of data on diakinesis/MI. Firstly we felt that the individual identification of each bivalent in the female meiotic material that we have studied was not possible with banding or other

TABLE 1

Harvest times and hours of incubation (range maximal)

Mammal	Diakinesis/MI	MII A*	MII B**
Guinea pig (dioestrous)	8	14	0
Ewe (anoestrous)	16–26	23–26	29–48
	(24)	(24)	(46)
Cow (anoestrous)	8–26	19–27	30–48
	(24)	(24)	(46)
Macaca (random)	19–31	24–30	41–48
	(26)	(27)	(48)
Baboon (random)	16–25	24–26	48
	(24)	(24)	
Human (random)	21–26	24–30	43–48
	(24)	(26)	(46)

* First harvest peak.
** Second harvest peak.

available techniques. Hence all observations on chiasma frequency and distribution must be presented for groups of bivalents assigned to their appropriate complement on total length and probable centromere position. Secondly, when seeking these stages, harvesting during the early part of the known culture times did not automatically yield cells in the earlier stages of diakinesis, and thirdly, the chiasmata counts represent minimal estimates, particularly in what may be termed "terminalized" bivalents. Cells were selected for scoring at D/MI which were judged to be complete and free from overlap. They were examined at × 1200 with Zeiss bright light optics. Each bivalent was measured with an optical micrometer, and the chiasmata counted and assigned to a position in the top, central or distal third of the bivalent. In the case of acrocentric chromosomes the term "first" was equivalent to proximal in relationship to the centromere. These observations were later rechecked using centromere stained preparations and photomicrographs.

3. RESULTS

(a) *Diakinesis/MI*

Table 2 is a summary of the chiasma frequencies. Analysis of these data using the least significant difference test (Snedecor, 1956) revealed that guinea pig, cow, and ewe chiasma frequencies were all smaller than those of the primates; there was no difference between human and baboon, and the monkey differed from all others.

Guinea pig. The scoring by groups of the chiasmata on the 32 bivalents of this subtelocentric and acrocentric complement with a submetacentric X is shown in table 3. As described by Cohen and Pinsky (1966), only the X, the subtelocentric chromosomes 1 and 2, and the submetacentric chromosomes 3 and 4 could be individually identified. The remainder were grouped by size. The distribution of these chiasmata (table 4) was obtained by scoring each identified bivalent with reference to the loca-

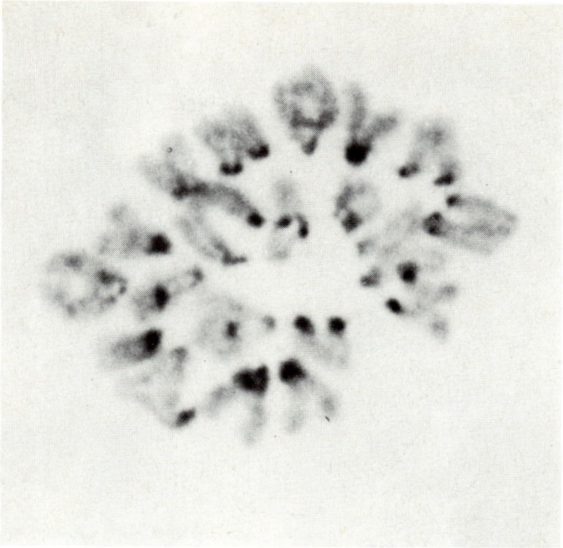

FIG. 1.—Mouse oocyte diakinesis MI stained for centromeres (dark spots). × 8125.

TABLE 2

Chiasma frequencies

Animal	No. Cells	Mean chiasmata/bivalent	Range	S.D.
Guinea Pig	28	1.04	1.00–1.38	0.09
Ewe	123	1.39	1.07–1.96	0.21
Cow	144	1.23	1.00–1.73	0.14
Macaca	194	1.62	0.86–2.43	0.29
Baboon	20	2.00	1.62–2.57	0.25
Human	27	1.89	1.39–2.39	0.25

TABLE 3

Chiasma distribution at diakinesis/metaphase I in the normal guinea pig oocyte

Bivalent group	Average chiasmata/bivalent range
1–2	2.57–1.82
3–4	1.29–1.25
5–14	1.36–1.04
15–24	1.21–1.04
25–31	1.14–1.04
X	1.75

TABLE 4

Distribution on bivalents of chiasmata in guinea pig oocytes. Total bivalents = 898

	No. bivalents	%
Singles		
proximal	5	0.6
central	21	2.3
distal	707	79.0
Doubles		
Central^2	11	1.2
proximal/distal	102	11
central/distal	8	0.9
proximal/distal	18	2.0
Triples		
proximal/central^2	11	1.2
proximal/central/distal	10	1.1
central^2/distal	1	0.1
proximal/distal^2	1	0.1
Quadruples		
proximal^2/distal^2	1	0.1

tion of chiasmata on the proximal, central or distal third, and to whether the combinations of chiasmata occurred as single, double, triple, etc. It can be seen that the single distal chiasma predominated in this complement (79 %), the proximal/distal was the commonest double (11 %), and a single proximal with two central chiasmata was the commonest triple (1.2 %).

The distribution of the various combinations by bivalent groups is shown in table 5. It can be seen that the single distals were found in groups 5–31 whilst the proximal/distal doubles were found on groups 1–2, 5–14, and 15–24. The triples and quadruples were found on the two largest bivalents and the X.

Ewe. This complement contains 3 large metacentric autosomes and an acrocentric X which is the largest of the remainder of the karyotype (fig. 2a). The average chiasma frequency per bivalent for the ewe was 1.39. The range per bivalent group is seen in table 6. The distribution of the chiasmata (table 7) showed a preponderance of distal singles (62 %) proximal/distal doubles (17.3 %), some proximal/central/distal triples (2.1 %), and quadruples made up of proximal^1, central^2, distal^1 (2.8 %). Consideration of the distribution of these on the bivalents (table 8) showed the single distal chiasma to be on all groups from 5 onwards, the P^1/D^1 doubles on the 5–10 group, and the triples and quadruples, etc. on the larger metacentric bivalents and the X.

Cow. Another Bovidae oocyte, the cow, is shown in fig. 2b. The complement is composed of 30 bivalents, 29 acrocentric and one large submetacentric X. The average chiasma frequency per bivalent was 1.23 compared with 1.8 per bivalent reported for the bull (Popescu, 1971). The range per bivalent group for the cow is presented in table 9. The distribution among the 1410 bivalents (table 10) was composed primarily of single distals (68.7 %), proximal/distal doubles (12.3 %), and

TABLE 5

Distribution on bivalent groups of chiasmata in guinea pig oocytes

Bivalent groups	Chiasma types											
	% singles			% doubles				% triples				% quads.
	P*	C*	D*	C^2	P/D	C/D	P/C	P^1/C^2	$P^1/C^1/D^1$	C^2/D^1	P^1/D^2	P^2/D^2
1–2	20	5	1	27	18	13	22	82	80	100	0	100
3–4	40	5	5	18	8	17	11	0	0	0	0	0
5–14	20	33	33	55	25	25	5	0	0	0	0	0
15–24	0	10	35	0	30	13	0	0	0	0	0	0
25–31	0	0	25	0	0	16	0	0	0	0	0	0
X	20	48	0.1	0	3	13	39	18	20	0	100	0
Total bivalents	5	21	707	11	102	8	18	11	10	1	1	1

* P = proximal; C = central; D = distal; superscript = number of chiasma.

TABLE 6

Chiasma distribution at diakinesis/metaphase I in the normal ewe oocyte

Bivalent group	Average chiasmata/bivalent range
1–3	3.83–3.25
X	2.25
5–10	1.78–1.33
11–16	1.28–1.13
17–22	1.15–1.00
23–27	1.03–1.00

TABLE 7

Distribution on bivalents of chiasmata in ewe oocytes total bivalents = 1107

	No. bivalents	%
Singles		
proximal	16	1.4
central	26	2.3
distal	692	62.0
Doubles		
central^2	9	0.8
proximal/distal	192	17.3
central/distal	37	3.3
proximal/central	30	2.7
Proximal^2		
Triples		
proximal^1/central^2	9	0.8
proximal^1/central^1/distal^1	24	2.1
central^2/distal^1	6	0.5
proximal^1/distal^2	3	0.3
Quadruples		
proximal^2/central^1/distal^1	4	0.4
proximal^1/central^1/distal^2	4	0.4
proximal^1/central^2/distal^1	31	2.8
proximal^2/central^0/distal^2	13	1.2
Quintuples		
proximal^2/central^2/distal^1	2	0.2
proximal^2/central^1/distal^2	3	0.3
proximal^1/central^3/distal^1	2	0.2
proximal^1/central^2/distal^2	5	0.5
proximal^2/central^0/distal^3	1	0.1
Sextuples		
proximal^2/central^2/distal^2	2	0.2

TABLE 8

Distribution on bivalent groups of chiasmata in ewe oocytes

Bivalent groups	Chiasma types: % singles			% doubles				% triples			
	P^1	C^1	D^1	C^2	P^1/D^1	C^1/D^1	P^1/C^1	P^1/C^2	$P^1/C^1/D^1$	C^2/D^1	P^1/D^2
1–3	0	0	0	11	11	5	3	22	75	50	67
X	0	0	0.1	22	8	51	3	56	13	50	33
5–10	63	54	11	67	53	24	60	22	8	0	0
11–16	25	38	27	0	15	16	30	0	0	0	0
17–22	13	8	32	0	8	3	0	0	4	0	0
23–27	0	0	29	0	0	0	3	0	0	0	0
Total bivalents	16	26	692	9	192	37	30	9	24	6	3

Bivalent groups	Chiasma types: % quadruples				% quintuples					% sextuples
	$P^2/C^2/D^1$	$P^1/C^1/D^2$	$P^1/C^2/D^1$	$P^2/C^0/D^2$	$P^2/C^2/D^1$	$P^2/C^1/D^2$	$P^1/C^3/D^1$	$P^1/C^2/D^2$	$P^2/C^0/D^3$	$P^2/C^2/D^2$
1–3	100	100	100	100	100	100	100	100	100	100
X	0	0	0	0	0	0	0	0	0	0
5–10	0	0	0	0	0	0	0	0	0	0
11–16	0	0	0	0	0	0	0	0	0	0
17–22	0	0	0	0	0	0	0	0	0	0
23–27	0	0	0	0	0	0	0	0	0	0
Total bivalents	4	4	31	13	2	3	2	5	1	2

TABLE 9

Chiasma distribution at diakinesis/metaphase I in the normal cow oocyte

Bivalent group	Average chiasmata/bivalent range
1–6	2.18–1.47
7–12	1.44–1.17
13–18	1.15–1.09
19–24	1.09–1.00
25–29	1.04–1.00
X	2.53

TABLE 10

Distribution on bivalents of chiasmata in cow oocytes
Total bivalents = 1410

	No. bivalents	%
Singles		
proximal	18	1.3
central	60	4.3
distal	968	68.7
Doubles		
$central^2$	21	1.5
proximal/distal	173	12.3
central/distal	44	3.1
proximal/central	59	4.2
$proximal^2$	3	0.2
Triples		
$central^3$	1	0.1
$proximal^1/central^2$	12	0.8
$proximal^1/central^1/distal^1$	37	2.6
$central^2/distal^1$	4	0.3
$proximal^1/distal^2$	2	0.1
Quadruples		
$proximal^1/central^2/distal^1$	4	0.3

$P^1/C^1/D^1$ triples (2.6 %). Assignment of these chiasmata to bivalent groups (table 11) showed the distal singles to be largely on the 13–29 groups, whilst the P^1/D^1 doubles were found on groups 1–6, and the $P^1/C^1/D^1$ triples on the 1–6 and the X. One structural rearrangement was seen in this series representing one individual in approximately 260 cows. A quadrivalent (fig. 3a) considered to represent a presumptive reciprocal translocation was found in 3 cells and 2 unequal chromosomes were found in 2 second metaphase preparations (fig. 3b). As noted before, absence of specific identification of bivalents prohibited positive assignment of the involved chromosomes but we believe by size they may be 3/4 and 22/24. We know nothing of the clinical characteristics of the donor cow.

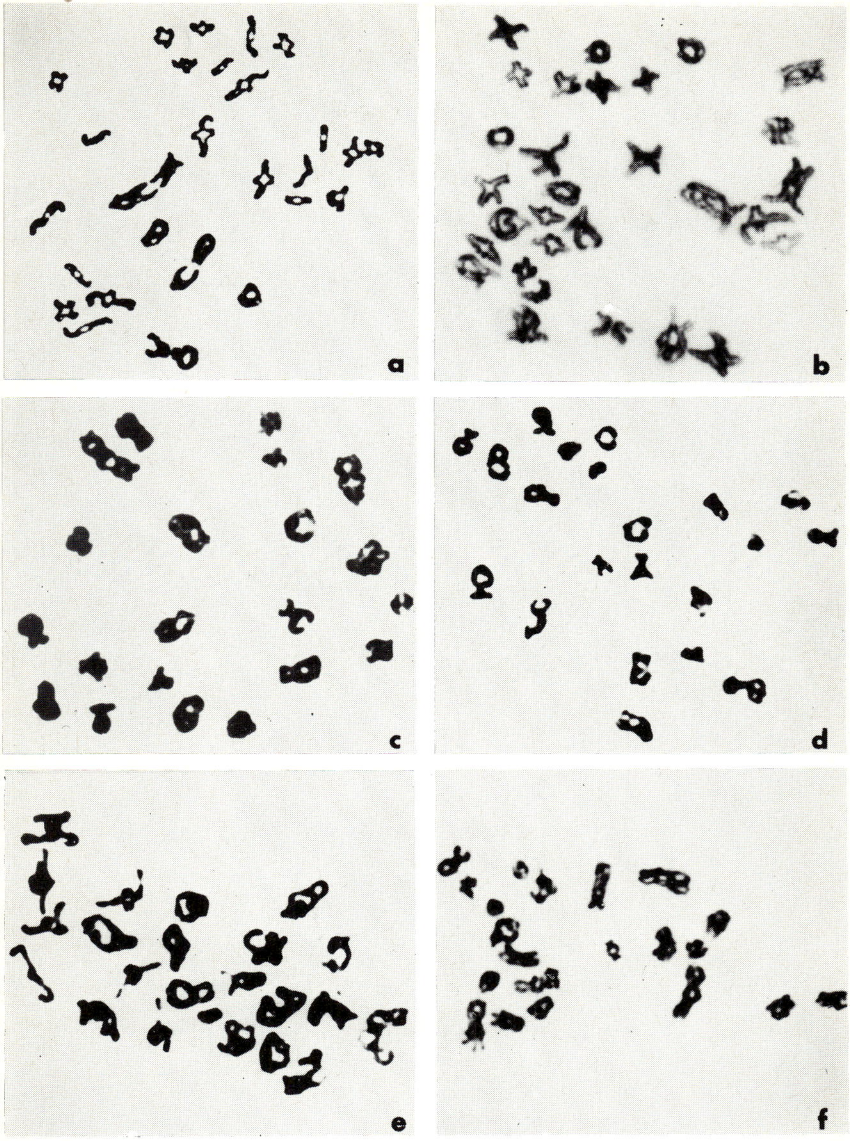

FIG. 2.—Diakinesis MI oocytes: (a) sheep, × 3240; (b) cow, × 2810; (c) monkey, × 2810; (d) baboon, × 3240; (e) marmoset, × 3240; (f) human, × 3750.

Macaca. The complement (fig. 2c) is notable for a clear marker bivalent with a deep secondary constriction near the centromere, and the remainder of the karyotype composed of meta or submetacentric bivalents; the X chromosome is metacentric and of about the same size as the marker. The average chiasma frequency of the pooled data for *Macaca mulatta* and *Nemestrina* was 1.62 per bivalent compared with 2.0 as reported for the male *Macaca* (Chiarelli and Egozcue, 1967). The range

TABLE 11

Distribution on bivalent groups of chiasmata in cow oocytes

Bivalent groups	Chiasma types: % singles			% doubles						% triples				% quads.
	P*	C*	D*	C^2	P^1/D^1	C^1/D^1	P^1/C^1	P^2	C^3	P^1/C^2	$P^1/C^1/D^1$	C^2/D^1	P^1/D^2	$P^1/C^2/D^1$
1–6	39.0	43.0	7.6	61.9	44.5	43.1	55.9	33.0	100	75	53.7	75	50	50
7–12	50.0	30.0	17	33.3	27.8	40.8	23.8	66.0	0	0	5.4	0	0	0
13–18	11.0	17.0	24.3	4.8	10.4	11.4	11.9	0	0	0	0	0	0	0
19–24	0	10	27.2	0	5.8	0.2	3.4	0	0	0	0	0	0	0
25–29	0	0	23.8	0	1.1	0.2	0	0	0	0	0	0	0	0
X	0	0	0	0	10.4	0	8.5	0	0	25	40.5	25	50	50
Total bivalents	18	60	968	21	173	44	59	3	1	12	37	4	4	4

* P = proximal; C = central; D = distal; superscript = number of chiasma.

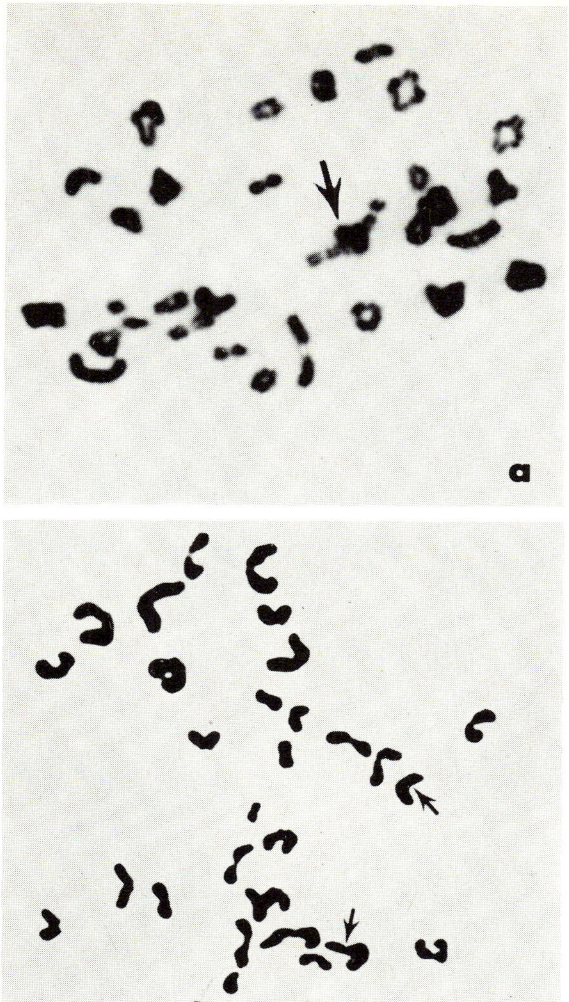

FIG. 3.—Diakinesis MI cow oocyte with (a) quadrivalent (arrow); (b) MII oocyte with 2 unequal chromosomes; arrows indicate centromeres. × 5000.

per bivalent group is noted in table 12. The data on distribution of chiasmata for this and subsequent species are annotated in thirds of the bivalent—first third (F), central third (C), and distal third (D). This seemed to us to be the most informative way of expressing the distribution within this largely metacentric and submetacentric complement where explicit bivalent identification was not available, and where assignment to the p or q arms would be potentially inaccurate and also fail to indicate chiasmata near the centromere. The distribution by groups (table 13) was thus predominantly F^1/D^1 doubles (43 %), distal singles (20 %), $F^1/C^1/D^1$ triples (13 %), and $F^1/C^2/D^1$ quadruples (5.0 %). The F^1/D^1 doubles (table 14) were found in groups

TABLE 12

Chiasma distribution at diakinesis/metaphase I in the normal monkey oocyte

Bivalent group	Average chiasmata/bivalent range
1–6	2.88–1.88
7–12	1.85–1.13
13–14	0.85–0.63
15–17	2.67–1.25
18–19	0.52–0.35
M	2.12
X	2.35

TABLE 13

Distribution on bivalents of chiasmata in monkey oocytes. Total bivalents = 889

	No. bivalents	%
Singles		
first^1	74	8
central^1	14	1.6
distal^1	178	20
Doubles		
central^2	7	0.8
first^1/distal^1	382	43
central^1/distal^1	24	2.7
first^1/central^1	12	1.3
Triples		
first^1/central^2	17	2.0
first^1/central^1/distal^1	113	13
central^2/distal^1	8	0.9
first^1/distal^2	5	0.5
first^2/distal^1	1	0.1
Quadruples		
first^2/central^1/distal^1	2	0.2
first^1/central^1/distal^2	3	0.3
first^1/central^2/distal^1	43	5.0
first^2/distal^2	3	0.3
Quintuples		
first^2/central^1/distal^2	1	0.1
first^1/central^3/distal^1	2	0.2

1–12 and 15–17 which are also large metacentrics, the distal singles on the 7–12 group, the triples $F^1/C^1/D^1$ on 1–6, and quadruples $F^1/C^2/D^1$ on the 1–6 group. The central chiasmata on the marker were on the presumed long arm.

Baboon. The D/M^1 of the female baboon, *P. papio* (Thorington), oocyte is shown in fig. 2d. The karyotype is similar to that of *Macaca* with a characteristic marker

TABLE 14

Distribution on bivalent groups of chiasmata in monkey oocytes

Bivalent groups	Chiasma types: % singles			% doubles				% triples					% quadruples				% quintuples	
	F^1	C^1	D^1	C^2	F^1/D^1	C^1/D^1	F^1/C^1	F^1/C^2	$F^1/C^1/D^1$	C^2/D^1	F^1/D^2	F^2/D^1	$F^2/C^1/D^1$	$F^1/C^1/D^2$	$F^1/C^2/D^1$	F^2/D^2	$F^2/C^1/D^2$	$F^2/C^3/D^1$
1–6	12	21	16	43	35	25	8	53	57	38	40	100	100	33	70	100	100	100
7–12	31	21	40	57	34	33	25	18	9	13	0	0	0	0	2	0	0	0
13–14	19	21	11	0	5	0	0	0	0	0	0	0	0	0	0	0	0	0
15–17	23	21	14	0	13	21	42	24	19	13	40	0	0	33	16	0	0	0
18–19	11	7	12	0	1	0	0	0	0	0	0	0	0	0	0	0	0	0
M	2.7	7	4	0	5	13	17	6	7	0	20	0	0	33	9	0	0	0
X	1	0	2	0	7	8	8	0	9	38	0	0	0	0	2	0	0	0
Total bivalents	74	14	178	7	382	24	12	17	113	8	5	1	2	3	43	3	1	2

and the larger metacentric group 15–17. The average chiasma frequency per bivalent was 2.00. The range per bivalent group is presented in table 15. The distribution in this species (table 16) was predominantly as first^1/distal^1 doubles (32%), distal singles (26%), and first^1/central^1/distal^1 triples (18%). The F^1/D^1 doubles (table 17) were found in the 7–12 group, distal singles in 7–12, 13–14, and 18–19, whilst the triples $F^1/C^1/D^1$ were on the 1–6 and the marker and X.

Marmoset. The New World monkey, the white-lipped marmoset, *Saguinus nigricollis*, was studied in a few specimens (fig. 2e). The average chiasma frequency for 63 marmoset oocytes was 1.97 per bivalent. The sparsity of data prohibited making

TABLE 15

Chiasma distribution at diakinesis/metaphase I in the normal baboon oocyte

Bivalent group	Average chiasmata/bivalent range
1–6	3.50–2.00
7–12	1.95–1.39
13–14	1.22
15–17	3.21–1.55
18–19	1.05–0.89
M	2.62
X	2.44

TABLE 16

Distribution on bivalents of chiasmata in baboon oocytes. Total bivalents = 363

	No. bivalents	%
Singles		
first	5	1.4
central	14	3.9
distal	96	26
Doubles		
central^2	5	1.4
first^1/distal^1	116	32
central^1/distal^1	21	5.8
first^1/central^1	3	0.8
Triples		
first^1/central^2	6	1.6
first^1/central^1/distal^1	67	18
central^2/distal^1	3	0.8
first^1/central^0/distal^2	3	0.8
Quadruples		
first^1/central^1/distal^2	2	0.6
first^1/central^2/distal^1	21	5.8
Quintuples		
first^2/central^2/distal^1	1	0.3

TABLE 17

Distribution on bivalent groups of chiasmata in baboon oocytes

Bivalent groups	Chiasma types: % singles			% doubles				% triples				% quadruples		% quintup.
	F	C	D	C^2	F^1/D^1	C^1/D^1	F^1/C^1	F^1/C^2	$F^1/C^1/D^1$	C^2/D^1	$F^1/C^0/D^2$	$F^1/C^1/D^2$	$F^1/C^2/D^1$	$F^2/C^2/D^1$
1–6	20	21	1	40	24	29	33	67	55	100	33	0	67	100
7–12	60	50	36	40	40	29	67	17	3	0	33	0	0	0
13–14	20	7	26	0	7	0	0	0	0	0	0	0	0	0
15–17	0	21	5	20	16	24	0	17	11	0	33	0	33	0
18–19	0	0	31	0	2	0	0	0	0	0	0	0	0	0
M	0	0	0	0	5	10	0	0	13	0	0	50	0	0
X	0	0	0	0	7	10	0	0	12	0	0	50	0	0
Total bivalents	5	14	96	5	116	21	3	6	67	3	3	2	21	1

the potentially interesting comparisons with the Old World monkeys on frequency and location of chiasmata. However, analysis revealed a predominance of single distals (34.9 %) and $F^1/C^1/D^1$ triples (26.9 %).

Human. The human female oocyte D/MI is shown in figure 2f. The patients were from 26–49 years of age and the average chiasma frequency per bivalent calculated from 621 bivalents was 1.89 compared with 1.61–2.26 reported by others (Yuncken, 1968; Edwards, 1970). The range of groups is seen in table 18.

Analysis of distribution (table 19) revealed a predominance of single distals (37.4 %), first third and distal third doubles (34.8 %), and triples made up of $first^2$, $central^0$, and $distal^1$ (5.8 %). When examined by bivalent groups (table 20) the single distals were found on the 21–22 and 13–15 bivalents, the F^1/D^1 doubles on the 6–12 group, and $F^2/C^0/D^1$ triples on the X.

One individual showed a clear pair of univalents in two first metaphase cells (fig. 4). Six other MI's were normal and no MII's were seen. She was a 30 year old gravida 7 with 5 normal pregnancies and 2 abortions. The mitotic complement from short-term ovarian cultures revealed 29 cells which were 46 XX and one cell which was a 45 XXG^-.

X Chromosome. Table 21 summarizes the chiasma frequencies on the X by species. The maximum was found in the human oocyte and the minimum in guinea pig. Table 22 summarizes the chiasma locations by species. The single distal predominated in guinea pig, ewe, and cow, first and distal third doubles in *Macaca* and baboon, and single distals in human.

(b) *Second metaphase*

As noted in table 23, analysis was made in MII cells of the number and morphology of chromosomes for ewe (708), cow (612), *Macaca* (314), baboon (76), and human (411). Abnormalities were noted in 2 cow, 1 *Macaca*, 3 baboon, and 6 human cells.

Morphology of the ewe, cow, monkey, baboon, and human MII oocytes is seen in figure 5. No abnormal cells were seen in the ewe oocytes. Other than the aforementioned presumed translocation cells in which 2 MII's contained unequal chromosomes, no abnormal cow cells were seen. One monkey cell previously reported (Jagiello et al., 1973) with 22 bodies at MII, due probably to separated chromatids, was

TABLE 18

Chiasma distribution at diakinesis/metaphase I in the normal human oocyte

Bivalent group	Average chiasmata/bivalent range
1–3	4.00–2.89
4–5	2.46–2.11
X	2.76
6–12	2.22–1.67
13–15	1.55–1.45
16–18	1.55–1.34
19–20	1.22–1.11
21–22	1.11–1.00

TABLE 19

Distribution on bivalents of chiasmata in human oocytes. Total bivalents = 621

	No. bivalents	%
Singles		
first[1]	21	3.4
central[1]	0	0
distal[1]	231	37.4
Doubles		
central[2]	0	0
first[1]/distal[1]	216	34.8
central[1]/distal[1]	24	3.9
first[1]/central[1]	0	0
Triples		
first[1]/central[2]	3	0.5
first[1]/central[1]/distal[1]	27	4.3
central[2]/distal[1]	0	0
first[1]/central[0]/distal[2]	12	1.9
first[2]/central[0]/distal[1]	36	5.8
Quadruples		
first[1]/central[2]/distal[1]	6	0.9
first[1]/central[1]/distal[2]	15	2.4
first[2]/central[0]/distal[2]	5	0.9
first[2]/central[1]/distal[1]	12	1.9
Quintuples		
first[1]/central[2]/distal[2]	6	0.9
first[2]/central[1]/distal[2]	6	0.9

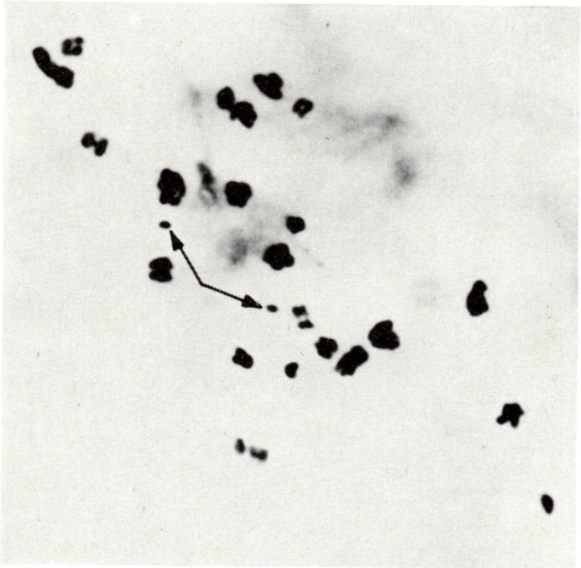

FIG. 4.—Human diakinesis/MI with 2 univalents (arrows). × 3750.

TABLE 20

Distribution on bivalent groups of chiasmata in human oocytes

Bivalent groups	% singles F^1	C^1	D^1	% doubles C^2	F^1/D^1	C^1/D^1	F^1/C^1	% triples F^1/C^2	$F^1/C^1/D^1$	C^2/D^1	$F^1/C^0/D^2$	$F^2/C^0/D^1$
1–3	0	0	0	0	8.3	0	0	0	55.5	0	25.0	0
4–5	14	0	6.5	0	5.6	0	0	0	22.2	0	50.0	8.3
X	0	0	0	0	2.8	0	0	0	22.2	0	0	58.4
6–12	43	0	14.2	0	57.0	12.5	0	100	0	0	0	33.3
13–15	0	0	20.8	0	6.9	75	0	0	0	0	25.0	0
16–18	43	0	16.9	0	13.9	12.5	0	0	0	0	0	0
19–20	0	0	19.5	0	4.2	0	0	0	0	0	0	0
21–22	0	0	22.1	0	1.4	0	0	0	0	0	0	0
Total bivalents	21	0	231	0	216	24	0	3	27	0	12	36

Bivalent groups	% quadruples $F^1/C^2/D^1$	$F^1/C^1/D^1$	$F^2/C^0/D^2$	$F^2/C^1/D^1$	% quintuples $F^1/C^2/D^2$	$F^2/C^1/D^2$
1–3	50	100	100	50	100	100
4–5	50	0	0	50	0	0
X	0	0	0	0	0	0
6–12	0	0	0	0	0	0
13–15	0	0	0	0	0	0
16–18	0	0	0	0	0	0
19–20	0	0	0	0	0	0
21–22	0	0	0	0	0	0
Total bivalents	6	15	6	6	6	6

TABLE 21

Chiasma frequency/X

Guinea pig	1.75
Ewe	2.25
Cow	2.53
Monkey	2.35
Baboon	2.44
Marmoset	2.30
Human	2.76

TABLE 22

Summary of chiasma locations

Mammal	Chiasma locations	%
Guinea pig	a. single, distal	79.0
	b. double, proximal/distal	11.0
Ewe	a. single, distal	62.0
	b. double, proximal/distal	17.3
Cow	a. single, distal	68.7
	b. double, proximal/distal	12.0
Macaca	a. double, first $\frac{1}{3}$/distal $\frac{1}{3}$	43.0
	b. single, distal	20.0
Baboon	a. double, first $\frac{1}{3}$/distal $\frac{1}{3}$	32.0
	b. single, distal	26.0
Human	a. single, distal	37.0
	b. double, first $\frac{1}{3}$/distal $\frac{1}{3}$	34.8

a = most frequent; b = second most frequent.

TABLE 23

Assessment of MII oocytes

Mammal	No. cells scored	No. abnormal cells
Ewe	708	0
Cow	612	2
Macaca	314	1
Baboon	76	3
Human	411	6

seen out of 314 cells examined, (one individual in 66 studied). One individual out of the 12 baboons studied was found to have 11 MII's with 21 chromosomes and 3 with 22 chromosomes. Ovarian mitotic analysis also revealed 2 cell lines with 34 cells with 42 chromosomes and 6 cells with 43 chromosomes, the extra chromosome being a presumptive 21. Banding of the mitotic chromosomes and further study of the pedigree is in progress since this baboon had an obstetrical history of 7 pregnancies,

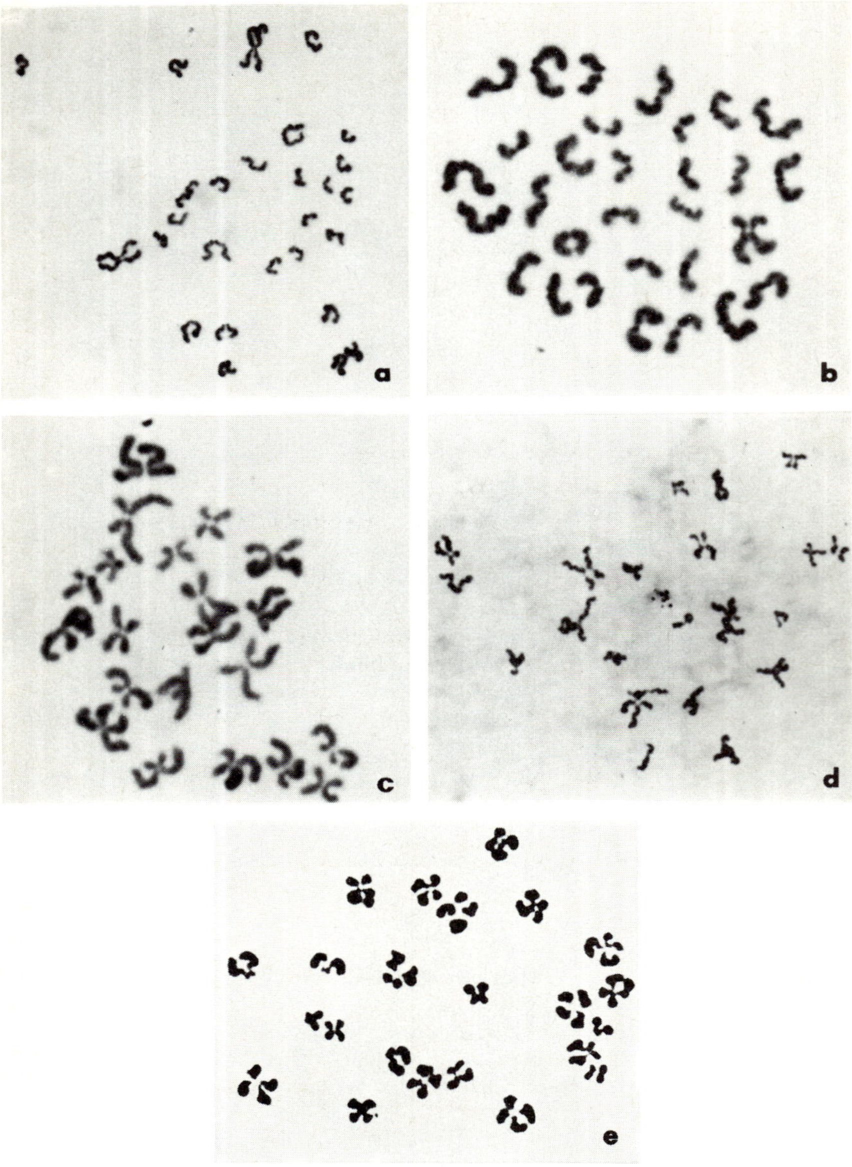

FIG. 5.—MII oocytes: (a) sheep, × 3240; (b) cow, × 5620; (c) monkey, × 5620; (d) baboon, × 2810; (e) human, × 3750.

2 normal births, with 2 induced stillbirths and 3 spontaneous abortions. Observations on 411 human second metaphase cells were made. In four instances one cell was seen with 24 bodies from patients aged 26, 42, 46, and 50 years and two were seen from an individual who was 49. There was nothing atypical in their clinical histories. No conclusions could be made other than that a total of 6 out of 411 human MII's probably contained a separation of a small chromosome.

4. SUMMARY

1. It would appear that the *in vitro* maturation of mammalian oocytes can be used for obtaining certain meiotic data on first and second metaphase complements.

2. Verification of these data must be made with *in vivo* material.

3. Improvement of bivalent and chromosome identification with banding or other techniques is essential and assessment of chiasma characteristics in foetal material fundamental to a more accurate concept of the number and distribution of chiasmata.

Acknowledgments. This study was supported by research grants from the NIH-NICHD, the Ford Foundation, and the National Foundation—March of Dimes. The cooperation of the attending and resident staffs of the Department of Obstetrics and Gynecology of the Columbia University—Presbyterian Hospital Medical Center, and the Laboratory for Experimental Medicine and Surgery in Primates of New York University is gratefully acknowledged.

5. REFERENCES

CHANDLEY, A. C., and FLETCHER, J. M. 1973. Centromere staining at meiosis in man. *Humangenetik*, *18*, 247–252.

CHIARELLI, B., and EGOZCUE, J. 1967. The meiotic chromosomes of two *Macaca*. *Caryologia*, *20*, 339–346.

COHEN, M. M., and PINSKY, L. 1966. Autosomal polymorphism via a translocation in the guinea pig, *Cavia porcellus* L. *Cytogenetics (Basel)*, *5*, 120–132.

EDWARDS, R. G. 1970. Human population cytogenetics. *Pfizer Medical Monographs*, *5*, 9–21.

FORD, C. E., and HAMERTON, J. L. 1956. The chromosomes of man. *Nature (Lond.)*, *178*, 1010–1023.

HENDERSON, S. A., and EDWARDS, R. G. 1968. Chiasma frequency and maternal age in mammals. *Nature (Lond.)*, *217*, 22–28.

HULTÉN, M. 1974. Chiasma distribution at diakinesis in the normal human male. *Hereditas*, *76*, 55–78.

JAGIELLO, G. M. 1969. Some cytologic aspects of meiosis in female guinea pig. *Chromosoma (Berl.)*, *27*, 95–101.

JAGIELLO, G. M., DUCAYEN, M. B., MILLER, W. A., LIN, J. S., and FANG, J. S. 1973. A cytogenetic analysis of oocytes from *Macaca mulatta* and *Nemestrina* matured *in vitro*. *Humangenetik*, *18*, 117–122.

JAGIELLO, G. M., MILLER, W. A., DUCAYEN, M. B., and LIN, J. S. 1974. Chiasma frequency and disjunctional behavior of ewe and cow oocytes matured *in vitro*. *Biol. Reprod.*, *10*, 354–363.

KLINGER, H. P., KAVA, H. W., and HACHAMOVITCH, M. 1970. Chromosome studies in human female meiosis. *Ann. N. Y. Acad. Sci.*, *171*, 431–439.

POLANI, P. E. 1972. Centromere localization at meiosis and the position of chiasmata in the male and female mouse. *Chromosoma (Berl.)*, *36*, 343–374.

POPESCU, C. P. 1971. Les chromosomes méiotiques du boeuf *(Bos Taurus* L.*)*. *Ann. Genét. Sél. anim.*, *3*, 125–143.

SNEDECOR, G. W. 1956. *Statistical Methods*, p. 251. Iowa State University Press, Ames, Iowa.

TARKOWSKI, A. K. 1966. An air drying method for chromosome preparation from mouse eggs. *Cytogenetics (Basel)*, *5*, 394–400.

YUNCKEN, C. 1968. Meiosis in the human female. *Cytogenetics (Basel)*, *7*, 234–238.

HETEROCHROMATIN, MICRONUCLEOLI, AND RNA CONTAINING BODY IN THE PACHYTENE AND DIPLOTENE STAGES OF THE HUMAN OOCYTE

A. STAHL, J. M. LUCIANI, R. GAGNÉ, M. DEVICTOR, and A. M. CAPODANO

Laboratoire d'Histologie—Embryologie II, Faculté de Medicine, 27, Bd. Jean Moulin, 13385 Marseille, Cedex 4, France

1. INTRODUCTION

Few investigations have been undertaken on the human oocyte pachytene and diplotene stages, which is the opposite situation to the corresponding stages in Amphibian and insect oocytes. The earliest investigations (Von Winiwarter, 1901; Swezy and Evans, 1930; Andres and Vogel, 1936) were carried out with the help of histological techniques. It was necessary to wait for the results of Ohno et al. (1961, 1962), Manotaya and Potter (1963), and Kindred (1963) to benefit from the contribution of modern cytological techniques. However, only chromosome morphology was described. Baker and Franchi (1967) were the first to study the human oocyte chromosomes with the help of both cytochemical and ultrastructural techniques.

Several hundreds or thousands of nucleoli are elaborated in the Amphibian oocyte and follow well described processes (MacGregor, 1965; Callan, 1966; Gall, 1968, 1969). The oocyte nucleus in the insects also contains a very large number of nucleoli (Kunz, 1967*a*, and *b*).

In a former study we worked out a numeration of nucleoli at various stages of the human oocyte during meiotic prophase: At the pachytene stage, 1–2 nucleoli per cell can be observed, and at the diplotene stage, most nuclei contain 2–3 large size nucleoli (Stahl and Luciani, 1972). However, we had already observed the existence of some micronucleoli (Luciani and Stahl, 1971) and demonstrated that the main nucleoli are in contact with the satellites or secondary constrictions of the acrocentric chromosomes, when the micronucleoli do not show this typical localization. Since those preliminary observations we have had the possibility to notice, using more sensitive techniques, that the number of micronucleoli can be high. The staining techniques for constitutive heterochromatin permitted us to show close connections between micronucleoli and heterochromatin. They also revealed the existence of a complex RNA containing body which is distinct from the nucleoli.

2. MATERIAL AND METHODS

Our observations were made on 7 human fetuses, $4\frac{1}{2}$ months (1), 5 months (1), $5\frac{1}{2}$ months (2), 6 months (2), and $8\frac{1}{2}$ months old, respectively. The ovaries were prepared following the technique of Luciani et al. (1974). Immediately after removal, the ovaries were dipped into an isotonic saline solution (Hanks or TC 199). Some of them were cut up into this solution and fixed with methanol-acetic acid (3/1) and others were directly cut up into the fixative. The cells were separated afterwards by passage through a 45% acetic acid solution. The spreading was carried out on pre-cooled slides.

The following cytological and cytochemical techniques were used: Giemsa staining at pH7; aceto-orcein, fluorescence after acridine orange and quinacrine mustard staining, Feulgen reaction, the Arrighi and Hsu technique for heterochromatin (1971), G11 technique (Gagné and Laberge, 1972; Bobrow et al., 1972). Treatment by 1‰ ribonuclease for 2 or 4 hours at 37° preceded the staining of a number of slides. Hydrolysis in 1N HCl at 60° for 7 minutes was carried out on a few slides before staining by the G11 technique.

3. OBSERVATIONS

(a) *Pachytene stage*

The oocyte nucleus shows 1 to 2 main nucleoli. They are connected with the satellites or secondary constrictions of D and G group bivalents. The association of a nucleolus with the extremity of several acrocentric chromosomes was seen. Micro-nucleoli were rarely observed at this stage.

In the preparations stained with the Arrighi and Hsu technique or by Giemsa at pH 11, a complex body was observed: it was composed of a purplish red spherule (fig. 1) frequently surrounded by a more lightly stained substance whose staining

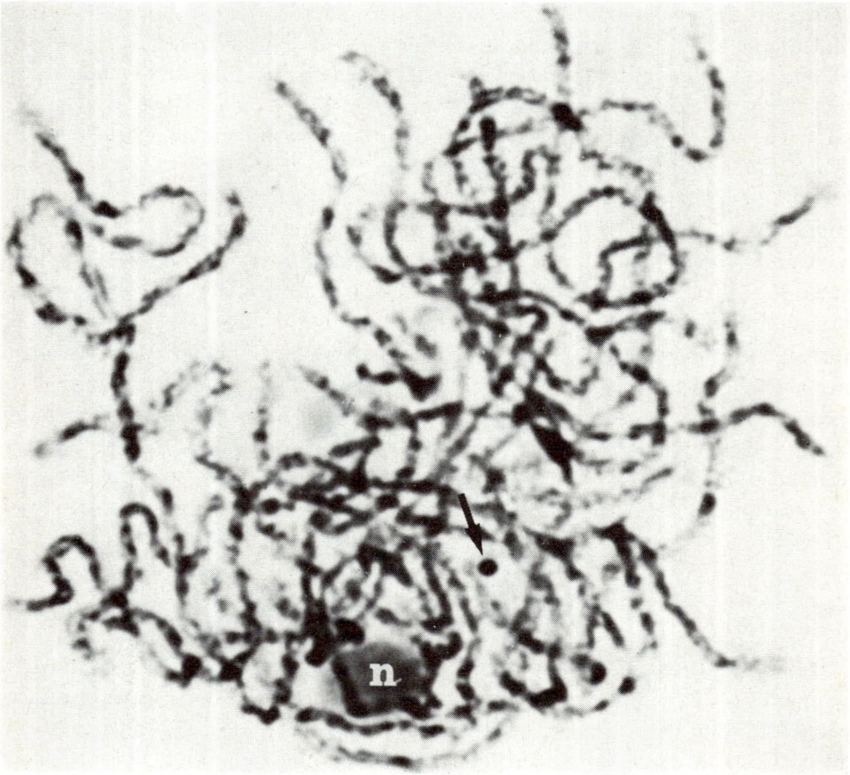

FIG. 1.—Pachytene stage (5 month fetus). Presence of a dark stained body (arrow) revealed by the G11 technique (n = nucleolus). × 1920.

properties were similar to those of nucleoli. This body was also visible in the leptotene and zygotene nuclei. The frequency of the body varied in the ovarian material studied between 16.1% and 38.40%. Various staining trials had shown that the optimum staining affinity of the body with Giemsa was between pH 10 and pH 11.5. The best preparations were obtained at pH 10.5 where the cell morphology was better preserved than at higher pH and where the chromosome No. 9, as well as other types of heterochromatin, were not stained.

The body is autonomous in most cells. However, in a small number of cells it seems to be attached to a chromosome by a more or less pointed pedicle. The chromosome is a large submetacentric which we have been unable to identify.

The results of the cytochemical investigations are summarized in the table.

The presence of RNA in the peripheral substance appears to be well established. The central spherule does not present any change in its stainability after treatment of the slides by ribonuclease. It gives a weak positive Feulgen reaction. After acridine orange staining, the spherule, in some instances, assumes a yellow-green colour whereas the peripheral substance is red, but this result, which corroborates the Feulgen reaction data, is not constant. There is a possibility that the spherule con-

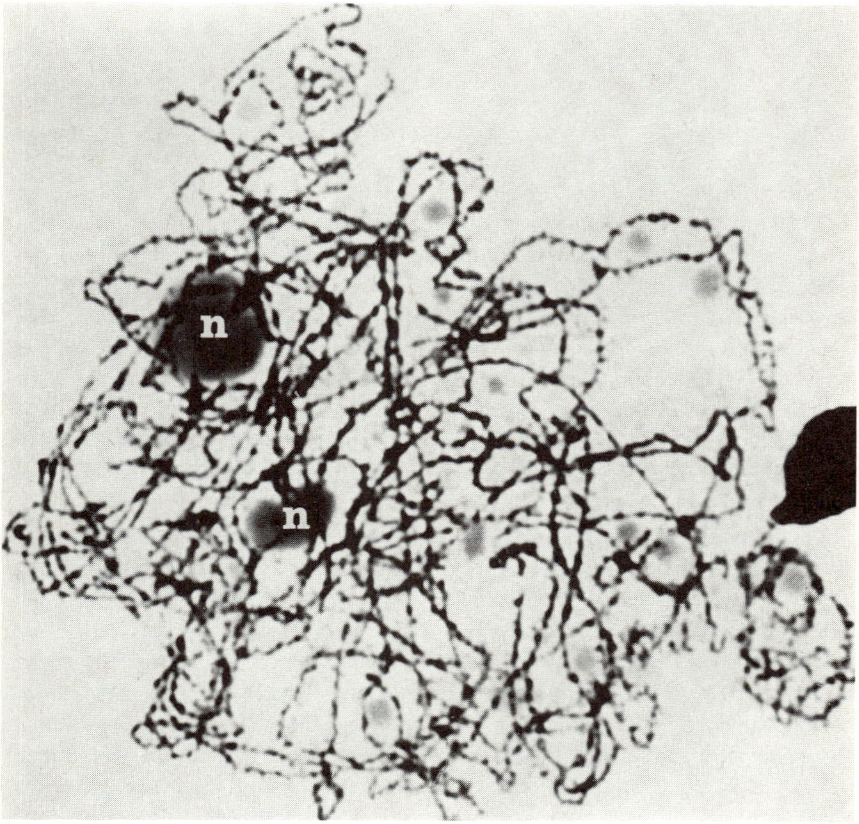

FIG. 2.—Diplotene stage (6 month fetus). Two main nucleoli (*n*) and 12 micronucleoli are visible. Aceto-orcein staining. × 1920.

TABLE

RNA containing complex body: staining and cytochemical properties

Technique	Central part	Peripheral material
Arrighi and Hsu (1971)	purple	blue
G11	purple	pink
HCl-Hydrolysis + G11	purple	0
Quinacrine mustard	0	0
Aceto-orcein	pale	0
Giemsa (pH = 7)	pale	0
Acridine orange	A: yellow	A: red
	B: red	B: red
	C: 0	C: red
RNase + A.O	yellow	0
RNase + G11	purple	0
Feulgen	pale pink	0

tains a small quantity of DNA which is too small to produce a really positive cytochemical reaction.

(b) *Diplotene stage*

The complex body was also observed at this stage but at a lower frequency. Most of the time, it was confined to the central spherule. The peripheral RNA containing substance rarely persisted. The body sometimes showed a duplication in the form of two small spherules close to each other.

The most distinctive changes involved the nucleoli. The main nucleoli, 2 or 3 in number, were more voluminous and basophilic than at the pachytene stage, their average diameter being 6.9 μm. They were associated with the satellites and the secondary constrictions of the acrocentric chromosomes.

Numerous micronucleoli with an average diameter of 1.6 μm were present (fig. 2). They were visible after Giemsa staining and particularly after acridine orange staining. In addition to the main nucleoli at least 2 or 3 micronucleoli were observed in each oocyte. In a large number of oocytes, varying between 10% and 50% according to the ovary studied, we counted at least fifteen micronucleoli and some oocytes had up to 40 micronucleoli.

The micronucleoli do not appear to be connected with the acrocentric chromosomes. The preparations stained either by the Arrighi and Hsu or G11 technique showed that the majority of micronucleoli were spatially related to the regions of heterochromatin in a different way to classical nucleolar organizers. The most frequent associations were found with centromeric heterochromatin. The heterochromatin is first seen as strongly stained circular bodies when the homologous chromosomes are still paired in the centromere region. One then sees adjoining this spherule a micronucleolus which seems to emerge from it (figs. 3 and 4a,b). When the centromeres have already undergone desynapsis the centromeric heterochromatin presents itself as two little spherical masses situated at the same relative level on the homologous chromosomes. In this instance, one sees a micronucleolus between the masses corresponding to the centromeres.

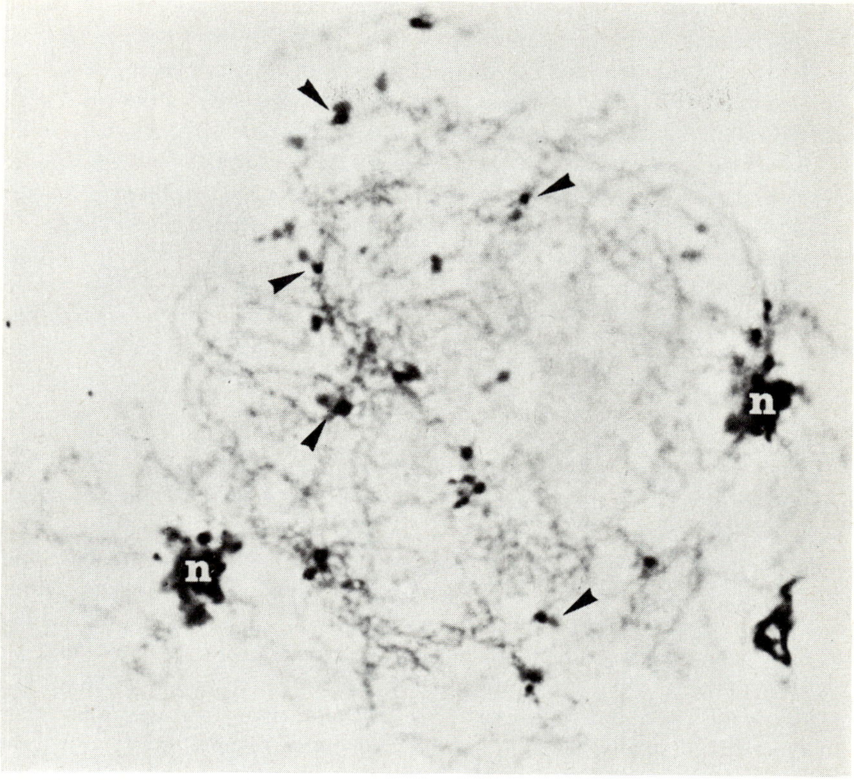

FIG. 3.—Diplotene stage (6 month fetus). Micronucleoli connected with centromeric heterochromatin (arrows). Denaturation with 0.07 N NaOH; renaturation with 2 × SSC. Giesma staining (n = main nucleoli). × 2050.

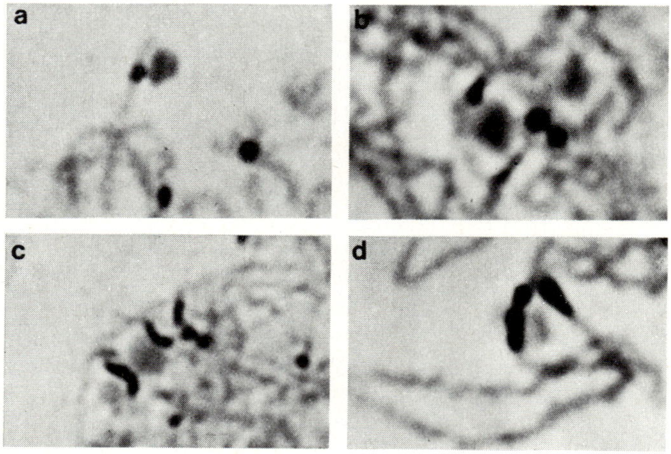

FIG. 4.—Details of diplotene nuclei showing relationships between micronucleolar material and heterochromatic segments. Denaturation with 0.07 N NaOH; renaturation with 2 × SSC. × 3200. (a) and (b)—Micronucleoli connected with centromeric heterochromatin. (c) and (d)—Micronucleoli included between two heterochromatic segments.

On the preparations stained by the Arrighi and Hsu technique a micronucleous was often observed situated between two parallel heterochromatic segments (fig. 4c), or between the two arms of a fork-shaped heterochromatic structure (fig. 4d). These structures may correspond to the secondary constrictions of chromosomes A1, C9, and E16. However, the technique does not allow us to distinguish one from the other.

The G11 technique selectively stains the C9 heterochromatin. When the two chromosomes are still paired in the secondary constriction area the heterochromatin presents itself in the form of a purple body which is sometimes associated with a micronucleolus. After the two heterochromatic regions of chromosome C9 have desynapsed, they adopt the shape of either two separate spherules or two parallel segments. Micronucleolar material was frequently associated with these structures (fig. 5). Other dispersed micronucleoli were visible in the same nucleus (fig. 5).

4. DISCUSSION

Our observations reveal that the oocyte chromosomes synthesise a large body of nucleolar material, and that the synthesis is amplified during the diplotene stage. The appearance of numerous micronucleoli is suggestive, although at a much lower scale, of the ribosomal cistron amplification described in the Amphibian oocyte. We feel that, as in the latter, this phenomenon corresponds to an increased production of ribosomal RNA in connection with an oocyte growth phase. There is, however, an important difference to the system in Amphibians: with these, the multiple copies of the genes coding for ribosomal RNA separate from the chromosomes and move towards the nuclear membrane in the shape of extrachromosomal nucleolar bodies. The only structure present in the human oocyte resembling this body is the complex body found at the pachytene stage. Should the presence of DNA in this body be confirmed, it would present a definite analogy with the Amphibian extra-chromosomal nucleolar organizers.

The elaboration of nucleolar material by heterochromatic regions raises difficulties because it clashes with the classical notion of heterochromatin genetical inactivity. This idea is strengthened by the absence of complementary RNA for the mouse DNA satellite (Walker et al., 1969; Flamm et al., 1969).

Cytological observations, however, are not lacking which describe the elaboration of nucleoli at the contact of heterochromatin: such is the case in the Teleostean oocyte (Yamamoto, 1956; Arndt, 1960; Chouinard, 1963) and in the insect oocyte (Weber, 1971). The cytological and biochemical observations agree as far as the latter is concerned: for example in the oocyte of *Acheta domesticus* a heterochromatic structure, the "DNA-body," which contains satellite DNA, shows an amplification of ribosomal cistrons and assumes the synthesis of ribosomal RNA at the pachytene and diplotene stages (Lima-de-Faria, 1969; Lima-de-Faria et al., 1973). Satellite DNA also codes for the ribosomal RNA in the Amphibian oocytes (Gall, 1969) and a satellite DNA which codes for 9 S m RNA, that is to say for the histone messenger, has also been described (Kedes and Birnstiel, 1971; Pardue, 1974).

Numerous satellite DNA families have been isolated in man. The complementary RNA of type II satellite DNA selectively hybridizes with the centromeric region of A1, C9, and E16 chromosomes (Jones and Corneo, 1971). Saunders et al. (1972*a*, *b*) have isolated repetitive fractions which show a preferential hybridization, one with

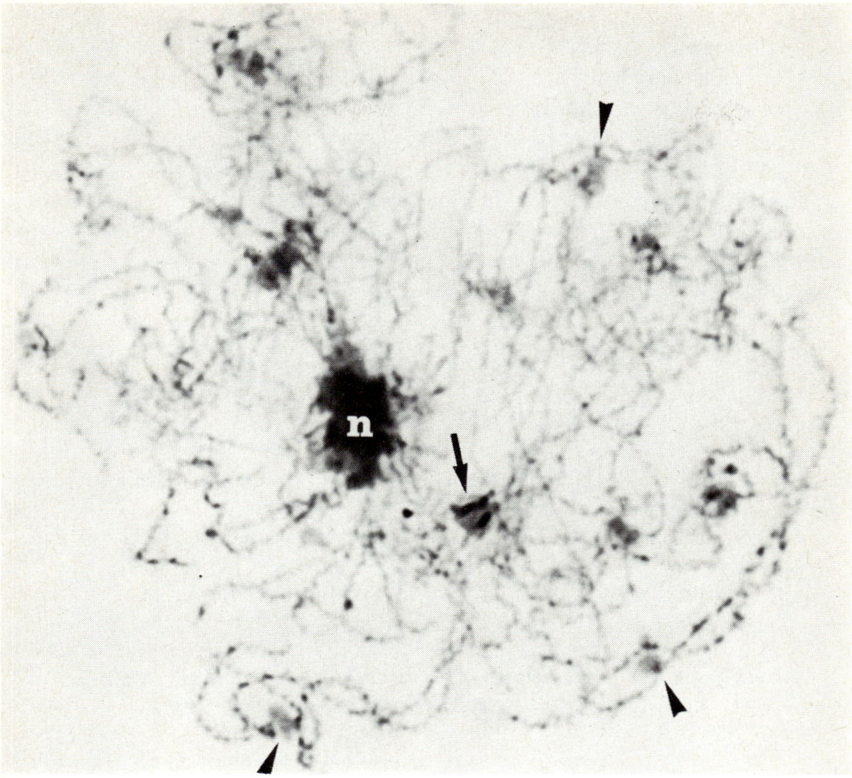

FIG. 5.—Diplotene stage (6 month fetus). Micronucleolar material associated with C9 heterochromatin (arrow). Short arrows indicate dispersed micronucleoli (*n* = main nucleolus). × 2000.

the heterochromatin of chromosome A1 and the other with the heterochromatin of chromosome C9. In contrast to mouse heterochromatin, which is made of a single satellite DNA only, the heterochromatin of man displays large heterogeneity in composition and properties (Saunders et al., 1972*b*). The heterochromatin of chromosome C9 is particularly complex and the centromeric regions of other chromosomes are also far from being composed of a single fraction of repetitive DNA.

We do not exclude the possibility that of the several kinds of satellite DNA present in the centromeric region, one of them assumes a purely structural role, and another, at least in the oocyte is capable of being transcribed into ribosomal RNA. The complexity of C9 heterochromatin encourages us to put forth the hypothesis that one of its components codes for RNA, which would show morphological evidence of translation by the elaboration of nucleolar-type material.

5. CONCLUSIONS

1. The diplotene stage of the human oocyte is characterized by the appearance of numerous micronucleoli while the main nucleoli at the same time become more voluminous.

2. The micronucleoli arise at the contact of heterochromatic regions and differ from the nucleolar organizers on acrocentric chromosomes. They are connected in part to centromeric heterochromatin including various secondary constrictions and in particular that of chromosome C9.

3. There is also a complex body distinct from the nucleoli which contains some RNA. Its central region has a peculiar constitution which perhaps contains DNA.

4. The diplotene stage shows chromosomes which are both morphologically individualized and visible but yet sufficiently despiralized to be genetically active and permit DNA transcription. This condition appears to be a widespread phenomenon in that it has been observed in species very far from man.

6. REFERENCES

ANDRES, A. H., and VOGEL, I. I. 1936. Karyologische Studien der Menschenovogenese. I. Embryonale Ovogenese. *Z. Zellforsch. Mikroskop. Anat., 24,* 552–568.

ARNDT, E. A. 1960. Die Aufgaben der Kerne während der Oogenese der Teleosteer. *Z. Zellforsch. Mikroskop. Anat., 51,* 356–378.

ARRIGHI, F. E., and HSU, T. C. 1971. Localization of heterochromatin in human chromosomes. *Cytogenetics (Basel), 10,* 81–86.

BAKER, T. G., and FRANCHI, L. L. 1967. The structure of the chromosomes in human primordial oocytes. *Chromosoma (Berl.), 22,* 358–377.

BOBROW, M., MADAN, K., and PEARSON, P. L. 1972. Staining of some specific regions of human chromosomes, particularly on secondary constriction of No. 9. *Nat. New Biol., 238,* 122–124.

CALLAN, H. G. 1966. Chromosomes and nucleoli of the axolotl, *Ambystoma mexicanum. J. Cell. Sci., 1,* 85–108.

CHOUINARD, L. A. 1963. Sites of formation of the extra nucleoli during early oocyte growth in the freshwater teleost, *Salvelinus fontinalis* Mitchill. *Can. J. Zool., 41,* 997–1010.

FLAMM, W. G., WALKER, P. M. B., and MCCALLUM, M. 1969. Some properties of the single strands isolated from the DNA of the nuclear satellite of the mouse *(Mus musculus). J. Mol. Biol., 40,* 423–443.

GAGNÉ, R., and LABERGE, C. 1972. Specific cytological recognition of the heterochromatic segment of number 9 chromosome in man. *Exp. Cell Res., 73,* 239–242.

GALL, J. G. 1968. Differential synthesis on the genes for ribosomal RNA during amphibian oogenesis. *Proc. Natl. Acad. Sci. U.S.A., 60,* 553–560.

GALL, J. G. 1969. The genes for ribosomal RNA during oogenesis. *Genetics, 61* (Suppl.), 121–132.

JONES, K. W., and CORNEO, G. 1971. Location of satellite and homogeneous DNA sequences on human chromosomes. *Nat. New Biol., 233,* 268–271.

KEDES, L. H., and BIRNSTIEL, M. L. 1971. Reiteration and clustering of DNA sequences complementary to histone messenger RNA. *Nat. New Biol., 230,* 165.

KINDRED, J. E. 1963. The chromosomes of the ovary of the human fetus. *Anat. Rec., 147,* 295–311.

KUNZ, W. 1967*a*. Funktionsstrukturen im Oocytenkern von *Locusta migratoria. Chromosoma (Berl.), 20,* 332–370.

KUNZ, W. 1967*b*. Lampenbürstenchromosomen und multiple Nukleolen bei Orthopteren. *Chromosoma (Berl.), 21,* 446–462.

LIMA-DE-FARIA, A. 1969. DNA replication and gene amplification in heterochromatin. In *Handbook of Molecular Cytology,* (LIMA-DE-FARIA, ed.), pp. 277–325. North Holland Publishing Company, Amsterdam-London.

LIMA-DE-FARIA, A., JAWORSKA, H., and GUSTAFSSON, T. 1973. Release of amplified ribosomal DNA from the chromomeres of Acheta. *Proc. Natl. Acad. Sci. U.S.A., 70,* 80–83.

LUCIANI, J. M., and STAHL, A. 1971. Rapports des nucleoles avec les chromosomes méiotiques de l'ovocyte foetal humain. *C.R. Acad. Sci. (Paris), 273,* 521–524.

LUCIANI, J. M., DEVICTOR-VUILLET, M., GAGNÉ, R., and STAHL, A. 1974. An air-drying method for first meiotic prophase preparations from mammalian ovaries. *J. Reprod. Fertil., 36,* 409–411.

MACGREGOR, H. C. 1965. The role of lampbrush chromosomes in the formation of nucleoli in amphibian oocytes. *Q. J. Microsc. Sci., 106,* 215–228.

MANOTAYA, T., and POTTER, E. L. 1963. Oocytes in prophase of meiosis from squash preparations of human fetal ovaries. *Fertil. and Steril., 14,* 378–392.

OHNO, S., KLINGER, H. P., and ATKIN, N. B. 1962. Human oogenesis. *Cytogenetics (Basel), 1,* 42–51.

PARDUE, M. L. 1974. Repeated DNA sequences in the chromosomes of higher organisms. In *Birth Defects* (A. G. MOTULSKY and W. LENZ, eds.), pp. 32–43. Excerpta Medica Amsterdam.

SAUNDERS, G. F., SHIRAKAWA, S., SAUNDERS, P. P., ARRIGHI, F. E., and HSU, T. C. 1972*a*. Populations of repeated DNA sequences in the human genome. *J. Mol. Biol., 63,* 323–334.

SAUNDERS, G. F., HSU, T. C., GETZ, M. J., SIMES, E. L., and ARRIGHI, F. E. 1972*b*. Locations of a human satellite DNA in human chromosomes. *Nat. New Biol., 236,* 244–246.

STAHL, A. and LUCIANI, J. M. 1972. Nucleoli and chromosomes: their relationships during the meiotic prophase of the human fetal oocyte. *Humangenetik, 14,* 269–284.

SWEZY, O., and EVANS, H. M. 1930. The human ovarian germ cells. *J. Morph. and Physiol, 49,* 543–578.

WALKER, P. M. B., FLAMM, W. G., and MCLAREN, A. 1969. Highly repetitive DNA in rodents. In *Handbook of Molecular Cytology* (LIMA-DE-FARIA, ed.), pp. 53–66. North-Holland Publishing Company, Amsterdam–London.

WEBER, F. 1971. Korrelierte Formveränderungen von Nukleolus und nukleolusassortiertem Heterochromatin bei der Gattung *Carabus (Coleoptera). Chromosoma (Berl.), 34,* 261–273.

WINIWARTER, H. VON. 1901. Recherches sur l'ovogenèse et l'organogenèse de l'ovaire des mammifères (Lapin et Homme). *Arch. Biol., 17,* 33–199.

YAMAMOTO, K. 1956. Changes in the nucleus of the oocyte of *Liopsetta obscura* with special reference to the activity of the nucleolus. *J. Fac. Sci. Hokkaido Univ.* Ser. VI Zool., *12,* 375–389.

MALE STERILITY AND DOUBLE HETEROZYGOSITY FOR ROBERTSONIAN TRANSLOCATIONS IN MOUSE

E. P. EVANS

Medical Research Council, External Scientific Staff,
Sir William Dunn School of Pathology, University of Oxford,
South Parks Road, Oxford, U.K.

Until recently all the individuals examined from every mouse colony showed 40 acrocentric chromosomes the meiotic segregation of which was remarkably regular. But following the discovery of four Robertsonian translocations in laboratory stocks (Evans et al., 1967; Léonard and Deknudt, 1967; White and Tjio, 1968; Baranov and Dyban, 1971), and a further ten in feral populations (Gropp et al., 1970, 1972), nearly all the acrocentrics have now been found combined in pairs as metacentrics. In a Robertsonian heterozygote, the trivalent formed at meiosis often shows irregular segregation, and a high frequency of nullosomic and disomic metaphase II cells is produced. Many workers, including ourselves, have used such Robertsonian heterozygotes to produce trisomic embryos. We have also used them to show that nullosomic sperm are capable of fertilisation to give zygotes which develop to the time of implantation (Ford and Evans, 1974).

The use of animals heterozygous for a single Robertsonian translocation has the disadvantage that two different disomic or nullosomic gametes can arise, one for each arm of the metacentric, and so produce two different types of trisomic and monosomic zygotes which are not immediately karyotypically distinguishable. This problem can be overcome by using mice doubly heterozygous for Robertsonian translocations which have a homologous arm (fig. 1). The chromosomes concerned can form a quadrivalent at meiosis (fig. 2). This may undergo regular segregation to give normal metaphase II counts of 20 chromosome arms including one metacentric (fig. 3). Alternatively it may segregate irregularly so that the two (adjacent) metacentrics go to one pole and the two acrocentrics to the other. The consequences of such irregular segregation are reflected in the occurrence of abnormal second metaphases of two types, one with both metacentrics and a total of 21 chromosome arms (fig. 4), the other with 19 acrocentric chromosomes only (fig. 5). The point of special interest about these cells is that the extra chromosome arm in the first type is (automatically) identified as the arm shared by the two metacentrics, and that the chromosome arm absent from the second type is (presumptively) also this homologous short arm. The latter inference is negative and there is always the possibility in the individual cell that the missing chromosome is attributable to non-disjunction of an independent bivalent or to artefact consequent upon damage during preparation.

White et al. (1972) and Gropp and Kolbus (1974) used this method to produce and study specific trisomy in the mouse. We know that nullisomic sperm are functional and that embryos can proceed to the implantation stage whether they are monosomic, diploid, or trisomic for a particular chromosome (Ford and Evans, 1974). In the present work we have mated male and female mice doubly heterozygous for the same

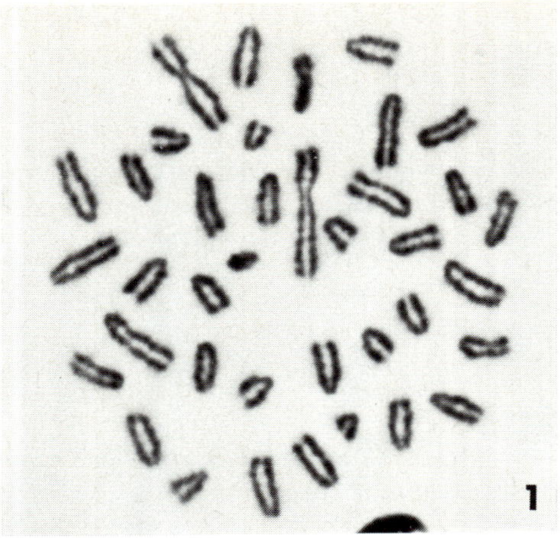

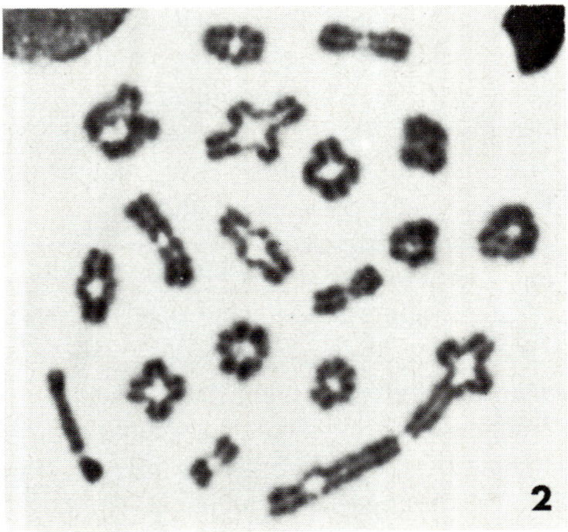

FIG. 1.—A spermatogonial mitosis with two Robertsonian metacentrics having a homologous short arm.

FIG. 2.—The quadrivalent formed by the two metacentrics at metaphase I.

Robertsonians to study the prospects of nullisomic zygote formation and development.

The metaphase II observations of White et al. (1972) in male double heterozygotes indicate the expected frequency of nullosomic gametes to be 0.17. Assuming the frequency of irregular segregation in double heterozygote females to be at least as great, approximately 3% nullosomic zygotes might be expected from the intercross. This frequency is low and there is no assurance that in other types of double heterozygotes it would even be as high. Nevertheless, though searching for nullosomic zygotes is arduous, we decided it was worthwhile. We had the means to establish three different types of the mice required. This we did but we encountered a difficulty of an unexpected kind.

The three types were produced in the sequential order shown in fig. 6. The terminology used is the one recommended by the Subcommittee on Cytogenetics of the

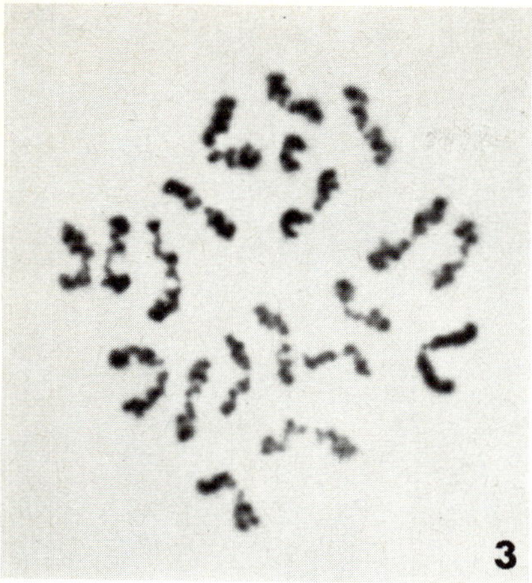

3

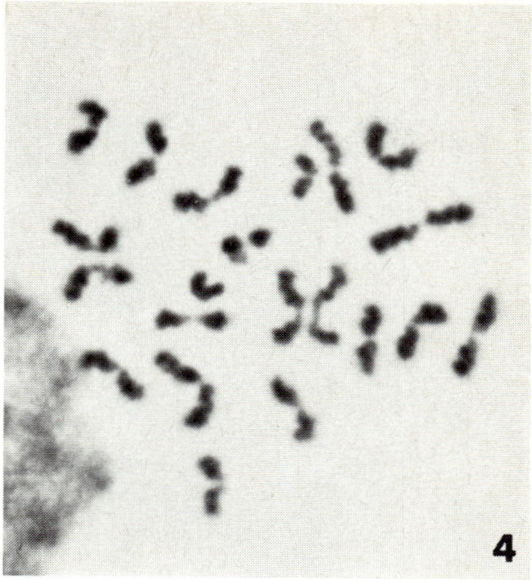

4

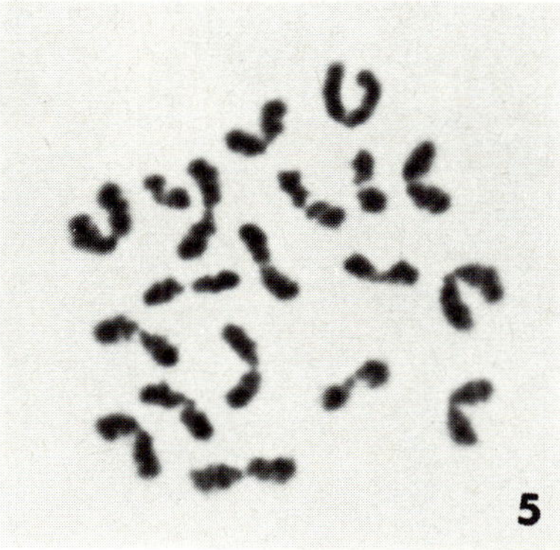

5

FIG. 3.—Normal metaphase II count of 20 chromosome arms including one metacentric following the regular segregation of the quadrivalent.

FIG. 4.—Abnormal metaphase II count of 21 chromosome arms including both metacentrics following the irregular segregation of the quadrivalent.

FIG. 5.—Abnormal metaphase II count of 19 chromosome arms with no metacentric following the irregular segregation of the quadrivalent.

Committee on Standardized Genetic Nomenclature for Mice (Mouse News Letter, No. 50, 1974), Robertsonian translocation being denoted by the symbol Rb. Animals of the first type, heterozygous for Rb(9;14) 6 Bnr and Rb(9;19) 163H, were intercrossed when sexually mature at the age of eight weeks. Females with copulation plugs were killed at gestational day 3 when they should have been carrying preimplantation embryos approximating to the 32-cell stage of cleavage. However, degenerate eggs only were found in the four females examined. This infertility might have been a fault of the males, or the females, or conceivably of both. To resolve the problem, one of the males was killed at the age of nine weeks and was found to have considerably reduced testis weights, 35 mg as against an expected 100 mg, and reduced spermatogenic activity with only a few sperm being produced. A further nine males aged between 9 and 14 weeks were examined and all gave the same picture. Female fertility was tested by mating the females to normal males and then killing

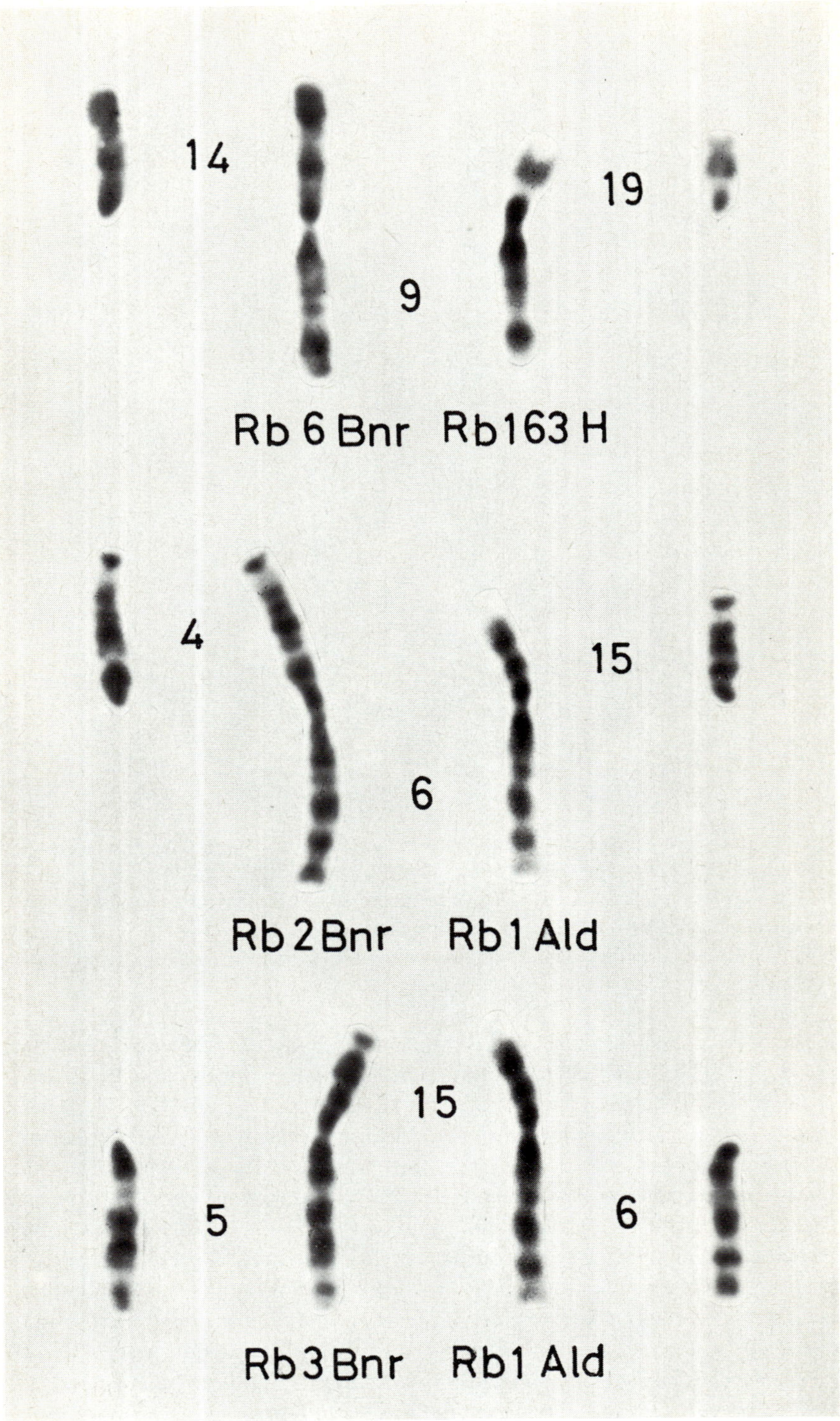
14
9
19
Rb 6 Bnr
Rb163 H
4
6
15
Rb 2 Bnr
Rb 1 Ald
15
5
6
Rb 3 Bnr
Rb 1 Ald

for pre-implantation embryos on gestational day 3. On this basis the three females tested proved fully fertile.

In the second type of animal, heterozygous for Rb(4;6) 2 Bnr and Rb(6;15) 1 Ald, five males within an age range of 6 to 28 weeks were killed and examined, and all gave evidence of sterility. Testis weights were reduced to between 15 and 40 mg, spermatogenic activity was reduced, and few sperm were being produced.

The first male examined from the third type, heterozygous for Rb(5;15) 3 Bnr and Rb(6;15) 1 Ald, suggested that the same sterility phenomenon was occurring. Admittedly, the male was only four weeks of age but even at this age he should have been producing many sperm and the testis weight should have been much higher than the 19 mg recorded. Recently, however, five of his brothers were mated and the breeding tests indicated that they were fertile to some degree. Moreover, metaphase II observations in one of these males indicate that 15% nullosomic sperm were being produced so it may yet be possible to obtain zygotes with a zero dosage for chromosome 15.

It therefore appears from our observations that combining certain Robertsonian translocations with a homologous arm may lead to male sterility in the mouse. This is by no means the only chromosomal phenomenon associated with sterility; eight other categories were listed by Ford et al. (1973), a ninth was found by Slizynski and quoted by Carter et al. (1956), a tenth was described by Purnell (1973). Our observations therefore constitute an eleventh type. The 10 types previously defined are:

1. X-autosome translocations;
2. Y-autosome translocations;
3. Single reciprocal translocations;
4. Multiple reciprocal translocations;
5. Insertional translocations;
6. Tertiary trisomy;
7. Failure of association of X and Y in meiotic prophase;
8. Sex chromosome trisomics which include XXY and XYY;
9. Double heterozygosity for certain reciprocal translocations involving a common chromosome;
10. Spontaneous univalence.

These ten types show a whole range of effects on the testis from a complete absence of spermatogenic cells as in the case of a XXY mouse (Cattanach, 1961) to the progressive decline of spermatogenesis apparently commencing from any one of a variety of points. Because of the insufficient information that is available regarding the histological manifestation of sterility little is known about the nature of the decline and it is still not clear whether complete arrest of spermatogenesis with absence of all later stages may occur in some instances. In our experience, certain animals in some of the categories listed above produced no sperm at all; others produced sperm to normal levels but were nevertheless full steriles. Many exhibit features similar to the ones described here: a reduction in testis weight accompanied

---

FIG. 6.—ASG banded partial karyotypes of the three different types of mice produced. The chromosomes involved are numbered according to the standard karyotype recommended by the Committee on Standardized Genetic Nomenclature for Mice (1972).

by a severe decline in the number of cells which reach the primary spermatocyte stage with the consequent production of few sperm.

No satisfactory explanation has been put forward for the other forms of male infertility and we are unable to offer one for the sterility in our double Robertsonian heterozygotes. It is notable that males singly heterozygous for the Robertsonian translocations used are fully fertile as far as the production of zygotes is concerned, and also that multiple Robertsonian heterozygotes in which no two metacentric chromosomes share a homologous arm are similarly fertile. Our observation is paralleled by the one reported by Slizynski and mentioned by Carter et al. (1956): males doubly heterozygous for certain reciprocal translocations that involved a heterozygotes of both types exhibited the typical semi-sterility of reciprocal translocation heterozygotes in the mouse. These double translocation heterozygotes, both Robertsonian and reciprocal, have a common feature in that both commonly form long, chain multivalents at meiosis. However, even if further observations should establish that this property is significant, present knowledge does not suggest a plausible hypothesis that could relate the formation of long multivalents to sterility. Similar multivalents are formed in our third type of animal, heterozygous for Rb (5;15) 3 Bnr and Rb(6;15) 1 Ald, and also in the double heterozygotes produced by White et al. (1972) and Gropp and Kolbus (1974) and yet in these instances the males proved fertile.

Our intention is to produce further animals of the same kind but using reciprocal crosses to previous ones and parents of a different origin wherever possible. The study of these animals should tell us whether male sterility is an invariable property of particular combinations of Robertsonian translocations or whether it is sensitive to the residual genetic background.

Acknowledgement. I am indebted to Dr. C. E. Ford for his valuable advice during the preperation of this manuscript, to Mrs. J. Whittenbury for her skill in producing the required animals, and to Mr. M. D. Burtenshaw for his assistance at all times.

REFERENCES

Baranov, V. S., and Dyban, A. P. 1971. Embryogenesis and peculiarities of karyotype in mouse embryos and centric fusion of chromosomes (Robertsonian translocation). *Ontogenese Akad. Nauk. SSSR, 2,* 164–175.

Carter, T. C., Lyon, M. F., and Phillips, R. J. S. 1956. Further genetic studies of eleven translocations in the mouse. *J. Genet., 54,* 462–472.

Cattanach, B. M. 1961. XXY mice. *Genet. Res., 2,* 156–157.

Committee on Standarized Genetic Nomenclature for Mice. 1972. Standard karyotype of the mouse, *Mus musculus. J. Hered., 63,* 69–72.

Evans, E. P., Lyon, M. F., and Daglish, M. 1967. A mouse translocation giving a metacentric marker chromosome. *Cytogenetics (Basel), 6,* 105–119.

Ford, C. E., and Evans, E. P. 1974. Non-expression of genome unbalance in haplophase and early diplophase of the mouse and incidence of karyotypic abnormality in post-implantation embryos. In *Symp. Les Accidents Chromosomiques de la Reproduction* (A. Boué et C. Thibault, eds.), pp. 271–285. Institut National de la Santé et la Recherche Médicale.

Ford, C. E., Burtenshaw, M. D., Clegg, H. M., and Evans, E. P. 1973. *Mouse News Letter,* No. 49, 43.

GROPP, A., and KOLBUS, V. 1974. Exencephaly in the syndrome of trisomy No. 12 of the foetal mouse. *Nature (Lond.)*, *249*, 145–147.

GROPP, A., TETTENBORN, V., and LEHMAN, E. VON. 1970. Chromosomenvariation vom Robertson'schen Typus bei der Tabakmaus, *M. poschiavinus*, und ihren Hybriden mit der Laboratoriumsmaus. *Cytogenetics (Basel)*, *9*, 9–23.

GROPP, A., WINKING, H., ZECH, L., and MULLER, H. 1972. Robertsonian chromosomal variation and identification of metachromosomes in feral mice. *Chromosoma (Berl.)*, *39*, 265–288.

LÉONARD, A., and DEKNUDT, G. H. 1967. A new marker for chromosome studies in the mouse. *Nature (Lond.)*, *214*, 504–505.

PURNELL, D. 1973. Spontaneous univalence at male meiosis in the mouse. *Cytogenet. Cell Genet.*, *12*, 327–335.

WHITE, B. J., and TJIO, J.-H. 1968. A mouse translocation with 38 and 29 chromosomes but normal N.F. *Hereditas*, *58*, 284–296.

WHITE, B. J., TJIO, J.-H., VAN DE WATER, L. C., and CRANDALL, C. 1972. Trisomy for the smallest autosome of the mouse and identification of the T1Wh translocation chromosome. *Cytogenetics (Basel)*, *11*, 363–378.

GAMETIC ANEUPLOIDY IN MOUSE HYBRIDS

E. CAPANNA
Institute of Comparative Anatomy, Rome University, Rome, Italy

1. INTRODUCTION

The role played by the heterozygosity for Robertsonian changes in producing gametic aneuploidy in mice were first emphasized by Evans et al. (1967), White and Tijo (1967), and Leonard and Decknudt (1967). They demonstrated that heterozygosity for only one Robertsonian chromosome, and consequently only one trivalent in the first meiotic diakineses, does not produce gametic aneuploidy or at most a very low frequency of unbalanced gametes.

On the contrary, the gametic aneuploidy revealed by Tettenborn and Gropp (1970) in the *Mus musculus* × *Mus poschiavinus* hybrids is much more striking; here the heterozygosity involves seven metacentric Robertsonian chromosomes, and the consequent seven trivalents segregate to produce over 50% unbalanced male gametes.

In spite of all these observations, interest in this particular problem has not decreased as is demonstrated by the recent paper of Ford and Evans (1973) in which they brought a new variable to bear on the problem; they demonstrated different frequencies of non-disjunction for different Robertsonian chromosomes.

Since I have had the opportunity of finding and studying some interesting *Mus musculus* specimens with a 22-chromosome complement, arising from 9 homozygous Robertsonian fusions, I considered it useful to contribute some data on the gametic unbalance present in the 22 chromosome × 40-chromosome mouse hybrids.

Since reports on this 22-chromosome *Mus musculus* have been published only in a preliminary note (Capanna et al., 1973*a*), it will be necessary to give a brief description of this finding.

2. THE 22-CHROMOSOME MOUSE

Following the advice given to us by Prof. Gropp in 1972, we collected information on Italian populations of *Mus musculus*. Besides the normal 40-chromosome populations and one polymorphic population (Capanna et al., 1973*b*), we found a 22-chromosome homomorphous population.

At present 38 specimens have been examined karyologically. They were trapped in 9 places in an extensive area of the Central Apennines which is about 150 kilometers in diameter and reaches the Adriatic coast. The karyotype (see fig. 1) is composed of 9 pairs of metacentric chromosomes, one pair of small acrocentrics, and one heteromorphic sexual pair: the fundamental number (F.N.) is 40.

In testicular preparations, the diakinesis displays 9 large bivalents, with 2 or 3 chiasmata, one small bivalent, and the sex-bivalent.

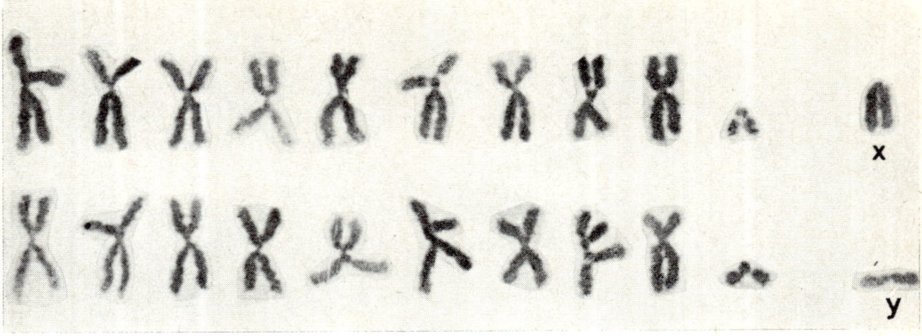

FIG. 1.—The 22-chromosome karyotype of the Apennine mice.

It is worth pointing out that in two villages situated a few kilometers apart along the southwest boundary between the areas of distribution of the 40- and the 22-chromosome forms, we caught several specimens with hybrid karyotypes. These had a F.N. of 40 but diploid numbers of $2n = 39, 38, 37, 36$, and 34.

The trypsin-Giemsa banding pattern of the 22-chromosome karyotype indicates that none of the centric fusions found in the 7 metacentrics of *Mus poschiavinus* or in the Alpine populations of *Mus musculus* (Gropp et al., 1972) has been found in this Apennine mouse.

The possibility of hybridization between 40- and 22-chromosome individuals is suggested by the very large number of hybrids easily obtained under breeding conditions. These F_1 hybrids have 31 chromosomes, which at diakinesis of the male meiosis arrange themselves to form 9 trivalents, a small bivalent, and the sex bivalent. F_2 hybrids, on the other hand, are very hard to obtain; in fact although 20 female F_1 hybrids were mated with male F_1 hybrids, only in four cases did the pregnancies develop to term. The number of births was in all cases very low, with three offsprings from one female, two from another, and only one from the other two. Although fertility is also low in the F_2 hybrids, F_3 hybrids can be obtained more easily than F_2.

3. THE MEIOSIS OF HYBRID MALES

Now we examine the results of the analysis of the second metaphases of the male meiosis which offers an explanation of low fertility in hybrids. The table shows data from observations on 8 hybrids with 31 chromosomes and 4 animals from each parental strain. Specimens and preparations were randomly selected and all the second metaphases present in the random samples counted. Approximately 30% of the male gametes produced by the hybrids were balanced.

This finding was not unexpected: Tettenborn and Gropp (1970) found 50% of aneuploid gametes in male hybrids with 7 Robertsonian heterozygosities, i.e., *Mus musculus* × *Mus poschiavinus* hybrids, and therefore 70% of unbalanced gametes in a hybrid with 9 Robertsonian chromosomes is acceptable. A further finding of Tettenborn and Gropp (1970) has been confirmed, viz., that the metacentrics tend to be equally divided in the two second spermatocytes. In our case, the 9 metacentrics tend to be divided 4 and 5 or, less frequently, 6 and 3. Other combinations are rare or completely lacking (fig. 3).

TABLE

Number of chromosome arms scored in secound meiotic metaphase of parental and hybrid mice

	Code of animals	Haploid fundamental number (No. of chromosome arms)							
		−18	18	19	20	21	22	+22	Total
31-chromosome hybrids	SW × SLF 5/2	6	8	18	16	6	4	8	66
	SW × SLF 5/8	8	4	6	9	6	2	2	37
	SW × SLF 5/13	6	8	6	15	—	3	2	40
	SW × SLF 5/16	2	4	—	12	11	—	3	32
	SW × SLF 5/18	—	3	5	10	4	—	—	22
	R 34 × SLF 11/1	10	4	9	15	10	3	3	54
	R 34 × SLF 11/2	12	5	10	16	9	—	—	52
	SFC × R 35/5	8	6	13	10	6	1	—	44
	Total	52	42	67	103	52	13	18	347
	Percent	*14.99*	*12.10*	*19.30*	*29.68*	*14.99*	*3.76*	*5.18*	100
22-chromos.	SLF 4	—	—	—	54	—	1	—	55
	SLF 5	—	—	1	41	—	—	—	42
	SLF 9	1	—	—	28				29
	AQ 2	—	—	—	42	1	—	1	44
	Total	1	1	1	165	1	1	1	170
	Percent	*0.58*	*0.58*	*0.58*	*97.05*	*0.58*	*0.58*	*0.58*	100
40-chromos.	CAL 9	—	—	1	46	—	—	—	47
	SW 3	1	—	1	48	—	—	—	50
	SIC 13	—	—	—	53	—	—	—	53
	R × VT/1	—	1	2	46	—	—	1	50
	Total	1	1	4	192	—	—	1	200
	Percent	*0.50*	*0.50*	*2.00*	*96.50*	—	—	*0.50*	100

4. DISCUSSION

It is clear that fertility in a 22 × 40-chromosome hybrid is very low and, in any case, less than that of a *Mus musculus* × *Mus poschiavinus* hybrid. In fact we can state that the reproductive fitness of a hybrid, i.e., the probability of forming euploid zygotes, corresponds to the square of the frequency of its balanced gametes. Figure 4 shows the frequencies of the aneuploid gametes and the reproductive fitness plotted against the increasing degree of Robertsonian heterozygosity. An important conclusion emerges: sterility in a hybrid is *not* an absolute but rather a relative concept which would be better expressed in terms of the probability of producing genetically balanced zygotes. For example, this probability in our 31 chromosome hybrid is 8 %, but rises to 17 % in the *Mus poschiavinus* × *Mus musculus* hybrids and gradually increases as the degree of Robertsonian heterozygosity decreases.

However, in theory the possibility exists that genetic information can filter through the barrier built up by Robertsonian changes, even in the face of 9 translocations. This theory may be a reality as our F_2 and F_3 laboratory hybrids and the finding of natural hybrid populations demonstrate. In fact, even if the trivalents have few

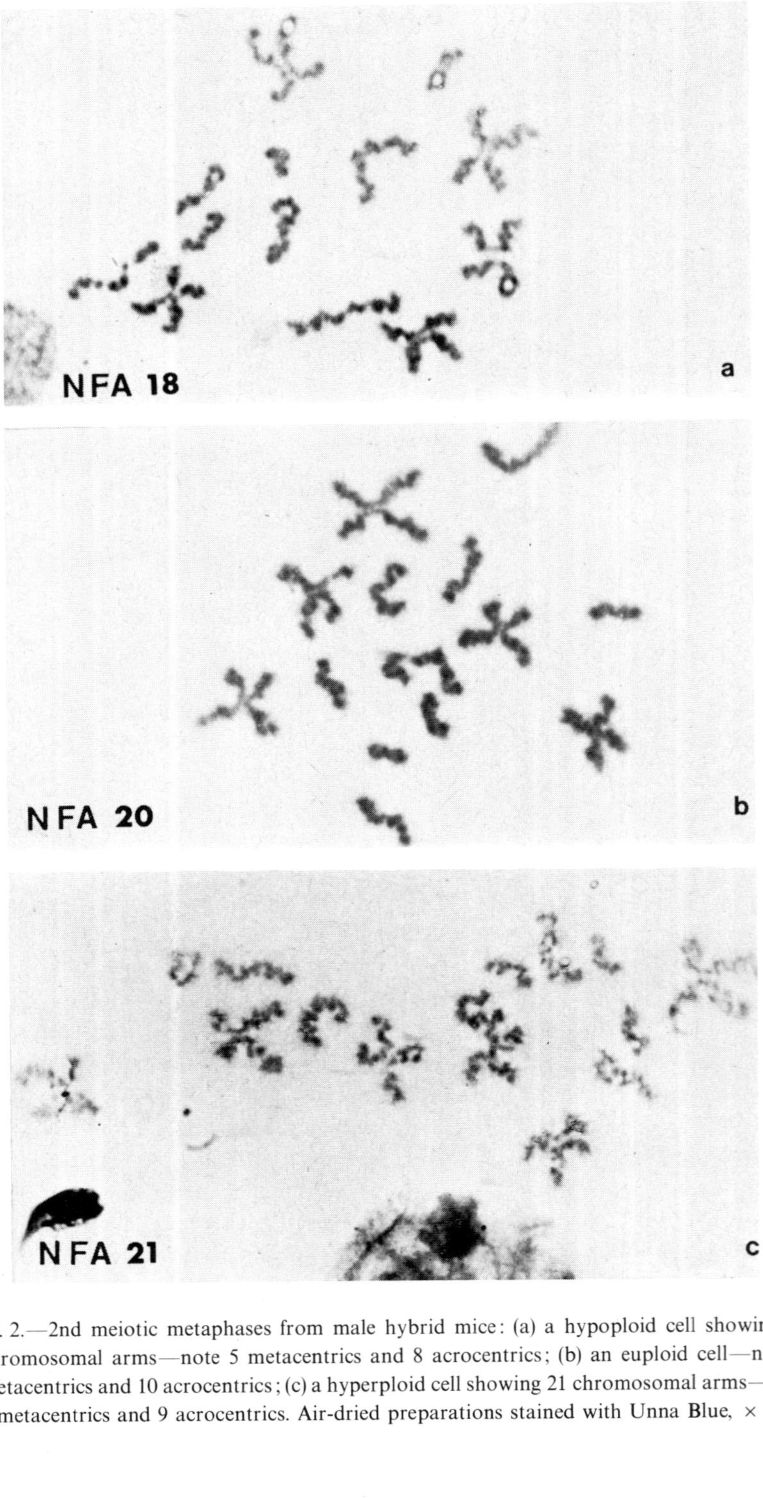

FIG. 2.—2nd meiotic metaphases from male hybrid mice: (a) a hypoploid cell showing 18 chromosomal arms—note 5 metacentrics and 8 acrocentrics; (b) an euploid cell—note 5 metacentrics and 10 acrocentrics; (c) a hyperploid cell showing 21 chromosomal arms—note 6 metacentrics and 9 acrocentrics. Air-dried preparations stained with Unna Blue, × 2000.

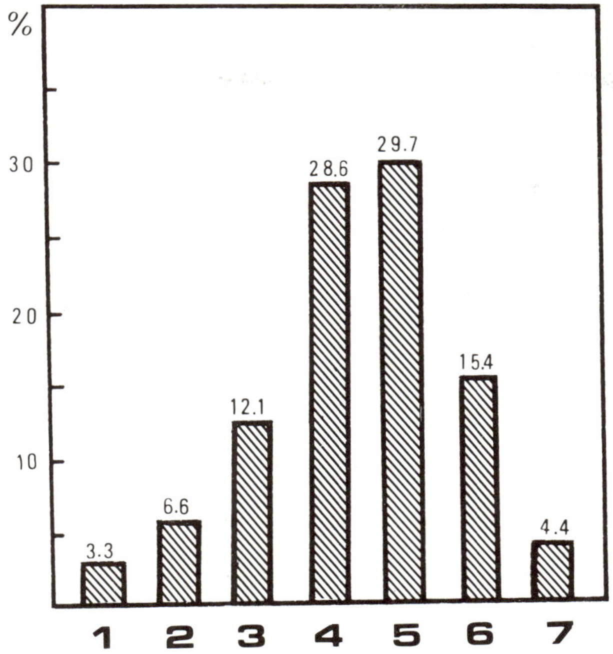

FIG. 3.—Histogram of the distribution of the metacentrics in the gametes of the male hybrids.

chiasmata, crossing over can transfer genetic material from the metacentrics to the homologous acrocentrics. It should not be forgotten that the equal division of metacentrics in sister gametes rapidly decreases heterozygosity in the progeny of back-crosses and, consequently, increases their reproductive probability.

It is possible, therefore, to hypothesize that once the bottleneck of the F_1 has been overcome, the probability of transferring genetic material from one Robertsonian transformed population to another is no longer negligible. Do *Mus musculus* populations with 22 and 40 chromosome complements share in a common gene pool? Do *Mus poschiavinus* and other *Mus musculus* polymorphic Alpine populations share in the same common gene pool? In other words, what is the probability of a gene crossing the reproductive barrier built up by 9 or 7 Robertsonian fusions? What level of reproductive fitness in hybrids should be taken as the limits for considering two parental populations as being sufficiently genetically separate to be considered as belonging to two different species? (Dobzhansky, 1950). The taxonomical separation between *Mus musculus* and *Mus poschiavinus* has only been reexamined following the chromosomal data of Gropp (Gropp et al., 1970); in fact Miller (1912) considered *Mus poschiavinus* and *Mus musculus musculus* to be synonymous. Are the Apennine populations of mice described here to be classified as *Mus musculus*? Although from the morphological point of view this name is correct, perhaps we should look for another specific name for these populations.

However, basic to considerations of the taxonomic consequences of hybrid fertility, we have to verify the effectiveness of the Robertsonian barrier. Qualitative

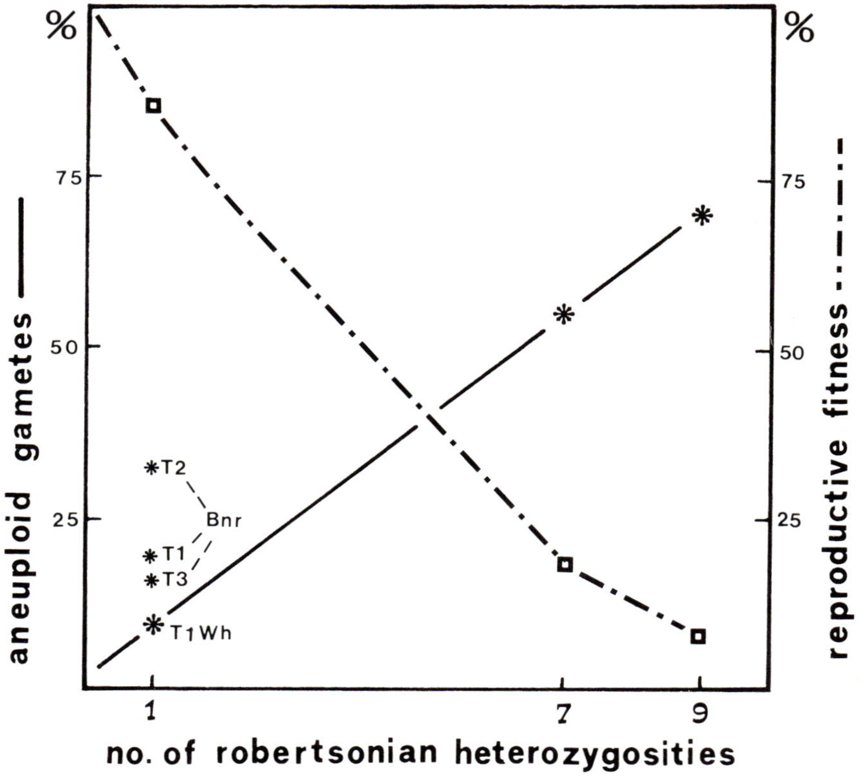

FIG. 4.—The frequencies of the aneuploid male gametes (solid line) and the reproductive fitness (dotted line) are plotted against the number of Robertsonian translocations. T_1 Wh indicates the frequency reported by White and Tijo (1967); T_1 Bnr, T_2 Bnr, and T_3 Bnr indicate different frequencies reported by Ford and Evans (1973) for different Robertsonian translocations.

and quantitative analyses on the gene frequencies in the two gene pools on either side of the Robertsonian barrier would undoubtedly contribute to a better understanding of this problem. Our study group, in fact, is planning research along these lines.

5. SUMMARY

1. A wild population of *Mus musculus* L. in the Central Apennine was found to have a 22-chromosome complement; 9 pairs of centric fusions transformed the 40-chromosome karyotype of the mouse into the 22-chromosome karyotype found. Natural hybrid populations (2n = 39, 38, 37, 36, and 34) have been found in two villages along the boundary between the areas of distribution of the 40- and 22-chromosome forms.

2. In order to evaluate the role played by the Robertsonian changes in creating a genetic isolation and, consequently, in speciation, the meiotic pattern was investigated in laboratory hybrids obtained by crossing 22-chromosome with 40

chromosome mice. The analysis of the 2nd meiotic metaphases demonstrates that 70% of the male gametes show aneuploid—both hyper- and hypoploid— arrangements of the chromosome arms.

6. REFERENCES

CAPANNA, E., CIVITELLI, M. V., and CRISTALDI, M. 1973*a*. Una popolazione appenninica di *Mus musculus* L. caratterizzata da un cariotipo a 22 cromosomi. *Rend. Acc. Naz. Lincei, ser. 8, 54,* 981–984.

CAPANNA, E., CIVITELLI, M. V., and CRISTALDI, M. 1973*b*. Chromosomal polymorphism in an Alpine population of *Mus musculus*. *Boll. Zool., 40,* 379–383.

DOBZHANSKY, T. 1950. Mendelian populations and their evolution. *Am. Nat., 84,* 401–409.

EVANS, E. P., LYON, M. L., and DAGLISH, M. 1967. A mouse translocation giving a metacentric marker chromosome. *Cytogenetics (Basel), 6,* 105–119.

FORD, C. E., and EVANS, E. P. 1973. Robertsonian translocations in mice: segregational irregularities in male heterozygotes and zygotic unbalance. In *Chromosomes Today, 4* (J. WAHRMANN and K. R. LEWIS, eds.), pp. 387–397. Israel Universities Press, Jerusalem, and John Wiley & Sons, New York.

GROPP, A., TETTENBORN, U., and LEHMANN, E. von. 1970. Chromosomenvariation vom Robertson'schen Typus bei der Tabakmaus, *M. poschiavinus*, und ihren Hybriden mit der Laboratoriumsmaus. *Cytogenetics (Basel), 9,* 9–23.

GROPP, A., WINKING, H., ZECH, L., and MULLER, H. 1972. Robertsonian chromosomal variation and identification of metacentric chromosomes in feral mice. *Chromosoma (Berl.), 39,* 265–288.

LEONARD, A., and DEKNUDT, G. H. 1967. A new marker for chromosome studies in the mouse. *Nature (Lond.), 214,* 504–505.

LEONARD, A., and DEKNUDT, G. H. 1969. Etude d'une translocation de type Robertsonien chez les souris de race AKR. *Acta Zool. Pathol. Antverpiensia, 48,* 43–57.

MILLER, G. S. 1912. *Catalogue of the Mammals of West Europe*. Trustees of the British Museum (Nat. History), London.

TETTENBORN, U., and GROPP, A. 1970. Meiotic non-disjunction in mice and mouse hybrids. *Cytogenetics (Basel), 9,* 272–283.

WHITE, B. J., and TIJO, J. H. 1967. A mouse translocation with 38 and 39 chromosomes but normal F.N. *Hereditas, 58,* 284–296.

CHANGES IN THE FORM OF THE POLYTENE X CHROMOSOME IN *PHRYNE (SYLVICOLA) CINCTA* —CAUSES AND FUNCTIONAL SIGNIFICANCE

B. ERICH WOLF and STEPHEN SOKOLOFF

Institute of Genetics, Free University of Berlin, and
Max Planck Institute of General Biology, Abt. Berman, Tübingen, W. Germany

1. INTRODUCTION

The appearance of the polytene X chromosome in Phryne (Diptera, Nematocera, Phryneidae) varies considerably (Wolf, 1957, 1970). It differs not only from one individual to another, but even among the cells of the same organ (fig. 2). The form depends on the tightness of the bundle of the chromatid equivalents, which seems to increase with greater polytenization. Certain environmental conditions, e.g., moisture, seem to directly influence the bundling (see 3(c)). Other factors such as the rearing temperature and the extent of crowding act indirectly. As will be shown, they do not directly change the bundling density, but rather affect the larval development, thereby apparently determining the degree of polyteny attained prior to pupation.

In large, highly-polytene cells of cold-reared females, the X is euchromatic. It looks like a "normal" giant chromosome; deeply-stained transverse bands alternate with poorly-stained interbands (in slides with carmine or orcein), and the width is not greater than that of the autosomes in the same nucleus (fig. 1a). In smaller cells the X has an entirely different form which we designate as diffuse (= unclearly banded) or beta-heterochromatic. Here it is much wider than the autosomes and shorter in proportion to them than it is in the euchromatic state; it can even be wider than long or square-shaped (fig. 1b). The distinction between bands and interbands is poorly defined, so that the chromosome stains with nearly the same intensity throughout a considerable portion of its length; lightly where there are few bands in the euchromatic condition, more heavily where there are many (fig. 1b: compare proximal and distal parts of the chromosome).

Usually the X is neither completely diffuse nor completely euchromatic, but intermediate in form. Except in the tiniest cells the autosomes are primarily euchromatic, but certain short segments behave like the X (Wolf, 1970).

Two types of X chromosome have been described in *Phryne cincta*, X_a and X_b (fig. 1a–d). Both can be found in euchromatic, intermediate, and diffuse states (Wolf, 1963; Wolf and Sokoloff, 1973). X_b contains a small alpha-heterochromatic band near its proximal end (alpha-1). In addition, X_a has two much larger ones near its distal end (alpha-2 and alpha-3; fig. 1c–d). When X_a occurs together with X_b in female heterozygotes (X_aX_b) a complicated series of proximal inversions becomes evident while the distal segments remain unpaired (see figs. 6 and 8b, c in Wolf, 1963).

Alpha-heterochromatin, unlike beta, never euchromatizes in Phryne giant chromosomes. It stains heavily with carmine or orcein, is usually vacuolized, and is frequently the site of weak points, ectopic pairing and alpha-migration (Wolf and Sokoloff, 1973). In contrast to beta-heterochromatin it is long-replicating (fig. 8).

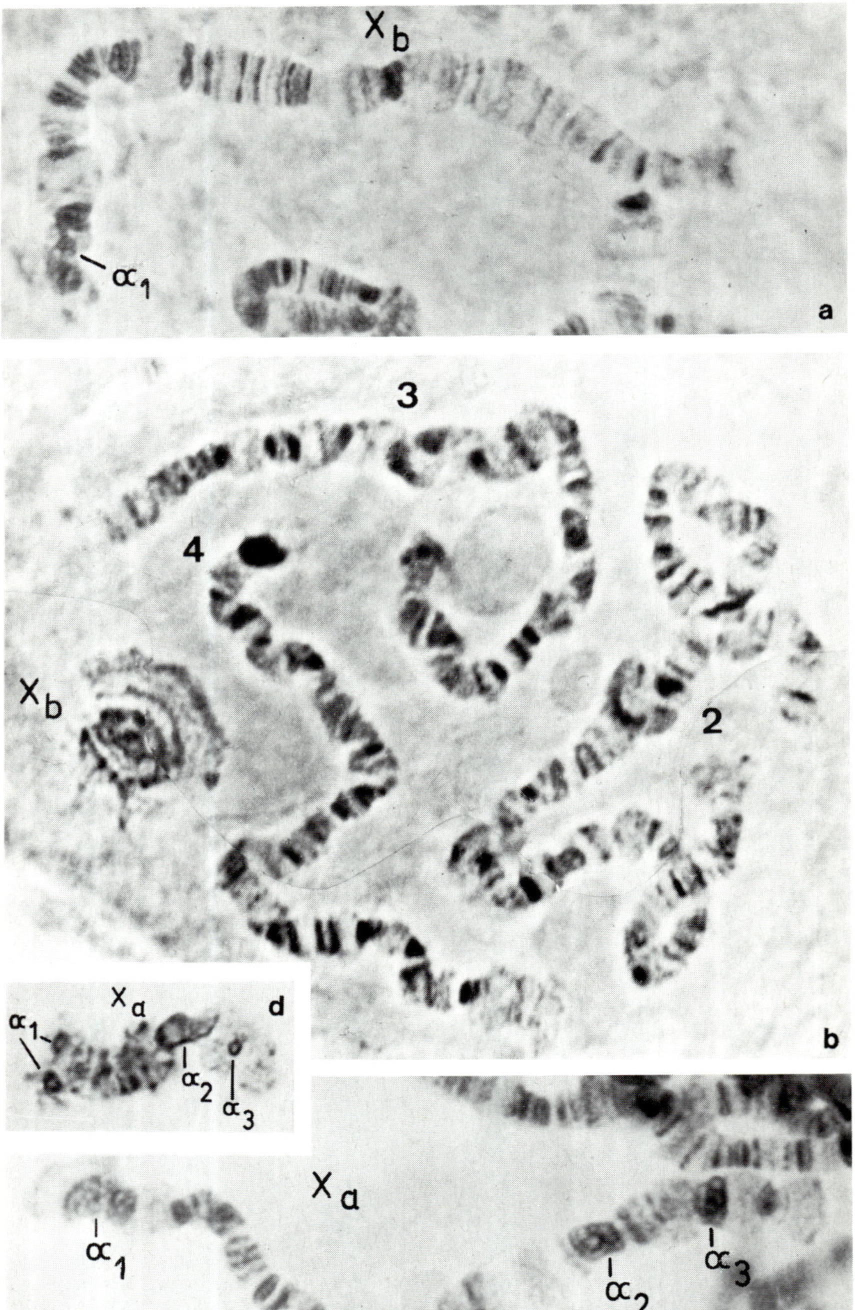
X_b
α_1
a
3
4
X_b
2
b
X_a
α_1
α_2
α_3
d
X_a
α_1
α_2
α_3
c

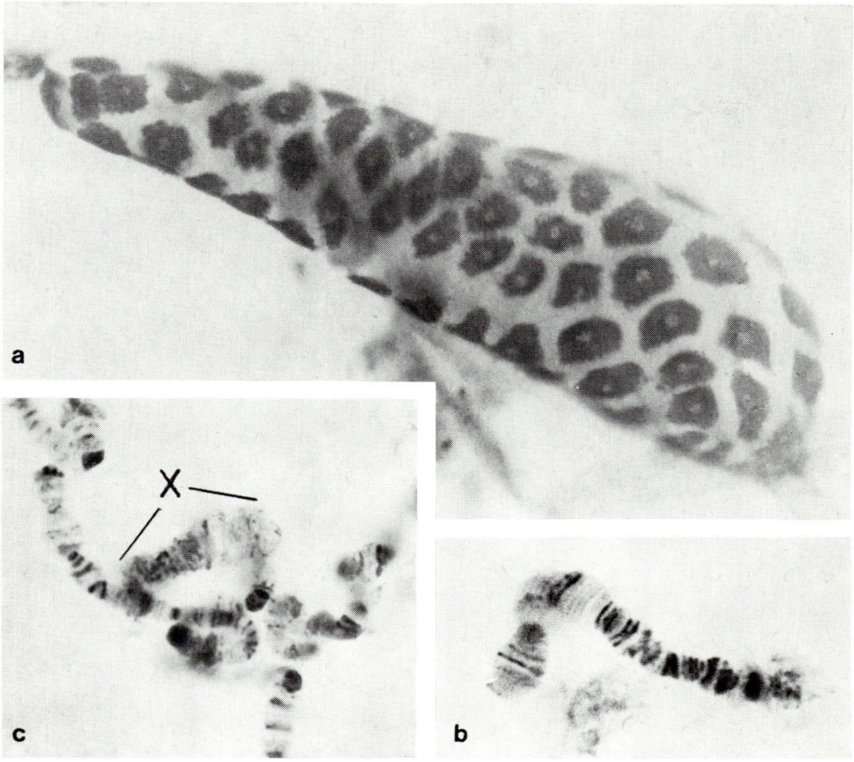

FIG. 2.—(a) One of the two salivary glands from a larva raised at 10°C. Notice how much cell size varies. × 150. (b) Largely euchromatic X from salivary gland of an almost late ♀. Relative length 52 units. × 910. (c) Another X from the same pair of salivary glands as the one in 2b. Diffuse; relative length 19 units. × 910.

In young larvae the X is always diffuse and remains more or less in this state until it attains a high degree of polyteny. It never becomes very euchromatic in the salivary glands of larvae held at 20°C. Larvae kept in colder uncrowded cultures attain a larger terminal size but their development is slower (larval life: 20 days at 18–20°C, 5 months at 2–5°C). The salivary gland is twice as long in late 8–10°C larvae as in comparable 17–22°C individuals; this is taken as a measure of larval size (Wolf, 1957). In the largest salivary gland cells of late-stage 2°C uncrowded females the X is entirely or largely euchromatic, but smaller cells from the same organ contain shorter Xs in which at least certain segments are considerably more diffuse (fig. 2). The X varies even more in the larval mid-gut; here it tends to euchromatize in the largest

---

FIG. 1.— × 1170. (a) An euchromatic Berlin-type X (X_b) from salivary gland of a late ♀ larva raised at 2°C. α_1 = alpha-heterochromatin in kinetochore region. (b) Entire nucleus with a very diffuse b-type X from salivary gland of a late ♀ larva raised at 18–22°C. (c) An euchromatic alpine type of X chromosome (X_a) with α_1 and two extra alpha-heterochromatic loci (α_2 and α_3). From salivary gland of a cold-raised larva. (d) A very diffuse X_a from salivary gland of a medium-sized larva raised at 17°C.

cells even in 20°C individuals. The Xs of the weakly polytene Malpighian gland, in contrast, are always tiny and diffuse. In all types of polytene cells the hemipolytene (= hemiploid) X of the male is always more diffuse than the comparable X of a female sibling from the same culture.

It was our intention in this study to show how and why various factors affect the X's appearance. Autoradiographs with ^{3}H-uridine and ^{3}H-thymidine were made to determine whether different forms correspond to different functional states. Finally a survey of the literature revealed that such changes in form are not confined to Phryne, but reflect structural properties common to all polytene chromosomes.

2. METHODS AND MATERIALS

Standard stocks of *Phryne cincta* without inversions or alpha-heterochromatic supernumerary chromosomes were employed (Wolf, 1961, 1963).

Culture methods: they were basically the same as described in Wolf 1957, except that yeast was added to the food only in yeast-feeding experiments. The imagines were paired in mating vessels 8.5 cm high and 3.3 cm in diameter. A 1.8% agar slanted at ca. 45° ran along one side and across the floor; a piece of kleenex dipped in a weak (ca. 2%) honey solution was affixed to the other side. Fertilized females deposited their eggs on the agar. After larvae appeared the agar was transferred to a glass culture dish 6.5 cm high and 11 cm in diameter which contained the standard food: cooked potatoes mixed with sterilized sawmeal. 2–5°C and 10°C cultures were raised as described by Wolf and Sokoloff (1973), except that the 18°C step was omitted in cultures used for autoradiography, and the animals were mated at 10–13°C.

Preparation methods: squash preparations and sexing of larvae are as in Wolf and Sokoloff (1973).

Effect of crowding: a large number of larvae was reared at 10°C in a mating glass. Slides were made after some pupae appeared, at which time the entire culture was one single tangle of larvae with little food between them. Controls were taken from comparable uncrowded culture vessels (dimensions of glasses: see above). Crowding had the same effect in 15°C and 2°C cultures, but no measurements were taken there.

Effect on euchromatization of exposure to 22°C: a 5 month old 2–5°C culture without pupae was divided into two parts. The control was kept at 2°C, the tested part at ca. 22°C (room temperature). After 5 days most of the larvae in 22°C had pupated; the rest were dissected, along with controls.

Effect of water and an aqueous solution on euchromatization: late 15°C larvae were placed in distilled water or a 4.1 g/l solution of $MgCl_2 \cdot 6H_2O$ for 36–48 hours. The liquid was shallow enough for the larva to bring its tail to the surface to breathe. The larvae survived without apparent damage. Controls were left in the food substrate which was originally solid but by the late developmental stages had been partially converted by the larvae into a puddinglike consistency; the larvae seem to prefer the liquefied portions of the culture-medium.

Effect of yeast feeding: 42g of yeast were added to the standard food in a culture vessel and young larvae were held there at 20°C. Control glasses contained standard food. Slides were made after some larvae had pupated.

Lengths of chromosomes: the chromosome was traced with a drawing prism and its

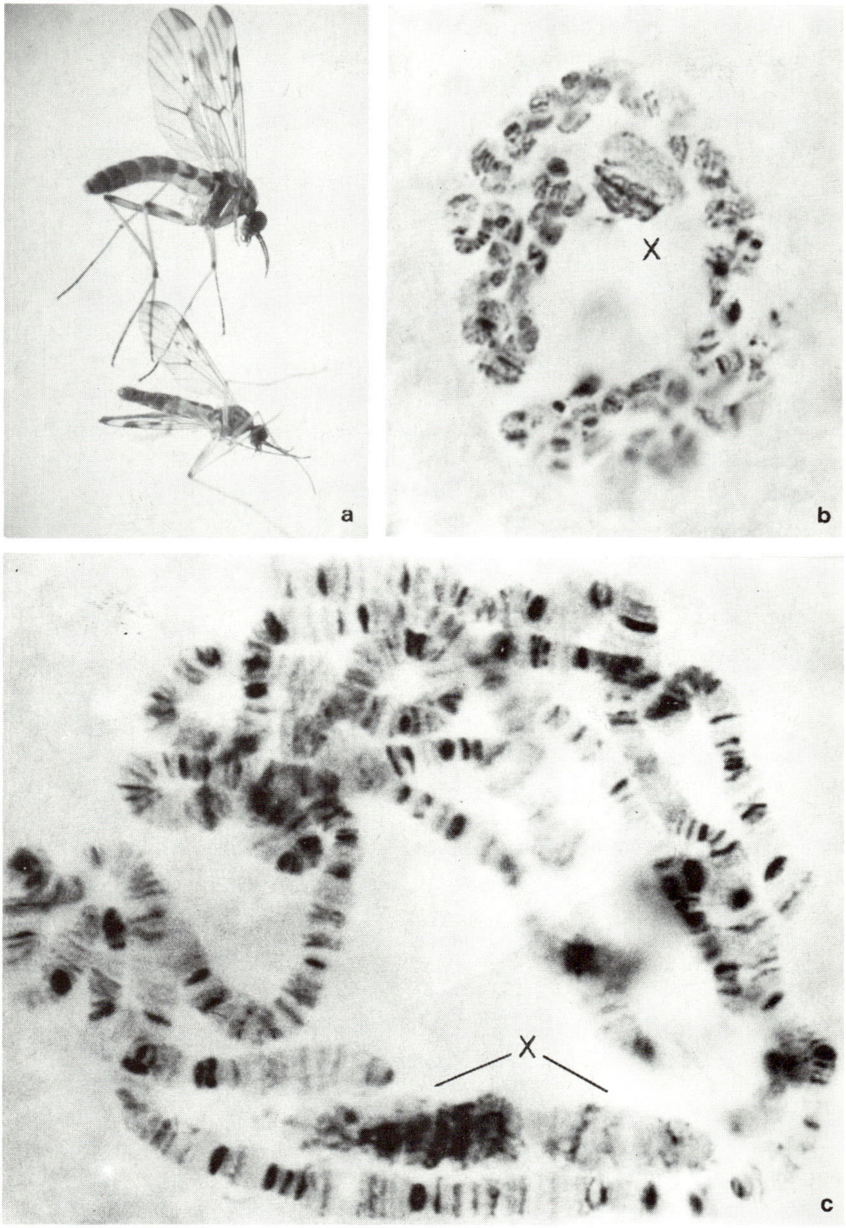

FIG. 3.—(a) Small ♂ imago from a crowded culture (below), and larger ♂ imago from an uncrowded culture, both raised at 10°C. × 3.7. (b) Average X from salivary gland of crowded late 10°C ♀ larva. × 530. (c) Average X from salivary gland of uncrowded late 10°C ♀ larva. × 940.

length, given in relative units (1 unit = 1.5 microns), determined with a cartographic curve-measuring device.

Translocations (experiment N. Israelewski—see acknowledgement): 3–24 hour old male imagines containing mostly mature sperm were irradiated with 1000–3000 R. They were paired with untreated females and the progeny was analyzed for chromosomal aberrations.

Autoradiographs: larvae were dissected in the incubation medium and left to incubate in vitro at 22°C; 5°C animals were dissected immediately after removal from the cold room. Incubation involved 10 min. in 9 mg NaCl and 0.1 m Ci ^{3}H-uridine/ml or 5 min. in 9 mg NaCl and 0.5 m Ci ^{3}H-thymidine/ml. Material fixed in ethanol glacial acetic acid (3:1) was pre-stained in carmine acetic acid and differentiated in 45% acetic acid. Squashes were made on chromalaun gelatine slides and siliconized cover glasses removed after freezing in CO_2-snow. After 3 min. in propanol and overnight in formaldehyde ethanol (3:1) slides were coated with Kodak AR-10 stripping film and exposed for 10–11 days. The film was developed in Kodak D-19, washed with H_2O, held 5 min. in Agfa fixer, 20 min. in running water, and dipped in 60% ethanol. The material was stained with a solution of chromalaun and gallocyanin for 90 min. and differentiated in water (Arcos-Teran, 1972).

3. RESULTS

(a) *Effect of crowding*

Phryne raised at cold temperatures do not always develop euchromatic salivary gland X chromosomes. Larvae kept at 10°C under crowded conditions develop up to twice as slowly as comparable uncrowded larvae, but remain small. If crowding is not too extreme, some of the tiny larvae develop into diminutive pupae and imagines. Prepupal larvae have small salivary gland cells with extremely diffuse Xs, much shorter than those of comparable uncrowded individuals (fig. 3, table 1). Similar results are obtained at 2°C, but no measurements have been made. Cold in itself does not euchromatize the X, but is only one of the conditions necessary for the attainment of high polyteny, which in turn leads to euchromatization.

(b) *Effect of warmth on euchromatic X*

Once the salivary gland X has become highly polytene it remains euchromatic even when larvae are exposed to high temperatures. Five days at 22°C had no noticeable effect on the X chromosomes of larvae taken from 5°C (fig. 4, table 2). High temperatures do not make the X more diffuse.

(c) *Euchromatization by exposure to distilled water or salt solution*

The level of polyteny is not the only factor affecting the X's form. Exposure to a 4.1 g/1 $MgCl_2 \cdot 6H_2O$ solution results in euchromatization (fig. 5, table 3) although the treatment does not affect the polyteny. It does not seem to be the salt which euchromatizes the X but rather the water in which it is dissolved; in a subsequent experiment an average lengthening of 50% was found after 2 days exposure to distilled water, 44% after exposure to the above-mentioned salt solution (n = 60 chromosomes, 10 from each of 6 individuals in each of the situations tested). In the water experiment larvae from a rather crowded 15°C culture were exposed at 22°C, instead of at 15°C.

TABLE 1

Effects of crowding on length (relative units) of X chromosome in salivary glands of five prepupal females reared at 10°C. Values (shortest-mean-longest) based on ten chromosomes per individual. Five females studied from each culture.

Crowded culture	Uncrowded culture
4–5.6–8	12–17.3–25
4–5.7–8	14–17.3–21
4–6.6–10	15–18.2–24
6–7.0–9	15–21.2–28
6–9.3–14	18–23.0–31
6.8 mean of all 50 Xs	19.4

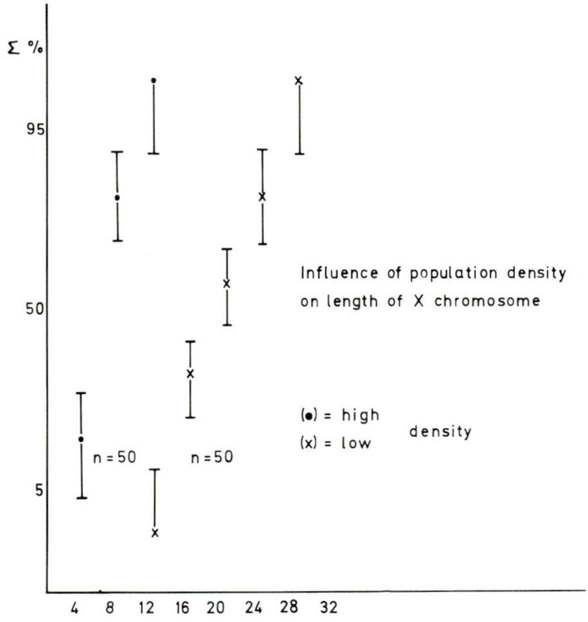

Horizontal: relative length of X (see Materials and Methods). Vertical: % X chromosomes not shorter than value in horizontal. Vertical lines from • and × = 2-fold margin of error. Results: significant difference between crowded and uncrowded.

(d) *Yeast feeding*

Adding a large amount of a relatively protein-rich component (yeast) to the potato food did not noticeably euchromatize the Xs of 20°C individuals. Since this was apparent upon observation, the chromosome length was not measured.

(e) *Effect of translocation onto euchromatic autosome on form of X (experiment by Norbert Israelewski)*

Reciprocal heterozygous X-autosomal translocations were found in progeny after

TABLE 2

Effect of 5 days at 22°C on length (relative units) of X chromosome in salivary glands of pre-pupal females reared at 2°C. Values based on ten chromosomes per individual. Results from seven treated and seven control individuals.

Held at 2°C	After 5 days at 22°C
24–30.8–41	27–31.0–42
25–34.4–42	23–31.8–42
25–35.2–43	27–35.2–46
26–35.2–47	28–35.4–45
26–35.9–50	26–34.4–45
29–36.2–43	25–39.5–51
30–37.0–42	28–39.6–51
34.9 mean of all 70 Xs	35.2

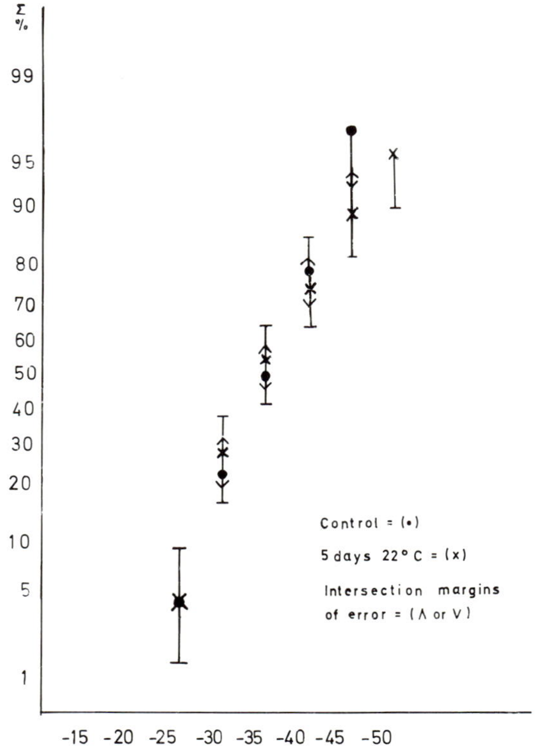

Horizontal: relative length of X. Vertical: % X chromosomes not shorter than value in horizontal. Vertical lines from • and × = 2-fold margin or error. Results: no significant changes after 5 days at 22°C.

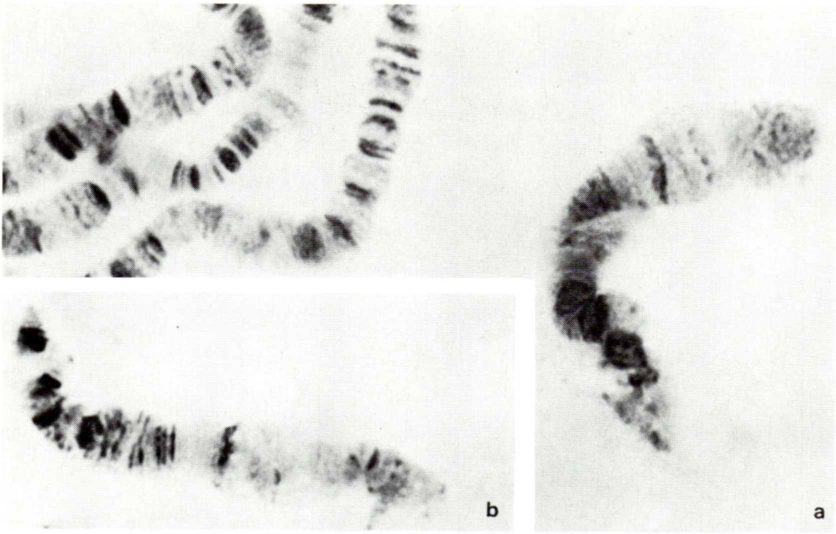

FIG. 4.— × 780. (a) Average X from salivary gland of nearly late ♀ larva raised at 2–5°C. Relative length 37 units. (b) Same as 4a, but after 5 days at 22°C. Relative length 39 units. Exposure to 22°C did not affect chromosomal form.

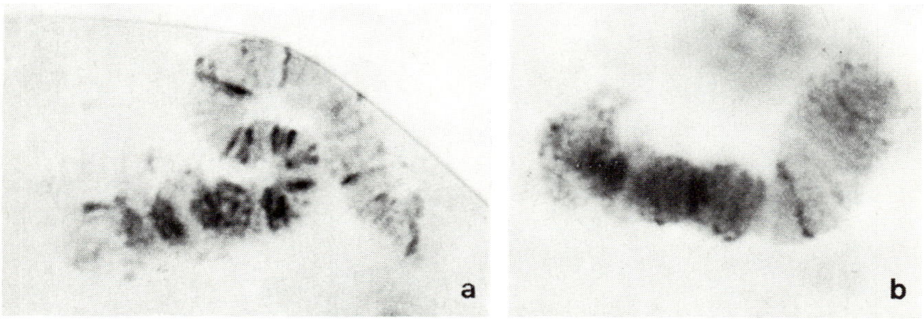

FIG. 5.— × 950. (a) Average X from salivary gland of almost late 15°C ♀ larva after 2 days in 4.1 g/1 $MgCl_2 \cdot 6H_2O$. Relative length 37 units. (b) Control. Average X from salivary gland of almost late 15°C ♀ larva. Relative length 24 units.

irradiation of spermatozoa. The form of the X is independent of the form of the autosome onto which it is translocated; it is diffuse in smaller cells, more euchromatic in larger ones (fig. 6a, b) (Israelewski, 1975).

(f) ^{3}*H-uridine incorporation*

The X shows the same pattern of transcriptive activity whether it is diffuse or euchromatic. The diffuse X does not behave like a puff (see Beermann, 1962).

In cells with significant levels of uridine incorporation all the chromosomes are marked along their entire lengths, with the exception of some alpha-heterochromatic loci (fig. 7). Two patterns are found. In one of them puffs, sites of intense incorporation

TABLE 3

Effect of 2-day in vivo *treatment with 4.1 g/l of $MgCl_2$-$6H_2O$ on length (relative units) of X chromosome in salivary glands of males (Series 1) and females (Series 2–4). Values based on 10 chromosomes per individual. Twelve treated and twelve control larvae studied. Treated chromosomes are, on average, 36% longer in males and 32% in females.*

Series	Control	Treated
1	13–18.9–26	20–24.5–35
	16–19.3–26	19–27.5–38
	19.1 mean of 20 ♂ Xs	26.0
2	22–24.9–27	29–34.6–48
	21–26.2–34	28–34.9–39
	25–31.3–38	28–37.1–46
3	22–26.4–32	26–32.5–40
	19–26.7–33	29–33.2–41
	25–31.3–38	21–35.6–43
	23–31.5–44	27–37.2–47
4	16–21.2–28	30–38.9–49
	21–28.6–34	26–39.0–51
	21–28.9–37	33–42.5–66
	27.7 mean of 100 ♀ Xs	36.6

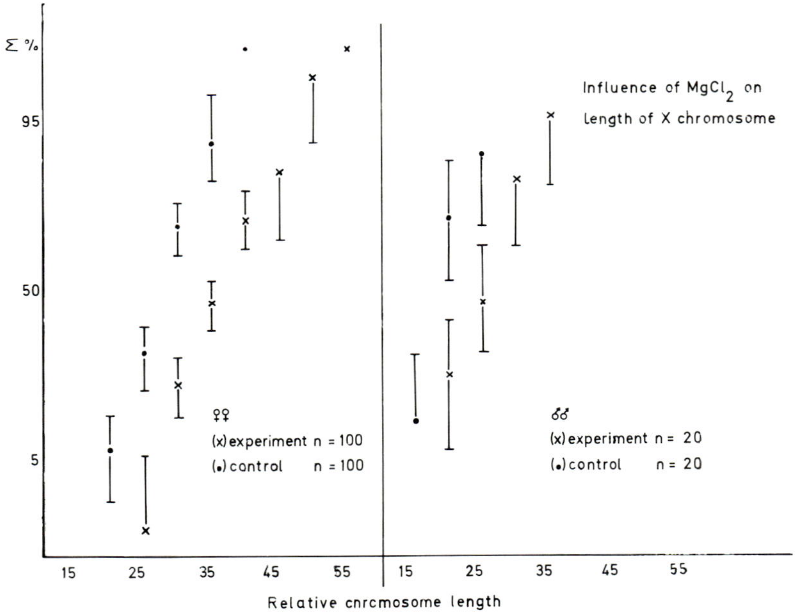

Horizontal: relative length of X. Vertical: % X chromosomes not shorter than value in horizontal. Vertical lines from • and × = 2-fold margin of error. Results: X significantly longer after 2 days in $MgCl_2$ solution.

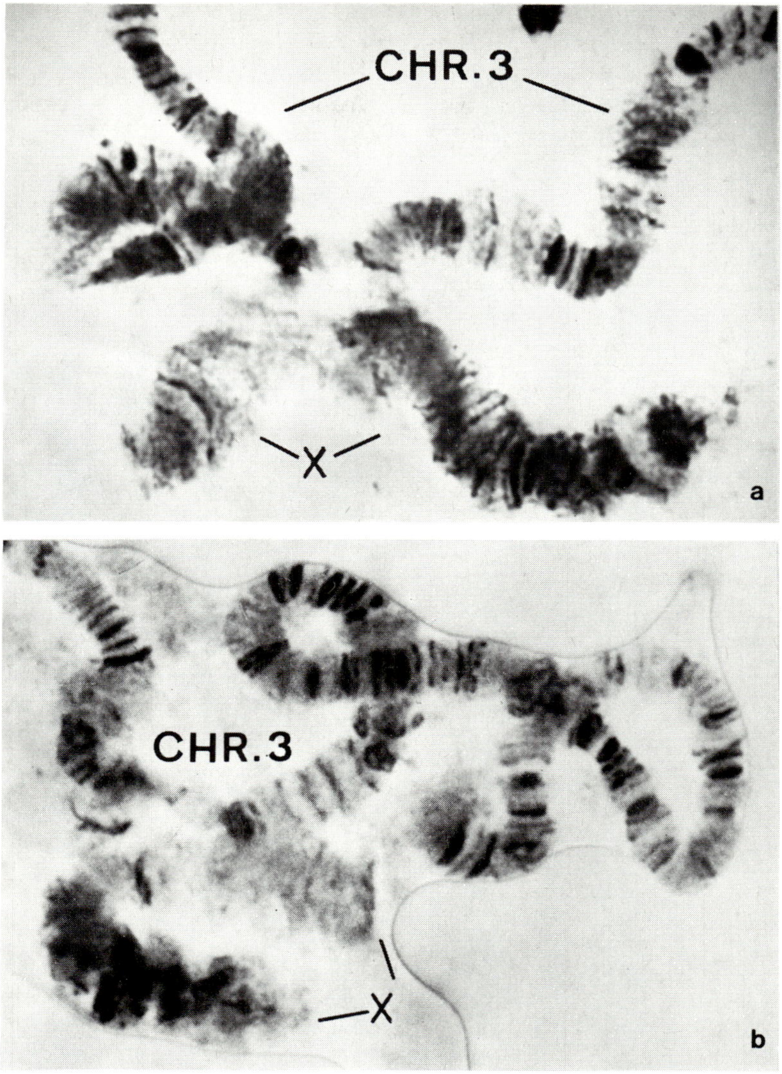

FIG. 6.— × 1700. (a) A heterozygous reciprocal translocation between the weakly-banded distal region of the X and the a-arm of chromosome 3 in a 5°C ♀. The X is somewhat euchromatic. (b) Same as 6a, but another cell with a more diffuse X.

alternate with less active "interpuffs". Two relatively short segments of the X, one in the distal end of the proximal region and one after the first third of the distal region, are as active as autosomal puffs; the rest of the X behaves like the "interpuffs". This pattern has only been found in some nuclei of 20°C larvae with diffuse Xs (fig. 7a). The second pattern is associated with low total incorporation. With the exception of some unmarked alpha-heterochromatic loci (alpha-2 of X chromosome) silver grains are rather evenly distributed along the X and the autosomes, puffs either not occurring or only being weakly indicated (fig. 7b–d). Only this pattern was found in nuclei with euchromatic X chromosomes (fig. 7c, d). This is probably because these larvae always came from 5°C cultures and were incubated immediately after being brought to 22°C, which resulted in a low rate of incorporation. Larvae with euchromatic salivary gland Xs were always handled like that, since it was erroneously believed that longer exposure to 22°C would make the X more diffuse. However, the same pattern is also often found in some of the nuclei with diffuse Xs (fig. 7b). Both patterns can occur in the same 20°C individual.

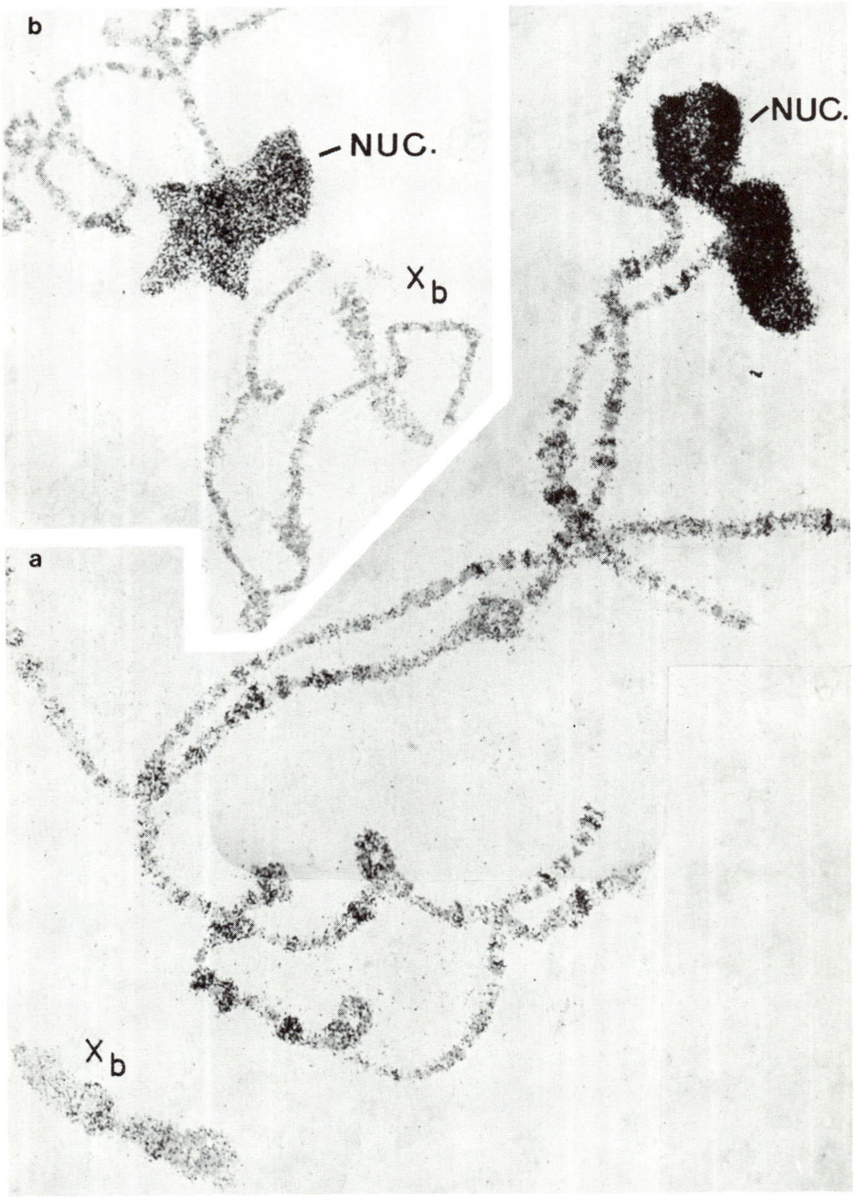

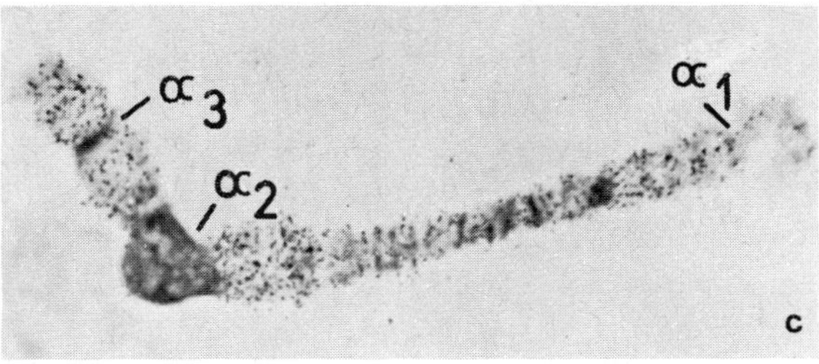

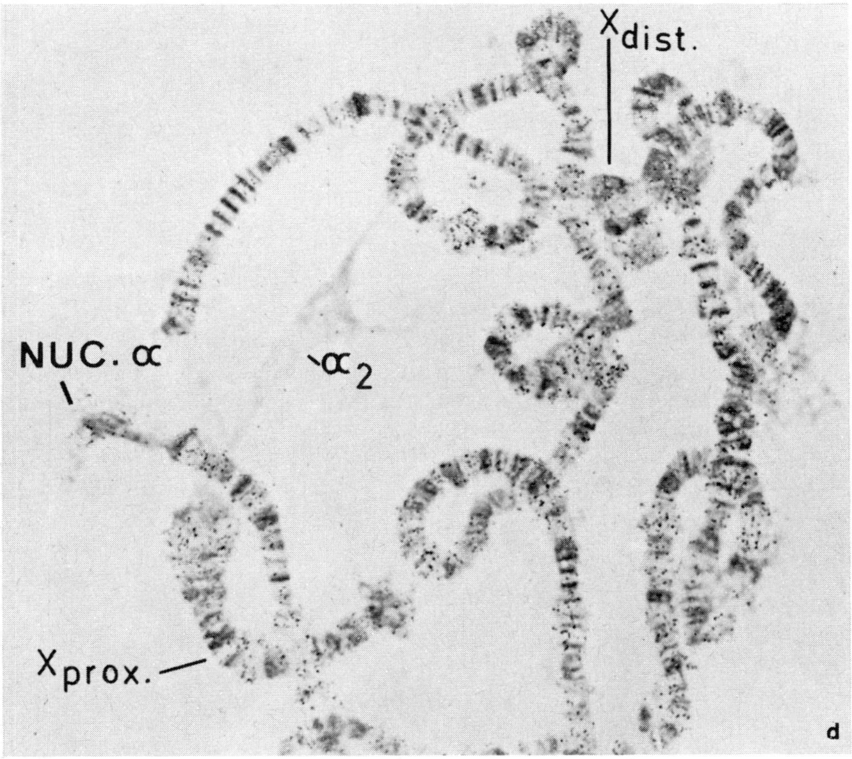

FIG. 7.—(a) Nucleus with X_b. Puff-interpuff pattern. Larva raised at 20°C. Nuc. = nucleolus. × 430. (b) Nucleus with X_b. Low-incorporation pattern. Larva raised at 20°C. × 430. (c) X_a with low-incorporation pattern. Larva raised at 5°C. × 670. (d) X_a fragmented at α_2-locus from larva raised at 5°C. Fragments: X prox., X dist.; Nuc. α = alpha-heterochromatin of nucleolus organizer. × 670.

The nucleolus is usually intact in the salivary gland cells of 20°C individuals (fig. 7a, b). In the corresponding cells of 5°C larvae it has usually been ripped away from its alpha-heterochromatic organizer (fig. 7c). The consistency of alpha heterochromatin depends upon the culture temperature (see Wolf and Sokoloff, 1973).

(g) ^{3}*H-thymidine incorporation*

Whether diffuse or largely euchromatic, the X always shows basically the same pattern of ^{3}H-thymidine incorporation as the autosomes in the same cell. When the X is totally marked, so are the autosomes and when only alpha-heterochromatic segments are marked, this is true in both the X and the autosomes (fig. 8).

The incorporation patterns in *Phryne* are similar to those of other Diptera, e.g., *Drosophila melanogaster* (Arcos-Terán, 1972; Rudkin, 1972). A morphological series can be constructed: (1) continuous marking along the entire length of the genome, (2) only bands are marked, but not interbands, (3) only some bands, generally the thicker ones, are marked, (4) only the alpha-heterochromatic chromosomal segments are marked. These patterns were found in both 20°C larvae with diffuse X chromosomes and 10°C prepupal larvae with largely euchromatic Xs.

4. DISCUSSION

(a) *Form changes in other species*

The peculiar changes in chromosomal form described in *Phryne cincta* are not confined to this species, but seem to reflect structural properties common to all giant chromosomes.

When larvae of other dipteran species are raised at abnormally low temperatures they generally grow quite large and have thick, tightly bundled and clearly banded giant chromosomes. This has been observed in *Drosophila melanogaster* (Wolf, unpublished) and *Chironomus tentans* (Sass, personal communication). Exposure to cold also increases the bundling in the polytene nurse-cell chromosomes of *Calliphora* (Bier, 1959), and in the polytene chromosomes of the leguminous plant

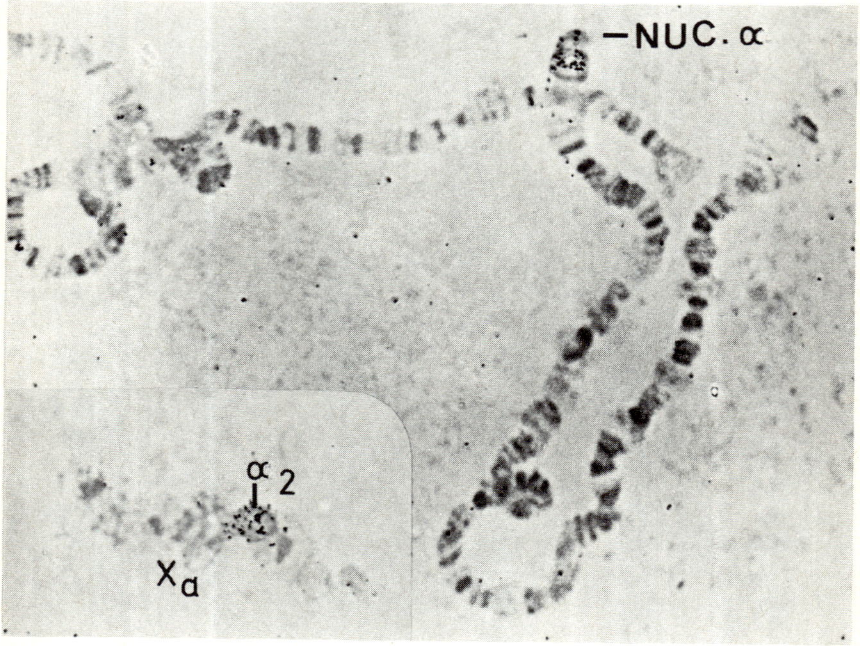

FIG. 8.—Autoradiograph: late marking pattern. Only α_2 of a-type X and nucleolar alpha (Nuc. α) are marked. 5 min. *in vitro* at 22°C in ^{3}H-thymidine. Late ♂ larva raised at 20°C. × 1340.

Phaseolus vulgaris (Nagl, 1969). In *Phaseolus* a return to the optimal temperature causes a reversion to a loosely bundled condition without euchromatic banding; this is not the case in *Phryne* (see 3b).

In *Phaseolus coccineus* the degree of bundling and clarity of banding generally increase with the level of polyteny. However, different cells at the same level vary among themselves, showing that other factors are involved (Nagl, 1962). The assertion that a greater transcriptive activity is associated with the less-banded condition in *Phaseolus* has to our knowledge not been strictly proven (Nagl, 1969, 1970).

Under pathological conditions the giant chromosomes of many dipterans assume a form similar to that of the diffuse *Phryne* X. In lethal strains of *D. melanogaster* (ltl tumorigenic) and *D. hydei* the polytene chromosomes in many tissues are wider, shorter, and less clearly banded than normally. The hemipolytene male X shows an especially altered appearance and can be completely diffuse. These changes in form are only found in larvae past the normal pupation age which later die without further metamorphosis.

In *Phryne* diffuse chromosomes are generally found in small, less-polytene cells. In some other insects they are characteristic of enormous cells which, after infection, have attained unusually high polyteny (*Rhynchosciara angelae, Sciara ocellaris*: Pavan and Basile, 1966; Pavan, 1967; Pavan and da Cunha, 1969; *Chironomus anthracinus*: Keyl, 1960). In the process of polytenization both the length and the width of the chromosomes increase enormously. The X is the first chromosome to become diffuse; it can assume this form in cells where the autosomes are still banded (e.g., fig. 4 in Pavan and da Cunha, 1969). It was not stated whether the X's behavior is identical in both sexes. The diffuse chromosomes of the Sciaridae have been described as puffs, and it was asserted that a change in the transcriptive activity is responsible for the altered chromosomal form (Pavan and da Cunha, 1969). As far as we know this has never been proven. Uridine incorporation has been shown in infected salivary gland cells of *R. angelae* (fig. 3 in Pavan, 1967), but no comparison was made with the incorporation in normal cells.

In *Drosophila melanogaster* euchromatic segments are morphologically altered when transposed to the proximity of centromeric heterochromatin in XO males reared at 18°C (Ananiev and Gvozdev, 1974). The nature of these changes varies from cell to cell: loss of a banded segment, appearance of an unusually thick band, lack of puffing in a normally puffed locus, or breaking up of a band into dots. These changes, which are taken together and described as "heterochromatization," are correlated with a high incidence of late replication and reduced uridine incorporation. Other authors described a more convincing heterochromatization in the same species as a result of similar chromosomal rearrangements (Wargent and Hartmann-Goldstein, this volume, pp. 109–116). A translocated segment showed changed replicative behavior, but this was also true when it did not look heterochromatic.

(b) *A note on transcriptive activity in Phryne and a structural model for the diffuse X*

Alterations in chromosomal form are often correlated with changes in transcriptive activity. In puffing, single bands become diffuse and at the same time hyperactive with respect to uridine incorporation (Beermann, 1962). The hemipolytene X of the male in *Drosophila melanogaster* is somewhat more diffuse than the female X and in proportion to its DNA content incorporates more ^{3}H-uridine (dosage compensation: Mukherjee and Beermann, 1965; Ananiev et al., 1974). It was hypothesized that the diffuse Phryne-X would behave like a puff. However, incorporation of ^{3}H-uridine as determined by the density of silver grains on the autoradiogram was no more intense in that chromosome than in the autosomes of the same cell. The same is true for the euchromatic X. This density can be taken as a measure of relative activity since the ratio of the area of the X to that of the autosomes seems to remain roughly constant whether the X is diffuse or euchromatic. It is true that the euchromatic X in the female is not wider than the autosomes and the diffuse salivary gland X in the late-stage uncrowded 20°C females is about three times wider (fig. 7). However, this increase in relative width is counterbalanced by a decrease in relative length: proportional to a given autosome the diffuse X of 20°C females is about three times shorter than the euchromatic X of 2°C females (Wolf, 1957).

The diffuse X does not act like a puff. The possibility that the diffuse form is accompanied by a slightly different transcriptive activity than the euchromatic form cannot, on the basis of this study, be completely excluded but these changes, if they do occur, are relatively minor.

Although unclear banding is common to both of them, puffing and chromosomal "diffusion" seem to be two entirely different processes. In puffs the chromomeres become de-condensed and unraveled into long, fine threads. In diffusion the chromomeres perhaps remain condensed, but lose contact with the corresponding chromomeres of other chromatids. It is apparent that individual chromatids are shorter and spaced further apart in the diffuse form.

(c) *Apparent under-replication*

Morphological observations led to the suggestion that alpha-heterochromatic regions in *Phryne*, especially alpha-2 of the X_a (fig. 8), are under-replicated (Rudkin, 1972). However, precisely these loci have been found to be intensely- and long-replicating in late larvae, so that an under-replication seems improbable. DNA-containing material has been seen sometimes to leave these loci (Wolf and Sokoloff, 1973); this could account for the apparent under-replication.

5. SUMMARY

1. In large, highly-polytene cells the X is euchromatic, with clearly defined bands and interbands. In smaller cells it is shorter and wider, and its banding pattern is less distinct (diffuse form).

2. When larvae are raised at 20°C they remain small and have only diffuse salivary gland Xs. When raised at 2°C the larvae grow larger and some of their salivary gland cells become big enough to contain euchromatic Xs. However, more-diffuse Xs can be found in the same gland.

3. Under crowded conditions, larvae remain small and their Xs remain diffuse, even at 2°C.

4. Exposure of the larvae to high temperatures does not make their euchromatic Xs more diffuse.

5. Placing the larvae in distilled water or in aqueous salt solutions makes their Xs longer and more euchromatic.

6. The form of the X depends on the tightness of bundling of its chromatids, and this generally increases with the level of polytenization. Crowding and culture temperature do not directly affect the bundling, but only determine the degree of polyteny which is attained before pupation. In contrast, exposure to distilled water, for example, directly influences the bundling without changing the degree of polyteny.

7. The X can retain a diffuse form even when it is translocated onto an euchromatic autosome.

8. Whether diffuse or euchromatic, the X incorporates ^{3}H-uridine with the same intensity as the autosomes of the same cell. The diffuse X does not behave like a puff.

9. The replication of the X, whether it is diffuse or heterochromatic, is always in step with that of the autosomes of the same cell.

10. Similar changes in form are found in other insect larvae, usually under pathological conditions. They probably reflect structural properties common to all polytene chromosomes.

11. It is proposed that the chromomeres remain condensed in diffuse chromosomes, but lose contact with the corresponding chromomeres of neighboring chromatids.

Acknowledgement. We would like to thank Prof. Wolfgang Beermann for his continuing support, Dipl.-Biol. Norbert Israelewski (doctoral student of B. W. Wolf) for allowing us to publish some of his results and photos, Dr. Elisabeth Wolf for the tests of statistical significance and the graphs, and Miss I. Sommerau for her technical assistance.

Part of this study was done under the direction of Prof. W. Beermann in partial fulfillment of the requirements for the degree of doctor of science.

6. REFERENCES

Ananiev, E. V., and Gvozdev. 1974. Changed pattern of transcription and replication in polytene chromosomes of *Drosophila melanogaster* resulting from eu-heterocromatin rearrangement. *Chromosoma (Berl.), 45,* 173–191.

Ananiev, E. V., Faizullin, L. Z., and Gvozdev. 1974. The role of genetic balance in control of transcription rate in the chromosome of *Drosophila melanogaster. Chromosoma (Berl.), 45,* 193–201.

Arcos-Terán, L. 1972. DNS-Replication und die Natur der spät replizierenden Orte im X-Chromosom von *D. melanogaster. Chromosoma (Berl.), 37,* 233–296.

Beermann, W. 1962. *Riesenchromosomen. Propoplasmatologia VI D.* Springer, Vienna.

Bier, K. 1959. Quantitative Untersuchungen über die Variabilität der Nährzellkernstruktur und ihre Beeinflussung durch die Temperatur. *Chromosoma (Berl.), 10,* 619–653.

Breugel, F. M. A. van, and Bos, H. J. 1969. Some notes on differential chromosome activity in *Drosophila. Genetica (The Hague), 40,* 359–378.

Israelewski, N. 1975. X-ray induced visible alterations on the giant chromosomes of *Phryne cincta* (Nematocera, Diptera): Relation of radiation sensitivity to pronuclear chromosome structure. *Chromosoma* (in press).

Keyl, H. G. 1960. Erhöhung der chromosomalen Replikationsrate durch Mikrosporidieninfektion in den Speicheldrüsenzellen von *Chironomus. Naturwissenschaften, 9,* 212–213.

Kobel, H. R., and Breugel, F. M. A. van. 1967. Observations on ltl (lethal tumerous larvae) of *Drosophila melanogaster. Genetica (The Hague), 38,* 305–327.

Lezzi, M., and Robert, M. 1972. Chromosomes isolated from unfixed salivary glands of *Chironomus.* In *Developmental Studies on Giant Chromosomes* (W. Beermann, ed.). Springer, Berlin, Heidelberg.

Mukherjee, A. S., and Beermann, W. 1965. Synthesis of ribonucleic acid by the X-chromosome of *Drosophila melanogaster* and the problem of dosage compensation. *Nature (Lond.), 207,* (4998), 785–786.

Nagl, W. 1962. 4096-Ploidie und "Riesenchromosomen" im Suspensor von *Phaseolus coccineus. Naturwissenschaften, 11,* 261–262.

Nagl, W. 1969. Banded polytene chromosomes in the legume *Phaseolus vulgaris. Nature (Lond.), 221,* (5175), 70–71.

Nagl, W. 1970. Temperature-dependent functional structures in the polytene chromosomes of *Phaseolus,* with special reference to the nucleolus organizers. *J. Cell. Sci., 6,* 87–107.

Pavan, C. 1967. Chromosomal changes induced by infective agents. *Triangle, 8,* 42–48.

Pavan, C., and Basile, R. 1966. Chromosome changes induced by infections in tissues of *Rhynchosciara angelae. Science (Wash. D. C.), 151,* (3717), 1556–1558.

Pavan, C., and da Cunha, A. B. 1969. Chromosomal activities in *Rhynchosciara* and other Sciaridae. *Annu. Rev. Genet., 3,* 425–450.

Rodman, T. C. 1964. The larval characteristics and salivary gland chromosomes of a tumorigenic strain of *Drosophila melanogaster. J. Morphol., 115,* (3), 419–445.

Rudkin, G. T. 1972. Replication in polytene chromosomes. In *Developmental Studies on Giant Chromosomes* (W. Beermann, ed.). Springer, Berlin, Heidelberg.

Wargent, J. M., and Hartmann-Goldstein, I. J. 1976. Replication behavior and morphology of a rearranged chromosome region in *Drosophila.* This volume, pp. 109–116.

Wolf, B. E. 1957. Temperaturabhängige Allozyklie des polytänen X-Chromosoms in den Kernen der Somazellen von *Phryne cincta. Chromosoma (Berl.), 8,* 396–435.

Wolf, B. E. 1961. Y-Chromosom und überzählige Chromosomen in den polytänen Somakernen von *Phryne cincta* M. (Diptera). Verh. Dtsch. Zool. Saarbrücken.

Wolf, B. E. 1963. Kontrolle des Crossing over vom temperaturbedingten Allozykliegrad und vom alpha-Heterochromatin des X-Chromosoms bei *Phryne cincta. Chromosoma (Berl.), 13,* 646–701.

Wolf, B. E. 1970. Structure and function of alpha- and beta-heterochromatin—results on *Phryne cincta. The Nucleus,* Supplement, 145–160.

Wolf, B. E., and Sokoloff, S. 1973. Migration of alpha-heterochromatin from the giant X chromosome of the gnat *Phryne cincta.* In *Chromosomes Today, 4,* (J. Wahrman and K. R. Lewis, eds.), pp. 129–142. Israel Universities Press, Jerusalem and John Wiley & Sons, New York.

REPLICATION BEHAVIOUR AND MORPHOLOGY OF A REARRANGED CHROMOSOME REGION IN *DROSOPHILA*

J. M. WARGENT and I. J. HARTMANN-GOLDSTEIN
Department of Genetics, University of Sheffield, U.K.

1. INTRODUCTION

Heitz (1928) first defined heterochromatin as that chromatin which is condensed at interphase and prophase. Later the distinction was made between constitutive heterochromatin, present in homologous chromosones, and facultative heterochromatin which results for example from inactivation of one of the two X chromosomes in female mammals (Brown, 1966). Constitutive heterochromatin, which best fits Heitz's definition, is relatively inactive in protein synthesis (Yunis and Yasmineh, 1972) and differs from euchromatin in base composition (e.g. Jones, 1970; Pardue and Gall, 1970). Heterochromatic regions undergo DNA-replication later than euchromatin (Lima-de-Faria, 1969).

In *Drosophila*, chromosome morphology and gene activity are affected by the position of a chromosome segment in the genome. Thus examination of salivary gland chromosomes shows that euchromatin transposed to the vicinity of heterochromatin may assume heterochromatic appearance and the variegated phenotype of these individuals indicates that the genes newly adjacent to the heterochromatin are inactivated in some cells (for review see Lewis, 1950). It is therefore a matter of interest whether the replication behaviour in such rearranged regions is also affected. Several inversions and translocations investigated autoradiographically in salivary gland preparations failed to show differences from the homologous non-rearranged regions (Barr et al., 1968; Valencia and Plaut, 1970; Evgeniev et al., 1972). Comparing two inversion strains, we observed differences in the Feulgen-DNA content of homologous bands near the heterochromatic breakpoint (Wargent et al., 1974) and have now undertaken further investigations into the replication behaviour of rearranged chromosome regions adjacent to heterochromatin. Here we present observations which indicate that a region subject to heterochromatic position effect, i.e., which can undergo gene suppression and a change in morphology, can also differ from the homologous non-rearranged region in the duration of replication.

2. MATERIALS AND METHODS

The strain T(1:4) $w^{m258\text{-}21}$/In(1) dl-49 *w lz* of *D. melanogaster*, used for this investigation, carries a reciprocal translocation with breaks in the euchromatic part of the X chromosome between bands 3E5 and 3E6 (band terminology according to the salivary gland chromosome map of Bridges, 1938) and in chromosome 4 in the heterochromatic region 101F (Lindsley and Grell, 1968). Females heterozygous for the translocation show variegation for X-linked characters whose loci are situated near the breakpoint, and examination of the larval salivary gland chromosomes reveals that the affected region can undergo heterochromatisation (Hartmann-Goldstein, 1967).

Salivary glands from female white prepupae reared at 15°C ± 0.2° were excised in insect Ringer. The glands were incubated for five minutes in 40μl of the Ringer solution containing tritiated thymidine (Radiochemical Centre, Amersham, sp. act. 20C/mMole) at a concentration of 50μ/ml. A drop of 3:1 ethanol-acetic acid was added, the glands were transferred to fresh acid-alcohol for 30–40 sec, stained with orcein, and squashed in 45% acetic acid. Suitable nuclei were photographed with bright field optics and a Zeiss planapochromat objective (NA 1.32). Coverslips were removed using liquid nitrogen and the material was postfixed for 16 hr in a mixture of 10% ethanol in 10% formalin. Slides were then rinsed in distilled water and covered with Kodak AR10 autoradiographic film. After 14 days exposure at 8°C the film was developed in Kodak D19 and the nuclei were rephotographed with phase contrast or bright field optics.

From the observed background grain count it was calculated that the presence of three or more silver grains in an area equal to that of subsections 3A and 3C of the X chromosome signified isotope incorporation with greater than 99% probability. Accordingly, a minimum of three grains over a given chromosome subsection or band group was taken to indicate the presence of label. Specificity of the tritiated thymidine as a label for DNA was checked with DNAase (Sigma, London) following the procedure of Howard and Plaut (1968). No incorporation of precursor was observed in DNAase-treated material. The possibility was also investigated of positive and negative chemographic effects due to interaction between material or stain and autoradiographic emulsion (Rogers, 1967). No evidence of chemography was obtained.

3. RESULTS

After a five minute pulse of tritiated thymidine, between 30% and 60% of nuclei show significant precursor incorporation, the intensity of labelling varying markedly between adjacent nuclei of a squash preparation. Nuclei with discontinuous patterns of label were selected (figs. 1 and 2) and included in the sample of 74 nuclei from 27 individuals. Label associated with subsections 3A, 3B, and 3D, and with band groups 3C1–4, 3C5–7, 3C8–11, and 3E1–5 was recorded for nuclei in which both non-translocated and translocated homologues were amenable to analysis. In heterochromatised regions, individual subsections or band groups cannot always be identified (fig. 3). In these instances, nuclei were selected in which the density and distribution of label over the heterochromatised region was such as to permit the assumption that all subsections within the heterochromatised region were labelled. Although some preselection of nuclei is unavoidable, the number of nuclei discarded was small, and there is no evidence from the results presented here, or from further analyses to be published elsewhere, that any significant bias has been introduced. In some nuclei homologous subsections showed asynchronous incorporation of thymidine. Fig. 4 shows labelling in euchromatic regions 1A through to 2A of the translocated homologue, but no significant incorporation in the homologous region of the nontranslocated chromosome. Similar asynchrony in region 3A can

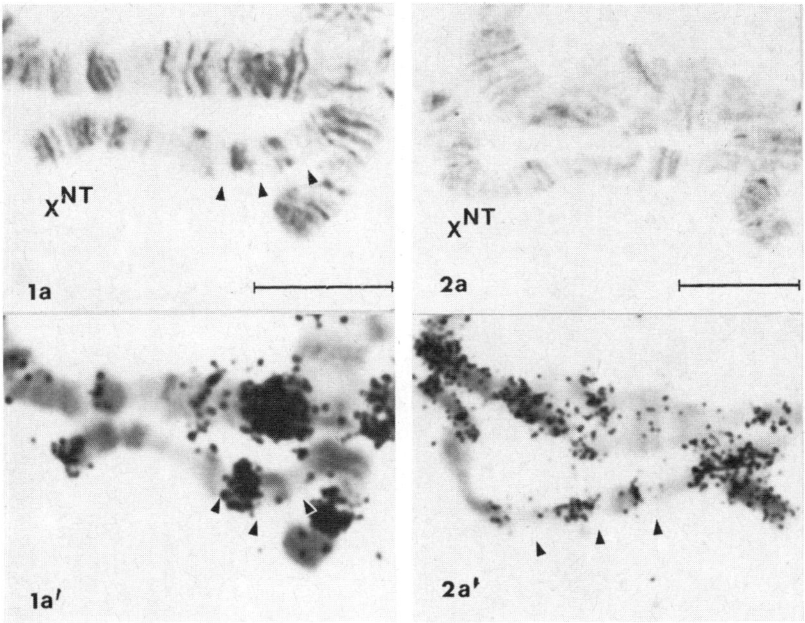

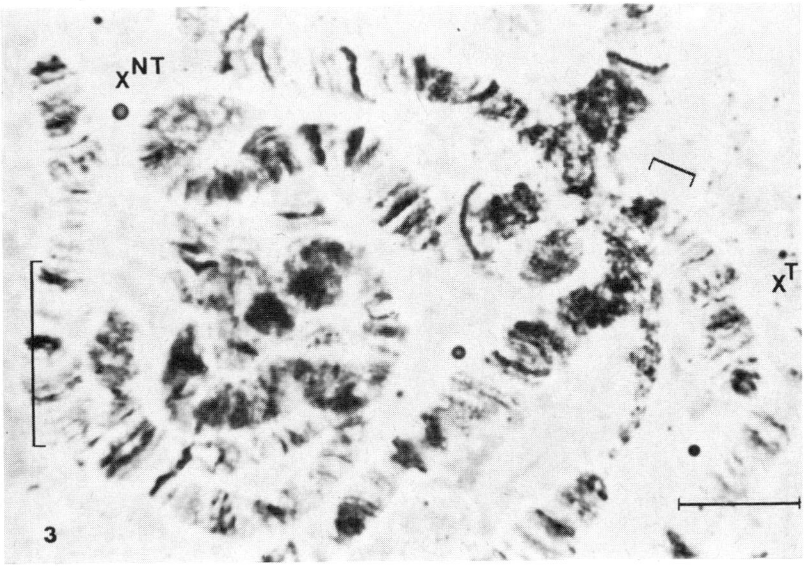

FIGS. 1–2.—(a) Tip of non-translocated X-chromosome (X^{NT}). (a′) Corresponding autoradiograph showing discontinuous labelling pattern. Arrows indicate regions 3A1–4, 3Cl–6, and 3D5 to 3E2. Bar represents 10μm.

FIG. 3.—Part of nucleus showing non-translocated (X^{NT}) and translocated (X^{T}) X-homologues. Brackets indicate regions 3A1 to 3E5 inclusive, which are euchromatic in X^{NT} but heterochromatised in X^{T}. Individual bands in the heterochromatised region cannot be identified. Bar represents 10μm.

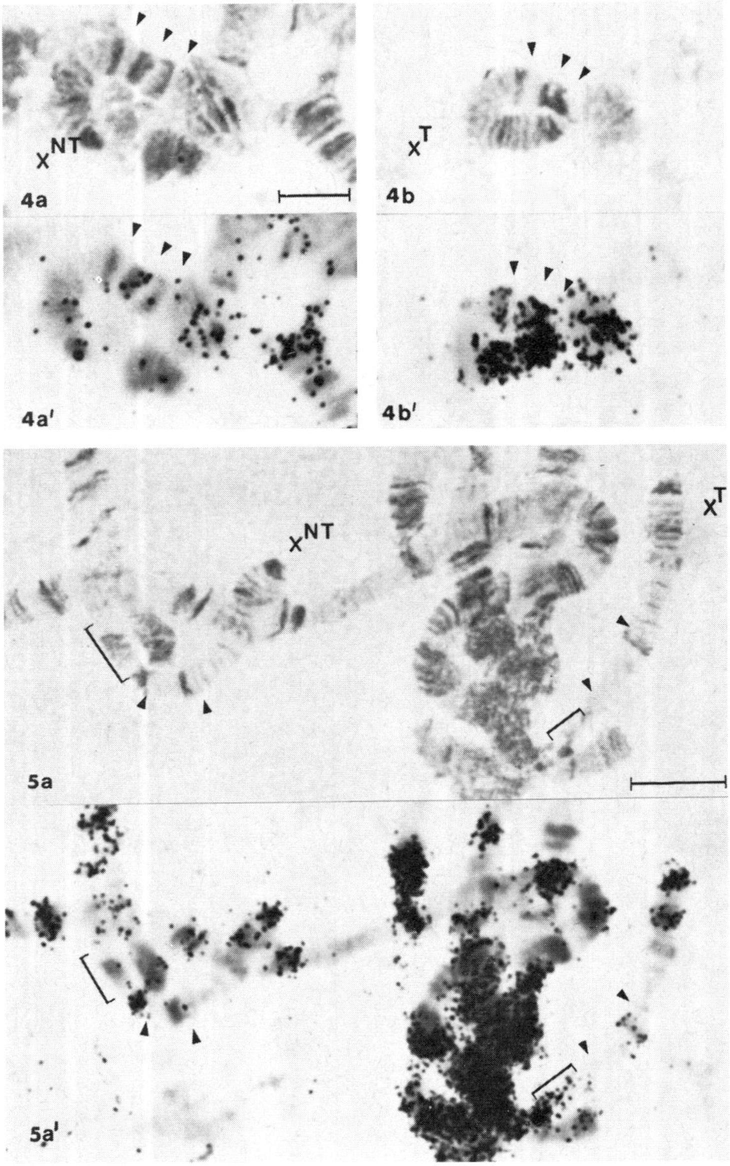

FIG. 4.—(a) Tip of non-transolcated (X^{NT}) X-chromosome and (b) euchromatic translocated (X^{T}) homologue. (a′) and (b′) show corresponding autoradiographs. Arrows indicate regions 3A1–4, 3C1–6, and 3D5 to 3E2. Asynchronous incorporation is observed in regions 3A1–4 and 3D5 to 3E2. Bar represents 10μm.

FIG. 5.—(a) Non-translocated (X^{NT}) and translocated (X^{T}) homologues. (a′) Corresponding autoradiograph. Arrows indicate regions 3A1–4 and 3C1–6. Region 3D1 to 3E5 (brackets) is heterochromatised in X^{T}. Differential incorporation is observed in euchromatic regions 1A through to 2A, in 3A1–4, and in the heterochromatised region, 3D1 to 3E5.

be seen in fig. 5. Differential incorporation was also observed between homologous subdivisions where the corresponding region was heterochromatised in the translocated chromosome (fig. 5).

In table 1, we compared the labelling frequencies in each subdivision (column 1), classified in the translocated homologue according to whether the relevant region is euchromatic or heterochromatised. Labelling frequencies were calculated as a proportion of the total number of chromosomes observed in each category. Comparison between individual subdivisions of the non-translocated and translocated heterochromatised homologues reveals that for each subdivision the labelling frequency in the translocated chromosome is higher, significantly so in the three subdivisions nearest to the break. If labelling frequency is taken as an index of the duration of replication (Howard and Plaut, 1968), these observations indicate that when a region becomes heterochromatised the time during which replication occurs is extended. Only four nuclei were found which showed heterochromatisation extending to include subsection 3B and in only two nuclei was 3A included in the compacted region. Comparisons of the frequencies for 3A and 3B, taken separately, are therefore meaningless. Since all other subdivisions analysed show the same phenomenon, however, we see no reason to suppose that 3A and 3B contradict the above conclusion.

Turning now to the comparison between labelling frequencies in the non-translocated and the translocated homologues when the latter has retained its euchromatic morphology: it can be seen from table 1 that when individual subdivisions are compared, the labelling frequency for the three subdivisions nearest the breakpoint is higher in the translocated chromosome, but not significantly so. But if all subdivisions are considered together, the chi^2 values seem to suggest a trend towards larger differences nearer the breakpoint. The apparent trend was tested statistically taking into account the direction, i.e., sign, of differences by using the appropriately signed value of $\sqrt{\chi^2} = \chi$ (Maxwell, 1961). Results are presented in table 2. The

TABLE 1

Labelling frequencies (f) of specified chromosome subdivisions, i.e. number of labelled subdivisions divided by total observed (N). NT: Subdivisions in non-translocated X chromosome. T_{HET} and T_{EU} : Heterochromatised and euchromatic subdivisions respectively of the translocated homologue

	NT		T_{HET}				T_{EU}			
Subdivision	N	f	N	f	χ^2	P	N	f	χ^2	P
3A	72	0.42	2	1.0	—	—	70	0.38	0.14	NS
3B	72	0.25	4	0.75	—	—	68	0.26	0.04	NS
3C 1–4	70	0.56	21	0.76	2.04*	NS	49	0.59	0.14	NS
3C 5–7	69	0.58	23	0.83	3.54*	NS	46	0.56	0.02	NS
3C 8–11	63	0.30	25	0.72	12.86	<0.001	38	0.42	1.49	NS
3D	60	0.35	32	0.59	5.05	<0.025	28	0.43	0.66	NS
3E	60	0.32	33	0.61	7.32	<0.01	27	0.41	0.68	NS

*Applying Yates' continuity correction.

TABLE 2

Effect of distance from chromosome breakpoint on relative labelling frequency

Subdivision		Distance from breakpoint (arbitrary scale)	T_{EU} χ*
3A		7	−0.38
3B		6	+0.20
3C	1–4	5	+0.38
3C	5–7	4	−0.15
3C	8–11	3	+1.22
3D		2	+0.81
3E		1	+0.82

*$\chi = \sqrt{\chi^2}$, with sign allocated according to whether labelling frequency in translocated euchromatic homologue is greater than (+) or less than (−) that in the non-translocated chromosome subdivision (Maxwell, 1961, page 75 et seq.). Correlation coefficient (r) for distance from breakpoint vs. χ: 0.763 ($P < 0.05$ for 5 degrees of freedom).

largest positive χ values are near the breakpoint. The significant correlation between χ value and distance from the breakpoint confirms the presence of trend and supports the subjective impression conveyed by table 1. We interpret these observations to indicate that when a euchromatic region is situated adjacent to heterochromatin its period of replication is extended beyond the time taken when in its usual position contiguous with euchromatin.

4. DISCUSSION

For many years Schultz advocated the idea that the function of heterochromatin has to do with the nucleic acid metabolism of the cell. He suggested (1965) that the late replication characteristic of heterochromatin is accomplished by a compaction of the chromosome template. This formulation implies that a change to the compacted state of chromatin which gives a chromosome or chromosome segment its characteristic heterochromatic stainability is a prerequisite for a change in the time at which replication of the heterochromatised region takes place. It would follow that a region which replicates out of phase with euchromatin should also differ in appearance. On the assumption that increased labelling frequency indicates a longer period of replication, the results presented here show that at least some compacted regions have extended replication by comparison with the homologous euchromatic regions. But the results also seem to indicate that in the rearranged chromosome regions closest to the heterochromatin, whatever their appearance, take longer to replicate than their counterparts in the non-translocated position. Apparently the replication time can be affected by the position in the genome and is not necessarily associated with the morphological appearance of the region concerned. This view is supported by the observations of Halfer et al. (1969), who found that when different rearrangements were studied separate segments of the heterochromatic Y chromosome varied in time of replication relative to each other, whereas the appearance of the segments remained the same in all rearrangements. Halfer et al. concluded that there is no strict correlation between the time at which replication occurs and intense stainability. Roberts (1972) observed that when the heterochromatic fourth chromosome is moved by translocation away from the vicinity of the chromocenter, basal 4R becomes more polytenic while retaining its dense staining, showing that underreplication and heavy staining are separable. Recently Ananiev and Gvozdev (1974), investigating the replication behaviour in an euchromatic duplication attached to heterochromatin, reported a significant difference in intensity and frequency of labelling in the duplication as compared with the homologous region in the normal chromosome, attributable to an induction of delayed replication in euchromatic regions by nearby heterochromatin. One may conclude that a change in condensation of a chromosomal region is not a prerequisite for a change in the replication behaviour of that region. In fact, the results presented here would be consistent with the view that extended replication precedes compaction. The reason for the absence of position effect on replication in the rearrangements studied by Barr et al. (1968), Valencia and Plaut (1970), and Evgeniev et al. (1972) is not clear. Ananiev and Gvozdev (1974) only detected differences when using lowered temperature and absence of the Y chromosome to enhance position effect, and they suggest that the negative results obtained in the previous work "are possibly explained by the slight extent of variegation in the *Drosophila* stocks used." Low culture temperature was also utilised in our experiments.

We would emphasize that by extended replication we are not implying that the region is late labelling. Evidence that heterochromatised regions of polytene chromosomes do not necessarily complete replication later than euchromatic regions will be presented elsewhere.

5. SUMMARY

1. In *Drosophila* euchromatin can be induced to assume a heterochromatic appearance by its relocation to the vicinity of heterochromatin.

2. By autoradiography, we compared labelling patterns in homologous regions of translocated and nontranslocated salivary chromosomes after *in vitro* incubation in tritiated thymidine. The duration of replication of translocated heterochromatised regions, and of translocated euchromatic regions adjacent to the break, is extended compared with homologous nontranslocated regions.

Acknowledgement. The authors are grateful to M. A. Williams for advice on autoradiographic procedures and analysis, and to D. J. Goldstein for helpful discussions. The work was carried out during the tenure of a British Empire Cancer Campaign Research Grant.

6. REFERENCES

Ananiev, E. V., and Gvozdev, V. A. 1974. Changed pattern of transcription and replication in polytene chromosomes of *Drosophila melanogaster* resulting from eu-heterochromatin rearrangement. *Chromosoma (Berl.), 45,* 173–191.

BARR, H. J., VALENCIA, J. I., and PLAUT, W. 1968. On temporal autonomy of DNA replication in a chromosome translocation. *J. Cell Biol., 39,* 8a.

BRIDGES, C. B. 1938. A revised map of the salivary gland X-chromosome of *Drosophila melanogaster. J. Hered.* (Suppl.), *29,* 11–13.

BROWN, S. W. 1966. Heterochromatin. *Science (Wash. D.C.), 151,* 417–425.

EVGENIEV, M. B., LUBBENIKOVA, E. I., and SHAPIRO, I. M. 1972. Autoradiographic study of replication pattern in polytene salivary gland chromosomes of *Drosophila melanogaster. C. R. Acad. Sci. (USSR), 204,* 215–217.

HALFER, C., TIEPOLO, L., BARIGOZZI, C., and FRACCARO, M. 1969. Timing of DNA replication of translocated Y chromosome sections in somatic cells of *Drosophila melanogaster. Chromosoma (Berl.), 27,* 395–408.

HARTMANN-GOLDSTEIN, I. J. 1967. On the relationship between heterochromatization and variegation in *Drosophilia,* with special reference to temperature sensitive periods. *Genet. Res., 10,* 143–159.

HEITZ, E. 1928. Das Heterochromatin der Moose 1. *Jahrb. wiss. Bot., 69,* 762–818.

HOWARD, E. F., and PLAUT, W. 1968. Chromosomal DNA synthesis in *Drosophila melanogaster. J. Cell Biol., 39,* 415–429.

JONES, K. W. 1970. Chromosomal location of mouse satellite DNA in individual cells. *Nature (Lond.), 225,* 912–916.

LEWIS, E. B. 1950. The phenomenon of position effect. *Adv. Genet., 3,* 73–115.

LIMA-DE-FARIA, A. 1969. DNA replication and gene amplification in heterochromatin. In *Handbook of Molecular Cytology* (LIMA-DE-FARIA, ed.), pp. 227–325. North Holland Publ. Co., Amsterdam and London.

LINDSLEY, D. L., and GRELL, E. H. 1968. Genetic Variations of *Drosophila melanogaster.* Carnegie Inst. Washington. Publ. No. 629.

MAXWELL, A. E. 1961. In *Analysing qualitative data* (Methuen's monographs on applied probability and statistics). Methuen and Co. Ltd., London.

PARDUE, M. L., and GALL, J. G. 1970. Cytological localization of DNA complementary to ribosomal RNA in polytene chromosomes of *Diptera. Chromosoma (Berl.), 29,* 268–290.

ROBERTS, P. A. 1972. A possible case of position effect on DNA replication in *Drosophila melanogaster. Genetics, 72,* 607–614.

ROGERS, A. W. 1967. In *Techniques of Autoradiography.* Elsevier, Amsterdam.

SCHULTZ, J. 1965. Genes, differentiation and animal development. In *Genetic Control of Differentiation and Development, Brookhaven Symp. Biol.,* No. 18, 116–147.

VALENCIA, J. I., and PLAUT, W. 1970. Further studies on temporal autonomy of DNA replication in chromosome rearrangements. *J. Cell Biol., 47,* 216a.

WARGENT, J. M., HARTMANN-GOLDSTEIN, I. J., and GOLDSTEIN, D. J. 1974. Relationship between DNA content of polytene chromosome bands and heterochromatisation in *Drosophila. Nature (Lond.), 248,* 55–57.

YUNIS, J. J., and YASMINEH, W. G. 1972. Model for mammalian constitutive heterochromatin. *Adv. Cell Mol. Biol., 2,* 1–46.

GENOME ORGANIZATION IN HIGHER PLANTS

R. N. JONES

Department of Agricultural Botany, University College of Wales, Aberystwyth, Wales, U.K.

1. INTRODUCTION

There are large differences in the number and size of chromosomes between different eukaryotic species (Darlington, 1937). Blackburn (1933) for example, recorded a maximum size (volume) range for chromosome complements of 66,000:1 in angiosperms and quantitative assessments of DNA variation by Feulgen microspectrophotometry established a general correlation between chromosome volumes and nuclear DNA amounts. The amounts of DNA in higher plant nuclei are excessive in relation to the estimated requirements. It has been suggested, for example, that 200,000 genes would be a sufficient genetic endowment to "make and run" one human being (Comings, 1972), and there is no reason to believe that a plant would require any more than this. Yet, the DNA present per haploid nucleus in flowering plants is enough to make from 700,000 (in flax) up to 98,000,000 (*Fritillaria davisii*) genes of 1000 base pairs long. It is evident now that although all genes are composed of DNA, the DNA of eukaryotes is complex, relative to that of prokaryotes, and all of it is not accommodated in the form of conventional genes. Cytologists have long known, of course, that certain classes of chromatin, such as heterochromatin and B-chromosomes, are conspicuously "emply" in terms of their major gene content, but only lately have we come to realise that as little as 10% of the eukaryote genome may actually exist in the form of *unique sequence* DNA coding for RNA and functional polypeptide chains. I will first consider the general causes of DNA variation in plants, and then look in more detail at the nature and function of the so-called "junk" fraction.

2. GENOME AMPLIFICATION

Each species has a unique genotype inscribed in its basic chromosome complement. In many cases, however, the genes of this basic set are repeated by way of established changes in the number of whole chromosome sets or even in individual chromosomes. Often, additional chromosomes showing no homology with any member of the basic A-chromosome set may occur in variable numbers. These are the B-chromosomes, so named on the basis of their apparent redundancy, lack of homology with the A's, and their non-Mendelian system of inheritance.

(a) *Polyploidy and aneuploidy*

Polyploidy contributes much to the excessive DNA amounts present in some plant species. Estimates put the percentage of polyploid angiosperms as high as

30–35 per cent (Stebbins, 1950). In some families like the Gramineae the figure may reach 70 per cent (Stebbins, 1956). Even-numbered multiples of C-values predominate since these are less mechanically disadvantageous at meiosis than are the odd-numbered multiples. Very high ploidy levels may be attained in some cases, e.g., *Andropogon*, 18x (Stebbins, 1956), and we may look upon these as cases of repetitive or multiple genomes. Aneuploids resulting from the irregular segregation do not make such a significant contribution to genome amplification, although we may consider them as repetitive chromosomes which afford some measure of continuous variation intermediate between that of the discontinuous polyploids.

(b) *B-chromosomes*

B-chromosomes as a source of chromosome repetition are much more relevant to the present discussion because there is considerable doubt about the nature of their DNA, both in respect of its composition and function. No major gene effects are known in B-chromosomes, notwithstanding a few cases such as the control by whole B's over homoeologous pairing of A-chromosomes in synthetic species hybrids (Evans and Macefield, 1973; Dover and Riley, 1972) and the control over their own non-disjunction property by the B's in Maize (Ward, 1973), which is confined to a particular localized euchromatic region of the B. But we do not know whether these particular activities can be attributed to individual Mendelian genes. There are also a few instances where B's are claimed to have nucleolus organizer regions (Powell and Burton, 1966; Schulz-Schaeffer, 1966). In general, though, their cytological behaviour, genetic effects, and widespread non-essentiality, are more indicative of a regulatory role akin to that of repetitive A-chromosome DNA, than to purveyors of genes proper, essential for the normal processes of growth and reproduction. Because of this likeness in function to redundant A-chromosome DNA their distribution, effects, and DNA composition will be considered in some detail.

Distribution. B-chromosomes are presently known in over 600 species of angiosperms (see table), divided equally between 12 monocotyledonous and 35 dicotyledonous families (although they probably occur much more commonly than this). Contrary to earlier opinions there is no preference for certain individual families. Those families which have the most B-containing species in them, usually have the most species anyway. If anything at all can be said about their distribution pattern

TABLE

B-chromosome distribution in angiosperm families

Family	Ploidy level and no. of species								Total	No. sp. known*	Percent with B's
	2X	3X	4X	5X	6X	7X	8X	?			
Monocotyledons											
Amaryllidaceae	27	1	3	—	1	—	—	4	36	395	9.1
Araceae	3	—	—	—	—	—	—	—	3	280	1.1
Bromeliaceae	1	—	—	—	—	—	—	—	1	86	1.2
Commelinaceae	13	—	4	—	—	—	—	2	19	240	7.9
Cyperaceae	1	—	—	—	—	—	—	1	2	562	0.4
Gramineae	66	2	34	1	16	1	6	13	139	3287	4.2

Table (contd.)

Iridaceae	4	—	1	—	—	—	—	1	6	488	1.2
Juncaceae	1	—	—	—	—	—	—	—	1	117	0.9
Liliaceae	76	4	7	2	2	—	1	1	93	1769	5.3
Musaceae	1	—	1	—	—	—	—	—	2	62	3.2
Orchidaceae	10	1	1	—	1	—	—	2	15	980	1.5
Zinigiberaceae	2	—	—	—	—	—	—	—	2	78	2.6
	205	8	51	3	20	1	7	24	319		
Dicotyledons											
Aceraceae	1	—	—	—	—	—	—	—	1	35	2.9
Boraginaceae	1	1	1	—	1	—	—	—	4	295	1.4
Campanulaceae	15	—	2	—	1	—	—	3	21	413	5.1
Chenopodiaceae	—	—	1	—	—	—	—	—	1	17	5.9
Compositae	76	4	18	1	8	2	6	22	137	4175	3.3
Convolvulaceae	1	—	—	—	—	—	—	—	1	157	0.6
Cornaceae	1	—	1	—	—	—	—	—	2	42	4.8
Crassulaceae	3	—	1	—	—	—	—	1	5	322	1.6
Cruciferae	19	3	3	—	2	—	1	—	28	794	3.5
Cucurbitaceae	1	—	—	—	—	—	—	—	1	115	0.9
Epacridaceae	3	—	—	—	—	—	—	—	3	104	2.9
Euphorbiaceae	2	—	—	—	—	—	—	—	2	255	0.8
Geraniaceae	3	—	—	—	—	—	—	—	3	150	2.0
Labiatae	3	—	1	—	—	—	1	—	5	634	0.8
Luraceae	2	—	1	—	—	—	—	—	3	31	9.7
Leguminosae	11	—	—	—	—	—	—	1	12	2460	0.5
Loranthaceae	6	—	—	—	—	—	—	—	6	117	5.1
Malvaceae	1	—	2	—	—	—	—	1	4	442	0.9
Moraceae	1	—	—	—	—	—	—	—	1	218	0.5
Onagraceae	11	—	1	—	—	—	—	2	14	406	3.4
Plantaginaceae	3	—	4	—	—	—	—	—	7	108	6.5
Polemoniaceae	12	—	—	—	—	—	—	—	12	115	10.4
Polygonaceae	1	—	—	—	—	—	—	—	1	352	0.3
Portulacaceae	—	—	—	—	—	—	—	1	1	72	1.4
Primulaceae	6	—	1	—	—	—	—	—	7	364	1.9
Ranunculaceae	8	—	1	—	1	1	—	1	12	827	1.5
Rhamnaceae	1	—	—	—	—	—	—	1	2	40	5.0
Rosaceae	—	—	1	—	—	—	—	1	2	1436	0.1
Salicaceae	1	—	—	—	—	—	—	—	1	170	0.6
Saxifragaceae	3	—	—	—	—	—	—	—	3	339	0.9
Schrophulariaceae	6	—	—	—	—	—	—	2	8	767	1.0
Solanaceae	3	—	—	—	—	—	—	—	3	631	0.5
Umbelligerae	1	—	—	—	—	—	—	—	1	675	0.1
Verbanaceae	1	—	—	—	—	—	—	—	1	179	0.6
Violaceae	2	—	1	—	—	—	—	—	3	269	1.1
	209	8	40	1	13	3	8	36	318		
Total	414	16	91	4	33	4	15	60	637		

* Number of species known cytologically, from Federov, 1969.

it is that they may be rarer in some primitive woody families than they are in herbaceous ones. Seventy-two per cent of all plus-B species are diploid and the remainder polyploid (fig. 1), so that in relative terms they are about as frequent in polyploids as they are in diploids (about two thirds of angiosperms are diploid). The number of B's found within members of individual species varies from zero to as many as 30 in *Zea mays*. The tolerance of many species for quite high numbers of B's is remarkable. In rye the 2C nuclear DNA amount in normal diploid individuals (2n = 2x = 14) is about 18.9 picograms. This can be increased by the presence of B's, in units of 1.05, up to 27.2 picograms when 8 B's are present. The comparable figures for maize are 11.0 and 27.5 picograms, respectively. This kind of situation can undoubtedly be found over and over again throughout various angiosperm families. At the population level, if we express the variation between individuals in terms of DNA amounts, instead of B-chromosome number, we find in rye, for instance, that the populations are highly polymorphic in respect of their nuclear DNA amounts (fig. 2). The immediate causes for the polymorphism can be readily traced to the non-Mendelian system of inheritance followed by the B's, but it is the genetic consequences of the system which are of much greater interest. The average DNA amount per individual will vary from population to population depending on the B-frequency. The significance of these differences between populations can only be assessed when we know what sort of physiological and genetic consequences are contingent upon this intraspecific variation in B-chromosome DNA.

Effects. Some of the consequences of B-chromosome activity are quite fundamental to cell and nuclear activity. Measurements of mitotic cycle times in root meristem cells of rye (Ayonoadu and Rees, 1968) and *Puschkinia libanotica* (Barlow, 1973) show that average cycle times are increased more or less additively with increasing numbers of B's. The cellular organization of the root meristems is also altered. In rye the presence of each additional B-chromosome decreases the number of cells

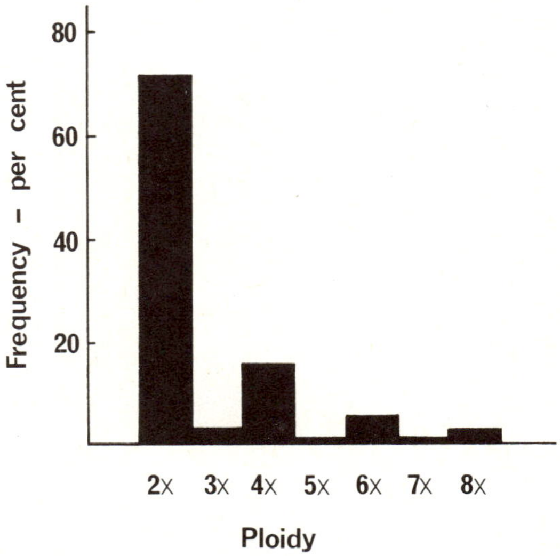

FIG. 1.—Distribution of B-chromosome containing species according to polyploidy.

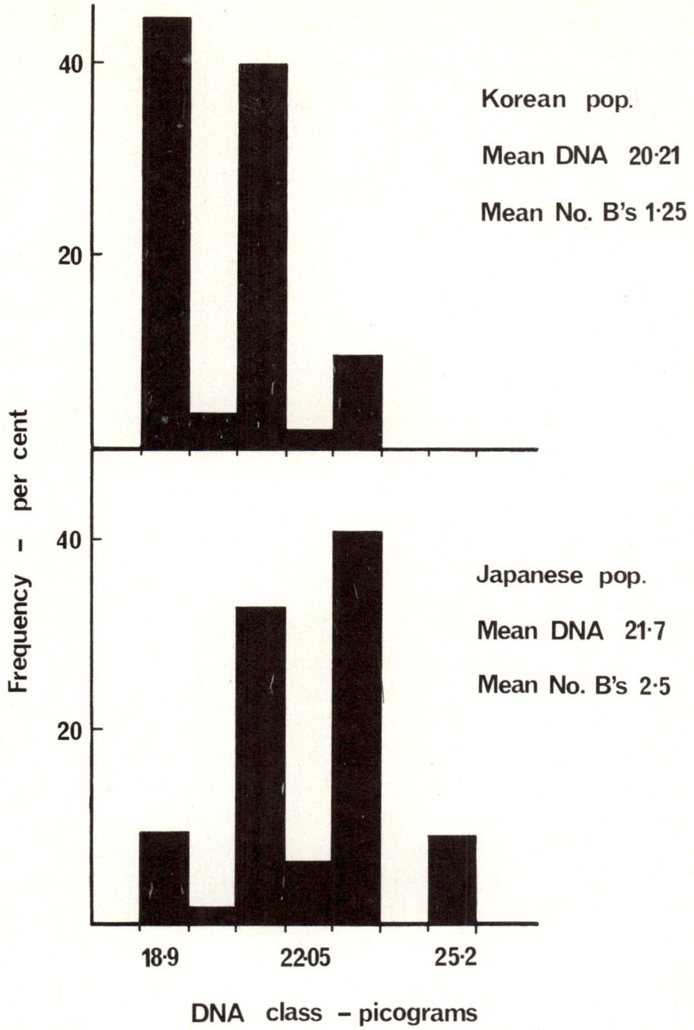

FIG. 2.—Distributions of 2C nuclear DNA values (picograms) among plants of B-chromosome rye (*Secale cereale*) populations from Korea (B-frequency data from Müntzing, 1957) and Japan (B-frequency data from Kishikawa, 1965).

per mg fresh weight by an average of 11.5% (John and Jones, 1970) (Fig. 3). It is not surprising therefore to find that B-chromosomes suppress vegetative vigour and delay the onset of flowering. The whole life cycle of the plant may thus be "regulated" through the presence of this "redundant" DNA. Populations containing these B's are "physiologically polymorphic" in respect of their vegetative and reproductive characteristics. Quite apart from these quantitative physiological effects, there is, too, an extended range of genetic variation resulting from the influence of the B's on the frequency and distribution of chiasmata in the A-chromosome bivalents (Jones, 1975). This latter effect is considered by some (Rhoades and Dempsey,

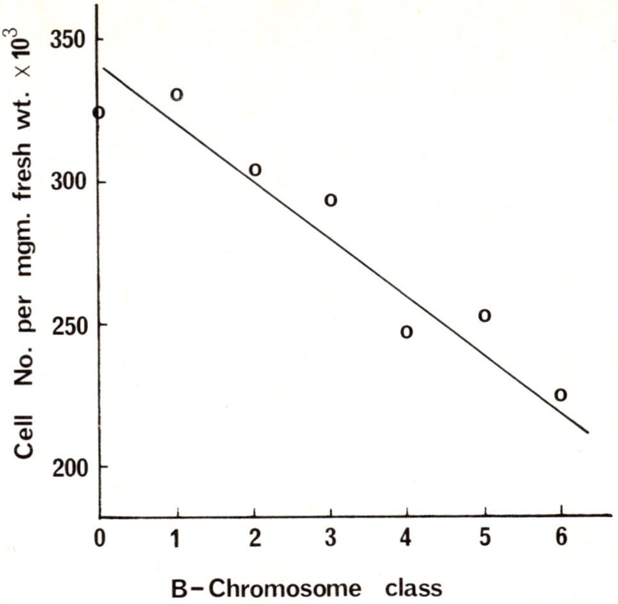

FIG. 3.—Mean cell number per mg fresh weight of root tip meristem, plotted against B-chromosome class. The material is from an experimental B-chromosome rye population.

1972) to be yet another manifestation of the basic alteration to cell cycle time. It is argued that the critical molecular events occurring at the time of recombination can be modified in those plants carrying B's by the additional time made available through the increase in division time. Naturally, in view of these considerations, it is urgent that we should attempt to analyse the nature of this B-chromosome DNA and discover how this redundant component of the genome compares in its molecular organization with that of the A-chromosomes. Before doing this, however, some aspects of A-chromosome DNA which relate specifically to quantitative variation in diploids will be considered.

(c) *A-chromosomes*

Surveys of several genera of diploid angiosperms revealed considerable divergence in nuclear DNA amounts, even between quite closely related species of identical chromosome number. In *Lathyrus* there is a threefold difference between species with the highest and lowest 2C DNA amounts (Rees and Hazarika, 1969). *Anemone* has a fivefold variation (Rothfels et al., 1966) and *Vicia* sevenfold (Rees et al., 1966). In the genus *Allium* detailed information is available about the distribution of DNA differences between the chromosomes of the complement (Jones and Rees, 1968). Two species, *Allium cepa* and *Allium fistulosum*, can be hybridised although the former has 27% more DNA. In the F_1 hybrid all the bivalents are heteromorphic, and this is evidence that all the chromosomes of the complement are involved in accommodating the extra DNA in *A. cepa*. Pachytene analysis reveals furthermore that the extra material in *A. cepa* is highly localized to one or two sites only within the chromosomes. These duplicated portions form large unpaired loops in otherwise perfectly paired homologues. At the cytological level therefore, in this case at least, the amplified portion of the genome is highly localized within individual chromosomes, but widely distributed throughout the complement.

The occurrence and distribution of quantitative DNA variation in angiosperms are now well enough documented for us to point to certain general trends and consequences. Within individual families and genera the evidence indicates that increasing specialization is accompanied by a reduction in chromosome number and size, and a decrease in DNA amounts. Stebbins discussed this matter in some detail (1966) and suggested a regulatory role for some DNA in terms of climatic and physiological adaptation. Species with high chromosome number and large DNA amounts are found preferentially in colder parts of the world, and have a lower metabolic rate and longer life cycle than those of more temperate regions. It is certainly the case that cell division rate is closely correlated with DNA amount (Evans et al., 1972) and with cell size (Martin, 1966). Both of these effects of course are fundamental and inevitably find expression by way of variation in the duration of life cycles. Bennett (1972) presented the case for this relationship with some forcefulness. Nagl (1974) has now added another variable to the argument by his findings that nuclear DNA amounts can be increased by the addition of heterochromatin without necessarily lengthening the cell cycle. The quality as well as the quantity of DNA is evidently important.

3. REPETITIVE DNA

DNA responds to heat treatment by melting or denaturing at certain critical temperatures. The melting profile can be monitored by measuring the changes in UV light absorption over a range of temperatures, and it reflects the DNA composition of particular species. Sequences with a higher C + G content require a higher temperature to induce strand separation. When melted DNA is slowly cooled under controlled conditions the single stranded molecules reassociate to reform a duplex structure virtually identical to the original molecule (Marmur and Doty, 1961). The kinetics of this reassociation process were first presented by Britten and Kohne (1966, 1968) who also discovered certain important properties of eukaryotic DNA's relating to the *rate* of reassociation. In prokaryotes the situation is relatively simple. When the DNA is sheared into small pieces, melted, and then allowed to reassociate, it does so at one rate. All the individual pieces are unique, and the time measured for the reassociation of half the DNA pieces varies inversely to the number of different pieces originally present. If one genome is twice the size of another then its rate of reassociation will be half as fast. This simple relation does not hold for eukaryotes. Their DNA has turned out to be complex and to have a number of different fractions with differing rates of reassociation, the fastest of which may reassociate up to a million times more quickly than the slowest. These measurable differences in reassociation rates, which reflect differences in the concentration of complementary sequences, constitute the main evidence for the existence of repetitive DNA. Evidently, a variable fraction of the genome (about one third on average) occurs in the form of nucleotide sequences which are repeated from a thousand to a million times per cell. Sometimes more than one type of sequence may be present, so that "families" of sequences are found which differ in their length and complexity as well as degree of repetitiveness. Very little is known in plants about the nature of this repetitive DNA. All the fundamental questions about the informational content and functional activity remain unanswered. We know a little about the extent to which it occurs in some genera. In six species of *Vicia* investigated by Chooi (1971), the degree of repetition varied between 15 and 38%. In conifers the proportion of repetitive DNA per genome is greatest in species with the highest DNA content (Miksche and Hotta, 1973). The proportion of repetitive DNA per genome in *Anemone* varies from 53 to 67%, and shows no correlation with either DNA per cell or the relative amounts of heterochromatin (Cullis and Schweizer, 1974). Analysis of the DNA of diploid and polyploid wheat species by Mitra and Bhatia (1973) has shown that the rapidly reassociating fraction comprises about 67, 74, and 80% of the total DNA in 2x (*Triticum monococcum*), 4x (*T. turgidum*) and 6x (*T. aestivum*) species, respectively. The DNA of wheat is therefore excessively repetitive, and has an estimated fragment size of about 450 nucleotide pairs long.

(a) *Satellite DNA*

Meselson et al. (1957) demonstrated that DNA of different composition could be separated by banding in dense salt gradients. Calcium chloride density centrifugation of DNA can be used to separate a "satellite" fraction (heavy or light) which generally has a strikingly rapid rate of reassociation. This satellite component of the repetitive DNA has been more thoroughly studied in plants than has the repetitive DNA in general. Coudray et al. (1970) compiled a list of species with satellite DNA which contained four monocotyledonous and 18 dicotyledonous species. In every case the satellite was C + G rich and with a greater buoyant density than the mainband DNA. Ingle et al. (1973) subsequently presented an extensive survey of the species distribution of satellite DNA's in higher plants. No satellite fraction was found in any of the 11 monocotyledons, but one was present in 27 out of the 59 dicotyledons. Satellite DNA was particularly prevalent in some species of the families Cucurbitaceae and Rutaceae, but otherwise there were no obvious correlations with the degree of evolutionary advancement, or any other significant pattern. Ingle et al., however, drew attention to the fact that the lack of a satellite component in the monocotyledons should be considered in the light of the known difference between monocotyledons and dicotyledons with respect to their cell cycle times. The average cycle time is 4 hours longer in dicotyledons than in monocotyledons (Evans and Rees, 1971). The fraction of the genome present as a satellite varies considerably, from zero in many cases, up to as high as 44%, as in the cucumber. Values of the order of 15–20% are quite common. So far only two species are known where the buoyant density of the satellite is less than that of the main bond DNA, flax and *Lobularia*, both in different families. Satellite DNA's from different species may behave quite differently with respect to their renaturation kinetics, some renaturing 30 times as fast as other. The satellite of the Muskmelon accounts for 30% of the total DNA (Bendich and Anderson, 1974). One third of this satellite fraction is high melting with a C + G content of 60%, while the other two thirds melts at a temperature of 8° lower and has a C + G content of 42%. The high temperature melting component has reassociation characteristic suggesting that it exists in the form of a simple repeating sequence about 380 nucleotides long, present some 6.1×10^5 times. The other component is about 1000 times more complex and is repeated only about

310 times. Pearson et al. (1974) studied the satellite DNA fraction of nine different melon varieties, using DNA extracted from several different tissues throughout the plant. The percentage satellite is different from the different varieties, but in addition to that there is variation in the percentage between different tissues within individual varieties. The satellite forms a higher percentage of the genome in meristematic tissues (i.e., seed and root tips) than in the mature differentiated cells of the fruit, leaves, and cotyledons. Further, in the cucumber, the variation in percentage satellite is correlated with a difference in the heterochromatin content of nuclei. Heterochromatin is under replicated in the fruit.

(b) *Ribosomal Cistrons*

Ribosomal geues account for only a minute fraction of total nuclear DNA, but their function is vital and all the more interesting on account of variations in the extent of their multiplicity both between and within species. In the artichoke (*Helianthus tuberosus*) there are about 260 ribosomal genes per haploid chromosome complement. This number is small compared with some other species such as *Pisum sativum* with 3,900 and *Allium cepa* with 6,650 (Ingle and Sinclair, 1972). In *Vicia* species the number of rRNA genes per 2C nucleus has been shown to vary between 2,500 and 9,500. The highest numbers are found in the species with the highest DNA amounts but there is no fixed relationship between DNA amount and rRNA gene multiplicity (Maher and Fox, 1973). An interesting case of intraspecific variation in rRNA gene number has been reported for *Hyacinthus orientalis* where a wide range of polyploid and aneuploid chromosome numbers may be found. Timmis et al. (1972) found that the number of copies of rRNA genes per nucleolar organizer is significantly lower in the aneuploid than in the euploid varieties. The difference is of the order of 20%. In *Triticum aestivum* there is also variation in the number of rRNA genes between different genotypes. Using aneuploids with deletions or additions of chromosomes bearing nucleolar organizers Mohan and Flavell (1974) found clear departures from the correlation between the number of rRNA cistrons and the number of nucleolar organizers. In *Zea mays* on the other hand a straightforward cytologically visible duplication of the nucleolus organizer region leads to a doubling of the numbers of ribosomal genes from 17,000 in the normal diploid to 34,000 in the strain carrying the duplication (Phillips et al., 1971). One of the interesting properties of these repetitive ribosomal cistrons is that the nucleotide sequences have been conserved throughout evolution relative to the rest of the genome. But here again there is some suggestion that there may be differences between the monocotyledons and dicotyledons, in this case with respect to the C + G content of their rRNA genes (Vodkin and Katterman, 1971).

(c) *B-Chromosome DNA*

The specialized cytological behaviour and genetic properties of B-chromosome suggest that their DNA sequences may differ from those of A-chromosomes. They are frequently heterochromatic, sometimes so much so (*Puschkinia libanotica*) that they can be observed in a highly contracted condition in interphase nuclei. In about half the recorded cases however this is not the case and their coiling sequence is identical to that of the A's.

Information about the heterochromatic status of chromosomes can be obtained by giemsa staining after alkali denaturation and reassociation of the DNA of somatic metaphase chromosomes in 2XSSC. Darkly stained giemsa bands on the chromosome correspond to locations of constitutive heterochromatin (Gill and Kimber, 1974). Such an analysis for the somatic complement of Japanese rye is presented in figures 4 and 5. Each of the seven A-chromosomes can be individually identified by their unique banding profiles. The B-chromosome banding pattern reveals constitutive heterochromatin at two locations which are of particular interest. The large band (two in favourable preparations) at the end of the long arm spans the site of the "controlling element" for nondisjunction, as well as the region in which chiasmata invariably occur. The centromeric band spans the site at which sister chromatids "stick" together during the nondisjunction process. In addition of course the banding arrangement of the B confirms its nonhomology with the A-chromosomes.

The first biochemical analysis of B-chromosome DNA was made in grasshoppers (Gibson and Hewitt, 1972) where they were found to contain a high proportion of repetitive sequences which could be separated as a satellite by neutral CsCl density gradient centrifugation. The heterochromatic B's of maize, by contrast, were found

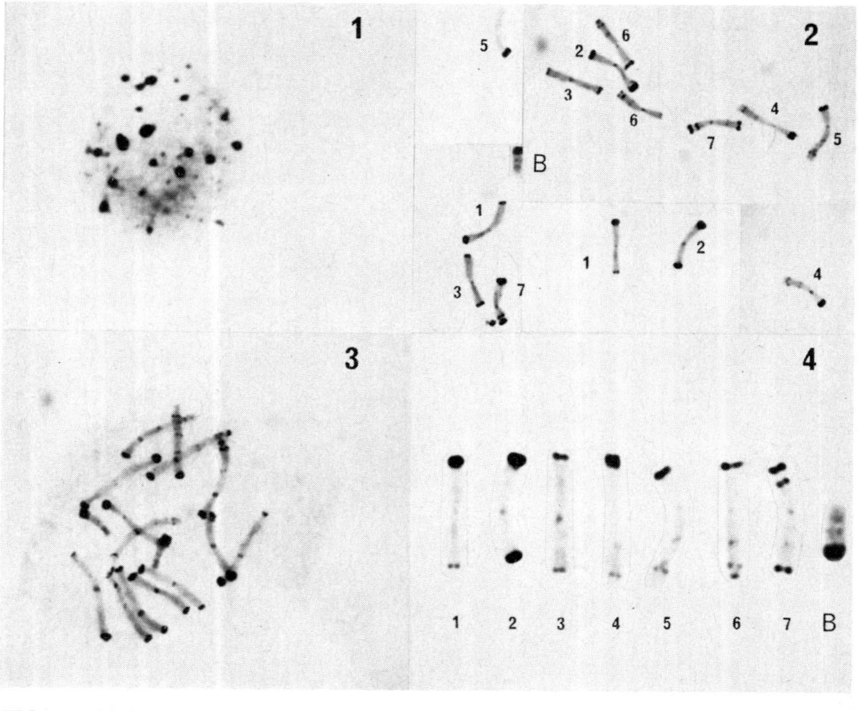

FIG. 4.—The Giemsa C-banding profile in B-chromosome Japanese rye (*Secale cereale*). (1) Giemsa stained interphase heterochromatin. (2) Composite photograph of c-mitosis showing the seven homologous pairs of A-chromosomes and a single B. There is some variation between the homologous pairs, as in pair 6 which are both from the same cell. (3) A complete chromosome complement including 2 B's. (4) The giemsa profiles of the seven A-chromosomes and the B-chromosome of Japanese rye.

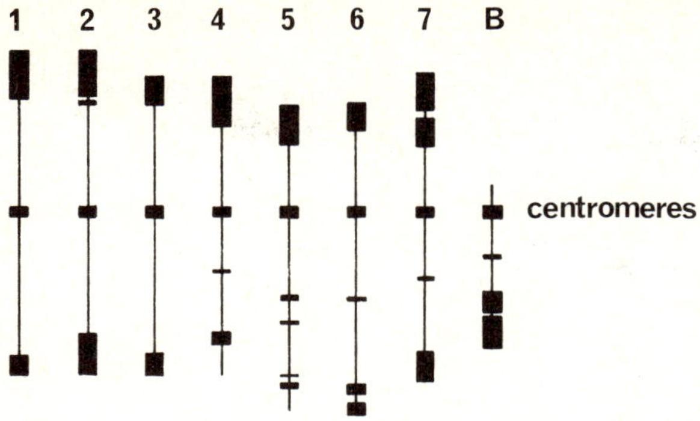

FIG. 5.—Diagrammatic interpretation of the giemsa c-band karyotype in Japanese rye (*Secale cereale*), identifying each of the seven A-chromosomes and the B. Chromosome seven carries the nucleolus organiser region between the two large bands on the short arm. (The classification is based on that of Verma and Rees, 1974.)

to have a DNA composition very closely related to that of the A's (Chilton and McCarthy, 1973). The DNA's from plants with and without B's were indistinguishable in their buoyant density in CsCl gradients and had identical renaturation kinetics. In rye, likewise (Timmis et al., 1975) the nuclear DNA from 0B and 6B plants is resolved by CsCl equilibrium centrifugation into a single fraction at a buoyant density of 1.702 g cm^{-3}. No distinct satellite or asymmetry of the band is detectable. The B-chromosomes appear to have a similar C + G composition to that of the A-chromosome complement. When the DNA's are compared by Ag^+/CS_2SO_4 analysis, however, some components can be resolved from the 6B plant DNA which are not shown in caesium chloride. These sequences account for only 3% of the 6B genome out of a total DNA contribution of the B's of 25%, and therefore represent some 12% of the B-chromosome DNA. Analysis of the melting profile revealed that the B-chromosome DNA has a slightly greater C + G content than that of the A's. The proportion of highly repeated sequences in rye, as determined from the renaturation kinetics is approximately 10% of the genome and this amount is found to be identical in both the 0B and 6B plants. Evidently the B-chromosomes contain a similar proportion of fast renaturing DNA to that of the A-chromosomes. It is clear now that in the two cases examined to date there is no convincing evidence that the DNA of the B-chromosome of plants differs in composition or degree of repetition from that of the A-chromosomes. It seems likely therefore that these B's must possess a large amount of unique sequence DNA, possibly in the form of functional genes.

4. CONCLUSIONS

The means by which genome amplification can come about in higher plants are varied, ranging from the relatively low order of amplification of whole chromosome complements as in polyploidy, where all genes and nucleotide sequences are coincidently amplified, down to the very specialized situation where short sequences of nucleotides are preferentially multiplied thousands if not millions of times. All these different mechanisms lead to variation in the quantity of DNA, and thus they have a common consequence. Mitotic cycle times and cell size are very closely correlated with nuclear DNA amount. Hence the quantity by itself is important. There are some deviations from this relationship which must be heeded, not least among which is the difference in behaviour between monocotyledons and dicotyledons. Evans et al. (1972) showed that the average cycle time is four hours longer in the dicotyledons than it is in the monocotyledons, while Nagl (1974) proposed that heterochromatin can vary independently of cycle time to some extent. But in general it remains a fact that more DNA means a longer cycle time, a larger cell size, and an increase in the life cycle. Since repetitive DNA can account for up to 80 per cent of the total DNA amount, we must conclude that this fraction too is implicated in this regulatory role. Plants may be relatively indifferent to the quality of variable DNA insofar as it regulates the cell and life cycle, but in other respects the nature and effects matter very much indeed. Polyploids for example have to tolerate considerable inconvenience to their meiotic system, so much so in many cases that they have had to resort to asexual means of reproduction to overcome it. B-chromosomes impose an even greater burden upon individuals. Sterility is so rife in many B-containing populations that a fairly large proportion of the individuals never manage to reproduce at all. But for the population as a whole there is greater flexibility than with polyploidy. The range of DNA variation is more continuous and is easily adjusted from generation to generation by changes in the B-frequency. The mechanism of this adjustment may involve changes in the frequency of non-disjunction in gametophytes, variation in the amount of elimination at meiosis or differential mortality of seedlings under conditions or environmental stringency (Rees and Hutchinson, 1974). Many species have also evolved systems of B-chromosome inheritance that trade on this inherent instability and specifically exclude the B's from selected tissues or organs. Repetitive DNA avoids the complications of both polyploidy and B-chromosome systems. The repetitive material is an integral part of the basic chromosome complement, and as such has no disadvantageous consequences for chromosome behaviour and reproductive fitness.

5. REFERENCES

AYONOADU, U., and REES, H. 1968. The regulation of mitosis by B-chromosomes in rye. *Exp. Cell Res., 52,* 284–290.

BARLOW, P. W. 1973. In *The Cell Cycle in Development and Differentiation* (M. BALLS and F. S. BILLET, eds.), pp. 133–165. Cambridge University Press.

BENDICH, A. J., and ANDERSON, R. S. 1974. Novel properties of satellite DNA from muskmelon. *Proc. Natl. Acad. Sci. U.S.A., 71,* 1511–1515.

BENNETT, M. D. 1972. Nuclear DNA content and minimum generation time in herbaceous plants. *Proc. R. Soc. Lond. Biol. Sci., 181,* 109–135.

BLACKBURN, K. B. 1933. Notes on the chromosomes of the duckweeds (Lemnaceae) introducing the question of chromosome size. *Proceedings of the University of Durham Philosophical Society, 9,* 84–90.

BRITTEN, R. J., and KOHNE, D. E. 1966. Nucleotide sequence repetition in DNA. *Carnegie Inst. Wash. Year Book, 65,* 78–106.

BRITTEN, R. J., and KOHNE, D. E. 1968. Repeated sequences in DNA. *Science (Wash. D.C.), 161,* 529–540.

CHILTON, M. D., and MCCARTHY, B. J. 1973. DNA from maize with and without B-chromosomes: a comparative study. *Genetics, 74,* 605–614.

CHOOI, W. Y. 1971. Comparison of the DNA of six *Vicia* species by the method of DNA-DNA hybridisation. *Genetics, 68,* 213–230.

COMINGS, D. E. 1972. The structure and function of chromatin. *Adv. Hum. Genet., 3,* 237–431.

COUDRAY, Y., QUETIER, F., and GUILLE, E. 1970. New compilation of satellite DNA's. *Biochim. Biophys. Acta, 217,* 259–267.

CULLIS, C. A., and SCHWEIZER, D. 1974. Repetitious DNA in some *Anemone* species. *Chromosoma (Berl.), 44,* 417–421.

DARLINGTON, C. D. 1937. *Recent Advances in Cytology,* 2nd ed. J. and A. Churchill Ltd., London.

DOVER, G. A., and RILEY, R. 1972. Prevention of pairing of homoeologous meiotic chromosomes of wheat by an activity of supernumerary chromosomes of *Aegilops. Nature (Lond.), 240,* 159–611.

EVANS, G. M., and MACEFIELD, A. J. 1973. The effect of B-chromosomes on homoeologous pairing in species hybrids. I. *Lolium temulentum* × *Lolium perenne. Chromosoma (Berl.), 41,* 63–73.

EVANS, G. M., and REES, H. 1971. Mitotic cycles in dicotyledons and monocotyledons. *Nature (Lond.), 233,* 3510–351.

EVANS, G. M., REES, H., SNELL, C. L., and SUN, S. 1972. The relationship between nuclear DNA amount and the duration of the mitotic cycle. *Chromosomes Today, 3,* 24–31.

FEDEROV, A. A. 1969. Chromosome numbers of flowering plants. Academy of Sciences of the USSR, Leningrad.

GIBSON, I., and HEWITT, G. 1972. Interpopulation variation in the satellite DNA from grasshoppers with B-chromosomes. *Chromosoma (Berl.), 38,* 121–138.

GILL, B. S., and KIMBER, G. 1974. The Giemsa C-banded karyotype of rye. *Proc. Natl. Acad. Sci. U.S.A., 71,* 1247–1249.

INGLE, J., PEARSON, G. G., and SINCLAIR, J. 1973. Species distribution of nuclear satellite DNA in higher plants. *Nat. New Biol., 242,* 193–197.

INGLE, J., and SINCLAIR, J. 1972. Ribosomal RNA genes and plant development. *Nature (Lond.), 235,* 30.

JOHN, P. C. L., and JONES, R. N. 1970. Molecular heterogeneity of soluble proteins and histones in relationship to the presence of B-chromosomes in rye. *Exp. Cell Res., 63,* 271–276.

JONES, R. N. 1975. B-chromosome systems in flowering plants and animal species. *Int. Rev. Cytol., 40,* 1–100.

JONES, R. N., and REES, H. 1968. Nuclear DNA variation in *Allium. Heredity, 23,* 591–605.

KISHIKAWA, H. 1965. Cytogenetic studies of B-chromosomes in rye, *Secale cereale* L. in Japan. *Agric. Bull. Saga Univ., 21,* 1–81.

MAHER, E. P., and FOX, D. P. 1973. Multiplicity of ribosomal RNA genes in Vicia species with different nuclear DNA contents. *Nat. New Biol., 245,* 170–172.

MARMUR, J., and DOTY, P. 1961. Thermal renaturation of deoxyribonucleic acids. *J. Mol. Biol., 3,* 585–594.

MARTIN, P. G. 1966. Variation in the amounts of nucleic acids in the cells of different species of higher plants. *Exp. Cell Res., 44,* 84–94.

MESELSON, M., STAHL, F. W., and VINOGRAD, J. 1957. Equilibrium sedimentation of macromolecules in density gradients. *Proc. Nat. Acad. Sci. U.S.A., 43,* 581–588.

MIKSCHE, J. P., and HOTTA, Y. 1973. DNA base composition and repetitious DNA in several conifers. *Chromosoma (Berl.), 41,* 29–36.

MITRA, R., and BHATIA, C. R. 1973. Repeated and non-repeated nucleotide sequences in diploid and polyploid wheat species. *Heredity, 31,* 251–262.

MOHAN, J., and FLAVELL, R. B. 1974. Ribosomal DNA cistron multiplicity and nucleolar organizers in hexaploid wheat. *Genetics, 76,* 33–44.

MÜNTZING, A. 1957. Frequency of accessory chromosomes in rye strains from Iran and Korea. *Hereditas, 43,* 682–685.

NAGL, W. 1974. Role of heterochromatin in the control of cell cycle duration. *Nature (Lond.), 249,* 53–54.

PEARSON, G. G., TIMMIS, J. N., and INGLE, J. 1974. The differential replication of DNA during plant development. *Chromosoma (Berl.), 45,* 281–294.

PHILLIPS, R. L., KLEESE, R. A., and WANG, S. S. 1971. The nucleolar organizer region of Maize (*Zea mays* L.): chromosomal site of DNA complementary to ribosomal RNA. *Chromosoma (Berl.), 36,* 79–88.

POWELL, J. B., and BURTON, G. W. 1966. Nucleolar organising accessory chromosomes in pearl millet. *Crop Sci., 6,* 131–134.

REES, H., CAMERON, F. M., HAZARIKA, M. H., and JONES, G. H. 1966. Nuclear variation between diploid angiosperms. *Nature (Lond.), 211,* 828–830.

REES, H., and HAZARIKA, M. H. 1969. Chromosome evolution in *Lathyrus*. *Chromosomes Today, 2,* 158–165.

REES, H., and HUTCHINSON, J. 1974. Nuclear DNA variation due to B-chromosomes. In *Cold Spring Harbor Symposium on Quantitative Biology (1973), 38,* 175–182.

RHOADES, M. M., and DEMPSEY, E. 1972. On the mechanism of chromatin loss induced by the B-chromosomes of Maize. *Genetics, 71,* 73–96.

ROTHFELS, K., SEXSMITH, E., HEIMBURGER, M., and KRAUSE, M. L. 1966. Chromosome size and DNA content of species of *Anemone* L. and related genera (Ranunculaceae). *Chromosoma (Berl.), 20,* 54–74.

SCHULZ-SCHAEFFER, J. 1966. A possible origin of B-chromosomes. *Zeitschrift fur Pflanzenzücht., 55,* 21–28.

STEBBINS, G. L. 1950. *Variation and Evolution in Plants.* Columbia University Press.

STEBBINS, G. L. 1956. Cytogenetics and evolution of the grass family. *Am. J. Bot., 43,* 890–905.

STEBBINS, G. L. 1966. Chromosome variation and evolution. *Science (Wash. D.C.), 152,* 1463–1469.

TIMMIS, J. N., SINCLAIR, J., and INGLE, J. 1972. Ribosomal RNA genes in euploids and aneuploids of *Hyacinth. Cell Differ., 1,* 335–339.

TIMMIS, J. N., INGLE, J., SINCLAIR, J., and JONES, R. N. 1975. The genomic quality of rye B-chromosomes. *J. Exp. Bot., 26,* 367–378.

VERMA, S. C., and REES, H. 1974. Giemsa staining and the distribution of heterochromatin in rye chromosomes. *Heredity, 32,* 118–122.

VODKIN, M., and KATTERMAN, F. R. H. 1971. Divergence of ribosomal DNA sequences within angiosperms. *Genetics, 69,* 435–451.

WARD, E. J. 1973. Nondisjunction: localisation of the controlling site in the maize B-chromosome. *Genetics, 73,* 387–391.

OBSERVATIONS ON THE REPEATED SEQUENCE DNA OF 'A' AND 'B' CHROMOSOMES OF GENOTYPES IN THE TRITICINAE WITH CONTRASTING PATTERNS OF MEIOTIC CHROMOSOME PAIRING

GABRIEL A. DOVER

Department of Genetics, University of Cambridge, U.K.

1. INTRODUCTION

Genetic analysis of the control of meiotic chromosome pairing in the Triticinae has revealed a complex set of interactions of 'A' and 'B' (supernumerary) chromosomes in their effect on pairing behaviour (Dover and Riley, 1972*a*, *b*; Vardi and Dover, 1972; Dover, 1973*a*). In particular, 'B' chromosomes reduce the high levels of homoeologous (multivalent) pairing normally associated with the absence of chromosome 5B of *Triticum aestivum* in *T. aestivum* × *Aegilops* spp. hybrids (Dover and Riley, 1972*b*). A 'B' chromosome restriction of homoeologous pairing has also been found in interspecific hybrids of *Lolium* (Evans and Macefield, 1972).

The mechanism of homologous chromosome recognition prior to synapsis is unknown, although results obtained with the use of spindle inhibitors applied during the last pre-meiotic mitosis in *T. aestivum* suggest a mechanism involving nuclear microtubules at this stage of development (Dover and Riley, 1973; Driscoll et al., 1967). The 'B' chromosomes of *Aegilops* spp. affect pairing, in certain instances, and also disrupt the normal functioning of the pre-meiotic spindles (Vardi and Dover, 1972).

It has been suggested (Walker, 1971; Yunis and Yasmineh, 1971; Flamm, 1972; Jones, 1973) that a possible function for highly repeated sequence DNA localized around the centromeres is the control of centromeric activity, chromosome movement, and chromosome pairing.

Genotypes within the Triticinae, having contrasting patterns of meiotic pairing, lend themselves ideally to an investigation of this suggestion. If the control of pairing involves a class of highly repetitive simple-sequence DNA, then a discrete species of DNA specific to 'B' chromosomes might be found, that is associated with the 'B' chromosome effect on meiotic pairing. Although no additional DNA fraction differing from 'A' chromosome DNA has been found in genotypes of maize carrying 'B' chromosomes (Chilton and McCarthy, 1973) and in rye plants with 'B' chromosomes (Rimpau and Flavell, 1976), 'B' chromosome specific satellite DNA has been reported in grasshoppers (Gibson and Hewitt, 1972).

2. MATERIALS AND METHODS

(a) *Genotypes*

Triticum aestivum var. Chinese Spring.

Aegilops speltoides (with zero to six 'B' chromosomes).

Aegilops mutica (with zero to four 'B' chromosomes).

Plants were grown singly in continuous light at 20°C. The 'B' chromosomes of *Ae. speltoides* and *Ae. mutica* preferentially segregate to the apex during zygote development and only the stems and leaves contain 'B' chromosomes (Mochizuki, 1964). The number of 'B' chromosomes in each plant was determined by cytological examination at first meiotic metaphase. Tillers were cut and the plants allowed to regenerate for a second harvest. Tissue from first and second harvest was bulked for each plant before extraction of DNA. Single plant extractions were made from 'B'-chromosome-containing plants and in plants containing no 'B' chromosomes extractions were carried out singly or in bulk.

(b) *Isolation of DNA*

Total DNA was extracted using a method based on Stern (1968) and on Marmur (1961), without the use of phenol for deproteinisation. This modification was introduced to avoid preferential extraction of d(A-T)n repetitive DNA by phenol (Morgan and Wells, 1968).

Plant material was frozen and crushed in liquid N_2, ground to a powder in a Molinex coffee mill, and ground further with a mortar in an equal volume of 0.33 M NaCl, 0.1 M EDTA, 1% sodium lauryl sulphate, 0.2% diethyl pyrocarbonate and acid washed sand. The mixture was shaken in 2 volumes of chloroform containing 1% 2-octanol and centrifuged for 5 min at 7,500 × *g*. The aqueous phase was heated to 70°C for 5 min; cooled in ice and deproteinised with chloroform/2-octanol after addition of 1 M sodium perchlorate. DNA was spooled from the aqueous phase with 2 volumes of ethanol and dissolved in 1 × SSC. The solution was treated with α-amylase (100 μg/ml), ribonuclease Tl (50λ/100ml), pancreatic ribonuclease (200 μg/ml), and protease (500 μg/ml). After treatment with enzymes the solution was deproteinised three times with chloroform 2-octanol (24:1) and dialysed against 0.12 M phosphate buffer (PB) at pH 6.8. DNA was collected by centrifugation at 115,000 × *g* for 16 hr. The pellet was dissolved in 0.12 M PB or 0.1 × SSC and sheared to a mean size of 300 base pairs with sonication. Fragment sizes were determined by velocity sedimentation in 1 M NaCl in a Centriscan 75 analytical centrifuge, using the method of Studier (1965).

(c) *Iodination of DNA with* I^{-125}

Total DNA was iodinated basically as described by Mizuno and MacGregor (1974) with modifications suggested by Dr. Mizuno. A reaction mixture of 100 μg of heat-denatured DNA, 3mCi of I^{125} (Radiochemical Centre, > 14 Ci/mg 5m Ci/50 μl of dilute NaOH, adjusted to 6×10^{-5}M Na_2SO_3 and 0.26 N H_2SO_4), 4.5×10^{-4} M KI and 2.25×10^{-3} M $TlCl_34H_2O$ (in 0.30 M Na acetate–0.12 M acetic acid, pH 5.0) was incubated for 50 min at 70°C. Reaction was terminated with 0.4 N NaOH and Na_2SO_3 10^{-2}M and incubated at 60°C for 20 min. Unattached iodine was removed on a 1.0 × 36 cm Sephadex G-50 (medium grade) column. The DNA-I^{125} fraction was eluted with 0.08 M PB and bound to hydroxyapatite (HAP) also washed with 0.08 M PB. The bound DNA was released with 0.5 M PB, dialysed against water and radioactivity determined by liquid scintillation counting on the ^{3}H-channel using a toluene-triton X-100 based scintillation cocktail.

(d) *Isopycnic centrifugation in CsCl gradients*

A solution of 10 μg of sample DNA plus 0.5 μg of marker DNA, *Pseudomonas aeruginosa*, buoyant density 1.726 g cm^{-3} (gift of Dr. John Sulston, M.R.C., Cambridge), in 0.6 ml 10m M Tris-HCl pH 7.5 was brought to an initial density of 1.700 g cm^{-3} with CsCl and centrifuged at 44,000 r.p.m. for 20 hr at 25°C in the analytical Centriscan 75 ultracentrifuge. Buoyant densities and % G + C composition were calculated according to Mandel et al. (1968).

(e) *Thermal denaturation*

Sheared DNA samples of average size 300 base pairs were melted in 0.1 × SSC or 0.12 M PB in an electrically heated block at a constant rise in temperature of 0.5°C per min. Experiments were designed to minimize environmental fluctuations between successive melts. Three samples of DNA of each genotype were melted simultaneously and changes in optical density (hyperchromic shift) and temperature were monitored continuously. Thermal stability profiles of the change in OD as a percentage of the total change were plotted at 0.5°C intervals. Differentiation of these profiles, giving the mean percentage change in OD between consecutive temperatures, was derived and plotted by computer. Differences in the melting characteristics of genotypes could be confused with environmental differences between melts. To eliminate this possibility samples of each genotype were also melted simultaneously in consecutive experiments and mean derived curves plotted for each genotype. This method allowed for the separation of experimental and sample-to-sample variation. Consistent differences between samples could, therefore, be compared to genotypic differences.

(f) *DNA/DNA hybridization in solution*

Sheared I^{125}-labelled samples of DNA were mixed with sheared unlabelled DNA in 0.12 M PB at a ratio of 1:3000. The mixture was heat-denatured, cooled in ice to 60°C and incubated at 60°C (T_m 25°C) for periods of time to allow renaturation of either highly repetitive ('C_0t' 10^{-2}, moles l^{-1} sec^{-1}) or highly repetitive plus moderately repetitive DNA ('C_0t' 100, moles l^{-1} sec^{-1}) only. Incubation times were calculated from reassociation rates published for *T. aestivum* (Bendich and McCarthy, 1970; Smith and Flavell, 1974) and *Aegilops* spp (Dover, unpublished). After incubation, the DNA mixture was fractionated into single- and double-stranded DNA by passage through a water-jacketed column of 0.5 g HAP in 0.12 M PB at 60°C. Single-stranded DNA was eluted with 3 × 2 ml washes of 0.12 M PB. Homo- and heteroduplexes of bound DNA were denatured by raising the column temperature, at 2°C intervals, from 60°C to 96°C. Denatured single-stranded DNA was eluted with 3 × 2 ml 0.12 M PB at each temperature. Optical density and radioactivity of each eluant were determined. Thermal elution profiles are given below for labelled (heteroduplex) and unlabelled (homoduplex) DNA from mixtures initially incubated to 'C_0t' values of 10^{-2} and 100. Mean percentage heteroduplex formation was calculated from experiments at which the relative percentages of bound labelled and unlabelled DNAs were determined at 60°C and 96°C only. This effectively eliminates overestimation of optical density and radioactivity of bound DNA due to accumulation of high background effects when calculated from separate 2°C intervals. A check on the efficiency of renaturation at the chosen stringency of conditions was obtained by further melting and incubation to 'C_0t' 100 of the single-stranded DNA not binding to HAP at the first incubation. After the second incubation 94–96% of the DNA eluted as single-stranded DNA.

3. RESULTS

Changes in mean T_m of DNA extracted from *Ae. speltoides* (0–6 'B' chromosomes), *Ae. mutica* (0–4 'B' chromosomes) and *T. aestivum* are given in table 1. There was a decrease in T_m of *Ae. speltoides* DNA with increasing numbers of 'B' chromosomes. This difference persisted in melting experiments designed to eliminate environmental fluctuation (see Materials and Methods). This decrease represents a fall in G + C% of total DNA from 45.6% (0– 'B' chromosomes) to 44.9% (3– 'B' chromosomes) to 43.4% (6– 'B' chromosomes). This small but consistent difference associated with 'B' chromosomes was similarly revealed by a decrease in buoyant density observed in *Ae. speltoides* DNA with 'B' chromosomes (fig. 1). There was a decrease in buoyant density from 1.705 g cm^{-3} to 1.703 g cm^{-3}, corresponding to a shift in G + C% from 45.9% to 43.8%. 'B' chromosome associated changes in T_m and buoyant density were not as strong in *Ae. mutica* DNA with or without 'B' chromosomes. There was a slight increase in buoyant density in the presence of *Ae. mutica* 'B' chromosome DNA (fig. 2). However, these small changes in the mean T_m cannot be linearly correlated with increasing amounts of *mutica* 'B' chromosome DNA (table 1).

Differentiation of thermal stability profiles reveals the percentage change in optical density between consecutive temperatures; narrow Gaussian peaks are indicative of discrete homogeneous fractions of DNA dissociating over a range of temperature relative to their G + C% composition (Huguet and Jouanin, 1972). A small (A-T)-rich DNA fraction (< 5%) with a characteristic melting peak (arrowed

TABLE 1

Mean melting temperatures (T_m°C) and untransformed standard errors of native DNAs of T. aestivum, Ae. speltoides *(with or without 'B' chromosomes), and* Ae. mutica *(with or without 'B' chromosomes) randomised and denatured in 0.1 × SSC or 0.12 M PB (see Materials and Methods).*

Source of DNA		Solvent	T_C(°C)	%G + C
Ae. speltoides	+ zero-'B's	0.1 × SSC	72.6 ± 0.20	45.6
"	+ 3-'B's	0.1 × SSC	72.3 ± 0.59	44.9
"	+ 6-'B's	0.1 × SSC	71.7 ± 0.32	43.4
"	+ zero-'B's	0.12 M PB	88.0 ± 0.35	
T. aestivum		0.12 M PB	87.3 ± 0.21	
Ae. mutica	+ zero-'B's	0.12 M PB	90.7 ± 0.20	
"	+ 2-'B's	0.12 M PB	90.1 ± 0.10	
"	+ 4-'B's	0.12 M PB	91.4 ± 0.14	

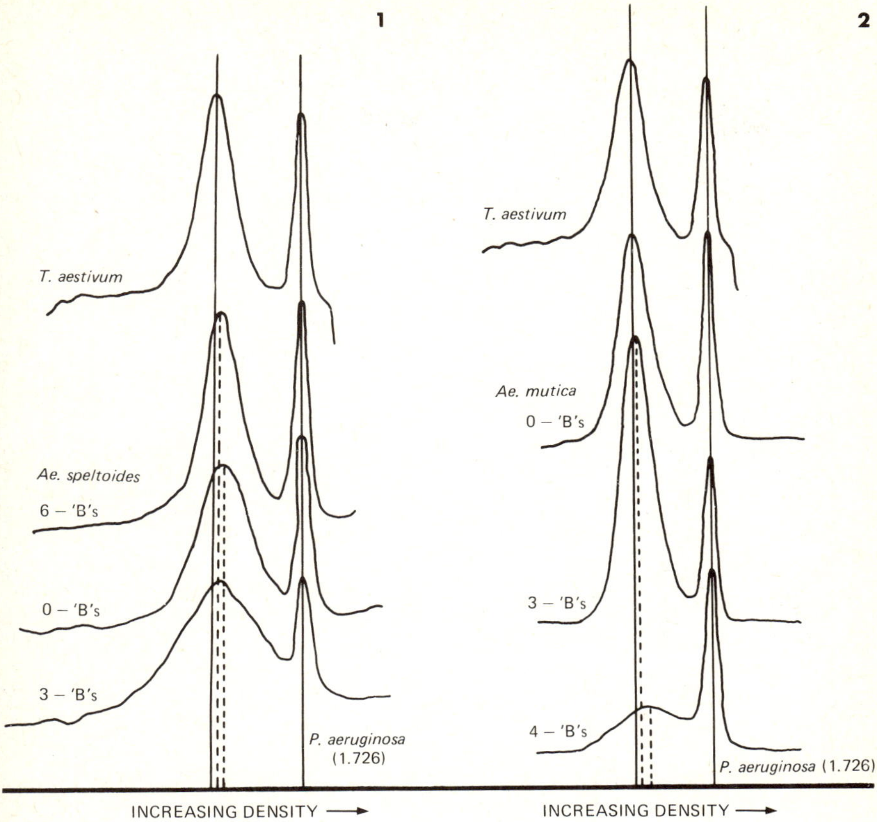

FIGS. 1 and 2.—Buoyant density patterns of DNA from *T. aestivum*, *Ae. speltoides* (with or without 'B' chromosomes), and *Ae. mutica* (with or without 'B' chromosomes). Buoyant densities were calculated relative to *Pseudomonas aeruginosa* (1.726 g cm^{-3}).

in figs. 3, 5, and 6) was only observed in the DNA extracted from plants having 'B' chromosomes. This peak persisted despite the randomisation of genotypes over successive melts (figs. 5 and 6) (see Materials and Methods). However, the overall melting profile of the DNA of individuals with 6–'B' chromosomes (representing 30% of the nuclear DNA) was similar to that of the DNA of zero-'B' individuals (figs. 3–6). No additional peak in derived melting profiles of DNA extracted from *Ae. mutica* could be associated with the presence of 'B' chromosomes (figs. 7–9). Simultaneous thermal denaturation of DNA extracted from populations of zero-'B' plants of *Ae. speltoides*, *Ae. mutica* and *T. aestivum* had very similar derived melting profiles (figs. 10, 11, and 12).

The mean percentage and standard errors of the degree of reassociation of excess sheared unlabelled DNA of *T. aestivum* and sheared labelled DNA of *Ae. speltoides* with or without 'B' chromosome DNA, incubated to 'C_0t' 10^{-2} and 'C_0t' 100, are given in tables 2 and 3. The percentage heteroduplex formation was not significantly altered with the addition of 30% 'B' chromosome DNA in 6-'B' chromosome genotypes reassociated to either 'C_0t' value. At 'C_0t' 100 the level of heterologous

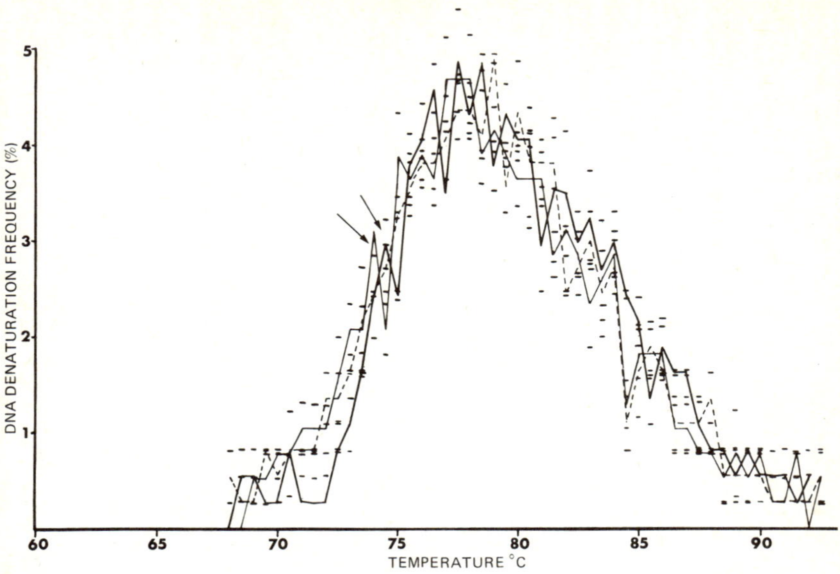

FIG. 3.—Mean derived curves and standard errors from thermal denaturation profiles of DNA from genotypes of *Ae. speltoides* with zero-, 3- and 6-'B' chromosomes. Three samples of each genotype were melted simultaneously in 0.1 × SSC. The frequency of dissociating DNA molecules between temperatures t_2 and t_1 were calculated with the relation $(A_{(t_1)} - A_{(t_2)})/(A_{(t_n)}) - A_{(t_1)}) \times 100$. $A_{(t_1)(t_2)....(t_n)}$ are the absorbance values measured at temperatures t_1 and t_2, etc. Interval $(t_2 - t_1)$ was 0.5°C. Arrow indicates small (A-T) n-rich DNA fraction associated with genotypes carrying 'B' chromosomes (continuous lines). Genotype with zero-'B' chromosomes (broken line).

TABLE 2

Percentage duplex formation between repeated nucleotide sequences of T. aestivum *DNA and* Ae. speltoides *DNA with or without 'B' chromosomes, incubated to 'C_0t' 100 moles l^{-1} sec^{-1}. Figures in parentheses represent homoduplexes of unlabelled DNA. Other figures represent heteroduplex and homoduplex formation between labelled DNA and unlabelled DNA. Standard errors are indicated*

	I^{-125}-labelled DNA		
Unlabelled DNA	*T. aestivum*	*Ae. speltoides* + zero-'B' chromosomes	*Ae. speltoides* + 6-'B' chromosomes
T. aestivum	62.6 ± 1.2 (79.1 ± 0.1)	66.5 ± 0.6 (82.0 ± 0.2)	66.30 ± 0.8 (82.3 ± 0.4)
Ae. speltoides + zero-'B' chromosomes	68.7 ± 0.1 (78.1 ± 0.1)	66.6 ± 4.3 (77.5 ± 0.9)	65.5 ± 3.7 (76.3 ± 0.7)

association was as high as homologous association of labelled *T. aestivum* DNA hybridized to excess unlabelled *T. aestivum* DNA. At 'C_0t' 10^{-2} heterologous association was just over half that of the relative homologous association. The mean fall in melting temperature (ΔT_m) between homoduplexes and heteroduplexes formed

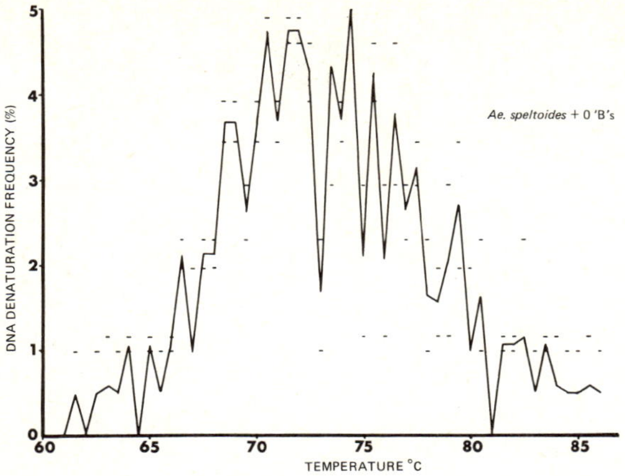

4

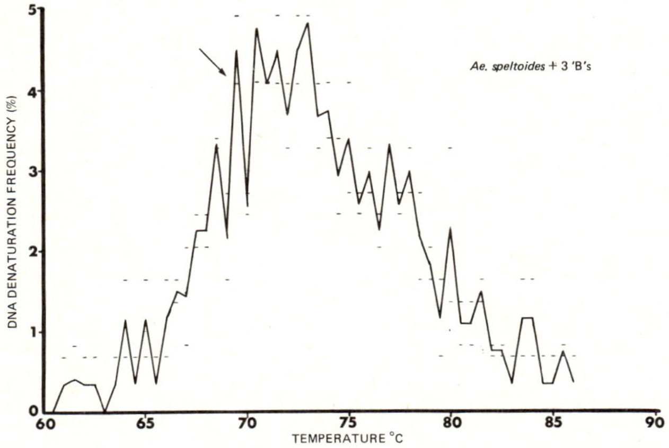

5

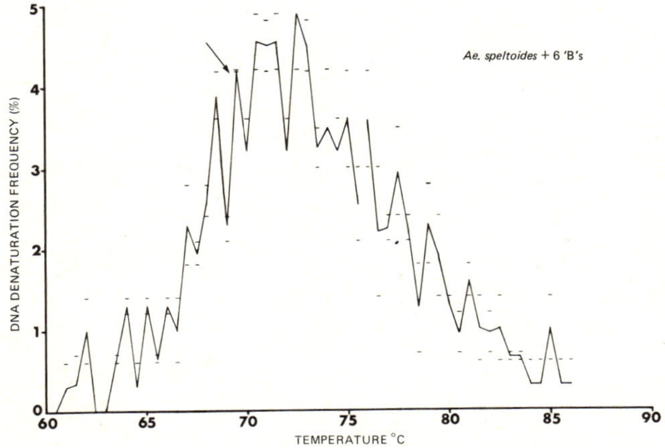

6

FIGS. 4–6.—Mean derived curves and standard errors from thermal denaturation profiles of DNA from genotypes of *Ae. speltoides* with zero-, 3-, and 6-'B' chromosomes. Genotypes were denatured simultaneously over three consecutive melts in 0.1 × SSC (see Materials and Methods). See legend to figure 3 for derivation of curves. Arrows indicate DNA fraction in 3- and 6-'B' chromosome DNA, not found in zero-'B' chromosome DNA.

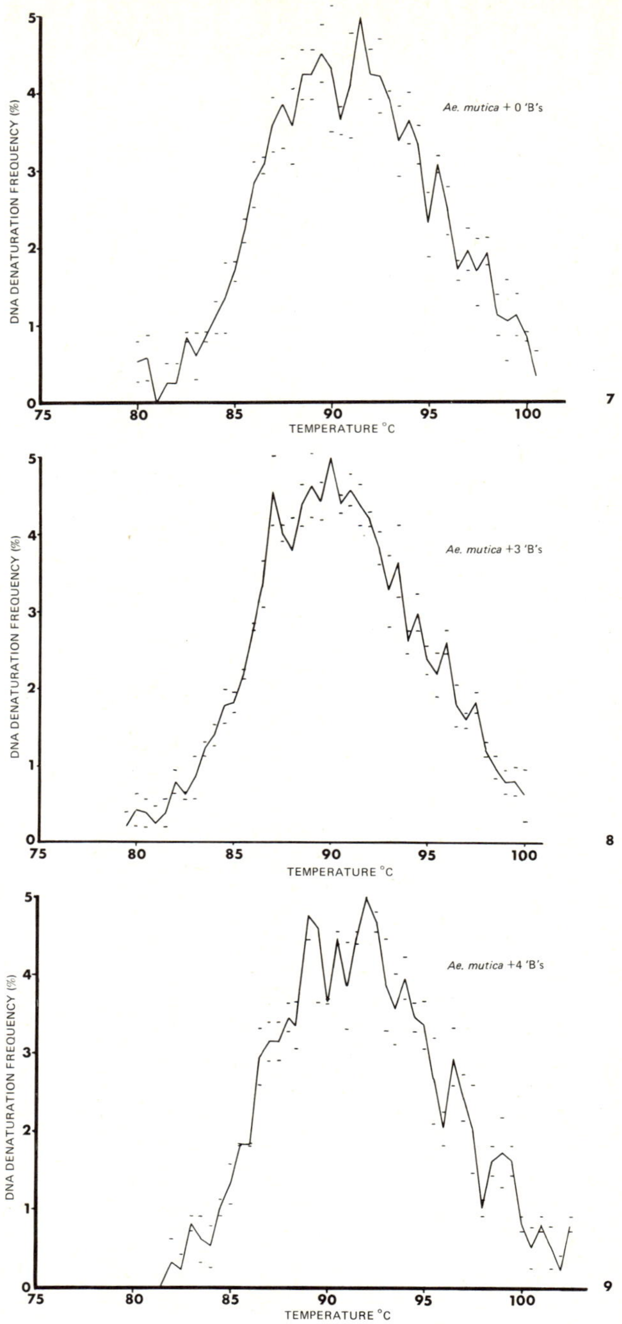

FIGS. 7–9.—Mean derived curves and standard errors from thermal denaturation profiles of DNA from genotypes of *Ae. mutica* with zero-, 3-, and 4-'B' chromosomes, melted in 0.12 M PB. For randomisation of genotypes and derivation of curves see legend to figures 3 and 4–6.

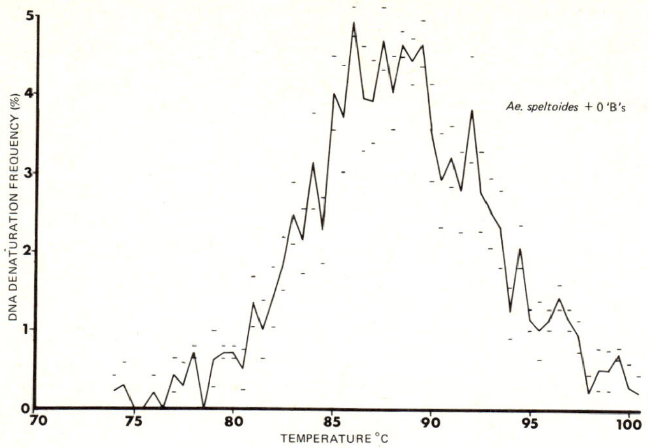

10

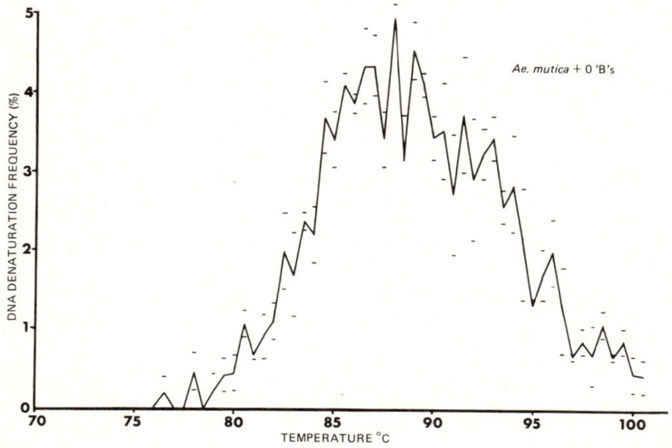

11

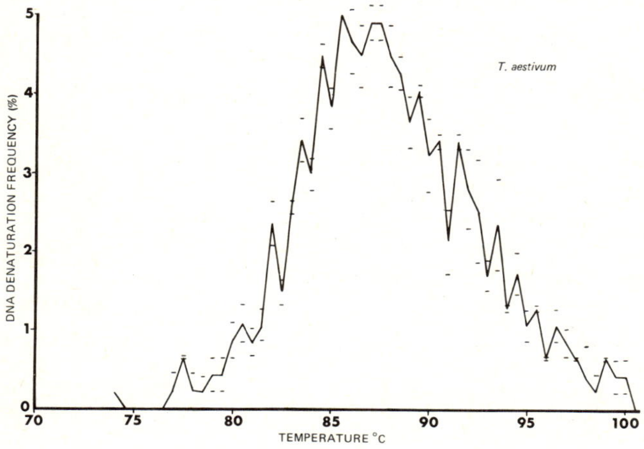

12

FIGS. 10–12.—Mean derived curves and standard errors from thermal denaturation profiles of DNA from *T. aestivum*, *Ae. speltoides*, and *Ae. mutica*, melted in 0.12 M PB. For randomisation of genotypes and derivation of curves see legend to figures 4, 5, and 6.

TABLE 3

Percentage duplex formation between repeated nucleotide sequences of T. aestivum *and* Ae. speltoides *DNA with or without 'B' chromosomes incubated to 'C_0t' 10^{-2} moles l^{-1} sec^{-1}. Figures in parentheses represent homoduplexes of unlabelled DNA. Other figures represent heteroduplex and homoduplex formation between labelled DNA and unlabelled DNA. Standard errors are indicated*

	I^{-125}-labelled DNA		
Unlabelled DNA	*T. aestivum*	*Ae. speltoides* + zero-'B' chromosomes	*Ae. speltoides* + 6-'B' chromosomes
T. aestivum	5.5 ± 0.6 (11.5 ± 0.6)	2.9 ± 0.2 (11.3 ± 0.6)	2.2 ± 1.1 (10.5 ± 0.3)
Ae. speltoides + zero-'B' chromosomes		4.0 (16.62)	3.8 (15.7)

TABLE 4

Differences in melting temperatures (ΔT_m, °C) between homologous and heterologous duplexes of I^{-125}-labelled and unlabelled DNA incubated in 0.12 M PB at 60°C to 'C_0t' 100 moles l^{-1} s^{-1}.

	I^{-125}-labelled DNA			
Unlabelled DNA	*T. aestivum*	*Ae. speltoides* + zero-'B' chromosomes	*Ae. speltoides* + 6-'B' chromosomes	*Ae. mutica* + zero-'B' chromosomes
T. aestivum		2.1 2.5 $\bar{x} = 2.3$	2.5	
Ae. speltoides + zero-'B' chromosomes	2.3			
Ae. mutica + zero-'B' chromosomes				3.9 3.1 $\bar{x} = 3.5$

in hybridizations of excess *T. aestivum* DNA to *Ae. speltoides* DNA was 2.3°C irrespective of the presence or absence of 'B' chromosome DNA (table 4).

Mean percentage heteroduplex formation and ΔT_m in reciprocal hybridizations (labelled DNA of *T. aestivum* incubated in a ratio of 1:3000 with unlabelled DNA of *Ae. speltoides* with and without 'B' chromosomes) are also shown in tables 2, 3, and 4. The level and thermal stability of heteroduplex formation was not significantly affected by the direction of the hybridization.

Results obtained from DNA/DNA hybridizations using *Ae. mutica* DNA are shown in table 5. There was a relatively large difference in the level of reassociation at 'C_0t' 100 between wheat DNA and *Ae. mutica* DNA (without 'B' chromosomes) and wheat DNA and *Ae. mutica* DNA (with 'B' chromosomes). However, the low

TABLE 5

Percentage duplex formation between repeated nucleotide sequences of T. aestivum *DNA and* Ae. mutica *DNA with or without 'B' chromosomes, incubated to 'C_0t' 100 moles l^{-1} sec^{-1}. Figures in parentheses represent homoduplexes of unlabelled DNA. Other figures represent heteroduplex and homoduplex formation between labelled DNA and unlabelled DNA. Standard errors are indicated*

	I^{-125}-labelled DNA		
Unlabelled DNA	*T. aestivum*	*Ae. mutica* + zero-'B' chromosomes	*Ae. mutica* + 4-'B' chromosomes
T. aestivum	62.6 ± 1.2 (79.1 ± 0.1)	59.7 ± 0.3 (78.2 ± 0.7)	* 14.2 ± 1.22 (78.6 ± 0.1)
Ae. mutica + zero-'B' chromosomes		58.3 (77.4)	* 18.2 (67.2)
Ae. mutica + 4-'B' chromosomes			* 23.5 ± 0.4 (75.5 ± 1.1)

* See text for discussion.

level of homologous association of labelled *Ae. mutica* DNA (with 'B' chromosomes) to excess *Ae. mutica* DNA (without 'B' chromosomes) calls for caution in the interpretation of these results. Further extraction and iodination of *Ae. mutica* DNA (with 'B' chromosomes) needs to be made to verify the nature of this difference.

There were no significant reciprocal differences in the percentage heteroduplex formation between the DNA of *T. aestivum* and the DNA of *Ae. mutica* (without 'B' chromosomes).

The ΔT_m between homoduplexes and heteroduplexes of excess wheat DNA hybridized to labelled *Ae. mutica* DNA (without 'B' chromosomes) (table 4) was 3.5°C. Thermal elution curves for reassociated repetitive DNA of excess wheat DNA hybridized to labelled *Ae. speltoides* DNA (with or without 'B' chromosomes) and for the reciprocal hybridization are shown in figures 13–16. The elution profiles show that dissociation of homoduplexes and heteroduplexes occurred over a wide range of temperatures; individual peaks indicated several species of DNA melting at optimum temperatures, that were determined by base composition and degree of base mis-matching. The number and positions of peaks remained constant for the dissociation of homoduplexes and heteroduplexes in any one experiment, irrespective of the presence of 'B' chromosome DNA and of the direction of hybridization.

4. DISCUSSION

Equilibrium centrifugation in CsCl gradients, controlled comparative thermal denaturations, cross-hybridization in solution allowing for heteroduplex formation, and thermal elution of dissociated heteroduplexes have not revealed a major species of DNA specific to 'B' chromosomes. The small yet consistent (A-T)n- rich DNA associated with the DNA of genotypes of *Ae. speltoides* with 'B' chromosomes, observed as a discrete peak in derived denaturation profiles, could contribute to the

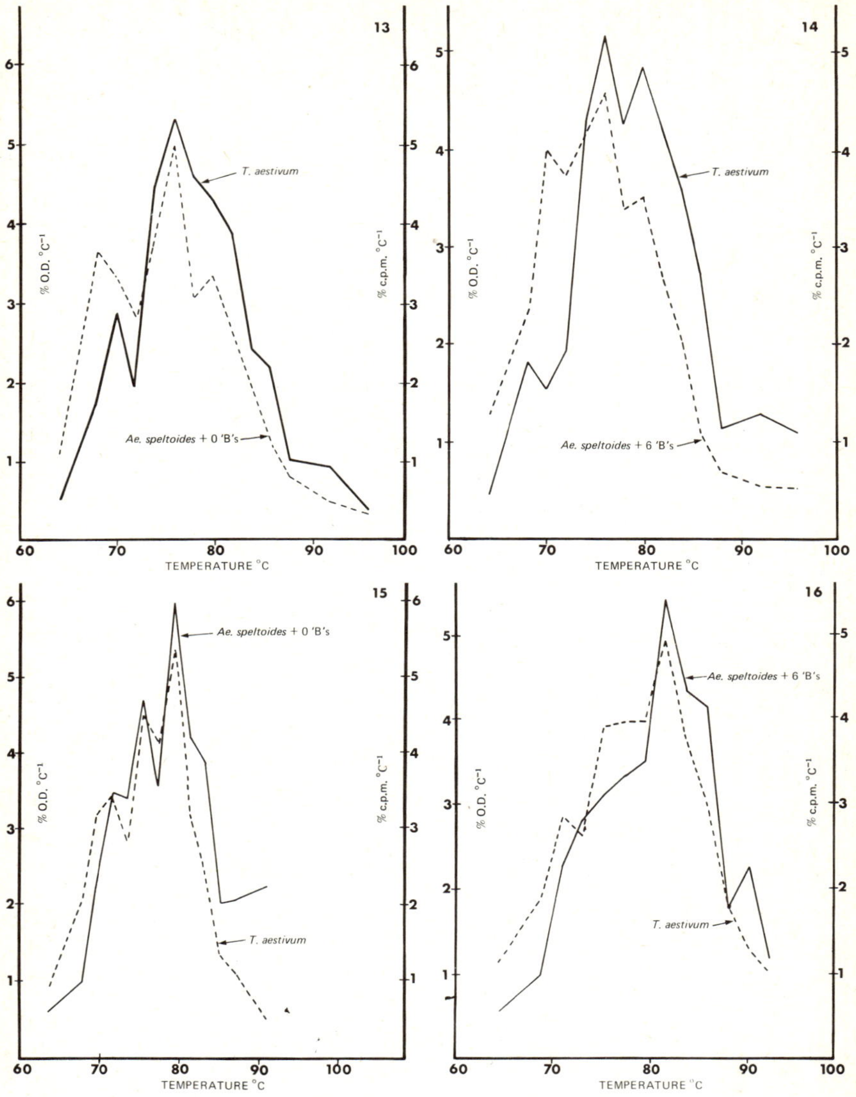

FIGS. 13–16.—Thermal dissociation profiles of highly repeated and moderately repeated homoduplexes (continuous lines) and heteroduplexes (broken lines) of excess DNA of one species hybridized to labelled DNA of the other species, to 'C_0t' 100 moles l^{-1} sec^{-1} at 60°C in 0.12 M PB.

small reduction in G + C% composition of total DNA, reflected in lower T_m's and lighter buoyant densities of 'B' chromosome carrying plants. However, this small DNA fraction cannot account for all of the additional 30% 'B' chromosome DNA in 6–'B' chromosome individuals. The overall similarities in the melting characteristics of the DNA extracted from *Ae. speltoides* (with or without 'B' chromosomes), *Ae. mutica* (with or without 'B' chromosomes), and *T. aestivum* show that the greater proportion of 'B' chromosome DNA appears to contain a spectrum of sequences not unlike 'A' chromosome DNA of the three species.

This conclusion is supported by the high levels of heteroduplex formation, relative to that of labelled *T. aestivum* DNA hybridized to excess *T. aestivum* DNA, under incubation conditions allowing for the reassociation of highly repetitive and moderately repetitive DNA ('C_0t' 100 moles l^{-1} sec^{-1}), irrespective of the presence of 'B' chromosome DNA and of the direction of hybridization. This latter result indicates that there are no additional classes of DNA present in one species not having homologous counterparts in the other species. However, under incubation conditions allowing for reassociation of highly repetitive DNA only ('C_0t' 10^{-2} moles l^{-1} sec^{-1}) the percentage heteroduplex formation between *T. aestivum* DNA and *Ae. speltoides* DNA (with or without 'B' chromosomes) is just over half that of the percentage relative homoduplex formation. Not all of the highly repetitive sequences present in *T. aestivum* are present in *Ae. speltoides*, and the presence of 'B' chromosomes does not alter the relative percentage hybridization at this 'C_0t' value.

Thermal elution profiles of hybrid molecules between *T. aestivum* and *Ae. speltoides* (with or without 'B' chromosomes), incubated to 'C_0t' 100, show that the 'B' chromosomes do not introduce a class of DNA unable to associate with *T. aestivum* DNA. There are no major differences, of the sort observed between the DNA of several rodents (Rice, 1972), in the optimum temperatures for the dissociation of varying species of DNA of either homo- or heteroduplexes in either direction of hybridization.

It would appear that 'B' chromosomes do not carry an additional highly repetitive or moderately repetitive DNA that might be responsible for the dramatic 'B'-induced reduction of homoeologous pairing observed in *T. aestivum* × *Aegilops* ssp. hybrids lacking wheat chromosome 5B or for the 'B' chromosome-induced disruption of mitotic and meiotic spindles in hybrids (Vardi and Dover, 1972; Dover, 1973*a*, *b*). We should be cautious in interpreting these results as firm evidence for a lack of involvement of repetitive DNA in meiotic pairing. It is possible that a fraction of 'B' chromosome specific DNA would be resolved in density gradients after suitable weighting with actinomycin-D, Ag^+ or Hg^+ ions. *In situ* hybridization of the DNA of genotypes of *Ae. speltoides* or *Ae. mutica*, with 'B' chromosomes, to chromosomes of *T. aestivum* might reveal discrete areas of hybridization to centromeres or to wheat chromosome 5B. Experiments of this kind are under way. It is arguable that the 'B' chromosome effect on the meiotic pairing of 'A' chromosomes is due to the observed similarities in the spectrum of DNA sequences rather than to their differences. Maize 'B' chromosomes and rye 'B' chromosomes, both having measurable effects on chiasma frequency, have been found to be similar to DNA composition to their respective 'A' chromosome DNA (Chilton and McCarthy, 1973; Rimpau and Flavell, this volume, pp. 147–157). Alternatively the 'B' chromosome effects might reside in coding sequences not resolvable with the techniques currently employed for DNA characterization.

Two unresolved questions remain: the function of highly repetitive species—specific chromosomally-localized DNA (of which one suggested role in meiotic pairing is not generally borne out by the present results) and the cellular mechanism of homologous chromosome recognition. A small amount of repeated sequence

DNA has been shown to be synthesized during pachytene in *Lilium* which, although possibly associated with meiotic recombination (Smyth and Stern, 1973), would not, in itself, be responsible for the control of homologous pairing shown to occur during the premeiotic interphase in locusts and wheat (Buss and Henderson, 1971; Dover and Riley, 1973; Bennett et al., 1974).

5. SUMMARY

1. Total DNA has been extracted from genotypes of *Triticum aestivum* and *Aegilops* spp. with supernumerary 'B' chromosomes that have a pronounced effect on the levels of meiotic chromosome pairing in intergeneric hybrids.

2. Analysis of the spectrum of highly repeated and moderately repeated sequence DNA of 'A' and 'B' chromosomes within the species group has shown that, with the exception of an (A-T)n-rich DNA associated with the 'B' chromosomes of one species, 'B' chromosomes do not carry a major class of DNA not present on 'A' chromosomes.

3. The results are discussed with reference to the suggested role of highly repetitive (satellite) DNA in meiotic chromosome pairing.

Acknowledgement. I am indebted to Dr. John Barrett for writing the computer programme used in analysis and plotting of the melting data. I thank Professor R. Riley of the Plant Breeding Institute for seed and greenhouse facilities and Dr. Richard Flavell for much useful discussion and reading of the manuscript. Also many thanks are due to Mr. Andy Holmes for technical assistance.

6. REFERENCES

Bendich, A. J., and McCarthy, B. J. 1970. DNA comparisons among some biotypes of wheat. *Genetics, 65,* 567–573.

Bennett, M. D., Dover, G. A., and Riley, R. 1974. Meiotic duration in wheat genotypes with or without homoeologous meiotic chromosome pairing. *Proc. R. Soc. B., 187,* 191–207.

Buss, E. M., and Henderson, A. S. 1971. Induced bivalent interlocking and the course of meiotic chromosome synapsis. *Nat. New Biol., 234,* 243–246.

Chilton, M. D., and McCarthy, B. J. 1973. DNA from maize with and without 'B' chromosomes: a comparative study. *Genetics, 74,* 605–614.

Dover, G. A. 1973*a*. The genetics and interactions of 'A' and 'B' chromosomes controlling meiotic chromosome pairing in the Triticinae. *Proc. 4th Int. Wheat. Genet. Symp.,* 653–667.

Dover, G. A. 1973*b*. On pores and pairing. In *Chromosomes Today, 4* (J. Wahrman and K. R. Lewis, eds.), pp. 197–204. Israel Universities Press, Jerusalem, and John Wiley & Sons, New York.

Dover, G. A., and Riley, R. 1972*a*. Variation at two lòci affecting homoeologous meiotic chromosome pairing in *Triticium aestivium* × *Aegilops mutica* hybrids. *Nature (Lond.), 235,* 61–62.

Dover, G. A., and Riley, R. 1972*b*. The prevention of pairing of homoeologous meiotic chromosomes of wheat by a genetic activity of supernumerary chromosomes of *Aegilops. Nature (Lond.), 240,* 159–161.

Dover, G. A., and Riley, R. 1973. The effect of spindle inhibitors applied before meiosis on meiotic chromosome pairing. *J. Cell Sci., 12,* 143–161.

Driscoll, C. J., Darvey, N. L., and Barber, H. N. 1967. Effect of colchicine on meiosis of hexaploid wheat. *Nature (Lond.), 216,* 687–688.

Evans, G. M., and Macefield, A. J. 1972. The suppression of homoeologous pairing by 'B' chromosomes in a *Lolium* species hybrid. *Nature (Lond.), 236,* 110–111.

FLAMM, W. G. 1972. Highly repetitive sequences of DNA in chromosomes. *Int. Rev. Cytol. 32,* 1–43.

GIBSON, I., and HEWITT, G. 1972. Interpopulation variation in the satellite DNA from grasshoppers with 'B' chromosomes. *Chromosoma, Berl.,* 38, 121–138.

HUGUET, T., and JOUANIN, L. 1972. The heterogeneity of wheat nuclear DNA. *Biochim. Biophys. Acta, 262,* 431–440.

JONES, K. W. 1973. Satellite DNA. *J. Med. Genet., 10,* 273–281.

MANDEL, M., SCHILDKRAUT, C., and MARMUR, J. 1968. Use of CsCl density gradient analysis for determining the guanine plus cytosine content of DNA. In *Methods in Enzymology* (L. GROSSMAN and K. MOLDAVE, eds.), *12B,* pp. 184–195. Academic Press.

MARMUR, J. 1961. A procedure for the isolation of deoxyribonucleic acid from microorganisms. *J. Mol. Biol., 3,* 208–218.

MITRA, R., and BHATIA, C. R. 1973. Repeated and non-repeated nucleotide sequences in diploid and polyploid wheat species. *Heredity, 31,* 251–262.

MIZUNO, S., and MACGREGOR, H. C. 1974. Chromosomes, DNA sequences, and evolution in salamanders of the genus *Plethodon. Chromosoma (Berl.), 48,* 239–296.

MOCHIZUKI, A. 1964. Further studies on the effect of accessory chromosomes on chromosome pairing. *Jap. J. Genet, 39,* 356–362.

MORGAN, A. R., and WELLS, R. D. 1968. Specificity of the three-stranded complex formation between double-stranded DNA and single-stranded RNA containing repeated nucleotide sequences. *J. Mol. Biol., 37,* 63–80.

RICE, N. R. 1972. Changes in repeated DNA in evolution. In *Evolution of Genetic Systems* (H. H. SMITH ed.), *Brookhaven Symp. Biol., 23,* 44–79.

RIMPAU, J., and FLAVELL, R. 1976. The repeated sequence DNA of 'B' chromosomes of rye. In this volume, pp. 147–157.

SMITH, D. B., and FLAVELL, R. 1974. The relatedness and evolution of repeated nucleotide sequences in the genomes of some Graminiae species. *Biochem. Genet., 12,* 243–256.

SMYTH, D. R., and STERN, H. 1973. Repeated DNA synthesized during pachytene in *Lilium henryi. Nat. New Biol., 245,* 94–96.

STERN, H. 1968. Isolation and purification of plant nucleic acids from whole tissues and from isolated nuclei. In *Methods in Enzymology* (L. GROSSMAN and K. MOLDAVE eds.), Vol. XIIb, pp. 100–112. Academic Press.

STUDIER, F. W. 1965. Sedimentation studies of the size and shape of DNA. *J. Mol. Biol., 11,* 373–390.

VARDI, A., and DOVER, G. A. 1972. The effects of 'B' chromosomes on meiotic and premeiotic spindles and chromosome pairing in *Triticium/Aegilops* hybrids. *Chromosoma (Berl.), 38,* 367–385.

WALKER, P. M. B. 1971. Origin of satellite DNA. *Nature (Lond.), 229,* 306–308.

YUNIS, J. J., and YASMINEH, W. G. 1971. Heterochromatin, satellite DNA and cell function. *Science (Wash. D.C.), 174,* 1200–1209.

THE REPEATED SEQUENCE DNA OF B CHROMOSOMES OF RYE

J. RIMPAU and R. B. FLAVELL

Department of Cytogenetics, Plant Breeding Institute, Cambridge, CB2 2LQ, U.K.

1. INTRODUCTION

Supernumerary B chromosomes in rye influence many morphological (Müntzing, 1963) and nuclear characters (Jones and Rees, 1968). Although they are not necessary for normal development, some populations tend to preserve B chromosomes, even if they are disadvantageous for the individuals carrying them. Thus rye B chromosomes have an adaptive value (Rees and Ayonoadu, 1973). Though some of the effects of B chromosomes have been well characterized little is known about their origin or their relatedness to the A chromosome complement. Kranz (1971) suggested, on the basis of cytological observations, that B chromosomes may have arisen by fragmentation of A chromosomes. However, they do not pair with A chromosomes at meiosis. The investigation described here was designed to characterize B chromosome DNA in order to obtain additional information about the origin and function of the B chromosomes. Special emphasis was placed on the repeated sequence DNA fraction since it constitutes the major part of the total DNA of cereal chromosomes (80%) and is so far the best examined fraction of cereal DNA. Smith and Flavell (1974) showed, by DNA/DNA hybridization experiments, that some of the repeated sequence DNA in cereals is common to oats, wheat, and rye while some is species specific. This offered the possibility of characterizing the B chromosome DNA by hybridizing it not only to the DNA of rye A chromosomes but also to the DNAs of wheat and oats. Rye B chromosome DNA has also been characterized with respect to the number of DNA sequences specifying the 18 and 25S ribosomal RNAs.

2. METHODS AND MATERIALS

Rye B chromosomes from two different populations in two different genetic backgrounds were used in these experiments. The rye plants with B chromosomes came from a population derived from *Secale vavilovi* × *Secale cereale*, the B chromosome source being *S. vavilovi* (Jones, personal communication). Rye plants without B chromosomes were segregants from this population. The wheat plants with B chromosomes were essentially the standard hexaploid wheat genotype "Chinese Spring" with B chromosomes from a Transbaikal spring rye (Müntzing, 1973). Wheat plants without B chromosomes were of the variety "Chinese Spring".

The DNAs were extracted and purified from green plant tissue as described in detail elsewhere (Smith and Flavell, 1974). For the rRNA/DNA experiments the DNAs were further purified by preparative caesium chloride equilibrium centrifugation (Flamm et al., 1966).

DNA/DNA hybridization experiments were carried out by incubating sheared, melted, unlabelled DNA with sheared, melted, ^{3}H-labelled DNA of the same or different species in 0.12 M phosphate buffer at 60°C to a C_0t of 50 (C_0t = initial concentration of DNA in moles per litre × incubation time in seconds). These conditions allow essentially all of the repeated sequence DNA of the cereals to reanneal whilst most of the single or few copy sequence DNA remains single stranded (Smith and Flavell, 1974). The proportions of unlabelled and ^{3}H-labelled DNAs (3000:1) were chosen to minimize self-reannealing of ^{3}H-labelled molecules so that all ^{3}H-labelled duplexes consisted of an unlabelled strand and a ^{3}H-labelled strand. Buoyant density distributions were determined in preparative and analytical caesium chloride gradients, in caesium chloride + Actinomycin D gradients, and in caesium sulphate gradients as described by Flamm et al. (1966) and Peacock et al. (1974). Ribosomal RNA/DNA hybridizations were carried out in 6 × SSC (SSC = 0.15 M sodium chloride, 0.015 M sodium citrate) at 70°C for 3 hr as described in detail by Mohan and Flavell (1974).

3. OBSERVATIONS

(a) *Proportion of repeated sequence DNA in B chromosomes*

To determine this proportion DNAs from the wheat and rye lines with and without four rye B chromosomes were sheared, melted (100°C, 15 min), incubated to C_0t 50, and the single and reannealed double stranded fractions separated by hydroxyapatite (HAP) chromatography. As table 1 shows there was no gross change in the percentage homoduplex formation, though the presence of four B chromosomes increases the DNA contents of wheat and rye by 22% and 11.6%, respectively. Thus the proportions of repeated sequence DNA in A and B chromosomes are similar.

TABLE 1

Proportion of repeated sequence DNA in the genomes of wheat and rye with and without four B chromosomes of rye: the sonicated denatured DNAs were incubated in 0.12 M phosphate buffer at 60°C to a C_0t of 50 and the single and double stranded DNAs separated on hydroxyapatite columns by washes with 0.12 M and 0.5 M phosphate buffer, respectively. The figures are corrected for 20% hypochromicity of reannealed double stranded DNA in the 0.5 M phosphate fraction and for any OD_{260} in sonicated native DNA which did not adhere to hydroxyapatite in 0.12 M phosphate buffer. Each value is the mean and standard deviation of the mean proportion of the DNA isolated in the double stranded fraction

B chromosome number	Wheat	Rye
0	75 ± 0.9	79 ± 0.9
4	75 ± 1.1	76 ± 0.9

Melting curves of the homoduplexes were obtained from HAP chromatography by raising the temperature of the HAP column in 4°C steps and fractionating the melted homoduplexes at each step. Figure 1a, b shows that the derived melting profiles were not different when B chromosome DNA was included with the A chromosome DNA. The broad melting profiles with T_ms (T_m = temperature at

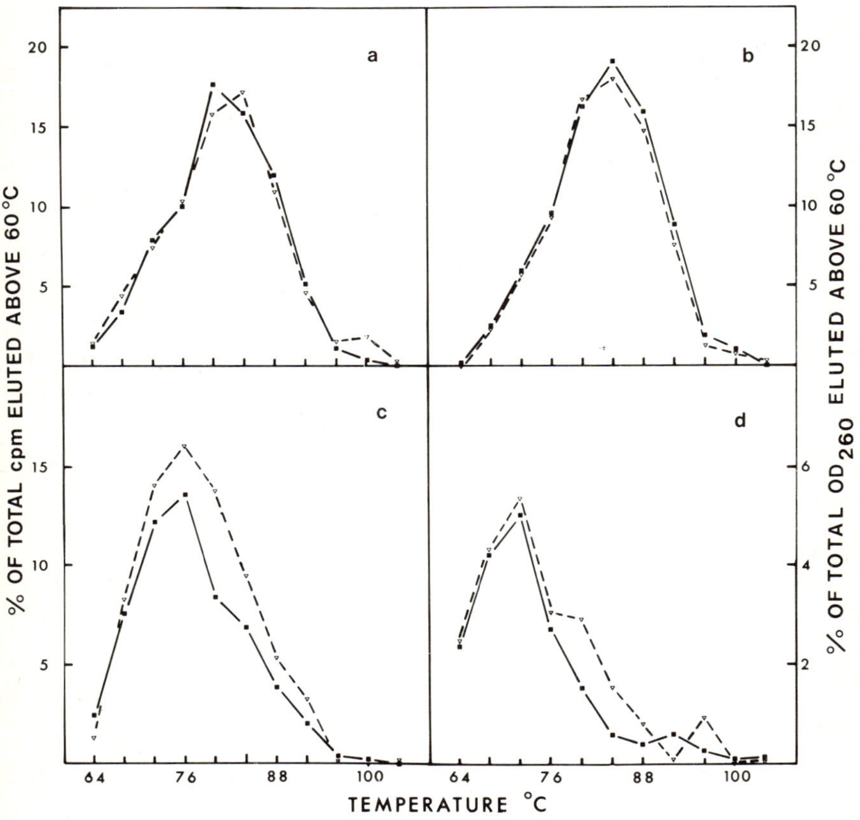

FIG. 1.—Thermal elution profiles from hydroxyapatite of homologous and heterologous duplexes. Mixtures (3000:1) of denatured, sonicated, unlabelled and ^{3}H-labelled DNAs were incubated in 0.12 M phosphate buffer at 60°C to C_0t 50. The duplexes formed were melted on hydroxyapatite columns by increasing the temperature of the columns in 4° steps and eluting and fractionating the melted DNAs. The elution profiles are derived by plotting against temperature the percentage of total counts or OD_{260} eluted.

DNA + DNA combinations

(a) ■ Wheat + Wheat; ∇ Wheat/4B + Wheat/4B;
(b) ■ Rye + Rye; ∇ Rye/4B + Rye/4B;
(c) ■ Wheat + Rye*; ∇ Wheat/4B + Rye*;
(d) ■ Wheat + Oats*; ∇ Wheat/4B + Oats*.

(a) and (b) represent homoduplex melting (optical density measurements).
(c) and (d) represent heteroduplex melting (radioactivity measurements).
* ^{3}H-labelled DNAs.

which 50% of the DNA melts) considerably below that of native DNA indicate that the repetitious sequence DNA in rye B chromosomes is as heterogeneous in base sequence as that of A chromosomes of wheat and rye.

(b) *Base composition of B chromosome DNA*

DNAs of plants carrying 0, 2, 4, or 8 B chromosomes were centrifuged to equilibrium in preparative and analytical caesium chloride gradients, in analytical caesium chloride + Actinomycin D gradients (DNA: Actinomycin D = 3:1) and caesium sulphate gradients. These three types of gradients were chosen since they have proved useful in fractionating out satellites from DNAs of other genomes (Peacock et al., 1974). In all these gradients, DNAs with and without B chromosomes were indistinguishable in their buoyant density distributions (figs. 2 and 3) indicating the similarity in base composition of fragments from rye A and B chromosomes.

(c) *Families of repeated sequence DNA in rye A and B chromosomes*

The repeated sequence DNAs of the wheat and rye lines carrying rye B chromosomes were characterized by hybridization to the DNAs of wheat, rye, and oats in all the possible combinations. From the analysis of the percentages of DNA duplexes formed (table 2) the repeated sequence fractions of rye A and B chromosome DNAs and of wheat and oats DNAs can be divided into six groups (table 3).

Group I contains those sequences which are present in all the DNAs tested. This was concluded from hybridizing a mixture of ^{3}H-labelled wheat and ^{3}H-labelled rye DNAs to unlabelled oats DNA. Since no additional heteroduplexes formed compared with the oats + ^{3}H-labelled rye DNA combination (table 2),

TABLE 2

Percent duplex formation between repeated nucleotide sequences of wheat and rye DNA with and without B chromosomes and oats DNA: unlabelled and ^{3}H-labelled sonicated, denatured DNAs were incubated in 0.12 M phosphate buffer at 60°C to C_0t 50 and the amount of hybridization determined by the percentage of counts retained on hydroxyapatite at 60°C in 0.12 M phosphate buffer. The figures are corrected for the proportion of counts in native ^{3}H-labelled DNA not retained on hydroxyapatite at 60°C in 0.12 M phosphate buffer. Each value is the mean and standard deviation of the mean proportion of the DNA isolated in the double stranded fraction. Those values without standard deviations involve fewer than three replicates

	Unlabelled DNA					
^{3}H-labelled DNA	Wheat		Rye		Oats	Wheat +Rye†
	0B	4B	0B	4B		
Wheat	74 ± 0.5	74 ± 1.3	60 ± 1.4	62 ± 0.8	45	79
Rye/0B	64 ± 0.6	73 ± 0.7*	77 ± 2.3	80 ± 2.6	55	82
Rye/2B	61	77	80	85	58	
Oats	24 ± 0.1	29 ± 0.4**	25 ± 1.9	25 ± 2.0	77	23
Wheat + Rye†	77		84		49	

† 1:1 mixture of DNAs.

* Significantly different from Wheat/0B + ^{3}H Rye/0B DNA at 5% level of probability.

** Significantly different from Wheat/0B + ^{3}H Oats DNA at 0.1% level of probability.

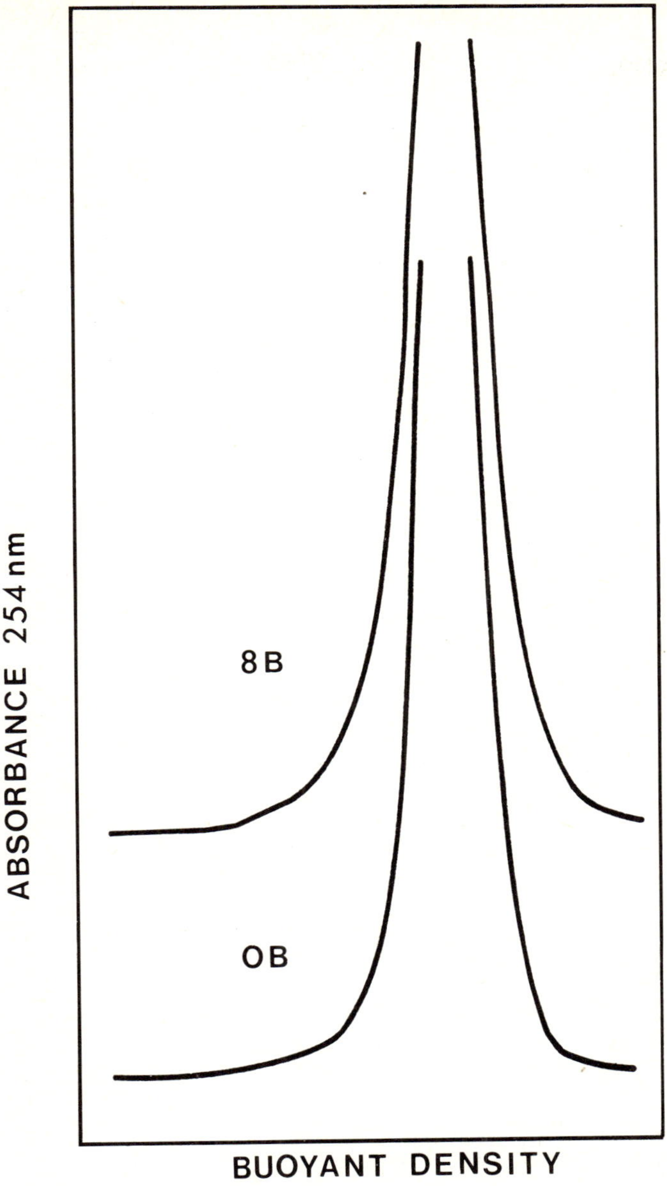

FIG. 2.—Analytical caesium chloride + Actinomycin D gradient analysis of rye DNA with and without 8 B chromosomes. Highly purified rye DNAs, with and without 8 B chromosomes, were mixed with CsCl solution (in 10 mM Tris-HCl, 1 mM EDTA, pH 8.0) and Actinomycin D-solution (2 mg Actinomycin D in 4 ml of the same buffer) to give a final OD of 0.3, a final density of 1.66 g/cc, and a final DNA:Actinomycin D ratio of 3:1. This DNA concentration was approximately twice that normally used so that any satellites would be easier to detect. Centrifugation was at 40,000 rpm at 20°C for 30 hr in a Centriscan Analytical Ultracentrifuge (MSE Ltd.).

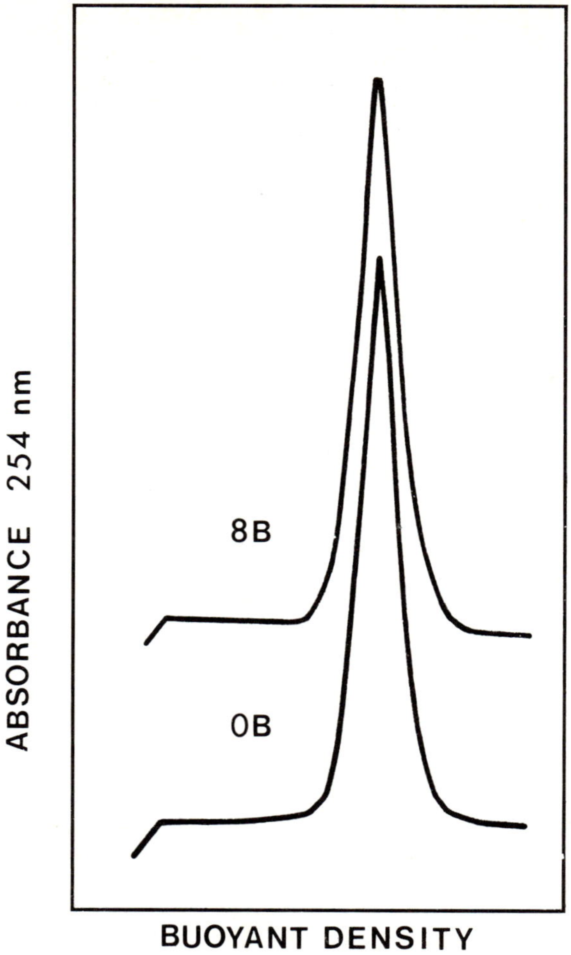

FIG. 3.—Analytical caesium sulphate gradient analysis of rye DNA with and without 8 B chromosomes. Highly purified rye DNAs, with and without 8 B chromosomes, were mixed with a Cs_2SO_4 solution (in 10 mM Tris-HCl, pH 8.0) to give a final OD_{260} of 0.15 and a final density of 1.43 g/cc. Centrifugation was at 40,000 rpm at 20°C for 30 hr in a Centriscan Analytical Ultracentrifuge (MSE Ltd.).

all those sequences which wheat and oats have in common must also be present in rye. Group I contains the major proportion of the repeated sequences of rye A and B chromosomes (59–66%) and also of wheat (61%) but only a relatively small proportion of the oats repetitious sequence DNA (31%).

Group II contains sequences which are present in rye A and B chromosomes and in wheat but not in oats DNA. Their existence is based on the higher percentage of heteroduplexes in the wheat + rye DNA combination than in the wheat + oats DNA and rye + oats DNA combinations (table 2).

Group III represents a small proportion of the rye A and B chromosome and oats

TABLE 3

Groups of repeated sequences and their proportions in the repeated sequence DNA fractions of rye A and B chromosomes, wheat, and oats: the values are the proportions of the total repeated sequence DNA in each group(s) calculated from the percentage duplexes shown in table 2. The groups probably represent more than one and in some cases (Groups I, II, and VI) many families

DNA	Proportion of groups of related sequences in the repetitious DNA fraction					
	I	II	III	IV	V	VI
Rye (A chromosome)	83		17*		—	—
Rye (B chromosome)	79		21		—	—
Wheat	61	20	7	—	12	—
Oats	31	—	7	—	—	62

* Groups III and IV of rye A chromosomes may include approximately 5% of the total repeated sequence DNA not present in rye B chromosomes.

DNA which is not present in wheat and accounts for the heteroduplexes formed between oats and rye B chromosome DNA (29%) but not in the wheat/OB + oats combination (24%) (table 2).

Groups IV, V, and VI are species-specific for rye, wheat, and oats, respectively. They represent all those sequences not belonging to Groups I, II, and III and account for the differences between the percentages of homoduplex formation and heteroduplex formation with each of the other DNAs (table 2).

Group III sequences were characterized further by their thermal stabilities. Whilst most of the sequences of A and B chromosome DNAs (Groups I and II) are similar in their base sequence heterogeneity (fig. 1a, b), Group III sequences form heteroduplexes which can be identified in derived melting profiles by their higher thermal stability than most other heteroduplexes (fig. 1c, d).

(d) *Ribosomal DNA sequences in rye B chromosome DNA*

DNAs from the wheat and rye lines carrying 0, 2, 3, or 4 B chromosomes were denatured, immobilized on nitrocellulose filters, and incubated with ^{3}H-labelled rRNA. The numbers of rRNA genes in each line were calculated from the percentage of rRNA hybridized to DNA. Figure 4 shows the relationship between the number of rye B chromosomes and the number of rRNA genes in wheat. The addition of four chromosomes to wheat increased the number of rRNA genes by 2700, demonstrating that each of these B chromosomes carries approximately 700 rRNA genes. The numbers of rRNA genes in single plants of rye carrying 0, 2, 3, or 4 B chromosomes are shown in figure 5. The slope of the linear regression line indicates that there is no relationship between the number of B chromosomes and number of rRNA genes (correlation coefficient = 0.17; P = 47.2%). However, the differences within each group of plants with the same number of B chromosomes are highly significant in all four cases, indicating heterogeneity in this population for the

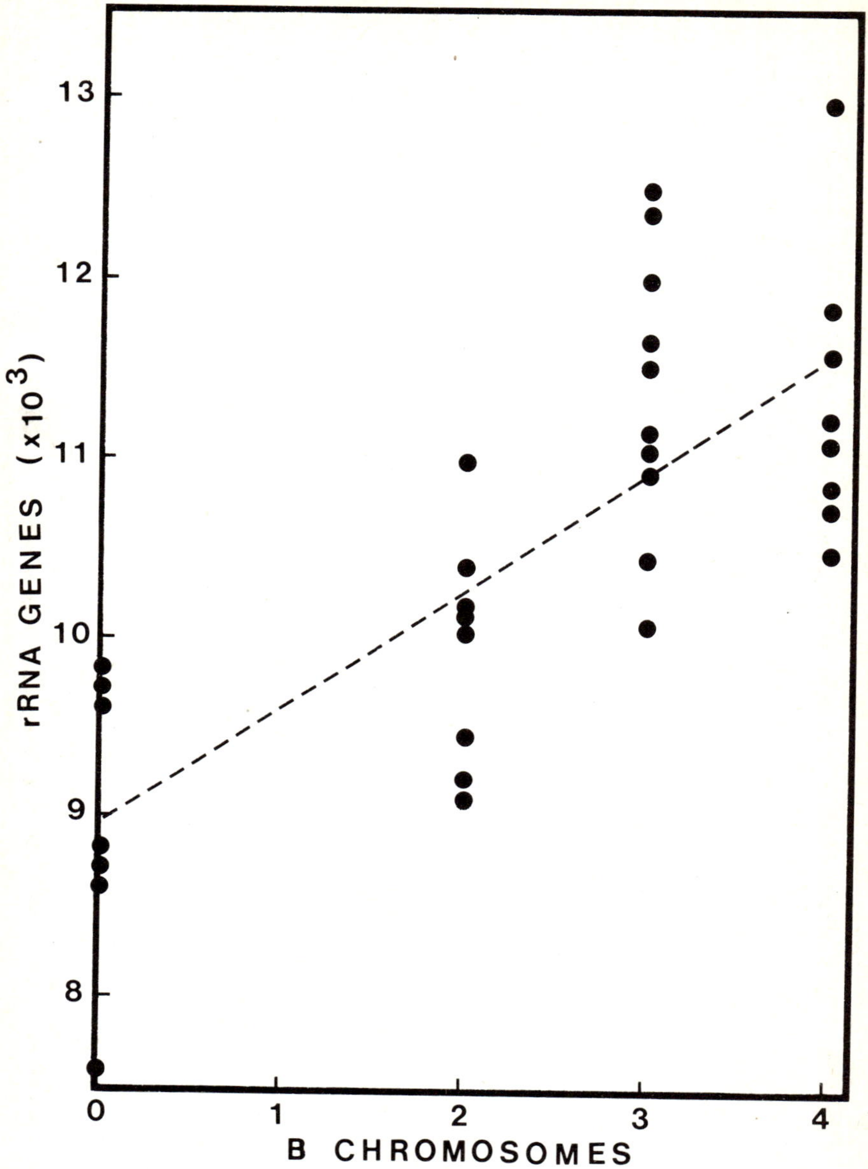

FIG. 4.—Effect of rye B chromosomes on rRNA gene number in wheat. Each point comes from a single nitrocellulose filter incubated with 5μg/ml ^{3}H-labelled rRNA for 3 hr at 70°C in 6 × SSC. The number of rRNA genes was calculated from the RNase-resistant rRNA bound to each filter and the amount of filter-bound DNA (Mohan and Flavell, 1974).

number of rRNA genes located on the A chromosomes. Thus, the repeated sequence DNAs of the two rye B chromosome types tested are different insofar as only the B chromosomes in the wheat line, which originated independently from those in the rye line, carry rRNA genes.

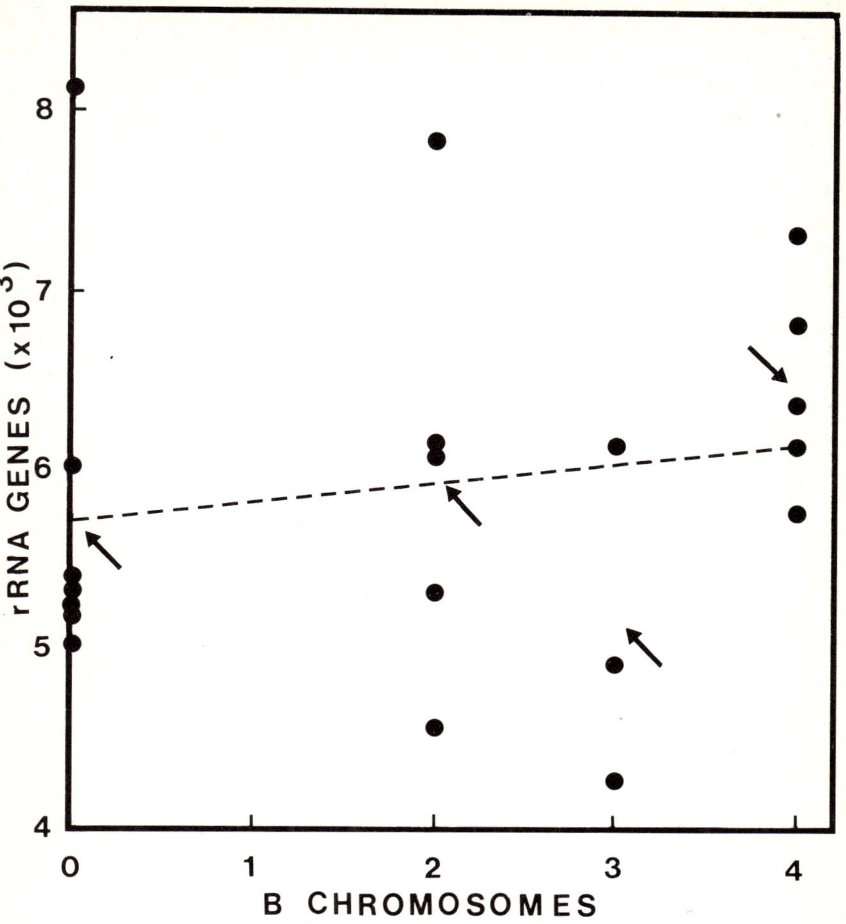

FIG. 5.—Effect of rye B chromosomes on rRNA gene number in rye. Each point is the mean of 6, 12, or 18 hybridizations in three experiments as described in figure 4. The standard error of each mean is approximately 200 genes. The arrows indicate the means of plants with the same number of B chromosomes.

4. CONCLUSIONS

All the data presented suggest a high degree of similarity between the DNAs of A and B chromosomes of rye in (1) the proportions of repeated and single or few copy sequences they contain, (2) the heterogeneity within the families of related sequences, (3) their buoyant density distributions under different centrifugation conditions, and (4) their division into groups of families of related sequences. These results indicate that rye B chromosome DNA originated from rye A chromosome DNA. Similar results have been reported for B chromosomes in maize (Chilton and McCarthy, 1973), *Aegilops speltoides* and *Aegilops mutica* (Dover, 1976).

When did B chromosomes arise? The Group III sequences form duplexes with a higher thermal stability than Group I and II sequences (fig. 1c, d). We conclude therefore that Group III sequences are evolutionary younger than those of Group I and II on the assumption that family divergence is a measure of the evolutionary age of the family (Britten, 1970). Since wheat does not contain Group III sequences, they were probably amplified in rye A chromosomes after diploid rye diverged from the diploid wheats (see Smith and Flavell, 1974). Consequently, the presence of Group III sequences in B chromosome DNA suggests that B chromosomes arose after rye diverged from wheat and after Group III sequences were amplified in rye A chromosomes. How and from where did B chromosomes arise? Kranz (1971) suggested from cytological observations that B chromosomes arose by a fragmentation process of A chromosome(s). Our finding of rDNA sequences on one of the two B chromosome types suggests that these particular B chromosomes arose as fragments from the nucleolar organizer region of a satellited chromosome of the rye A chromosome complement. It is not surprising that the other B chromosome type does not carry rDNA sequences, since such a fragmentation process is unlikely to have been restricted to one chromosome segment. The presence of all the groups of repeated sequences of rye A chromosomes in both types of B chromosome implies a general interspersion of all types of repeated sequences in at least those parts of the rye A chromosomes which gave rise to the B chromosomes.

5. SUMMARY

1. DNAs isolated from wheat and rye plants with and without rye B chromosomes have been compared.

2. The presence of B chromosome DNA made no significant difference to the proportion of repeated sequence DNA in the genomes and no differences in buoyant density distributions could be detected in caesium chloride, caesium chloride + Actinomycin D, or caesium sulphate analytical gradients when 30% of the DNA was of B chromosome origin.

3. From DNA/DNA hybridization experiments involving the repeated sequence DNA fraction of the rye, rye + B, wheat, wheat + B, and oat genomes, the rye A and rye B chromosomes could be divided into two groups. The proportions of the repeated sequence DNA in each of the groups was similar for rye A and B chromosomes.

4. These results indicate that rye A and B chromosome DNAs are very similar.

5. B chromosomes from one source, but not another, have been shown to possess ribosomal RNA genes.

Acknowledgement. We are grateful to Mr. Derek Smith for helpful discussions and to Mr. Michael O'Dell for extracting some of the DNAs. J. Rimpau is on leave from the Institut für Pflanzenzüchtung of the University of Göttingen and supported by the Deutsche Forchungsgemeinschaft.

6. REFERENCES

BRITTEN, R. J. 1970. Observed properties of repeated DNA sequences. *Carnegie Inst. (Wash). Year Book, 68,* 376–378.

CHILTON, M. D., and MCCARTHY, B. J. 1973. DNA from maize with and without B chromosomes: a comparative study. *Genetics, 74,* 605–614.

DOVER, G. A. 1976. Observations on the repeated sequence DNA of 'A' and 'B' chromosomes of genotypes in the Triticinae with contrasting patterns of meiotic chromosome pairing. This volume, pp. 131–145.

FLAMM, W. G., BOND, H. E., and BURR, H. E. 1966. Density gradient centrifugation of DNA in a fixed angle rotor. *Biochim. Biophys. Acta, 129,* 310–319.

JONES, R. N. Genotypes of the rye population carrying B chromosomes. Personal communication.

JONES, R. N., and REES, H. 1968. The influence of B-chromosomes upon the nuclear phenotype in rye. *Chromosoma (Berl.), 24,* 158–176.

KRANZ, A. R. 1971. Cytogenetik des B-Chromosomen. II. Mitotische und meiotische Assoziationen in wilden und primitiven Roggen. *Z. Pflanzenzücht, 66,* 317–330.

MOHAN, J., and FLAVELL, R. B. 1974. Ribosomal RNA cistron multiplicity and nucleolar organisers in hexaploid wheat. *Genetics, 76,* 33–44.

MÜNTZING, A. 1963. A. Effects of accessory chromosomes in diploid and tetraploid rye. *Hereditas, 49,* 361–426.

MÜNTZING, A. 1973. Effects of accessory chromosomes of rye in the gene environment of hexaploid wheat. *Hereditas, 74,* 41–56.

PEACOCK, W. J., BRUTLAG, D., GOLDRING, E., APPELS, R., HINTON, C. W., and LINDSLEY, D. L. 1974. The organization of highly repeated DNA sequences in *Drosphila melanogaster* chromosomes. *Cold Spring Harbor Symp. Quant. Biol., 38,* 405–422.

REES, H., and AYONOADU, U. 1973. B chromosome selection in rye. *Theor. Appl. Genet., 43,* 162–166.

SMITH, D. B., and FLAVELL, R. B. 1974. Relatedness and evolution of repeated nucleotide sequences in the genomes of some Graminae species. *Biochem. Genet, 12,* 243–256.

DIFFERENTIAL PERFORMANCE OF PREFERENTIAL PAIRING OF THREE OAT GENOMES

G. LADIZINSKY

Faculty of Agriculture, The Hebrew University, Rehovot, Israel

1. INTRODUCTION

Genome homology between two diploid species is usually determined from the pattern of chromosome pairing in the hybrid; the less regular the meiosis the more divergent the genomes. Occasionally, an interspecific diploid hybrid which displays an appreciable amount of chromosome pairing gives rise to an amphidiploid having predominantly bivalents resulting from preferential pairing. This kind of pairing is usually attributed to 1) difference in the chromosome architecture of the two genomes, or 2) genic determination. Induction of preferential pairing by chromosome rearrangement has been demonstrated in trisomic corn (Doyle, 1963) and barley (Tsuchiya, 1969). On the other hand, no preferential pairing was noted in translocation heterozygotes of rye (Sybenga, 1966) and *Anthoxanthum odoratum* (Jones, 1964) when their chromosome number was doubled.

Genic control of preferential bivalent pairing in polyploid plants was demonstrated first in wheat (Riley, 1958; Sears and Okomoto, 1958) and recently also in the tetraploid oat *A. barbata* (Ladizinsky, 1973). In neither case, however, is it yet clear whether the genes affecting preferential pairing already exist at the diploid level or arise after polyploidization. The present paper attempts to elucidate the nature of preferential pairing by studying the potential of three closely related diploid oat species *Avena strigosa*, *A. prostrata*, and *A. longiglumis* to pair preferentially in the presence of an alien genome.

2. MATERIALS AND METHODS

The genomes of the three diploid oat species *A. strigosa* (S), *A. prostrata* (P), and *A. longiglumis* (L) were combined in different ratios and at three ploidy levels as follows:

Diploid hybrids	LP	SP	SL
Chromosome doubling	↓	↓	↓
Amphidiploids	LLPP	SSPP	SSLL
Triploids	× LL → LLP; × PP → LPP	× SS → SSP; × LL → SPL; × PP → SSP	× SS → SSL; × LL → SLL
Tetraploids with three genomes	LLPP × SSPP → LPSP	LLPP × SSLL → LPSL	SSPP × SSLL → SPSL

By this procedure 1:1, 1:2, 2:1, and 2:2 genome ratios were obtained between all species pairs. Moreover, the three genomes were combined in a triploid and in three different tetraploids, in each of which another genome was present in double dose.

The amphidiploids were obtained by treating the diploid hybrids at the stage of 6–8 tillers with a 0.2% aqueous colchicin solution. Tubes containing the solution were placed on cut tillers for 8 hours. Triploid hybrids were obtained by crossing the amphidiploids to their diploid parents. As embryos of the triploid die 14–16 days after pollination, 12-day-old embryos were excised and planted in embryo culture. The medium was prepared according to Davies (1960) but was slightly modified by using 8% sucrose and adding 0.2 g casein hydrolysate per liter.

Anthers were fixed in 3:1 absolute ethanol-acetic acid, stored in 70% ethanol, and stained with acetocarmine. In each hybrid combination 2–5 different plants were examined. Usually 30 pollen mother cells (P.M.C.s) were scored in each plant.

3. RESULTS AND DISCUSSION

(a) *A. prostrata and A. longiglumis*

The majority of the chromosomes in *A. longiglumis* × *A. prostrata* hybrid (LP) paired as bivalents (fig. 1a). In 35% of the P.M.C.s 7 bivalents were formed of which 4 were ring-shaped, which indicates appreciable similarity in the chromosome architecture of the two genomes. Univalents were occasionally formed in the hybrid but did not exceed 6 per cell. The difference in the chromosomes of these two species is therefore due mainly to partial lack of homology. Differentiation through chromosome rearrangement is negligible in this case. A single trivalent or quadrivalent was observed only in 12% of the P.M.C.s.

This chromosome relationship was further emphasized when P and L genomes were combined at the triploid level. The frequency of trivalents, bivalents, and univalents in LLP and LPP triploid combinations was typical of an autotriploid (fig. 1a), and was consistent with the pairing pattern of the diploid hybrid.

In the LLPP amphidiploid where each of the two genomes was presented in double dose, bivalents were the most frequent configuration. Yet 33% of the chromosomes were associated in multivalents, particularly quadrivalents. Assuming that the six chromosomes of the diploid hybrid that formed rod bivalents or were even left unpaired, later paired as bivalents in the amphidiploids, the rate of multivalents for the remainder of the chromosomes is typical of an autotetraploid.

(b) *A. strigosa and A. prostrata*

The majority of the chromosomes in the SP diploid hybrid were associated in multivalents. Bivalents were rare and mostly rod-shaped. The most common configuration was 3III + V but chains of VI and VII chromosomes were also observed. The multivalent frequency in this hybrid indicates that S and P genomes differ from each other by at least 5 chromosome rearrangements.

Considering the pairing pattern of the diploid hybrid, the predominant bivalent pairing in both SSP and SPP triploids is significant (fig. 1b). Further, most of the bivalents, in both triploids, were ring-shaped. Multivalents were not only less frequent but also smaller in size. Chains of V chromosomes were the biggest multivalents observed but in very low frequency.

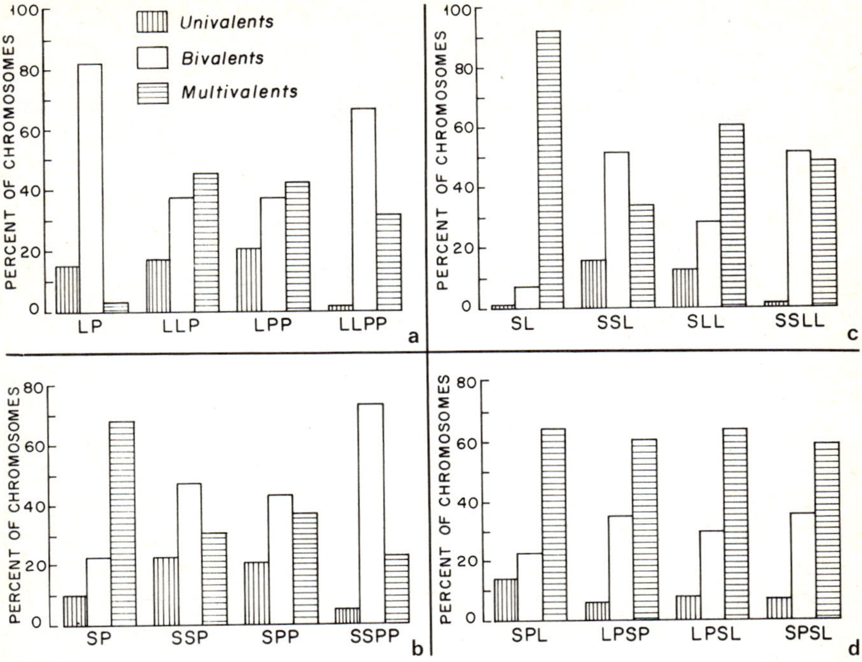

FIG. 1.—Frequency of univalents, bivalents, and multivalents in diploid, triploid, and tetraploid hybrids involving the following diploid ($x = 7$) oat species: a) *A. longiglumis* (L) and *A. prostrata* (P); b) *A. strigosa* (S) and *A. prostrata*; c) *A. strigosa* and *A. longiglumis*; d) triploid and tetraploids involving the three diploid oats.

Bivalent pairing was even more extreme in the SSPP amphidiploid (fig. 1b). In 32% of the cells 14II or 12II + IV were observed. Preferential bivalent pairing in the SSPP amphidiploid was also supported by genetic evidence. The *A. strigosa* parent of the amphidiploid had a pubescent leaf sheath, a characteristic governed by the dominant allele of a single gene (Dyck, 1966). The *A. prostrata* parent had a glabrous leaf sheath. As expected, both the diploid hybrid and the amphidiploid were pubescent. Seven hundred seeds collected from the amphidiploid were sown and all the 685 emerging seedlings were also pubescent. Lack of segregation in this case resulted most probably from preferential bivalent pairing.

(c) *A. strigosa and A. longiglumis*

The meiosis of the SL diploid hybrid was characterized by complex multivalents (fig. 1c). About 90% of the chromosomes were associated in multivalents, some of which were formed by VIII chromosomes. In this hybrid too, 3III + V was the most frequent configuration, indicating that the S genome differs also from L by 5 chromosome rearrangements.

When S and L genomes were combined in a triploid, a marked difference in the pairing pattern of the SSL and SLL triploid was found (fig. 1c). In the former about 50% of the chromosomes paired as bivalents. The mode of pairing was very similar to that found in the SSP and SPP triploids. By contrast, the majority of chromosomes in the SLL triploid were associated in multivalents, some of which were composed of VI chromosomes.

The conspicuous difference in the pairing pattern of SLL and SSL triploids indicates that bivalent pairing in the latter could not be a consequence of the difference in the chromosome arrangement of the two genomes. It is more likely that it was induced by a factor located in the S genome which operates in disomic conditions. Since S also differs from the P genome by V chromosome rearrangements, it could be that the bivalent pairing in the SSP triploid was due to the same S genome factor. It is also possible that a similar factor exists in the P genome, hence the bivalent pairing in the SPP triploid and in the SSPP amphidiploid. It is obvious, however, that these two factors are not identical, since they behave differently in the presence of the L genome.

In SSLL amphidiploid pairing was very irregular, bivalents and multivalents occurring at about the same rate (fig. 1c) with some of the multivalents being composed of VI or even VII chromosomes. The attainment of bivalent pairing in SSL but not in SLL triploids indicates that this characteristic has no dominant effect but is rather of a quantitative nature. Further, the marked difference in the pairing pattern of SSLL and SSPP amphidiploids suggests a quantitative effect and also some kind of interaction. The latter was best shown when the three genomes were combined in the SPL triploid and in LPSP, LPSL, and SPSL tetraploids. In these 4 synthetic polyploids meiosis was very irregular and about 60% of the chromosomes were involved in multivalents (fig. 1d). This high frequency in SPL triploids indicates a better affinity between the chromosomes of the S genome and those of either P or L than between the chromosomes of the latter two genomes. While this might explain the irregular pairing in LPSP and LPSL tetraploids which contained a single S genome, the high multivalent rate in SPSL is more ambiguous. In this particular tetraploid one might expect predominantly bivalent pairing due to pairing between the two S genomes and between P and L chromosomes similar to that occurring in their diploid hybrid. It could be that the irregular pairing in SPSL resulted from an inappropriate genetic balance preventing the expression of the S genome factor.

The capability of S and probably of P, but not of the L genome, to undergo preferential pairing is evolutionary significant; it might affect the chance for each of these species to participate in the formation of allopolyploids in nature. Hybridization between two species possessing genes that can cause preferential pairing would give rise, following doubling of the chromosome number, to a meiotically relatively stable amphidiploid, regardless of the pairing pattern of their diploid hybrid. Even if meiosis would not be perfectly regular in this raw amphidiploid, it would facilitate development of a more elaborate genetic mechanism that would enhance bivalent pairing in the new polyploid. It could be that most natural allopolyploids evolved from diploid species that possessed genes for preferential pairing. Some of the available examples are most indicative: The tetraploid oat *A. barbata* is cytologically an allopolyploid but its bivalent pairing is controlled by a single recessive gene (Ladizinsky, 1973). The diploid *A. strigosa* has evidently participated in the formation of *A. barbata* (Ladizinsky and Zohary, 1971) and, as shown in the present study, this diploid species has a gene for preferential pairing. Despite the difference in the mode of action of these two genes it is very likely that their combination facilitated the establishment of preferential bivalent pairing in the raw *A. barbata* line.

The situation in the genus *Aegilops* is also worth mentioning. This genus is composed of 23 species; 10 are diploids, the rest are polyploids and grouped in two distinct clusters. The diploid *Ae. squarrosa* participated in the formation of all the polyploids of one cluster while *Ae. umbellulata* contributed to all those of the second cluster. These two species were therefore named pivotal genomes by Zohary and Feldman (1962). In both clusters the chromosome relationships between the genomes of two ordinary species are generally similar to those existing between them and the pivotal genome (Kihara, 1949). Since no allopolyploid that combines two ordinary diploids is available, one might conclude that the type of chromosome relationships between two *Aegilops* diploid species has little to do with their chance of forming a stable allopolyploid. It could be that the two pivotal genomes of the genus *Aegilops*, besides many other important traits, also possess genes that promote preferential pairing. Therefore, any raw amphidiploid that includes these genomes would be relatively advantageous owing to its stable meiosis.

4. SUMMARY

1. The potential of the genomes of three diploid oat species, *Avena strigosa* (S), *A. prostrata* (P), and *A. longiglumis* (L) to undergo preferential pairing was studied from the meiotic behavior of all the possible hybrid combinations of triploids and tetraploids containing 1:2, 2:1, 1:1:1, 2:2, 1:1:2 genomic ratios.

2. S and probably also P genomes can pair preferentially in synthetic polyploids of specific genomic combinations.

3. Bivalent pairing in SSL but not in SLL triploids indicated that preferential pairing in this case was due to genetic factors and not to a difference in the chromosome arrangement.

4. It was suggested that this genetic factor has a quantitative effect and can be expressed in a specific genomic combination.

5. The significance of the diploid species possessing genes for preferential pairing to the evolution of allopolyploids was indicated.

5. REFERENCES

Davies, D. R. 1960. The embryo culture of interspecific hybrids of *Hordeum*. *New Phytol.*, *59*, 9–14.

Doyle, G. G. 1963. Preferential pairing in structural heterozygotes of *Zea mays*. *Genetics*, *48*, 1011–1027.

Dyck, P. L. 1966. Inheritance of stem rust and other characteristics in diploid oats *Avena strigosa*. *Can. J. Genet. Cytol.*, *8*, 444–450.

Jones, K. 1964. Chromosomes and the nature and the origin of *Anthoxanthum odoratum* L. *Chromosoma (Berl.)*, *15*, 248–274.

Kihara, H. 1949. Genomanalyse bei Triticum und Aegilops. IX. Systematischer Aufbau der Gattung Aeglilops auf genomanalytischer Grundlage. *Cytologia (Tokyo)*, *14*, 135–144.

Ladizinsky, G. 1973. Genetic control of bivalent pairing in the *Avena strigosa* polyploid complex. *Chromosoma (Berl.)*, *142*, 105–110.

Ladizinsky, G., and Zohary, D. 1971. Notes on species delimitation, species relationships and polyploidy in Avena L. *Euphytica*, *20*, 380–395.

RILEY, R. 1958. Chromosome pairing in haploid wheat. *Proc. 10th Intern. Congr. Genet., 2,* 234–235.

SEARS, E. R., and OKOMOTO, M. 1958. Intergenomic chromosome relationships in the hexaploid wheat. *Proc. 10th Intern. Congr. Genet., 2,* 258–259.

SYBENGA, J. 1966. Reciprocal translocation and preferential pairing in autotetraploid rye. In *Chromosomes Today, 1* (C. D. DARLINGTON and K. R. LEWIS, eds.), pp. 66–71. Oliver and Boyd, Edinburgh and London.

TSUCHIYA, T. 1969. Cytogenetics of a new type of barley with 16 chromosomes. *Chromosoma (Berl.), 26,* 130–139.

ZOHARY, D., and FELDMAN, M. 1962. Hybridization between amphidiploids and the evolution of polyploids in the wheat (*Aegilops-Triticum*) group. *Evolution, 16,* 44–61.

CHROMOSOME PAIRING IN SOME TRIPLOID AND TRISPECIFIC HYBRIDS IN *LOLIUM-FESTUCA* AND ITS PHYLOGENETIC IMPLICATIONS*

PREM P. JAUHAR

Welsh Plant Breeding Station, Aberystwyth, Wales

1. INTRODUCTION

Perennial ryegrass (*Lolium perenne* L.), Italian ryegrass (*L. multiflorum* Lam.), and meadow fescue (*Festuca pratensis* Huds.) are important diploid ($2n = 14$) species of temperate grassland, each possessing some distinctive agronomically superior features. Combining the genomes of these species could be an effective means of producing hybrids and derivatives of high agronomic potentiality. A thorough understanding of the cytogenetic relationships between these species would, however, be a prerequisite to formulating rational crossing programmes. This also poses a fascinating problem from the phylogenetic standpoint.

The regular formation of seven bivalents in diploid hybrids between these species shows their close phylogenetic proximity. In order to study the nature of chromosome differentiation in them, different triploid hybrids incorporating two genomes of one species and one of the other were synthesized. Also some trispecific hybrids combining the genomes of all the three species were made. The nature of chromosome pairing in these hybrids and its phylogenetic implications are discussed here.

2. MATERIAL AND METHODS

A wide range of material of perennial and Italian ryegrasses and meadow fescue was used to make various hybrids:

(i) *Diploid hybrids.* Diploid hybrids between *Lolium perenne* and *L. multiflorum* could be made very easily in either direction. Hybrids between these species and *Festuca pratensis*, however, could be made more easily when *Lolium* was used as the female parent. Nevertheless, several hybrids between *F. pratensis* and the two *Lolium* species could be obtained in both directions with and without embryo culture.

(ii) *Triploid hybrids.* The following triploid ($2n = 21$) hybrids were made by carrying out hand emasculation and pollinations in the glasshouse. Although several hybrids could be obtained by using the embryo culture technique, a few were obtained even without it.

* This paper is dedicated with admiration and affection to Professor P. T. Thomas, C. B. E., on his retirement, who has done so much to advance the cause of plant breeding and in helping to train numerous students from all over the world.

A. *F. pratensis* (2x) × *L. perenne* (4x)

a. *F. pratensis* Bf 55 (36) × *L. perenne* S. 24 CR 66 (2)
(2n = 14 + 1B) Colchicine-induced autote-
(Les Croisetes, Switzerland) traploid at the Station
(2n = 28)
Hybrid 2n = 21

b. *F. pratensis* BG 55 (11) × *L. perenne* S. 24 CR 66 (2)
(2n = 14) (2n = 28)
(Les Croisetes, Switzerland)
Hybrid 2n = 21

B. *F. pratensis* (2x) × *L. multiflorum* (4x)

a. *F. pratensis* Bf 924 (56) × *L. multiflorum* Bb 28/71 (8)
(2n = 14 + 1B) (2n = 28)
(North Italy)
Hybrid 2n = 21

b. *F. pratensis* Bf 924 (56) × *L. multiflorum* Bb 28/71 (6)
(2n = 14 + 1B) (2n = 28)
(North Italy)
Hybrid 2n = 20 + 1B

C. *L. perenne* (2x) × *L. multiflorum* (4x)

a. *L. perenne* Ba 8973 × *L. multiflorum* Bb 28/71 (10)
(2n = 14 + 1B) (2n = 28)
(Algeria)
Hybrid 2n = 21

b. *L. perenne* Ba 8973 × *L. multiflorum* Bb 28/71 (8)
(2n = 14 + 1B) (2n = 28)
(Algeria)
Hybrid 2n = 21

(iii) *Trispecific hybrids.* Several trispecific hybrids were synthesized by Mr. E. J. Lewis of the Herbage Breeding Department using the methods described in Lewis and Jauhar (1974). Only the following trispecifics were used in this study:

a. (*L. perenne* × *F. pratensis*) × *L. multiflorum*
(4x = 28) (2n = 14)

Two different hybrids with 3x = 21 chromosomes were studied.

b. (*L. multiflorum* × *F. pratensis*) × *L. perenne*
(4x = 28) (2x = 14)

Three different hybrids with 3x = 21 chromosomes were studied. In the trispecific crosses the station-bred varieties of *L. perenne* (S. 24), *L. multiflorum* (S. 22) and *F. pratenis* were used. Herbarium specimens of most of the parents used in this hybridization have been prepared.

Abbreviations. The following abbreviations have been used in this paper: *Lolium perenne*—Lp; *Lolium multiflorum*—Lm; *Festuca pratensis*—Fp. The three types of auto-allotriploids are abbreviated as Fp LpLp, Fp LmLm, and Lp LmLm; and trispecific hybrids as LpFp Lm and LmFp Lp. The gap between two genomic designations indicates the contributions from the female (given first) and male parents.

(iv) *Embryoculture technique.* Spikelets from the different crosses were harvested 14 days after the last pollination. Immature caryopses were removed under sterile conditions and treated with 0.1 % solution of mercuric chloride for about 5 minutes and then washed 3 or 4 times with sterile distilled water. The immature embryos were then excised under aseptic conditions and cultured on nutrient agar medium (Davies, 1960) and grown in the dark in an incubator at 24°C. After 7–10 days some embryos started developing into tiny plantlets and were then given artificial light until they reached 2-leaf stage. The seedlings were then transferred to John Innes compost and grown to maturity. At the initial stages they were covered with inverted funnels and later with cellophane paper until they were established.

(v) *Meiotic studies.* For meiotic analysis heads emerging from the flag leaf were fixed in 6:3:1 Carnoy's fluid to which a few drops of ferric chloride had been added. The anthers were stained with 1.5 % acetocarmine or Snow's carmine (Snow, 1963). A combined staining with Snow's carmine and 1.5 % acetic orcein also gave a very good differentiation between chromosomes and cytoplasm.

Pollen fertility was calculated by their stainability with 1 % cotton blue in lactophenol and was based on 500–1000 pollen grains.

3. RESULTS

(a) *Diploid hybrids*

Meiosis in diploid (2n = 14) hybrids, *L. perenne* × *L. multiflorum*, *F. pratensis* × *L. perenne*, and *F. pratensis* × *L. multiflorum* was regular with most PMC's having seven bivalents. Both rod- and ring-bivalents were formed, and some rings had more than two chiasmata.

(b) *Triploid hybrids*

The three types of triploid (2n = 21) hybrids incorporating two genomes of one species and one of another, viz. *F. pratensis* (2n = 14) × *L. perenne* (2n = 28)—designated as Fp LpLp, *F. pratensis* (2n = 14) × *L. multiflorum* (2n = 28)—designated as Fp LmLm, and *L. perenne* (2n = 14) × *L. multiflorum* (2n = 28)—designated as Lp LmLm, showed more or less a similar trend of chromosome pairing resulting largely in trivalents. Their range and mean chromosome configurations and chiasmata per cell are recorded in the table and salient meiotic features are described below:

(i) *Fp LpLp* (3x = 21). Meiosis in two triploid hybrids of this chromosomal constitution was characterized by the formation of a large number of trivalents, and so there was little indication of preferential pairing of the Lp chromosomes. Of 90 cells scored in two hybrids there was not one without trivalents, and a maximum of seven trivalents (fig. 6) was found in nine cells, while 17 cells had $6_{III} + 1_{II} + 1_{I}$ (fig. 4). Thus, these auto-allotriploids behaved meiotically like an autotriploid. All shapes of trivalents like V-, chain-, and frying pan-types were observed (figs. 1, 4, 6). Frying pan trivalents with four chiasmata were also common, and some trivalents were somewhat heteromorphic (fig. 1).

Univalents ranged from 0–5 and they generally lagged at anaphase, sometimes underwent division, and did not seem to get included at the poles.

Pollen fertility, as judged by their stainability with 1% cotton blue in lactophenol, was 44.2% (range in 4 plants 40.4 to 50.3%).

(ii) *Fp LmLm* (2n = 21). Two hybrids of this genomic composition were studied, one of which had a B-chromosome derived from the *Festuca* parent. The B-chromo-

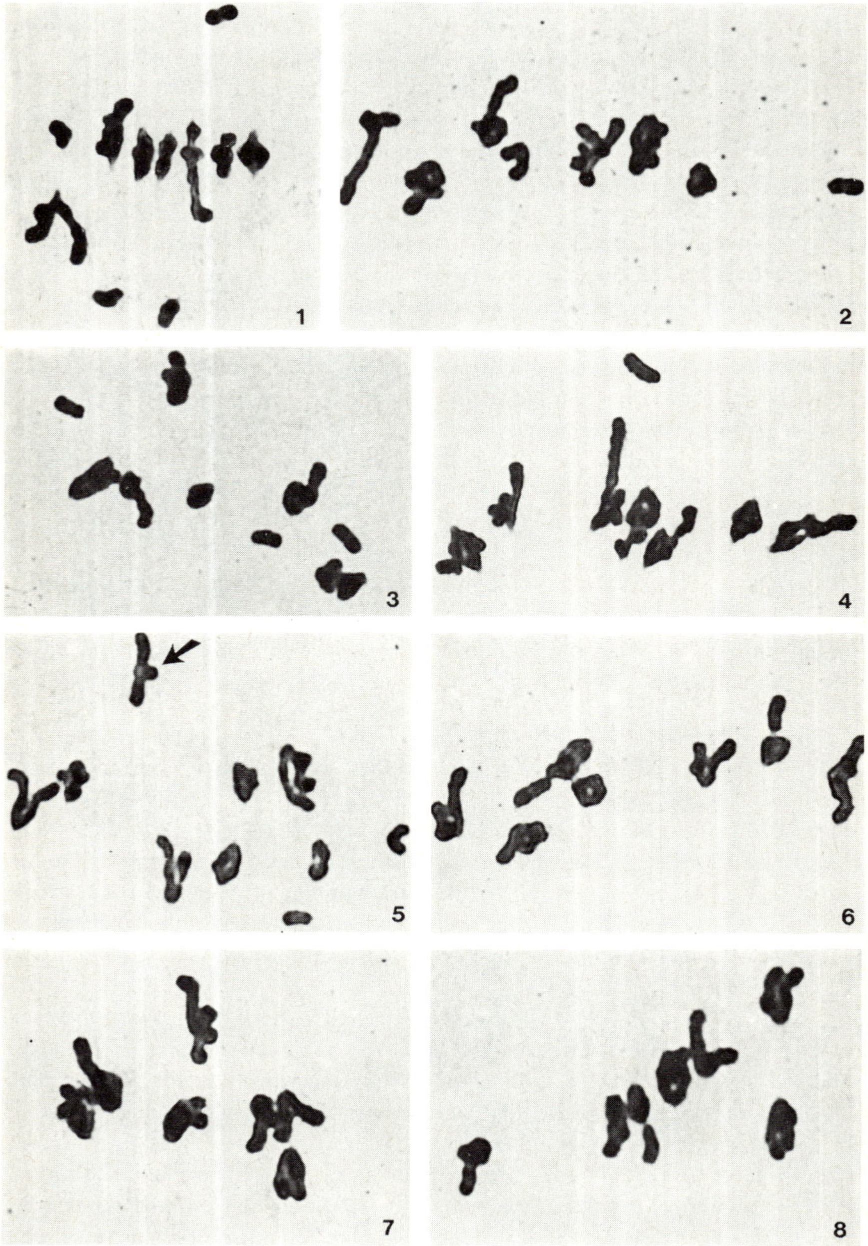

some hybrid had only 20 normal chromosomes instead of the 21 expected. The trend of chromosome pairing in the two hybrids was, however, very similar with a preponderance of trivalents (fig. 3). The 21 chromosome hybrid showed as many as six trivalents in four of the 30 cells scored. Frying pan trivalents with four chiasmata were also observed in some cells. The mean chiasmata per cell and per paired chromosome were 15.67 and 0.835, respectively. Pollen fertility could be calculated in one plant and was 38.8%.

(iii) *Fp LmLm* (2n = 20 + 1B). In this hybrid, despite the presence of a B-chromosome transmitted through the female gamete, a large number of trivalents was formed (table). As many as six trivalents (the highest theoretically possible) were observed in three of the 40 cells scored. The mean chiasmata per cell and per paired chromosome were 15.73 and 0.869.

At anaphase lagging and dividing univalents were observed. The lagging B-chromosome sometimes divided and each chromatid was included at the two poles.

(iv) *Lp LmLm* (2n = 21). Though the Lp parent used had one B-chromosome, it was not transmitted to the two hybrids studied here. As in the triploid hybrids reported above, chromosomes in the auto-allotriploids of this genomic constitution also paired predominantly as trivalents. There was no evidence of preferential pairing of Lm chromosomes. A maximum of seven trivalents (fig. 7) was observed in three, and six trivalents in eight of the 60 cells analysed. Thus these hybrids again behaved like an autotriploid. Only two cells had a quadrivalent each. Pollen fertility as calculated in one plant was 48.5 per cent.

(c) *Trispecific hybrids*

Five different intergeneric hybrids incorporating the two *Lolium* species and *Festuca pratensis* were analysed to study the pairing behaviour of the three genomes in a common background.

(i) *LpFp Lm* (3x = 21). In the two hybrids of this genomic constitution there was free pairing between the chromosomes of the three species resulting in a high

FIGS. 1–8.—Chromosome configurations at metaphase I in the different auto-allotriploids and trispecific hybrids. FIG. 1.—Balanced pairing (two homologous sets with the third homoeologous set) in the Fp LpLp auto-allotriploid hybrid with $3_{III} + 4_{II} + 4_{I}$. FIG. 2.—LmFp Lp trispecific hybrid with $5_{III} + 2_{II} + 2_{I}$, a case of balanced pairing with 5 intergenomal trivalents (one univalent is overlapping a trivalent in the centre). FIG. 3.—4_{III} + $3_{II} + 3_{I}$ in Fp LmLm hybrid. Note 4_{III} between four homologous pairs of Lm and four chromosomes of Fp, three ring bivalents between the Lm chromosomes and 3_{I} of Fp. FIG. 4.—$6_{III} + 1_{II} + 1_{I}$ in Fp LpLp hybrid; 6_{III} are obviously between 6 pairs of Lp and 6 chromosomes of Fp, 1 ring II between Lp chromosomes and 1_{I} of Fp. FIG. 5.—Unbalanced pairing in Fp LmLm showing $3_{III} + 5_{II} + 2_{I}$; 3_{III} are between 3 pairs of Lm and 3 Fp chromosomes, 4 ring II are obviously between Lm chromosomes and 2_{I} of Fp. The 5th bivalent (presumably the top rod bivalent marked with an arrow) must have resulted from intragenomal pairing of Fp chromosomes. FIG. 6.—7_{III} (2_{III} overlapping) in Fp LpLp auto-allotriploid showing complete pairing between 7 homologous sets of Lp with the 7 homoeologous chromosomes of Fp. FIG. 7.—7_{III} (2_{III} overlapping) in Lp LmLm triploid showing complete pairing between 7 homologous pairs of Lm and the 7 homoeologous chromosomes of Lp. FIG. 8.—7_{III} in the LpFp Lm trispecific hybrid showing complete pairing between the three genomes. Note the different types of trivalents (V- and frying pan-shaped).

TABLE

Chromosome pairing in some triploid and trispecific hybrids in Lolium-Festuca

Hybrids	No. of cells analysed	Mean and range of chromosome configurations VI	V	IV	III	II	I	B chrs.	Xta/ cell
Triploid									
(i) Fp LpLp	90	0.02	—	0.02	4.87	2.09	1.96	—	15.69
		(0–1)		(0–1)	(2–7)	(0–6)	(0–5)		
(ii) Fp LmLm	30	—	—	0.03	3.76	3.70	2.20	—	15.67
		—		(0–1)	(1–6)	(1–7)	(0–5)		
(iii) Fp LmLm	40	—	—	—	3.60	3.65	2.23	1	15.75
					(1–6)	(1–7)	(0–5)		
(iv) Lp LmLm	60	—	—	— 0.03	3.86	3.28	2.65	—	14.80
				(0–1)	(1–7)	(0–7)	(0–5)		
Trispecific									
(i) LpFp Lm	150	—	—	0.07	4.15	2.93	2.38	—	15.24
				(0–1)	(0–7)	(0–9)	(0–6)		
(ii) LmFp Lp	225	0.01	0.01	0.04	4.23	2.80	2.41	—	14.39
		(0–1)	(0–1)	(0–1)	(1–7)	(0–7)	(0–8)		

Lp = *Lolium perenne*; Lm = *Lolium multiflorum*; Fp = *Festuca pratensis*
All the hybrids, except (iii) Fp LmLm (3x = 20 + 1B), had 3x = 21 chromosomes.
Genomic contributions from male and female parents are separated by a gap.

frequency of trivalents (table). Out of a total of 150 cells analysed, five had seven trivalents (fig. 8) and 31 had six trivalents each. A quadrivalent each was recorded in 11 cells. Different anaphasic abnormalities resulting from multivalents and univalents were observed.

(ii) *LmFp Lp* (3x = 21). In three hybrids of this chromosomal constitution high intergenomal chromosome pairing led to the formation of a large number of trivalents (fig. 2). Of a total of 225 cells scored, 21 had 7_{III}, 22 had 6_{III}, and 49 had 5_{III},with a mean of 4.23_{III} per cell. Thus these trispecifics (apparently genomic allotriploids), as the two described above, behaved meiotically as autotriploids. A few higher chromosome configurations were also observed. Two plants produced a mean of 32.4% stainable pollen.

(d) *The nature of chromosome pairing in the auto-allotriploid and trispecific hybrids*
(i) *Intergenomal or homoeologous pairing.* Intergenomal pairing was very high in the three different types of auto-allotriploids and the trispecific hybrids resulting mostly in trivalents. In the auto-allotriploids, the two homologous sets of chromosomes paired with the third related or homoeologous set to form trivalents. Thus pairing was mostly restricted to the homologous and homoeologous sets resulting in balanced pairing, and the number of univalents was equal to the number of bivalents formed. For example, in cells having $4_{III} + 3_{II} + 3_{I}$ (fig. 3) the 4_{III} can be attributed to the synapsis of four homologous pairs and the four homoeologous

partners from the third genome, 3_{II} must have resulted from the three homologous pairs, the three remaining chromosomes of the third set being left unpaired as univalents. Similarly, configurations of $5_{III} + 2_{II} + 2_{I}$ and $6_{III} + 1_{II} + 1_{I}$ (fig. 4) could be explained as cases of balanced pairing resulting from homoeologous and homologous pairing.

In the trispecific hybrids or allotriploids having all three apparently different genomes from the three species, pairing was restricted to the homoeologous sets resulting largely in trivalents. Thus when all the seven homoeologous sets paired, seven trivalents were formed (fig. 8). A lesser number of trivalents, depending upon the complete homoeologous sets involved in pairing, was always accompanied by the appropriate number of bivalents and univalents. These cases of balanced pairing, e.g., $6_{III} + 1_{II} + 1_{I}$, or $5_{III} + 2_{II} + 2_{I}$ (fig. 2), or $4_{III} + 3_{II} + 3_{I}$, were predominant in all the trispecific hybrids analysed.

(ii) *Intragenomal pairing.* Apart from balanced pairing restricted only to homologous or homoeologous sets of chromosomes, there was some evidence for intragenomal or inter-homoeologous pairing, i.e., pairing between non-related chromosomes in the auto-allotriploid and allotriploid hybrids. Chromosome configurations higher than trivalents (see table) could have been formed only if such a pairing occurred. The formation of, for example, $3_{III} + 5_{II} + 2_{I}$ (fig. 5) in some cells of Fp LmLm hybrids could be explained as follows: 3_{III} resulted from pairing between three pairs of homologous (Lm) and three homoeologous (Fp) chromosomes, 4_{II} could easily result from the remaining four strictly homologous (Lm) pairs, and 2_{I} could belong to the Fp genome because they have no partners, but the fifth bivalent (presumably the top rod) can be explained only if two Fp chromosomes paired. Such cases of unbalanced pairing were recorded in about 9% of the cells in the two LpFp Lm and in 17.8% of the cells in the three LmFp Lp trispecifics.

4. DISCUSSION

Several interspecific and intergeneric hybrids have been studied between *L. perenne* L., *L. multiflorum* Lam., and *Festuca pratensis* Huds. (Peto, 1934; Crowder, 1953; Jenkin, 1954, 1955; Carnahan and Hill, 1955; Essad, 1956; Wit, 1959, 1964; Hertzsch, 1960; Hill and Carnahan, 1962, and others). However, phylogenetic relationships between these three important species are still far from clear. Among others, Peto and Jenkin studied chromosome pairing in diploid hybrids between these species and found mostly bivalents. In the present study also the diploid hybrids, *F. pratensis* × *L. perenne*, *F. pratensis* × *L. multiflorum*, and *L. perenne* × *L. multiflorum*, formed mostly seven bivalents, showing thereby a close phylogenetic proximity of the three species. It has been suggested, however, that chromosome pairing in hybrids cannot be taken as a true index of phylogenetic relationships. Darlington (1937) stressed the undesirability of basing phylogenetic relations on counts of bivalents and univalents in the hybrids, and suggested that the chromosome pairing in the amphidiploids was a more realistic test of homology (see Darlington, 1963).

An additional approach to studying chromosome differentiation in these species is to analyse chromosome pairing in the triploid hybrids where one genome is present in a double dose and another in its haploid state. It should be a critical test of affinity because the internal homologies of the chromosomes of different genomes can be best revealed by their competition for pairing in such auto-allotriploids.

(i) *Chromosome pairing in the auto-allotriploids.* In all the three auto-allotriploids with different genomic constitutions, viz. Fp LpLp, Fp LmLm, and Lp LmLm, the two homologous sets of chromosomes paired with the third related or homoeologous set to form mostly trivalents, and there was hardly any evidence of preferential pairing in any of the auto-allotriploids. They all behaved meiotically as autotriploids, indicating thereby that the Lp, Lm, and Fp chromosomes are highly homologous with one another, so much so that the chromosomes of one genome are capable of pairing with those of another, despite the presence of their own homologues. Since even a small amount of differentiation can lead to preferential pairing (see Stebbins, 1950), it would appear that there is little differentiation of chromosomes of these three species, or the chromosomal differentiation is much too low to permit preferential pairing. Carnahan and Hill (1955) and Hill and Carnahan (1962) also found trivalents in the auto-allotriploids produced by crossing diploid *L. perenne* (2n = 14) as female with autotetraploid (2n = 28) *F. elatior* L. (*F. pratensis* Huds.), providing evidence that chromosomes from the two genera paired even when the *Festuca* complement was present in duplicate.

While intergenomal pairing was very high and resulted in balanced pairing restricted only to homologous and homoeologous sets of chromosomes, the occurrence of intragenomal pairing in 15% of the cells of some auto-allotriploids shows that some cryptic interchanges may have resulted in the restructuring of certain chromosomes in some populations. It is plausible to assume that minor translocations have played some role in the evolution of these species of *Lolium* and *Festuca.*

(ii) *Pollen fertility in the auto-allotriploids.* Another remarkable feature of the auto-allotriploids was their fairly high pollen fertility as judged by their stainability with cotton blue. It was 44.2% in Fp LpLp, 38.8% in Fp LmLm, and 48.5% in Lp LmLm. Normally both diploid and triploid hybrids between distinct species are completely or highly sterile (see Stebbins, 1952; Carnahan and Hill, 1961; Dewey, 1974; Sakamoto, 1974). The diploid hybrids LpFp and LmFp are almost entirely pollen sterile despite their regular meiotic pairing with seven bivalents. But the chromosomal nature of their sterility is confirmed by the restoration of high fertility on chromosome doubling. It would appear therefore that cryptic structural hybridity (Stebbins et al., 1946) of the parental chromosomes might be responsible for sterility in these diploid intergeneric hybrids. However, the chromosomal divergence is too low to hinder the production of seven bivalents in them.

But when two doses of Lp or Lm genomes are present with one of Fp, fairly high pollen fertility is obtained in the auto-allotriploids. This could be due at least partly to the formation of balanced gametes. Configurations of $2_{III} + 5_{II} + 5_{I}$, or $3_{III} + 4_{II} + 4_{I}$ in Fp LpLp hybrids, for example, could on anaphasic separation lead to the production of 7 chromosome gametes. It is reasonable to assume that bivalents in these cells are between Lp chromosomes; 5_{II} of Lp would separate 5:5 to the two poles and 5_{I} presumably of Fp could lag and fail to reach the poles, as is generally observed in these hybrids; the 2:1 disjunction of 2_{III} could therefore easily produce some gametes with 7 chromosomes most of which would be from the Lp parent. A small proportion of pollen grains might even happen to have all the 7 Lp chromosomes, though the probability of the formation of such balanced gametes would be low. Hence some of the apparently fertile pollen grains would have Fp chromosomes also. In view of the tremendous variation in the size of stainable grains it would not be unreasonable to assume that unbalanced gametes, like 6-, 8- and perhaps 9-chromosome gametes, may also be stainable and presumably functional. Since the chromosomes of the two species are highly homologous and genetically related, it is likely that a small mixture of Fp chromosomes in these gametes is tolerated. Such a mixture of Lp and Lm chromosomes in pollen grains is perhaps better tolerated in Lp LmLm triploids (fertility 48.5%). The pollen grains containing mixtures of apparently different, but presumably genetically compatible, chromosomes may be stainable and seemingly functional.

Normally the triploids, more so the triploid hybrids (Dewey, 1974), are largely pollen sterile. Fairly high pollen stainability in the present intergeneric and interspecific auto-allotriploids would further indicate close phylogenetic relatedness of the parental species. Hill and Carnahan (1962), however, recorded a mean of 9.7% "good" pollen in triploid intergeneric hybrids between *L. perenne* (2n) and *F. elatior* (4x). In some autotriploids of *Dactylis glomerata* synthesized by crossing tetraploids with diploid subspecies, Jones and Borrill (1962) recorded a mean of 43% pollen fertility, though a few plants had over 90% fertility (Borrill, personal communication). They also got high female fertility in these triploids as judged by their ability to produce seeds when crossed with both diploid and triploid cytotypes. Carroll (1966) recorded 83.6% stainable pollen in autotriploid (3x = 15) *Anthoxanthum ovatum*, and he attributed it to the selective assortment of chromosomes to the two poles being probably subject to a degree of genetic control. In some autotriploids produced by crossing induced tetraploids with diploids in *Agropyron*, pollen stainability ranged from 21 to 87%, while the 21-chromosome triploids derived by crossing *A. cristatum* × *A. desertorum* produced 23% stainable pollen (Dewey and Pendse, 1967).

(iii) *B-chromosome and homoeologous pairing in Fp LmLm hybrids.* The trend of chromosome pairing in the two Fp LmLm hybrids, one of which had a B-chromosome derived from the *Festuca* female parent, is almost exactly similar (table), the mean chiasmata per cell being 15.67 and 15.75 for the hybrids without and with a B-chromosome, respectively. It is realized, however, that the comparison of multivalents and chiasma frequency per cell in the two hybrids may not be entirely valid because one hybrid had 21 chromosomes and the other had 20 + 1B. But even if mean chiasmata per paired chromosome are compared, they are 0.835 and 0.869 for the 1B- and 0B-chromosome hybrids. The B-chromosome therefore did not seem to suppress homoeologous pairing or reduce in any way chiasma formation.

B-chromosomes have been reported to suppress homoeologous chromosome pairing in some hybrids of *Lolium* species (Evans and Macefield, 1972) and *Lolium-Festuca* hybrids (Bowman and Thomas, 1973). In the present study, however, no such effect of a B-chromosome was noticeable. It may, however, be emphasized that the B-chromosome in the present study was derived from the *Festuca* parent, while in the previous reports the B's came from the Algerian *Lolium perenne* parent. It would thus appear that the B's from only certain sources may have regulatory effects on chromosome pairing.

(iv) *Chromosome pairing in trispecific hybrids.* In all the intergeneric hybrids involving the two *Lolium* species and *Festuca pratensis*, namely, two of LpFp Lm constitution and three of LmFp Lp constitution, the chromosomes paired predominantly as trivalents (table, figs. 2, 8). Thus all these trispecific allotriploids behaved meiotically like true autotriploids, suggesting again that there is very little differentiation of the chromosomes of the three genomes. On the basis of the formation of 5_{III} in a 19-chromosome trispecific hybrid, Lewis and Jauhar (1974) concluded that the three genomes were highly homologous.

Whilst in the majority of the cells there was intergenomal, balanced pairing restricted to homoeologous sets to form only trivalents, or trivalents with corresponding number of bivalents and univalents, 15.3% of the cells in the two FpFp Lm hybrids and 17.8% of the cells in the three LmFp Lp hybrids showed unbalanced pairing which could be explained only if intragenomal and/or interhomoeologue pairing (pairing between non-related chromosomes) occurred. Multivalents higher than trivalents could also result from both homoeologous as well as intragenomal pairing, which shows structural hybridity for segmental interchange in some chromosomes. Such a segmental interchange could easily have occurred as a consequence of crossing over between the *Lolium* and *Festuca* chromosomes which had paired before the formation of gametes in the maternal amphidiploid parents used in this study.

(v) *Taxonomic and phylogenetic implications of chromosome pairing*

a. *Lolium* hybrids. *Lolium perenne* and *L. multiflorum* cross reciprocally as easily as two populations or varieties of the same species. The diploid hybrids between them show perfect chromosome pairing with 7_{II} and are pollen fertile. These results are in agreement with the previous reports on these species (Peto, 1934; Jenkin, 1954, 1955; Naylor, 1960). Thus these two species of *Lolium* interbreed freely, are completely interfertile, and there is no barrier to gene exchange. The Lp LmLm triploid hybrids behave meiotically like autotriploids forming up to 7_{III}, the Lm chromosomes pairing with Lp chromosomes despite the presence of their strictly homologous partners. Moreover, synthetic amphidiploids LpLpLmLm form quadrivalents rather commonly (up to a maximum of 5_{IV} recorded by the writer) and can better be considered as "intervarietal autotetraploids" (Stebbins, 1957) or "intraspecific autotetraploids" (Jauhar and Joshi, 1969) rather than allotetraploids. On the basis of all these data, and considering the concept of biological Linnaean species (see Jauhar and Joshi, 1970), there is hardly any justification for the retention of *L. perenne* and *L. multiflorum* as separate species. They differ only with respect to certain superficial characters of the inflorescence, like number of florets per spikelet, glume length, or awning which could in fact differentiate even different varieties of a species.

b. *Lolium-Festuca* hybrids. The fact that *Festuca pratensis* crosses fairly easily with *L. perenne* and *L. multiflorum* both as male and female parent, the two diploid intergeneric hybrids form mostly 7_{II}, and in the Fp LpLp and Fp LmLm auto-allotriploids, and LpFp Lm and LmFp Lp allotriploids that the chromosomes pair largely as trivalents, shows a close phylogenetic proximity of the three species. Essad (1956) produced amphidiploids from two F_1 hybrids between *L. perenne* ($2n = 14$) and *F. pratensis* ($2n = 14$), and found that nearly half the chromosomes of the amphidiploids paired as quadrivalents or as trivalents with univalents. Thus he found a means of 2.89 IV + (III + I) in 100 cells of the two amphidiploids in contrast to the means of 3_{IV} + (III + I) observed in the autotetraploid *L. perenne* produced by chromosome doubling of the same parent as used in the amphidiploids. Quadrivalents have also been observed in the synthetic LpLpFpFp and LmLmFpFp amphidiploids in this station. The occurrence of trivalents in the Fp LpLp and Fp LmLm auto-allotriploids and of quadrivalents in the LpLpFpFp and LmLmFpFp amphidiploids provides incontrovertible evidence that Fp chromosomes are highly homologous with Lp and Lm chromosomes—so much so that they pair despite the presence of their own truly homologous partners. There is thus no effective isolation barrier to gene exchange between the Fp-Lp and Fp-Lm chromosomes. There is little evidence, therefore, that *F. pratensis* is sufficiently isolated either from *L. perenne* or *L. multiflorum* as to deserve a specific rank in a separate genus.

Several species of *Lolium* cross rather easily with those of *Festuca* (Crowder, 1953; Jenkin, 1955; Carnahan and Hill, 1955; Wit, 1959; Essad, 1964; Hill and Carnahan, 1962; Hill and Buckner, 1962; Lewis, 1966). Based on the relative ease with which species of *Lolium* and *Festuca* cross, Terrell (1966) suggested that the two genera should be united. Careful taxonomic studies by Stebbins (1956) have shown that *L. perenne* is in fact more similar to *F. pratensis (F. elatior)* than it is to other species of *Lolium.* Also *F. pratensis* in most of its morphological characters resembles *L. perenne* more than it does other species of *Festuca.* Based on these morphological studies coupled with those on cross-compatibility, Stebbins argued that the genus *Lolium* was merely a section of the large, diverse genus *Festuca,* a view which has largely been shared by Tutin (1956) and Löve (1963). The present studies further point to the need for considerable taxonomic revision of the whole *Lolium-Festuca* complex. Whether or not *Lolium* should be merged with *Festuca,* there is at least irrefutable evidence that *L. perenne, L. multiflorum,* and *F. pratensis* are closely related phylogenetically.

5. SUMMARY

1. Chromosome pairing in different diploid (2n = 14), triploid (2n = 21), and trispecific (2n = 21) hybrids between *Lolium perenne, L. multiflorum,* and *Festuca pratensis* was analysed.

2. The diploid hybrids—FpLp, FpLm and LpLm—formed mostly seven bivalents. The six auto-allotriploids of three different genomic constitutions behaved like autotriploids. The chromosomes paired largely as trivalents and there was little evidence for preferential pairing. Evidently the Lp, Lm, and Fp chromosomes are highly homologous.

3. Pollen fertility in some of the auto-allotriploids was fairly high and was attributed partly to balanced gamete formation and partly to genetic compatibility of the parental chromosomes in the pollen grains.

4. The trend of chromosome pairing in the two Fp LmLm triploids, one of which had 20 chromosomes plus a B-chromosome derived from the Fp parent, was similar. The B-chromosome did not seem to suppress homoeologous pairing or reduce chiasma formation in this hybrid.

5. All five trispecific hybrids also behaved as autotriploids, the chromosomes pairing predominantly as trivalents. Some intragenomal or interhomoeologue pairing resulting in multivalents, however, suggested some structural hybridity

for segmental interchange in some chromosomes, which could easily have occurred from intergenomal pairing of chromosomes in the maternal amphidiploid parents used to make the trispecifics.

6. The three species are clearly closely related phylogenetically, having possibly evolved from a common ancestor. It was inferred that *L. perenne* and *L. multiflorum* are much too close to deserve specific ranks and are so closely related to *F. pratensis* that there is little justification for their being in a separate genus.

Acknowledgement. I wish to thank Professor P. T. Thomas, C. B. E., Director of the Welsh Plant Breeding Station, and Dr. Hugh Thomas for their interest and unfailing help in this study and for critically going through the manuscript. Discussions from time to time with Dr. Martin Borrill and Mr. Elfed Lewis during the course of this investigation were very helpful and are gratefully acknowledged. Thanks are also due to Miss Sheila McLardy for typing the manuscript neatly and promptly.

Note added in proof

Further studies by the author have shown that B-chromosomes even from the Algerian *Lolium perenne* parent do not suppress homoeologous pairing in several diploid auto-allotriploid and amphidiploid hybrids between *Lolium* and *Festuca* species. It would appear therefore that the breeding significance of B-chromsomes has been overemphasized by Evans and Macefield (1972) and by Bowman and Thomas (1973).

6. REFERENCES

Bowman, J. G., and Thomas, H. 1973. B chromosomes and chromosome pairing in *Lolium perenne* × *Festuca arundinacea* hybrid. *Nat. New Biol., 245,* 80–81.

Carnahan, H. L., and Hill, H. D. 1955. *Lolium perenne* L. × tetraploid *Festuca elatior* L. triploid hybrids and colchicine treatments for inducing autoallohexaploids. *Agron. Jour., 47,* 258–262.

Carnahan, H. L., and Hill, H. D. 1961. Cytology and genetics of forage grasses. *Bot. Rev., 27,* 1–162.

Carroll, C. P. 1966. Autopolyploidy and the assortment of chromosomes. *Chromosoma (Berl.), 18,* 19–43.

Crowder, L. V. 1953. Interspecific and intergeneric hybrids of *Festuca* and *Lolium. J. Hered., 44,* 195–203.

Darlington, C. D. 1937. *Recent Advances in Cytology.* Churchill Ltd., London.

Darlington, C. D. 1963. *Chromosome Botany and Origins of Cultivated Plants.* Allen and Unwin Ltd.

Davies, D. R. 1960. The embryo culture of inter-specific hybrids of *Hordeum. New Phytol., 59,* 9–14.

Dewey, D. R. 1974. Hybrids and induced amphiploids of *Elymus canadensis* × *Agropyron libanoticum. Am. J. Bot., 61,* 181–187.

Dewey, D. R., and Pendse, P. C. 1967. Cytogenetics of crested wheat grass triploids. *Crop Sci., 7,* 345–349.

Essad, S. 1956. Analyse cytogénétique de deux amphidiploides *Lolium perenne* L. × *Festuca pratensis* Huds. *Compt. Rend. Acad. des Sciences (Paris), 243,* 670–672.

Essad, S. 1964. Étude comparative des hybrides réciproques *Lolium perenne* L. × *Festuca pratensis* Huds. et de leur descendance. *Ann. Amelior Plant (Paris), 14,* 295–308.

Evans, G. M., and Macefield, A. J. 1972. Suppression of homoeologous pairing by B chromochromes in a *Lolium* species hybrid. *Nat. New Biol., 236,* 110–111.

HERTZSCH, W. 1960. Kreuzungen innerhalb der Gattung *Festuca* und zwischen den Gattungen *Festuca* und *Lolium*. *Z. Pflanzenzücht.*, *44*, 301–318.

HILL, H. D., and BUCKNER, R. C. 1962. Fertility of *Lolium-Festuca* hybrids as related to chromosome number and meiosis. *Crop Sci.*, *2*, 484–486.

HILL, H. D., and CARNAHAN, H. L. 1962. *Lolium perenne* × induced tetraploid *Festuca elatior* L. and hybrids with *Festuca arundinacea* Schreb. *Crop Sci.*, *2*, 245–248.

JAUHAR, P. P., and JOSHI, A. B. 1969. Cytotaxonomic investigations in the *Panicum maximum* complex—III. Cytological features, chromosome diminution and evolution of the karyotype. *Cytologia (Tokyo)*, *34*, 222–233.

JAUHAR, P. P., and JOSHI, A. B. 1970. The concept of species and "microspecies". *Taxon*, *19*, 77–79.

JENKIN, T. J. 1954. Interspecific and intergeneric hybrids in herbage grasses, IV–VIII. *J. Genet.*, *52*, 239–331.

JENKIN, T. J. 1955. Interspecific and intergeneric hybrids in herbage grasses, XVI–XVIII. *J. Genet.*, *53*, 380–486.

JONES, K., and BORRILL, M. 1962. Chromosomal status, gene exchange and evolution in *Dactylis*. 3. The role of the inter-ploid hybrids. *Genetica*, *32*, 296–322.

LEWIS, E. J. 1966. The production and manipulation of new breeding material in *Lolium-Festuca*. Proc. 10th Intern. Grassld Congr. Helsinki, pp. 688–693.

LEWIS, E. J., and JAUHAR, P. P. 1974. A trispecific hybrid in *Lolium-Festuca*. *Z. Pflanzenzücht.*, *71*, 299–306.

LÖVE, A. 1963. Cytotaxonomy and generic delimitation. In *Symposium on Biosystematics. Regnum Veg.*, *27*, 45–51.

NAYLOR, B. 1960. Species differentiation in the genus *Lolium*. *Heredity*, *15*, 219–233.

PETO, F. H. 1934. The cytology of certain intergeneric hybrids between *Festuca* and *Lolium*. *J. Genet.*, *28*, 113–156.

SAKAMOTO, S. 1974. Integeneric hybridization among three species of *Heteranthelium*, *Eremopyrum* and *Hordeum*, and its significance for the genetic relationships within the tribe Triticeae. *New Phytol.*, *73*, 341–350.

SNOW, R. 1963. Alcoholic hydrochloric acid-carmine as a stain for chromosomes in squash preparations. *Stain Technol.*, *38*, 9–13.

STEBBINS, G. L., JR. 1950. *Variation and Evolution in Plants*. Columbia Univ. Press, New York.

STEBBINS, G. L., JR. 1952. Species hybrids in grasses. *Proc. 6th Intern. Grassland Congr. Pennsylvania*, 247–253.

STEBBINS, G. L., JR. 1956. Taxonomy and the evolution of genera, with special reference to the family Gramineae. *Evolution*, *10*, 235–245.

STEBBINS, G. L., JR. 1957. Genetics, evolution and plant breeding. *Indian J. Genet.*, *17*, 129–141.

STEBBINS, G. L., JR., VALENCIA, J. I., and VALENCIA, R. M. 1946. Artificial and natural hybrids in the Gramineae, tribe Hordeae. I. *Elymus*, *Sitanion* and *Agropyron*. *Am. J. Bot.*, *33*, 338–351.

TERRELL, E. E. 1966. Taxonomic implications of genetics in ryegrasses *(Lolium)*. *Bot. Rev.*, *32*, 138–164.

TUTIN, T. G. 1956. Generic criteria in flowering plants. *Watsonia*, *3*, 317–323.

WIT, F. 1959. Hybrids of ryegrass and meadow fescue and their value for grass breeding. *Euphytica*, *8*, 1–12.

WIT, F. 1964. Natural and experimental hybrids of ryegrass and meadow fescue. *Euphytica*, *13*, 294–304.

VARIATION OF GIEMSA BANDING PATTERNS IN THE CHROMOSOMES OF *ANEMONE BLANDA* L

G. E. MARKS

John Innes Institute, Colney Lane, Norwich, U.K.

1. INTRODUCTION

The chromosome complement of *Anemone blanda* has been shown to have Giemsa stained bands amounting to approximately 22% of the total length (Marks and Schweizer, 1974). The haploid complement consists of 4 acrocentric and 4 submeta-metacentric chromosomes all of which have bands (fig. 1).

Except for the short arms of chromosomes 2 and 3 which are stained there are no terminal bands. There are also no centromeric bands. In the material described by Marks and Schweizer (1974) two variants of chromosome 8 were found differing in the presence or absence of a single band. Plants homomorphic for both variants and one heteromorphic for the variants were found. Finding this single difference prompted an investigation into the amount and kind of variation in Giemsa banding within *Anemone blanda* the results of which form the basis of this report.

2. MATERIALS AND METHODS

Thirty plants of *Anemone blanda* were grown from tubers supplied by W. Blom and Son Ltd., Holland. All individuals were seedlings and there was no replication due to cloning. This was clear because the small tubers had no cut surfaces which show when tubers are subdivided. Preparations were made from root-tips as follows.

1) Pre-treat in 0.10% aqueous colchicine for $1\frac{1}{2}$ hr.
2) Fix in ethanol/glacial acetic acid (3:1) for 12 hr.

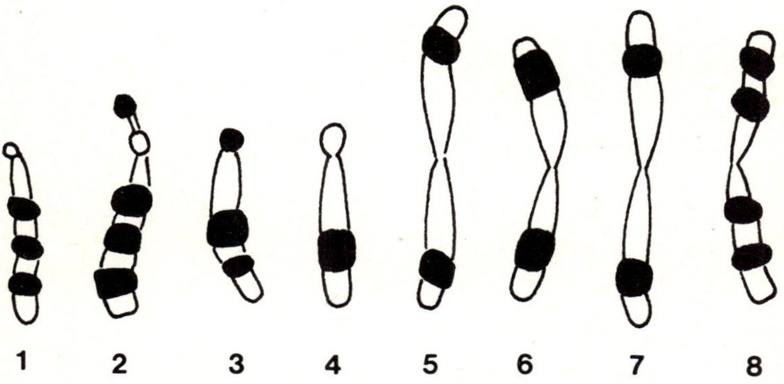

FIG. 1.—Haploid karyotype of *Anemone blanda* showing banding pattern found by Marks and Schweizer (1974).

3) Hydrolyze roots in 45% acetic acid at 60°C for 20 minutes. This step was introduced as a means of softening the root-tips for squashing but subsequently it was found to be the most critical stage influencing the differentiation of bands with Giemsa.

4) Transfer to distilled water at room temperature and squash in 45% acetic acid at room temperature. Root-tips should be soft enough to give excellent dispersal and spread of cells with minimum of pressure. No adhesive is necessary as there is no subsequent loss of cells if the squashing and spreading is satisfactory. This is checked under phase contrast. Slides require no heating.

5) Remove coverslip using dry-ice method and dry slide on a warm hotplate.

6) Immerse slide in a saturated solution of Barium hydroxide at room temperature for 5–10 minutes.

7) Wash in tap water for 1 hr.

8) Incubate slide in × 2 SSC at 60°C for 1 hr.

9) Rinse in distilled water and stain in 2% Giemsa (G. T. Gurr's R66 "improved" stock solution diluted × 50 with M/15 Sorensen phosphate buffer pH 6.9).

10) Check progress of staining after 5 minutes. Preparations are usually optimally stained within 1 hr.

11) Rinse rapidly and dry slide on hotplate for 12 hr.

12) Rinse in Euparal Essence and mount in Euparal. This procedure was found to give consistently good results with *Anemone blanda* and also proves to be very reliable with a number of other species.

3. RESULTS

Variants of all the chromosomes were found with the exception of chromosome 4 (fig. 2).

The banding pattern in the karyotype of an individual was constant. It could not be altered by growing plants in a range of temperatures (+4° to +30°C) and, while modifications of the staining procedure affected the extent of differentiation, they did not alter the pattern.

A random distribution of the variant chromosomes found could produce 216 unique karyotypes. The patterns found in the 30 karyotypes analyzed suggest, however, that randomness is not the case (table).

At the chromosome level there is either a complete absence or a great shortage of heteromorphic combinations whereas at the karyotype level there is clearly a concurrence of certain variants. Within the population there is a dimorphism for two karyotypes. The first (Type A) has a preponderance (81.7%) of *a* variants whereas the second (Type B) has a preponderance (67.7%) of *b* variants. The two karyotypes also differ markedly in band number and this represents a difference in the total amount of banding for whereas about 22% of karyotype A is banded the value for type B is around 36% (fig. 3).

4. DISCUSSION

Since we do not know the exact origin and nature of this population we cannot account for the reasons which brought about this dimorphism of karyotypes. However, certain features are clear.

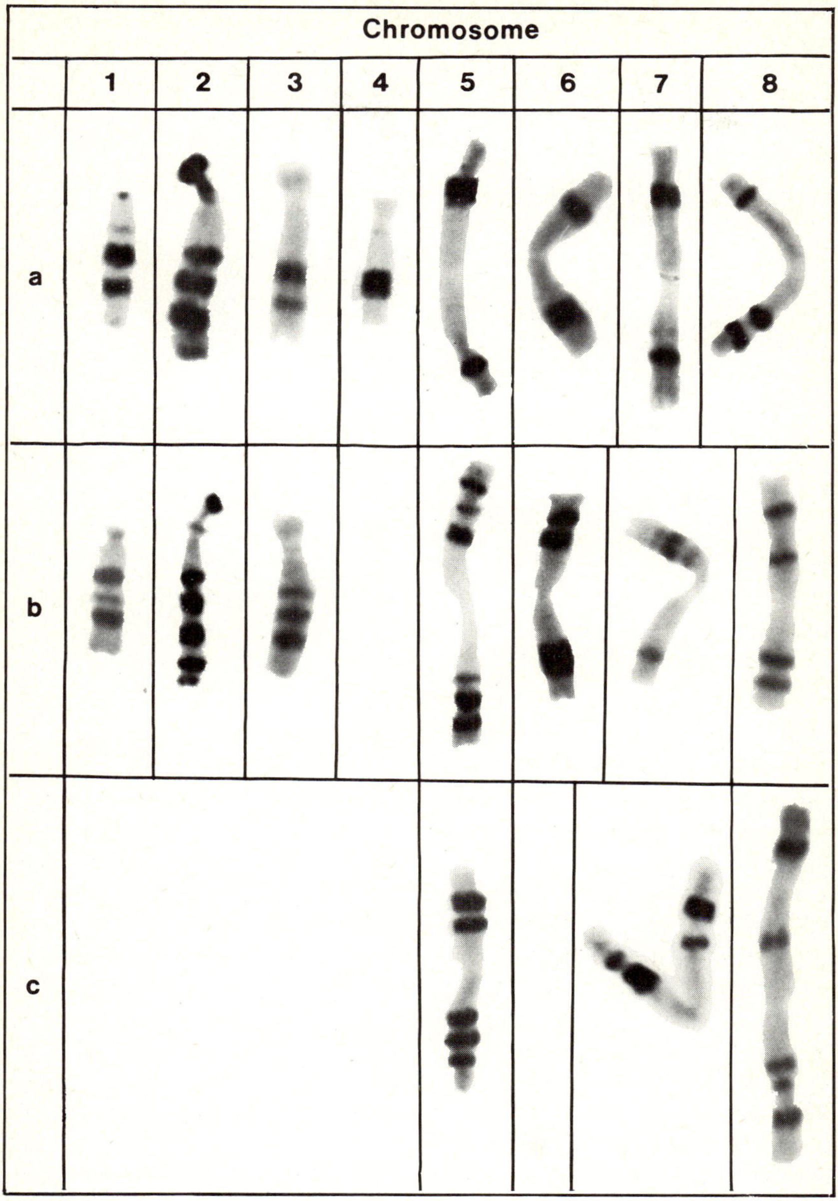

FIG. 2.—Variant chromosomes found in a population of 30 plants.

(a) There is no replication due to cloning as previously stated.

(b) A history of continuous selfing would account for the preponderance of homomorphic pairs but it cannot account for the concurrence of particular variants.

(c) The plants show much variation for flower colour and leaf morphology which suggests many genotypes derived from an essentially outbreeding population.

We cannot yet account for the origin of the different variant chromosomes. It

TABLE

Distribution of variant chromosomes throughout the karyotypes of 30 plants. Chromosome 1 and chromosome 4 excluded because the variant of chromosome 1 was only observed once and no variants of chromosome 4 were found

Number of plants	Chromosome 2	3	5	6	7	8	Bands per 2n complement
10	aa	aa	aa	aa	aa	bb	30
2	aa	aa	aa	bb	aa	bb	34
2	aa	aa	aa	aa	aa	(bc)	31
1	aa	aa	aa	aa	aa	(ab)	32
15 (4)							
9	bb	bb	bb	bb	cc	cc	52
1	bb	bb	bb	bb	bb	bb	50
1	bb	bb	cc	bb	bb	aa	48
1	bb	bb	bb	(ab)	bb	aa	47
1	bb	(ab)	(bc)	(ab)	(ac)	bb	46
1	bb	bb	cc	(ab)	aa	bb	45
1	bb	bb	bb	(ab)	cc	cc	51
15 (7)							

is already clear, however, that chiasmata are not involved because these are extremely localized proximal to the centromere and do not coincide with banded regions (Marks, 1974). Also apart from the difference between chromosomes, 1a and 1b, which could be due to an inversion, there is no clear indication amongst the other chromosomes that chromosome rearrangements are responsible for producing variants. This conclusion will be checked by studying meiosis in all the plants.

Vosa (1973*a*) described Giemsa banding polymorphism in a population of twenty plants of *Scilla sibirica*. There were numerous variants of all chromosomes the majority being differences in band length but all plants examined were unique in the banding patterns of their karyotypes. In *Tulbaghia leucantha* also all plants in two wild populations had unique fluorescence patterns (Vosa, 1973*b*). The variants are thought to arise from chromosome rearrangements and the results to be consistent with the hypothesis of a freely inbreeding population with selection acting against hetermorphic chromosome pairs. However, Vosa (1973*a*) states that in *Allium pulchellum* certain band patterns are peculiar to given populations. But since there is no exact information about the population structure of these Liliaceous species or of *Anemone blanda* we cannot make a meaningful comparison of the results.

In *Anemone blanda* the paradox of having much variation in banding patterns between chromosomes and little variation in patterns between karyotypes argue for considerable interdependence between certain variants within a karyotype implying in turn an adaptive significance to certain combinations reflected in the banding patterns themselves.

Seeds have been obtained from crossing plants with Type A and Type B karyotypes as readily as from crossing those with the same karyotype. Cross-incompatibility

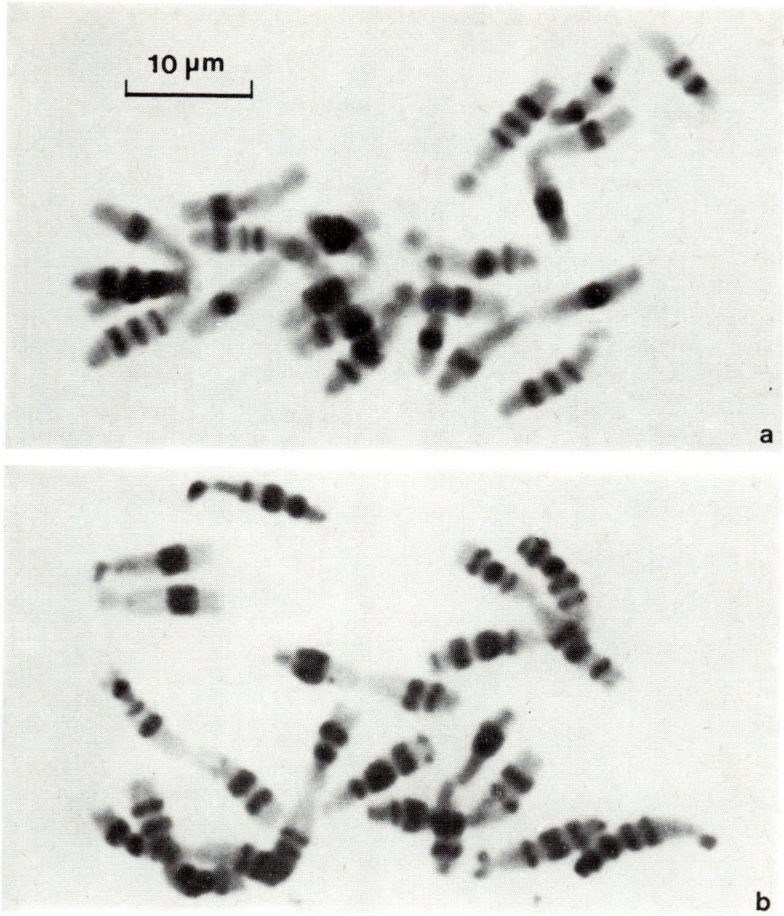

FIG. 3.—Type A (*a*) and Type B (*b*) karyotypes of *Anemone blanda.*

therefore does not maintain the distinction between the two karyotypes. The distribution of banding patterns obtained in the progenies of these crosses should indicate the kind and extent of preferential survival although understanding the adaptive value of a particular banding pattern must wait until the role of the bands themselves is understood.

5. SUMMARY

1. An analysis of Giemsa stained bands in the karyotypes of thirty plants of *Anemone blands* shows considerable variation between chromosomes.
2. This variation is conserved, however, to give two types of karyotypes from which it is argued that there is considerable interdependence of chromosomes within each karyotype.
3. Whether this interdependence is due directly to differences within the bands themselves or whether the bands merely reflect some other underlying cause is not known.

Acknowledgement. I would like to acknowledge the assistance of Mrs. S. Negus in making the chromosome preparations.

6. REFERENCES

MARKS, G. E. 1974. Giemsa banding of meiotic chromosomes in *Anemone blanda L. Chromosoma (Berl.)*, *49*, 113–119.

MARKS, G. E., and SCHWEIZER, D. 1974. Giemsa banding: Karyotype differences in some species of *Anemone* and in *Hepatica nobilis*. *Chromosoma (Berl.)*, *44*, 405–416.

VOSA, C. G. 1973*a*. Heterochromatin recognition and analysis of chromosome variation in *Scilla sibirica*. *Chromosoma (Berl.)*, *43*, 269–278.

VOSA, C. G. 1973*b*. Quinacrine fluorescence analysis of chromosome variation in *Tulbaghia leucantha*. In *Chromosomes Today*, *4* (J. WAHRMAN and K. R. LEWIS, eds.), pp. 345–349. Israel Universities Press, Jerusalem, and John Wiley & Sons, New York.

HETEROCHROMATIN CLASSIFICATION IN *VICIA FABA* AND *SCILLA SIBIRICA*

CANIO G. VOSA

Botany School, Oxford, U.K.

1. INTRODUCTION

Recent advances in techniques for the study of the linear differentiation of chromosomes have given a new insight into the problem of heterochromatin. Several distinct types have been recognized in plants and animals on the basis of enhanced or reduced fluorescence when stained with fluorochromes, sensitivity to cold and positive or negative response when stained with Giemsa or other cytological stains after various pretreatments (Vosa, 1970, 1972, 1973*a*, *b*; Vosa and Marchi, 1972).

The present study is concerned with an investigation into the location and nature of heterochromatin in the chromosomes of *Vicia faba* and *Scilla sibirica.*

2. MATERIALS AND METHODS

The material consisted of seeds of the commerical variety of *Vicia faba* (2n = 12) 'Bunyards Exhibition' and of bulbs of *Scilla sibirica* (2n = 12). Seeds and bulbs were grown suspended in glass beakers of distilled water at room temperature.

Actively growing root-tips pretreated in an aqueous solution of 0.05% colchicine for 4–6 hr at room temperature were prepared by the following methods:

1. Normal squash preparations stained with Feulgen or acetic-orcein: fixation in 1:3 acetic alcohol followed by 6 min hydrolysis in 1N HCl at 60°C.

2. Fix in 1:3 acetic alcohol overnight, squashing in 45% acetic acid, and staining in alcoholic solutions of either quinacrine (Q), 0.5%, quinacrine mustard (QM), 0.05%, or Hoechst 33258, 0.02%. Staining at room temperature for 2–5 min.

3. As in method 2 but staining in aqueous solution of ethidium bromide (EB), 0.02%, at room temperature for 2 min.

4. Fix in 1:3 acetic alcohol overnight followed by 25–30 sec in 1 N HCl at 60°C; squash in 45% acetic acid; denature in a saturated solution of barium hydroxide for 5 min at room temperature; wash in distilled water, 6 min hydrolysis in 1N HCl at 60°C; stain in Feulgen.

5. As method 4 but without the second hydrolysis and stain in quinacrine or Hoechst 33258.

6. As method 5 but stain in Giemsa (0.5% at pH 6.8).

7. Fix and treat as in the preceding methods but after the barium step wash in distilled water and incubate in 2 × SSC for 1 hr at 60°C, stain in 0.5% Giemsa (pH 6.8) or acetic-orcein at room temperature.

8. As in 7 but stain in quinacrine or Hoechst 33258.

9. Fix in 1:3 acetic alcohol overnight; hydrolysis in 0.2N HCl at 60°C for 5

min; wash in distilled water; denature in barium; incubate in 2 × SSC for 1 hr at 60°C; stain in Giemsa.

10. Fix in 45% acetic acid for 15 min at room temperature followed by the same steps as the preceding method.

3. RESULTS

The results of the various staining methods are illustrated in figure 1a and b. In order to facilitate the evaluation of the different methods only one easily identifiable chromosome from each of the two species has been analyzed, namely the M-chromosome of *Vicia faba* (fig. 1a) and chromosome 3/7 (fig. 1b) of *Scilla sibirica* (Vosa, 1973*a*).

The maximum number of bands in the M-chromosome of *V. faba* is seven and they have been numbered progressively from the band distal to the nucleolar organizer (fig. 2a).

(a) *Vicia faba*

Method 1: The chromosome is stained evenly along its length with the secondary constriction appearing as an unstained gap. In about half of the metaphases a small area of denser strain, often delimited by a small unstained gap, is seen near the centromere in the long arm of the chromosome and corresponds to band 7.

Method 2: Q, QM and Hoechst 33258 give the same results: relatively low fluorescence along the chromosome with four clearly enhanced fluorescence bands, one in the long arm adjacent to the centromere (band 7) and three in the short arm (bands 3, 4, and 5). The centromere (band 6) is unstained (Caspersson et al., 1968, 1969; Vosa, 1970; Vosa and Marchi, 1972).

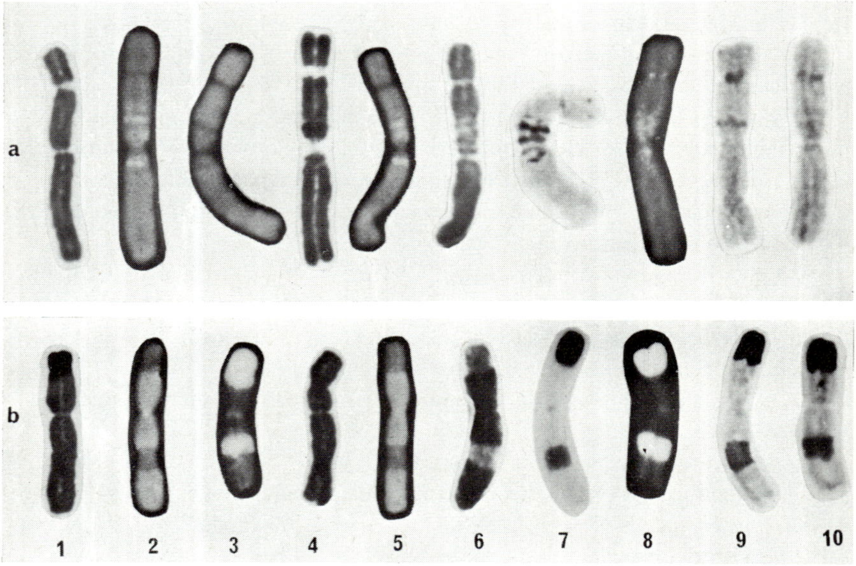

FIG. 1.—The results of the ten staining methods outlined in the text on the H-segments of the M-chromosome of *Vicia faba* (a) and on chromosome 3/7 of *Scilla sibirica* (b).

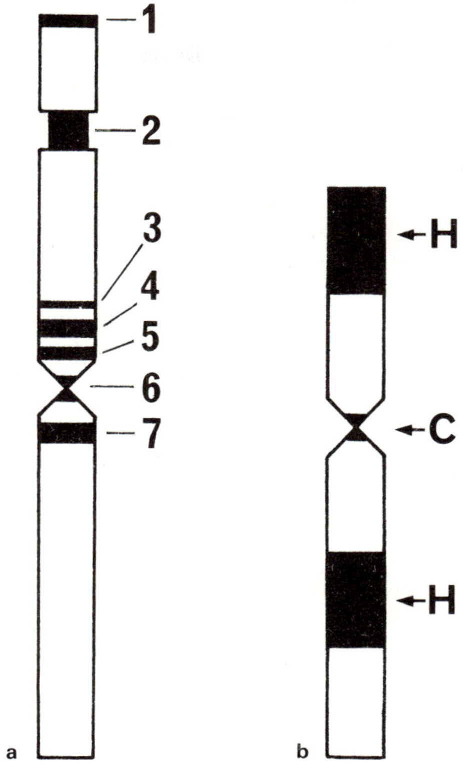

FIG. 2.—Diagrammatic representation of the H-segments location in the M-chromosome of *Vicia faba* (a) and on chromosome 3/7 of *Scilla sibirica* (b).

Method 3: EB gives fairly intense red-orange fluorescence with unstained bands at the nucleolar constriction and at bands 4 and 7 (Vosa, 1970).

Method 4: Deep staining along the chromosome with clear gaps at bands 2, 4, 6, and 7.

Method 5: The same result as method 2.

Method 6: Dark staining along the chromosome with clear, unstained gaps at bands, 2, 3, 4, 5, 6 and 7.

Method 7: Faint staining along the chromosome with darkly stained bands at 1, 2, 3, 4, 5, 6 and 7.

Method 8: Enhanced fluorescence bands at 2, 3, 4, 5, and 7. The centromere (band 6) appears as an unstained gap.

Method 9: Faint staining along the chromosome with a thick, deeply stained band at the nucleolar organizer (band 2) and at band 4.

Method 10: Faint staining along the chromosome with deeply stained bands at the nucleolar constriction (band 2) and at band 7 and a clear gap at band 3.

(b) *Scilla sibirica*

Method 1: The chromosome is stained evenly but in the region of the H-segments the chromatids are not fully separated and "stick" together with a decrease in width.

Method 2: Q, QM, and Hoechst 33258 give the same results: two regions of reduced fluorescence, one terminal in the short arm and the other about the middle of the long arm. In addition, in preparations which have been left overnight or longer, a thin enhanced fluorescence band is visible at the centromere.

Method 3: A complete reversal of the fluorescence pattern of method 2 with the centromere appearing as an unstained gap (Caspersson et al., 1969; Vosa, 1970, 1973*a*).

Method 4: Same results as method 1.

Method 5: Same results as method 2 except that the enhanced centric band is not visible.

Method 6: Dark staining with the exception of the H-segments which appear understained and narrower.

Method 7: Giemsa: faint staining with deeply stained segments at the same position as in methods 2 and 3. In addition a thin dark band is visible at the centromere. Orcein: as with Giemsa but no centric band.

Method 8: Enhanced fluorescence segments at the same position as the reduced fluorescence of method 2, with the centromere fluorescing brightly.

Method 9: The same results as with method 7 but no centric band.

Method 10: As with method 9.

4. DISCUSSION

The results show that all the bands in the M-chromosome of *V. faba* differ from one another. Those at the nucleolar constriction and at the centromere, obtainable with methods 8, 9 and 10 and with method 7, respectively, consist of two separate segments on either side of an unstained gap. In most metaphases they are not separately visible owing to chromosome condensation and swelling and give the impression of a single band.

In *S. sibirica* there are only two kinds of differential segments: one confined to the centromere and the other to the H-segments.

Some of the most striking results are those obtained with methods 4, 5 and 6. In *Vicia*, after barium treatment, Feulgen staining reveals only two bands (4 and 6) as "gaps". Although band 2 may be present it may not be distinguishable because of its contiguity with the nucleolar constriction. There is no differentiation in the chromosome of *Scilla*. Quinacrine and quinacrine mustard after barium, give essentially the same results in both plants as without treatment except that the centric band in *Scilla* is not visible. After barium, Giemsa staining gives "gaps" or regions of reduced stainability coupled with a reduction in width of the chromosomes in the region of the H-segments. If the alkali treatment differentially removes the chromatin moieties (proteins and/or DNA) responsible for positive banding, this subtraction cannot be complete because the Q-staining pattern is not altered significantly. Alkali treatment followed by incubation in SSC and by Giemsa or fluorescence staining (methods 7 and 8) highlights the problems involved in band production. With these methods there is a complete reversal of the banding patterns in both species when the stain used is Giemsa and in the case of *Scilla* also acetic-orcein (Vosa, 1973*b*). But with quinacrine or Hoechst 33258 the differences (enhanced versus reduced fluorescence) between the H-segments of *Vicia* and *Scilla* are clearly demonstrated. In *Vicia* the pattern is unchanged except that the nucleolar band (band 2) is now visible, but in *Scilla* the reduced and enhanced band, intercalary, terminal, and centric, respectively, are now all enhanced. This reversal of reactivity in *Scilla* H-segments indicates the fundamental differences in the composition of the heterochromatin in the two plants and, of course, points to the drastic changes produced by the SSC incubation.

The mechanism of C-banding must involve restoration of the stain affinity of the H-segments after the barium treatment, while the stainability of the other chromosome regions is decreased. The alkali denaturation process must also induce a degree of dissociation in the euchromatin which, however, maintains its affinity for the stain. The SSC incubation "reanneals" the H-segments which then stain intensely and at the same time dissolves away the DNA and/or the protein components from the euchromatin. This dissolution is consistent with various studies which have shown considerable loss of chromosomal DNA and proteins during SSC incubation. It has been estimated that the complete C-banding technique, comparable with the methods considered here, on average removes about 60% of chromosomal DNA and that this DNA is preferentially extracted from the euchromatic regions (Comings et al., 1973; Hsu and Arrighi, 1973; Pathak and Arrighi, 1973).

According to Weisblum and de Haseth (1972) and Ellison and Barr (1972), AT-base pair sequences enhance Q-fluorescence while GC-base pairs effectively quench it. Thus Q-fluorescence may be used for the detection of AT-rich or GC-rich chromosome regions. There is a limitation in this technique because of the quenching effect of GC-base pairs when interspersed regularly in an otherwise AT-rich region (Weisblum, 1973*a*). The fluorochrome Hoechst 33258, which according to Weisblum (1973*b*) shows enhanced fluorescence in the presence of repetitive AT-base pairs regardless of GC-pairs interspersion, can be used to classify the differential segments of *Vicia* and *Scilla*. Thus bands 3, 4, 5, and 7 in the M-chromosome of *Vicia* and the centric region of *Scilla* are AT-rich, while the intercalary and distal H-segments of *Scilla* and possibly the secondary constriction (band 2) and the pericentric region of *Vicia* are GC-rich.

Only the complete C-banding technique (method 7), which includes alkali denaturation and incubation in hot SSC, reveals all seven differential segments in the M-chromosome of *V. faba*. The thin band distal to the nucleolar organizing region (band 1) and the centric band (band 6) are positively revealed only by this method, which is to be considered the most useful for chromosome identification. In most methods the bands that are contiguous with the nucleolar constriction and with the centromere may be present but impossible to detect with certainty, because of this contiguity, when negatively stained. The staining reaction of the nucleolar organizer is interesting and it is revealed only four of the methods employed in this investigation, all involving some kind of acid treatment or hydrolysis. Comparable results with differential staining of the nucleolar organizing region have been obtained by Takehisa (1968), Takehisa and Utsumi (1973), and also by Döbel et al. (1973).

Band 4 is observable either as positive or negative in all methods except method 1. Its most interesting behaviour is seen in methods 9 and 10 when it may be positive or negative, respectively, while the other band present (band 2) is always positive.

It is evidently very sensitive to the acid fixation of method 10. Band 7 is the most consistently seen except in the methods involving prolonged acid hydrolysis, such as method 9 and the method employed by Döbel et al. (1973) with 5 min hydrolysis in 0.2N HCl or the method used by Schweizer (1973) which involves 6 hr "maceration" in 45% acetic acid.

The bandings patterns induced by cold treatment in *Vicia faba* are somewhat inconsistent and give variable results, but for the most part correspond to the bands revealed by the methods used in this investigation. In the M-chromosome they include probably all three bands in the nucleolar arm (bands 3, 4 and 5), possibly fused together to form a single "gap", and band 7 in the long arm. Evans and Bigger (1961) also found an intercalary band in the long arm. This band has been observed in a few plants in some varieties of *Vicia*, including the one used in this investigation, in quinacrine-stained preparations (Vosa and Marchi, 1973), but it has not been detected with any of the methods considered here. In trypsin-treated preparations (Döbel et al., 1973) only three bands, corresponding to band 2, 4 and 5 of the present study, could be consistently seen, and a fourth (band 7) in only 10% of the chromosomes. In *Scilla sibirica*, the H-segments can be revealed only after drastic and prolonged cold treatment (Baumann, 1971) and correspond exactly to the regions of reduced fluorescence (Vosa, 1973*a*).

Experiments with treatments which are thought to exclude DNA denaturation, such as prolonged exposure to high concentration of urea, have led to the suggestion that the C-banding patterns may be due to differential chromatin condensation (McKay, 1973). An indication of a situation of this kind is given by the careful observation of the Feulgen-stained chromosomes (method 1). The area of denser stain near the centromere of the M-chromosome of *Vicia* and the sticking of the chromatids in the region of the H-segments in *Scilla* are evidence of a differential chromatin organization. Further data in this direction are provided by the electron and visible light microscopy studies of La Cour and Wells (1974) in *Fritillaria lanceolata* and in *Scilla sibirica*. In *F. lanceolata*, where the H-segments show enhanced fluorescence and are stained positively by a Giemsa method (Schweizer, 1973), the heterochromatin is distinguishable at all stages of the nuclear cycle by being less opaque to electrons. This is thought to be due to the less tight packing of the chromatin fibrils and to their lower intrinsic opacity. This finding seems to be consistent with a persistent incomplete condensation of the H-segments in this species. La Cour and Wells (1974) found that the heterochromatin in *S. sibirica* was recognizably different from that of *F. lanceolata* in that fibrils have the same degree of electron opacity as those in the euchromatin and are more tightly packed. The authors suggest that the enhancement and quenching of fluorescence may not necessarily be due to repetitive AT- or GC-base sequences, respectively. They postulate that the degree of chromatin spiralization or condensation could be the governing factor: more fluorochrome may lodge in the less tightly packed H-segments of *F. lanceolata*, hence enhanced fluorescence, while in the tightly coiled H-segments of *S. sibirica* the amount of fluorochrome between the chromatin fibrils may be negligible, giving reduced fluorescence. While the value of this hypothesis remains to be tested, it is worth considering the suggestion of Yunis and Yasmineh (1971) and that the degree of heterochromatin condensation may be affected by the repetitiveness of its DNA constituent. Possibly the two factors—chromatin condensation and the repetitiveness and bias of its base composition—are responsible for the differences in fluorescence intensity.

The precise chemical constitution of the chromatin fractions represented by the various bands is not known. Because all methods used, with the exception of some of the fluorescence techniques, include steps that may result in selective protein extraction and/or denaturation, it is probable that protein distribution and molecular nature are paramount in determining band differentiation. The straight Q, QM, EB, and Hoechst 33258 techniques do not include steps which drastically alter the protein configuration of the chromosomes. Thus the fluorescence patterns may be determined by the location, concentration, and molecular constitution of specific chromosomal proteins, together with the underlying DNA-base constitution. The various other staining patterns may be dependent on protein and/or DNA extraction, displacement and/or denaturation.

5. SUMMARY

1. Various staining techniques have been used to identify several types of heterochromatin.

2. Heterochromatic segments of seven different kinds have been found in the M-chromosome of *Vicia faba* and two in the chromosome of *Scilla sibirica.* These H-segments differ in their reactivity to fluorochromes and to Giemsa, orcein and Feulgen after various treatments.

3. The segments adjacent to the nucleolar constriction in the M-chromosome of *V. faba* are very sensitive to mild acid hydrolysis, becoming apparent only after this kind of treatment.

4. All other H-segments show differential reactivity when treated with acid or alkali. They are thought to consist of repetitive sequences of DNA composed exclusively of AT or GC nucleotides, or of repetitive sequences where the relative proportion of AT:GC may be biased either way in various patterns.

5. The overlying protein component of the chromosomes may play a part in the differentiation of the H-segments.

6. REFERENCES

Caspersson, T., Farber, S., Foley, G. E., Kudynowski, J., Modest, E. J., Simonsson, E., Wagh, U., and Zech, L. 1968. Chemical differentiation along metaphase chromosomes. *Exp. Cell Res., 49,* 219–222.

Caspersson, T., Zech. L., Modest, E. J., Foley, G. E., Wagh, U., and Simonsson, E. 1969. Chemical differentiation with fluorescent alkylating agents in *Vicia faba* metaphase chromosomes. *Exp. Cell Res., 58,* 147–152.

Comings, D. E., Avelino, E., Okada, T. A., and Wyandt, H. E. 1973. The mechanism of C- and G-banding of chromosomes. *Exp. Cell Res., 77,* 469–493.

Döbel, P., Rieger, R., and Michaelis, A. 1973. The Giemsa banding patterns of the standard and four reconstructed karyotypes of *Vicia faba. Chromosoma (Berl.), 43,* 409–422.

Ellison, J. R., and Barr, H. J. 1972. Quinacrine fluorescence of specific chromosome regions. Late replication and high AT content in *Samoaia leonensis. Chromosoma (Berl.), 36,* 357–390.

Evans, J. H., and Bigger, T. R. L. 1961. Chromatid aberrations induced by gamma irradiation.

II. Non-randomness of chromatid aberrations in relation to chromosome length in *Vicia faba* root-tip cells. *Genetics, 46,* 277–289.

HSU, T. C., and ARRIGHI, F. E. 1973. Service of *in situ* nucleic acid hybridization to biology. *Nobel Symposium, 23,* pp. 307–314. Academic Press, New York.

LA COUR, L. F., and WELLS, B. 1974. Fine structure and staining behaviour of heterochromatic segments in two plants. *J. Cell. Sci., 14,* 505–521.

MCKAY, R. D. G. 1973. The mechanism of G- and C-banding in mammalian metaphase chromosomes. *Chromosoma (Berl.), 44,* 1–14.

PATHAK, S., and ARRIGHI, F. E. 1973. Loss of DNA following C-band procedures. *Cytogenet. Cell Genet., 12,* 414–422.

SCHWEIZER, D. 1973. Differential staining of plant chromosomes with Giemsa. *Chromosoma (Berl.), 40,* 307–320.

TAKEHISA, S. 1968. Heterochromatic segments in *Vicia* revealed by treatment with HCl-acetic acid. *Nature (Lond.), 217,* 567–568.

TAKEHISA, S., and UTSUMI, S. 1973. Visualization of metaphase heterochromatin by the denaturation-renaturation Giemsa staining method. *Experientia (Basel), 29,* 120–121.

VOSA, C. G. 1970. Heterochromatin recognition with fluorochromes. *Chromosoma (Berl.), 30,* 366–372.

VOSA, C. G. 1972. La struttura cromosomica alla luce delle nuove tecniche citologiche. *Inf. Bot. Ital., 4,* 103–114.

VOSA, C. G. 1973*a*. Heterochromatin recognition and analysis of chromosome variation in *Scilla sibirica*. *Chromosoma (Berl.), 43,* 269–278.

VOSA, C. G. 1973*b*. Acetic-orcein, a new stain for the detection of constitutive heterochromatin in plant and animal chromosomes. *Exp. Cell Res., 79,* 463–465.

VOSA, C. G., and MARCHI, P. 1972. Quinacrine fluorescence and Giemsa staining in plants. *Nat. New Biol., 237,* 191–192.

VOSA, C. G., and MARCHI, P. 1973. On the quinacrine fluorescence and Giemsa patterns of the chromosomes of *Vicia faba*. *G. bot. Ital., 106,* 151–159.

WEISBLUM, B. 1973*a*. Why centric regions of quinacrine-treated mouse chromosomes show diminished fluorescence. *Nature, 246,* 150–151.

WEISBLUM, B. 1973*b*. Fluorescent probes of chromosomal DNA structure: three classes of acridines. *Cold Spring Harbor Symp. Quant. Biol., 38,* 441–449.

WEISBLUM, B., and DE HASETH, P. L. 1972. Quinacrine a chromosome stain specific for Deoxy-adenylate-Deoxythymidylate-rich regions. *Proc. Natl. Acad. Sci. U.S.A., 69,* 629–632.

WEISBLUM, B., and DE HASETH, P. L. 1973. Nucleotide specificity of the quinacrine stain reaction for chromosomes. In *Chromosomes Today, 4* (J. WAHRMAN and K. R. LEWIS, eds.), pp. 35–51. Israel Universities Press, Jerusalem and John Wiley & Sons, New York.

YUNIS, J. T., and YASMINEH, W. G. 1971. Heterochromatin, satellite DNA and chromosome structure. *Science, 174,* 1200–1209.

INTERCHROMOSOMAL ASSOCIATION IN *VICIA FABA* INDUCED BY 4-AMINOURACIL

VERONICA STOIAN[1], PETRE RAICU[1] and ROBERT GORENFLOT[2]

[1]*Laboratorul de Genetica, Universitatea din Bucuresti, Aleea Portocalilor 1–3, Romania*

[2]*Laboratoire de Taxonomie végétale experimentale et numerique associé au C.N.R.S., Universite de Paris XI, Batiment 362, 91.405 Orsay, France*

1. INTRODUCTION

In recent studies (Wagenaar, 1968, 1969; DuPraw, 1970), connections and associations between mitotic chromosomes were observed in telophase, early interphase, prophase, and metaphase. These were telomeric (end-to-end), centromeric, and interstitial connections (side-by-side). These connectives may not be fortuitous and they could be related to the possible existence of relatively fixed positions for chromosomes in a given metaphasic plate. Those positions are probably determined by the homology of chromosomes. Independently, these connectives are related to the possible existence of a suprachromosomal organization of the nuclear genetic material.

An analysis of the effect of 4-aminouracil on *Vivia faba* suggested that interchromosomal associations may be induced which we have attempted to make visible by several procedures: (i) in squash preparations by DNA-specific Feulgen stain, (ii) on slides with isolated chromosomes, seen under the scanning electron microscope, and (iii) on slides with isolated chromosomes, viewed by the specific staining of chromosomal protein.

2. MATERIAL AND METHODS

Demonstrating the existence of mitotic associations, following treatment with 4-aminouracil required special techniques of chromosome preparation, in addition to routine methods.

Thus, lateral roots of *Vicia faba*, about 2–2.5 cm long, were treated with a solution of 4-aminouracil (10^{-2}M) for 2 hr at a temperature of 23 ± 1°C. One part of a root was used for Feulgen staining and the other part for chromosome isolation.

To study mitotic associations in metaphase squash preparations, material pre-treated with 0.05% colchicine was fixed in 1:3 acetic alcohol at hourly intervals for six hours after treatment. Staining based on the Schiff reaction was used.

For chromosome isolation 4-aminouracil-treated meristematic tips were fixed after colchicine pre-treatment in 5% formaline solution, in neutral phosphate buffer 0.006 M for 1 hour at 2°C. This was followed by homogenization in a mortar and filtration through a nylon tissue with meshes of only 25 μm. Fixative was added to the homogenate and centrifuged at 200 g (aprox. 1000 rpm), 3–4 times for 5 minutes. The material was spread on very clean slides and dried in the air.

Some of the slides with isolated chromosomes were prepared for study under the scanning electron microscope while others were stained to reveal chromosomal protein by the method of alkaline bromophenol blue.

Slides for study under the electron microscope were prepared as follows (Scheid and Traut, 1971): to facilitate visualization of chromosomes, a drop of acetic carmine was placed on the slide and the optical microscope was first used. Slides were then quickly washed with distilled water, passed for 10 min through absolute alcohol and dried in vacuum. Surfaces of about 10 mm/10 mm which contained selected chromosomes were cut with a diamond and then covered with carbon and gold conductor layers.

To stain chromosomal protein, slides with isolated chromosomes were hydrolyzed for 15 min at 90°C in a 5% trichloracetic acid solution (TCA) and then washed in distilled water for 5 min. Staining was made with 0.1% alkaline bromophenol blue for 10 min. Mounted slides were analyzed under the optical microscope.

3. RESULTS AND DISCUSSION.

The table, based on cytological analyses of squash preparations in the optical microscope, presents the frequency of the three types of chromosome connectives at various recovery periods after the treatment. The frequency of the end-to-end (telomeric) and centromeric associations is high, and there is no proportionality between their frequency and the recovery time.

Several chromosomes, usually 5–6, can form radial configurations by centromeric connectives (fig. 1). Associations of 2 or 3 chromosomes linked end-to-end are also found (fig. 2). These associations always occur between the S chromosomes which suggests either a certain homology between them or proximity at metaphase.

Such homology and mitotic association is not surprising if account is taken of the make-up of the karyotype in this species. Thus, the karyotype formula is as follows (Natarajan and Upadhya, 1964): M, Sa, Sb_1, Sb_2, Sb_3, Sc. It seems, therefore, that at least 3 chromosome pairs (Sb_1, Sb_2, Sb_3) are very similar in length (8.6, 8.1, and 7.9 μm, respectively) and distribution of heterochromatic areas. Radial configurations at metaphase in *Vicia faba* were also observed by Kihlman (1952, unpub.). While Hsu (1967) found centromeric connections in *Oppossum*.

Proof of the positive existence and maintenance of these mitotic associations was supplied by the method of isolated chromosomes seen under the scanning

TABLE

Influence of the 4-aminouracil on the chromosomes of Vicia faba

Time after treatment	Metaphase analyzed	Normal, %	Abnormal with/without connections, %	Connections, % end-to-end	centromeric	interstitial
3	85	88.30	11.70	1.85	6.48	0.92
4	121	63.19	36.81	6.61	14.04	4.13
5	98	65.20	34.80	12.24	10.20	2.04
6	122	68.06	31.94	12.29	8.19	7.37

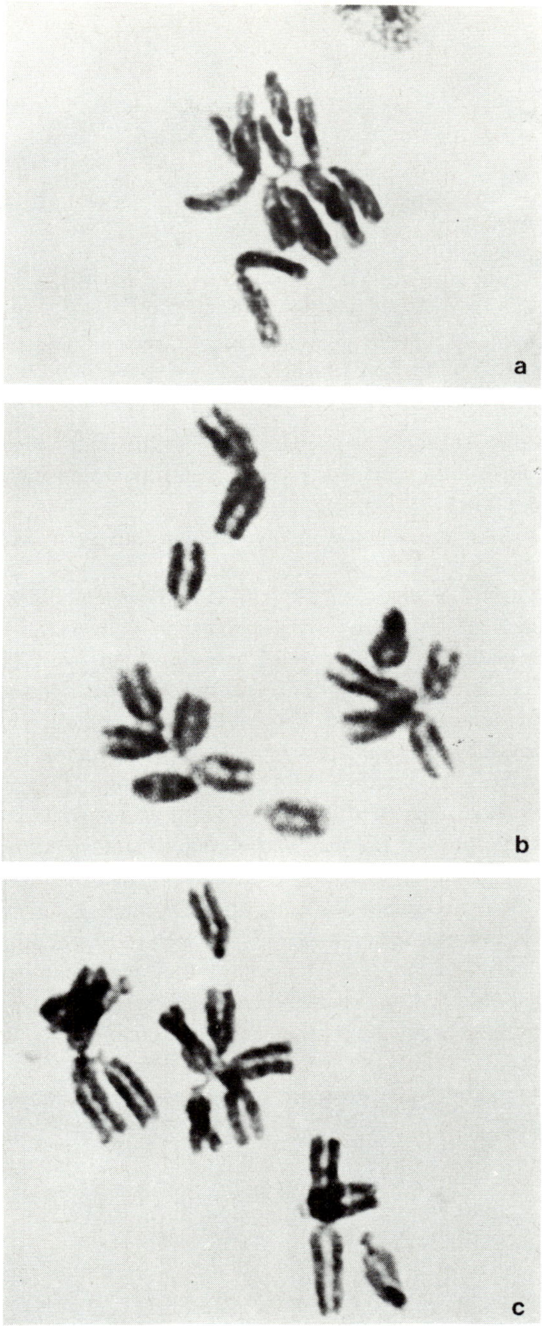

FIG. 1.—Mitotic associations (chromosome-to-chromosome) induced by 4-aminouracil, where all S chromosomes (*a*) or most of them (*b* and *c*) are oriented with the centromere inside and are connected by centromeric or interstitial connectives (revealed by Feulgen staining).

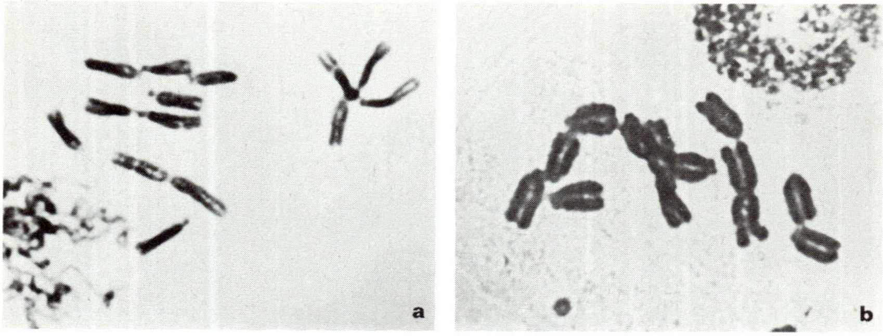

FIG. 2.—Chromosome-to-chromosome connectives of the end-to-end type induced by 4-aminouracil (revealed by Feulgen staining).

electron microscope. The fact that these connections are maintained after the whole procedure used for isolation involving several centrifugations entitles us to believe that they are not artefacts (fig. 3).

These mitotic associations could involve protein, DNA, or both chromosomal components.

On the basis of DNase digestion, Hoskins (1968) considers that DNA is an important component of chromosome-to-chromosome connectives between mitotic chromosomes in man. By specific staining, our investigations indicated that basic protein is an important component of these connectives, at least to the same extent as DNA. It would appear, therefore, that these chromosome-to-chromosome connectives have the same structural characteristics as the chromatid fibers which make up chromosomes (i.e. are formed of DNA and protein) (fig. 4).

Many authors have suggested that these mitotic associations arise because chromosome distribution on the metaphasic plate is not fortuitous but relatively fixed and probably based on homology to a certain extent (German, 1964; Kumar and Natarajan, 1966; Rao and Natarajan, 1967; Raicu et al., 1972). The proof that homologous chromosomes in somatic cells are close to one another was obtained by studying the effects of radiation and other mutagenic agents on chromosomes.

Thus it has been observed that chromosome exchanges in *Vicia faba* mostly occur among homologous chromosomes (Rao and Natarajan, 1967). Further, the fre-

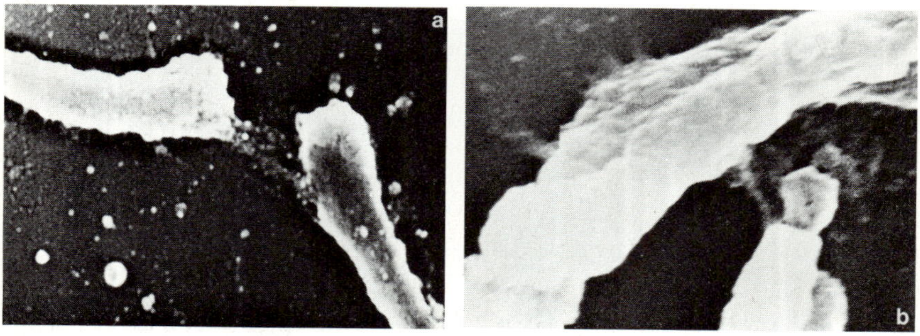

FIG. 3.—Mitotic associations seen under the scanning electron microscope in preparations of isolated chromosomes.

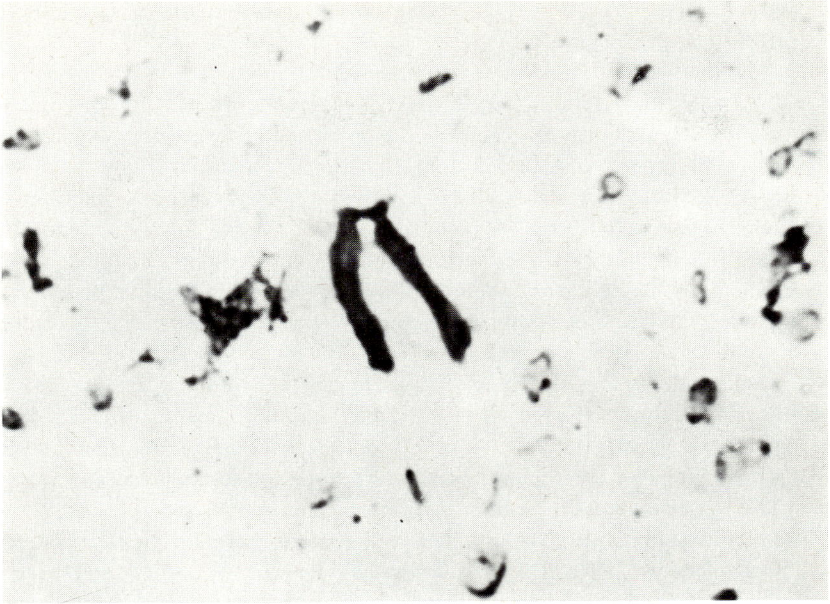

FIG. 4.—Chromosome-to-chromosome connectives, viewed by specific staining for chromosomal basic proteins in preparations of isolated chromosomes.

quency of the somatic crossing-over in fungi and yeasts is increased by the action of some mutagenic treatments such as radiation and alkylating agents, while mitomycin C induces a high frequency of homologous exchanges in human leucocytes (Shaw and Cohen, 1965). Rao and Natarajan (1967) account for the high frequency of homologous exchanges as the result of somatic associations in the interphase, which are maintained throughout the mitotic cycle. Thus, homologous chromosomal exchanges can be accounted for by the proximity of some chromosomes in interphase, which sometimes continues throughout the cellular cycle.

In our material, the associations could have been induced by 4-aminouracil or the treatment could simply have maintained those already present in interphase. We suppose that both processes occur, especially the latter, since connections are otherwise difficult to see at metaphase.

The agent employed is an analogue of uracil which acts mainly on chromosome ends, and some theoretical considerations are relevant to its mode of action. Thus if it is accepted that analogues of uracil prevailingly act on chromosome regions rich in A-T base sequences, producing various types of chromosomal exchanges by thymine substitution, we can suppose that 4-aminouracil also acts at the same levels in yielding mitotic associations. If we allow that 4-aminouracil specifically acts on chromosome regions rich in A-T, it is not surprising that there is a high frequency and end-to-end connectives, since telomers are known to be rich in A-T base sequences (Hsu, 1963).

The effect of 4-aminouracil especially in telomeric regions of the chromosomes does not contradict the commonly found sensitivity of heterochromatic regions to chemical agents, since Ohno (1970), considers that the nature of chromosome telomers is heterochromatic.

The fact that we also found interstitial connectives supports Hsu's (1963) conclusion that "interstitial telomers" can exist. But we do not know whether these mitotic associations depend solely on centromeres or telomeres or whether they can be distributed throughout the chromosome length as Wagenaar (1969) maintains. Feldman (1966) states, however, that the presence of centromeres is sufficient for somatic association to occur.

The hypothesis that, in a given metaphase plate, chromosomes hold determined places and homologous chromosomes lie close together was advocated on the basis of the somatic associations observed. The possible existence of a suprachromosomal structure has also been discussed on the basis of these associations. Thus, these chromosome connectives appear to include "nonsense" DNA very rich in adenine-thymine similar to that discovered in man, mice, and other mammals which could be genetically inactive (DuPraw, 1970). It is supposed that the single folded chromatin fiber is not confined to single chromosomes but extends to several formed of a single giant DNA-protein molecule both longitudinally and transversally.

The relationship between the associations considered here and "sticky" chromosomes produced by chemicals and radiations is not clear.

Stickiness induced in the chromosomes of higher organisms by radiation and chemicals is probably due to the breaking of DNA fibers. The formation of hydrogen bridges between broken ends to give chromosomes which look sticky under the optical microscope is facilitated if the fragments involved contain simple DNA sequences (DuPraw, 1972).

4. SUMMARY

1. Chromosome-to-chromosome connections were induced and/or revealed in *Vicia faba* by means of 4-aminouracil. Such associations can be end-to-end, side-by-side, and centromeric (radial configurations).

2. These interchromosomal associations are maintained in chromosomes isolated for observation by scanning electron microscopy.

3. Selective staining, for DNA and protein, shows that both these components are involved in the chromosome-to-chromosome connectives.

4. The high incidence of associations in telomeric regions rich in AT base sequences suggests that 4-aminouracil affects only these regions, probably by thymine substitution.

5. In *Vicia faba* such associations are observed more often between S-type chromosomes. This corroborates some very recent hypotheses, on a) the non-random disposal of chromosomes in the metaphase plate, and b) the theory of the suprachromosomal organization of the genetic material.

Acknowledgement. The authors are grateful to H. Couderc (CNRS) for his assistance with the scanning electron microscope and for the excellent photographs. We also thank Dr. F. Quetier for providing us with the method for isolated chromosomes and Prof. Dr. M. Ionescu-Varo for the method of staining chromosomal proteins.

5. REFERENCES

DuPraw, E. J. 1970. In *DNA and Chromosomes*, pp. 186–204. Holt, Rinehart and Winston, Inc.

DuPraw, E. J. 1973. Stages in chromosome evolution; the chromatid twins and how they grew. In *Evolution of Genetic Systems, Brookhaven Symp. Biol., 23,* 230–249.

Feldman, M. T., Mello-Sampoia, and Sears E. R. 1966. Somatic association in *Triticum aestivum. Proc. Natl. Acad. Sci. U.S.A., 56,* 1192–1199.

German, J. L. 1964. Cytological evidences for crossing over *in vitro* in human lymphoid cells. *Science, 144,* 298–301.

Hoskins, G. C. 1968. Sensitivity of micrurgically removed chromosomal spindle fibres to enzyme disruption. *Nature (Lond.), 217,* 748–750.

Hsu, T. C. 1963. Longitudinal differentiation of chromosome and the possibility of interstitial telemers. *Exp. Cell. Res.* (Suppl.), *9,* 73–85.

Kihlman, B. A. 1952. Induction of chromosome change with purine derivated. Uppsala, unpublished.

Kumar, S., and Natarajan, A. T. 1966. Kinetics of two break chromosomes and the spatial arrangement of chromosome strands in interphase nucleus, *Nature (Lond.), 209,* 769–797.

Natarajan, A. T. and Upadhya, M. D. 1964. Localised chromosome breakage induced by ethylmethane sulphonate and hydroxylamine in *Vicia faba. Chromosoma (Berl.), 15,* 156–169.

Ohno, S. 1970. *Evolution by Gene Duplication.* Springer Verlag.

Raicu, P., Vladescu, B., and Kirillova, M. 1970. Distribution of chromosomes in metaphase plates of *Mesocricetus newtoni. Genet. Res., 15,* 1–6.

Rao, N. R., and Natarajan, A. T. 1967. Somatic association in relation to chemically induced chromosome association in *Vicia faba. Genetics, 57,* 821–835.

Scheid, W. and Traut, H. 1971. Visualisation by scanning electron microscopy of achromatic lesions ("gaps") induced by X-rays in chromosomes of *Vicia faba. Mutat. Res., 11,* 253–255.

Shaw, M. W., and Cohen, M. M. 1965. Specific effects of viruses and antimetabolites on mammalian chromosomes. In *The Chromosomes-Structural and Functional Aspects.* Miami.

Wagenaar, E. B. 1968. Attached chromosome ends at interphase in *Allium cepa* and *Crepis capilaris. Can. J. Genet. Cytol., 10,* 769.

Wagenaar, E. B. 1969. End-to-end chromosome attachment in mitotic interphase and their possible significance to meiotic chromosome pairing. *Chromosoma (Berl.), 26,* 410.

THE ROLE OF PROTEINS AND DYES IN CHROMOSOME BANDING

A. T. SUMNER

M.R.C. Clinical and Population Cytogenetics Unit, Western General Hospital, Edinburgh, U.K.

1. INTRODUCTION

Although the mechanism of G-banding of chromosomes is far from being understood in terms of chromosome structure and chemical composition, it is now strongly advocated that it depends primarily on the relationship between the DNA and chromosomal proteins, probably non-histones (Comings et al., 1973; Sumner et al., 1973; Sumner and Evans, 1973), and not on any variation in concentration of DNA or protein along the chromosome. Two critical questions for the further understanding of this problem concern the nature of the linear differentiation of the chromosomal proteins, and how this affects the dye-binding properties of the chromosomal DNA. Zakharov et al. (1971), Kato and Yosida (1972) and Utakoji (1973) have all shown that G-banding can be produced by reagents which affect protein sulphydryl or disulphide groups, and further work has indicated a differential distribution of these groups along chromosomes (Sumner, 1974). These studies are amplified in this paper, together with a consideration of how dye-binding properties might be affected.

Q-banding does not appear to be affected by the sulphydryl reagents which affect G-banding. Indeed, it is widely held that Q-banding is primarily a consequence of differences in base composition along the chromosomes, though other factors may also be involved (Pachmann and Rigler, 1972; Ellison and Barr, 1972; Selander and de la Chapelle, 1973; Weisblum and de Haseth, 1972; Weisblum, 1973). We have previously pointed out some objections to this simple hypothesis (Evans and Sumner, 1973), and it seems probable that chromosomal proteins must be involved in Q-banding also. In this paper further objections will be raised against a mechanism based solely on base composition, and evidence presented that proteins are also involved.

2. PROTEIN DISULPHIDES AND SULPHYDRYLS, AND CHROMOSOME BANDING

In the ASG technique for the production of G-bands on chromosomes, the fixed chromosome preparations are incubated in 2 × SSC at 60°C (Sumner et al., 1971). If a reagent which breaks protein disulphide bands is added to the SSC solution no banding is produced, the chromosomes appear swollen, and stain palely with Giemsa (Sumner, 1974). Such results are obtained with 2-mercaptoethanol, thioglycolate, or dithiothreitol (fig. 1a), but banding is obtained on suitable control preparations. On the other hand, if chromosome preparations are treated prior to the ASG

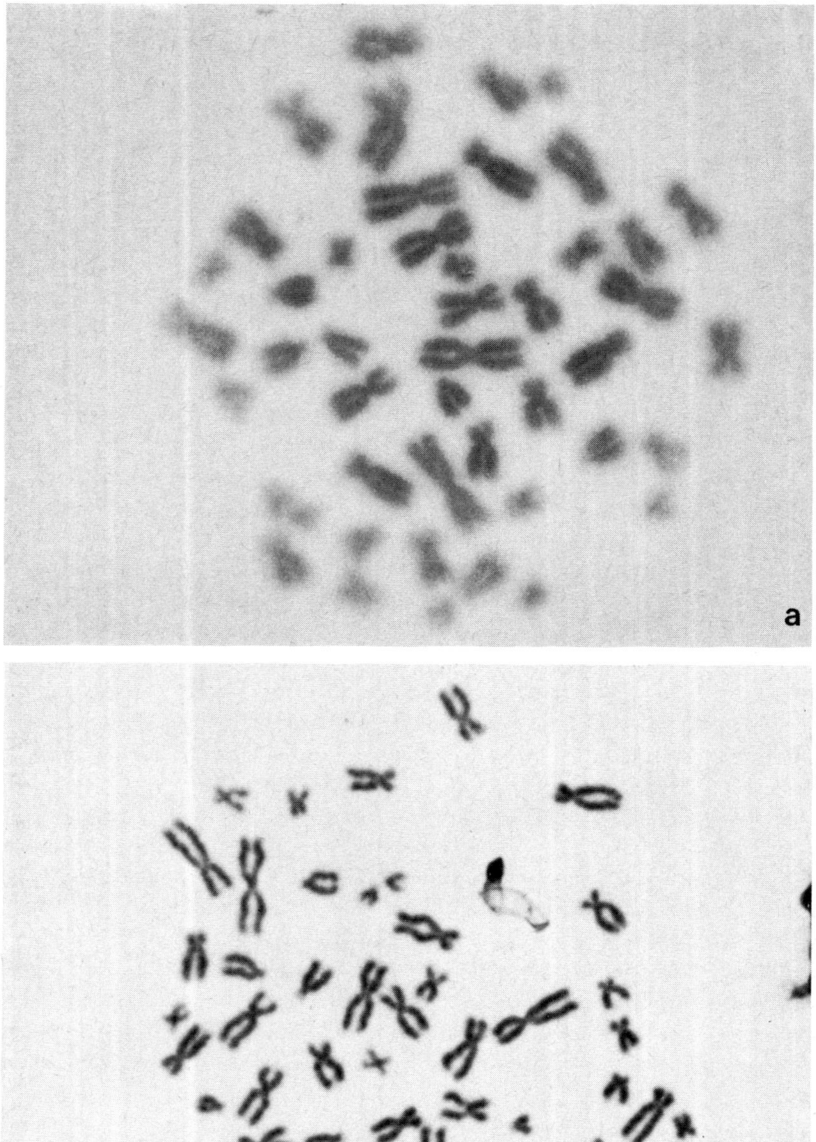

FIG. 1.—a) Human metaphase chromosomes, treated according to the ASG technique for G-bands, but with 1M 2-mercaptoethanol added to the 2 × SSC. Note uniform pale staining and fuzzy swollen appearance. b) Human metaphase chromosomes, treated with 0.001M mercuric chloride in 70% ethanol for 3 days, followed by the ASG technique. Note the uniform dark staining and lack of swelling.

procedure with reagents wich cross-link protein sulphydryls, again no banding is produced. This time the chromosomes are not swollen, and are darkly stained (Sumner, 1974). This type of result can be obtained with mercuric chloride, mercuric chloride followed by iodine, or with *bis*-(acetato-mercurimethyl) dioxane (fig. 1b).

We may interpret these results as follows. The proteins of fixed metaphase chromosomes contain sulphur, which in some microscopically visible regions is predominantly cross-linked to form disulphide bonds, and in other regions is mainly present as free protein sulphydryls. Those regions which are rich in disulphides stain darkly, because the cross-linking maintains the chromosomal DNA in the compact state necessary for strong Giemsa staining. Regions rich in sulphydryls have insufficient cross-linking to maintain them in a compact state when treated with a variety of reagents, and then stain weakly. This would account for the apparent lack of specificity of agents which produce G-bands; breaking of any type of chemical bond would be adequate. Hot saline (Sumner et al., 1971) or urea (Kato and Yosida, 1972) would be expected to break hydrogen bands, while proteases (Finaz and de Grouchy, 1971; Seabright, 1971) break peptide links between specific amino acid residues; treatment with alkali (Sumner et al., 1971; Schnedl, 1971) would tend to disrupt ionic links.

It has also been reported that G-bands may be produced by reagents which break disulphide bonds (Zakharov et al., 1971; Kato and Yosida, 1972; Utakoji, 1973). This could be interpreted to mean that weakly staining bands are rich in disulphides, whereas dark bands are rich in some type of bond which is unaffected by these treatments. This is contrary to the results given above. The possibility of inducing G-bands by reagents which split disulphides was therefore re-investigated. 2-mercaptoethanol (1M) or dithiothreitol (0.1M) were dissolved in 2 × SSC, 1M sodium chloride, or 50% methanol, and slides were treated for 1 hour to 6 days at room temperature (22°C) or at 37°C before staining with Giemsa. Ethylene glycol and erythritol, respectively, were used as control substances. Although in many cases G-bands appeared, to be followed by C-bands or a complete loss of banding after prolonged treatment, no significant differences were found between chromosomes treated with mercaptoethanol or dithiothreitol, and the controls. The authors cited above do not appear to have described results from control procedures, and it is conceivable that the G-banding they obtained was not due to the breakage of disulphide bonds, but was caused by other components of their incubation media. For example, Utakoji (1973) used cupric sulphite at pH 9 as a specific reagent to oxidize both sulphydryls and disulphides, yet mild alkalinity alone is known to produce banding (Patil et al., 1971; Kato and Moriwaki, 1972).

A differential distribution of sulphydryls and disulphides along chromosomes related to the banding patterns may be correlated with a number of other observations about banding. Positive Q- and G-bands are known to be late replicating regions of chromosomes (Ganner and Evans, 1971). Late replication has been linked with genetic inactivity and heterochromatin, and genetically inactive chromatin is rich in protein disulphides (Sadgopal and Bonner, 1970).

Two distinct ageing phenomena may also be explained. It is well known that G-bands cannot usually be induced in chromosome preparations after a few months. Exposure to air would cause the sulphydryls of the negative G-bands to autoxidize to disulphide cross-links, resulting in uniform dark staining. On the other hand, chromosomes uniformly stained with Giemsa and mounted sometimes develop G-bands during storage (Evans et al., 1973; Zuelzer et al., 1973); this may be attributed to reduction of the dye by the concentrations of sulphydryl groups in the regions of the negative bands.

Since Giemsa stains DNA (Sumner and Evans, 1973), the quantity of dye bound to the chromosomes should not be directly affected by the state of sulphydryl and disulphide groups in the associated protein. However, as shown earlier in this paper, breaking disulphide bands causes the chromosomes to swell (see also Dounce et al., 1973). This will affect the concentration of DNA in the chromosomes, and we have previously indicated that binding of Giemsa to DNA is concentration dependent. Preliminary results of further studies confirm not only that Giemsa binding varies with concentration of DNA, but does so in a most irregular fashion (fig. 2). This type of variation helps to explain not only G-banding (although the mechanism is probably more complicated), but also the fact that R-banding can be produced on chromosomes by relatively minor changes in technique.

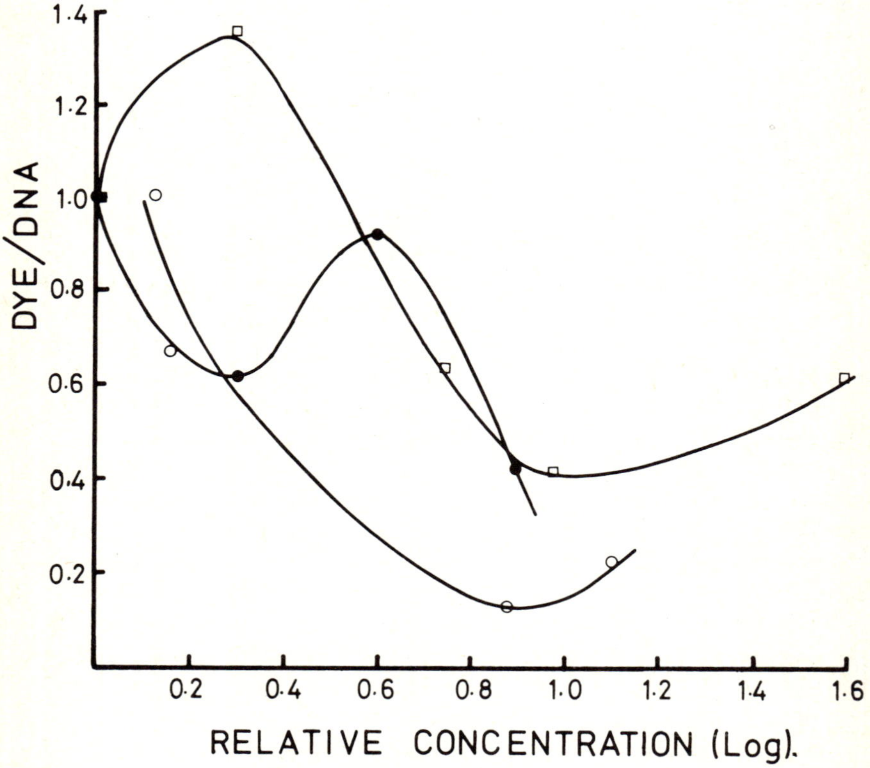

FIG. 2.—Dependence of Giemsa binding on DNA concentration. DNA-gelatine films, containing different relative concentrations of DNA, were prepared according to Sumner and Evans (1973). The amount of the magenta Giemsa compound bound to a given amount of DNA is not constant, but varies irregularly with the concentration of DNA.

3. BASE COMPOSITION AND Q-BANDING

So far no evidence has been obtained that breaking disulphides or cross-linking sulphydryls in chromosomal proteins has any significant effect on Q-banding. This is consistent with the view, now widely held, that Q-banding is primarily a consequence of differences in base composition. In fact, the evidence for this hypothesis is rather limited, and there are several observations against it.

(a) *Evidence for the importance of base composition in Q-banding*

Evidence that Q-banding patterns are a consequence of variation in base composition of chromosomal DNA comes from three sources. In dilute DNA solutions, quinacrine, or quinacrine mustard fluorescence is enhanced by DNA rich in adenine-thymine (AT) base pairs, and quenched by guanine (G) (Pachmann and Rigler, 1972; Weisblum and de Haseth, 1972; Selander and de la Chapelle, 1973). Immunofluorescent staining of chromosomes produces a pattern similar to Q-banding when anti-adenosine is used, and under appropriate conditions a reverse pattern can be obtained with anti-cytidine (Dev et al., 1972; Schreck et al., 1973). Finally, in some species of *Drosophila* and related genera, certain chromosome regions which are believed to contain very AT-rich DNA show brilliant quinacrine fluorescence (Blumenfeld and Forrest, 1971; Barr and Ellison, 1971; Ellison and Barr, 1972).

(b) *General arguments against the importance of base composition in Q-banding*

If the level of quinacrine fluorescence were related only to DNA base composition, Q-banding would not occur unless there were adequate variation of base composition along the chromosomes. It is difficult to obtain an accurate figure for the base composition of strongly and weakly fluorescent bands; however, Tobia et al. (1970) have obtained values for late and early replicating DNA, which may be regarded as equivalent (Ganner and Evans, 1971). Early replicating DNA (negative Q bands) contain 56.4% AT, and late replicating DNA (positive Q bands) 61.3% AT. Thus, brightly fluorescent chromosome regions contain 8.7% more AT than dimly fluorescent regions. Since the relationship between quinacrine flurescence and base composition for naturally occurring DNAs is approximately linear (Selander and de la Chapelle, 1973), and even poly d(GC) shows some fluorescence, brightly fluorescent bands would not be more than about 8% brighter than dim bands if base composition were the sole cause of the difference. Such a small difference would be almost impossible to distinguish, and is indeed much smaller than published values for differences in fluorescence intensity (Caspersson et al., 1970). A similar objection applies to studies with fluorescent antibodies to the different nucleotides in DNA (Dev et al., 1972), suggesting that the distribution patterns obtained in these experiments may be largely determined by factors such as the accessibility of the DNA bases.

(c) *Quinacrine fluorescence of chromosomal regions of known base composition*

The technique of *in situ* hybridization has now been used to localize many different DNA fractions of known base composition onto chromosomes. Although it is not possible to say that a particular chromosomal region contains exclusively those DNA fractions which have been hybridized to it, it is reasonable to suppose that they constitute the major part of the DNA in such regions.

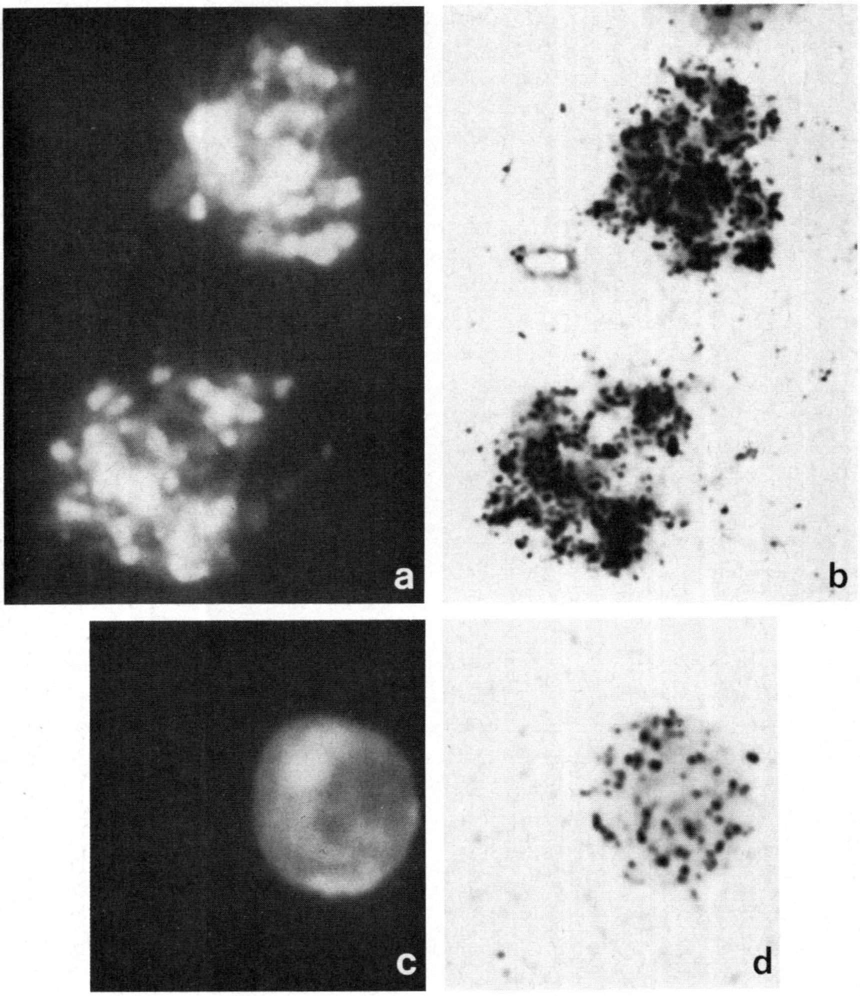

FIG. 3.—*In situ* hybridization of *Cancer pagurus* light satellite DNA. a,c) Quinacrine fluorescence patterns. b,d) Autoradiographs showing distribution of light satellite DNA. a,b) Pachytene cells from testis; autoradiographic label is over both brightly and dimly fluorescent regions, although not all dim regions are labelled. c,d) Sperm; the amount of bright fluorescence is much less than in pachytene cells, and the label is almost uniformly distributed over bright and dim regions.

The Q-banding properties of the centromeric regions of mouse chromosomes are particularly interesting in this connection. These regions contain predominantly mouse satellite DNA (Pardue and Gall, 1970), which is AT rich (33% GC), yet they show dim fluorescence with quinacrine. It has been suggested that this discrepancy could be a consequence of the base sequence of the satellite DNA; if sufficient GC base pairs were interspersed between the AT pairs, then the overall effect might be that of quenching the fluorescence (Weisblum, 1973). The base sequence of mouse satellite DNA is in fact partially known (Southern, 1970): the repeating unit consists of 8 to 13 nucleotides, and includes the sequence TTTTTC. Such a sequence ought to be particularly favourable for enhancement of quinacrine fluorescence.

Strong evidence against the importance of base composition in Q-banding would be the existence of two chromosomal regions having the same DNA composition, but differing in their fluorescence properties. Such a pair are the secondary constriction region of chromosome 9, and the distal part of the long arm of the Y chromosome in man. The former does not fluoresce with quinacrine, while the latter fluoresces brilliantly; yet both regions contain human satellite DNA fractions 1, 2, 3, and 4 (Evans et al., 1974).

To study further the relationship between base composition and Q fluorescence, we have carried out *in situ* hybridization experiments on the edible crab (*Cancer pagurus*) (Sumner et al., in press). These crabs have a large satellite DNA fraction which is almost entirely poly d(AT); their nuclei also show regions of intense Q fluorescence. Although some of the satellite DNA turns out to be localized in highly fluorescent regions, there is also significant labelling in dim regions (fig. 3a, b). Moreover, the pattern of labelling and fluorescence is not constant from one cell type to another. Crab sperm show relatively little fluorescence (fig. 3c), and a uniform pattern of labelling (fig. 3d).

4. EVIDENCE FOR INVOLVEMENT OF PROTEINS IN Q-BANDING

The fact that Q-banding patterns do not, in several respects, agree with what is known about the DNA base composition of chromosomes, suggests that the other main component of fixed chromosomes, protein, must be involved. However, this is essentially negative evidence. To provide positive evidence, one should be able to show that changes in chromosomal proteins affect Q-banding. Natarajan and Gropp (1972) found that the centromeric heterochromatin of the mouse, which is only weakly fluorescent at metaphase, shows strong fluorescence in interphase nuclei, but that this specific fluorescence can be abolished by treatment with trypsin. We have noted above the great difference in the Q fluorescence patterns of sperm and other nuclei of the crab. It may be significant that during spermiogenesis in crabs, basic proteins are lost completely, leaving only acidic proteins. In this respect, crab sperm differs not only from most other sperm, but also from all other crab cells.

So far the evidence for involvement of proteins in Q-banding is largely negative, being based on the realization that differential excitation and quenching by DNA of different base composition cannot explain all the observations. There seems little doubt that further work will provide more direct evidence for the role of chromosomal proteins in Q-banding. An important finding is that G-banding, but apparently not Q-banding, is very much affected by the state of chromosomal protein disulphides and sulphydryls. The similarity of G- and Q-banding patterns has always suggested a common underlying mechanism, but in this respect this does not seem to be true.

5. SUMMARY

1. Evidence is presented which suggests that disulphide cross-linking maintains areas of G-banding in a compact state.
2. The general effect of the numerous and apparently nonspecific G-banding

pretreatments employed is to break down proteins in chromosomal regions rich in sulphydryl bonds. These regions stain weakly and the disulphide-rich regions stain strongly with Giemsa.

3. It is pointed out that Q-banding differentiation cannot be adequately explained on the basis of base composition alone, and *in situ* hybridization data are presented showing a lack of correlation between the distribution of intensely fluorescent chromatin and its AT content. It is suggested that chromosomal proteins must also play a role in Q-banding.

6. REFERENCES

BARR, H. J., and ELLISON, J. R., 1971. Quinacrine staining of chromosomes and evolutionary studies in *Drosophila*. *Nature (Lond.), 233,* 190–191.

BLUMENFELD, M., and FORREST, H. S. 1971. Is *Drosophila* dAT on the Y chromosome? *Proc. Natl. Acad. Sci. U.S.A., 68,* 3145–3149.

CASPERSSON, T., ZECH, L., JOHANSSON, C., and MODEST, E. J. 1970. Identification of human chromosomes by DNA-binding fluorescent agents. *Chromosoma (Berl.), 30,* 215–227.

COMINGS, D. E., AVELINO, E., OKADA, T. A., and WYANDT, H. E. 1973. The mechanism of C- and G-banding of chromosomes. *Exp. Cell Res., 77,* 469–493.

DEV, V. G., WARBURTON, D., MILLER, O. J., MILLER, D. A., ERLANGER, B. F., and BEISER, S. M. 1972. Consistent pattern of binding of anti-adenosine antibodies to human metaphase chromosomes. *Exp. Cell Res., 74,* 288–293.

DOUNCE, A. L., CHANDA, S. K., and TOWNES, P. L. 1973. The structure of higher eukaryotic chromosomes. *J. Theor. Biol., 42,* 275–285.

ELLISON, J. R., and BARR, H. J. 1972. Quinacrine fluorescence of specific chromosome regions. Late replication and high A:T content in *Samoaia leonensis*. *Chromosoma (Berl.), 36,* 375–390.

EVANS, H. J., and SUMNER, A. T. 1973. Chromosome architecture: morphological and molecular aspects of longitudinal differentiation. In *Chromosomes Today, 4* (J. WAHRMAN and K. R. LEWIS, eds.), pp. 15–33. Israel Universities Press, Jerusalem, and John Wiley & Sons, New York.

EVANS, H. J., BUCKLAND, R. A., and SUMNER, A. T. 1973. Chromosome homology and heterochromatin in goat, sheep and ox studied by banding techniques. *Chromosoma (Berl.), 42,* 383–402.

EVANS, H. J., GOSDEN, J. R., MITCHELL, A. R., and BUCKLAND, R. A. 1974. Location of human satellite DNAs on the Y chromosome. *Nature (Lond.), 251,* 346–347.

FINAZ, C., and DE GROUCHY, J. 1971. Le caryotype humain après traitement par l' α-chymotrypsine. *Ann. Génét., 14,* 309–311.

GANNER, E., and EVANS, H. J. 1971. The relationship between patterns of DNA replication and of quinacrine fluorescence in the human chromosome complement. *Chromosoma. (Berl.), 35,* 326–341.

KATO, H., and MORIWAKI, K. 1972. Factors involved in the production of banded structures in mammalian chromosomes. *Chromosoma (Berl.), 38,* 105–120.

KATO, H., and YOSIDA, T. H. 1972. Banding patterns of Chinese hamster chromosomes revealed by new techniques. *Chromosoma (Berl.), 36,* 272–280.

NATARAJAN, A. T., and GROPP, A. 1972. A fluorescence study of heterochromatin and nucleolar organization in the laboratory and tobacco mouse. *Exp. Cell Res., 74,* 245–250.

PACHMANN, V., and RIGLER, R. 1972. Quantum yield of acridines interacting with DNA of defined base sequence. A basis for the explanation of acridine bands in chromosomes. *Exp. Cell Res., 72,* 602–608.

PARDUE, M. L., and GALL, J. G. 1970. Chromosomal localization of mouse satellite DNA. *Science (Wash. D.C.), 168,* 1356–1358.

PATIL, S. R., MERRICK, S., and LUBS, H. A. 1971. Indentification of each human chromosome with a modified Giemsa stain. *Science (Wash. D.C.), 173,* 821–822.

SADGOPAL, A., and BONNER, J. 1970. Proteins of interphase and metaphase chromosomes compared. *Biochim. Biophys. Acta., 207,* 227–239.

SCHNEDL, W. 1971. Banding pattern of human chromosomes. *Nat. New Biol., 233,* 93–94.

SCHRECK, R. R., WARBURTON, D., MILLER, O. J., BEISER, S. M., and ERLANGER, B. F. 1973. Chromosome structure as revealed by a combined chemical and immunochemical procedure. *Proc. Natl. Acad. Sci. U.S.A., 70,* 804–807.

SEABRIGHT, M. 1971. A rapid banding technique for human chromosomes. *Lancet, ii,* 971–972.

SELANDER, R-K, and DE LA CHAPELLE, A. 1973. The fluorescence of quinacrine mustard with nucleic acids. *Nat. New Biol., 245,* 240–244.

SOUTHERN, E. M. 1970. Base sequence and evolution of guinea-pig α-satellite DNA. *Nature (Lond.), 227,* 794–798.

SUMNER, A. T. 1974. Involvement of protein disulphides and sulphydryls in chromosome banding. *Exp. Cell Res., 83,* 438–442.

SUMNER, A. T., and EVANS, H. J. 1973. Mechanisms involved in the banding of chromosomes with quinacrine and Giemsa. II. The interaction of the dyes with the chromosomal components. *Exp. Cell Res., 81,* 223–236.

SUMNER, A. T.. EVANS, H. J., and BUCKLAND, R. A. 1971. New technique for distinguishing between human chromosomes. *Nat. New Biol., 232,* 31–32.

SUMNER, A. T., EVANS, H. J., and BUCKLAND, R. A. 1973. Mechanisms involved in the banding of chromosomes with quinacrine and Giemsa. I. The effects of fixation in methanol-acetic acid. *Exp. Cell. Res., 81,* 214–222.

SUMNER, A. T., MITCHELL, A. R., and GOSDEN, J. R. The relationship of nuclear quinacrine fluorescence to DNA base composition in the edible crab, *Cancer pagurus. Cytobios.* (in press).

TOBIA, A. M., SCHILDKRAUT, C. L., and MAIO, J. J. 1970. Deoxyribonucleic acid replication in synchronized cultured mammalian cells. I. Time of synthesis of molecules of different average guanine + cytosine content. *J. Mol. Biol., 54,* 499–515.

UTAKOJI, T. 1973. Differential staining of human chromosomes after oxidation treatment. In *Chromosome Identification—Technique and Applications in Biology and Medicine* (T. CASPERSSON and L. ZECH, eds.), pp. 346–349. Academic Press, New York.

WEISBLUM, B. 1973. Why centric regions of quinacrine-treated mouse chromosomes show diminished fluorescence. *Nature (Lond.), 246,* 150–151.

WEISBLUM, B., and DE HASETH, P. L. 1972. Quinacrine, a chromosome stain specific for deoxyadenylate-deoxythymidylate-rich regions in DNA. *Proc. Natl. Acad. Sci. U.S.A., 69,* 629–632.

ZAKHAROV, A. F., SELEZNEV, J. V., BENJUSCH, V. A., BARANOVSKAYA, L. I., and DEMINTSEVA, V. S. 1971. Differentiation along human chromosomes in relation to chromosome identification. *Excerpta Med. Int. Congr. Ser., 233,* 193.

ZUELZER, R. T., OTTENBREIT, M., INOUE, S., and ZUELZER, W. W. 1973. Banding in old chromosome preparations. *Lancet, ii,* 270.

DIFFERENTIAL FLUOROCHROMING OF MAMMALIAN CHROMOSOMES WITH PROTEIN-SPECIFIC DANSYL CHLORIDE AND N-BROMOSUCCINIMIDE

TADASHI UTAKOJI

Department of Pathology, Cancer Institute, Toshima-ku, Tokyo 170, Japan

1. INTRODUCTION

The fact that protein-specific reagents such as trypsin (Ridler, 1971) and sulfitolytic agents (Utakoji, 1973), and some of the protein-denaturing agents (Kato and Moriwaki, 1972) can be successfully applied in G-banding procedures strongly implies the involvement of chromosomal proteins in G-band formation. However, relatively few attempts have been reported which demonstrate directly the protein distribution in the chromosome. Information about the protein-DNA complex in metaphase chromosomes would be important for elucidating the chemical organization of mammalian chromosomes as well as for analyzing the basis of differential staining of metaphase chromosomes. A study of the chemical background of chromosome bandings may be regarded as a molecular distribution study within a single mammalian metaphase chromosome. Well-defined chemical specificity of the staining reaction and high sensitivity of the detection of changes in chromosome preparations caused by the staining procedures appear to be prerequisites for such studies.

1-Dimethylaminonaphthalene-5-sulfonyl chloride (abbreviation: dansyl chloride) was employed in our current study on the distribution of proteins within a single chromosome, since dansyl chloride appeared to meet the above-described prerequisites. Dansyl chloride reacts with amino acids, peptides, and proteins, and the resulting sulfonamide conjugates are intensely fluorescent under ultraviolet irradiation (Hartley and Massey, 1956; Chen, 1967). It does not react with nucleic acids and their components (Ringertz, 1968; Rosselet and Ruch, 1968).

N-Bromosuccinimide is also known to cause proteins to fluoresce in the presence of phosphate (Brand and Shaltiel, 1963). The detailed mechanism of the reaction has not yet been elucidated, but histidines and tryptophans in peptides and proteins are responsible mainly for the fluorescence. Neighboring residues to the histidine in peptides are known to influence the intensity of the fluorescence upon treatment with N-bromosuccinimide (Brand and Shaltiel, 1963).

In the present report differential staining of L-cell chromosomes with dansyl chloride, and the chromosome fluorescence upon treatment with N-bromosuccinimide will be presented.

2. MATERIALS AND METHODS

(a) *Chromosome preparations*

Mouse-derived L-cell metaphases were harvested with 0.2% trypsin, hypotonically treated with 0.075 M KCl for 15 min at room temperature (20°–25°C), and fixed with methanol-acetic acid mixture (3:1). Ordinary air-dried chromosome spreads were made without heating or flaming.

(b) *Staining with dansyl chloride*

Dansyl chloride solution in acetone (1.2%) was mixed with the same volume of 0.2 M acetate buffer at pH 5.0, of 0.2 M phosphate buffer at pH 7.0, and of 0.2 M $NaHCO_3$ in water (pH of resulting mixture about 9.5), respectively, to compare the effect of pH on the formation of fluorescent conjugates. Slides were stained overnight at 37°C, washed with 50% acetone in water, air-dried, and sealed with Eukitt (O. Kindler, Freiburg). Some slides were treated with 10 mM NaCl for 24 hr at 4°C or with 0.2 N HCl for one hr at room temperature before dansyl chloride staining (Utakoji and Matsukuma, 1974).

Dansyl chloride-stained slides were observed with a Zeiss fluorescence microscope fitted with a vertical illuminator, super-pressure mercury lamp, BG 12 + BG 38 exciter filters, and a barrier filter 50.

(c) *Staining with N-bromosuccinimide*

N-Bromosuccinimide was dissolved to 0.1 mM in 0.1 M Sørensen's phosphate buffer at pH 7.4. Air-dried chromosome preparations were treated with this solution for 15 min at room temperature (20°–25°C), washed with running tap water for about 30 sec, air-dried, and sealed with Eukitt which contained 1% 2,6-di-*tert*-butyl-*p*-cresol as an antioxidant. Chromosome fluorescence was examined under the same observing conditions as for the dansyl chloride-stained preparations.

3. RESULTS AND DISCUSSION

(a) *Fluorescence of dansyl chloride-stained chromosomes*

Metaphase chromosomes in untreated control slides, when stained with dansyl chloride, showed a relatively uniform and bright yellowish green fluorescence. There was no apparent difference in the fluorescence intensity either within or between chromosomes of the same metaphase plate. With regard to the fluorescence intensity of chromosomes stained at three different pH values, there were no distinct differences in the brightness of the chromosomes. However, it appeared that the fluorescence of the chromosomes stained at pH 9.5 was the brightest, and that the chromosome fluorescence stained at pH 5 was slightly less bright than that stained at higher pH values.

When chromosome preparations were treated with 0.2 N HCl before dansyl chloride-staining, the fluorescence was generally reduced, except at the centromeric regions. This indicates that an amount of acid-soluble protein existed in the air-dried chromosomes, especially in the euchromatic parts of the L-cell chromosome arms. This finding is contrary to some observations reported previously (Comings et al., 1973; Sumner et al., 1973; Vogel et al., 1974), but we believe that this reflects the high sensitivity of the protein-fluorochroming by dansyl chloride.

When the chromosome preparations were stained with dansyl chloride at pH 9.5 after treatment with 10 mM NaCl for 24 hr at 4°C, the fluorescence in chromosomes was less bright than that in control slides. The centromeric regions of each chromosome and several interstitial regions of particular chromosomes showed distinctly brighter fluorescence than the rest of the chromosome regions, as presented in figure 1. In these slides treated with 10 mM NaCl, chromosome regions other than the above-described brighter segments exhibited subtle differences in their fluorescence intensity. The differences were, however, too small to permit comparison of the differentiation to G-bands even from photographic records. It was noted that the chromosomes were swollen and the contour of the chromatid was brighter than the chromatid itself (Utakoji and Matsukuma, 1974).

(b) *Chromosome fluorescence on the treatment with N-bromosuccinimide*

The bluish white fluorescence of L-cell chromosomes treated with N-bromosuccinimide was very dull compared with the fluorescence of chromosomes stained with dansyl chloride. However, the intensity of the fluorescence was rather stable and remained at approximately the same intensity for relatively long periods of observation. The fluorescence appeared to be relatively uniform along the chromosome length (fig. 2), especially in freshly made chromosome preparations. When chromosome spreads kept for more than several days were treated with N-bromosuccinimide, the fluorescence at the centromeric regions of L-cell chromosomes, particularly the centromeric regions of some bi-armed chromosomes, appeared to be darker than the rest of the chromosome regions. It may be regarded as the re-

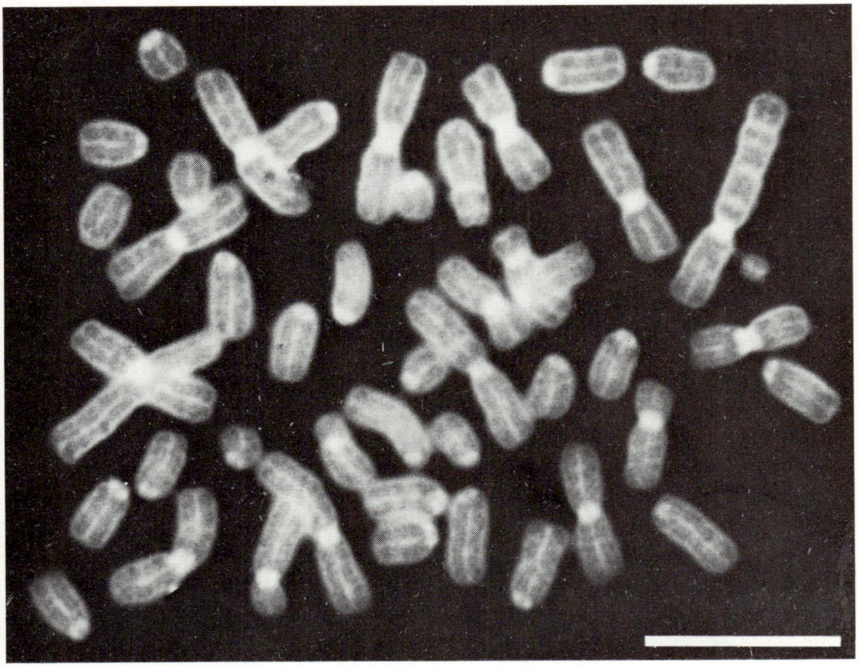

FIG. 1.—A metaphase plate stained with dansyl chloride after treatment with 10 mM NaCl for 24 hr at 4°C. Although this treatment of air-dried chromosomes with 10 mM NaCl produces G-bands with Giesma staining, only centromeric regions, several other interstitial regions of chromosome arms, and contours of chromatids are stained fluorescent (scale 10 μm).

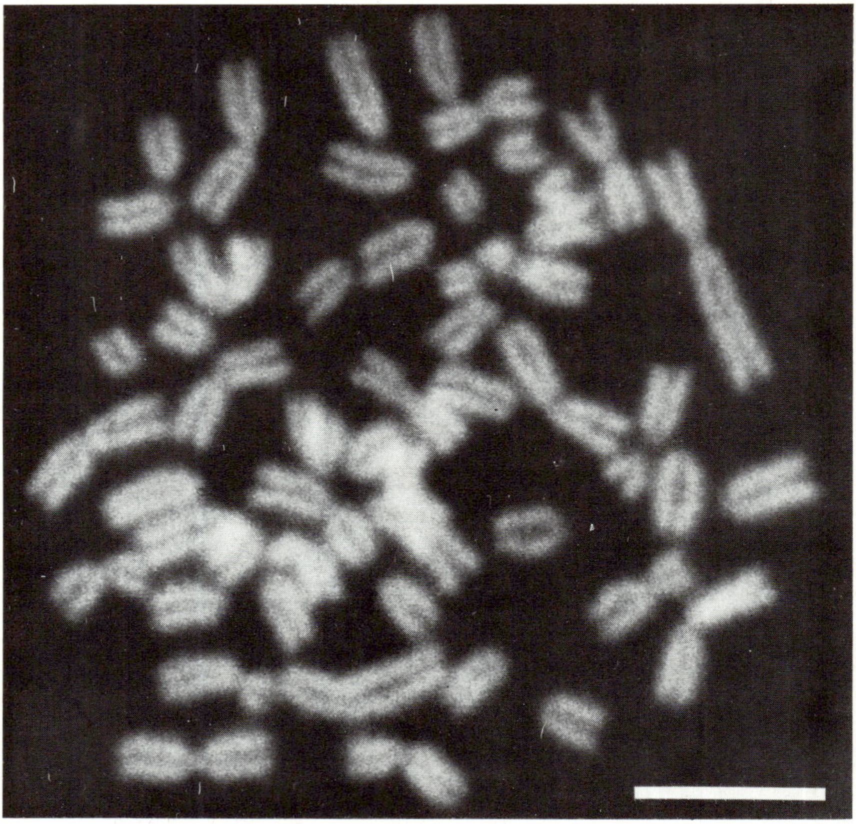

FIG. 2.—A metaphase plate treated with N-bromosuccinimide. The bluish white fluorescence, which was reported to be histidine residue specific, is dull. The fluorescence at the centromeric regions in some bi-armed chromosomes appears to be darker than that in other regions of chromosome arms (scale 10μm).

versed pattern of the fluorescence observed in 10 mM NaCl-treated and dansyl chloride-stained chromosomes. Chromosomes treated with 10 mM NaCl and with 0.2 N HCl, respectively, did not show any appreciable fluorescence after treatment with N-bromosuccinimide.

4. CONCLUSIONS

1. From the above observations of the chromosome fluorescence in the preparations stained with dansyl chloride and with N-bromosuccinimide it can be concluded that a particular protein (or proteins) is associated with the centromeric regions of L-cell chromosomes.

2. The protein is insoluble in 0.2 N HCl and may be classified as a non-histone protein. This particular protein is not fluorescent or only weakly fluorescent after treatment with N-bromosuccinimide.

3. The reason for the weaker fluorescence in the centromeric regions is as yet unknown. However, suggested explanations are:

(a) This peculiar non-histone protein contains only few histidine residues.

(b) The amount of histidine in this protein is not significantly different from that in other proteins distributed along the chromosome arms, but the tertiary structure of the protein is different. This results in a weakening of the fluorescence emission after treatment with N-bromosuccinimide.

(c) Association of this protein with the A-T-rich repetitious DNA distributed mainly in the centromeric regions of mouse chromosomes may cause fluorescence quenching for reasons unknown.

Acknowledgements. This study was supported in part by research grants from the Ministry of Education, Japan, and from the Princess Takamatsu Cancer Research Fund. Appreciation is extended to Dr. H. Sugano of this institute for his advice and encouragement, and to Miss A. Sekiguchi for her skillful technical assistance throughout this study.

5. REFERENCES

BRAND, L., and SHALTIEL, S. 1963. Appearance of fluorescence on treatment of histidine residues with N-bromosuccinimide. *Biochim. Biophys. Acta, 75,* 145–148.

CHEN, R. F. 1967. Fluorescence of dansyl amino acids in organic solvents and protein solutions. *Arch. Biochem. Biophys., 120,* 609–620.

COMINGS, D. E., AVELINO, E., OKADA, T. A., and WYANDT, H. E. 1973. The mechanism of C- and G-banding of chromosomes. *Exp. Cell Res., 77,* 469–493.

HARTLEY, B. S., and MASSEY, V. 1956. The active centre of chymotrypsin. I. Labelling with a fluorescent dye. *Biochim. Biophys. Acta., 21,* 58–70.

KATO, H., and MORIWAKI, K. 1972. Factors involved in the production of banded structures in mammalian chromosomes. *Chromosoma (Berl.), 38,* 105–120.

RIDLER, M. A. C. 1971. Banding patterns of metaphase chromosomes in Down's syndrome. *Lancet, ii,* 354–356.

RINGERTZ, N. R. 1968. Cytochemical demonstration of basic proteins by dansyl staining. *J. Histochem. Cytochem., 16,* 440–441.

ROSSELET, A., and RUCH, F. 1968. Cytofluorometric determination of lysine with dansyl chloride. *J. Histochem. Cytochem., 16,* 459–466.

SUMNER, A. T., EVANS, H. J., and BUCKLAND, R. A. 1973. Mechanisms involved in the banding of chromosomes with quinacrine and Giemsa. I. The effects of fixation in methanol-acetic acid. *Exp. Cell Res., 81,* 214–222.

UTAKOJI, T. 1973. Differential staining of human chromosomes treated with potassium permanganate and its blocking by organic mercurials. In *Chromosomes Today, 4* (J. WAHRMAN and K. R. LEWIS, eds.), pp. 53–59. Israel Universities Press, Jerusalem, and John Wiley & Sons, New York.

UTAKOJI, T., and MATSUKUMA, S. 1974. Fluorescent staining of L-cell chromosomes and chromocenters with 1-dimethylaminonaphthalene-5-sulfonyl chloride and G-bandings. *Exp. Cell Res., 87,* 111–119.

VOGEL, W., FAUST, J., SCHMID, M., and SIEBERS, J.-W. 1974. On the relevance of non-histone proteins to the production of Giemsa banding patterns on chromosomes. *Humangenetik, 21,* 227–236.

CHROMOSOME CONDENSATION AND DIFFERENTIAL STAINING

R. D. G. MCKAY

MRC Mammalian Genome Unit, Department of Zoology, University of Edinburgh, West Mains Road, Edinburgh, U. K.

1. INTRODUCTION

The discovery of different techniques for staining chromosomes differentially has provoked a great deal of discussion and experimental work. Initial hypotheses attributed the differential staining to differences in base composition with quinacrine staining (Caspersson et al., 1968) and to differential rates of reassociation of repeated DNA in the case of G- and C-bands (Sumner et al., 1971; Arrighi and Hsu, 1971). Although these interpretations have been extensively modified there is still a great deal of controversy in this field and a profusion of explanations for the many different techniques. In this paper I would like to present evidence that leads to a hypothesis which includes most, if not all, of these disparate observations in a single framework. I propose that the differential staining is due to a differential packing of chromatin rather than to a primary property such as the base composition DNA or the repetitive nature of the DNA.

I will first examine, in some detail, the evidence that G-bands are caused by the differential distribution of chromatin and then show how the other staining patterns can be accounted for by the same mechanism. The many different explanations for G-bands rest on the variety of treatments that are thought to induce them. This makes the necessity of particular post-fixation treatments very important as the interpretation is derived from these steps.

2. METHODS OF OBTAINING G-BANDS

Most methods of obtaining G-bands are based on treating the fixed chromosome in one of a variety of ways before staining them (Sumner et al., 1971; Kato and Moriwaki, 1972; Kato and Yosida, 1972; Lee et al., 1973; Seabright, 1972; Utakoji, 1972; see Nilsson, 1973). This type of treatment is illustrated in line 1 of table 1. More recently the living cells have been exposed to some agent in the G2 phase prior to metaphase and the fixed chromosomes are then simply stained in order to obtain G-bands (table 1, line 2) (Hsu et al., 1973).

While this treatment certainly has some effect on the chromosomes and may enhance banding, the simple conclusion that it directly causes banding is unlikely to be true, since G-bands can be obtained on fixed chromosomes without any treatment other than staining (table 1, line 3; figs. 1a and 2; McKay, 1973; Yunis and Sanchez, 1973).

It might be thought that the staining procedure itself causes G-bands, but this is also not a necessary step as bands corresponding to G-bands can be observed by

TABLE 1

Diagram of the different types of technique for obtaining G- and Q-bands (S, G_2 and M refer to stages of the cell cycle.)

G BANDS

1. S—G_2—M ⟶ fixed ⟶ treated ⟶ stained
2. S—G_2—M ⟶ fixed ⟶ stained
   treated
3. S—G_2—M ⟶ fixed ⟶ stained
4. S—G_2—M ⟶ fixed

Q BANDS

1. S—G_2—M ⟶ fixed ⟶ stained

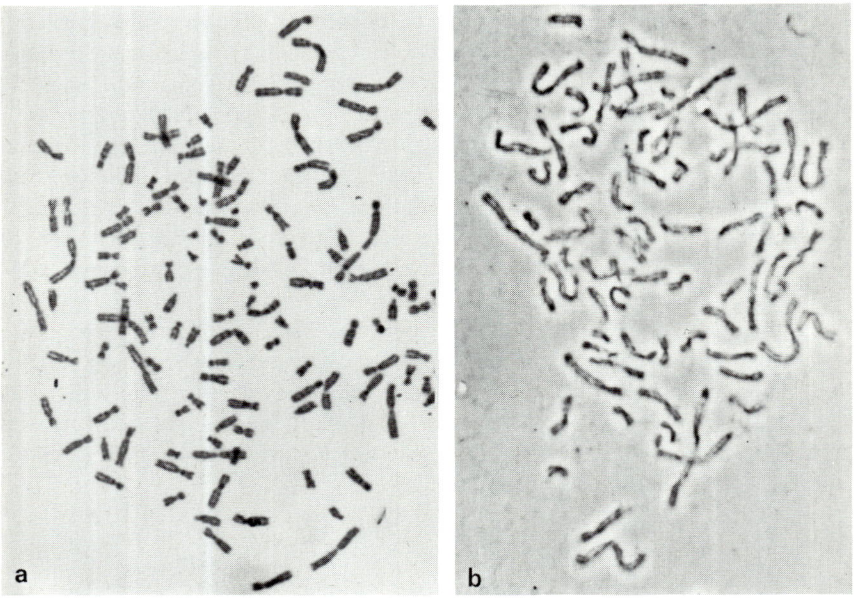

FIG. 1.—The chromosomes of the HeLa cell line showing G-bands (a) and phase bands (b). The G bands were obtained by staining fixed chromosomes (table 1, line 3). The phase bands shown are on a fixed, untreated metaphase spread (table 1, line 4). The methods have been reported previously for mouse L cells (McKay, 1973).

phase contrast microscopy of the fixed chromosomes ("phase bands"; table 1, line 4; fig. 1b; McKay, 1973). Although postfixation treatment and staining do affect chromosome structure, these observations make it extremely difficult to interpret the effect of treatments either after fixation or in the G2 phase.

3. THE BASIS OF G-BANDS

The different techniques for obtaining G-bands (table 1) appear to represent a complex situation but one which can be resolved by considering the nature of G-

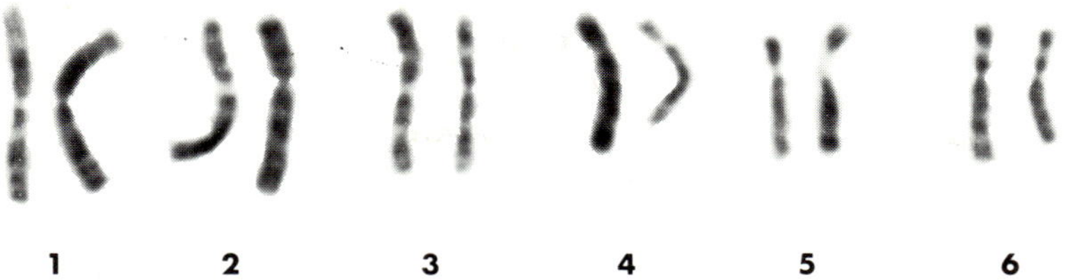

FIG. 2.—A partial human karyotype from cultured peripheral lymphocytes. The G-bands were obtained simply by staining fixed chromosomes.

bands. The observation of bands by phase contrast microscopy allows one to investigate the distribution of chromatin without any intervening biochemical treatment. Ultraviolet microscopy in the wavelength 260 ± 5 nm reveals the distribution of DNA, which absorbs light of this wavelength maximally. The DNA distribution has been shown to correspond to the G- and phase bands (McKay, 1973). This confirms the results of Kato and Moriwaki (1972), Rodman and Tahiliani (1973), and Yunis and Sanchez (1973) who showed the presence of bands by Feulgen staining, which is also specific for DNA. It appears then that the G-bands correspond to a differential distribution of chromatin. I have proposed that this differential distribution is caused by a differential condensation of chromatin *in vivo* (McKay, 1973). The evidence for this derives firstly, from the fact that the method of preparing fixed chromosomes can be altered radically but the phase bands are still observed, and secondly, from the correspondence between G-bands and pachytene chromosome chromomeres as shown by Ferguson-Smith and Page (1973); the pachytene chromomeres are known to occur *in vivo* as they have been observed in living cells. It seems probable that pachytene chromomeres and G-bands correspond to the same structure.

Treatments which interfere with chromosome condensation are known to lead to chromosomes with regions which are extended (Woodward and Swift, 1964; Zhakarov and Egolina, 1972). G-bands which are obtained by treatment of the living cells in the G2 phase of the cell cycle may also be caused by an alteration in this process of condensation (table 1, line 2; Hsu et al., 1973; Meisner et al., 1973).

It is still necessary, however to explain the role of postfixation treatment (table 1, line 1). It is a familiar observation, particularly in the presence of colchicine, that chromosomes appear to be uniformly contracted. If colchicine is omitted much more chromosome structure can be seen in individual cells. Although the G-banding pattern is stable in development (Burkholder and Comings, 1972), chromosome morphology can change dramatically and reversibly after fixation (McKay, 1973). Polyvalent cations seem to have an important role in maintaining chromosome structure (McKay, 1973). The azure component of Giemsa stain is a polyvalent cation and it may be this moiety, interacting with chromatin, that is the basis of the stain's action. One would expect a polyvalent cation to assist in packing negatively charged DNA molecules. It is clear then that even after fixation the distribution of chromatin can be reversibly changed and it is probably by altering the chromatin distribution that postfixation treatments act. The specificity of the G-banding pattern, however, appears to reside within the chromosome and not in the dye or the preceding treatment.

The formation of G-bands by this variety of techniques can then be accounted for by a single mechanism, differential chromosome condensation. This is a process which can be modified *in vivo* or revealed after the chromosomes have been fixed. This proposition has interesting biological and clinical implications. The similarity between G-bands and meiotic chromomeres (Ferguson-Smith and Page, 1973) suggests that we are now able to reveal, in mitotic metaphase chromosomes, the same types of structures that have aroused so much interest in other cells. What, for instance, is the genetic significance of this arrangement? Is there any functional unity between genes in a G-band as there appears to be for a band in *Drosophila* polytene chromosome (Judd and Young, 1973). The clinical significance of this hypothesis is that one may see changes in the banding pattern which are not due to major genetic changes, such as deletions, but are caused by alterations in the pattern of condensation. The clinical consequences of this type of genetic change are unclear.

4. OTHER TYPES OF DIFFERENTIAL STAINING

There is an increasing amount of evidence indicating that other types of differential staining (Q-, R-, T-, and C-bands) can be explained by the same mechanisms of chromosome condensation.

Q-bands

The initial reports of differential staining with quinacrine mustard attributed this to the specificity of the mustard group for the base guanine (Caspersson et al., 1968). It was shown later that quinacrine hydrochloride, which lacked this group, gave the same banding pattern (Evans et al., 1971). Further cytological and biochemical work suggested that the quinacrine reveals regions rich in the bases adenine and thymine (Ellison and Barr, 1972; Weisblum, 1973). While this hypothesis does not necessarily conflict with the differential distribution of chromatin, there are strong reasons for criticizing the base composition theories (Bostock and Christie, 1974). Recently Golomb and Bahr (1974*a*) have observed regular chromomeric structures in mitotic chromosomes by scanning electron microscopy. It should be noted that these structures were observed without any fixation in methanol-acetic acid, special treatment, or staining. The distribution of chromatin is almost identical to the fluorescence after quinacrine staining (Golomb and Bahr, 1974*b*). Golomb and Bahr's work appears to have revealed "phase" bands and shown these to be complementary to Q-bands. It has already been shown that phase bands are complementary to G-bands (McKay, 1973) and that G-bands are very similar to Q-bands (Evans et al., 1971). In a number of cases phase, Q- and G-bands appear to be the same structures and this makes a strong case for including Q-bands in the class of differential staining phenomena that are caused by differential chromatin condensation.

C-bands

C-bands were first observed using techniques of *in situ* hybridization (Arrighi and Hsu, 1971; Pardue and Gall, 1970;Jones, 1970) and this led to the view that the differential staining was due to the differential reassociation of highly repeated sequences of DNA. That this is not the case was shown by the fact that C-bands can be obtained after treatment with 8 M urea dissolved in Sørensen's buffer and staining in Giemsa (McKay, 1973). This treatment does not denature DNA or chromatin in solution (Britten et al., 1969; cited by Thomas et al., 1970). It was concluded that C-bands are caused by a differential destruction of chromosome morphology (McKay, 1973). A number of reports suggest that this destruction is due to the loss of DNA from the euchromatic chromosome arms (Comings et al., 1973; Hsu and Arrighi, 1973; Pathak and Arrighi, 1973). This explanation of C-bands fits very well with the hypothesis presented here, because the C-banding procedures are thought to be altering the relative distribution of chromatin along the chromosome, the heterochromatic regions being more tightly packed *in vivo* and more resistant to the post-fixation treatment. So here again the differential staining is a result of the differences in condensation in the cell.

It has often been shown that C-bands occupy those regions of the chromosome that contain least material in phase contrast (the primary and secondary constrictions) or by Feulgen staining (Vosa, 1976). These are surprising observations and might be thought to contradict the mechanism of C-banding proposed above. If it is really the material in the secondary constrictions that stains in C-banding, then there may be something peculiar about the primary characteristics of these regions. That this is not the case is shown by observations on chromosomes in which the centromere is extended.

The administration of BrdU to mouse L cells in late S phase leads to marked extension of the centromeres, which is particularly obvious in metacentric chromosomes

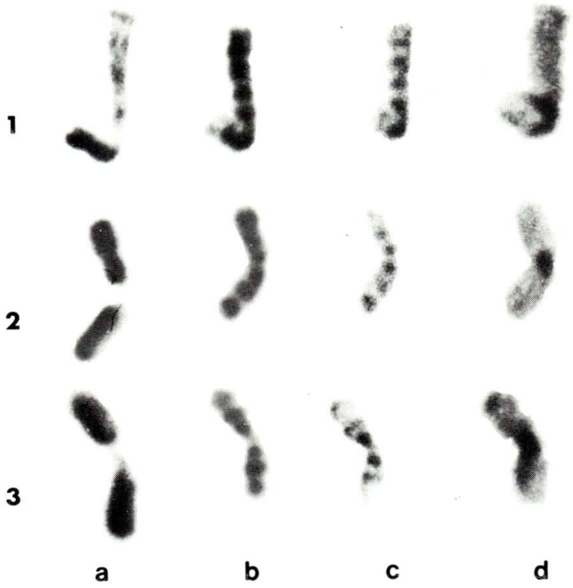

FIG. 3.—Mouse L cell chromosomes showing the extended centromeres obtained after treatment with BdrU (400 μg/ml, in the last quarter of S phase). Column *a* shows these chromosomes in phase contrast. The chromosomes were then treated with 8 M urea dissolved in Sørensen's buffer for 1 hr (b) and 3 hr (c) and subsequently stained with Giemsa. There appears to be a gradual shift from the G- to the C-bands which are clear after a C-banding procedure (Sumner, 1972). Note the shift of stain into the extended centromere.

(Stewart, 1973). This material allows the shift of staining with C-banding to be closely analyzed. In figure 3 the changes of staining with increasing lengths of incubation in 8 M urea are shown. The extended centromeres can be seen in the phase contrast photomicrograph. After short treatment in 8 M urea the G-bands can be seen. As this treatment is extended the G-bands gradually disappear leaving the C-bands still separated by the extended centromere in the metacentric chromosomes. After further treatment with the barium hydroxide C-banding procedure (Sumner, 1972) only the extended region is darkly staining. This shift in staining pattern also occurs on the marker chromosome found in L cells but much more readily (fig. 4).

As I have argued that Giemsa staining represents the relative distribution of chromatin, it is rather surprising that the region of the chromosome that contains least material to start with ends up with relatively more. There are three possible explanations for this change: 1. material is either a) lost from the arms or b) made non-stainable; 2. material in the extended regions greatly increases its ability to bind dye; 3. there is an actual shift of staining material into the extended centromere. Which of these explanations is correct is of some interest for two reasons. Firstly,

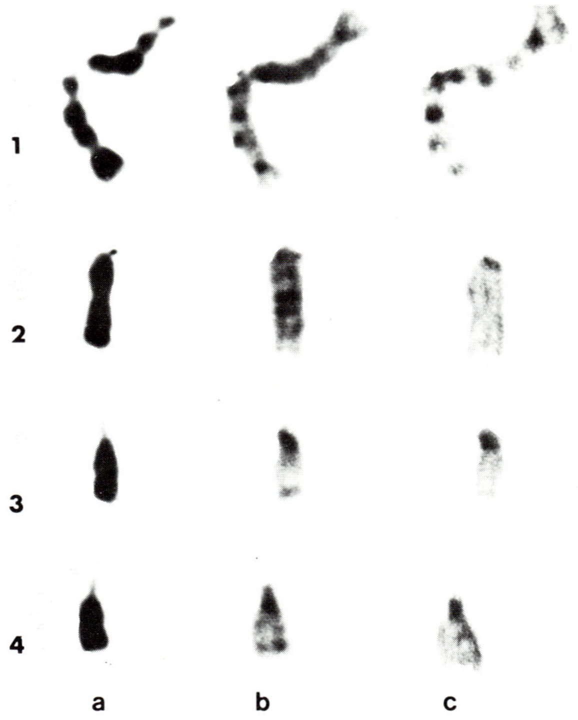

FIG. 4.—BdrU treated mouse L cell chromosomes. (a) phase contrast; (b) after 1 hr 8 M urea treatment; (c) after C-banding (Sumner, 1972). Note the shift of stain into the secondary constrictions of the marker chromosome (a) even after 1 hr of the 8 M urea treatment. With the same treatment the other chromosomes are G-banded (2). In the two telocentric chromosomes (3 and 4) the extended centromere can be clearly seen in phase contrast (a), and it is this region that is intensely stained after C-banding (c).

if explanation 1b or 2 is correct then there is no stoichiometry between the distribution of chromatin and the Giesma pattern, and secondly, if the third explanation is true then a great deal of care must be taken in interpreting experiments which are designed to localize particular DNA sequences on the chromosome, as these treatments may be altering the linear distribution of DNA. Further experiments should distinguish between these possibilities, but for the present it seems very likely that C-bands are due to preferential DNA loss from the euchromatic regions.

R- and T-bands

The question arises as to whether this type of shift in staining pattern is in any way related to R- and T-bands. RecentlyDutrillaux and Covic (1974) have analyzed the factors leading to G-, R-, T-, and C-bands. They found that by altering such simple parameters as salt concentration, temprature, and pH it was possible to obtain a sequential change of banding pattern. They conclude that there is a progressive destruction of chromosome structure that gives rise to the patterns in the order G, R, T and C. This evidence correlates very well with the hypothesis that the banding patterns are based on differential chromatin condensation and the progressive disruption of this organization.

It is clear from the data presented here that any hypothesis that is based on differential staining of particular components of chromatin will have to correct for differences in the gross distribution of chromatin and changes in this distribution caused by the treatment itself. For as Lezzi (1970) has shown in polytene chromosomes, precise alterations in the pattern of condensation can result from simple changes in the environment. It is clear from Lezzi's work that these changes can be reversible and it may be that the changes in mitotic chromosomes are also reversible. It appears that disulphide bonds may be involved in maintaining chromosome structure (Sumner, 1976) as well as reversible ionic bonds (McKay, 1973).

It appears that it is possible to account for all the different banding patterns by the single hypothesis of differential condensation of chromatin. This suggests that further understanding of the mechanism of staining requires a knowledge of the chemical basis of chromosome contraction.

5. SUMMARY

1. It is clear that there are important differences of opinion over the mechanism of chromosome banding patterns. There are a number of different positions; the differential staining is often attributed to the specificity of the dye (Ellison and Barr, 1972; Weisblum, 1973; Caspersson et al., 1968; Arrighi and Hsu, 1971; Sumner et al., 1971). The selective extraction of protein and DNA has also been argued as the basis of G- and C-bands (Comings et al., 1973; Hsu and Arrighi, 1973; Pathak and Arrighi, 1973). The differential condensation of chromatin has also been suggested as the mechanism of banding (McKay, 1973; Meisner et al., 1973; Yunis and Sanchez, 1973).

2. This paper presents and reviews evidence for the condensation hypothesis. It is suggested that differential condensation of chromatin is an explanation for G-, Q-phase, R-, T-, and C-bands.

3. This does not completely exclude other hypotheses but it significantly influences the interpretation of data presented in their favour.

4. The biological and clinical implications of the chromosome condensation hypothesis are discussed.

Acknowledgements. I should like to thank all the members of this unit for their advice. In addition I am grateful to Miss J. Stewart for allowing me to use her work on BdrU treated L cells, Dr. M. J. Moses in whose laboratory the HeLa cells were prepared, and Dr. M. A. Ferguson-Smith who supplied the human lymphocyte chromosomes. This work was supported by a Medical Research Council scholarship.

6. REFERENCES

ARRIGHI, F. E., and HSU, T. C. 1971. Localisation of heterochromatin in human chromosomes. *Cytogenetics (Basel), 10,* 81–86.

BOSTOCK, C. J., and CHRISTIE, S. 1974. Quinacrine fluorescent staining of chromosomes and its relation to DNA base composition. *Exp. Cell Res., 86,* 157–161.

BRITTEN, R. J., PAVICH, M., and SMITH, J. 1969. In *Carnegie Inst. Wash. Year Book, 68,* 400–406.

BURKHOLDER, G. D., and COMINGS, D. E. 1972. Do Giesma banding patterns of chromosomes change during development? *Exp. Cell Res., 75,* 268–271.

CASPERSSON, T., FARBER, S., FOLEY, G. E., KUDYNOWSKI, J., MODEST, E. J., SIMONSSON, E., WAUGH, U., and ZECH, L. 1968. Chemical differentiation along metaphase chromosomes. *Exp. Cell Res., 51,* 626–636.

COMINGS, D. E. AVELINO, E., OKADA, T. A., and WYANDT, A. E. 1973. The mechanism of C and G banding of chromosomes. *Exp. Cell Res., 77,* 469–493.

DUTRILLAUX, B., and COVIC, M. 1974. Etude de facteurs influenceant la denaturation thermique menagee des chromosomes. *Exp. Cell Res., 85,* 143–153.

ELLISON, V. R., and BARR, H. J. 1972. Quinacrine fluorescence of special chromosome regions. *Chromosoma (Berl.), 36,* 375–390.

EVANS, H. J., BUCKTON, K. E., and SUMNER, A. T. 1971. Cytological mapping of human chromosomes: Results obtained with quinacrine fluorescence and acetic-saline-Giemsa techniques. *Chromosoma (Berl.), 35,* 310–325.

FERGUSON-SMITH, M. A., and PAGE, B. M. 1973. Pachytene analysis in a human reciprocal (10:11) translocation. *J. Med. Genet., 10,* 282–287.

GOLOMB, H. M., and BAHR, G. F. 1974*a*. Human chromatin from interphase to metaphase. *Exp. Cell Res., 84,* 79–87.

GOLOMB, H. M., and BAHR, G. F. 1974*b*. Correlation of the fluorescent banding pattern and ultrastructure of a human chromosome. *Exp. Cell Res., 84,* 121–126.

HSU, T. C., and ARRIGHI, F. E. 1973. In *Chromosome Identification: Techniques and Applications in Biology and Medicine* (T. CASPERSSON and L. ZECH, eds.), *Nobel Symp., 23,* 307–314. Academic Press, New York.

HSU, T. C., PATHAK, S., and SHAFER, D. A. 1973. Chromosome crossbanding by treating cells with chemical agents before fixation. *Exp. Cell Res., 79,* 484–487.

JONES, K. W. 1970. Chromosomal localisation of mouse satellite DNA in individual cells. *Nature (Lond.), 225,* 912–915.

JUDD, B. H., and YOUNG, M. W. 1973. An examination of the one cistron: one chromomere concept. *Cold Spring Harbor Symp. Quant. Biol., 38,* 441–449.

KATO, H., and MORIWAKI, K. 1972. Factors involved in the production of banded structures in mammalian chromosomes. *Chromosoma (Berl.), 38,* 105–120.

KATO, H., and YOSIDA, T. H. 1972. Banding patterns of Chinese hamster chromosomes revealed by new techniques. *Chromosoma (Berl.), 36,* 272–280.

LEE, C. L. Y., WELCH, J. P., and LEE, S. H. S. 1973. Banding of human chromosomes by protein denaturation. *Nat. New Biol., 241,* 142–143.

LEZZI, M. 1970. Differential gene activation in isolated chromosomes. *Int. Rev. Cytol., 29,* 127–168.

McKAY, R. D. G. 1973. The mechanism of G and C banding in mammalian metaphase chromosomes. *Chromosoma (Berl.), 44,* 1–14.

MEISNER, L. F., CHUPREVICH, T. W., and INHORN, S. L. 1973. Giemsa banding specificity. *Nat. New Biol., 245,* 145–147.

NILSSON, B. 1973. A bibliography of literature concerning chromosome identification. *Hereditas, 73,* 259–270.

PARDUE, M. L., and GALL, J. G. 1970. Chromosomal localisation of mouse satellite DNA. *Science (Wash. D.C.), 168,* 1356–1358.

PATHAK, S., and ARRIGHI, F. E. 1973. Loss of DNA following C banding procedures. *Cytogenet. Cell Genet., 12,* 414–422.

RODMAN, T. C., and TAHILIANI, S. 1973. The Feulgen banded karyotype of the mouse. *Chromosoma (Berl.), 42,* 37–56.

SEABRIGHT, M. 1972. The use of proteolytic enzymes for the mapping of structural rearrangement in the chromosomes of man. *Chromosoma (Berl.), 36,* 204–210.

STEWART, J. 1973. *The effect of 5-BUDR on the chromosomes of mouse L. cells.* B.Sc. Thesis, Department of Zoology, University of Edinburgh.

SUMNER, A. T. 1972. A simple technique for demonstrating centromeric heterochromatin. *Exp. Cell Res., 75,* 304–306.

SUMNER, A. T. 1976. The role of proteins and dyes in chromosome banding. This volume, pp. 201–209.

SUMNER, A. T., EVANS, H. J., and BUCKLAND, R. A. 1971. A new technique for distinguishing between human chromosomes. *Nat. New Biol., 232,* 204–210.

THOMAS, C. A., HAMKALO, B. A., MISRA, D. N., and LEE, C. S. 1970. Cyclisation of eukaryotic DNA fragments. *J. Mol. Biol., 51,* 621–632.

UTAKOJI, T. 1972. Differential staining of human chromosomes stained with potassium permanganate. *Nature (Lond.), 239,* 168–170.

VOSA, C. G. 1976. Heterochromatin classification in *Vicia faba* and *Scilla sibrica.* This volume, pp. 185–192.

WEISBLUM, B. 1973. Fluorescent probes of chromosomal DNA structure. *Cold Spring Harbor. Symp. Quant. Biol., 38,* 441–449.

WOODWARD, J., and SWIFT, H. 1964. The DNA content of cold treated chromosomes. *Exp. Cell Res., 34,* 131–137.

YUNIS, J. J., and SANCHEZ, O. 1973. G banding and chromosome structure. *Chromosoma (Berl.), 44,* 15–23.

ZHAKAROV, A. F., and EGOLINA, N. A. 1972. Differential spiralisation along mammalian mitotic chromosomes. *Chromosoma (Berl.), 38,* 341–365.

ELECTRON MICROSCOPY OF HUMAN BANDED AND PREMATURELY CONDENSED CHROMOSOMES

H. G. SCHWARZACHER, F. RUZICKA, and K. SPERLING

Histologisch-Embryologisches Institut, University of Vienna,
Boltzmann-Institut für Leukämieforschung, Vienna,
and Genetisches Institut, Free University, Berlin

1. INTRODUCTION

Electron microscopy of chromosomes is handicapped by numerous artefacts inherent in the methods of preparation. Although banding procedures may cause particular artefacts, some persistently found structural features of banded chromosomes will be briefly reported here.

2. MATERIALS AND METHODS

(a) *Whole mount chromosome preparation*

Routine chromosome preparations from normal human fibroblast and peripheral blood cultures (pretreated with hypotonic solution, fixed in acetic acid-alcohol, dropped on glass slides, and air dried) were coated with a carbon film. This film was floated off together with the adhering cells in 0.2% fluoric acid and then picked up on electron microscope grids. In this way the chromosomes and cell nuclei can be studied *in toto.*

(b) *Premature condensation of chromosomes*

Premature condensation of interphase chromosomes was achieved by fusing

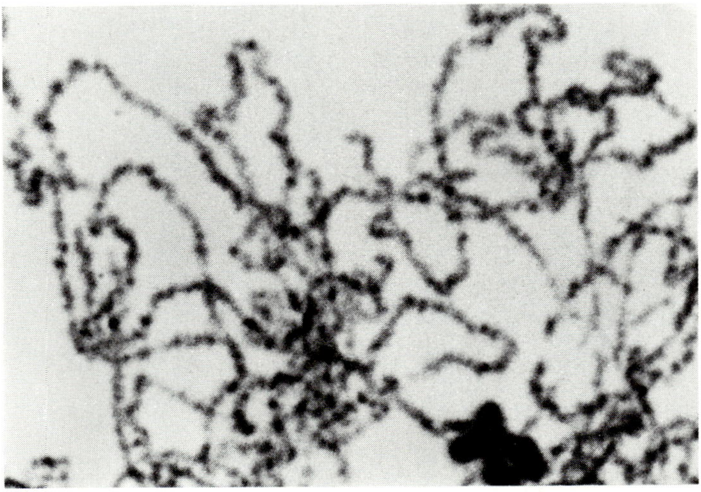

FIG. 1.—Light-microscopic picture of prematurely condensed chromosomes after G-band staining. Very fine banding pattern. × 2,800.

partly synchronized HeLa cells arrested in metaphase with unsynchronized human fibroblasts. The synchronization was carried out with thymidine (2.5 mM for 18 hr) followed by colcemid (8 μg for 10 hr) 12 hr after thymidine release. The fusion was performed with inactivated Sendai-Virus. Chromosome preparations were made 30 min and 45 min after fusion.

3. RESULTS

(a) *Prematurely condensed chromosomes*

Chromosomes which have been prematurely condensed in G1 consist of very thin single threads. In G2 chromosomes two chromatids are present (Johnson and Rao, 1970). After G-band staining (fig. 1) a very fine pattern of small bands can be seen under the light microscope. It should be pointed out, however, that even in very thin and only slightly condensed chromosomes, the G-bands are limited in their fineness of appearance.

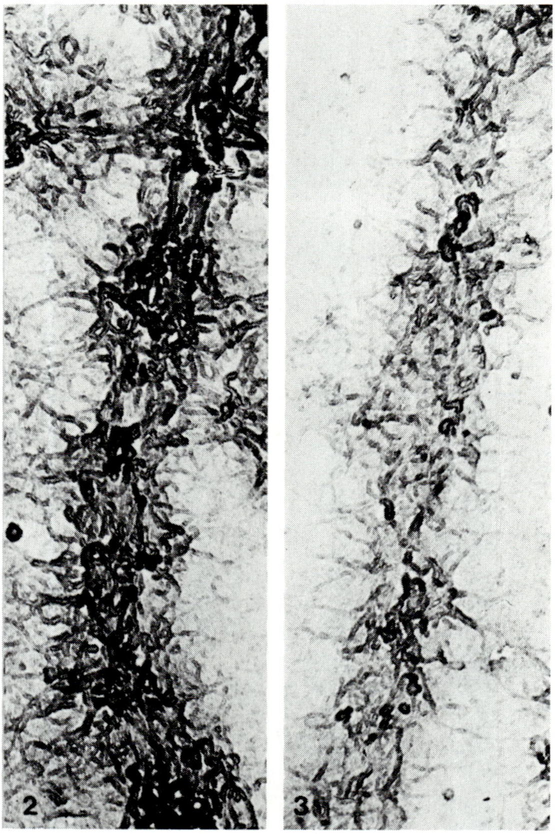

FIG. 2.—Part of prematurely condensed G2-chromosome of a rather high degree of condensation, comparable to early prophase. The G-bands are very clearly visible. × 26,000.

FIG. 3.—Part of a prematurely condensed G1-chromosome of a very low degree of condensation. Only one fibril may build up the chromosome. × 26,000.

Under the electron microscope, prematurely condensed chromosomes reveal the same fibrils as metaphase chromosomes and interphase nuclei. The fibrils are of the same size and irregularly folded in the same way (figs. 2 and 3). The G-banded regions appear to be thicker and contain more tightly packed fibrils, the fibrils themselves being darker stained. In rather strongly condensed chromosomes (fig. 2) this is particularly clearly visible. In the regions between the G-bands the fibrils may show a tendency to form elongated loops. This is considered to be an artefact caused by stretching during preparation. Very thin G1-chromosomes (fig 3) also show regions of stronger stained fibrils with tighter packing, presumably corresponding to G-banded regions. The fibrillar loops are irregular and rather short. They often reach out from the main axis of the chromatid, giving it a lampbrush-like appearance. The only structures visible are the fibrils with no trace of any "backbone" structure or a denser core fibril (see, e.g., Stubblefield, 1973). Also no remnants of the nuclear membrane are present.

Prematurely condensed chromosomes from the S-phase cell appear fractionated into very small particles (fig. 4). These particles correspond to condensed chromosome regions, whereas in the regions between them, the DNA is presumably maximally decondensed for replication (Rao and Johnson, 1973). Higher magnifications show again that the condensed chromosome regions are built up of irregularly

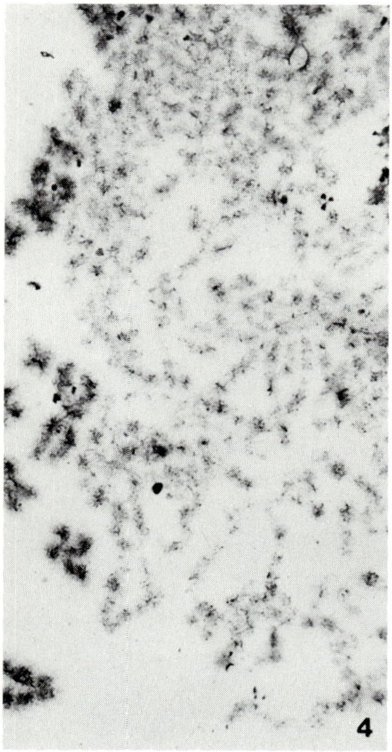

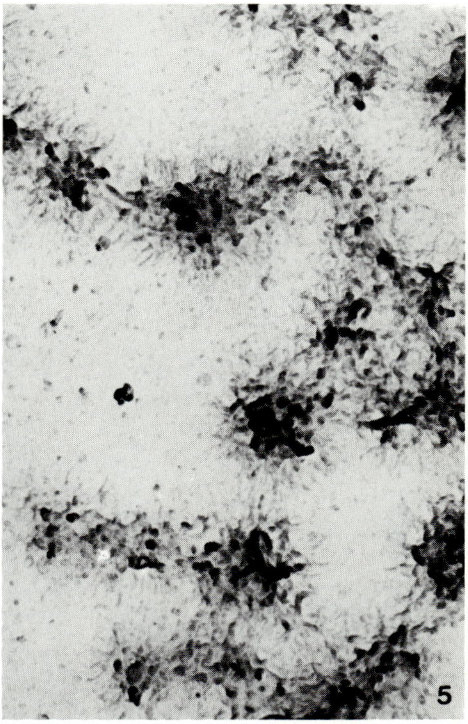

FIG. 4.—Prematurely condensed chromosomes in S-phase. Also some of the fused metaphase chromosomes are visible. × 2,400.

FIG. 5.—Prematurely condensed chromosomes in S-phase at higher magnification. Fibrillar bridges but not finer fibrils are detectable between condensed chromosome parts. × 22,000.

folded fibrils (fig. 5). Sometimes bridges of fibrils can be observed between the condensed parts. It is quite probable that these bridges originate from the fibrils which stick out from the condensed parts. Presumably, the method used is not suitable for demonstrating replicating DNA fibrils.

(b) *Metaphase chromosomes*

Metaphase chromosomes give a strong contrast, but structural details are hardly seen when they are examined without any further treatment (fig. 6). After G-band staining (using 0.07 M NaOH for 30 sec followed by incubation in phosphate buffer of pH = 6.0 at 59°C for 18 hr, according to Schnedl, 1971) the chromosomes appear to be built up of distinctly visible fibrils (fig. 7). In a previous paper (Ruzicka, 1974) it has already been shown that NaOH treatment causes swelling of the chromosomes. After the subsequent buffer treatment the swelling is reduced and fibrils become visible. After Giemsa staining the fibrils gain a lot in contrast.

The fibrils are irregularly folded and bent into short loops. In the G-band regions the fibrils are more strongly stained and the chromatids are also thicker, containing more tightly packed fibrils (fig. 7). The fibrils have a diameter of 300–600 Å. At high magnification a substructure can be observed consisting of either one folded or several parallel finer fibrils of about 30 Å thickness (for details, see Ruzicka and Schwarzacher, 1974).

Without doubt the fibrils between the chromatids and neighboring chromosomes are artefacts. Fibrillar loops reach out from the edges of the chromatids and can obviously stick together during the course of preparation. Similar fibrillar bridges are also seen between interphase nuclei, if they happen to come to lie close enough together in preparations.

(c) *Giemsa*-11 *stained chromosomes*

In preparations stained according to the Giemsa-11 method (Bobrow et al., 1972;

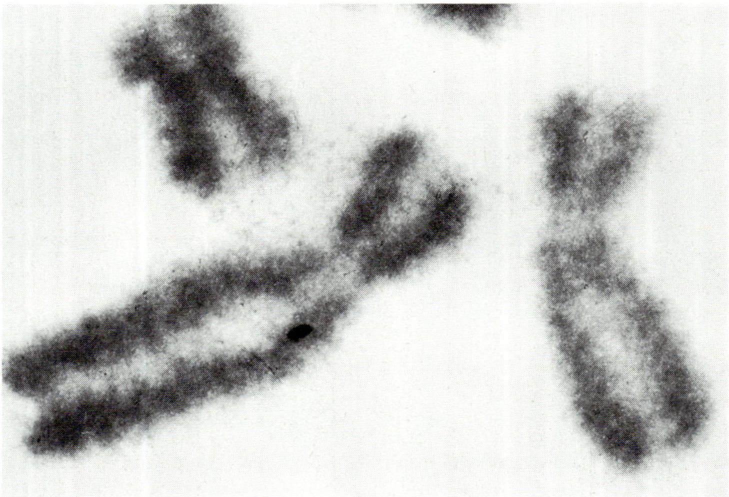

FIG. 6.—Metaphase chromosomes of a standard preparation without any special treatment and unstained. Faint suggestion of a fibrillar structure. × 10,000.

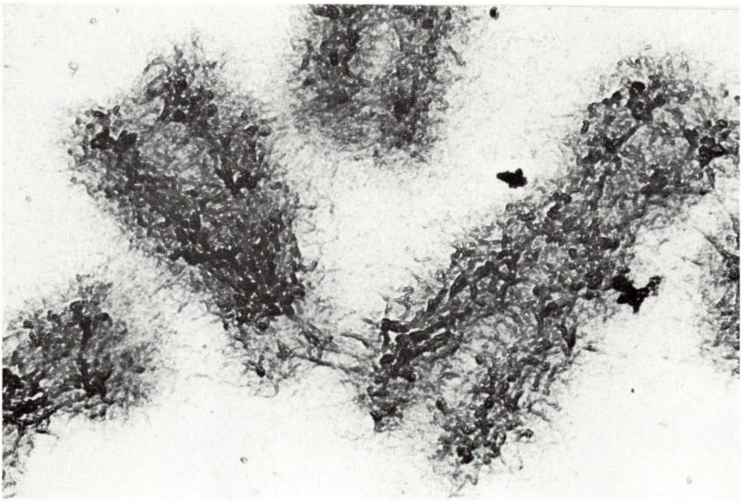

FIG. 7.—Metaphase chromosomes after G-band staining (method of Schnedl, 1971). Fibrils of at least 300 Å thickness are laid in numerous small loops. G-band regions are characterized by denser packing of fibrils as well as stronger contrast of the fibrils. Fibrillar bridges between chromatids and chromosomes are artefacts and are formed by the sticking together of fibrillar loops. × 10,000.

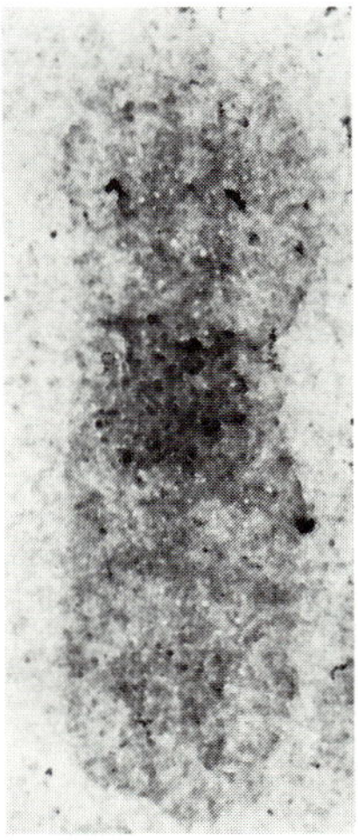

FIG. 8.—Chromosome No. 9 after Giemsa-11 staining. The fibrils appear to be swollen and faintly stained; only in the secondary constriction near the centromere are the fibrillar loops highly contrasted. × 5,000.

Gagné and Laberge, 1972) the chromosomes have a rather swollen appearance. Fibrils are faintly seen and fibrillar loops with a strong contrast are present only in the regions appearing red under the light microscope. In figure 8 a chromosome No. 9 is shown. It seems that fibrils are reconstituted and stained only in the region of the secondary constriction near the centromere. In contrast to the G-bands, the chromatids are not thicker in this region and the higher contrast is achieved solely by a stronger staining of the fibrils. The accumulation of the Giemsa stain may also be responsible for the larger diameter of the fibrils (up to 800 Å). The bromine atoms of the eosin component of the dye presumably causes the electron microscopic contrast.

4. DISCUSSION

A possible chromosome model

Electron microscopic investigations made with the aid of many different methods on chromosomes of many species have all revealed that fibrils are the main constituents of chromosomes. The diameter of such fibrils (which are also called the elementary fibrils) may vary with the method applied. Usually, values between 100 and 300 Å are given (e.g., Barnicot and Huxley, 1961; Wettstein and Sotelo, 1965; Wolfe, 1965; Du Praw, 1965; Lampert, 1969; Schwarzacher and Schnedl, 1969; Comings, 1972). The greater thickness of the fibrils in our preparations is presumably caused by a stronger swelling due to the treatment and by an accumulation of the Giemsa stain (Ruzicka and Schwarzacher, 1974).

Many authors reported that the elementary fibrils are composed of finer fibrils of a diameter which comes close to the value of the DNA double helix. It does not seem to be quite clear from these findings if there is only one or several such fine fibrils (DNA molecules) within an elementary fibril. However, there is no evidence against the assumption of there being only one fine fibril.

Therefore, the next important question is whether only one elementary fibril runs through from one end of a chromatid to the other, or several fibrils take part in its formation. Our pictures of thin prematurely condensed chromosomes are indeed very suggestive of the possibility of there being only one fibril laid in numerous small loops (fig. 9). At least we can say that there are no detectable signs of several parallel running fibrils and that the model of one fibril laid in long narrow loops parallel to the longitudinal axis of the chromatid (Du Praw, 1965) is very improbable.

So far, all models of multi-stranded chromatids or chromosomes consisting of elongated fibrillar loops (Ris, 1961; Osgood et al., 1964; Du Praw, 1965; Stubblefield, 1973) have been constructed using electron microscopic pictures of chromosomes spread on a water surface and dried at a critical temperature. This method causes a very severe stretching of the preparation. It is conceivable that the loops of the single elementary fibril may stick together and in this way produce pictures of parallel running fibrils.

Our preparations show that the G-bands are characterized by denser packing of the elementary fibril (as has been also shown by Bahr et al., 1973) as well as higher stainability (fig. 9).

As we see it, the step from the slightly condensed chromosome, in the form of a prematurely condensed chromosome, to a strongly condensed metaphase chromosome is performed, in part, by an increased folding of the fibril and packing of the loops. This leads to increased thickness of the chromatids and, partly through chromatid coiling, to the well-known major coils of metaphase chromosomes.

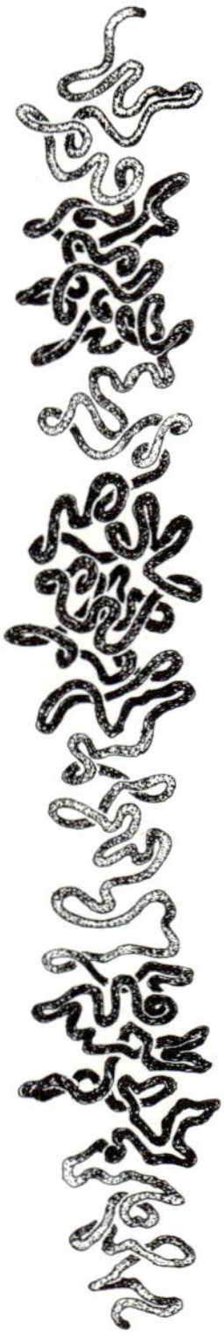

FIG. 9.—Model of a slightly condensed chromatid assuming that only one fibril runs from one end to the other. The darker regions correspond to G-bands.

5. SUMMARY

1. Total preparations of human chromosomes prepared as for Giemsa banding techniques were investigated with the electron microscope.

2. Metaphase chromosomes are composed of irregularly folded fibrils of at least 300 Å diameter. Fibrillar bridges between chromatids or between neighboring chromosomes are considered to be artefacts.

3. In G-banded regions the chromatids are thicker and the fibrils appear more strongly stained.

4. In preparations stained after the Giemsa-11 method only the regions corresponding to the red colored areas under the light microscope show strongly contrasted fibrils.

5. Prematurely condensed chromosomes, prepared after fusion of interphase cells with metaphases, reveal similar fibrils as metaphase chromosomes. G-banded regions are rather small but of finite size. Thin G1-chromosomes suggest that one chromatid is built up of only one fibril running from one end to the other folded in numerous short loops. Neither denser core fibrils nor any structures other than fibrils were seen. In prematurely condensed S-phase chromosomes no structures were seen between the condensed parts.

Acknowledgements. This work was supported by the "Fonds zur Förderung der wissenschaftlichen Forschung in Österreich," the "Krebsforschungsspende des Hern Bundespräsidenten Dr. h.c. Franz Jonas," and the "Forschungsfonds der Österreichischen Nationalbank."

6. REFERENCES

BAHR, G. F., MIKEL, U., and ENGLER, W. F. 1973. Correlates of chromosomal banding at the level of ultrastructure. In *Nobel Symp. 23. Chromosome Identification—Techniques and Application in Biology and Medicine* (T. CASPERSSON and L. ZECH, eds.). Academic Press, New York and London.

BARNICOT, N. A., and HUXLEY, H. E. 1961. The electron microscopy of unsectioned human chromosomes. *Ann. Hum. Gen., 25,* 253–258.

BOBROW, M., MADAN, K., and PEARSON, P. L. 1972. Staining of some specific regions of human chromosomes, particularly the secondary constriction of No. 9. *Nat. New Biol., 238,* 122–124.

COMINGS, D. E. 1972. The structure and function of chromatin. In *Advances of Human Genetics, 3* (H. HARRIS and K. HIRSCHHORN, eds.), pp. 237–431. Plenum Press, New York and London.

DU PRAW, E. J. 1965. Macromolecular organization of nuclei and chromosomes. A folded fibre model based on wholemount electron microscopy. *Nature (Lond.), 206,* 338–343.

GAGNÉ, R., and LABERGE, C. 1972. Specific cytological recognition of the heterochromatic segment of number 9 chromosome in man. *Exp. Cell Res.,* **73**, 239–242.

JOHNSON, R. T., and RAO, P. N. 1970. Mammalian cell fusion: Induction of premature chromosome condensation in interphase nuclei. *Nature (Lond.), 226,* 717–722.

LAMPERT, F. 1969. Feinstruktur und Trockengewicht menschlicher Chromosomen. Quantitative Elektronenmikroskopie. *Naturwissenschaften, 56,* 629–633.

OSGOOD, E. E., JENKINS, D. P., BROOKS, R. and LAWSON, R. K. 1964. Electron micrographic studies of the expanded and uncoiled chromosomes from human leucocytes. *Ann. N.Y. Acad. Sci., 113,* 717–726.

RAO, P. N., and JOHNSON, R. T. 1973. Induction of chromosome condensation in interphase cells. In *Advances in Cell and Molecular Biology, 3* (E. J. DU PRAW, ed.). Academic Press, New York.

RIS, H. 1961. Ultrastructure and molecular organization of genetic systems. *Canad. J. Genet. Cytol., 3,* 95–120.

RUZICKA, F. 1974. Effect of G-banding techniques on the ultrastructure of human chromosomes. *Humangenetik, 22,* 119–126.

RUZICKA, F., and SCHWARZACHER, H. G. 1974. The ultrastructure of human mitotic chromosomes and interphase nuclei treated by Giemsa banding techniques. *Chromosoma (Berl.), 46,* 443–454.

SCHNEDL, W. 1971. Banding pattern of human chromosomes. *Nat. New Biol., 233,* 93.

SCHWARZACHER, H. G., and SCHNEDL, W. 1969. Zur Ultrastruktur der Chromosomen des Menschen. *Humangenetik, 8,* 75–80.

STUBBLEFIELD, E. 1973. The structure of mammalian chromosomes. In *International Review of Cytology, 35* (G. H. BOURNE and J. F. DANIELLE, eds.). Academic Press, New York.

WETTSTEIN, R., and SOTELO, J. R. 1965. Fine structure of meiotic chromosomes. The elementary components of metaphase chromosomes of *Gryllus argentinus. J. Ultrastruct. Res., 13,* 367–381.

WOLFE, S. L. 1965. The fine structure of isolated metaphase chromosomes. *Exp. Cell. Res., 37,* 45–53.

CYTOGENETIC AND CYTOCHEMICAL OBSERVATIONS IN PATIENTS WITH THE SÉZARY SYNDROME

F. T. BOSMAN, W. A. VAN VLOTEN and P. L. PEARSON

*Laboratory for Pathology, Department of Dermatology, and Department of Anthropogenetics, Leiden University, Leiden, The Netherlands**

1. INTRODUCTION

The Sézary syndrome, originally described by Sézary and Bouvrain in 1938, is characterized by erythroderma with pruritus, lymphadenopathy, and the presence of abnormal cells in the skin and peripheral blood. These abnormal cells have a characteristic appearance with a large convoluted nucleus and a narrow rim of cytoplasm, containing PAS positive granules (Taswell and Winkelmann, 1961; Labaze et al., 1972). The convolutions of the nucleus cause the so-called cerebriform appearance of the nucleus in the electron micrograph (Lutzner and Jordan, 1968; Lutzner et al., 1973). These types of cells are also found in mycosis fungoides (Brownlee and Murad, 1970). Recent investigations mark the Sézary cell as an abnormal T lymphocyte (Shevach et al., 1974; Brouet et al., 1973).

Cytophotometric measurements of the DNA content of cells in the peripheral blood showed marked aneuploidy and polyploidy (Lutzner et al., 1973). Corresponding cytogenetic abnormalities have been found, consisting of hypoploidy and polyploidy (Crossen et al., 1971; Lutzner et al., 1973; Dewald et al., 1974). Löffler et al. (1974), however, described one patient with a normal karyotype. To date differential staining techniques have been used on three patients only (Lutzner et al., 1973).

In this paper we report the cytophotometric and cytogenetic observations on blood and infiltrate cells in the skin of three patients with the Sézary syndrome which have enabled a better characterization of the Sézary cell.

2. MATERIALS AND METHODS

Skin biopsies and blood samples were taken from three patients with the Sézary syndrome before cytostatic therapy was started. Skin imprint preparations and blood smears were stained with May-Grünwald-Giemsa and PAS. For ultrastructural study buffy coat pellets and skin biopsies were fixed in glutaraldehyde, postfixed in osmium tetraoxide, embedded in Epon and stained with lead citrate.

Cells were cytophotometrically scanned in Feulgen-stained skin imprints and blood smears with a Zeiss S.M.P. interfaced to a PDP 12 computer (van Vloten et al., 1974). Sixty cells from the skin imprints and 200 cells from the blood smears were randomly measured. Chromosome metaphase preparations were obtained from whole blood cultures with and without PHA stimulation after 72 and 24 hr

* Address for correspondence: W. A. van Vloten, Department of Dermatology, Academisch Ziekenhuis Leiden, Leiden, The Netherlands

culture time, respectively. These preparations were stained with a modified trypsine-Giemsa technique.

From each preparation 100 cells were counted and at least 100 abnormal cells karyotyped.

3. RESULTS

After PAS staining peripheral blood specimens of all three patients showed up to 15% abnormal lymphoid cells with PAS positive granules in the cytoplasm. The total white blood cell count was 8000 in patient GV, and 30,000 to 40,000 in patients MM and MS, showing definite lymphocytosis. The atypical cells of patient MM, with a diameter of 13–15 μ, had nuclei with a cerebriform appearance. In patients MS and GV the cells were smaller, the diameter varied from 8–10 μ, and had less pronounced nuclear indentations. Electron microscopy confirmed these light microscopic findings (fig. 1).

Skin biopsies of all three patients showed a dense infiltrate in the upper dermis containing several atypical lymphoid cells. In the lymph nodes and bone marrow of patient MM and MS the same atypical cells were found.

(a) *Cytophotometry*

DNA histograms from skin imprints of all three patients showed a wider variation of the diploid DNA range and a higher frequency of tetraploid cells than in control specimens. Although less pronounced, the DNA histograms of peripheral blood lymphocytes showed similar abnormalities (fig. 2).

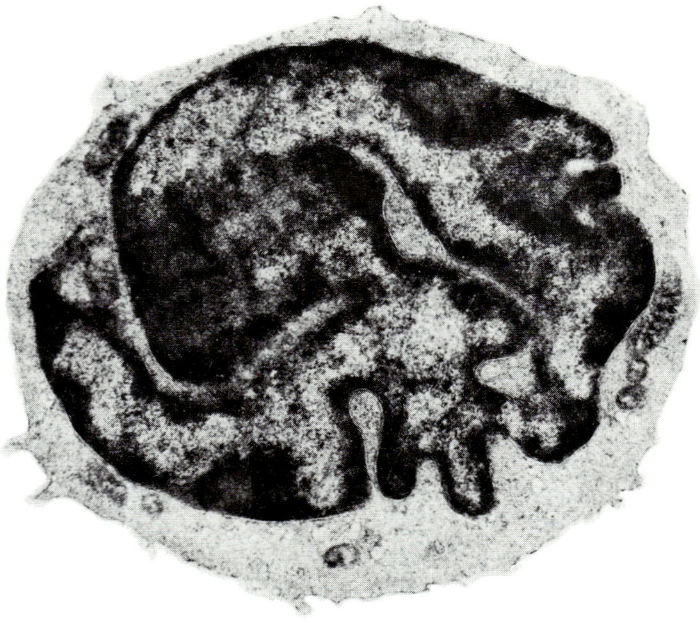

FIG. 1.—Electron micrograph of a typical so-called Sézary cell in the peripheral blood (courtesy of Dr. H. de Man).

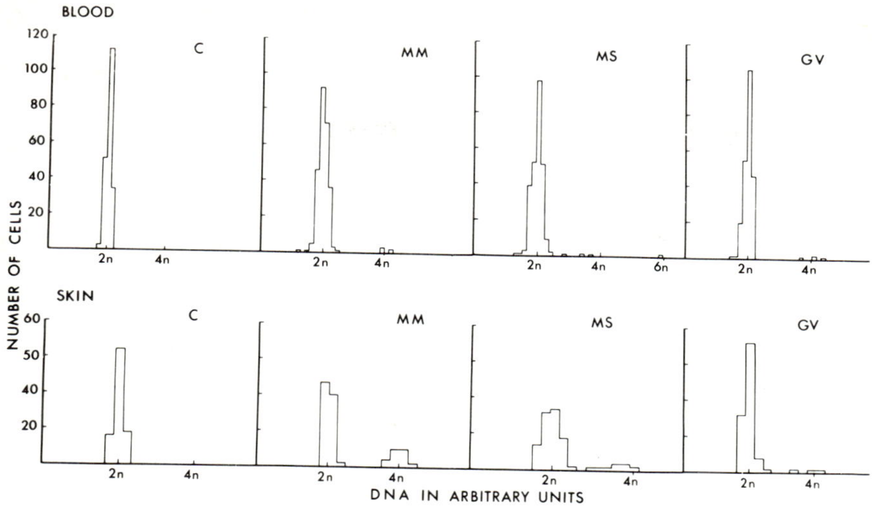

FIG. 2.—Histograms of Feulgen DNA measurements performed on cells in the peripheral blood and of infiltrate cells in the skin from three patients with the Sézary syndrome. A patient without any malignancy gives the control values C. For the patients with Sézary's syndrome tje histograms show aneuploidy and polyploidy.

(b) *Cytogenetics*

The peripheral blood lymphocytes of all three patients showed a subnormal response to PHA stimulation. In particular the blood cultures of patient MM resulted in a very low number of metaphases. From all patients more than one analysable culture was obtained. Bone marrow preparations could not be studied because of a dry tap in patient MM and MS, and in patient GV no bone marrow aspiration was performed. Table 1 summarizes the chromosome numbers in 100 counted metaphases. In patient MM definite aneuplody was found. Two hypodiploid cell clones could be identified (39 and 40 chromosomes). Moreover, a large number of hypotetraploid cells were found, which corresponds to a doubling of the n = 40 clone. In all these abnormal cells multiple double minute fragments were present. Furthermore multiple translocations were identified, and they varied considerably from cell to cell. The abnormal chromosomes found are summarized in figure 3 and table 2. In patient MS aneuploidy and some tetraploidy was found (table 1). Numerous translocations were present in the n = 47 cell line and also in the pseudodiploid cells. In patient GV the degree of aneuploidy was less than in the two other patients. A few polyploid cells were found. A small number of cells showed a translocation and an abnormal chromosome with a banding pattern resembling the pattern of a chromosome 2.

TABLE 1

Distribution of chromosome number per 100 *cells*

Patient	39	40	41	42	43	44	45	46	47	80	92
MM	30	46						14		10	
MS				5	2	7	30	42	7		7
GV						4	26	66	4		

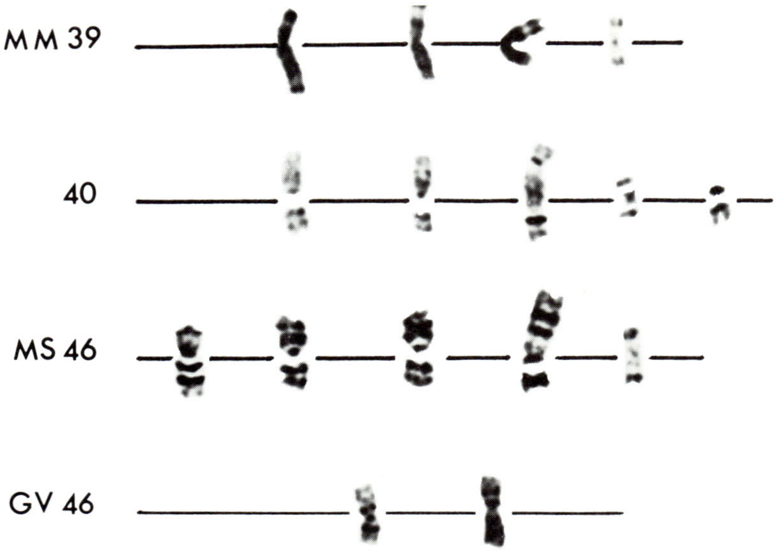

FIG. 3—Marker chromosomes of patient MM, MS and GV.

TABLE 2

Description of the abnormal chromosomes shown in figure 3 according to the Paris convention

39	t(4q;3p)(6q;3q)(9q;13q), iq17
40	t(9q;13q)(9q;14q)(9q;12q), iq17, ?
46	7+, t(9q;14q)(9q;15q)(11q;2q), iq17
46	t(Xq;10q), i?

4. DISCUSSION

DNA cytophotometry revealed aneuploidy and tetraploidy in all three patients in the infiltrate cells of the skin and to a minor degree in cells of the peripheral blood. The cytophotometric results are in mutual agreement with the cytogenetic results in that both show evidence of aneuploidy and polyploidy in all patients. In all three patients marker chromosomes as well as double minute fragments were found.

The chromosome abnormalities show a great variation between the different patients, however, marker chromosomes could be identified in most abnormal cells in all three patients. In all translocations the break points were localized in the centromere region with C and D group chromosomes being more involved than the other chromosomes. The occurrence of an isochromosome for the long arm of 17 in two patients was also described by Lutzner et al. (1973) in one patient. As the results show, it cannot be expected that widespread chromosome abnormalities which characterize the Sézary syndrome will be found. However, further careful cytogenetic investigation may show some localized patterns in the abnormalities found in the cells of affected patients.

5. SUMMARY

1. The Sézary syndrome is a rare disease characterized by generalized erythroderma with palmo-plantar hyperkeratosis, lymphadenopathy, and the presence of atypical lymphoid cells in the peripheral blood and in the skin.

2. Cytophotometrical determinations of the nuclear Feulgen-DNA content were performed on mononuclear cells in blood smears and on infiltrate cells in skin imprint preparations. Aneuploid and multiple (pseudo) tetraploid cells were found in all three patients.

3. Cytogenetic analysis was performed on blood cultures. In one patient hypodiploid clones were found with 39 and 40 chromosomes. In the other patients some aneuploidy and tetraploidy was found. The chromosomal abnormalities showed a wide variation between the patients.

4. The break points seem to be nonrandomly distributed, they were all located adjacent to the centromere, and C and D group chromosomes were more frequently involved.

6. REFERENCES

Brouet, J. C., Flandrin, G., and Seligman, M. 1973. Indications of the thymus-derived nature of the proliferating cells in six patients with Sézary's syndrome. *N. Engl. J. Med., 289,* 341–344.

Brownlee, T. R., and Murad, T. M. 1970. Ultrastructure of Mycosis fungoides. *Cancer, 26,* 686–698.

Crossen, P. E., Meller, J. E. L., Finley, A. G., Ravich, R. M. B., Vincent, P. C., and Gunz, F. W. 1971. The Sézary syndrome. *Am. J. Med., 50,* 24–34.

Dewald, G., Spurbeck, J. L., and Vitek, H. A. 1974. Chromosomes in a patient with the Sézary syndrome. *Mayo Clin. Proc., 49,* 553–557.

Labaze, J. J., Moscovic, E. A., Pham, T. D., and Azar, H. A. 1972. Histological and ultrastructural findings in a case of the Sézary syndrome. *J. Clin. Pathol. (Lond.), 25,* 312–319.

Löffler, H., Meyhöfer, W., Lange, R. H., Ehlers, G., and Remmele, W. 1974. Sézary syndrome. *Dtsch. Med. Wochenscr., 99,* 429–434.

Lutzner, M. A., and Jordan, H. W. 1968. The ultrastructure of an abnormal cell in Sézary's syndrome. *Blood, 31,* 719–726.

Lutzner, M. A., Emerit, I., Durepaire, R., Flandrin, G., Grupper, Ch., and Prunieras, M. 1973. Cytogenetic, cytophotometric and ultrastructural stydy of large cerebriform cells of the Sézary syndrome and description of a small-cell variant. *J. Natl. Cancer Inst., 50,* 1145–1162.

Sézary, A., and Bouvrain, Y. 1938. Erythrodermie avec présence de cellules monstrueuses dans le derme et le sang circulante. *Bull. Soc. Fr. Dermatol. Syphiligr., 45,* 254–260.

Shevach, E., Edelson, R., Frank, M., Lutzner, M., and Green, I. 1974. A human leukemia cell with both B and T cell surface receptors. *Proc. Natl. Acad. Sci. U.S.A., 71,* 863–866.

Taswell, H. F., and Winkelmann, R. K. 1961. Sézary syndrome—a malignant reticulemic erythroderma. *J. Amer. Med. Assoc., 177,* 465–472.

Van Vloten, W. A., van Duyn, P., and Schaberg, A. 1974. Cytodiagnostic use of Feulgen DNA measurements in cell imprints from the skin of patients with mycosis fungoides. *Brit. J. Dermatol., 91,* 365–371.

THE MONGOLOID PHENOTYPE IN MAN IS DUE TO TRISOMY OF THE DISTAL PALE G-BAND OF CHROMOSOME 21

J. WAHRMAN,[1] R. GOITEIN,[1] C. RICHLER,[1] B. GOLDMAN,[2] E. AKSTEIN,[2] and R. CHAKI[2]

[1]*Department of Genetics, The Hebrew University of Jerusalem, Israel*
[2]*Cytogenetics Laboratory, Sheba Medical Center, Tel-Hashomer, Israel*

1. INTRODUCTION

Fifteen years have passed since the important discovery that mongolism is associated with an extra chromosome 21 (Lejeune et al., 1959). Studies of the chromosomes in certain cases of translocation mongolism later showed that even without triplication of the *short* arm and satellite of chromosome 21, this syndrome is manifested in full. However, progress in delimiting the part of the *long* arm of the chromosome responsible for the appearance of Down's syndrome has been hindered by lack of differentiation along it by the then current staining procedures. The newer G-banding methods distinguish a proximal dark-staining band in the long arm of chromosome 21 and a pale distal one of about equal length. The findings reported here indicate that:

(1) Triplication of the pale band, or part if it, is responsible for production of the mongoloid phenotype.

(2) Monosomy for most or all of the dark band has no obvious physical effects, but is accompanied by mental retardation.

These conclusions agree with Niebuhr's (1974) and Lejeune's (personal communication) suggestions that the distal part of the long arm of chromosome 21 is implicated in Down's syndrome.

This paper is based on chromosomal analysis of a family seeking genetic advice because of the birth of one mentally retarded and two mongoloid children, followed by three spontaneous abortions. Amniocentesis combined with banded karyotype analysis made it possible to assure the parents of the birth of a chromosomally normal child.

2. CLINICAL AND CYTOGENETIC FINDINGS

Phenotypes and simplified diagrams of chromosomes 2 and 21 of the members of the family are given in figure 1. The mother, II-1, is a de-novo case of an apparently balanced 2/21 translocation. The breaks occurred in chromosome 21 at the transition between the dark band (21q21) and the light band (21q22), and in chromosome 2 toward the end of the long arm. Reliable cytological information is available for four of her children and doubtful data on two spontaneous abortions, leaving one unexamined abortus. In this sibship only one child, the last, had a normal karyotype.

Case histories of most members of the family have previously been reported (Schmidt et al., 1972). These authors suggested that the part of the G-chromosome deleted in the mother II-1 had been translocated to another chromosome, probably

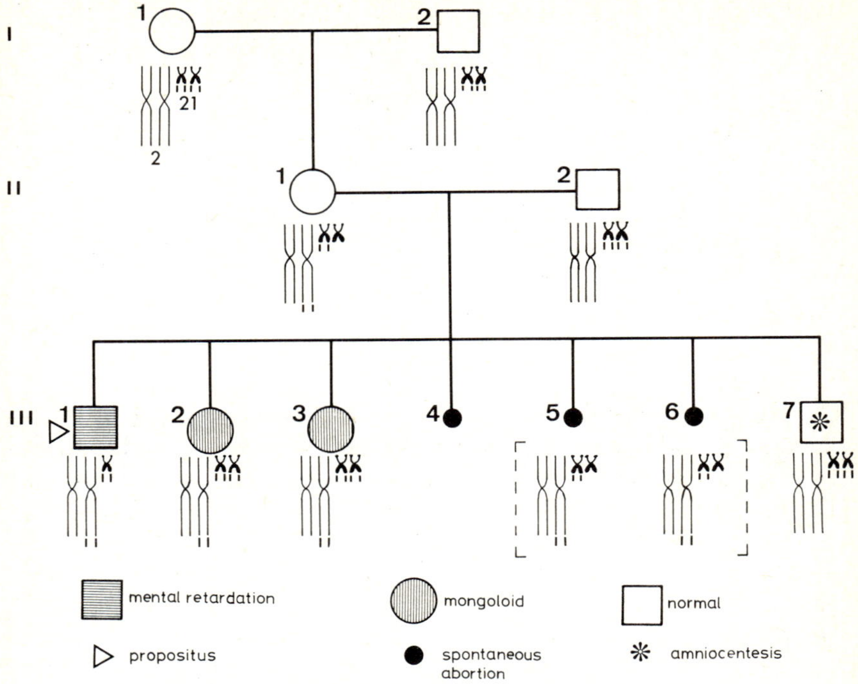

FIG. 1.—Pedigree of kindred and simplified partial karyotypes. Karyotypes in brackets may belong to II-1 (see Discussion), only the dark and light bands of the long arm of chromosome 21 are indicated.

of the C-group. The same unrecognized translocation chromosome was assumed to be present in her mentally retarded son, III-1, who was therefore monosomic for part of the G chromosome, and in her two mongoloid daughters, II-2 and III-3, whose karyotypes were indistinguishable from normal karyotypes.

Investigation of this family was resumed when the mother, II-1 (case H2213), came to another hospital concerned with the possible outcome of further pregnancies. Three pregnancies that followed terminated in spontaneous abortions and two of the abortuses (III-5 and III-6) were examined cytologically. During her seventh pregnancy amniocentesis was performed and Giesma-banding techniques were applied to cells from amniotic fluid cultures and to lymphocyte cultures of herself and her only living child (III-1).

Case II-1. The small G-chromosome, often participating in satellite associations, was found to be a deleted No. 21 possessing the short, satellited arm and the dark proximal band of the long arm, or most of it. In addition, one chromosome 2 had an extra short segment at the distal end of its long arm. In some cells a slight constriction could be seen between the main part of the long arm and the extra segment which appeared to include the distal pale band of No. 21 (figs. 2, 4, 5).

Case III-1. There were 45 chromosomes in all cells examined. The deleted No. 21 was missing and one chromosome 2 had an extra segment, indistinguishable from that of the mother (figs. 3–5). We interpret this karyotype as a partial monosomy for No. 21, involving the short satellited arm and the proximal dark band of the long arm.

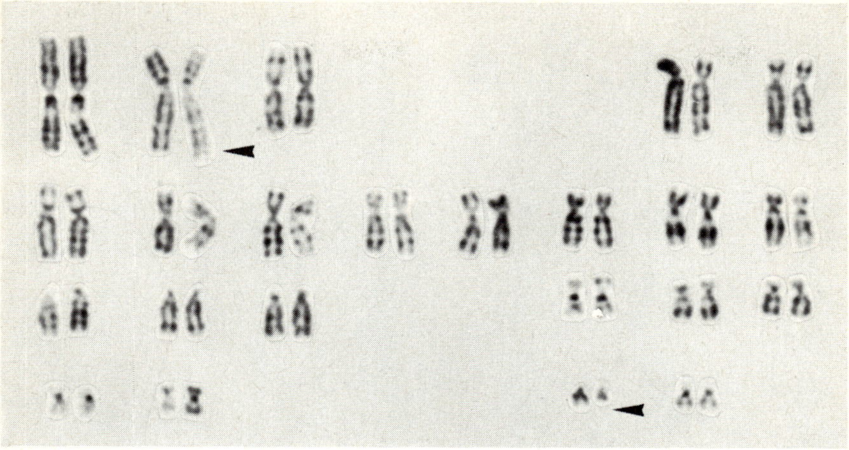

FIG. 2.—Karotype of II-1. The extra segment of chromosome 2 and the deleted chromosome 21 are indicated (arrows). Giemsa-banding.

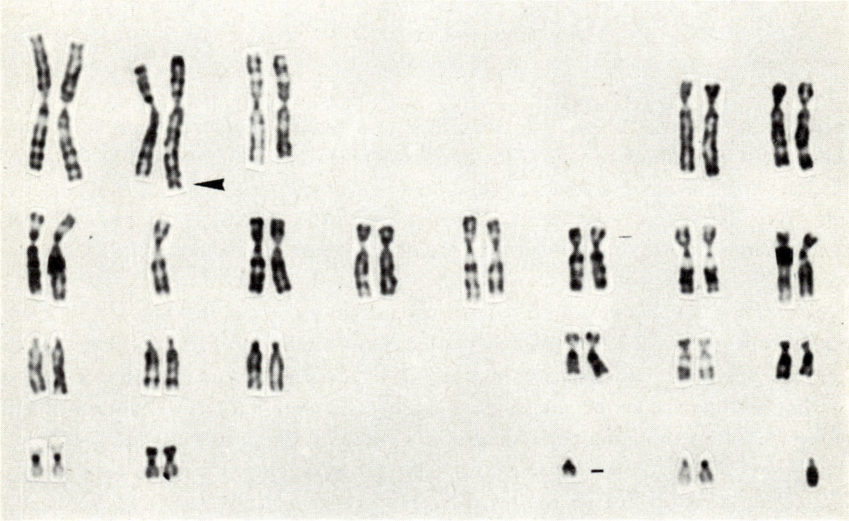

FIG. 3.—Karyotype of III-1, 45 chromosomes. The extra segment of chromosome 2 is indicated (arrow). Giemsa-banding.

To the published case report of the propositus (Schmidt et al., 1972) can be added that at the age of 7 his physical development was normal; IQ was 43 (Stanford-Binet L-M) but was possibly underestimated due to restlessness, difficulties in concentration, and lack of cooperation.

Case III-7. In 19 amniotic cells examined, chromosomes 2 and 21 were normal (figs. 4, 5). As could be predicted on the basis of this finding, a clinically normal child was born.

Cases III-2 and III-3. Giemsa-banding could no longer be applied as the two mongoloid girls died in infancy. Through the courtesy of the Cytogenetics Labora-

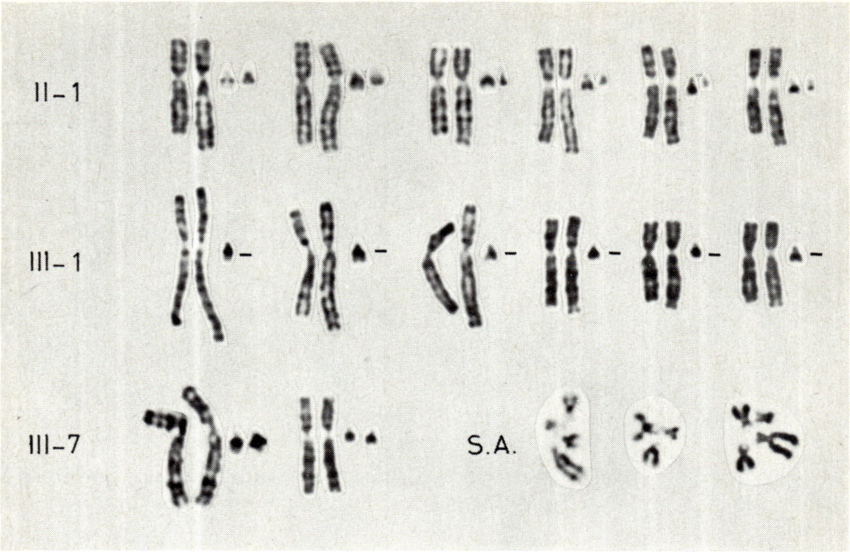

FIG. 4.—Partial karyotypes (chromosomes 2 and 21) of II-1, III 1, and III-7. Giemsa-banding. *S.A.*, satellite associations involving the deleted 21 from two cells of II-1 and one of III-6.

tory of Asaf Harofe Hospital we were able to examine the original orcein-stained slides. Examination of 42 cells of the two cases revealed a difference in the length of the long arms of chromosomes 2, while the G-chromosomes appeared to be normal (fig. 5). It thus seems that the chromosome 2 with the extra segment was inherited from the mother, and that this segment includes the part of chromosome 21 responsible for Down's syndrome.

Cases III-4, 5, 6. No information was available on the first of these three abortuses, but 23 orcein-stained karyotypes were obtained from cultures of the other two. In both cases all cells were female, had one deleted chromosome 21 like that of the mother and the marker chromosome 2 (fig. 5). Therefore karyotype analysis makes no contribution to an understanding of the cause of the abortions. The possibility that tissues of the mother were inadvertently grown in the cultures, at least in case *III*-6, is discussed below.

3. DISCUSSION

Mongolism is probably the best known chromosomal disorder. Even so the exact part of chromosome 21 responsible for the expression of the mongoloid phenotype when present in triplicate is still unknown. Phenotype-karyotype correlations in the family described here restrict the "critical mongoloid segment" to about 1/3 of chromosome 21, namely the distal pale band of the long arm, designated 21q22 by the Paris Conference (1971).

This restriction was deduced from the segregation of a rearrangement, involving chromosomes 2 and 21, transmitted by the mother, II-1. Banding techniques have permitted the conclusion that band 21q22 is missing from its original place in chromosome 21, and that chromosome 2 is enlarged by approximately the same length. The

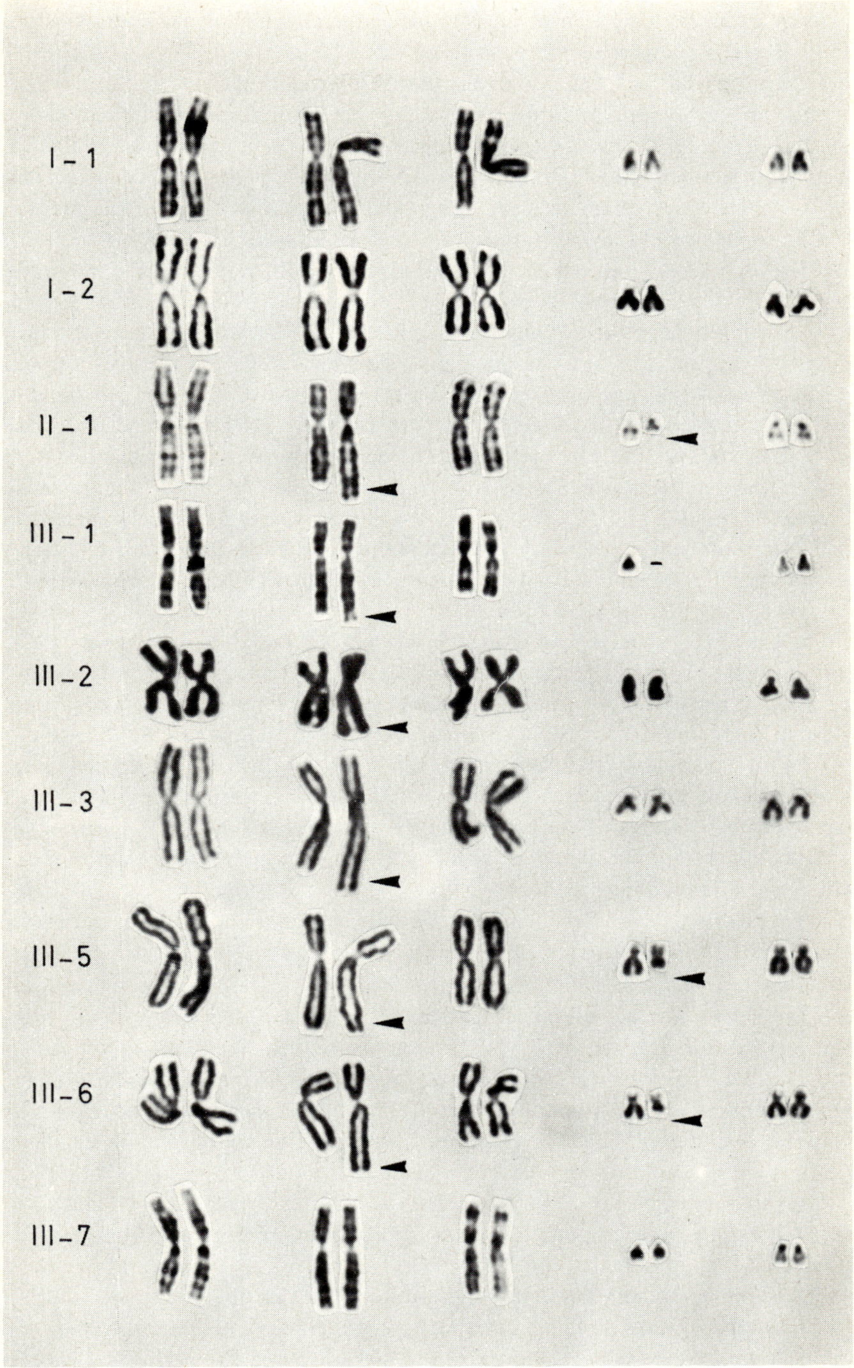

FIG. 5.—Partial karyotypes (chromosomes 1, 2, 3, 21, and 22) of members of the family and abortuses. I-1, II-1, III-1, and III-7—Giemsa-banding; all others—acetic-orcein.

simplest interpretation of this finding requires two chromosome breaks—one about halfway along the long arm of 21, perhaps at the dark/pale band boundary, and another in the telomere region of the long arm of 2—following which pieces were reciprocally exchanged. The true nature of this 2/21 rearrangement could, however, not be clarified. Some doubts arose whether this was a simple reciprocal translocation because the terminal segment of the elongated No. 2 was relatively darkly stained. It sometimes appeared as if the light band of No. 21 had been inserted proximally into the long arm, which would necessitate more than two breaks. Other break points in chromosome 21 could also be postulated. However, according to Savage et al. (1973) and Seabright (1973) induced chromosome breaks hardly ever occur in dark bands, and those which they scored in chromosome 21 would also fit our preferred interpretation. As it was impossible to identify exactly the kind of change, we have refrained from applying the structural designations recommended by the Paris Conference (1971). It seems sufficient to describe it as a transposition of the distal pale band of the long arm of No. 21 (21q22) to the long arm of No. 2. The genetic interpretations given here are applicable irrespective of the detailed mode of rearrangement.

The rearrangement was absent from the somatic karyotypes of the mother's parents, I-1 and I-2, and thus presumably arose in the germ-line of one of them. The significance of four out of 22 analyzed cells of the grandmother, I-1, containing acentric and dicentric chromosomes (involving in one cell two G-group chromosomes) is unknown.

The most likely arrangement of the chromosomes 2 and 21 of the mother, II-1, is given in figure 1 (where telomeres are not indicated). Such a translocation carrier will normally produce two types of balanced and at least four types of unbalanced oocytes (normal No. 2 and deleted No. 21, translocation No. 2 and normal No. 21, normal No. 2 with No. 21 completely lost, translocation No. 2 with No. 21 completely lost). The last two kinds of oocytes are presumably produced due to the loss, through asynapsis, non-disjunction, or lagging, of the small deleted No. 21. Gametes containing both the normal and the deleted No. 21 can, in principle, also be formed but will not be discussed here.

From these six zygotic combinations, three have been found amongst the sibs of generation III: one case of a normal karyotype (normal phenotype), two cases of a translocation No. 2 and normal No. 21's (mongoloids), and one case of a translocation No. 2 with only one normal No. 21 (mentally retarded but physically normal). The combinations of two normal No. 2's and one normal No. 21 (complete monosomy No. 21), or one normal No. 21 and one deleted No. 21 (monosomy for the light band only) were not yet found in this family; the first of these is presumably lethal while the second will probably cause so-called anti-mongolism (see, for example, Nevin et al., 1971).

The apparently normal karyotypes of the two abortus specimens, III-5 and III-6, were not helpful in determining the causes of abortion. Three explanations may be considered:

(1) The abortions were unrelated to chromosomal abnormalities.

(2) The karyotypes of the fetuses, although resembling those of the mother, were not identical with them, and thus genetically unbalanced (see, for example, Grouchy et al., 1966).

(3) The karyotypes were derived from maternal cells. The abortions were early

ones and the conceptuses were partially macerated: abortion III-5 occurred at the 15th week of pregnancy and III-6 at about the 6th week. It is quite possible that in the second case only maternal cells were grown; one may also doubt the fetal origin of cells obtained from the first.

From the phenotype-karyotype correlation of the surviving children it seems justified to conclude that the most important part of the genetic information of chromosome 21 resides in the pale band, that triplication of this information will cause Down's syndrome, and that this band is not involved in an obvious position effect. On the other hand, elimination of one copy of the short arm and the dark band of the long arm, that is about 2/3 of the total length of No. 21, had a relatively unspecific effect on the phenotype. This family supports previous inferences that triplication of the short arm of No. 21 is not essential for the manifestation of mongolism and also adds to this the dark band of the long arm. If our interpretation of the roles of the pale versus the dark bands is confirmed, it may have a more general implication, namely that genes with major effects are concentrated in light bands.

Other cases of monosomy for short arms and small proximal pieces of long arms of acrocentric chromosomes are known. Although short arms alone are dispensable, the additional loss of the proximal segment of certain of the long arms may lead to mental retardation and some somatic effects (see, for example, cases 15 and 16 of Leisti, 1971). On the other hand, partial trisomies of proximal segments of G chromosomes may either cause severe physical and mental effects (as in the proband of the family described by Macintyre et al., 1971) or none (as in the kindred reported by Day and Miles, 1965). In the first case it is, however, possible that chromosome 22, possessing a proximal light band, is involved. In some of these cases banding methods may be expected to provide a better resolution of the composition of the relevant chromosome segments.

From the practical point of view the most important problem in this and similar families lies in the prenatal distinction between fetuses with normal, balanced and unbalanced karyotypes. This is often a question of fine resolution of chromosome structure requiring banded preparations of good quality. Prior to the development of banding methods such decisions could rarely be made, unless chromosome shape was markedly affected, as in the cases of Kontras et al., 1966; Cohen and Davidson, 1967; Miller et al., 1970; Macintyre et al., 1971; and Wyandt et al., 1971. In another family (Day and Miles, 1965), as well as in ours when first studied (Schmidt et al., 1972), the chromosome changes were too small to be safely recognized by orcein-staining.

4. SUMMARY

1. Chromosome banding analysis of a kindred, in which a de-novo chromosome change occurred, revealed the translocation of the distal pale G-band of chromosome 21 to the long arm of chromosome 2.

2. A mother carrying a balanced karyotype gave birth to four children: two mongoloids who had an extra pale band of No. 21, a mentally retarded but physically normal son who was disomic for the pale band but monosomic for the dark band (and the short arm as well), and a phenotypically and chromosomally normal child which was karyotyped prenatally following amniocentesis.

3. With regard to the long arm of chromosome 21, karyotype-phenotype correlations indicate that (a) triplication of the pale band, or part of it, produces Down's syndrome, and (b) monosomy for the dark band has no obvious physical effects but is accompanied by mental retardation.

4. It is suggested that genes with major effects are concentrated in pale bands.

Addendum. After this paper was submitted the mother gave birth to another normal son whose normal chromosomes were prenatally ascertained.

5. REFERENCES

Cohen, M. M., and Davidson, R. G. 1967. Down's syndrome associated with familial (21q – ; 22q +) translocation. *Cytogenetics (Basel)*,*6,* 321–330.

Day, R. W., and Miles, C. P. 1965. Familial Down's syndrome with undetected translocation. *J. Pediatr., 67,* 399–409.

Grouchy, J. De., Aussannaire, M., Brissaud, H. E., and Lamy, M. 1966. Aneusomie de recombinaison: Three further examples. *Am. J. Hum. Genet., 18,* 467–484.

Kontras, S. B., Currier, G. J., Cooper, R. F., and Ambuel, J. P. 1966. Maternal transmission of a 21/1 translocation associated with Down's syndrome. *J. Pediatr., 69,* 635–639.

Leisti, J. 1971. Structural variation in human mitotic chromosomes. *Ann. Acad. Sci. Fenn. Ser. A IV Biol., 179,* 1–69.

Lejeune, J., Gautier, M., and Turpin, R. 1959. Les chromosomes humains en culture de tissus. *C. R. Hebd. Seances Acad. Sci. Ser. D Sci. Nat., 248,* 602–603.

Macintyre, M. N., Walden, D. B., and Hempel, J. M. 1971. Tertiary trisomy in a human kindred containing an E/G translocation. *Am. J. Hum. Genet., 23,* 431–442.

Miller, J. R., Dill, F. J., Corey, M. J., and Rigg, J. M. 1970. A rare translocation (47, XY, t(2p – ; 21q +), 21 +) associated with Down's syndrome. *J. Med. Genet., 7,* 389–393.

Nevin, N. C., MacLaverty, B., and Campbell, W. A. B. 1971. A child with a ring chromosome (46, XX, Gr). *J. Med. Genet., 8,* 231–234.

Niebuhr, E. 1974. Down's syndrome: The possibility of a pathogenetic segment on chromosome No. 21. *Humangenetik, 21,* 99–101.

Paris Conference. 1971. *Standardization in Human Cytogenetics.* Birth Defects: Original Article Series, *8:7* (1972). The National Foundation, New York.

Savage, J. R. K., Watson, G. E., and Bigger, T. R. L. 1973. The participation of human chromosome arms in radiation-induced chromatid exchange. *Chromosomes Today, 4* (J. Wahrman and K. R. Lewis, eds.), pp. 267–276. Israel Universities Press, Jerusalem, and John Wiley & Sons, New York.

Schmidt, R., Mundel, G., Rosenblatt, M., and Bat-Miriam Katznelson, M. 1972. Apparent G-monosomy, G-deletion, and incomplete Down's syndrome in a single family. *J. Med. Genet., 9,* 457–461.

Seabright, M. 1973. High resolution studies on the pattern of induced exchanges in the human karyotype. *Chromosoma (Berl.), 40,* 333–346.

Wyandt, H. E., Hecht, F., Lovrien, E. W., and Stewart, R. E. 1971. Study of a patient with apparent monosomy 21 owing to translocation: 45, XX, 21 –, t(18q +). *Cytogenetics (Basel), 10,* 413–426.

CHROMOSOME POLYMORPHISM IN A HUMAN NEWBORN POPULATION—PART I

HANSJAKOB MÜLLER and HAROLD P. KLINGER

Laboratory of Cell Genetics, Department of Genetics, and R. F. Kennedy Center for Research in Mental Retardation and Human Development, Albert Einstein College of Medicine, Bronx, New York 10461

1. INTRODUCTION

The chromosome banding methods (Paris Conference, 1971) allow the recognition of new polymorphic variants (Caspersson et al., 1971; Craig-Holmes and Shaw, 1971; Evans et al., 1971; Schnedl, 1971) as well as a more specific and detailed characterization of already known variants (see: Patau, 1961; Ferguson-Smith et al., 1962; Turpin and Lejeune, 1965; Lubs and Ruddle, 1970).

This study is an attempt to utilize the C-, Q- and G-chromosome banding methods in combination on the same metaphase cells, or on those of the same individual, to determine the incidence and racial distribution of polymorphic chromosome bands in karyotypes of an unselected newborn population.

2. MATERIAL AND METHODS

The 316 newborn babies included in the present series are part of a larger ongoing cytogenetic, anthropometric, and developmental study on the potential effects of maternal use of hormonal contraceptives on the subsequent conceptus (Klinger et al., 1974, 1975). The neonates were born at the Albert Einstein College Hospital, Bronx, New York, between January 1973 and May 1974. They were selected on a random basis according to a method described in greater detail in Klinger et al. (1975).

Chromosome preparations were made from umbilical cord blood according to a standardized air drying method whereby air temperature and humidity are kept constant (Klinger, 1972). Replicate slides from each case were stained with the banding techniques listed below within 3 to 6 days after preparation.

C-banding method: The technique of Sumner (1972) was used as follows: The preparations were treated for 10 min. in a saturated aqueous barium hydroxide solution at 50°C, rinsed in distilled water, and incubated for 60 min. in 2 × SSC (pH 7.2) at 60°C. The slides were then stained for one hour in a solution of one part of G.T. Gurr's Giesma R-66 to 25 parts of Gurr's phosphate buffer at pH 6.8.

Q-banding method: The preparations were stained in a 0.5% aqueous solution of quinacrine dihydrochloride (SIGMA) for 5 min, rinsed four times in distilled water, and mounted in a 0.95% sodium chloride solution. The stained slides were examined with the Zeiss UV epi-illumination fluorescence microscope fitted with a HBO 200 mercury lamp, BG 12 exciter, and 510 nm barrier filter.

G-banding method: The trypsin-method of Seabright (1971) as modified by Klinger (1972) was used.

All the cytogenetic as well as related contraceptive, clinical, anthropometric, ethnic, and other data were coded onto computer cards. This information was not known to the observer conducting the chromosome studies until the computer tabulations were completed. Correlations between the results of this study and the contraceptive, clinical, anthropometric and other data will be described in a future report.

3. DEFINITIONS AND SCORING SYSTEM

The morphologic chromosome variants occur principally within the regions termed "C-bands" which have arbitrarily been defined as constitutive heterochromatin (Paris Conference, 1971). They stain heavily with the C-band technique. In addition, when stained with quinacrine, this chromatin may appear to be divided into bands of varying length and position as well as intensity of fluorescence. In the human karyotype this is particularly conspicuous on chromosomes 3, 4, 13–15, 21, 22, and the Y. For this reason our study was concentrated on these regions, with the exception of that on the Y.

Because it is difficult to quantify *length variation* of chromosome bands by linear measurements only, we attempted to classify these in relation to clearly defined and consistent morphologic chromosome characteristics which alter little, and fairly proportionately, in relation to increasing contraction of the entire chromosome set as the cell proceeds through mitosis, or in response to technical treatment. Such cytogenetic landmarks were: the diameter of the chromatid, the short arm of chromosome 18, the long arm of chromosome 21, and the distinct Q-band 1q25. This scoring system was also chosen because it overcomes cell to cell or even chromosome to chromosome variations caused by stretching (peripheral location), twisting, unequal staining of chromosomes or parts of chromosomes, etc. Thus, it allows interindividual comparisons with a fair degree of objectivity.

The absolute *fluorescent intensity* of a quinacrine-stained chromosome, or a chromosome segment, is difficult to quantify objectively because it is dependent on many factors. These include a variety of technical and other conditions as well as the immediate environment (presence of other chromosomes or nuclei) and duration of UV-illumination. Various degress of fluorescent intensity were observed in the regions known to be subject to variation after Q-staining, some of these can be easily identified because of their conspicuously bright fluorescence. In the Paris Conference Report (1971), the intensity of such regions or bands is described as intense or brilliant. In the absence of densitometric measurements, and because of the factors considered above, the distinction between these two intensity levels is difficult in actual practice. As a consequence variable Q-bands which may fluoresce intensely or brilliantly will be referred to as "bright". However, in the case of the satellites, an effort was made to use the terms recommended by the Paris Conference, i.e., "negative," "pale," "medium," "intense" and "brilliant."

The chromosome complement of each subject was first determined from two cut-out and mounted karyotypes of the G-banded preparations. No cases with chromosome aberrations were found. In the next step, ten well-spread quinacrine-stained mitoses were examined by one of us under direct microscopic observation and the frequency, distribution and relative length of the "brightly" fluorescent bands were scored. Another ten cells, which had not been UV-irradiated, were then photographed on Kodak Panatomic-X film. Their position was recorded with the aid of an "England finder" (Graticules Ltd., London, England). The same mitoses were restained with the C-banding method, relocated, and photographed on Kodak High Contrast film. Because prolonged UV-illumination of the Q-stained chromosomes may occasionally impair the quality of the subsequent C-staining method, an untreated replicate slide was always stained with the C-banding method as a control, and additional metaphases were photographed.

The final classification of each variant was made from negatives of the same metaphase cell photographed after C- and Q-staining and projected side by side on one screen at an end magnification of about 9000 ×. The results of this analysis were cross-checked with those obtained from the direct observations of the Q-stained mitoses as well as from photographs of C-stained metaphases of the replicate slides.

Because of technical difficulties, it was not possible for some subjects to classify an adequate number of chromosomes of a particular type from the available karyotypes. These are noted in the tables as "not classifiable" and are not included in the percentage calculations.

4. RESULTS

When a variant band was detected on a homologue of a chromosome then, with minor technical exceptions, it was always found to be the same in all ten metaphases examined from that subject. This was also true when the findings from the projections were cross-checked with the records of the direct observations and the photographs of the extra C-stained non-irradiated metaphases. Therefore, to simplify matters, *we considered each partner of a homologous pair as one chromosome even though at least ten samples were examined.* As a consequence the data in tables 1 to 4 represent the analysis of chromosomes 1, 3, 4, 9, 13–15, 16, 21 and 22 of 316 homologous pairs or 623 "chromosomes." Only some of the findings are presented in this report; more extensive analyses including other chromosomes are dealt with in Müller et al. (1975).

(a) *C-band length variation on chromosomes* 1, 9 *and* 16

C-bands on some of the autosomes and the X are generally very small and variants, although sometimes distinguishable, are difficult to characterize with certainty (Paris Conference, 1971). This is not true for chromosomes 1, 9 and 16 where in addition to the centromeric chromatin the adjacent constriction, primarily on the long arm but to a variable degree also on the short arm (see below), stains heavily with the C-banding method (fig 1). The length variations in these regions are the basis of this study. The results given in table 1 on the distribution of position and length of the C-bands of these chromosomes indicate a considerable variation in the amount of C-chromatin which extends into the short arm in addition to that present on the long arm. In the case of chromosome 9, two out of 620 samples had more C-chromatin on the short than on the long arm. No cases with apparent inversions of the secondary constriction were found in chromosomes 16. All ten samples listed to have "about one third of the C-chromatin on p" had very small C-bands.

Two findings became apparent:

1. The Q-banding method alone is not suitable for the identification of length

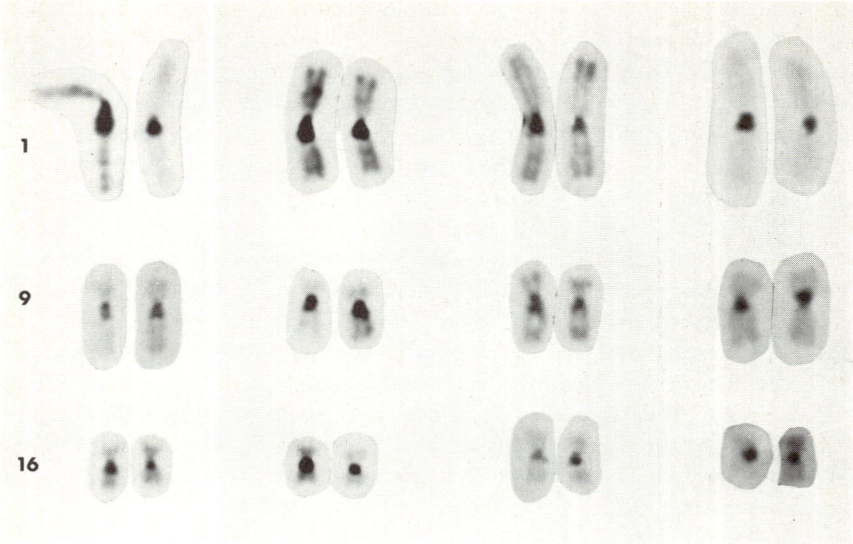

FIG. 1.—Samples of chromosomes 1, 9 and 16 from four different individuals (vertical columns) demonstrating variations in C-chromatin location and length.

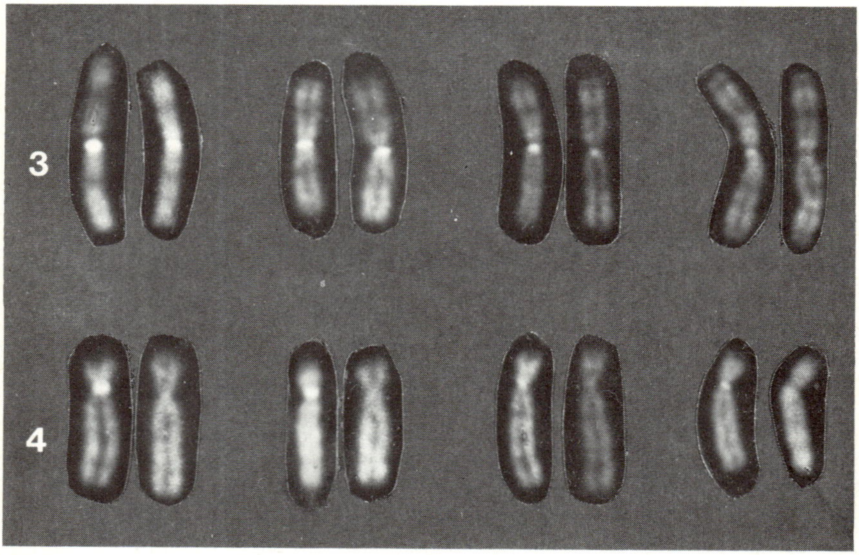

FIG. 2.—Samples of quinacrine stained chromosomes 3 and 4 from four different individuals demonstrating variations in the length of the brightly fluorescent bands at the centromeric region.

variants of the secondary constrictions. With this method it is often impossible to determine where such negative fluorescent regions end and an adjacent weakly fluorescent band begins. Also, chromosomes with "partial inversion" of the secondary constrictions cannot be identified if only the Q-banding method is used.

TABLE 1

Location and length of C-bands on chromosomes 1, 9 and 16 from 316 neonates. (Each unit in the "No." column represents the characteristics of one homologue of a pair determined from examination of 10 metaphase cells and confirmed from replicate preparations, also see text.)

	No. 1		No. 9		No. 16	
	No.	%	No.	%	No.	%
Extension of C-chromatin into p in addition to q						
No C-chromatin on p	333	53.2	259	41.8	540	86.5
Little C-chromatin on p	283	45.2	289	46.6	74	11.9
About one third of the C-chromatin on p	10	1.6	70	11.3	10	1.6
More C-chromatin on p than q	0		2	0.3	0	
Not classifiable*	6		12		8	
Length of the C-bands in respect to the length of 21q						
1/4 or less than 21q	4	0.6	3	0.5	154	24.7
About 1/2 of 21q	215	34.3	291	46.9	430	68.9
About equal to 21q	354	56.5	280	45.2	40	6.4
About 1 1/2 times 21q	42	6.7	40	6.5	0	
2 or more times 21q	11	1.8	6	1.0	0	
Not classifiable*	6		12		8	

* Not included in percentage calculations.

2. The variation of the C-stained region of these chromosomes is even greater if, in addition to length and location, unique features of variation in its structure are also considered. These regions are often divided into distinct segments of consistent pattern which are particularly evident in early metaphase.

(b) *Q-band variants on chromosomes* 3 *and* 4

The variability of the brightly fluorescent bands adjacent to the centromeric region on chromosomes 3 and 4 is demonstrated in table 2. A brightly fluorescent band was missing in 44.4% of the samples of chromosome 3 and in 86.6% of chromosome 4. Because these bands can be very thin, their detection is to a certain extent subject to the quality of the preparation, but this potential error was reduced by the examination of multiple cells. In addition to length and intensity of fluorescence these bands vary in respect to their specific locations: the brightly fluorescent band on chromosome 3 was, with one exception, always found on the long arm side of the centromere. In the case of chromosome 4, the brightly fluorescent band was located on the short arm in 40% of the samples, on the long arm in 40%, and in the remaining 20% was restricted to the immediate centromeric region. Furthermore, it was noted that when chromosome 3 showed a large and brightly fluorescent band, the whole C-region was large when stained with the C-banding method.

(c) *Variability of the acrocentric chromosomes*

The amount of variability within the acrocentric chromosomes is striking. Four

TABLE 2

Length of the brightly fluorescent band at the centromeric region of chromosomes 3 *and* 4 (*see also legend to table 1*)

	No. 3		No. 4	
Length of the band	No.	%	No.	%
None	272	44.4	528	86.6
Thin	151	24.7	74	12.1
Shorter than 1q25	125	20.4	6	1.0
About equal to 1q25	62	10.1	2	0.3
Longer than 1q25	2	0.3	0	
Not classifiable*	20		22	

* Not included in percentage calculations.

major segments vary independently: the centromeric region, the proximal part of the short arm, the secondary constriction or satellite stalk, and the satellite proper. Further variability is found when C- and Q-banding characteristics are compared. Although brightly fluorescent Q-stained regions tend to stain strongly with the C-method, this is not always true. However, when the discrepancy is observed it is consistent in all cells of an individual for that particular chromosome region.

Table 3 demonstrates the frequency of the different variants at the centromeric regions and the short arms of the acrocentric chromosomes. If the length of the short arms of the chromosomes 13–15 are compared, it is apparent that the short arm of chromosome 13 is more often shorter than that of chromosomes 14 or 15. Also, chromosome 13 more often has a small C-band. The length of the C-band in most of the karyotypes is clearly different between chromosomes 21 and 22. However, exceptions to this rule are apparent in table 3, indicating that the C-bands alone do not permit the two chromosome pairs to be identified in all cases.

The variability of satellites of the acrocentric chromosomes is demonstrated in table 4. The category "small to medium-sized satellites" needs special comment: For about one third of all chromosomes included in this group it was not possible to clearly identify the satellites in all metaphases examined, partly because the satellite stalk was very short. Consequently the non-satellited chromosomes are listed in table 4 but are not included in the percentage calculations.

As can be seen in table 4, chromosome 22 has strongly C-stained satellites more often than any of the other acrocentric autosomes. Negative to pale fluorescent satellites occur more frequently on chromosome 13 while intensely fluorescent satellites were more common on chromosomes 21 and 22. The observed polymorphism of the acrocentric chromosomes may be somehow related to the fact that these chromosomes do not undergo Robertsonian translocations or participate in satellite associations at random.

(d) *Distribution of the variants within the sample*

We attempted to determine whether the variants are distributed independently within the homologous pairs. The frequency of each concordant and discordant homologous pair of all neonates was first determined. The distribution of these observed concordant and discordant pairs was then compared with that of the expected

TABLE 3

Frequency of variants of the acrocentric chromosomes (see also legend to table 1)

	No. 13		No. 14		No. 15		No. 21		No. 22	
	No.	%	No.	%	No.	%	No.	%	No.	%
Length of the short arm in relation to length of 18p (based on Q-stained preparations)										
About 1/4 or less	200	31.7	38	6.0	48	7.6	274	43.6	206	32.8
About 1/4 to 1/2	418	66.3	515	81.7	467	74.1	344	54.8	409	65.1
About 1/2 or equal to 18p	11	1.7	75	11.9	110	17.5	10	1.6	12	1.9
Larger than 18 p	1	0.2	2	0.3	5	0.8	0		1	0.2
Not classifiable*	2		2		2		4		4	
Length of the centric C-band										
Small C-band**	183	29.6	90	14.6	54	8.7	534	86.1	48	7.7
Medium C-band†	229	37.1	407	66.2	332	53.7	62	10.0	418	67.4
C-band extended into p	190	30.7	113	18.4	215	34.8	23	3.7	143	23.1
Entire short arm stained	16	2.6	5	0.8	17	2.8	1	0.2	11	1.8
Not classifiable*	14		17		14		12		12	
Length and location of the brightly fluorescent centric or paracentric band										
No brightly fluor. band	157	25.6	594	97.1	595	97.5	594	97.1	395	64.5
Very thin band	107	17.4	4	0.7	3	0.5	8	1.3	33	5.4
Short band	126	20.5	4	0.7	2	0.3	6	1.0	78	12.7
Band extends into most or all of p	208	33.9	3	0.5	3	0.5	4	0.7	65	10.6
Brightly fluorescent band on p not in centric region	8	1.3	7	1.1	7	1.1	0		11	1.8
One band at the centromere and one in p	8	1.3	0		0		0		30	4.9
Not classifiable*	18		20		22		20		20	

* Not included in percentage calculations.

** Smaller or about equal to C-band on chromosome 2.

† About length of C-band on chromosome 6.

TABLE 4

Frequency of variants of the acrocentric chromosomes (see also legend to table 1)

	No. 13		No. 14		No. 15		No. 21		No. 22	
	No.	%	No.	%	No.	%	No.	%	No.	%
Size of the satellites only (diameter of chromatid = 1)										
No satellites	55	8.8	56	9.0	71	11.5	32	5.2	37	6.0
Small to medium sized sat. (less than 1)	544	87.5	511	81.9	495	80.0	538	86.8	522	84.6
Large satellites (about 1)	21	3.4	54	8.7	52	8.4	43	6.9	51	8.3
Very large (giant) sat. (more than 1)	2	0.3	3	0.5	1	0.2	7	1.1	7	1.1
Not classifiable*	10		8		13		12		15	
C-staining intensity of satellites										
No satellites*	55		56		71		32		37	
Faintly stained	418	81.3	385	77.2	384	79.5	409	76.0	325	62.9
Lightly stained (more than euchromatin)	79	15.4	85	17.0	79	16.4	103	19.1	134	25.9
Strongly stained	17	3.3	29	5.8	20	4.1	26	4.8	58	11.2
Not classifiable*	63		77		78		62		78	
Q-staining intensity of satellites (as per Paris Conference, 1971)										
No satellites*	55		56		71		32		37	
Negative to pale	286	51.9	198	35.6	220	41.0	219	37.8	196	34.1
Medium	156	28.3	220	39.6	204	38.0	200	34.5	172	30.0
Negative to medium**	57	10.3	61	11.0	61	11.4	55	9.5	47	8.2
Intense	23	4.2	47	8.5	36	6.7	74	12.8	121	21.1
Brilliant	29	5.3	30	5.4	16	3.0	32	5.5	38	6.6
Not classifiable*	26		20		24		20		21	

* Not included in percentage calculations.
** Distinction between negative, pale and medium not possible.

pairs, whereby the expected number of concordant and discordant pairs was based upon the observed distribution of the characteristics of all 632 homologues. The details of the calculations, as well as of the Chi Square test used, followed that of Mantel and Crittenden (1961). For most of the chromosomal variants the differences between the observed and the expected matched and unmatched pairs is consistent with random variation ($P > 0.30$). In the case of the location of C-chromatin on p and q of chromosome 9 the difference is at the $P = 0.10$ level. The only consistent exception involved the C-bands of the acrocentric chromosomes where concordance of length was significantly greater than expected ($P \leqq 0.05$). This may mean either that the length of this specific chromatin is for some reason unique to an individual, or more probably, that this chromatin, which has many unique features, is somehow subject to selective artifactual alterations which enhance equalization of length in the preparations.

(e) *Frequency of variants according to ethnic group*

Of the 316 newborns examined, 222 were white, 39 were black, and the others were of a different or mixed racial background. The frequency of the different variants was compared according to the two major ethnic groups of our sample. With only some minor exceptions no variants were restricted to only one of the ethnic groups (table 5). However, there was a trend for the neonates of the black population to have a higher frequency of brightly (intensely or brilliantly) fluorescent centric and paracentric chromatin than those of the white population. This applied to most of the chromosomes examined. The difference is statistically significant for chromosomes 3 ($P < 0.05$) and for both the short arm and satellite variants of 22 ($P < 0.01$) but not for the others. The short arms of chromosomes 14 and 15 may be exceptions to this trend, but the sample sizes here are very small. If the sizes of these bands, in addition to the intensity of their fluorescence were to be taken

TABLE 5

Incidence of the brightly variable Q-bands on specific chromosomes of 222 white and 39 black newborn babies

Chromosome homolog		White No.*	White %	Black No.*	Black %
Chromosome 3		230	54.4	50	67.5
Chromosome 4		50	12.8	13	17.6
Chromosome 13	short arm	316	73.8	59	79.7
	satellites	42	9.8	8	10.8
Chromosome 14	short arm	14	3.2	0	
	satellites	40	9.3	10	13.5
Chromosome 15	short arm	14	3.2	1	1.4
	satellites	32	7.4	6	8.1
Chromosome 21	short arm	15	3.5	4	5.4
	satellites	70	16.2	13	17.6
Chromosome 22	short arm	83	19.2	20	27.0
	satellites	103	23.9	28	37.8

* Not classifiable samples not included.

into account in the form of an "intensity-size index," then the differences shown in table 5 would very likely become more pronounced. This is now being analyzed in greater detail on a somewhat larger sample. It should also be stressed that the racial classification of our neonates is very likely not completely accurate since precise racial origins cannot be determined in many instances. It is therefore possible that greater differences would be found if populations of pure racial origin were examined.

5. DISCUSSION

The chromosomal variants which have been described are of both theoretical and practical interest. It was shown that chromosome polymorphism is frequent in man and that these characters are consistent in all cells of one individual. Family studies of others indicate that they are usually transmitted as simple Mendelian traits. Chromosome polymorphism is not unique to man; C-band variants have been described in the wild mouse (*Peromyscus maniculatus*, Duffy, 1972), laboratory mouse (*Mus musculus*, Dev et al., 1973), climbing rats (genus *Tylomys*, Pathak et al., 1973), and many other animals.

The observation that the constitutive heterochromatin contains numerous repeated DNA sequences (Pardue and Gall, 1970; Jones and Corneo, 1971; Saunders et al., 1972) has suported the long-held view that it is genetically inert. Therefore, the observed C- and Q-band polymorphisms might not be expected to show phenotypic expression. In addition, heterochromatic regions may show a wide variability in respect to base composition and sequences despite their highly repetitive nature (Henning and Walker, 1970; Sutton and McCallum, 1971, 1972). The latter may explain some of the variable staining properties we observed in the C-band regions. The repetitive nature of DNA in the heterochromatic regions makes it possible that they could undergo unequal crossing over between homologues during meiosis or interphase. However, this would probably result in a greater variability of the C-bands than has been observed. Detailed and extensive family studies would be required to resolve this point. Our own observations suggest that, if recombinational events occur in this region, they are not readily detectable. The proposal that certain chromosome variants may cause segregation distortion, as observed in families with a large C-block on chromosome 9 (Fitzgerald, 1973) needs further confirmation in similar families.

The high frequency of polymorphic chromosome characteristics observed here and by other workers, and the fact that they are heritable, makes them of considerable practical value in pedigree analyses, population studies, attempts at gene localizations, and in other somatic cell genetic investigations. These variants have already achieved considerable importance in prenatal diagnosis by allowing the distinction between maternal and fetal cells. They may gain general acceptance in paternity testing.

The trend for racial differences found in this study supports those of earlier reports (Lubs and Ruddle, 1971). Although more rigorous studies of larger samples or preferably of "pure" races would be required to determine whether these differences are significant, the current findings suggest that the cytogenetic markers may also be useful in ethnological and evolutionary studies.

6. SUMMARY

1. Replicate chromosome preparations of 316 unselected newborn babies were stained with the C- and Q-, as well as with the G-banding methods for the determination of the frequencies of different chromosome variants.

2. The variability in the C-staining regions (primary and secondary constrictions) of chromosomes 1, 9 and 16, of the variable Q-bands on chromosomes 3 and 4, and of the polymorphic segments of the acrocentric chromosomes was analyzed.

3. The combined use of the C- and Q-banding techniques allows the detection of many more chromosome variants than the conventional chromosome staining methods or any of the banding techniques used individually.

4. Racial differences were found in the frequencies of some variant types when chromosomes of black and white neonates were compared. The results reinforce the widely held view that the polymorphic chromosome characteristics are very useful markers in pedigree analyses, in population studies, in attempts at gene localizations, and in ethnologic and evolutionary studies.

Acknowledgements. We are grateful to Dr. Marvin Glasser for his help with the statistical analyses. This work was supported by the Center of Population Research, NICHD Contract No. 69-2129, by Grant No. M72.158 from the Population Council, N.Y., and by NIGMS Genetics Center Grant No. 19100. Hj. M. is a recipient of a fellowship from the "Stiftung für biologisch-medizinische Stipendien" of the Swiss Academy of Medical Sciences (1973) and the Swiss National Foundation (1974). H.P.K. holds NIGMS Research Career Program Award No. GM-25,260.

7. REFERENCES

Caspersson, T., Lomakka, G., and Zech, L. 1971. The 24 fluorescence patterns of the human metaphase chromosomes—distinguishing characters and variability. *Hereditas, 67,* 89–102.

Craig-Holmes, A. P., and Shaw, M. W. 1971. Polymorphism of human constitutive heterochromatin. *Science (Wash. D.C.), 174,* 702–704.

Craig-Holmes, A. P., Moore, F. B., and Shaw, M. W. 1973. Polymorphism of human C-band heterochromatin. I. Frequency of variants. *Am. J. Hum. Genet., 25,* 181–192.

Dev, V. G., Miller, D. A., and Miller, O. J. 1973. Chromosome markers in *Mus musculus:* strain differences in C-banding. *Genetics, 73,* 633–670.

Duffy, P. A. 1972. Chromosome variation in *Peromyscus:* a new mechanism. *Science (Wash. D.C.), 176,* 1333–1334.

Evans, H. J., Buckton, K. E., and Sumner, A. T. 1971. Cytological mapping of human chromosomes: results obtained with quinacrine fluorescence and the acetic-saline-Giemsa techniques. *Chromosoma (Berl.), 35,* 310–325.

Ferguson-Smith, M. A., Ferguson-Smith, M. F., Ellis, P. M., and Dickson, M. 1962. The sites and relative frequencies of secondary constrictions in human somatic chromosomes. *Cytogenetics, 1,* 325–343.

Fitzgerald, P. H. 1973. The nature and inheritance of an elongated secondary constriction on chromosome 9 of man. *Cytogenet. Cell Genet., 12,* 404–413.

Henning, W., and Walker, P. M. B. 1970. Variation in the DNA from two rodent families (Cricetidae and Muridae). *Nature (Lond.), 225,* 915–919.

Jones, K. W., and Corneo, G. 1971. Location of satellite and homogeneous DNA sequences on human chromosomes. *Nat. New Biol., 233,* 268–271.

KLINGER, H. P. 1972. Rapid processing of primary embryonic tissues for chromosome banding pattern analysis. *Cytogenetics, 11,* 424–435.

KLINGER, H. P., GLASSER, M., and KAVA, H. W. 1975. Contraceptives and the conceptus: Part I. Chromosome abnormalities of the fetus and neonate related to maternal contraceptive history. (Submitted for publication.)

KLINGER, H. P., KAVA, H. W., GLASSER, M., and KALLENBERGER, A. 1974. Cytogenetic, anthropometric and developmental studies of postcontraceptive reproduction in man—an interim report. In *Les Accidents Chromosomiques de la Reproduction* (A. BOUÉ and C. THIBAULT, eds.), pp. 371–389. Centre Int. de l'Enfance, Inst. Nat. Santé Recherche Médicale, 3, Rue Ison-Bonnat, Paris, France.

LUBS, H. A., and RUDDLE, F. H. 1970. Applications of quantitative karyotypy to chromosome variation in 4400 consecutive newborns. *Pfizer Foundation Series.* Edinburgh University Press.

LUBS, H. A., and RUDDLE, F. H. 1971. Chromosome polymorphism in American negro and white populations. *Nature (Lond.), 223,* 134–136.

MANTEL, N., and CRITTENDEN, L. B. 1961. Determination of Chi Square for comparing the number of matched pairs with its expectation. *J. Natl. Cancer Inst., 27,* 887–892.

MATSUI, S.-I., and SASAKI, M. 1973. Differential staining of nucleolus organisers in mammalian chromosomes. *Nature (Lond.), 246,* 148–150.

MÜLLER, H. J., KLINGER, H. P., and GLASSER, M. 1975. Chromosome polymorphism in a newborn population. II. Potentials of polymorphic chromosome variants for characterising the idiogram of an individual. *Cytogenet. Cell. Genet., 14* (in press).

PARDUE, M. S., and GALL, J. G. 1970. Chromosomal localization of mouse satellite DNA. *Science (Wash. D.C.), 168,* 1356–1358.

PARIS CONFERENCE. 1971. *Standardization in Human Cytogenetics. Birth Defects, Original Article Series VIII:*7 (1972). The National Foundation, New York.

PATAU, K. 1961. Chromosome identification and the Denver Report. *Lancet, i,* 933–934.

PATHAK, S., HSU, T. C., SHIRLEY, L., and HELM, J. D. 1973. Chromosome homology in the climbing rats, genus *Tylomys* (Rodentia: Cricetidae). *Chromosoma (Berl.), 42,* 215–228.

SAUNDERS, G. F., SHIRAKAWA, S., SAUNDERS, P. P., ARRIGHI, F. E., and HSU, T. C. 1972. Populations of repeated DNA sequences in the human genome. *J. Mol. Biol., 63,* 323–334.

SCHNEDL, W. 1971. Unterschiedliche Fluoreszenz der beiden homologen Chromosomen Nr. 3 beim Menschen. *Humangenetik, 12,* 59–63.

SEABRIGHT, M. 1971. A rapid banding technique for human chromosomes. *Lancet, ii,* 971–972.

SOUTHERN, E. M. 1970. Base sequence and evolution of guinea pig-satellite DNA. *Nature (Lond.), 227,* 794–798.

SUMNER, A. T. 1972. A simple method for demonstrating centromeric heterochromatin. *Exp. Cell Res., 75,* 304–306.

SUTTON, W. D., and MCCALLUM, M. 1971. Mismatching and the reassociation rate of mouse satellite DNA. *Nat. New Biol., 232,* 83–85.

SUTTON, W. D., and MCCALLUM, M. 1972. Related satellite DNA's in the genus *Mus. J. Mol. Biol., 71,* 633–636.

TURPIN, R., and LEJEUNE, J. 1965. *Les chromosomes humains. Caryotype normal et variations pathologiques.* Gauthier-Villars, Paris.

DOUBLE TRISOMIC CELLS FROM A BOY WITH CHRONIC MYELOPROLIFERATIVE DISORDER

C. C. LIN,[1,2] J. M. WHAUN[1] and J. B. DUNDAS[1]
[1]*Division of Pediatrics, Faculty of Medicine, University of Calgary, Calgary, Alberta, Canada*
[2]*Division of Medical Biochemistry, Faculty of Medicine, University of Calgary, Calgary, Alberta, Canada*

1. INTRODUCTION

A mildly anemic boy with splenomegaly thrombocytosis leucopenia was first seen by us in 1971. His marrow sample was hypercellular with some immature cells and numerous megakaryocytes and was thought at that time to have either a pre-leukemia or a myeloproliferative type marrow. Direct chromosome preparations from the marrow cells revealed a unique chromosome complement, with an extra chromosome in the C-group and an extra chromosome in the G-group in all twenty cells examined. The boy's routine lymphocyte culture had a normal male karyotype. In October 1972 he was found to have severe myelofibrosis. By May 1973, routine stain technique for chromosome analysis on his marrow cells had been repeated on three separate occasions, and each time a karyotype of 48, XY, C+, G+ was consistently found in ten to twenty cells examined. He was transfused several times and has been on androgenic therapy (50 mg oxymetholone, 4 times a day) for the past nine months. The boy, seen again recently, is now sixteen years old and continues to appear healthy. He has not had a blood transfusion for more than six months. Bone marrow was aspirated from left iliac crest at this time. Banded chromosome technique was used to identify the chromosome aberrations. Moreover, in an attempt to see whether the patient's cells with different chromosome complements may differ in response to their *in vitro* culture condition, we examined the chromosomes from short term cultures of marrow cells and peripheral lymphocytes using both phytohaemagglutinin (PHA) and Pokeweed mitogen (PWM) to stimulate cell proliferation.

2. MATERIALS AND METHODS

One ml of marrow was aspirated from the iliac crest and immediately transferred into two sterile 15 ml centrifuge tubes. Each tube contained 0.5 ml marrow and 10 ml of Hank's balance salt solution (Gibco) with 0.25 ml heparin. Colcemid in a final concentration of 0.1 μg/ml was added into one of the tubes for direct chromosome preparation. The other tube was centrifuged at 600 rpm for 10 min. After removing the supernatant and blood clot, the marrow cells were then resuspended in 2 ml of culture medium (Connaught CMLR-HB597). One ml of the cell suspension was then added into a culture bottle containing 9 ml of medium (Connaught) with 15% Fetal Calf Serum and 0.2 ml Phytohaemagglutinin (Wellcome). The remaining 1 ml of suspension was added into another culture bottle with the same culture medium but with 0.2 ml Pokeweed mitogen (Gibco) added. The cultures were incubated at 37°C for 72 hr. Two lymphocyte cultures from peripheral blood were set up following the routine procedures. However, in one of the cultures, instead of PHA, 0.2 ml of Pokeweed mitogen was added.

The procedure of chromosome preparation from uncultured cells and from short-term cultured cells was similar. The time of Colcemid treatment was $1\frac{1}{2}$ to $2\frac{1}{2}$ hr. The cells were then treated with a hypotonic solution, 0.075 M KCl for 25 to 30 minutes and fixed in methanol-acetic acid (3 : 1, vol/vol). Slides were prepared by an air-drying technique (Moorhead et al., 1960). Q-banding patterns were obtained by the method of Lin and Uchida (1973).

3. RESULTS AND DISCUSSION

Chromosome analysis was performed on 25 cells from uncultured marrow sample. All of them were found to have 48 chromosomes. The extra chromosomes appeared to be a chromosome 8 and a chromosome 21. Apart from the numerical aberration, each chromosome in the cell appeared to have normal Q-band patterns resulting in a double trisomic karyotype 48, XY, +8, +21 (see fig. 1) according to the nomenclature of the Paris Conference.

Numerous mitotic figures were found in both short term bond marrow cultures. Sixty cells examined from the marrow culture with PHA appeared to have a normal male karyotype, 46, XY, in every cell. However, two types of cell were found in 70

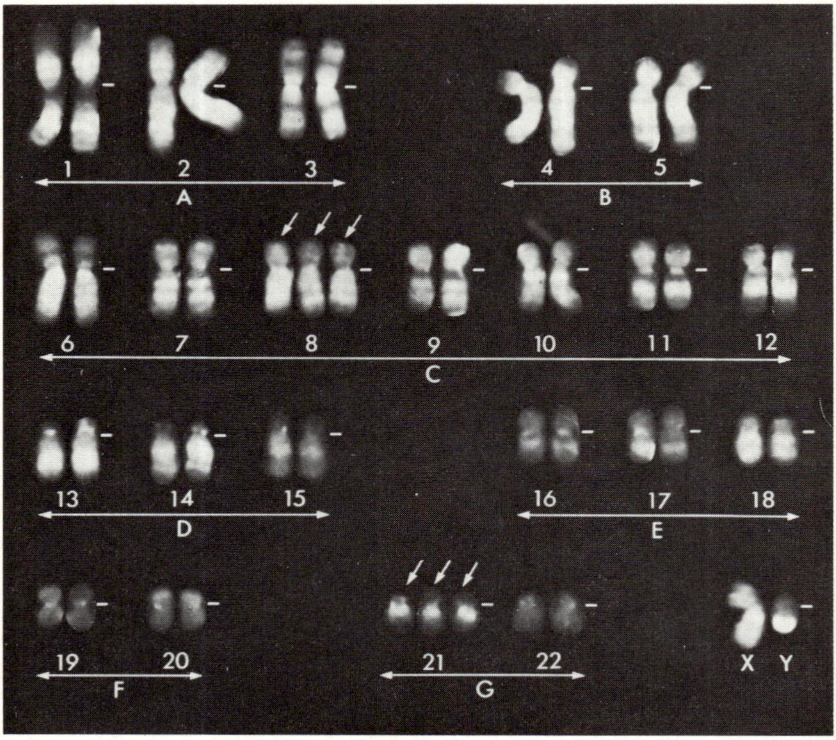

FIG. 1.—Q-banding karyotype of a double trisomic cell obtained from direct marrow preparations.

cells examined from marrow culture with Pokeweed mitogen. One type of cell had 48 chromosomes with a karyotype 48, XY, +8, +21 (63%), similar to the cell from direct marrow preparation; the other with 46 chromosomes had a karyotype of 46, XY, (37%) (see table).

Cells from peripheral lymphocyte culture with PHA again showed a normal male karyotype in all forty cells examined. The lymphocyte culture with Pokeweed mitogen was comparatively poor. Of the 40 cells karyotyped, 7 showed a karyotype of 48, XY, +8, +21 (17.5%) and the rest had a normal male karyotype (82.5%).

Apparently, cells undergoing proliferation in the boy's bone marrow were predominantly the double trisomic cells involving chromosomes 8 and 21. We are unable to identify what types of cell (or stem cells) in the marrow are the double trisomic cells. Our preliminary results from short term marrow culture indicate that the double trisomic cells and the cells with normal karyotype may have a difference in their response to *in vitro* cultures. The former only respond to cultures with Pokeweed mitogen, whereas the latter respond to cultures with Pokeweed or PHA.

Several cases have been reported in which an extra chromosome 8 was found in marrow cells of patients (Hellstrom et al., 1971; de la Chapelle et al., 1973; Rowley, 1973) with hematological disorders. Patients with trisomic 21 have been known to have a higher risk of leukemia. Recently, trisomic 21 has also been described in acute myelomonocytic leukemia (Brandt et al., 1974). These two chromosomes may bear factors which control the marrow cell proliferations. However, to our knowledge, it is the first case in which a double trisomic cell involving these two chromosomes was found to be associated with a myeloproliferative disorder.

4. SUMMARY

Double trisomic cells involving chromosomes 8 and 21 were found initially in the bone marrow of a boy with a chronic myeloproliferative disorder. Subsequent chromosome analysis on short term cultures with Pokeweed motogen from both marrow cells and peripheral lymphocytes revealed two types of cells: one with normal chromosome complement and the other with double trisomy 8 and 21. In contrast, on cultures with PHA, only cells with normal chromosome complement were seen. The preliminary results suggested that the trisomic cells and the normal cells may have differences in their response to mitogen in the *in vitro* culture condition.

TABLE

Chromosome analysis on 72 hours culture of marrow cells and peripheral lymphocytes with phytohaemagglutinin (PHA) and Pokeweed mitogen (PWM)

Cellculture	Karyotype	No. of cells examined	%
Marrow cells with PHA	46, XY	60	100
Marrow cells with PWM	46, XY	26	37
	48, XY, +8, +21	44	63
Lymphocytes with PHA	46, XY	40	100
Lymphocytes with PWM	46, XY	33	82.5
	48, XY, +8, +21	7	17.5

Acknowledgements. We wish to thank Miss M. Ursel and Miss L. Wilkie for excellent technical assistance. This work was supported in part by grant funds from the Medical Research Council of Canada.

5. REFERENCES

BRANDT, L., LEVAN, G., MITELMAN, F., OLSSON, I., and SJOGREN, U. 1974. Trisomy G-21 in adult myelomonocytic leukemia. *Scand. J. Haematol., 12,* 117–122.

DE LA CHAPELLE, A., SCHRODER, J., and VUOPIO, P. 1973. Cytogenetical and clinical aspects of trisomy 8 in bone marrow. In *Chromosome Identification* (T. CASPERSSON and L. ZECH, eds.), pp. 201–204. Academic Press, New York and London.

PARIS CONFERENCE. 1971. *Standardization in Human Cytogenetics.* Birth Defects, Original Article Series *8*:7 (1972). The National Foundation, New York.

HELLSTROM, K., HAGENFELDT, L., LARSSON, A., LINDSTEN, J., SUNDELIN, P., and TIEPOLO, L. 1971. An extra C chromosome and various metabolic abnormalities in the bone marrow from a patient with refractory sideroblastic anaemia. *Scand. J. Haematol., 8,* 293–306.

LIN, C. C., and UCHIDA, I. A. 1973. Fluorescent banding of chromosomes (Q-bands). In *Tissue Culture Methods and Applications* (P. F. KRUSE and M. K. PATTERSON, eds.), pp. 778–781. Academic Press, New York and London.

MOORHEAD, P. S., NOWELL, P. C., MELLMAN, W. J., BATTIPS, D. M., and HUNGERFORD, D. A. 1960. Chromosome preparations of leukocytes cultured from human peripheral blood. *Exp. Cell Res., 20,* 613–616.

ROWLEY, J. D. 1973. Nonrandom chromosomal abnormalities in leukemia. 16th Annual Meeting of Amer. Soc. Hemat. (abstract), p. 45.

CHROMOSOME IDENTIFICATION AND KARYOTYPIC EVOLUTION IN A HUMAN MELANOMA CELL LINE (MEL-41)

M. FRACCARO, F. LO CURTO, and SUSI SCAPPATICCI

Euratom Unit for Human Radiation and Cytogenetics at the Institute of General Biology of the Medical Faculty, University of Pavia, Italy

1. INTRODUCTION

Irrespective of their origin, established cell lines have some common characteristics such as heteroploid chromosome sets and varying degrees of karyotypic evolution. The chromosome banding techniques have greatly improved the analysis of these variables. Here, we report the essentials of the natural history of a cell line derived from a human tumor and give a preliminary description of its karyotypic variation and evolution.

2. MATERIALS AND METHODS

The cell line, designated MEL-41, was established in 1971 by Dr. G. Fossati (Instituto dei Tumori, Milan) after a few passages of primary cultures derived from a metastatic cutaneous melanoma from a female patient. It was melanotic up to the 30th passage and after that amelanotic. It was frozen at the 47th passage and the culture resumed in 1972, when we obtained it from Dr. Fossati.

Our stock cultures are grown in flasks with Eagle's minimal essential medium with 20% calf serum and antibiotics, and transferred by trypsinization. The cells are fibroblast-like (fig. 1) and the doubling time is approximately 20 hr. The cells are negative when stained by using a method for the detection of argentophilic granules. Chromosome preparations were made from cell suspensions and stained with orcein, quinacrine mustard for Q-bands, and Giemsa for G- and C-bands. The chromosome counts for the definition of the modal numbers were made on samples of 200 cells, selected on the basis of good spreading. The detailed chromosome analysis was made on two samples of 12 cells each.

3. RESULTS

Chromosome analysis was performed at the 48th passage and at the 150th passage. We estimated that approximately 550 cell generations had elapsed between the two passages.

(a) *Evolution of chromosome numbers*

The chromosome count distributions are given as diagrams in fig. 2. At the 48th passage the modal number was 60 in 56 cells (28%) with a second peak of 36 cells (18%) with 44 chromosomes. Thirty-three cells (16.5%) had more than 60 chromosomes. At the 150th passage the modal chromosome number was 42 in 49 cells (25%).

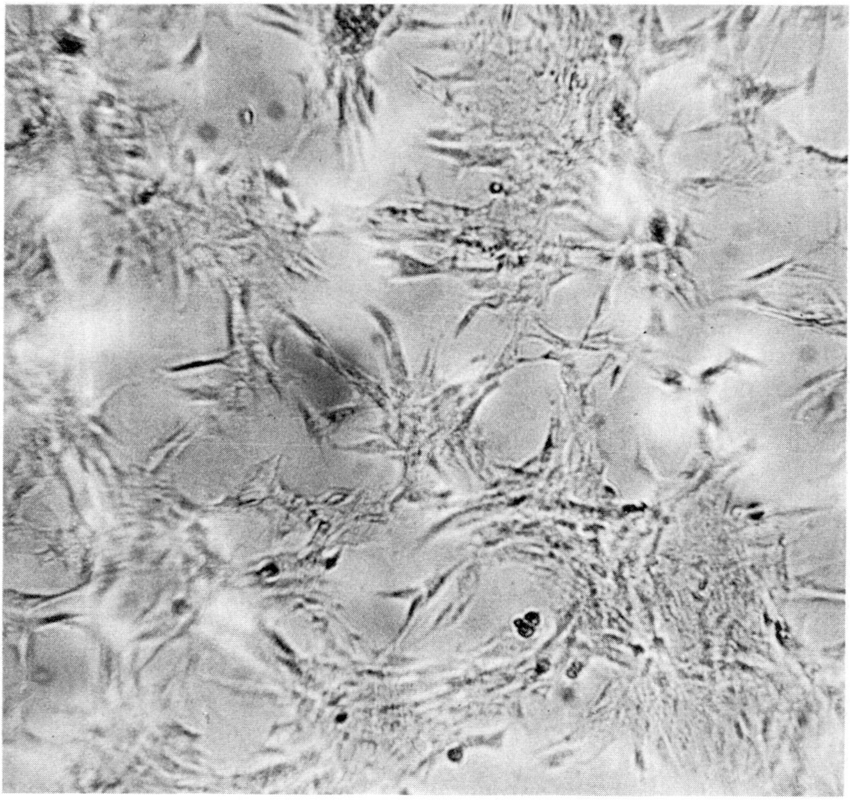

FIG. 1.—Appearance of live MEL-41 cells.

It should be noted that 64 cells (32%) had 40 and 41 chromosomes and that no cells with 60 chromosomes were present.

(b) *Karyotypic variation*

48th passage. We first classified the normal chromosomes present in each cell. They are set out in table 1. The cells around the modal chromosome number of 60 all have between 27 and 30 normal chromosomes, an average of 48% of the total complement (cells 6–12, table 1). Those around the chromosome number of 44 (cells 1–5, table 1) also have a range of 25–28 normal chromosomes, giving a higher mean proportion of normal chromosomes of 58%. Analysis of the normal chromosome distribution shows that the only chromosome consistently absent is the X. Chromosome 8 is present as a single copy in only one cell, chromosome 15 as a single copy in only three cells, and chromosome 3 as a single copy in 4 cells. A hierarchical classification of the normal chromosomes places chromosome 17 as the most frequent. It is present in all cells, in duplicate in 11 cells, and in triplicate in 1, followed by chromosomes 6 and 11 (in duplicate in 10 and as a single copy in 2). Chromosomes 2, 5, 7, 10, 13, 14, 16, 18, 19, 21 and 22 are present in all cells at various doses. Chromosomes 5, 10, 21 and 22 are present in all cells as a single copy. Because chromosome 9 is trisomic in 5 cells, it has a high total number of 23 copies in 10 cells.

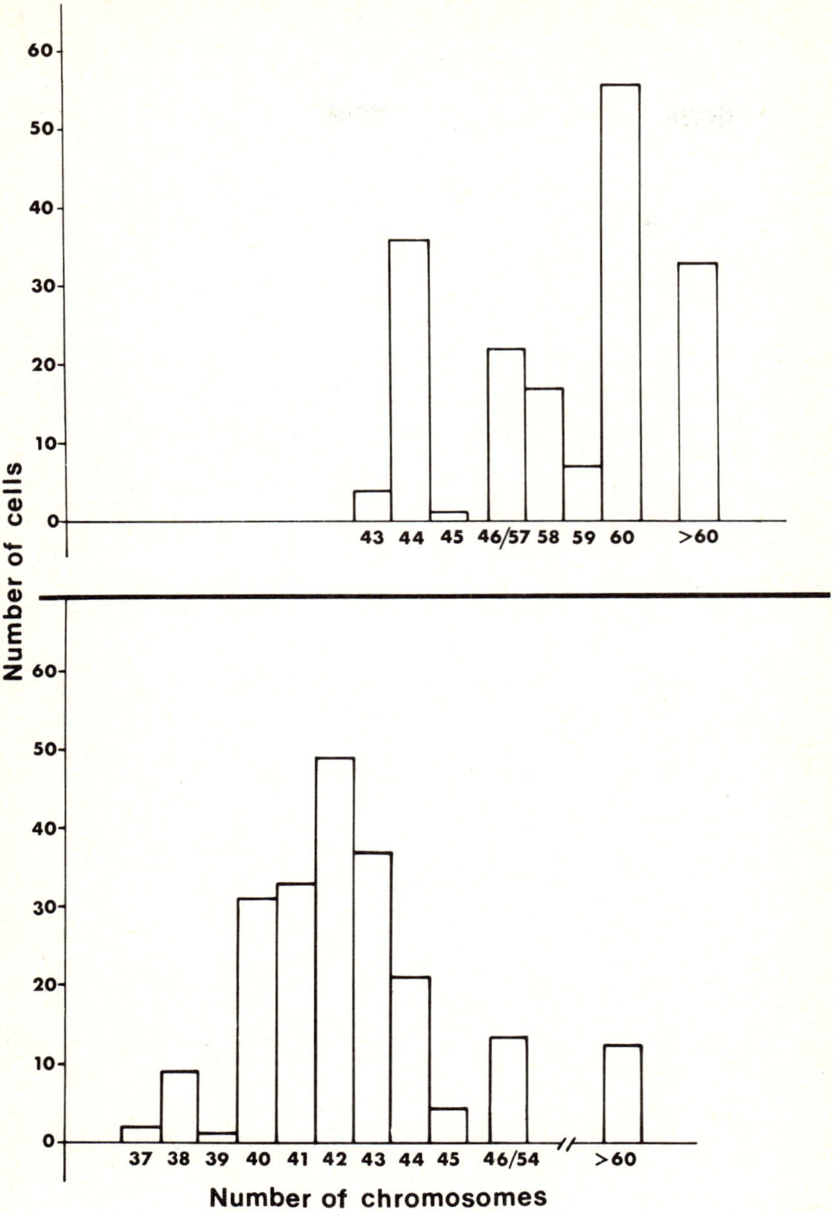

FIG. 2.—Distribution of chromosome counts in 200 cells from the 48th (above) and 150th (below) passage.

Next, we tried to identify the abnormal marker chromosomes in each cell by their Q-, G-, and C-bands. When this was possible, either entirely or in part, we gave them a denomination (A_1, A_2, etc.), as entered in table 2. We designated as U those chromosomes whose origin we could not trace but which were found consistently in several cells, and as NC the unclassified, unidentified, and sporadic abnormal chromosomes

TABLE 1

48th passage. Distribution of normal chromosomes present as such in each of 12 cells with chromosome numbers from 42 to 61

Cell no.	Normal Chromosome no.																							Total normal chrom.	Total chrom.	% normal chrom.
	1	2	3	4	5	6	7	8	9	10	11	12	13	14	15	16	17	18	19	20	21	22	X			
1		1	1	1	1	2	2		1	1	2	2	2	2		2	2	1	1		1	1		26	42	62
2		1	1	1	1	2	2			1	2	2	2	2		2	2	1	1	1	1	1		26	43	60
3		1	1	1	1	2	2		1	1	2	2	2	2		2	2	1	1	2	1	1		28	45	62
4	1	2			1	2	1	1	3	1	1	2	1	1		1	2	1	2	1	1	1		26	48	54
5		1	1	1	1	2	2			1	2		2	2		2	2	2	1	1	1	1		25	48	52
6	1	2		1	1	2	1		3	1	2	2	2	1		1	3	2	1	2	1	1		30	59	51
7	1	2		1	1	2	2		2	1	2	1	1	1	1	1	2	2	2		1	1		28	59	48
8		1		1	1	1	2		3	1	2	2	1	1	1	1	2	2	1	2	1	1		27	60	45
9	1	2		1	1	1	2		3	1	2	2	2	1		1	2	2	1	2	1	1		29	60	48
10	1	2		1	1	2	2		2	1	1	2	1	2	1	1	2	2	2	2	1	1		30	60	50
11	1	2		1	1	2	2		2	1	2	2	2	1		1	2	2	2	2	1	1		30	60	50
12	1	1		1	1	2	1		3	1	2	2	1	1		1	2	3	1	2	1	1		28	61	46
Total	7	18	4	11	12	22	21	1	23	12	22	21	20	17	3	16	25	21	16	17	12	12	0			

TABLE 2

48th passage. Distribution of the 19 partially or totally identified abnormal chromosomes in each of the 12 cells of table 1

Cell no.	A_1 7qi	A_2 6pi	A_3 16/1p	A_4 1p+	A_5 7q+	A_6 17q+	A_7 1q−/3p?	A_8 /12q	A_9 12q/2q	A_{10} 9q+	A_{11} 21/21	A_{12} 14/1q	A_{13} 21/8q	A_{14} 3p/5q	A_{15} ?/13	A_{16} 10p+	A_{17} inv 1/?	A_{18} inv 16	A_{19} 21q−/22	Total	Total chrom.
1	1	1	1	1		1		1				1		1					1	9	42
2	1	1	1	1	1	1		1	1			1	1	1					1	12	43
3	1	1	1	1		1		1				1		1					1	9	45
4		1	1	1	1	1	1	1	1			1	1	1	1	1	1	1	1	16	48
5		1	1	1	1	1	1	1		2			1	1	1	1	1	1		15	48
6	1	1	1	1	1	1	1	1	1	1	1	1	1	1	1	1	1	1	1	19	59
7	1	1	1	1	1	1	1	1	1	1	1	1	1	1	1	1	1	1	1	19	59
8	1	1	1	1	1	1	1	1	1	1	1	1	1	1	1		1	1	1	18	60
9	1	1	1	1		1	1	1	1	1	1	1	1	1	1		1	1	1	18	60
10	1	1	1	1	1	1	1	1	1	1	1	1	1	1	1	1	1	1	1	19	60
11	1	1	1	1	1	2	1	1	1	1		1	1	1	1	1	1	1	1	19	60
12	1	1	1	1	1	1	1	1	1	1	1	1	1	1	1		1	1		17	61
Total	10	12	12	12	9	13	9	12	9	9	6	11	10	12	9	6	9	9	10		

(table 5). As seen from table 2, we were able to identify 19 "A" chromosomes. It should be noted that the same A chromosomes are present both in cells with a chromosome number in the range 59–61 and those with 42–48 chromosomes. The sole exception to this is A_{11} which is present only in the 59–61 cells. Seven of the identified markers (A_2, A_3, A_4, A_6, A_8, A_9, A_{14}) are in fact present in all cells. All A chromosomes are present as a single copy per cell with the exception of A_6 and A_{10},

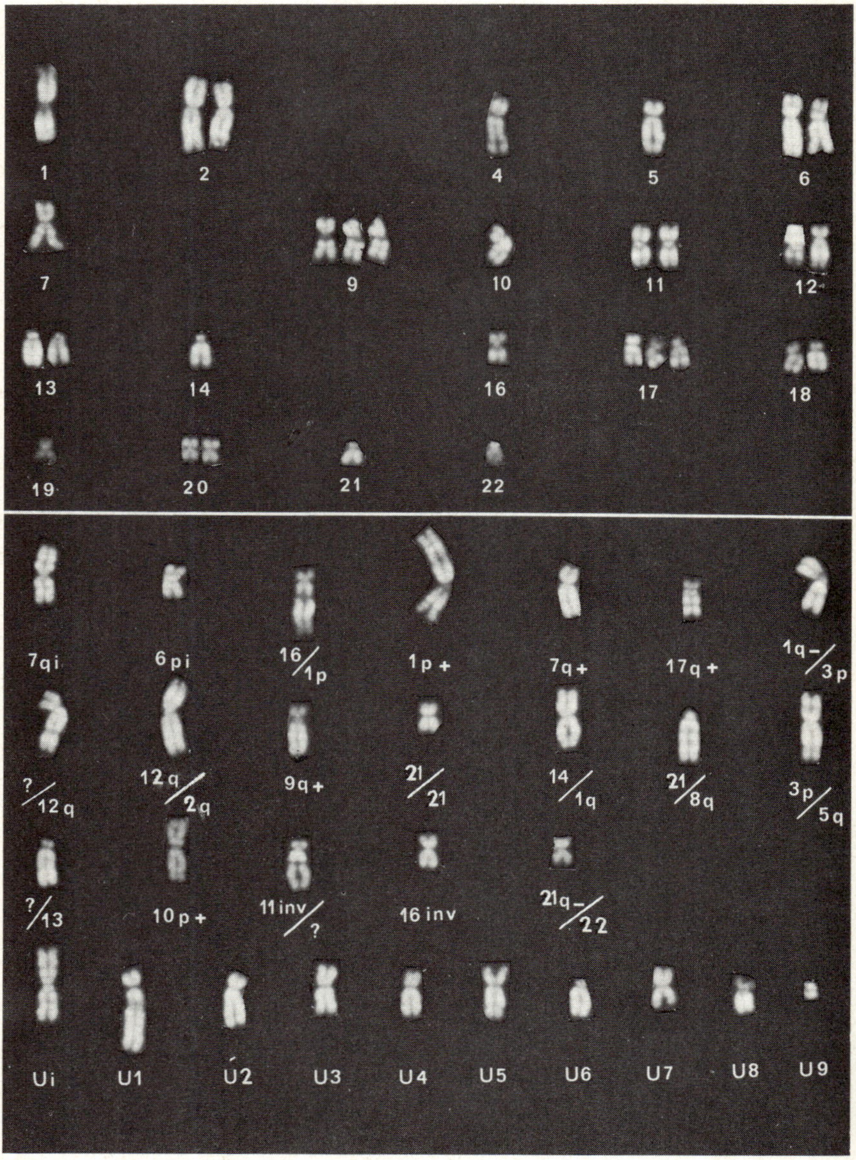

FIG. 3.—48th passage. Chromosomes of cell No. 6 of tables 1 and 2, stained with quinacrine mustard. Upper part: normal chromosomes. Lower part: first three lines are A_1 to A_{19}; last line are U_i and U_1 to U_9.

both of which were found in duplicate in one cell. The abnormal chromosomes were the product of translocation in eight instances, of isochromosome formation in three instances, and of inversion in one instance (table 2). In the others, only part of the abnormal chromosome could be identified. A representative cell with Q-bands illustrating these findings is reproduced in figure 3.

Taking into account the normal chromosomes and the identified segments of the abnormal ones found in each cell, we obtained a rough overall estimate of the number of copies of each chromosome and expressed this in terms of "excess" or "deficiency." As an example, we give in table 3 the detailed analysis of one cell and in table 4 the scores for all chromosomes and cells.

A definite excess of chromosome material is present for chromosomes 1, 6, 7, 9, 11, 12, 16 and 17 and a deficiency for chromosomes 3, 4, 5, 8 and 19, while for the

TABLE 3

48th passage. Example of detailed analysis of the cell No. 6 in tables 1 and 2

Chromosome no.	Description	Estimate of total chromosome material			Sign
1	1N; p, 1p + q, q−	2	+	pq−	+
2	2N; q	2	+	q	+
3	; p, q	1			−
4	1N	1			−
5	1N; q	1	+	q	−
6	2N; p_i	2	+	2p	+
7	2N; q_i, 1pq+	3	+	2q	+
8	; q			q	−
9	3N; 1pq+	4			+
10	1N; 1p + q	2			
11	2N; 1inv	3			+
12	2N; 1p + q, q	3	+	q	+
13	2N; q	2	+	q	+
14	1N; 1p + q	2			
15					
16	1N; 1pq+, 1inv	3			+
17	3N; 1pq+	4			+
18	2N;	2			
19	1N	1			−
20	2N	2			
21	1N; q−, q−, q	1	+	q 2q−	
22	1N; 1p+ q	2			
X					
Total	(30)	(43)			

* 1N, one normal chromosome present as such; p or q, entire or nearly entire arm present either as such or attached to another chromosome; p− or q−, deficient arm as such or attached to another chromosome; 1p+ q, entire chromosome with an extra segment attached to its short arm.

TABLE 4

48th passage. Synopsis of scores for excess (+), deficiency (−), equality or 2n (=), complete absence (0) of chromosome material for each chromosome in 12 cells. Obtained as exemplified in table 3

Chrom. no.	Cell no. 1	2	3	4	5	6	7	8	9	10	11	12	Sum of scores +	−	=	0	Overall score
1	=	=	−	+	−	+	+	−	+	+	+	+	7	3	2		+
2	−	−	−	+	−	+	+	−	+	+	+	−	6	6			=
3	−	−	−	−	−	−	−	−	−	−	−	−		12			−
4	−	−	−	0	−	−	−	−	−	−	−	−		11		1	−
5	−	−	−	−	−	−	−	−	−	−	−	−		12			−
6	+	+	+	+	+	+	+	−	−	+	+	+	10	2			+
7	+	+	+	=	+	+	+	+	+	+	+	+	11		1		+
8	0	−	0	−	−	−	−	−	−	−	−	−		10		2	−
9	−	0	−	+	=	+	+	+	+	+	+	+	8	2	1	1	+
10	−	−	−	=	=	=	=	−	−	=	=	−		6	6		−
11	=	=	=	=	+	+	+	+	+	=	+	+	7		5		+
12	+	+	+	+	−	+	−	+	+	+	+	+	10	2			+
13	=	=	=	−	+	+	+	−	+	−	+	−	5	4	3		+
14	+	+	+	=	=	=	−	−	−	=	−	−	3	5	4		−
15	0	0	0	0	0	0	−	−	0	−	0	0		3		9	−
16	+	+	+	+	+	+	+	+	+	+	+	+	12				+
17	+	+	+	+	+	+	+	+	+	+	+	+	12				+
18	−	−	−	−	=	=	=	=	=	=	=	+	1	4	7		−
19	−	−	−	=	−	−	=	−	−	=	=	−		8	4		−
20	−	−	=	−	−	=	0	=	=	=	=	=		4	7	1	−
21	−	+	−	+	−	−	+	+	+	+	−	+	7	5			+
22	=	=	=	=	−	=	=	=	=	=	=	−		2	10		−
X	0	0	0	0	0	0	0	0	0	0	0	0				12	0

other chromosomes the scores are more or less balanced. In general the scores are correlated with the presence of entire normal chromosomes (see table 1). Exceptions are the chromosomes 1 and 16 which are present as few entire chromosomes but are represented in overall excess by variously distributed segments.

The distributions of the U and NC chromosomes are set out in table 5 for each cell. We note that the relative proportion of the U chromosome is comparatively higher in the cells 59–61 than in the cells 42–48. The only chromosome consistently present in all cells is U_i, a metacentric chromosome composed of symmetrically equal arms and therefore thought to be an isochromosome.

150th passage. The normal chromsome distribution is given in table 6. The cells range in chromosome number between 40 and 44 and have a normal chromosome content of between 12 and 14, giving a rather constant proportion of 30% normal chromosomes. Twelve chromosomes are missing in all cells, namely Nos. 1, 3, 4, 5, 6, 8, 9, 11, 17, 19, 20 and the X chromosome. Chromosome 15 is found as a single copy in three cells, chromosome 22 in 10 out of 12, and chromosomes 12, 14 and 18 in 11 out of 12 cells. Chromosomes 2, 7, 10, 13, 16 and 21 are present in all cells. Chromosome 7 is found in duplicate in all but one cell and chromosomes 2 and 10 in single copy in all cells. Chromosome 7 is present in the highest number of copies (also frequent at the 48th passage); it is followed by chromosomes 13 (19 copies), 21 (17 copies) and 14 (16 copies). These chromosomes were also present in a relatively high number of copies at the 48th passage. Conversely, chromosomes 6, 9, 11 and 17, which were frequent at the 48th passage, are now entirely missing.

Thirteen A chromosomes were identified (table 7 and fig. 4) and these were all different from the A chromosomes of the 48th passage with the exception of A_3 which appears to be the same chromosome as A_9 in the previous passage. Conversely, A_5 is not equal to the A_{16} chromosome of passage 48 because the unidentified part is completely different.

With regard to the number of copies of A chromosomes, there is a major difference between the two passages. At the 48th passage all but one of the A chromosomes was present in single copy, while at the 150th passage several of them are often present in duplicate.

The U chromosomes present at the 48th passage were found in only 5 out of 12 cells and no new U chromosomes were identified. There is, however, a very high variation among the non-identified chromosomes classified as NC. The U chromosomes found are U_i, U_3, U_4, U_5, and U_7 (table 5). At the 150th passage there remains a significant excess of material of chromosomes 7 and 12. There is also an excess of chromosome 13 which is higher than the slight excess found for this chromosome at the 48th passage. All other chromosomes are deficient and have negative scores (table 8).

4. DISCUSSION

A formal analysis of karyotypic variation in the MEL-41 cell line revealed the following main facts. The proportion of normal chromosomes present in each cell is relatively constant among cells of the same sample. The proportion of 50% found in the 48th passage sample is similar to that found by us in other cell populations, namely human ascitic tumours (Tiepolo and Zuffardi, 1973) and two established lines of Chinese hamster CHEF-125 (Lo Curto et al., 1972) and human EUE (unpublished).

TABLE 5

48th and 150th passages. Distribution in each cell of the U (consistently non-identified) and NC (non-classified) chromosomes. The cells of the 150th passage not entered in the table had no U chromosomes

	Cell no.	U_i	U_1	U_2	U_3	U_4	U_5	U_6	U_7	U_8	U_9	Total	NC	Total	Total chromosomes
	1	1	–	–	–	–	–	–	–	–	–	1	6	7	42
	2	1	–	–	–	–	–	–	–	–	–	1	4	5	43
	3	1	–	–	–	1	1	–	–	–	–	3	5	8	45
	4	1	–	–	–	–	–	–	–	–	–	1	5	6	48
	5	1	1	–	–	–	–	–	1	–	–	3	5	8	48
48th	6	1	1	1	1	1	1	1	1	1	1	10	–	10	59
	7	1	1	1	1	1	1	–	1	1	1	9	3	12	59
	8	1	1	–	1	–	1	1	1	1	1	8	7	15	60
	9	1	1	–	1	–	1	–	1	1	1	7	7	14	60
	10	1	1	–	1	1	–	–	–	1	1	6	5	11	60
	11	1	1	–	1	1	–	1	1	1	1	8	3	11	60
	12	1	1	–	1	–	1	1	1	1	1	8	8	16	61
	1	1			1							2	13	15	40
	3								1			1	12	13	41
150th	5				1	1						2	13	15	42
	7					1			1			2	16	18	42
	9						1					1	20	21	44

TABLE 6

150th passage. Distribution of normal chromosomes present as such in each of 12 cells with chromosome number from 40 to 44

Cell no.	Normal chromosome no.																						Total normal chrom.	Total chrom.	% normal chrom.
	1	2	3	4	5	6	7	8	9	10	11	12	13	14	15	16	17	18	19	20	21	22	X			
1		1					2			1		1	2	1		1		1			2	1		13	40	32
2		1					2			1		1	2	1		1		1			1	2		13	41	32
3		1					2			1		1	2	1	1	1		1			1	2		14	41	34
4		1					2			1		1	2	1		1		1			2	1		13	41	32
5		1					2			1		1	2	1		1		1			1	2		13	42	31
6		1					2			1		1	1	2		1		1			2	1		13	42	31
7		1					2			1		1	1	2		1		1			2			12	42	29
8		1					2			1		1	2		1	2		2			1	2		15	42	36
9		1					1			1			1	2		1					1			8	42	19
10		1					2			1		1	1	2		1		1			2	1		13	43	30
11		1					2			1		1	1	2	1	1		1			1	2		14	43	33
12		1					2			1		1	2	1		1		1			1	1		12	44	27
Total		12					23			12		11	19	16	3	13		12			17	15	0			

TABLE 7

150th passage. Distribution of the 13 partially or totally identified abnormal chromosomes in each of the 12 cells of table 6

Cell no.	A_1 3p/1q	A_2 8p+	A_3 ?/12q	A_4 2q+	A_5 ?/13	A_6 11p+	A_7 12/12q	A_8 10q+	A_9 7p+	A_{10} 7q−	A_{11} 6q−	A_{12} 3p	A_{13} 2p+	Total	Total chrom.
1					2	2	1	2	1	1	2	1		12	40
2	1	1	1	1	1	1	2	1	1	1	2	1		14	41
3			1		1	1	1	1	2	2	2	2	1	14	41
4		1	1	1	2	1	1	1		1		1		10	41
5		1	1	1	2	1	1	2	1	1	2	1		14	42
6		1	1	1	2	1			1	1	1	1		10	42
7		1	1		1	1	1	2	1	1	2	1		12	42
8	1		1		3	1	1	1			2	2		12	42
9	1		1		2	1	1	2	1	2	2	1	1	15	42
10	1				2	1	1	1	1	1	2	1		11	43
11		1	1		1	1	1	2		1	2	1	1	12	43
12			1		2	2	1		1	1	2	1		11	44
Total	4	6	10	4	21	14	12	15	10	13	21	14	3		

TABLE 8

150th passage. As in table 4

Chrom.	Cell no.												Sum of scores				Overall
No.	1	2	3	4	5	6	7	8	9	10	11	12	+	–	=	0	score
1	0	–	0	0	0	0	0	–	0	–	–	–		5		7	–
2	–	=	=	=	=	=	–	–	–	=	–	=		5	7		–
3	–	–	–	–	–	–	–	–	–	–	–	–		12			–
4	0	0	0	0	0	0	0	0	0	0	0	0				12	0
5	0	0	0	0	0	0	0	0	0	0	0	0				12	0
6	–	–	–	0	–	–	–	–	–	–	0	–		10		2	–
7	+	+	+	+	+	+	+	+	+	+	+	–	11	1			+
8	0	–	0	–	–	–	–	0	0	–	0	0		6		6	–
9	0	0	0	0	0	0	0	0	0	0	0	0				12	0
10	=	=	=	=	+	–	+	=	–	=	=	+	3	2	7		+
11	=	–	–	–	–	–	–	–	=	–	–	–		10	2		–
12	+	+	+	+	+	–	+	+	+	+	+	–	10	2			+
13	+	+	+	+	+	+	=	+	+	=	+	–	9	1	2		+
14	–	–	–	0	–	=	=	=	–	=	0	=		5	5	2	–
15	0	0	–	0	0	0	0	0	0	–	–	0		3		9	–
16	–	–	–	–	–	–	–	–	–	–	=	–		11	1		–
17	0	0	0	0	0	0	0	0	0	0	0	0				12	0
18	–	–	–	–	–	–	–	–	–	–	=	–		11	1		–
19	0	0	0	0	0	0	0	0	0	0	0	0				12	0
20	0	0	0	0	0	0	0	0	0	0	0	0				12	0
21	=	=	–	=	–	=	=	=	–	–	–	–		6	6		–
22	–	–	=	–	=	–	0	–	–	=	=	0		6	4	2	–
X	0	0	0	0	0	0	0	0	0	0	0	0				12	0

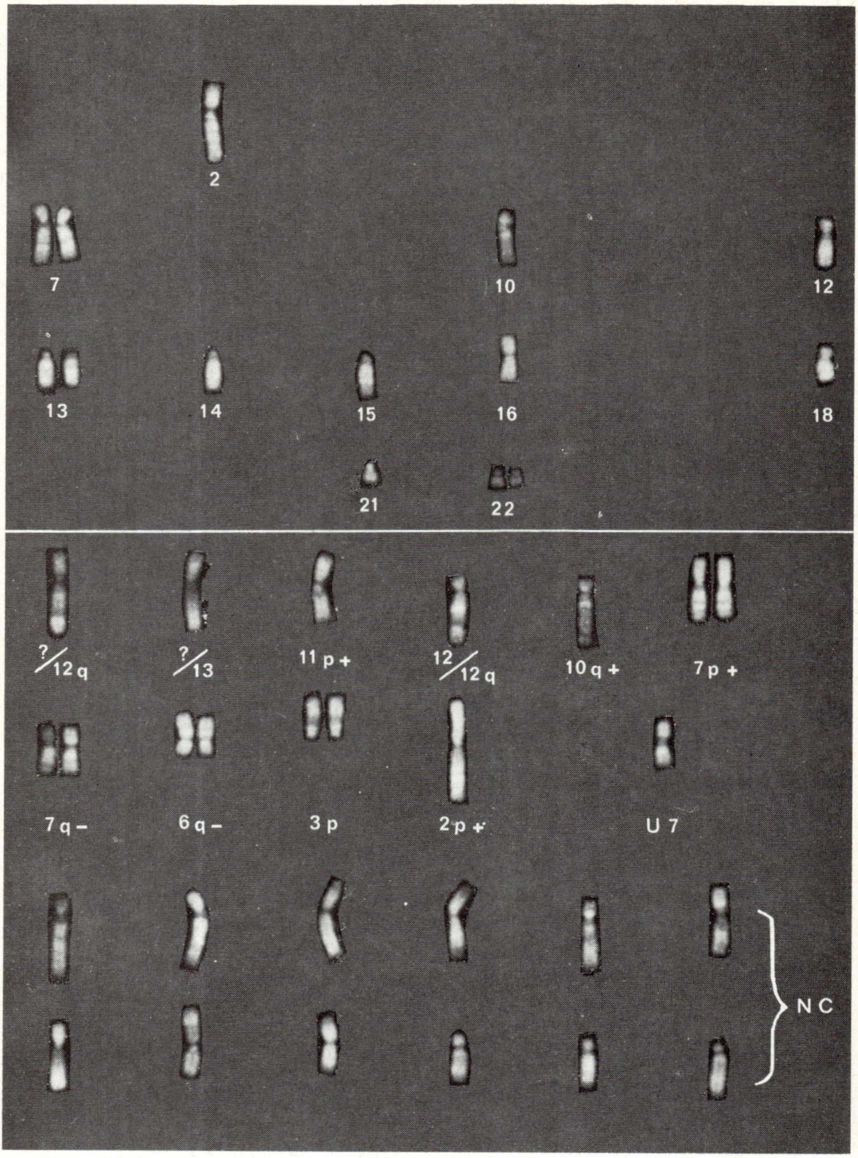

FIG. 4.—150th passage. Chromosomes of cell No. 3 of tables 6 and 7, stained with quinacrine mustard. Upper part: normal chromosomes. Lower part: first line are chromosomes A_3 and A_5 to A_9 ; second line A_{10} to A_{13} and U_7. The rest are all NC (non-classified) chromosomes.

It should be noted that in the few cell lines so far studied by banding techniques (see Echard, 1974, for a short review) the proportion of normal chromosomes per cell varies from 40% to more than 80%. Currently, it is possible to trace some of the distribution of chromosome segments involved in various rearrangements and therefore to obtain a rough estimate of the overall excess or deficiency of material for each chromosome. As seen by comparing the data in tables 1 and 4, there is a certain correlation between the number of entire chromosome copies and the excess or deficiency of the same chromosomes, but not always. For example, chromosome 1 is present as a complete chromosome in only seven out of twelve cells in the 48th passage sample, but because of the many rearrangements involving chromosome 1 there is an overall excess of chromosome 1 material. Of course, this exercise is easier when the exchanges which form the new abnormal chromosomes involve large sections of easily recognized arms, such as those of chromosome 1.

Another interesting finding in this cell line is the consistent presence of the same abnormal chromosomes between cells. Twenty-nine abnormal chromosomes were found in all cells analyzed, indicating that in some previous period of the evolution of the line, new chromosome rearrangements were fixed in the population. Clonal analysis should provide us with an estimate of the continued stability of these abnormal chromosomes.

In the other lines kept in our laboratory (CHEF-125, EUE) the chromosome modal number has remained relatively constant for many years. In the MEL-41 cell line there has occurred a dramatic shift in modal number from 60 to 42 chromosomes at about the 500th cell generation. Since at the 48th passage there was a second peak at 44 chromosomes, one would normally have concluded that, in the past, these cells with 44 chromosomes had had a selective advantage to give the new modal number of 42 in the 150th passage cells. Our analysis showed that this is probably not the case. The loss has been partly confined to the normal chromosomes which at the 150th passage were present as 30% of the total instead of the 50% found in the first sample. In fact, comparing the scores of table 4 with those of table 7 we see that nearly all chromosomes are deficient with the exception of chromosomes 7, 12, and 13 which have maintained an overall excess of material.

The rate of chromosome rearrangement must have been remarkable during the time lapse between the two passages. The identifiable abnormal chromosomes were completely different in the two lines with the exception of one (A_9 and A_3 in tables 2 and 7, respectively) which was present in both samples. Five out of ten U chromosomes were also present in both samples. Thus, it is not possible to decide whether the cells of the second sample arose from some specific clone present in the first one.

We think it likely that the karyotypic evolution of this line has taken place by successive and intricate steps, but we cannot exclude the possibility that the changes have occurred following relatively few structural rearrangements and selection for a range of them. Comparison within and between clonal variations should give us a more precise idea of the rate of karyotypic evolution. It also remains to be seen whether the dramatic change in the chromosome modal number in the MEL-41 cell line, a phenomenon that, in this extent, is unusual even in cell lines, is in some way correlated with the origin and/or some characteristic of the line itself.

5. SUMMARY

1. The amelanotic MEL-41 cell line established in 1971 from a human melanoma had a modal number of 60 chromosomes with a second mode of 44 chromosomes at the 48th passage.

2. After 550 cell generations the modal number was 42. Analysis by banding

techniques revealed: a) relative constancy of the proportion of normal chromosomes among cells of the same sample; b) there is a correlation between the number of normal chromosome copies and the overall excess or deficiency of the same chromosomes, but not always so. Some chromosomes are apparently deficient but when segments of the same chromosomes involved in rearrangements are individually traced they are found to be present with an excess of material; c) Abnormal new chromosomes are the product of translocation, inversion, deletion, and isochromosome formation, and several of them are consistently present in the majority of cells.

3. The dramatic change in the modal number between the two passages was probably due to successive and intricate steps, since it was possible to demonstrate that the modal cells in the second sample were not directly derived by selection of cells with the same chromosome number present in the first sample.

Note added in proof

Glucose 6-phosphate dehydrogenase activity in MEL-41 cells was demonstrated by electrophoresis on cellogel. The electrophoretic mobility of the enzyme was consistently and clearly different from those of type A (controls: HeLa cells) and type B (controls: Caucasian male and female red blood cells).

6. REFERENCES

ECHARD, G. 1974. Chromosomal banding patterns and karyotype evolution in three pig kidney cell strains (PK15, F, and RP). *Chromosoma (Berl.), 45,* 133–149.

LO CURTO, F., SCAPPATICCI, S., and FRACCARO, M. 1972. Chromosome identification in a Chinese hamster pseudodiploid cell line (CHEF-125). *Cytogenetics (Basel), 11,* 305–312.

TIEPOLO, L., and ZUFFARDI, O. 1973. Identification of normal and abnormal chromosomes in tumour cells. *Cytogenet. Cell Genet., 12,* 8–16.

LOCATION OF QUINACRINE MUSTARD-INDUCED CHROMATID EXCHANGE POINTS IN RELATION TO ASG BANDS IN HUMAN CHROMOSOMES

J. R. K. SAVAGE, T. R. L. BIGGER and G. E. WATSON
MRC Radiobiology Unit, Harwell, Oxon, England

1. INTRODUCTION

There is now considerable evidence that the presumptive exchange points for both chromosome-type aberrations induced by ionizing radiation in human cells (Caspersson et al., 1972; Bigger et al., 1972; Seabright, 1973*a*, *b*; Holmberg and Jonasson, 1973; San Roman and Bobrow, 1973) and for chromatid-type aberrations induced by radiation (Savage et al., 1973*b*; Jonasson and Holmberg, 1973) or mitomycin C (Morad et al., 1973) are located predominantly in the weakly fluorescing bands of quinacrine mustard (QM)- or Atebrine-stained chromosomes. These bands correspond to the light-staining bands (l-bands) found with the ASG and other similar Giesma staining methods (Evans et al., 1971).

This preferential location may be an artefact, arising from local stress and disorganization of normal chromosome contraction at the region of exchange, since achromatic lesions are frequently seen at exchange points in unbanded preparations. On the other hand, it may indicate a real regional difference in susceptibility to exchange along a chromosome arm, a difference which must therefore be present during interphase.

Fluorescence banding, which, in contrast to the Giemsa methods, requires no drastic pretreatment of the chromosomes, is thought to arise from a differential binding or concentration of the QM along the chromosome arm. If this differential concentration is characteristic of interphase chromosomes in living cells, then QM acting in its capacity as a monofunctional alkylating agent should induce the majority of aberrations in regions of high concentration, i.e., the brightly fluorescent Q bands corresponding to the dark Giemsa bands (d-bands).

This paper describes attempts to test this hypothesis, using both QM and atebrine, and a comparison is made with 250 Kv X-ray-induced chromatid aberrations.

2. MATERIALS AND METHODS

(a) *Quinacrine Mustard*

Quinacrine mustard dihydrochloride (Sigma, grade II, anhydrous M.W. = 541.8) was added to whole blood cultures of normal human female lymphocytes at 34–36 hr after PHA stimulation, and left in until harvest.

Being a monofunctional alkylating agent, it was anticipated that aberrations would only be found within a narrow concentration band, below which only normal cells would be present, and above which complete lethality would occur. Initially, therefore, medium concentrations of 10^{-4}M, 10^{-5}M, 10^{-6}M, 10^{-7}M and 10^{-8}M were tested and the expectation was confirmed. The region between 10^{-5}–10^{-6}M was selected for more detailed study, and the concentrations used for the main experiment were 5×10^{-5}M, 1×10^{-5}M, and 7.5×10^{-6}M, the last proving to be the most satisfactory.

QM produces considerable cell death, mitotic delay and cell perturbation, and metaphase preparations were made at various intervals between 50 and 72 hr from the initiation of culture.

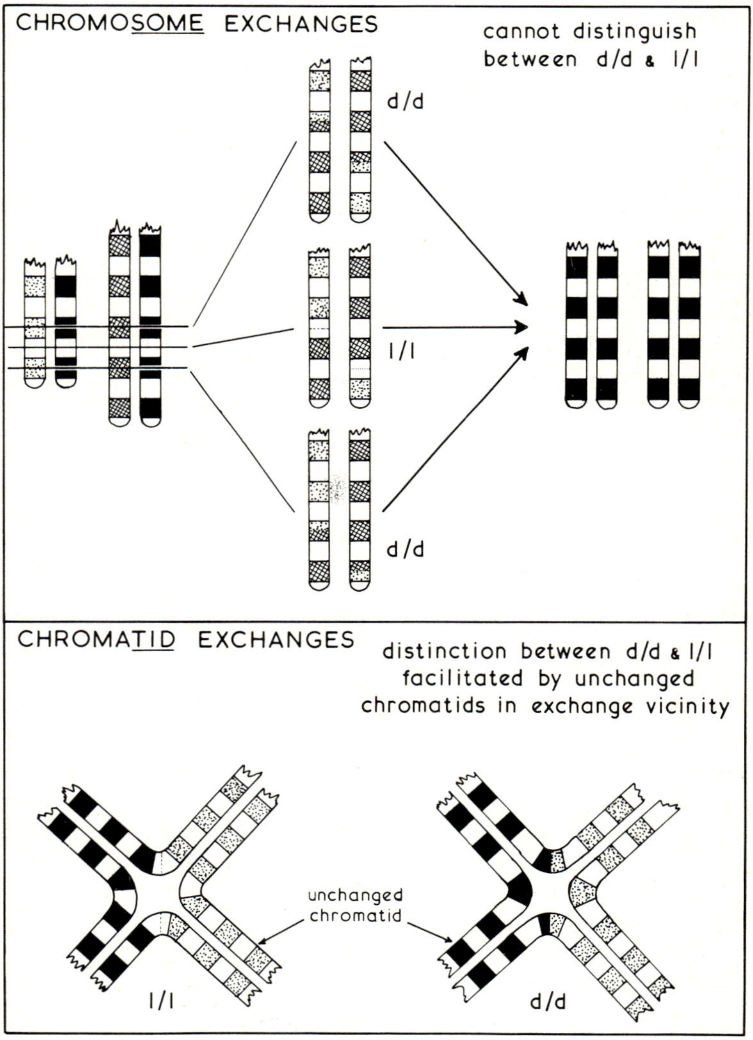

FIG. 1.—Locating presumptive exchange points in banded chromosomes. Chromosome-type exchanges are nearly always ambiguous, since both d/d and l/l exchanges can produce the same ultimate banding pattern and length changes. Chromatid-type exchanges have unchanged reference chromatids in the vicinity of the exchange region so that the point of exchange can be determined with considerable accuracy.

(b) *Atebrine* (George T. Gurr, Ltd., London, M.W. = 472.88)

Parallel experiments were performed in exactly the same way as for QM using final molar concentrations of 10^{-3}, 10^{-5}, 10^{-6}, 5×10^{-7}, 2.5×10^{-7} and 1×10^{-7}.

250Kv X-rays (14 mA, H.V.L. 12 mm Cu, dose-rate 100 rad/min): 400 rad were given at 35 hr post-stimulation, and cultures harvested 50–60 hr.

Air-dried preparations from all treatments were stored at room tememrature for at least one week, and then banded by the ASG technique (Sumner et al., 1971).

Slides were coded, randomised, and scored for mitotic index. Those with a reasonable number of metaphases were then scored in detail for all types of structural aberrations, the chromosomes involved being identified and the location of the presumptive exchange points determined in relation to the d and l G-bands, using the Harwell banding norm and numbering scheme (Bigger et al., 1972).

A note on scoring. The purpose of the experiment is to determine the position of the presumptive points of exchange in relation to ASG bands, and for this purpose, only certain types of aberration can give an unambiguous answer.

Three possible band combinations exist: both lesions in light bands (l/l), both in dark bands (d/d), and one in each (d/l).

For chromosome type aberrations, only true terminal deletions can give a clear distinction between lesions in l-versus d-bands, and these are fairly infrequent. The much more common exchange type aberrations (dicentrics, centric-rings, reciprocal translocations, and pericentric inversions) can seldom give a clear answer since the same banding pattern and length change can arise from a variety of d/d or l/l exchanges. This point is illustrated for a reciprocal translocation in figure 1.

Chromatid aberrations, in particular interchanges, are of much greater value, for in well-banded preparations all three band combinations, l/l, d/d and d/l, can be easily distinguished. This arises from the presence of unchanged chromatids in the vicinity of the points of exchange which can be used as referencing controls (see fig. 1).

Interchanges are common following ionizing radiation (table 1) but are relatively infrequent following QM treatment, chromatid intra-arm intrachanges being the predominant aberrations. Adopting Revell's classification (Revell, 1959; Savage et al., 1968) four distinct simple types can occur. In their complete form, all four cannot be scored with equal accuracy, but the eight incomplete forms (fig. 2) can all be seen. Types 2a and 2b tend to be underscored, however, in air-dried preparations, since the minute acentric deletion is usually dislodged from the region of intrachange. This means that 2a will more frequently be scored as 1a and 2b and, unless the deleted portion is large, will be overlooked.

All these incomplete types can be used to distinguish d/d and l/l, and provided the intercalary distance between exchange points is reasonably large, d/d can be distinguished from d/l since the latter leads to the creation of an additional band (fig. 2). In practice the intercalary distance was usually found to be very small (i.e., the loop is much smaller than indicated in fig. 2) and this distinction could not be readily made. In some cases it was obvious that the whole intrachange had taken place within a single band.

CH.29 table 1

TABLE 1

Summarized aberration scores

QM conc. (molar)	Fixation period (hr)	Total cells scored	Normal		Intrachanges 1	1a	b	2	3a + 3b	4	4a	4b	Inter-arm intrachange	Interchange	Isochromatid/chromatid interchange
5×10^{-5}	50–54	22	17	d/d											
				d/l											
				l/l					2	1					
1×10^{-5}	50–54	165	100	d/d		1			6	5	1		1		
				d/l				1							
				l/l	3	8			14	7	5	2	1	8	
7.5×10^{-6}	50–72	903	792	d/d	1	1			1	3	2	4		7	
				d/l				7							
				l/l		3	1		19	16	6	4	2	13	1
Totals		1090	909 (0.834)		4	13	1	8	42	32	14	10	4		
400 rad X-rays		50	11	l/l	6	3	1		14	16	6		2	40	1

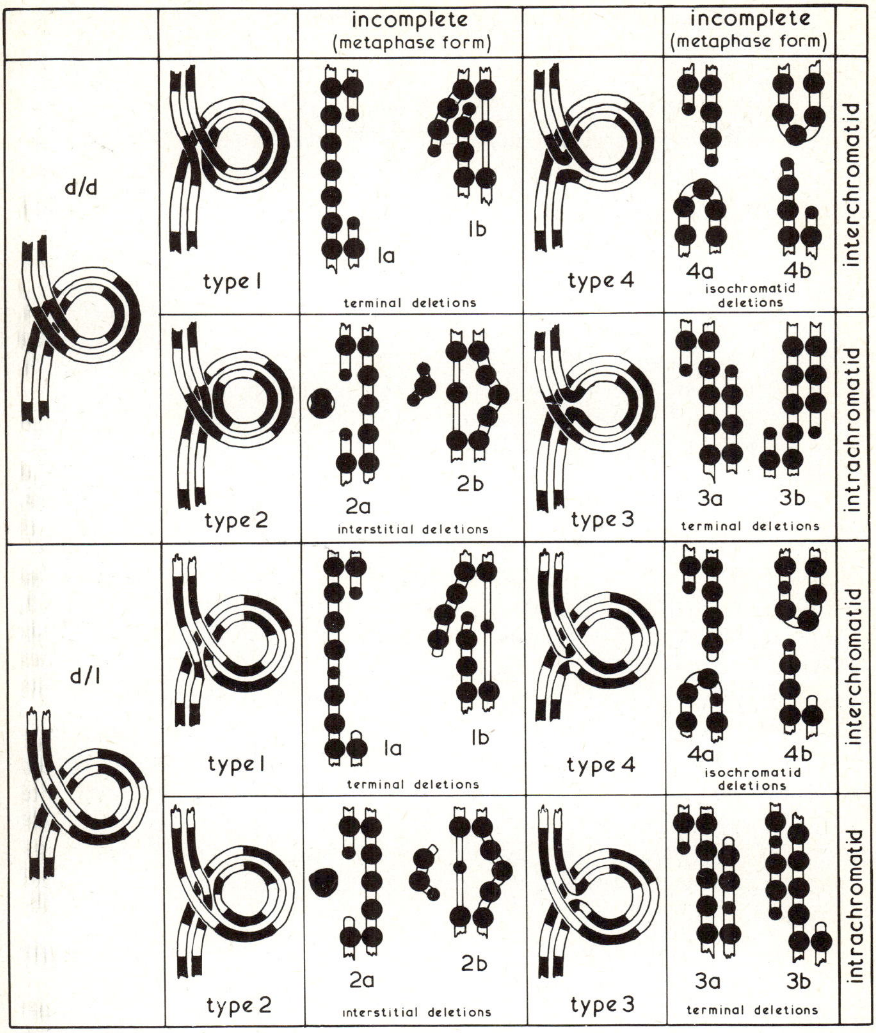

FIG. 2.—The eight incomplete simple chromatid intrachange types (after Revell, 1959) in banded chromosomes, illustrating the types scored for d-band versus l-band location of intrachange points. Only the combinations d/d and d/l are shown. d/l can be distinguished since it leads to the creation of an extra band. In practice, the loop region is much smaller than shown, and this distinction can rarely be made.

3. RESULTS

(a) *Atebrine*

At concentrations stronger than $\sim 10^{-6}$M there was a drastic reduction of the Mitotic Index (MI), indicating perturbation of the progress of cells towards division. Above $\sim 10^{-5}$M pycnosis and cellular disintegration were in evidence.

Below $\sim 10^{-6}$M, although there was some mitotic delay, the MI eventually rose to the level of the untreated controls.

Metaphases were examined for structural aberrations, and none were found.

(b) *Quinacrine Mustard*

A low level of chromatid aberrations was found, with 60–80% of the metaphases observed being normal, i.e., containing no visually detectable structural changes. The absolute quantitative scores per cell are, of course, meaningless in the presence of such a high degree of mitotic delay and cell perturbation (Savage and Papworth, 1973).

Table 1 summarizes the data; the incomplete intrachange numbers correspond to the types given in figure 2.

Considering the summed data from all treatments, a total of 33 interchanges and inter-arm intrachanges was observed, 6 of which were d/l and 1 was d/d. Therefore, 21.2% of interchanges involved at least 1 d-band. In terms of total exchange points involved, 8/66 (12.1%) were in d-bands.

A total of 124 intrachanges was observed, 80 of which were incomplete. Of these 80, 16 (20.0%) were judged to involve d-bands on the basis of the criteria of fig. 2, and no clear distinction between d/d and d/l exchanges could be made. It is impossible to make an accurate estimate on the basis of exchange points since in most cases only one of the two points can be recognized. However, on the basis of the points used for fig. 3, 18/94 (19.1%) were located in d-bands.

Since the majority of intrachange points were very close together, and a fair number appeared to be wholly within one band, it is probably legitimate to use the complete type 4 (isochromatid deletions with sister union) to obtain a further estimate of d involvement. However, caution must be exercised since, in the case of a sizable loop, the eccentric lesions of an l/l exchange could pull d-bands round to occupy terminal positions at metaphase, thus simulating a d/d exchange. This could lead to an overestimate of d-band participation. Thirty-two complete type 4 were observed, 8 (25.0%) of which were judged to involve d-bands.

Only 4 unambiguous complete type 1 were recorded, and one of these was clearly in a d-band.

Pooling these estimates (omitting type 2 from which no inference can be made) 33/149 = 22.15% of all the observed aberrations involved at least one d-band.

(c) *X-rays*

Previous work (Savage et al., 1973*b*) has shown that all presumptive chromatid interchange points are confined to the l-bands of the Harwell norm.

Fifty cells were scored (table 1) for intrachanges and 46 (24 incomplete) were recorded and classified as for the QM work. In no case was a d-band involved. Admittedly this is a small sample, but at face value it implies a d-band involvement of < 2%.

Distribution of presumptive exchange points

The location of all recorded exchange points in relation to the d- and l-bands of the Harwell norm is shown in figure 3. The overall distribution of points was tested in relation to the metaphase chromosome lengths (Paris Conference, 1971, weighted means of C and D columns) by Woolf's G-test. $\chi^2_{22} = 42.61$, $P = 0.0053$ indicate that the distribution is not according to expectation. Similarly, exchange points in

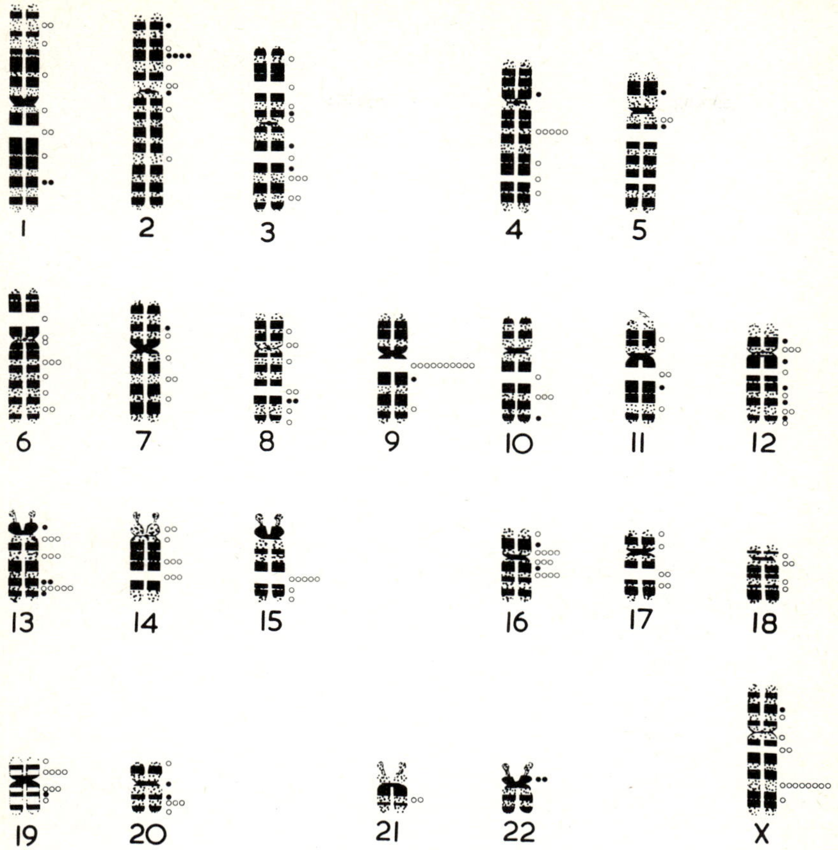

FIG. 3.—Location of chromatid aberration exchange points induced by quinacrine mustard in human female lymphocytes. Data for inter- and intrachanges have been pooled. Open circles = points located in light bands (l-bands); closed circles = points located in dark bands (d-bands). The banding pattern is the Harwell ASG norm (Bigger et al., 1972).

1-band versus chromosome length (χ^2_{22} = 49.40, P = 0.0007) and points in 1-bands versus numbers of 1-bands per chromosome, (χ^2_{22} = 48.86, P = 0.0008) show significant departures from expectation.

If exchange points are distributed between l-bands at random, then the relative numbers of l-bands having 0, 1, 2 . . . points should conform to a Poisson distribution with mean points per band 0.94. The observed distribution is significantly overdispersed, variance 2.08 (unit normal deviate 11.21, P very small). Thus, there is overwhelming evidence to suggest that some bands receive more exchange points than they should.

There are insufficient d-band lesions to make these tests.

Table 2 lists the d-bands involved with their frequency of participation, and shows also those known to be compound, i.e., resulting from the fusion of smaller d-bands during contraction from prophase to metaphase (Schnedl, 1971; Savage et al., 1973*a*).

TABLE 2

Dark G-bands (d-bands) involved in QM-induced chromatid aberrations

Numbering		Known	Intra-arm	Interchange
Harwell	Paris 1971	compound	intrachange	
2	1q 41		2	—
19	2 cen		1	—
21	2p 14 → 16	+	4	—
23	2p 24		1	—
26	3q 22 → 24	+	1	—
27	3q 13	+	1	—
30	3p 12	+	1	—
43	4p 13		1	—
51	5q 12		1	—
53	5p 14.1		1	—
68	7p 14		1	—
71	8q 23	+	2	—
79	9q 21	+	1	—
83	10q 25.3		—	1
92	11q 14	+	1	—
96	12q 24.2	+	—	1
97	12q 23		1	—
98	12q 21	+	1	—
100	12q 12		—	1
101	12p 12		1	—
102	13q 33		1	—
103	13q 31		—	2
106	13p 11 → q11		—	1
118	16q 11 → 12	+	1	—
120	16p 12	+	—	1
133	19q 13.2		1	—
137	20q 12		1	—
138	20 cen		1	—
144	22p 11		—	2
151	Xp 21	+	1	—
Totals	30	12	28	9

4. DISCUSSION

The exchange points of chromatid structural aberrations induced by QM are still predominantly in the pale G-bands, corresponding to the weakly fluorescing bands. About 22% of the aberrations involve dark bands.

It follows, therefore, that if a differential concentration of QM was present along the interphase chromosome at the time of aberration induction, it has not influenced the observed aberration distribution in the expected direction.

Ideally, the experiment should have been done using a short-duration "pulse" treatment with QM, but all our attempts to produce aberrations in this way failed.

The continuous presence of QM from 36 hr until the time of harvest may not have allowed the same degree of differential concentration to build up, so that the whole chromosome may have been uniformly at risk. The proportion of d-material (based on length measurements) in the Harwell norm is $\sim 41\%$ and probably less during interphase if l-regions relax more than d-regions. Thus l-regions present a bigger "target", but whether the unequal relaxation reduced the relative proportion of d-band to $\sim 22\%$ remains to be seen.

A second fact to consider is that many, if not most, of the d-bands observed at metaphase are compound, derived from the fusion of two or three smaller d-bands during chromosome contraction (Schnedl, 1971). An aberration observed in a d-band at metaphase could still, therefore, have arisen in an l-region, which is later lost in a d-band fusion.

As pointed out in the introduction, the predominant location of lesions in l-bands could still be an artefact. If the observed metaphase banding patterns are in any way related to coiling/contraction phenomena, then there is ample scope for coiling modification in the region of an exchange such that these regions more readily give rise to l-bands, the concomitant shift of the adjoining d-bands not being easily detectable. Moreover, with some kinds of exchange the chromatids involved may move relative to one another during the contraction process, so that the observed points of exchange may not be the original ones. This would be analogous to the terminalization movements of chiasmata.

All these arguments apply equally to radiation-induced aberrations which in our experience are never observed to occur in d-bands, i.e., we have never needed to subdivide a Harwell d-band to accommodate a radiation-induced chromatid aberration. A real difference between the location of QM and X-ray lesions may therefore exist.

With mitomycin C, Morad et al. (1973) found $\sim 14\%$ were preferentially located in d-bands, and there was an excess of exchange points in the secondary constriction regions of chromosomes 1, 9, and 16.

The amount of data for QM is not large enough to do a thorough analysis of distribution of exchange points, and for fig. 3 we have pooled interchange and intrachange data, and disregarded both QM concentration and sampling time. This procedure is not really legitimate in studies of aberration distribution. However, we do have evidence of an excess of lesions at the secondary constriction of chromosome 9, but not at those of chromosomes 1 or 16. There is also a curious excess at one position on the long arm of X (Xq24), which is not paralleled in the X-ray data (Savage et al., 1973*b*; Jonasson and Holmberg, 1973; Holmberg and Jonasson, 1973; Seabright, 1973*a*). In the absence of extensive data on the effect of sampling time, it is impossible to offer any explanation.

A final caution should be made on the subject of resolution in experiments of this kind, where chromosomal aberrations are used for locating exchange points. In molecular terms, the resolution available is extremely poor. The diploid content of human cells is ~ 5.8 pg (Abrahamson et al., 1973), and in B configuration this represents a total DNA length of $\sim 1.929 \times 10^9$nm (1.93m). The Harwell ASG banding norm has a total of 1304 chromatid bands, so that if we make the assumption of a uniform distribution of DNA between bands (which in reality is unlikely) the average length per chromatid band is 1.479×10^6nm, or 4.35×10^6 nucleotide pairs. This is a tremendous length, quite adequate for many structural changes to occur wholly within a band and to remain completely undetectable by normal visual methods.

5. SUMMARY

1. Evidence is accumulating that the observed exchange points for radiation-induced interchanges of both chromo*some* and chroma*tid* types are located almost exclusively in the pale-staining ASG bands of human chromosomes. These bands correspond closely to regions which show negative or weak fluorescence in the presence of quinacrine mustard (QM).

2. In view of the uneven distribution of QM fluorescence along chromosome arms, it is of interest to study the distribution of exchange points when QM is used as an alkylating agent to induce structural chromatid changes.

3. Using stimulated human female lymphocytes, presumptive exchange points for QM-induced inter- and intrachanges have been mapped in ASG banded cells.

4. The exchanges still occur predominantly in the pale bands, but a reasonable proportion ($\sim 22\%$) are unambiguously within dark ASG bands.

6. REFERENCES

ABRAHAMSON, S., BENDER, M. A., CONGER, A. D., and WOLFF, S. 1973. Uniformity of radiation-induced mutation rates among different species. *Nature (Lond.), 245,* 460–462.

BIGGER, T. R. L., SAVAGE, J. R. K., and WATSON, G. E. 1972. A scheme for characterising ASG banding and an illustration of its use in identifying complex chromosomal rearrangements in irradiated human skin. *Chromosoma (Berl.), 39,* 297–309.

CASPERSSON, T., HAGLUND, U., LINDELL, B., and ZECH, L. 1972. Radiation induced non-random chromosome breakage. *Exp. Cell Res., 75,* 541–543.

EVANS, H. J., BUCKTON, K. E., and SUMNER, A. T. 1971. Cytological mapping of human chromosomes: Results obtained with quinacrine fluorescence and the acetic-saline-Giemsa techniques. *Chromosoma (Berl.), 35,* 310–325.

HOLMBERG, M., and JONASSON, J. 1973. Preferential location of X-ray induced chromosome breakage in the R-bands of human chromosomes. *Hereditas, 74,* 57–68.

JONASSON, J., and HOLMBERG, M. 1973. Evidence for an inverse relationship between X-ray induced chromatid and chromosome breakage in human chromosomes. *Hereditas, 75,* 259–266.

MORAD, M., JONASSON, J., and LINDSTEN, J. 1973. Distribution of mitomycin C induced breaks on human chromosomes. *Hereditas, 74,* 273–282.

PARIS CONFERENCE. 1971. *Standardization in Human Cytogenetics. Birth Defects, Original Article Series, 8*:7 (1972). The National Foundation, New York.

REVELL, S. H. 1959. The accurate estimation of chromatid breakage and its relevance to a new interpretation of chromatid aberrations induced by ionizing radiations. *Proc. R. Soc. Lond. B. Biol. Sci., 150,* 563–589.

SAN ROMAN, C., and BOBROW, M. 1973. The sites of radiation-induced breakage in human lymphocyte chromosomes, determined by quinacrine fluorescence. *Mutat. Res., 18,* 325–331.

SAVAGE, J. R. K., and PAPWORTH, D. G. 1973. The effect of variable G_2 duration upon the the interpretation of yield-time curves of radiation-induced chromatid aberrations. *J. Theor. Biol., 38,* 17–38.

SAVAGE, J. R. K., PRESTON, R. J., and NEARY, G. J. 1968. Chromatid aberrations in *Tradescantia bracteata* and a further test of Revell's hypothesis. *Mutat. Res., 5,* 47–56.

SAVAGE, J. R. K., WATSON, G. E., and BIGGER, T. R. L. 1973*a*. A brief comparison of the Paris Conference (1971) and Harwell schemes for G-band numbering in human chromosomes. *Chromosoma (Berl.), 41,* 123–127.

SAVAGE, J. R. K., WATSON, G. E., and BIGGER, T. R. L. 1973*b*. The participation of human chromosome arms in radiation-induced chromatid exchange. In *Chromosomes Today, 4* (J. WAHRMAN and K. R. LEWIS, eds.), pp. 267–276. Israel Universities Press, Jerusalem, and John Wiley and Sons, New York.

SCHNEDL, W. 1971. Analysis of the human karyotype using a reassociation technique. *Chromosoma (Berl.), 34,* 448–454.

SEABRIGHT, M. 1973*a*. High resolution studies on the pattern of induced exchanges in the human karyotype. *Chromosoma (Berl.), 40,* 333–346.

SEABRIGHT, M. 1973*b*. Non-involvement of the human X chromosome in X-ray-induced exchanges. *Cytogenet. Cell Genet., 12,* 342–356.

SUMNER, A. T., EVANS, H. J., and BUCKLAND, R. A. 1971. New technique for distinguishing human chromosomes. *Nat. New Biol., 232,* 31–32.

PATTERNS OF INDUCED ABERRATIONS IN HUMANS WITH ABNORMAL AUTOSOME COMPLEMENTS

MARINA SEABRIGHT

Wessex Regional Cytogenetics Unit, Salisbury, England

Observations of X-ray induced lesions and exchanges, made in a study of the autosomes (excluding the X and Y chromosomes) from ten normal individuals, provided the basis for the assessment of data obtained from another study of subjects with autosomal anomalies.

A significantly higher number of lesions per cell was observed in a group which included individuals with extra chromosome material and two carriers of balanced translocations.

Bias may be introduced into the scoring procedure unless the preparations are coded and scored blind, but in the presence of extra or abnormal chromosomes it is impossible to be ignorant of the identity of the cell being scored. Therefore, a control experiment was carried out to establish the reliability of the scoring method using normal individuals. The first five normal individuals, which on initial scoring could be ordered in relation to the number of breaks per cell, were rescored blind. No significant variation in the ordering or mean number of breaks per cell was found when compared with the initial analysis.

Table 1 shows the mean number of lesions per cell from the ten normal individuals and from six subjects with autosomal anomalies.

It can be seen from this table that an increase was found whether or not extra chromatin was present in the cell, i.e. there was a significantly higher number of lesions not only in subjects with extra chromosome material (in two mongols and a father and his son who had a duplication of a portion of the long arm of chromosome 1) but also in the two carriers of balanced rearrangements, in which no extra chromatin was present.

Previously, it had been suggested that the increased number of breaks per cell observed in mongols was attributable to the presence of the extra chromosome. This simple hypothesis cannot explain the present observations. An alternative hypothesis is that the abnormal chromosomes, be they extra or rearranged, would themselves show a significantly higher number of lesions.

To test this second hypothesis it was necessary to examine the response of each individual autosome to the inducing agent.

A regression analysis was performed to examine the relationship between the relative length of the autosomes and the number of lesions per cell. In the normal subjects the relationship was a simple linear one (the number of lesions was proportional to the length). This is represented graphically in fig. 1.

The equation for the best fitting line was found to be $\hat{y} = 0.0215x + 0.0522$, $b = 0.0215 \pm 0.0034$.

TABLE 1

Karyotypes	Mean number of lesions/cell	"t" value	P
Normal (10 individuals)	3.4		
46, XY, t(21;21)	4.5	3.6	<0.1%
47, XY, +21	4.6	4.0	<0.1%
46, XY, (1) dup q12	4.2	2.6	<0.1%
46, XY, (1) dup q12	5.6	5.5	<0.1%
46, X, t(9; X)	4.9	5.0	<0.1%
46, X, t(15; Y)	6.0	5.2	<0.1%

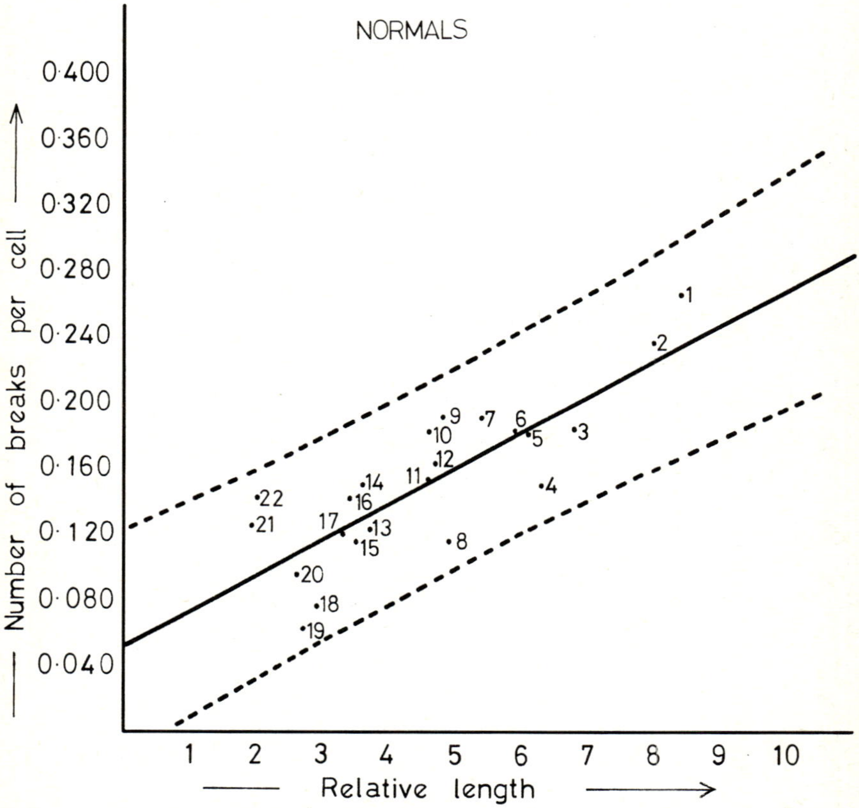

FIG. 1.—Relationship between length of autosomes and number of lesions per cell in normal subjects.

The behaviour of the autosomes from the abnormal subjects was examined, *excluding* the anomalous chromosomes. If these were responsible for the increased number of lesions, then the other autosomes should behave like the autosomes of normal people.

Regression analysis of the relationship between length and the total number of lesions was carried out separately for all six abnormal individuals. Joint regression analysis showed that the form of the relationship was homogeneous for the four subjects with extra chromatin. The best fitting line equation was $y = 0.0376x + 0.0283$, $b = 0.0376 \pm 0.0043$ and it is represented graphically in fig. 2. A comparison of this pooled estimate with that obtained from normal individuals showed a significant difference in position and slope and is shown in table 2.

The relationship between the length and total number of lesions was homogeneous for the two individuals with rearranged chromatin. The best fitting line was found

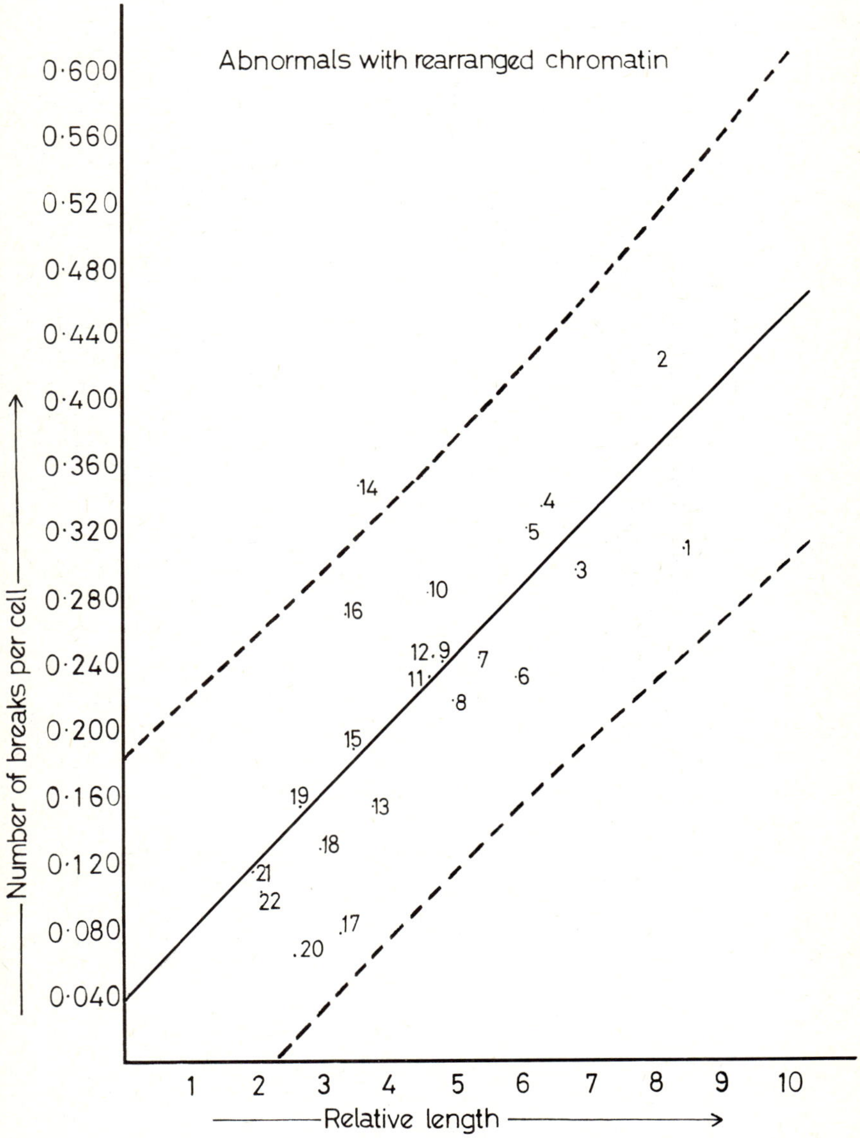

FIG. 2.—Relationship between length of autosomes and number of lesions per cell for four subjects with extra chromatin.

TABLE 2

Joint regression analysis. Normal v subjects with extra chromatin

Item	df	MSS	VR	P
Overall regression	1	0.1219		
Difference in position	1	0.0269	24.5	<0.1 %
Difference in slope	1	0.0091	8.3	1–0.1 %
Pooled residual	40	0.0011		
Total variation	43			

to have a equation of $\hat{y} = 0.0409x + 0.0399$, $b = 0.0409 \pm 0.0072$. This is represented graphically in fig. 3.

A comparison of this data with that obtained from normal individuals showed a significant difference in position and slope and is shown in table 3.

These analyses demonstrate that even the normal autosomes in the aberrant individuals show a significantly different pattern of breakage in relation to length than that observed in the autosomes of normal subjects.

A further analysis of the behaviour of each abnormal chromosome was compared to the normal autosomes of these individuals. Predictions were made as to the number of lesions to be expected in the affected chromosomes on the basis of the modified rates shown by the other autosomes. For instance, the actual number of lesions per cell observed in chromosomes 21 of the trisomic mongol was 0.3095. The number of units of chromatin at risk in the trisomic mongol is 2.85 as compared with 1.9 for a normal pair of 21s. On this basis, the expected number of lesions in 2.85 units of chromatin would be 0.1355 ± 0.0376 $t_{(20)} = 4.6$, $P < 0.1\%$.

A realistic estimate of the relative amount of chromatin in the 21; 21 translocation mongol would be in the order of 2.7 units. The observed number of lesions per cell was 0.2353. The expected number of lesions in 2.7 units of chromatin would be 0.1298 ± 0.0377 $t_{(20)} = 2.8$, $P = 2\text{–}1\%$. Therefore, there is a significant increase of the number of lesions observed in the 21 set over that to be expected from the behaviour of the other autosomes in individuals with extra chromosome material.

When the carriers of balanced translocations were studied, no evidence was found for any increased susceptibility in the rearranged chromosomes even at the points of translocation.

The average number of lesions per unit of autosome in all the abnormal individuals

TABLE 3

Joint regression analysis. Normals v subjects with rearranged chromatin

Item	df	MSS	VR	P
Overall regression	1	0.1359		
Difference in position	1	0.0634	28.8	0.1 %
Difference in slope	1	0.0133	6.1	5.1 %
Polled residual	40	0.0022		
Total variation	43			

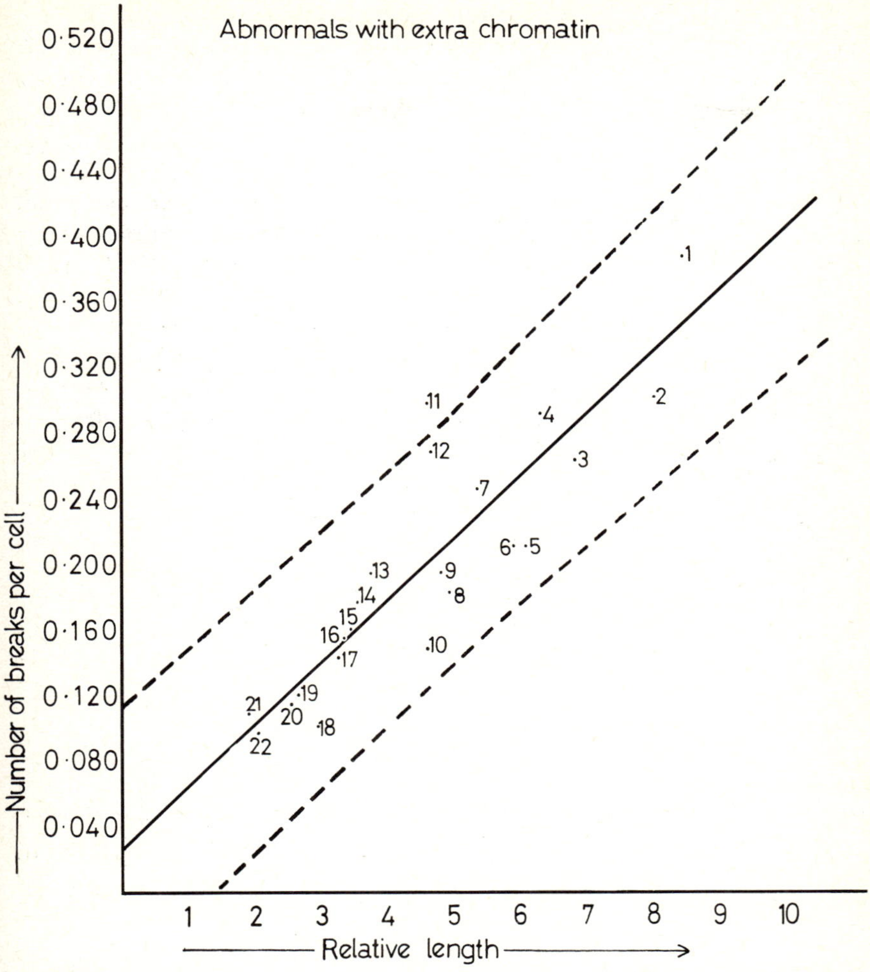

FIG. 3.—Relationship between length of autosomes and number of lesions per cell for two individuals with rearranged chromatin.

was 0.038. This is almost 50% higher than that found in normal subjects, which was 0.022. This increase was also found in the autosomes of individuals who had abnormal sex-chromosome complements (multiple Xs, double Y and even in an XO patient) where the average number of lesions per unit of chromatin was 0.039.

These analyses have therefore shown that either extra, missing, or rearranged material affects the whole of the chromosome complement in its response to X-rays.

It appears that *any* type of anomaly of the chromosomes may produce some disturbance of the metabolism of the cell. This disturbance may be responsible either for an increase in the fragility of the chromosomes or for a decreased ability to repair. There is a possibility that individuals who have congenitally abnormal karyotypes may be predisposed to neoplasm because of this variation. For instance, in conditions like Fanconi's anaemia, Bloom's syndrome, and ataxia telangiectasia the affected patients are prone to malignant disease, particularly leukaemia. These diseases are characterized cytologically by breaks and rearrangements of the chromosomes.

There is convincing evidence of an association between Down's syndrome and leukaemia. Holland et al. (1962) estimated that the frequency of leukaemia in mongols was 18 times that in the general population. It was formerly thought that chromosome 21 was involved in both mongolism and in the formation of the Philadelphia chromosome found in chronic myeloid leukaemia. Moreover, alkaline phosphatase is generally lncreased in blood polymorphs of mongols and decreased in chronic myeloid leukaemia. Since the demonstration by O'Riordan et al. (1971) that the Philadelphia chromosome is a deleted No. 22 and not No. 21, and because of all the types of leukaemia that may occur in mongols, chronic myeloid is the least common, the reason for the association between Down's syndrome and leukaemia remains unexplained. Other chromosome abnormalities like trisomies for D or E chromosomes or unbalanced translocations have very severe effects, so that the life span of the affected individuals is too short to show if any tendency to neoplasm may exist in these cases. A study of the incidence of cancer in those people who have anomalies of their sex-chromosomes and in those who carry balanced rearrangements may establish if there is an increased risk for malignancy in these individuals. A further experiment has been initiated to detect the pattern of spontaneous sister chromatid exchanges in individuals with anomalous karyotypes.

REFERENCES

HOLLAND, W. W., DOLL, R., and CARTER, C. O. 1962. The mortality from leukaemia and other cancers amongst patients with Down's syndrome mongols and amongst their parents. *Br. J. Cancer, 16,* 177–186.

O'RIORDAN, M. L., ROBINSON, J. A., BUCKTON, K. E., and EVANS, H. J. 1971. Distinguishing between the chromosomes involved in Down's syndrome (Trisomy 21) and chronic myeloid leukaemia (Ph_1) by fluorescence. *Nature (Lond.), 230,* 167–168.

TRANSLOCATIONS INDUCED BY IRRADIATION OF *LOCUSTA* SPERMATOZOA

B. LEIGH* **and D. ZOHARY**

Laboratory of Genetics, The Hebrew University, Jerusalem, Israel

1. INTRODUCTION

The migratory locust, *Locusta migratoria*, is a suitable animal for laboratory studies because it is easy to breed, lays eggs throughout the year, and has no obligatory diapause. Although meiotic cells in the testis have large, easily stainable chromosomes, genetic studies are difficult because of the lack of suitable mutant markers. One way of circumventing this problem would be to induce easily recognizable chromosomal rearrangements for use as markers. This requires the availability of a technique for karyotyping males without either killing or sterilizing them. The *Locusta* male has one X chromosome and 11 pairs of autosomes and many of the latter can be identified by their length and staining pattern.

2. MATERIALS AND METHODS

Locusta migratoria males were irradiated 7–8 days after the final moult, at the time when they reach sexual maturity. They were allowed to mate with virgin females for 3–4 days and then discarded. The F_1 progeny (hoppers) were kept at 28°C and given an abundant supply of food. When they reached third instar, the females were removed to prevent overcrowding. At 6–8 days after the final moult the males were scored for chromosomal rearrangements. They were anaesthetized with frozen CO_2 and held on a perspex platform with rubber bands. Using a razor blade, a small lateral incision was made immediately posterior to the testes and 5–10 testicular follicles were extracted with flame-sterilized watchmakers' forceps. The follicles were placed in insect Ringer and the incision was sealed with a mixture of bees' wax and Canada balsam. The males were marked for future identification and kept in a cage.

For quick screening, 2–3 follicles were stained with acetic orcein and squashed. The remaining follicles were fixed in 1:3 acetic alcohol for a later, more detailed examination.

Less than 10% of the males died within 14 days of the operation.

* Permanent Address: Department of Radiation Genetics and Chemical Mutagenesis, The State University of Leiden, and The J.A. Cohen Institue for Radiopathology and Radiation Protection, Leiden, The Netherlands.

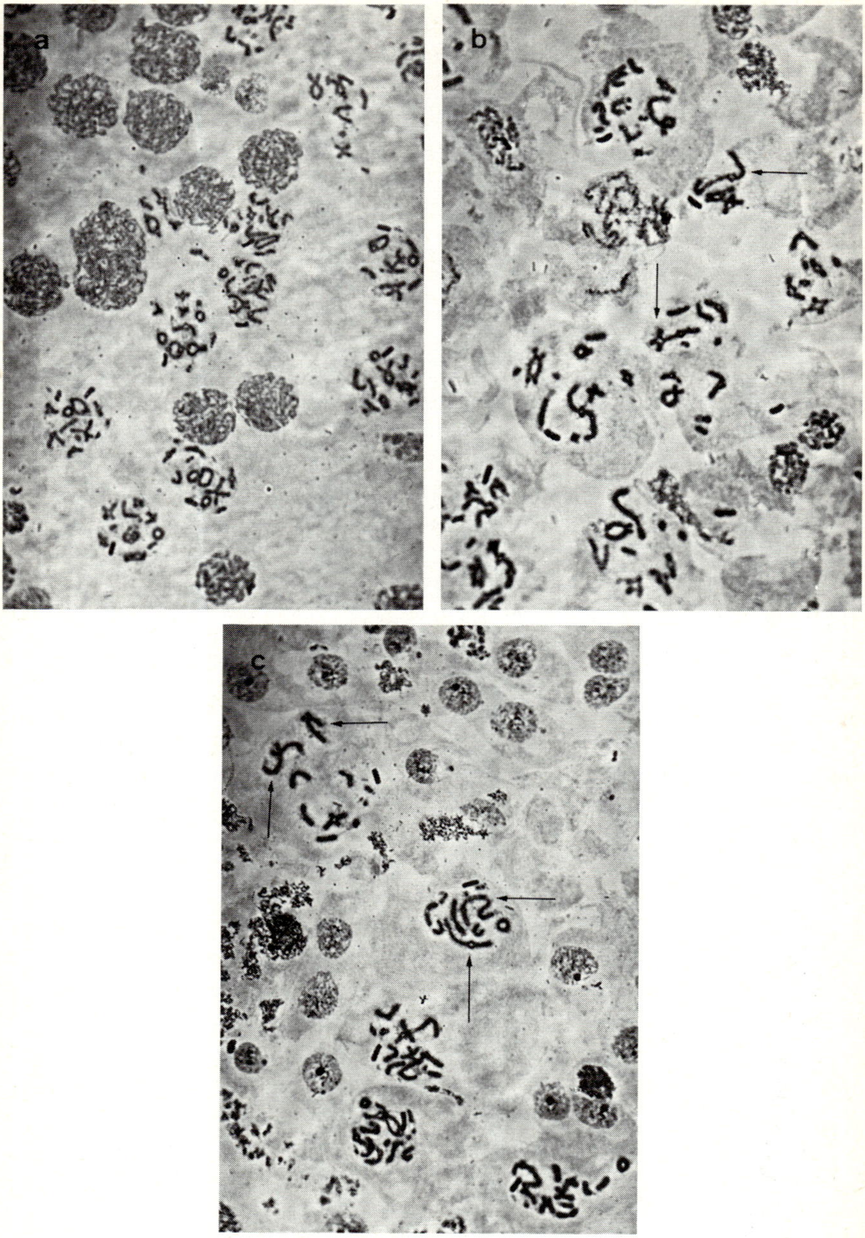

FIG. 1.—Diplotene cells: *a*—with a normal karyotype, *b*—with one reciprocal translocation, *c*—two reciprocal translocations.

3. RESULTS

The germ cells of *Locusta* males develop in synchronous cysts and each follicle contains many cysts at different stages of development. Most of the examined follicles contained one cyst of diplotene cells. The ease of detecting translocations in these cells is shown in figure 1. Figure 1a shows diplotene cells from a male with normal karyotype. There are several cells in which it is easy to count one X chromosome and eleven autosomal bivalents. Cells from a male heterozygous for one reciprocal translocation are shown in figure 1b, and from a male heterozygous for two reciprocal translocations in figure 1c. Except in the case of a mosaic, all the cells of a male will carry the same rearrangement(s) and it is not necessary to be able to score each nucleus.

By more careful study of the fixed material it is often possible to determine which chromosomes are involved in a rearrangement. In this case, the task is again simplified by the availability of many genetically identical cells. This is shown by the two nuclei in figure 2, which were both from the same cyst. In figure 2a it can be seen that there is a rearrangement but it is not possible to determine which chromosomes are involved. In figure 2b the three pairs of chromosomes can be identified as one of the two long chromosomes and the longest and shortest of the six medium length autosomes.

In one experiment, P_1 males were given an exposure of 1,5000 R. Of the 43 F_1 males examined, 26 were apparently normal, 10 carried one reciprocal translocation, 2 carried two reciprocal translocations, 1 carried a three-chromosomal interchange (fig. 2), and 3 carried a small inversion. The last category was identified by the presence of figures with a dicentric and an acentric loop in diplotene cells (fig. 3). The size of the inversion could be judged by the difficulty of identifying it in pachytene nuclei and the low frequency of double-loop configurations in diplotene nuclei, the latter resulting from crossing-over within the inversion.

The males from this experiment were not used for breeding, but in separate tests it was found that the removal of several follicles from the testis did not affect the fertility of the male.

4. DISCUSSION

In recent years the process of recombination has received ever-increasing attention from both theoretical and applied geneticists. There is a basic interest in elucidating

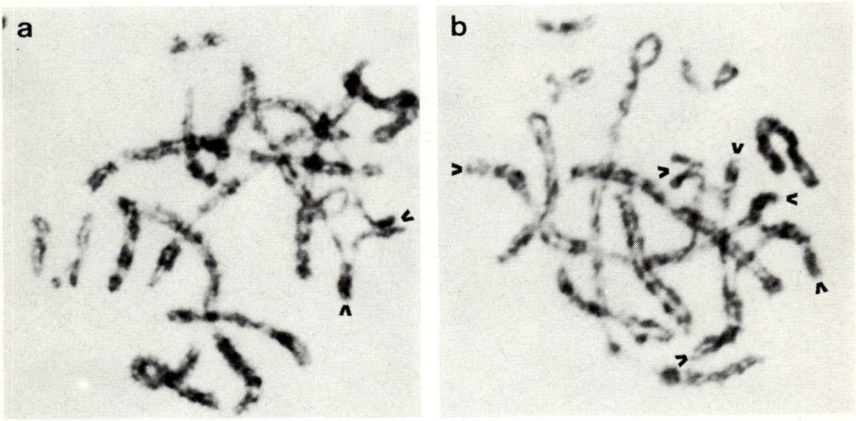

FIG. 2.—Pachytene nuclei containing the same rearrangement. It can be fully identified in *b* but not in *a*. Black v's mark the ends of the chromosomes which can be seen to be involved in the rearrangement.

the mechanism of meiotic crossing-over, which is still only vaguely understood (John and Lewis, 1965). There are also practical implications. An ability to control (enhance or restrict) the rates of recombination is of prime importance to the breeder. Several initial trials have been performed (Riley, 1966), but it is still desirable to find suitable systems (in higher plants and animals) for testing and checking various factors affecting meiotic crossing-over in a simple and effective way.

At present, the study of the processes involved in crossing-over in higher organisms is being carried out using biochemical techniques (Hotta et al., 1966; Hotta et al., 1968). Attempts are being made to correlate the replication of DNA and protein synthesis to chromosome synapsis.

One of the aims of the project reported here was to test the feasibility of using the cytological detection of heterozygous chromosomal aberrations in organisms with large chromosomes (such as *Lilium* and *Locusta*) for locating crossing-over immediately after its occurrence in meiosis. This technique is well illustrated in the works of Brown and Zohary (1953) and Peacock (1970).

In the work reported here it has been shown that it is possible to induce and maintain chromosome rearrangements in *Locusta*. This is a technique often used by *Drosophila* geneticists and is now potentially available for the genetic analysis of *Locusta*.

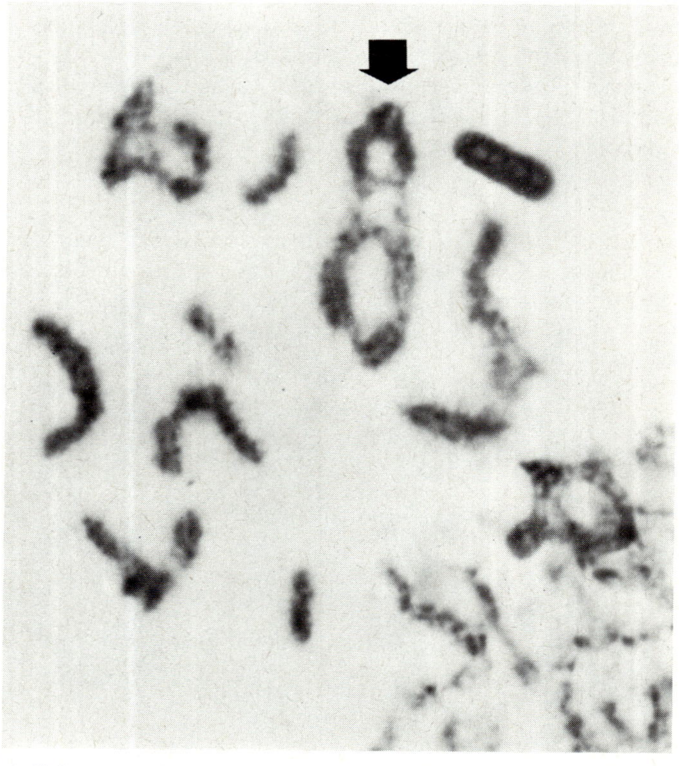

FIG. 3.—A diplotene nucleus with one chromosome showing the double loop configuration resulting from a cross-over within a region of inversion heterozygosity.

Acknowledgement We are grateful to the late Professor E. Goldschmidt who made it possible for the first author to spend a year at the Laboratory of Genetics of the Hebrew University in Jerusalem.

5. REFERENCES

BROWN, S. W., and ZOHARY, D. 1953. The relationship of chiasmata and crossing-over in *Lilium formosanum*. *Genetics, 40,* 850–873.

HOTTA, Y., ITO, M., and STERN, H. 1966. Synthesis of DNA during meiosis. *Proc. Natl. Acad. Sci. U.S.A., 53,* 357–362.

HOTTA, Y., PARCHMAN, L. G., and STERN, H. 1968. Protein synthesis during meiosis. *Proc. Natl. Acad. Sci. U.S.A., 56,* 1184–1191.

JOHN, B., and LEWIS, K. R. 1965. The meiotic system. *Protoplasmatologia VI/F/1,* 1–335. Springer, Wein.

PEACOCK, W. J. 1970. Replication, recombination, and chiasmata in *Goniaea australasiae* (Orthoptera: Acrididae). *Genetics, 65,* 593–617.

RILEY, R. 1966. Genetics and regulation of meiotic chromosome behaviour. *Sci. Prog., 54,* 193–207.

REPETITIVE DNA SEQUENCES IN ANIMALS, PARTICULARLY PRIMATES

K. W. JONES

Epigenetics Research Group, Institute of Animal Genetics, West Mains Road, Edinburgh

1. INTRODUCTION

The discovery of repetitive DNA sequences is undoubtedly the most important contribution to our understanding of the organization, structure, and evolution of the eukaryotic genome in this decade. It has upset all previous simplistic ideas about the relationship of genes to chromosome structure and has launched cytogenetics on a new voyage of discovery since, like most significant developments, it has raised many new and exciting questions. In this paper I will be concerned mainly with certain aspects of chromosome structure and evolution which are beginning to be illuminated through the study of highly repetitive DNA sequences in primates.

The functions, the genomal organization, and, in certain cases, the chromosomal localization of a few classes of repeated DNA sequences are known. Among these are the sequences coding for 28S, 18S ribosomal RNA (see for example Attardi and Amaldi, 1970; Wallace and Birnstiel, 1966; Henderson et al., 1972; Pardue and Birnstiel, 1973), 5S RNA (Brown et al., 1971; Pardue et al., 1973; Wimber and Steffenson, 1970), transfer RNA (Ritossa et al., 1966; Clarkson et al., 1973), and histone messenger RNA (Kedes and Birnstiel, 1971; Pardue and Birnstiel, 1973). Other types of repeated sequences, however, are of unknown function and thus, with certain exceptions difficult to purify for intensive study. This has led to the development of methods for kinetic analysis which have begun to reveal the general features of the organization, transcription, and evolution of such sequences, pioneered largely by Britten and his co-workers (Britten and Kohne, 1968; Britten and Davidson, 1971). The exceptional sequences are the so-called satellite, or more accurately, simple sequence DNAs which are inherently easy to purify (Flamm et al., 1968). Because of this, satellite DNAs have been intensively studied by such approaches as differential chromatin fractionation (e.g., Yasmineh and Yunis, 1969; Yasmineh and Yunis, 1970), base sequence analysis (Southern, 1970; Gall and Atherton, 1974), and *in situ* molecular hybridization (Jones, 1970; Hennig et al., 1970; MacGregor and Kezer, 1971). Because satellite DNAs appear to be transcriptionally inert and because their known nucleotide sequences contain insufficient information for protein synthesis, attention is currently focussed on their role in chromosome structure and evolution. In what follows I will describe and discuss some recent data from primate DNA studies which suggest a possible relationship between satellite DNA and other repetitive DNAs in evolution and which associate satellite DNA with the processes of speciation.

2. EVOLUTION OF REPETITIVE DNA IN PRIMATES

In the primates earlier workers, exemplified by Hoyer and Roberts (1967), showed that the homology between repeated DNA of various species is an exponential function of the time since their divergence, indicating that repeated DNA homology reflects evolutionary relationships. More recently Gummerson (1972) and Kohne (1970) have made more detailed studies of such relationships between complete primate genomes. Comparative C_0t analyses of DNA from a range of primates (fig. 1; table 1) show that there are very striking differences in the complexity of their

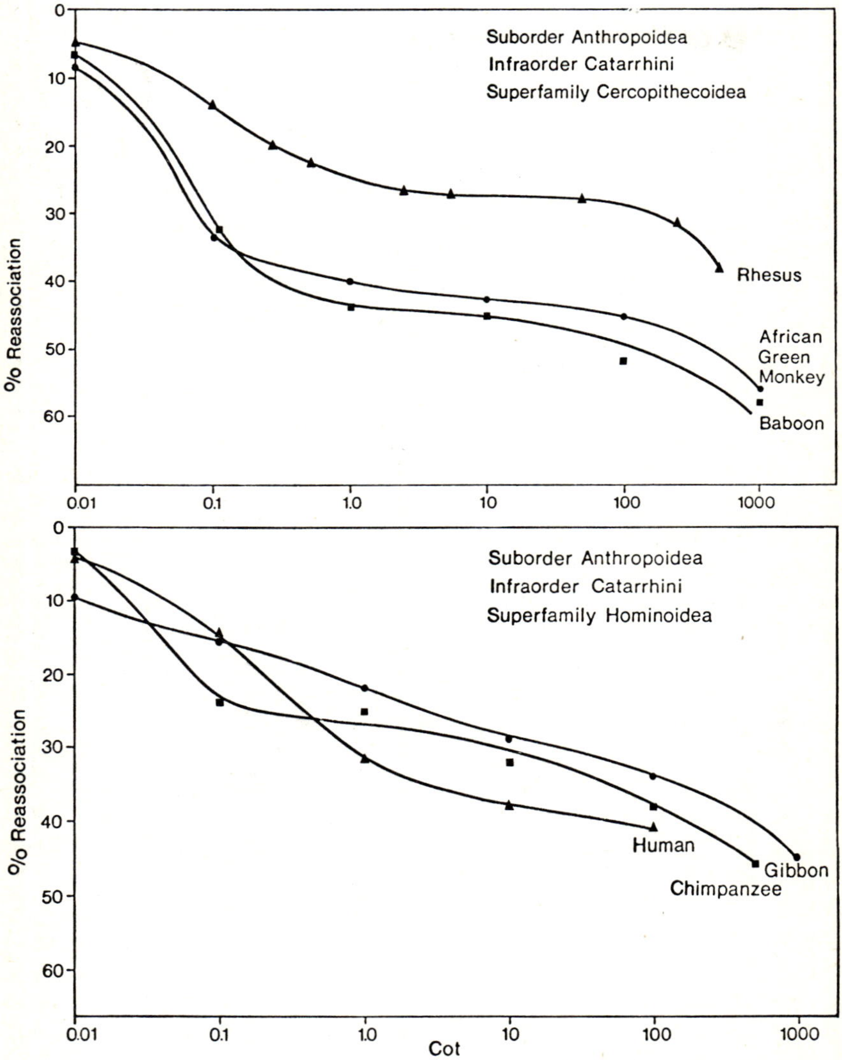

FIG. 1.—C_0t curves of the DNA isolated from representative primates. Significant differences can be seen in the genomal amounts of DNA reassociating at a C_0t of 0.1. The largest difference, amounting to over 50%, is seen between the rhesus monkey and the baboon (from Gummerson 1972).

TABLE 1

Stability fractionation of repeated DNA in primates

Animal	Percentage of total DNA which is repeated	C_0t_i10 Percentage of reassociated DNA eluted at the phosphate buffer concentrations given 0.16 M	0.19 M	0.3 M
Rhesus	29	20	36	44
African Green monkey	43	21	32	48
Baboon	47	20	41	39
Human	42	27	37	36
Chimp	39	22	37	41
Gibbon	31	22	39	39
Slow Loris	33	18	31	51

Isolated repeated DNA was reassociated in 0.12M phosphate buffer to C_0t_i10* and fractionated on hydroxyl-apatite. The extent of the reassociation ranged from 73% to 85%. The data are the average of four determinations. Despite large differences in the genomal percentages of repeated DNA (see also figure 1) the percentage of DNA eluted in the three stability classes is very similar in each species.

* C_0t_i = (1/fraction of total DNA represented by the reassociating DNA) × C_0t (adapted from Gummerson 1972).

repetitive DNAs. For example, the percentage of the total DNA which is repeated varies from 29% in the rhesus monkey to 47% in the baboon. This sort of complexity difference is found in plants (see p. 131) but unlike plants, which have also large variations in genome size, primates have similar sized genomes of around 3.4×10^{12} daltons (Britten and Davidson, 1971). To account for such variations in primates we must suppose either that such genomes are all growing at a steady rate or that mechanisms for loss and gain of sequences have come into a steady-state relationship (Gummerson, 1972). The picture is further complicated by the fact that the percentage of repeated sequences exhibiting high and low stability after reassociation is similar in all the genomes examined by Gummerson. He interprets this to mean that there is a selective advantage in maintaining a balance of diverged and non-diverged DNA in the genome. Whatever the mechanism, it seems that the rate of addition of new DNA to the genome remains fairly constant at around 0.12% of the human genome per million years (Kohne, 1970; Gummerson, 1972. Table 2 contains a comparison of data of Gummerson (1972) and of Kohne (1970) on the rate of addition of DNA to the genomes of primates. There is close agreement on a value of 0.11–0.12%, on average, of the human genome being added every million years. One mechanism for creating such new DNA is by saltation of a short nucleotide sequence to give rise to a simple sequence family (satellite) DNA (Britten and Kohne, 1968). But can such a mechanism account fully for all of the new DNA added to the genome? In what follows I will examine the extent to which present knowledge of human and primate satellite DNAs provides an answer to this question.

TABLE 2

Animals compared	% Undiverged sequences not held in common (% of genome)	Years since divergence ($\times 10^6$)	Gummerson's % of present genome added as undiverged sequences per 10^6 years	Kohne's % of present genome added as repeated DNA per 10^6 years
Human-Chimp	2.25	15–30	0.15–0.075	—
Human-Gibbon	2.35	30	0.078	0.07
Human-AGM	4.6	45	0.102	0.09
Human-Baboon	3.75	45	0.084	0.09
Human-Rhesus	5.17	45	0.115	0.09
Human-Slow Loris	7.18	75	0.104	0.28

3. SATELLITE DNA IN HIGHER PRIMATES

Satellite DNA appears to be confined to constitutive heterochromatin. This is shown by *in situ* hybridization, for example in the mouse (Jones, 1970; Jones and Robertson, 1970; Pardue and Gall, 1970) and in man (Jones and Corneo, 1971; Jones et al., 1973), confirming earlier suggestive evidence from chromatin fractionation studies (Yasmineh and Yunis, 1969). Subsequent studies of base sequence homologies in the satellite DNAs of higher primates (Jones et al., 1972) showed that satellite III in man is related by hybridization to DNA sequences in constitutive heterochromatin in all of the higher apes (table 3). The chromosomal regions involved (e.g., fig. 2) also exhibit differential staining by the Giemsa pH 11 procedure (reviewed by Pearson, 1972). In the gibbon and monkeys, both the staining reaction and the related satellite DNA sequences are undetectable, suggesting that both arose after the divergence of the ancestral form of the higher primates. The other human satellites so far studied, that is satellites I and II, are not detectable in the chimpanzee by molecular hybridization and are assumed to have arisen subsequent to the chimpanzee divergence. This assumption is supported by the lesser divergences (ΔT_m) of these latter satellite DNAs and by the fact that the chromosomal features concerned are absent from the homologous chromosomes of the chimpanzee. Thus the chimpanzee number I chromosome lacks a prominent heterochromatic block near the centromere, which contains satellite II in man, and the chimpanzee Y chromosome lacks a distal fluorescent portion which contains a high concentration of satellite I in man (fig. 3) (Jones, 1974; Jones et al., 1974). Interestingly, the gorilla Y does show a distal fluorescent region, but unfortunately nothing is presently known about the DNA satellites of this species aside from the presence of a human satellite III-related sequence. The essential point which emerges, however, is that it seems probable that the known satellite DNAs of man can be dated in evolution to a period not earlier than the man-gibbon divergence which is usually supposed, from palaeontological evidence, to have occurred about 30–40 million years ago. There are four known human satellite DNAs, I, II, III, and IV, contributing approximately 0.14, 0.6, 0.8% (table 4), and 2% (Corneo et al., 1972) of the human genome, respectively, giving a total of 3.54%. This amounts to an additional 0.09–

TABLE 3

Presence of DNA complementary to human satellite III cRNA in various species by filter hybridisation (species below the orangutan show background values indicating the occurrence of related DNA only in the higher primates)

Species	Counts/min ^3H per filter
Human	695
Chimpanzee	552
Orangutan	472
Baboon	70
Macaque	46
Marmoset	96
Vervet monkey	73
Mouse	64
Bacterium	57
Blank filter	34

TABLE 4

Complexity and genomal percentage of three human satellite DNAs as determined by rate hybridization at optimum temperature (T_{opt}) in 6 × SSC-30% formamide

Satellite	$T_{0.5}$(3μg/ml)	% of genome
I	48 sec	0.14
II	24 sec	0.6
III	16 sec	0.8

0.12% of DNA per million years; a value very close to that derived from the data of Kohne (1970) and Gummerson (1972) for the rate of addition of new DNA to primate genomes (table 2). This permits the suggestion that a significantly large proportion of the new DNA, and perhaps all of it, is added as simple sequence DNA. In this case one of the important functions of constitutive heterochromatin is to generate novel DNA. We do not presently understand why this occurs but the fact that each species has a different and characteristic satellite DNA pattern indicates a rapid spread of new DNA through a species (Walker, 1971). The simplest mechanism which could account for this, I suggest, would be one in which new DNA was only produced or tolerated during the process of speciation so as to be included in all of the initial members of a new species. At other times there would be strong selection pressure against saltatory events. Selection pressure would originate from the involvement of satellite DNA with constitutive heterochromatin which has been implicated in mechanisms of developmental homeostasis (see, for example, Schultz, 1965; Brown, 1966; Baker, 1968). The phenotypic changes which commonly accompany speciation might be expected to favour changes in constitutive hetero-

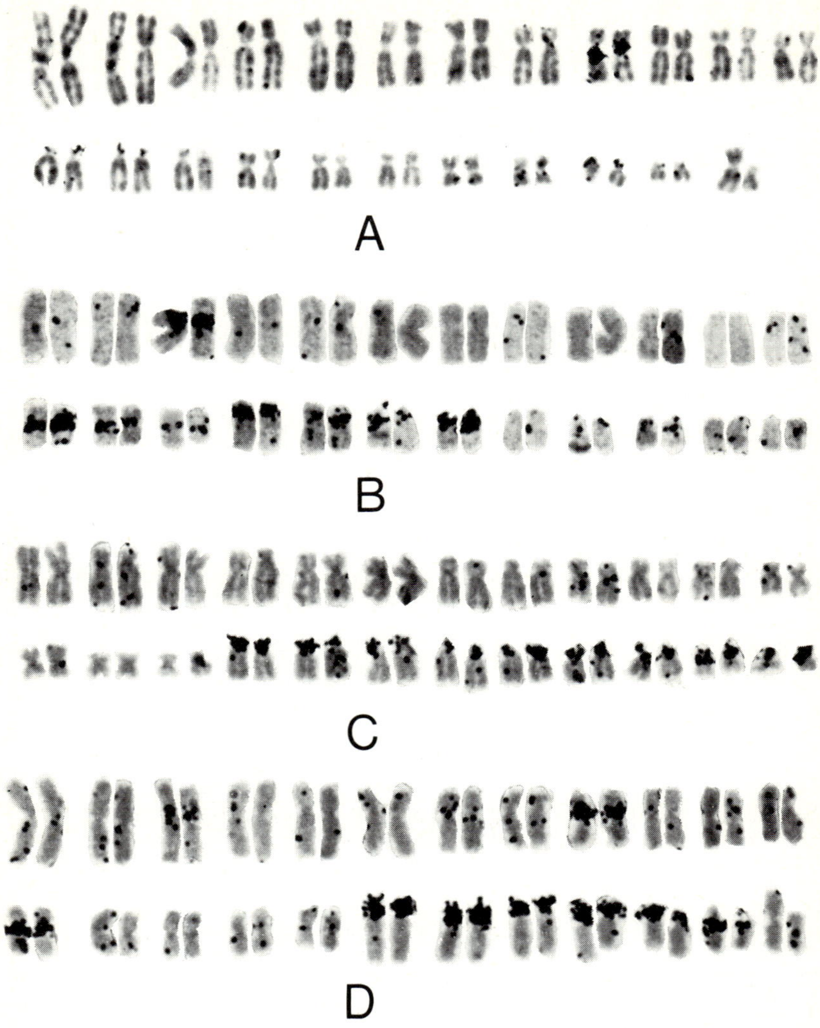

FIG. 2.—Summary of the hybridization *in situ* of human satellite III DNA cRNA to chromosomes of A, man; B, chimpanzee; C, orangutan; D, gorilla. The regions containing homologous DNA also stain differentially with Giemsa at pH 11.

chromatin as a mechanism of achieving a new homeostatic balance and thus encourage underlying saltatory processes leading to the generation of new satellites and perhaps the elimination of certain pre-existing ones. Once a new phenotype had been stabilized further alterations in heterochromatin would be disadvantageous. Such a mechanism would have interesting corollaries. For example, evolutionary alterations in satellite DNA may denote important speciation events. The occurrence of two satellite DNAs with different degrees of sequence divergence, and thus of likely different age, exclusively in man (Satellites I and II) may indicate that he has undergone at least two important evolutionary steps, involving the emergence of successive populations from small isolates, since diverging from the chimpanzee.

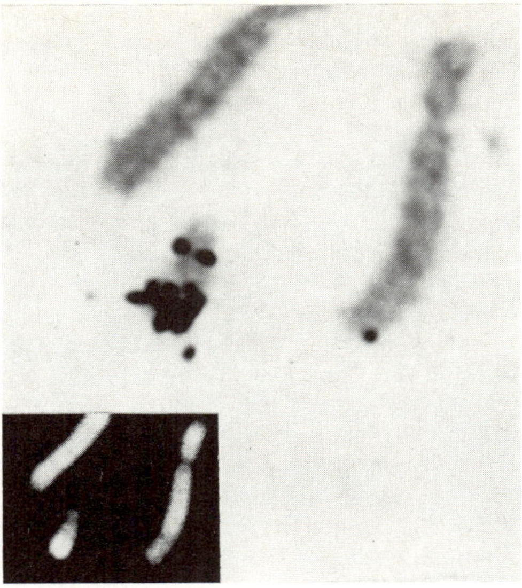

FIG. 3.—Hybridization of human satellite DNA I cRNA to the human Y chromosome. Inset is a fluorescence picture of the same field showing the bright distal portion which hybridizes intensively. A further satellite I rich region, represented by two grains, is seen closer to the centromeric region (from data of Jones, 1974; and Jones et al., 1974).

Such a suggestion is in accord with the existence of recently extinct, intermediate hominoid "species" in the palaeontological record (see, for example, Simons, 1964). Further, quantitative variation which occurs as heritable chromosomal polymorphism (Craig-Holmes et al., 1973) and which involves quantitative differences in satellite DNA on homologous chromosomes (Jones and Corneo, 1971) may be concerned with the wide range of normal phenotypes in modern man.

4. REFERENCES

ATTARDI, G., and AMALDI, F. 1970. Structure and synthesis of ribosomal RNA. *Annu. Rev. Biochem., 39,* 183–226.

BAKER, W. K. 1968. Position effect variegation. *Adv. Genet., 14,* 231–234.

BRITTEN, R. J., and DAVIDSON, E. H. 1971. Repetitive and non-repetititve DNA sequences and a speculation on the origins of evolutionary novelty. *A. Rev. Biol., 46,* 111–138.

BRITTEN, R. J., and KOHNE, D. E. 1968. Saltatory events in replication. *Carnegie Inst. Wash. Year Book, 68,* 83–85.

BROWN, D. D., WENSINK, P. C., and JORDAN, E. 1971. Purification and some characteristics of 5S DNA from *Xenopus laevis. Proc. Natl. Acad. Sci. U.S.A., 68,* 3175–3179.

BROWN, S. W. 1966. Heterochromatin. *Science (Wash. D.C.), 151,* 417–425.

CLARKSON, S. G., BIRNSTIEL, M. L., and PURDOM, I. F. 1973. Clustering of transfer RNA genes in *Xenopus laevis. J. Mol. Biol., 79,* 411–429.

CORNEO, G., ZARDI, L., and POLLI, E. 1972. Elution of human satellite DNA on a methylated albumin kieselguhr chromatographic column. *Biochim. Biophys. Acta, 269,* 201–204.

CRAIG-HOLMES, A. P., MOORE, F. B., and SHAW, M. W. 1973. Polymorphism of human C-band heterochromatin. I. Frequency of variants. *Am. J. Hum. Genet., 25,* 181–192.

FLAMM, W. G., BIRNSTIEL, M. L., and WALKER, P. M. B. 1968. Preparation and fractionation and isolation of single strands of DNA by isopycnic ultracentrifugation in fixed angle rotors. In *Sub-Cellular Components, Preparation and Fractionation* (G. BIRNIE and S. M. FOX, eds.), pp. 125–155. Butterworth, London.

GALL, J. G., and ATHERTON, D. D. 1974. Satellite DNA sequences in *Drosophila virilis*. *J. Mol. Biol., 85,* 633–664.

GUMMERSON, K. S. 1972. The evolution of repeated DNA in primates. Ph.D. Thesis. Johns Hopkins University, Baltimore, Maryland.

HENDERSON, A. S., WARBURTON, D., and ATWOOD, K. C. 1972. Location of ribosomal DNA in the human chromosome complement. *Proc. Natl. Acad. Sci. U.S.A., 69,* 3394–3398.

HENNIG, W., HENNIG, I., and STEIN, H. 1970. Repeated sequences in the DNA of *Drosophila* and their location in giant chromosomes. *Chromosoma (Berl.), 32,* 31–63.

HOYER, B. H., and ROBERTS, R. B. 1967. Studies of DNA homology by the DNA-agar technique. In *Molecular Genetics*. Academic Press, New York.

JONES, K. W. 1970. Chromosomal and nuclear location of mouse satellite DNA in individual cells. *Nature (Lond.), 225,* 912–915.

JONES, K. W. 1974. Primate satellite DNA. In *World Anthropology* (SOL TAX, ed.). Mouton, The Hague.

JONES, K. W., and CORNEO, G. 1971. Location of satellite and homogeneous DNA sequences on human chromromes. *Nat. New Biol., 233,* 268–271.

JONES, K. W., and ROBERTSON, F. W. 1970. Localisation of reiterated nucleotide sequences in *Drosophila* and mouse by *in situ* hybridisation by complementary RNA. *Chromosoma (Berl.), 31,* 331–345.

JONES, K. W., PROSSER, J., CORNEO, G., GINELLI, E., and BOBROW, M. 1972. Satellite DNA constitutive heterochromatin and human evolution. In *Modern Aspects of Cytogenetics: Constitutive Heterochromatin in Man. Symposia Medica Hoechst 6* (R. A. PFEIFFER, ed.), pp. 45–74.

JONES, K. W., CORNEO, G., GINELLI, E., and PROSSER, J. 1973. The chromosomal location of human satellite DNA. III. *Chromosoma (Berl.), 42,* 445–451.

JONES, K. W., PURDOM, I. F., PROSSER, J., and CORNEO, G. 1974. Chromosomal location of human satellite DNA. I. *Chromosoma (Berl.), 49,* 161–171.

KEDES, L. H., and BIRNSTIEL, M. L. 1971. Reiteration and clustering of DNA sequences complementary to histone messenger RNA. *Nat. New Biol., 230,* 165–169.

KOHNE, D. E. 1970. Evolution of higher organism DNA. *Q. Rev. Biophys., 3,* 327–375.

MACGREGOR, H. C., and KEZER, J. 1971. The chromosomal localisation of a heavy satellite DNA in the testis of *Plethodon c. cinereus. Chromosoma (Berl.)*, 33, 167–182.

PARDUE, M. L., and BIRNSTIEL, M. L. 1973. Cytological localisation of repeated gene sequences. In *Modern Aspects of Cytogenetics: Constitutive Heterochromatin in Man. Symposia Medica Hoechst 6* (R. A. PFEIFFER, ed.), pp. 75–85.

PARDUE, M. L., and GALL, J. G. 1970. Chromosomal localization of mouse satellite DNA. *Science (Wash. D.C.), 169,* 1356–1358.

PARDUE, M. L., BROWN, D. D., and BIRNSTIEL, M. L. 1973. Location of the genes for 5S ribosomal RNA in *Xenopus laevis. Chromosoma (Berl.), 42,* 191–203.

PEARSON, P. L. 1972. The use of new staining techniques for human chromosome identification. *J. Med. Genet., 9,* 264–275.

RITOSSA, F., ATWOOD, K. C., LINDSLEY, D. L., and SPIEGELMAN, S. 1966. On the chromosomal distribution of DNA complementary to ribosomal and soluble RNA. *Natl. Cancer Inst. Monogr., 23,* 449–472.

SCHULTZ, J. 1965. Genes, differentiation and animal development. *Brookhaven Symp. Biol., 18,* 116–147.

SIMONS, E. 1964. The early ancestors of man. *Sci. Am., 211,* 50–62.

SOUTHERN, E. M. 1970. Base sequence and evolution of guinea pig satellite DNA. *Nature (Lond.), 227,* 794–798.

WALKER, P. M. B. 1971. Origin of satellite DNA. *Nature (Lond.), 229,* 306–308.

WALLACE, H., and BIRNSTIEL, M. L. 1966. Ribosomal cistrons and the nucleolar organiser. *Biochim. Biophys. Acta, 114,* 296–310.

WIMBER, D. E., and STEFFENSON, D. M. 1970. Localisation of 5S RNA genes on *Drosophila* chromosomes by RNA-DNA hybridisation. *Science N.Y., 170,* 639–641.

YASMINEH, W. G., and YUNIS, J. J. 1969. Satellite DNA in mouse autosomal heterochromatin. *Biochem. Biophys. Res. Commun., 35,* 779–782.

YASMINEH, W. G., and YUNIS, J. J. 1970. Localisation of mouse satellite DNA in constitutive heterochromatin. *Expl. Cell Res., 59,* 69–75.

COMPARISON OF HUMAN AND NON-HUMAN PRIMATE CHROMOSOMES USING THE FLUORESCENT BENZIMIDAZOL AND OTHER BANDING TECHNIQUES

P. K. SETH[1], L. E. M. DE BOER[2], M. B. SAXENA[1] and S. SETH[1]
[1] *Department of Anthropology, University of Delhi, Delhi, India*
[2] *Institute of Genetics, State University, Utrecht, The Netherlands**

1. INTRODUCTION

Chromosomal variation within and between species permits reconstruction of the sequence of chromosomal events which accompany speciation. Thereby, it is possible to determine not only the nature of the differences but also the phylogenetic sequence in which they have occurred.

The primate karyological data is largely restricted to results obtained with conventional cytological techniques which do not permit identification of every chromosome. Further, these techniques fail to reveal small differences so that rearrangements that have little effect on overall length or arm ratios escape detection. This paper presents a comparison of *Pan*, *Aotes*, *Macaca*, and human chromosomes on the fluorescent and other banding techniques.

2. MATERIAL AND METHODS

5 ♂♂ and 6♀♀ *Macaca mulatta*, 1 ♀♀ *Pan troglodytes* and 1 ♂♂ *Aotes*, all adults, were used for these studies.

(a) *Bone marrow*

Cells of the bone marrow of macaques were incubated at 37°C in 0.2 μg/ml colcemide for 3 hr 45 min, and exposed to hypotonic solution (0.563% KCl) for 7 min prior to fixation in three changes of methanol : acetic acid (3:1) for a total period of 24 hr.

(b) *Lymphocyte cultures*

1. Chimpanzee and *Aotes* lymphocyte cultures, prepared and harvested in the usual manner, were exposed to 0.075 M KCl for 5 min and fixed in methanol : acetic acid (3:1) after two days of culturing. All slides were flame dried.

2. Chromosome spreads were obtained from *Macaca mulatta* lymphocyte cultures according to a modification of the technique described by Egozcue and de Egozcue (1966).

---

* Reprint requests to Dr. P. K. Seth, Cottage 7, Road 69, Punjabi Bagh, New Delhi—110026, India.

(c) *Fluorescence benzimidazol staining*

Slides were stained for 8 min in 0.04 μg/ml buffered benzimidazol derivative "Hoechst 33258" (Seth and Gropp, 1973). They were examined under a Zeiss fluorescence microscope using incident light from an HBO 200 W mercury lamp, BG 12 exciter filter, a KP 500 barrier filter, and a 63/1.3 oil objective. Well spread metaphases were photographed on Ilford FP4 film and developed in Microphen developer.

(d) *G-staining*

Some slides were incubated in 2 × SSC at 60°C for 60 min, photographed for benzimidazol fluorescence patterns, and then stained with Gurr's Giemsa (kindly supplied by Dr. K. W. Jones, Edinburgh) (Sumner et al., 1971).

3. RESULTS AND DISCUSSION

Longitudinal differentiation revealed by the benzimidazol derivative and Giemsa staining allowed recognition of every element in the chromosomal complements. A systematic comparison of human, *Pan troglodytes*, *Aotes*, and *Macaca mulatta* idiograms revealed few structural rearrangements.

(a) *Man* ($2n = 46$)–*chimpanzee* ($2n = 48$)

The karyotypes of man (fig. 1) and *Pan troglodytes* (fig. 2) differ mainly by the centric fusion of two chimpanzee acrocentric chromosomes corresponding to the

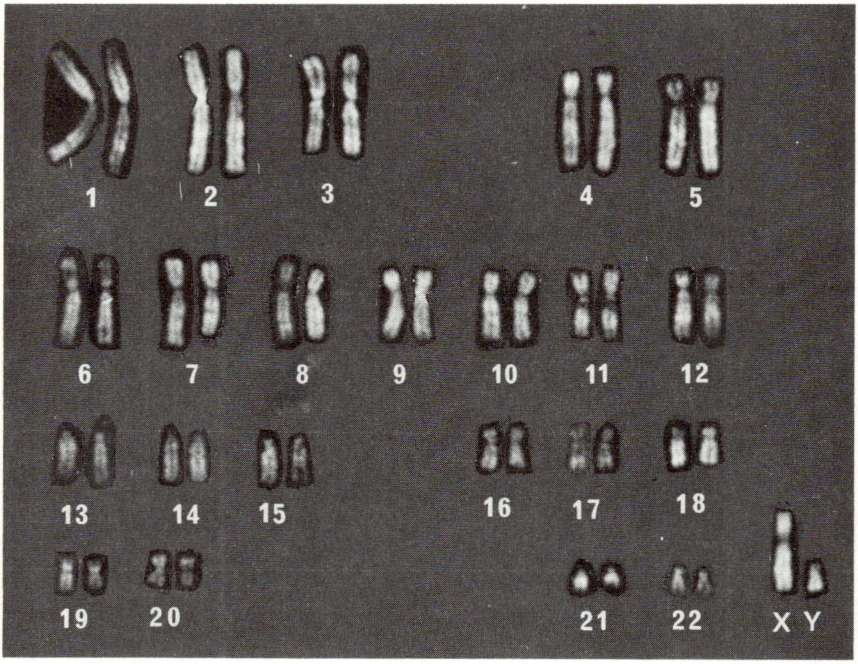

FIG. 1.—Man ♂♂ ($2n = 46$). Metaphase chromosomes stained with benzimidazol derivative 'Hoechst 33258'.

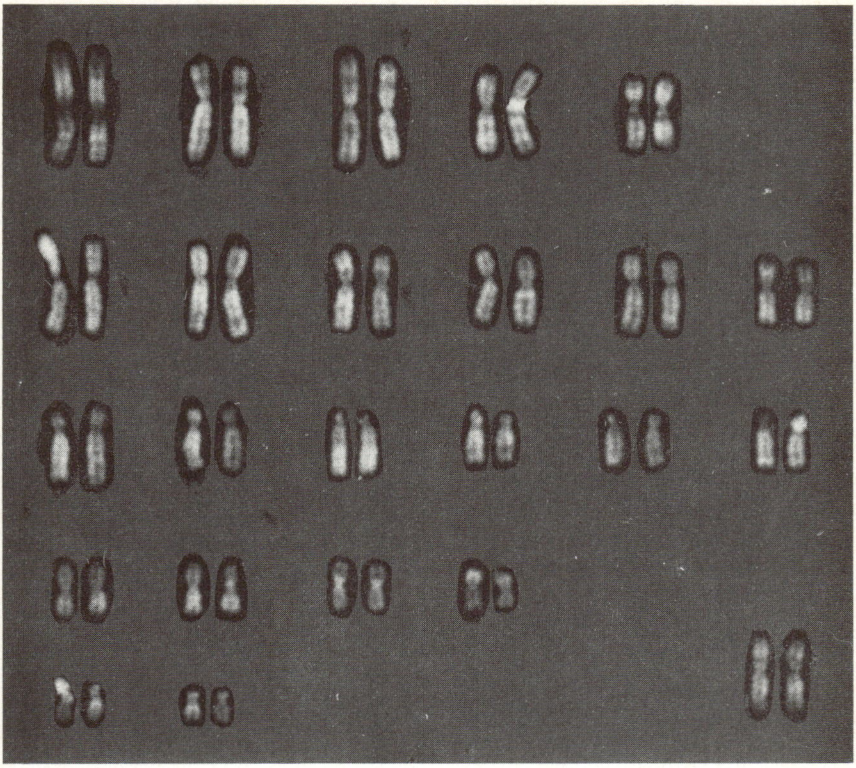

FIG. 2.—*Pan troglodytes* ♀♀ (2n = 48). Metaphase chromosomes stained with benzimidazol derivative.

human chromosome 2. Such a fusion would account for the difference in the chromosome number. This finding is contrary to a previous report (Chiarelli, 1972) that the human chromosome 1 resulted from the centric fusion of these two acrocentric chromosomes but supports the results of a re-examination (Chiarelli and Lin, 1972). *Pan* chromosome 1 has a paracentric band in the upper arm corresponding to the paracentric band in the lower arm of human chromosome 1. This difference in the banded 1q region in the two species perhaps led de Grouchy et al. (1972), Turleau et al. (1972), Bobrow and Madan (1973), and Warburton et al. (1973) to believe that the paracentric segment is missing in chimpanzee. We believe that this difference may be due to pericentric inversion, which would explain the reversal in arm ratios in *P. troglodytes* compared to that in man, a view supported by Egozcue et al. (1973).

Most of the human chromosomes are so similar to those of chimpanzee that homology is obvious despite slight differences. There seems to be general agreement among most workers that chromosomes 6–11, 13–16, and 19–22 have their homologues in the two species. Chromosomes 4, 5, 12, 17, and 18 seem to have undergone pericentric inversion in *P. troglodytes* but are otherwise similar to the corresponding human chromosomes.

(b) *Man* (2*n* = 46)–*Macaca* (2*n* = 42)

The topography of the bands in man (fig. 1) and *Macaca mulatta* (figs. 3, 4) is very similar with minor differences arising from a few simple structural rearrangements within the chromosomes (fig. 5). The chromosomes of *M. mulatta* which differ most are chromosomes 2, 8, 18, and the X. A comparison of the two karyotypes suggests that human chromosomes 21 and 22 evolved from the fission of chromosome 18 of *Macaca mulatta* (fig. 5). Likewise, it seems that human chromosome 18 and the 2q segment originated from Macaca chromosome 2. In addition, the two karyotypes differ by 3 pericentric and 2 paracentric inversions. These findings are in direct contrast to the report of Stock and Hsu (1973) who (i) propose an idiogram of Rhesus monkey on the basis of chromosomal morphology rather than the human idiogram pattern, and (ii) show homology for only 7 chromosomes for *Macaca mulatta* and man, i.e. chromosomes 1, 5, 12, 14, 15, X, and Y.

(c) *Chimpanzee* (2*n* = 48)–*Macaca* (2*n* = 42)

On the basis of banding patterns, all *Macaca* chromosomes (figs. 3, 4) except chromosome 8 have a homologue in *P. troglodytes* (fig. 2). In addition to these similarities, some important points of interest are revealed by a detailed comparison of the karyotypes of the two regarding the position and thickness of bands in some chromosomes. These differences are the result of some structural rearrangements in the chromosomes due to peri- and paracentric inversions. The chromosomes of *Macaca mulatta* (2n = 42) differ from the chromosomes of *Pan troglodytes* (2n = 48) by two pericentric inversions and 4 paracentric inversions. Besides these, the chimpanzee chromosomes 8, 15, 21, 22, and 'a' find no homologue in the *Macaca mulatta* chromosomes.

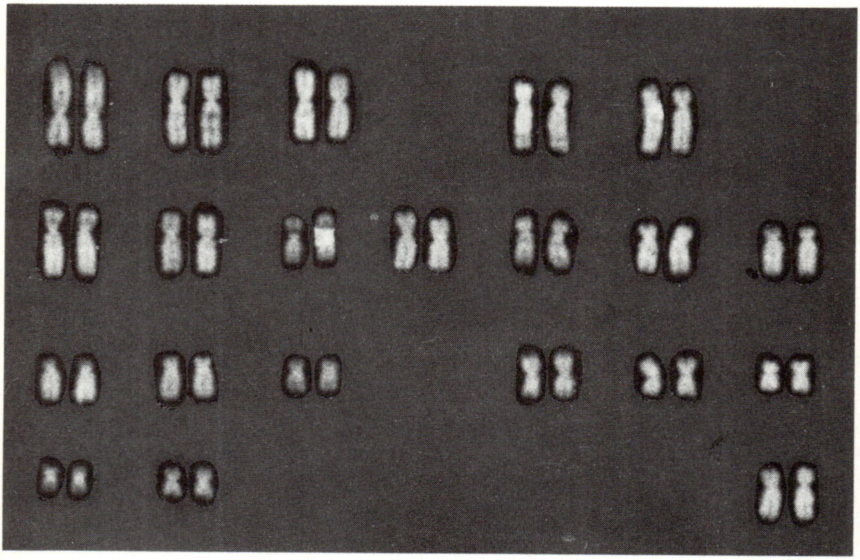

FIG. 3.—*Macaca mulatta* ♀♀ (2n = 42). Metaphase chromosomes stained with benzimidazol derivative 'Hoechst 33258'.

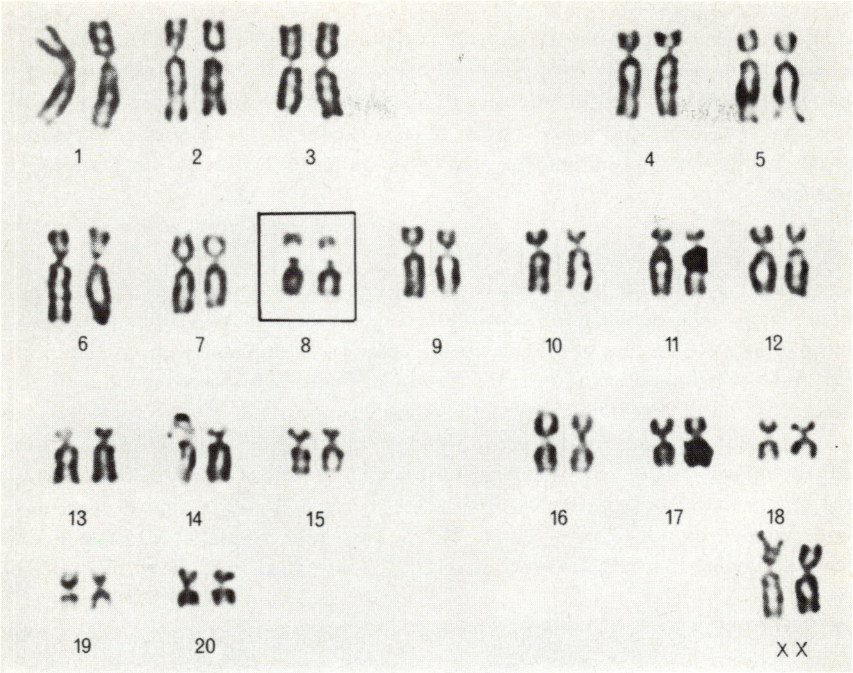

FIG.4.—*Macaca mulatta* ♀♀ (2n = 42). Metaphase chromosomes.

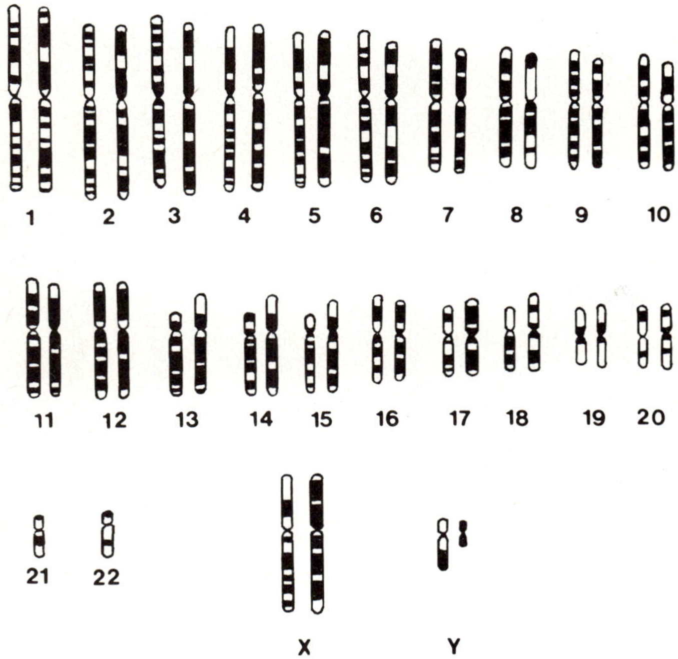

FIG. 5.—Comparison of idiograms of man and *Macaca mulatta*. Chromosomes on the left in each pair belong to man and those on the right belong to *Macaca*.

(d) *Aotus trivirgatus* ($2n = 51$)

Although banding patterns can be demonstrated along the length of all chromosomes of *Aotes* with the benzimidazol fluorescent technique (fig. 6), the paracentric bands on certain chromosomes vary in size and fluorescence intensity or are altogether non-fluorescing. Research is in progress for studying normal variations, structural polymorphism, and for possible homologies between *Aotes** and other primates.

4. COMMENTS

The presence of common centromeric DNA sequences among higher primates and man signifies the existence of an evolutionary mechanism which has potentiated the comparative success of this group in evolution. Compared with other groups, e.g., rodents, primates have conserved certain DNA families within their constitutive heterochromatin. The banding patterns of the chromosomes of *Pan troglodytes* are similar to those of man, of course with minor variations. Satellite A DNA of chimpanzee shares so many of the physical properties of human satellite III DNA that the original satellite sequence was presumably present in a common progenitor of both these primates (Prosser et al., 1973). This and cross-hybridization studies indicate underlying base sequence homology. It has also been demonstrated that

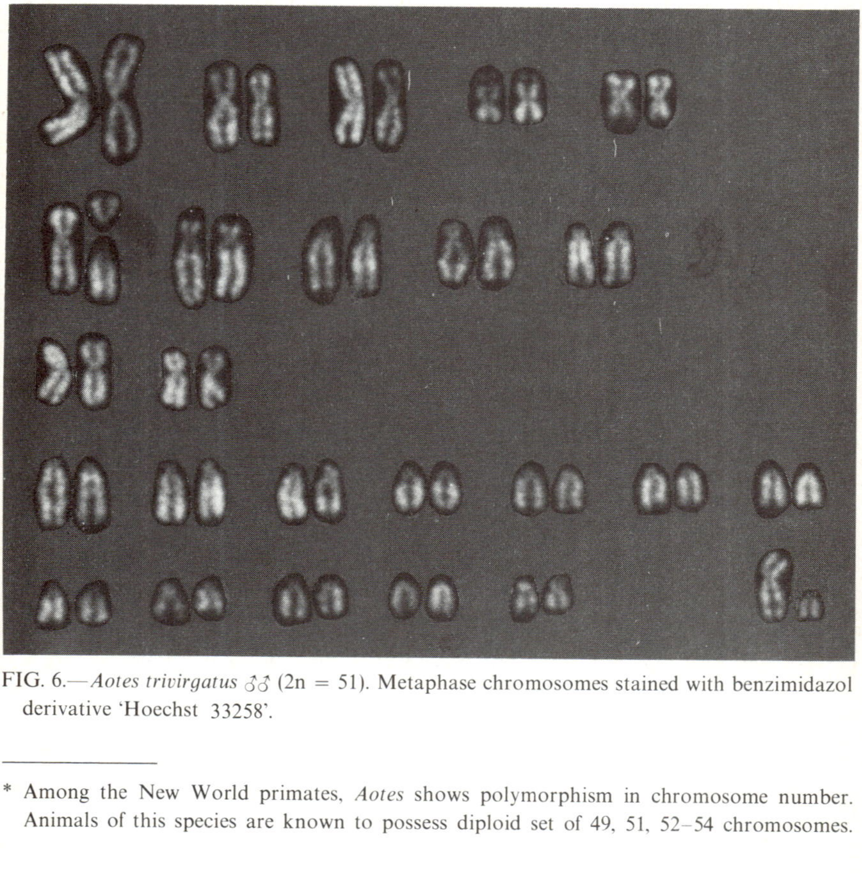

FIG. 6.—*Aotes trivirgatus* ♂♂ (2n = 51). Metaphase chromosomes stained with benzimidazol derivative 'Hoechst 33258'.

* Among the New World primates, *Aotes* shows polymorphism in chromosome number. Animals of this species are known to possess diploid set of 49, 51, 52–54 chromosomes.

the Giemsa and fluorescence staining variations in chromosome 1, 9, and 16 correspond to the molecular differences and similarities characteristic of the satellite DNA's of these chromosomes (Pearson, 1972; Evans et al., 1971; Bobrow et al., 1972; Gagné and Laberge, 1972; Bobrow and Madan, 1973). Jones (1973) has suggested that these differentially stained regions in chimpanzee and man retain features in common other than related satellite DNA. This indicates, especially because of chromatin similarities between man and chimpanzee (Pearson et al., 1973; Seth, 1974), that the intensely fluorescent polymorphisms arose somewhere in the ancestral line that gave rise to man.

De Grouchy et al. (1972) suggest that besides one set of Robertsonian fusion, a deletion in chromosome 12 had occurred. This feature is also corroborated by the recent work of Stock and Hsu (1973) who have demonstrated a nearly perfect homology for chromosome 12 in the Rhesus and the African Green monkey.

Detailed cross comparisons of the longitudinal chromosomal differentiation in man and chimpanzee with those of *Macaca mulatta* indicate that much of the *Macaca* genome can be matched to that of chimpanzee and man. There is evidence that in *in-situ* hybridization, satellite III DNA is not only homologous with the chimpanzee chromosome but a physically similar satellite DNA is also present in the chimpanzee (Prosser et al., 1973). This, therefore, suggests that the evolutionary divergence of man and chimpanzee took place after the origin of the original satellite III sequence. Systematic comparisons of the banding patterns of these three primates and the biochemical genetic assays of man and *Macaca* (Seth et al., 1975) demonstrate that the evolutionary divergences of man-Macaca and chimpanzee-Macaca predate the evolutionary divergence of man and chimpanzee. This observation should enable us to reconstruct the likely phylogenetic tree of the primates since it seems that so far they may be unique in possessing similar banding patterns. Together with biochemical and paleontological data, chromosomal observations will probably facilitate a better understanding of the origin of man.

Acknowledgement. The work reported here was partly aided by the Alexander von Humboldt-Stiftung, Bonn-Bad Godesberg, West Germany.

5. REFERENCES

BOBROW, M., and MADAN, K. 1973. A comparison of chimpanzee and human chromosomes using the Giemsa-11 and other chromosome banding techniques. *Cytogenet. Cell Genet.*, *12*, 107–116.

BOBROW, M., MADAN, K., and PEARSON, P. L. 1972. Staining of some specific regions of human chromosomes, particularly the secondary constriction of No. 9. *Nat. New Biol.*, *238*, 122–124.

CHIARELLI, B. A. 1972. Comparative chromosome analysis between man and chimpanzee. *J. Hum. Evol.*, *1*, 389–393.

CHIARELLI, B., and LIN, C. C. 1972. Comparison of fluorescence patterns in human and chimpanzee chromosomes. *Genen Phaenen*, *15*, 103–106.

EGOZCUE, J., and DE EGOZCUE, M. V. 1966. Simplified culture and chromosome preparations of primate leukocytes. *Stain Technol.*, *41*, 173–177.

EGOZCUE, J., CABALLIN, M. R., and GODAY, C. 1973. Banding patterns of the chromosomes of man and the chimpanzee. *Humangenetik*, *18*, 77–80.

EVANS, H. J., BUCKTON, K. E., and SUMNER, A. T. 1971. Cytological mapping of human chromosomes: Results obtained with Quinacrine fluorescence and the acetic-saline-Giemsa techniques. *Chromosoma (Berl.)*, *35*, 310–325.

GAGNÉ, R., and LABERGE, C. 1972. Specific cytological recognition of the heterochromatic segment of number 9 chromosome in man. *Exp. Cell. Res.*, *73*, 239–242.

DE GROUCHY, J., CATHERINE, T., MICHELLE, R., and KLEIN, M. 1972. Evolutions caryotypiques de l'homme et du chimpanze. Etude comparative des topographies de bandes apres denaturation menagee. *Ann. Genet.*, *15*, 79–84.

JONES, K. W. 1973. Annotation: Satellite DNA. *J. Med. Genet.*, *10*, 273–281.

PEARSON, P. L. 1972. The use of new staining techniques for human chromosome identification. *J. Med. Genet.*, *9*, 264–275.

PEARSON, P. L., GERAEDTS, J. P. M., and VAN DER LINDEN, A. G. J. M. 1973. Human chromosome polymorphism. In *Symp. Medica Hoechst 6, Modern Aspects of Cytogenetics: Constitutive Heterochromatin in Man* (R. A. PFEIFFER, ed.), pp. 201–213. F. K. Schattauer-Verlag, Stuttgart-New York. Symp. Schloß Reinhartshausen/Rein, June 18–20, 1972.

PROSSER, J., MOAR, M., BOBROW, M., and JONES, K. W. 1973. Satellite sequences in chimpanzee *(Pan troglodytes)*. *Biochim. Biophys. Acta*, *319*, 122–134.

SETH, P. K. 1974. Fluorescence banded patterns in chromosomes with a benzimidazol derivative: characterization of constitutive heterochromatin and AT concentration in chromosomal DNA. 1st Annual Conf. and Seminar on *Recent Trends in Population Genetics*, Bombay, Feb. 14–16, 1974.

SETH, P. K., and GROPP, A. 1973. Study of constitutive heterochromatin with a new and simplified fluorescence staining technique. *Genetica (The Hague)*, *44* (3), 485–495.

SETH, S., SETH, P. K., and SAXENA, M. B. 1975. Genetic variations in primates: red cell enzymes and serum proteins in *Macaca mulatta*. *Humangenetik*, *29*, 241–348.

STOCK, A. D., and HSU, T. C. 1973. Evolutionary conservation in arrangement of genetic material. A comparative analysis of chromosome banding between the *Rhesus macaque* (2n = 42, 84 arms) and the African green monkey (2n = 60, 120 arms). *Chromosoma (Berl.)*, 43, 211–224.

SUMNER, A. T., EVANS, H. J., and BUCKLAND, R. 1971. New technique for distinguishing between human chromosomes. *Nat. New Biol.*, *232*, 31–32.

TURLEAU, C., DE GROUCHY, J., and KLEIN, M. 1972. The human and chimpanzee karyotypes. *Medical Primatology, Proc. 3rd Conf. Exp. Med. Surg. Primates*, Pt. I, pp. 398–401, Lyon.

WARBURTON, D., FIRSCHEIN, I. L., MILLER, D. A., and WARBURTON, F. E. 1973. Karyotype of the chimpanzee, *Pan troglodytes*, based on measurements and banding pattern: comparison to the human karyotype. *Cytogenet. Cell Genet.*, *12*, 453–461.

CHROMOSOMES OF *PEROMYSCUS* (RODENTIA, CRICETIDAE). V. EVIDENCE OF PERICENTRIC INVERSIONS

F. E. ARRIGHI, A. D. STOCK and S. PATHAK

Department of Biology, The University of Texas System Cancer Center, M. D. Anderson Hospital, and Tumor Institute, Houston, Texas 77025, USA

1. INTRODUCTION

Heterochromatin, since its discovery more than 40 years ago (Heitz, 1928, 1933, 1934), has been studied by biologists from various angles. However, the greatest advance in our understanding of its nature came recently as the result of the *in situ* hybridization experiments (Pardue and Gall, 1970). By modifying this technique, Arrighi and Hsu (1971) observed a differential staining in human chromosomes, i.e., constitutive heterochromatin that stains more heavily than euchromatin. Further studies on many different life forms resulted in finding a positive correlation between constitutive heterochromatin (C-band) and the chromosomal localization of repetitive DNA.

As derivatives of the C-band technique, there emerged a number of methods which produced light and dark bands along the euchromatic chromosomes, now known as the G-band and R-bands. These techniques complement the results of the differential quinacrine fluorescence (Q-band) discovered by Caspersson et al. (1968, 1969) a few years earlier. These methods have become powerful tools for the identification of chromosomes and have helped the studies on chromosome evolution.

The present paper reports the cytological studies of 3 species of the American rodent genus *Peromyscus: P. eremicus, P. crinitus* and *P. leucopus.*

2. MATERIALS

The following animals were used in the present study. Skin fibroblast cultures were initiated for conventional air-dried preparations:

P. eremicus: 1♀ 7.0 mi N NE Oatman, Mohave Co., Arizona.
2♂ 7.5 mi N NE Oatman, Mohave Co., Arizona.
1♂ 9.3 mi N NE Oatman, Mohave Co., Arizona.
P. leucopus: 2♂, 3♀ 1 mi E Graford. Palo, Pinto Co., Texas.
1♂, 2♀ Arroyo, NE Tortugas Mts., Dona Ana Co., New Mexico.
2♀ NE Slope Tortugas Mts., Dona Ana Co., New Mexico.
1♀ 17 mi S SW Paducah, King Co., Texas.
P. crinitus: 5♀, 5♂ 7 mi N St. George, Washington Co., Utah.
1♀, 9 mi N NE Oatman, Mohave Co., Arizona.
2♀, 7 mi N NE Oatman, Mohave Co., Arizona.

The animals are either still living or skin and skulls have been prepared and the specimens stored in our laboratory.

3. CHROMOSOMES OF *PEROMYSCUS*

Hsu and Arrighi (1968) analyzed the chromosome constitutions of 20 of the more than 50 species of *Peromyscus*. All species studied had a diploid number of 48. However, the fundamental number or NF (Matthey, 1945) varies from 56 for *P. boylei* and *P. crinitus* to 96 for *P. eremicus* (based on female karyotypes). The NF of other species of this genus ranged between these two extremes. Hsu and Arrighi used the classic explanation, viz., the karyological changes were the results of pericentric inversions and translocations. However, Pathak et al. (1973) reported that in *P. eremicus*, all 48 short arms resulted from additions of heterochromatin. These authors went to the other extreme in their interpretation by projecting that probably the short chromosome arms of all *Peromyscus* are heterochromatic and that pericentric inversions were probably not involved in karyological evolution of this genus. We now have evidence to show that both addition of heterochromatic arms and pericentric inversions operate in the karyotypic evolution of the genus *Peromyscus*.

4. BANDING PATTERNS

The methods for C-banding followed that described by Arrighi and Hsu (1971) with the omission of the RNase treatment. G-banding was accomplished by modifying the technique described by Seabright (1971) and Wang and Federoff (1972).

The positive C-band areas of *P. crinitus* (fig. 1a) are only at the centromeres and the short arms of the 4 biarmed chromosomes, including the X. In males the Y chromosome is heterochromatic. All animals studied thus far have shown no variation from this pattern.

The positive C-band areas of *P. eremicus* (fig. 1b) include nearly all of the short arms as well as the centromere areas. In males the Y chromosome is heterochromatic.

The chromosomes of *P. leucopus* present an entirely different C-band pattern (fig. 1c). The fundamental number of this species varies considerably from population to population. However, the short arms of *P. leucopus* are not always heterochromatic including the short arm of the X chromosome. In fact, five of the largest chromosomes of figure 1c have euchromatic second arms. In addition, several pairs of chromosomes have interstitial or telomeric C-bands. In figure 1c one pair shows polymorphic C-bands. The Y chromosome is again heterochromatic.

Despite the differences in the C-band patterns (e.g., interstitial C-bands in *P. leucopus*), the G-band patterns of the three species are reasonably similar (fig. 2). Superficially these patterns may appear different from one another, but these differences, when closely examined, can be easily explained. Pathak et al. (1973) compared the G-bands of *P. crinitus* and *P. eremicus* and found that the bands in the euchromatic long arms are identical. When the G-bands of *crinitus* and *leucopus* are compared, it appears that a few sets of pericentric inversions can explain most of the differences. Figure 3 compares the G-band patterns of the nine longest chromosomes of *P. crinitus* and *P. leucopus*. The chromosome on the left of each pair is from *P. leucopus* while the one on the right is from *P. crinitus*. Except for an additional dark band in the long arm of chromosome 1 of *P. leucopus* (C-band, straight arrow), these two chromosomes have identical banding patterns.

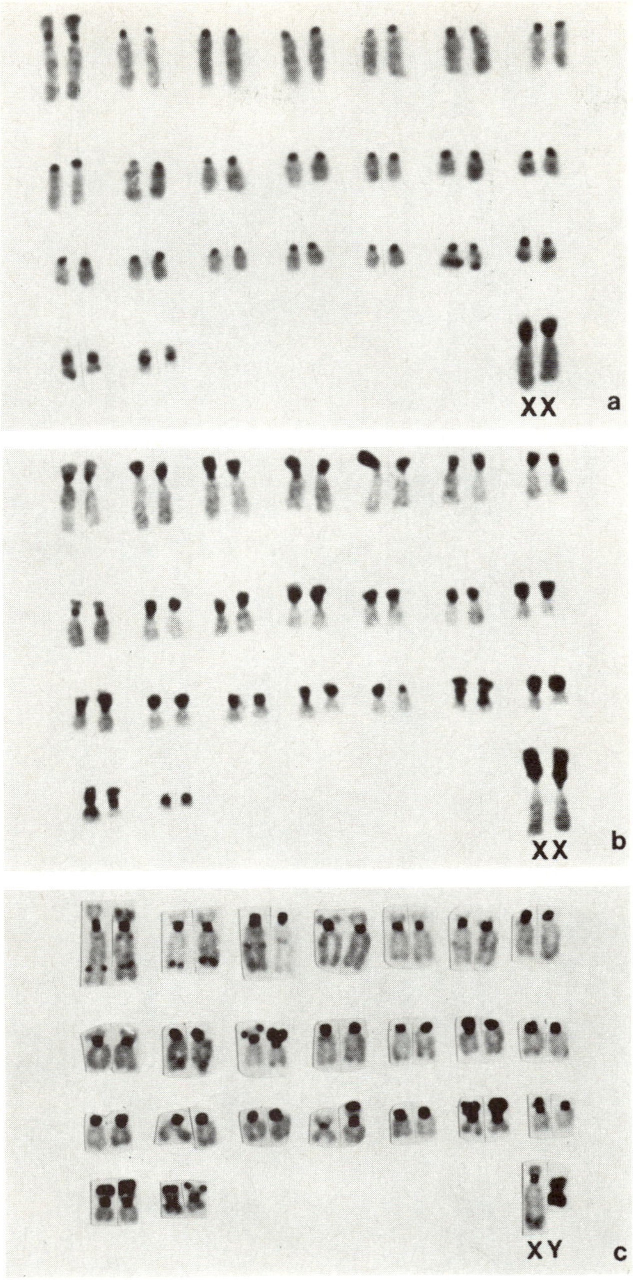

FIG. 1.—C band patterns. (a) *P. crinitus.* The C bands are confined to the centromere areas and 4 of the 8 short arms. (b) *P. eremicus.* All of the short arms are heterochromatic except 2 pairs. (c) *P. leucopus.* Many short arms are not heterochromatic. Both interstitial (chromosome 1) and telomere heterchromatin is present. Polymorphism in C-bands is seen in chromosomes 18, 21 and 22.

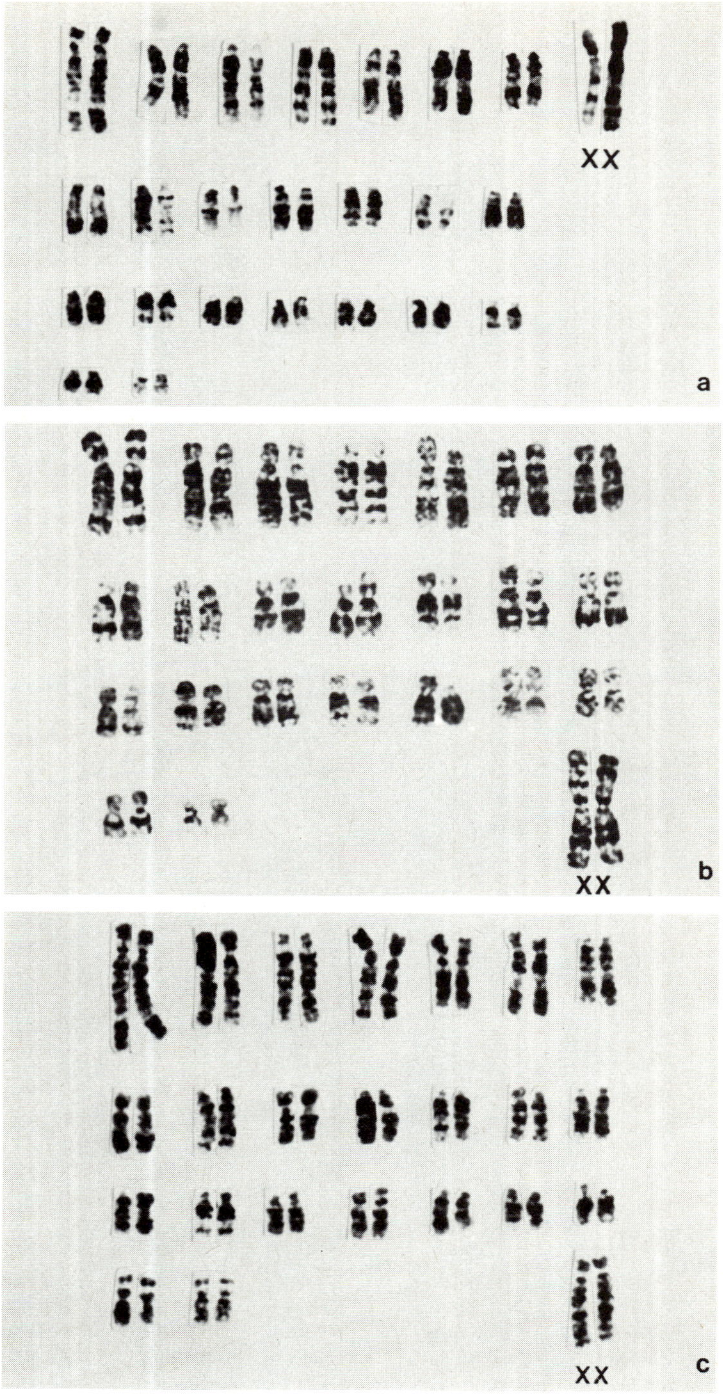

FIG. 2.—G band patterns. (a) *P. crinitus.* (b) *P. eremicus.* Note light and dark G-bands in short arms. (c) *P. leucopus.*

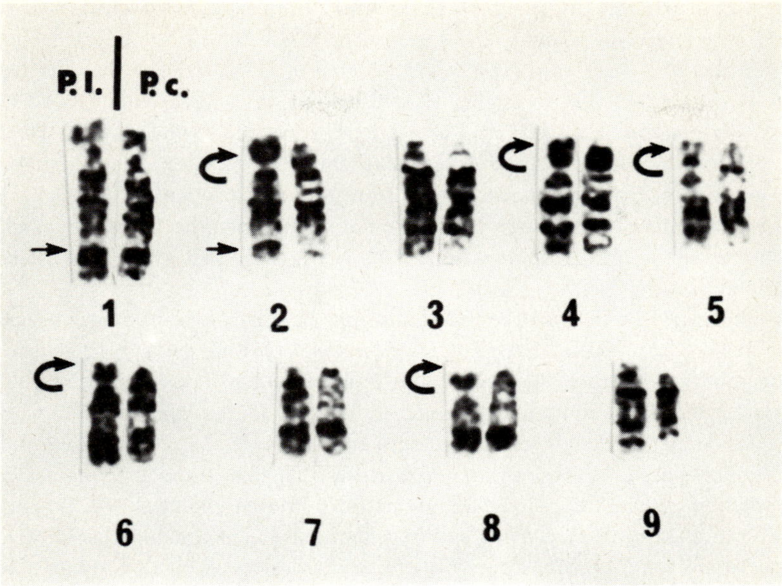

FIG. 3.—Comparison of G-bands of the 9 largest chromosomes of *P. leucopus* and *P. crinitus*. The chromosome on the left is from *P. leucopus* and the one on the right of each pair from *P. crinitus*. The straight arrows indicate the position of C-bands. The curved arrow indicates pericentric inversions.

Chromosome 2 of *P. leucopus* has a short arm which is not C-band positive. When the bands are compared to one of the chromosomes of *P. crinitus*, it is obvious that the short arm of *P. leucopus* No. 2 resulted from a pericentric inversion. If one cuts this short arm and reinverts it, then the G-bands of the two species are identical. The same is true for *P. leucopus* chromosomes 4, 5, 6 and 8. Chromosomes 3, 7 and 9 do not have euchromatic short arms and the G-bands of these chromosomes of the two species appear identical.

The G-banding pattern in constitutive heterochromatin can be observed in the short arms of *P. eremicus* (fig. 2b). Both light and dark G-bands occur. These are especially prominent in the short arm of the X chromosome. However, several of these short arms appear to have few dark bands.

5. DISCUSSION

Inspection of the C-band patterns shows considerable variation among the three species. The position of the C-bands may be confined mainly to the centromere areas as in *P. crinitus*, to additional short arms plus the centromere areas as in *P. eremicus*, or it may be located in various positions along the chromosomes as in *P. leucopus*.

There are numerous reports showing that repeated sequences are located in the C-band areas of chromosomes. The sequences as well as the G + C content of these satellite DNAs vary considerably even among members of the same genus such as

Mus (Sutton and McCallum, 1972). The DNA of *P. eremicus* has a hypersharp band at the heavy side of the main band in neutral CsCl density gradients. Isolation, purification, and characterization of the *P. eremicus* DNA indicate that it is repetitious in nature with slightly higher G + C content than main band DNA (R. W. Clark, personal communication). There was no such satellite band in the DNA of *P. crinitus*. *In situ* hybridization experiments show localization in the C-band area of *P. eremicus* with no localization in the chromosomes of *P. crinitus*. Filter hybridization experiments confirmed the lack of homology between the *P. eremicus* and the *P. crinitus* genomes in respect to this particular fraction (R. W. Clark, personal communication).

G-band analyses, on the other hand, indicate stability of chromosome organization for these three species. Even though these species belong to the same genus, they are members of different subgenera. Both *P. eremicus* and *P. crinitus* belong to the subgenus *Haplomylomys* while *P. leucopus* belongs to the subgenus *Peromyscus*. It is considered that the two subgenera have been separated for a long period of time. Even rodent species taxonomically separated further than these three species show considerable resemblance in G-banding patterns. Mascarello et al. (1974) analyzed the G-bands of species belonging to five genera and found considerable homology. Furthermore, the X chromosome of mammals has a very stable G-banding pattern and this chromosome can be identified by G-bands regardless of its morphology (Pathak and Stock, 1974). Their X chromosome study included 77 species belonging to 9 orders of mammals and specific bands could be observed whether the X was metacentric, submetacentric, or telocentric.

The structural stability as viewed by G-banding appears to be confined only to euchromatin. The constitutive heterochromatin, on the other hand, appears to be very flexible in amount and position among species, and this flexibility is even seen within a species. The role played by repeated nucleotide sequences and nucleotide clustering along chromosomes is unknown. In other species it is possible that the interstitial C-bands are the result of pericentric inversions or translocations involving the telomere of one chromosome and the centromere, including the C-band, of the second chromosome. However, in *Peromyscus* our evidence suggests that these bands arose as *in situ* events.

Acknowledgement. Supported in part by the National Foundation March of Dimes. The authors wish to thank Mr. F. Elder and Drs. M. R. Lee and J. Mascarello for donating a number of the rodents used in this study.

6. REFERENCES

Arrighi, F. E., and Hsu, T. C. 1971. Localization of heterochromatin in human chromosomes. *Cytogenetics (Basel)*, *10*, 81–86.

Caspersson, T., Farber, S., Foley, G. E., Kudynowski, J., Modest, E. J., Simonsson, E., Wagh, U., and Zech, L. 1968. Chemical differentiation along metaphase chromosomes. *Exp. Cell Res.*, *49*, 219–222.

Caspersson, T., Zech, L., Modest, E. J., Foley, G. E., Wagh, U., and Simonsson, E. 1969. DNA-binding fluorochromes for the study of the organization of the metaphase nucleus. *Exp. Cell Res.*, *58*, 141–152.

Heitz, E. 1928. Das Heterochromatin der Moose. *I. Jahrb. wiss. Bot.*, *69*, 762–818.

HEITZ, E. 1933. Die somatische Heteropknose bei *Drosophila melanogaster* und ihre genetische Bedeutung. *Z. Zellforsch. mikrosk. Anat., 20,* 237–287.

HEITZ, E. 1934. Über α und β-Heterochromatin sowie Konstanz und Bau der Chromomeren bei *Drosophila. Biol. Zbl., 54,* 588–609.

HSU, T. C., and ARRIGHI, F. E. 1968. Chromosomes of *Peromyscus* (Rodentia, Cricetidae). I. Evolutionary trends in twenty species. *Cytogenetics (Basel), 7,* 417–446.

MASCARELLO, J. T., STOCK, A. D., and PATHAK, S. 1974. Conservatism in the arrangement of genetic material in rodents. *J. Mammal., 55,* 695–704.

MATTHEY, R. 1945. L'evolution de la formule chromosomiale chez les vertébrés. *Experientia (Basel), 1,* 50–56:78–86.

PARDUE, M. L., and GALL, J. G. 1970. Chromosomal localization of mouse satellite DNA. *Science (Wash. D.C.), 168,* 1356–1358.

PATHAK, S., and STOCK, A. D. 1974. The X-chromosomes of mammals: Karyological homology as revealed by banding techniques. *Genetics, 78,* 703–714.

PATHAK, S., HSU, T. C., and ARRIGHI, F. E. 1973. Chromosomes of *Peromyscus* (Rodentia: Cricetidae). IV. The role of heterochromatin in karyotypic evolution. *Cytogenet. Cell Genet., 12,* 315–326.

SEABRIGHT, M. 1971. A rapid banding technique for human chromosomes. *Lancet, ii,* 971–972.

SUTTON, W. D., and MCCALLUM, M. 1972. Related satellite DNA's in the genus *Mus. J. Mol. Biol., 71,* 633–656.

WANG, H. C., and FEDEROFF, S. 1972. Banding in human chromosomes treated with trypsin. *Nat. New Biol., 235,* 52–53.

CHROMOSOMES AND DNA SEQUENCES IN SALAMANDERS

HERBERT C. MACGREGOR, SHIGEKI MIZUNO and MARCELA VLAD

Department of Zoology, School of Biological Sciences, University of Leicester, Leicester, England

1. INTRODUCTION

Plethodontid salamanders have large chromosomes, and they provide excellent material for the study of meiosis in the male and of lampbrush chromosomes in the female. They are, moreover, easily available in many parts of the United States. and they offer the added attraction to the molecular cytogeneticist in that their phylogeny has been well researched and carefully documented (Wake, 1966; Highton, 1962, 1972). We chose to study the genus *Plethodon* because all species have the same chromosome number, and because we knew from earlier studies (Macgregor and Walker, 1973) that there are species within the genus whose DNA values per haploid chromosome set differed by as much as twofold. We have studied four aspects of the genus: the size of the genome, the characteristics of the karyotype, the degree of commonness from species to species with respect to DNA sequences, and the number and general characteristics of chromomeres in the lampbrush chromosomes of species with widely different C values. We have asked specifically whether changes in the size of the *Plethodon* genome in the course of speciation have been accompanied by changes in the relative dimensions of the chromosomes, by changes in the repetitive or unique DNA sequences that constitute these genomes, or by changes in the number of chromomeres per haploid set of lampbrush chromosomes.

2. OBSERVATIONS

We have used 19 species of *Plethodon*, belonging to 3 species groups (Highton, 1962), ten of which feature in this account (table 1). Larger plethodons found in the Eastern parts of the United States are designated "Eastern large" plethodons, smaller Eastern species are called "Eastern small" plethodons, and species found in the Pacific North West are called "Western" plethodons (Highton, 1962).

The C value of *P. cinereus* was first determined biochemically with respect to *Xenopus laevis*. The methods employed have been described elsewhere (Mizuno and Macgregor, 1974). C values for all other species were then determined by microdensitometry of Feulgen-stained red blood cell nuclei, with reference to cells from *P. cinereus* prepared in the same way (Mizuno and Macgregor, 1974). C values for all 10 species are shown in table 1. We considered two aspects of these results to be useful and significant. First, the C values of all the Eastern species listed are between 18 and 23 pg. Secondly, the C values of the three Western species listed are substantially higher (36–39 pg).

In line with the C values and the constancy of chromosome number in the genus,

TABLE 1

C values (amount of DNA per haploid chromosome set) for 10 species of Plethodon

Group	Species	C(g × 10^{-12})
Eastern small	*cinereus*	20.0
	hoffmani	21.4
	nettingi	18.2
	richmondi	20.4
Eastern large	*wehrlei*	20.3
	glutinosus	22.5
	jordani	23.1
Western	*vehiculum*	36.8
	dunni	38.8
	elongatus	33.8

the chromosomes of Western species are larger. Our studies of the karyotypes of two Eastern and three Western species were intended to determine whether the relative lengths and centromere positions of corresponding chromosomes in different groups of species had changed in the course of evolution, along with the change in the total size of the genome. Karyotype analyses were carried out on lampbrush chromosomes and chromosomes in the early anaphase of the 2nd meiotic division from two Eastern and three Western species. Representative idiograms from one Eastern and two Western species are shown in figure 1. Our methods are described elsewhere (Mizuno and Macgregor, 1974). The idiograms together with an analysis of variance with respect to relative lengths have indicated that such karyotypic differences as exist between the species with respect to the relative dimensions of their chromosomes are small, and in all but three cases, insignificant. We find that only chromosome 2 in *P. cinereus* differs significantly from its counterpart in *P. dunni*, and chromosomes 5 and 11 in *P. cinereus* differ from their counterparts in both *P. dunni* and *P. vehiculum*. These observations have led us to the conclusion that despite large differences in genome size, the karyotypes of Eastern and Western species of *Plethodon* are remarkably similar.

Our experiments at the molecular level began with two predictions. The first was that closely related species would have similar DNA sequences, whereas the DNA of distantly related species would have less in common. Secondly, on the basis of Britten and Kohne's (1967) hypothesis about the production of repetitive DNA sequences and Britten and Davidson's (1969) hypothesis about functions of repetitive and unique DNA sequences, we predicted that in the course of evolution, repetitive DNA sequences would have changed more than unique DNA sequences. We set about testing these predictions by fractionating DNA from *P. cinereus* and from *P. vehiculum*, on the basis of reassociation kinetics, into repetitive and slowly reassociating components, and we examined the capacities of these DNAs to form stable hybrids with DNA from other species of *Plethodon* under specified experimental conditions.

DNA of *P. cinereus* can be categorized into: (i) a very fast reassociating fraction

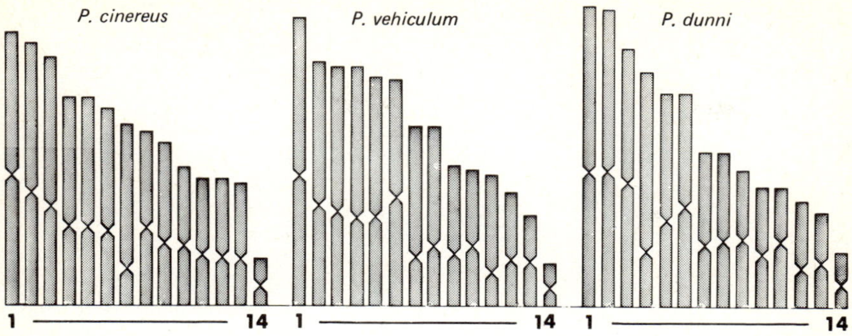

FIG. 1.—Idiograms constructed from relative lengths and centromere indices of lampbrush chromosomes in preparations made from oocytes of *P. cinereus*, *P. vehiculum*, and *P. dunni*. In terms of absolute size, the chromosomes of *P. vehiculum* and *P. dunni* are much larger than those of *P. cinereus*.

that comprises about 15% of the genome and completes its reassociation by C_0t 0.05; (ii) a fast reassociating fraction (the "repetitive" fraction used in our studies) that comprises about 30% of the genome and completes reassociation between C_0t 0.05 and 10; (iii) an intermediate fraction that comprises about 15% of the genome and completes reassociation between C_0t 10 and 10^3; and (iv) a slowly reassociating fraction (the "slow" fraction used in our studies) that comprises about 40% of the genome and is not completely reassociated by C_0t 3×10^4. We think that much of the DNA in the slow fraction consists of unique sequences. In contrast, about 80% of the genomes of the Western salamander, *P. vehiculum*, consists of repetitive sequences that reassociate by C_0t 10^3.

When labelled and sheared, repetitive DNA from *P. cinereus* was allowed to reassociate with unlabelled whole DNA from other species of *Plethodon*, three distinct levels of reassociation were observed, representing three levels of similarity between the repetitive DNA of *P. cinereus* and that of other species (table 2, columns 3 and 4). The highest level, shown with DNAs from other Eastern small species, was close to that of the homologous reassociation. The intermediate level, shown with DNAs from Eastern large species, was about 50% of the homologous level, and the lowest level, shown with DNA from Western species, was about 10% of the homologous level. This is to say that only about 10% of the nucleotide sequences in the *P. cinereus* repetitive fraction, which can form stable duplexes with homologous DNA under our experimental conditions, seem to be represented in the genome of Western species. This level did not change significantly even when the reassociation reaction was carried out to C_0t 10^3 (Mizuno and Macgregor, unpublished data). Moreover, such sequences as *P. cinereus* and Western species have in common, nevertheless differ with respect to 10–15% base substitutions.

Conversely, only 10% or less of the repetitive sequences in *P. vehiculum* seem to be present in the genomes of Eastern species, and in these common sequences there are 8–16% base substitutions (table 2, columns 5 and 6).

Our reassociation experiments show a clear correspondence between percentage similarity of repetitive sequences and taxonomic relatedness, as we had predicted.

TABLE 2

Relative levels of reassociation of ^{125}*I-repetitive fraction from* P. cinereus *(columns 3 and 4) or* P. vehiculum *(columns 4 and 5), or* ^{125}*I-"slow" fraction from* P. cinereus *(columns 7 and 8) with DNAs from various species in the genus* Plethodon

Unlabelled DNA from		Repetitive				Slow	
Group	Species	Relative level of reassociation (%) *P. cinereus* ^{125}I DNA	ΔT_m (C)	Relative level of reassociation (%) *P. vehiculum* ^{125}I DNA	ΔT_m (C)	Relative level of reassociation (%) *P. cinereus* ^{125}I DNA	ΔT_m (C)
Eastern small	*P. cinereus*	100		10.3	8.5	100	
	P. hoffmani	92.0	1.2	12.3	9.4	94.4	2.4
	P. nettingi	90.8	1.6	9.6	6.4	81.0	2.3
Eastern large	*P. wehrlei*	54.7	5.2	11.4	7.5	53.3	5.0
	P. glutinosus	52.4	4.9	9.6	9.3	53.0	5.0
	P. jordani	55.1	4.7	4.7	8.0	64.4	5.0
Western	*P. elongatus*	13.8	9.0	57.5	2.3	38.7	8.0
	P. dunni	12.1	9.3	81.6	1.2	32.4	8.6
	P. vehiculum	12.1	9.2	100		29.2	9.4

Reassociation of ^{125}I-repetitive fraction was carried out in 0.12M PB (equal volume mixture of 0.12M Na_2HPO_4 and 0.12M NaH_2PO_4, pH 6.8)–0.0028 M EDTA at 65°C to C_0t 10, which was determined by the concentration of unlabelled, sheared DNA. Reassociation of ^{125}I-"slow" fraction was carried out in 0.60M PB–0.0028M EDTA at 65°C to C_0t 10^4. Reassociation products were separated from single-stranded DNA by hydroxyapatite (HAP) column chromatography. Thermal stability of reassociation products was determined by the thermal elution from HAP-columns in 0.14M PB. T_m is the temperature by which 50% of the reassociation products were dissociated and eluted from the column. ΔT_m is the difference from the T_m of homologous reassociation products. T_m of hybrids between heterologous DNAs were always lower than that of homologous duplexes. It was assumed that 1°C decrease in T_m corresponds to the introduction of 1–1.5% base substitutions. Details of the experiments were described elsewhere (Mizuno and Macgregor, 1974).

Reassociations of labelled "slow" DNA from *P. cinereus* with unlabelled sheared whole DNA from other species gave similar results, in that three levels of similarity to the "slow" fraction of *P. cinereus* were found, and these correlated with taxonomic relatedness (table 2, columns 7 and 8). However, differences between Eastern and Western species with respect to their "slow" DNA were much less than with respect to repetitive DNA. As much as 40% of the level of homologous reassociation was attained between the "slow" sequences of *P. cinereus* and the DNAs of Western salamanders.

Our observations so far indicate that selection pressures favouring the conservation of unique sequences in salamander genomes have been greater than those operating on repetitive sequences, and we regard this as evidence in support of Britten and Davidson's (1969, 1973) notion of unique sequences as structural genes and repetitive sequences as having a less clearly definable, perhaps regulatory role in inheritance and development.

Our investigations of chromomeres on lampbrush chromosomes have been confined to three species: *P. cinereus*, *P. dunni*, and *P. vehiculum*. Specifically, we have asked whether the number of chromomeres per haploid set of lampbrush chromosomes is related to C value within the genus *Plethodon*. We have approached this problem by making preparations of lampbrush chromosomes from oocytes at a stage when the chromosomes are judged to be maximally extended and their lateral loops are well developed. Our method of preparing lampbrush chromosomes is described in detail elsewhere (Vlad and Macgregor, 1975). It is essentially that of Callan and Lloyd (1960) with one difference. The chromosomes are dissected out into an observation chamber of a kind that can be fitted into the swinging bucket of a Sorvall HB4 rotor, as used in conjunction with a Sorvall RC2B (Vlad and Macgregor, 1975). The chromosomes are then spun for 30 min. at 3,500 g. Centrifugation has the effect of flattening the chromosomes' axes against the bottom of the observation chamber, so that all parts of the axes are in one plane of focus when the preparation is examined with a microscope. Chromomeres are therefore more easily distinguishable and countable.

A preparation was selected for chromomere counts if it showed all 14 lampbrush bivalents, unstretched, unbroken, and distinguishable from one another. The entire preparation was then drawn to scale with the aid of a camera lucida attached to a Carl Zeiss UP1 phase contrast microscope. The total length in micrometers of the haploid set of lampbrush chromosomes was then calculated. After careful scrutiny of the chromosomes, 5 different regions were selected in which the chromomeres could easily be distinguished with the aid of a 100 × planapochromatic phase contrast objective and a carefully adjusted microscope. Chromomeres were drawn, photographed, and counted in these regions, and the number of discernible chromomeres per unit length of chromosome was determined. From the latter value and the total length of all lampbrush chromosomes, the total number of chromomeres in the haploid chromosome set was estimated. This method assumes that each discernible granule on a lampbrush chromosome axis is one chromomere, and it assumes that the distribution of chromomeres per unit length of lampbrush chromosome is the same in all parts of the chromosome set. We consider that both these assumptions are reasonable.

Our estimations of the number of chromomeres per haploid lampbrush chromosome set are shown in table 3. These data show that there are 55% more chromomeres per haploid lampbrush chromosome set in *P. vehiculum*, in which C = 36.8 pg, than there are in *P. cinereus*, in which C = 20 pg. Similarly, *P. dunni*, with a C value of 38.8 pg has 59% more lampbrush chromomeres than *P. cinereus*.

We recognize that the number of chromomeres that can be counted in a set of lampbrush chromosomes will depend to some extent on the state of extension of the chromosomes at the time of counting. Chromosomes from larger oocytes are likely to be past the stage of maximum extension, and some amalgamation of chromomeres will have taken place. In this connexion we wish to stress that our counts of chromomeres for *P. vehiculum* were made on chromosomes that were undoubtedly partially contracted and in which some amalgamation of chromomeres had certainly occurred. These counts were nonetheless substantially higher than counts made on fully extended chromosomes from *P. cinereus*, where little or no amalgamation of chromomeres could have taken place. Our conclusion is that Western plethodons with relatively high C values have many more chromomeres per set of lampbrush chromosomes than their Eastern relatives.

Our main observations may be summarized as follows. First, the genomes of Western salamanders are almost twice as large as those of Eastern ones. Secondly, the quantitative difference in DNA between the two kinds of animal is spread evenly through the whole chromosome set. Thirdly, Western plethodons have much more of their genome as repetitive DNA than Eastern ones. Fourth, Western plethodons have more chromomeres in their lampbrush chromosomes than Eastern ones. Finally, the repetitive DNA of Eastern plethodons has little in common with that of Western species.

3. THE CHROMOMERE

Let us now consider how these observations relate to ideas concerning the nature of a chromomere. Curve B in figure 2 is a C_0t curve for DNA from *Bacillus subtilis*. The C_0t value needed for reassociation of half of this DNA ($C_0t_{\frac{1}{2}}$) is 2.7. The C value for *P. cinereus* is 20 pg. The size of this animal's genome is therefore 1.2×10^{13} daltons. *B. subtilis* has a genome of 2.4×10^9 daltons (Wallace and Morowitz, 1973). The expected $C_0t_{\frac{1}{2}}$ for that part of the genome of *P. cinereus* that consists of unique sequence DNA should therefore be $2.7 \times (1.2 \times 10^{13})/(2.4 \times 10^9) = 13{,}500$. We have observed that the 40% of the genome of *P. cinereus* that reassociates above C_0t 10^3 does so with the kinetics of single components having a $C_0t_{\frac{1}{2}}$ of approximately 14,000. The latter value is close to the expected value, and so we may suppose that much of the DNA reassociating above C_0t 10^3 consists of unique sequences, and the remainder of the DNA in the genome is repetitive sequences.

The repetitive fraction of *P. cinereus* genome can be further subdivided into 15% (of the total genome) that reassociates below C_0t 0.05, 30% that reassociates between C_0t 0.05 and C_0t 10, and 15% that reassociates between C_0t 10 and C_0t 10^3. If we consider only the second fraction as moderately repetitive sequences, then the average C_0t value for this fraction is 1.8 (see fig. 2). On this basis we estimate that the average repetition frequency of this repetitive fraction is 13,500/1.8 = 7,500.

The sizes of the repetitive units in the *Plethodon* genome are less easily determined, but on the basis of our own experiments (Mizuno and Macgregor, 1974) and those

TABLE 3

Species and C value	Oocyte diameter, mm	Total chromomeres in all 5 measured segments	Total length of all 5 measured segments, μm	Mean distance between chromomeres, μm	Length of haploid chromosome set, μm	Number of chromomeres in haploid set	General characteristics of the lampbrush chromosomes
P. cinereus	1.4	410	779	1.90	7480	3936	Long and loopy
20 pg	1.8	294	610	2.07	6405	3087	Slightly contracted short loops
	1.9	388	854	2.20	6397	2904	Same
P. vehiculum	2.0	207	390	1.89	10391	5503	Slightly contracted short loops
36.8 pg	2.8	409	792	1.93	9700	5009	Same
	2.9	376	700	1.86	9054	4867	Same
P. dunni	1.9	264	560	2.12	13793	6502	Long and loopy
38.8 pg	2.4	326	780	2.39	10680	4469	Shorter chromosome, long loops
	2.6	310	700	2.26	10980	4862	Same
	2.8	171	340	1.99	10248	5154	Same

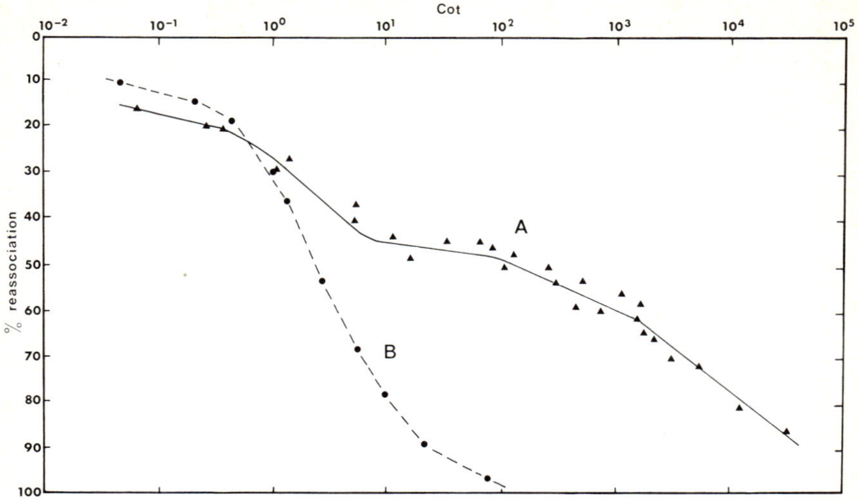

FIG. 2.—Reassociation kinetics (C_0t-curves) of total sheared DNA of *P. cinereus* (A) and *Bacillus subtilis* (B). DNAs were sheared into 460 average nucleotide residues per strand. Reassociation was carried out in 0.12M PB–0.0028M EDTA at 65°C after heat-denaturation. After incubating to various C_0t-values, extensively paired DNA fractions were eluted from HAP-column with 0.40M PB at 60°C. The per cent reassociation was expressed as the per cent distribution of the absorbance at 260 nm into the extensively paired DNA fraction.

of others (Lagowski et al., 1973; Bick et al., 1973; Davidson et al., 1973), we think it likely that their average length is about 300 nucleotide pairs. On this basis we may calculate that the amount of DNA in each family of well-matched repetitive sequences is about 7,500 × 300 nucleotide pairs, or 1.46×10^9 daltons (assuming 650 daltons per nucleotide pair). There are approximately 3,500 chromomeres per haploid set of lampbrush chromosomes in *P. cinereus*. Disregarding interchromomeric DNA, which probably represents less than 5% of the total genomic DNA, we can estimate that each half chromomere will contain $1.2 \times 10^{13}/3{,}500 (= 3.4 \times 10^9)$ daltons of DNA. We may therefore predict that in *P. cinereus* an average half chromomere and its loop will comfortably accommodate at least one family of moderately repetitive sequences.

We therefore propose a relationship between chromomeres and families of repetitive sequences, although perhaps not a simple 1:1 relationship. Secondly, because selection pressure favouring the conservation of repetitive sequences has been low in *Plethodon*, we propose that many chromomeres may contain DNA that has little genetic significance in the transcriptive sense. Lastly, we think that the difference in genome size between Eastern and Western plethodons is largely attributable to repetitive DNA, and we think that the increase in chromomere number that has accompanied increase in genome size in Western species reflects an increase in the number of different repetitive families in the genome. Of course, this idea would gain support from a demonstration that the diversity or variety of moderately repetitive sequences in the genome of a *P. vehiculum* or *P. dunni* is substantially greater than that found in the genome of *P. cinereus*. Such a situation is exceedingly hard to examine, but experiments are currently in progress to determine whether the repetitive sequences that Eastern and Western plethodons have in common are present with the same level of redundancy in the two groups.

4. SUMMARY

1. In salamanders of the genus *Plethodon* DNA per haploid chromosome set varies from species to species, but chromosome number and the relative dimensions of the chromosomes are the same in all species studied.

2. With respect to repetitive DNA sequences, closely related species have much in common, but distantly related species have only about 10% of the observed sequences in common.

3. The same applies to "unique" DNA sequences, but these seem to have been better conserved, and distantly related species may have as much as 40% in common.

4. Species of *Plethodon* with relatively large genomes nave a larger fraction of their genome as repetitive DNA, and have more chromomeres per haploid set of lampbrush chromosomes.

5. A relationship between chromomeres and families of repetitive DNA sequences is proposed, and it is suggested than many chromomeres may contain DNA that has little genetic significance in the transcriptive sense.

Acknowledgements. We thank Dr. James Kezer and Dr. R. Highton for their help. We acknowledge support from Science Research Council (grant no. BSR 44681).

5. REFERENCES

BICK, M. D., HUANG, H. C., and THOMAS, C. A. 1973. Stability and fine structure of eukaryotic DNA rings in formamide. *J. Mol. Biol., 77,* 75–84.

BRITTEN, R. J., and DAVIDSON, E. H. 1969. Gene regulation for higher cells: a theory. *Science (Wash. D.C.), 165,* 349–357.

BRITTEN, R. J., and KOHNE, D. E. 1967. Nucleotide sequence repetition in DNA. *Carnegie Inst. Wash. Year Book, 65,* 78–106.

CALLAN, H. G., and LLOYD, L. 1960. Lampbrush chromosomes. In *New Approaches in Cell Biology,* (WALKER, ed.), pp. 23–46. Academic Press.

DAVIDSON, E. H., and BRITTEN, R. J. 1973. Organization, transcription and regulation in the animal genome. *Q. Rev. Biol., 48,* 565–613.

DAVIDSON, E. H., HOUGH, B. R., AMENSON, C. S., and BRITTEN, R. J. 1973. General interspersion of repetitive with non-repetitive sequence elements in the DNA of Xenopus. *J. Mol. Biol., 77,* 1–23.

HIGHTON, R. 1962. Revision of North Americal salamanders of the genus Plethodon. *Bull. Fla. State Mus. Biol. Vol. 6,* 235–367.

HIGHTON, R. 1971. Distributional interactions among Eastern North American salamanders of the genus Plethodon. *Va. Polytech. Inst. State Univ. Res. Div. Monogr., 4,* 139–187.

LAGOWSKI, J. M., YU, M-Y. W., FORREST, H. S., and LAIRD, C. D. 1973. Dispersity of repeat DNA sequences in *Oncopeltus fasciatus,* an organism with diffuse centromeres. *Chromosoma (Berl.), 43,* 349–373.

MACGREGOR, H. C., and WALKER, M. H. 1973. The arrangement of chromosomes in nuclei of sperm from plethodontid salamanders. *Chromosoma (Berl.), 40,* 242–262.

MIZUNO, S., and MACGREGOR, H. C. 1974. Chromosomes, DNA sequences and evolution in salamanders of the genus Plethodon. *Chromosoma (Berl.), 48,* 239–296.

VLAD, M., and MACGREGOR, H. C. 1975. Chromomere number and its genetic significance in lampbrush chromosomes. *Chromosoma (Berl.), 50,* 327–347.

WAKE, D. B. 1966. Comparative osteology and evolution of the lungless salamanders, Family Plethodontidae. *Mem. South. Calif. Acad. Sci., 4,* 1–111.

WALLACE, D. C., and MOROWITZ, H. J. 1973. Genome size and evolution. *Chromosoma (Berl.), 40,* 121–126.

A CHROMOSOME STUDY ON TWO NEW JAPANESE POLYPLOID PARTHENOGENETIC WEEVILS (COLEOPTERA: CURCULIONIDAE)

YASUSHI TAKENOUCHI

Biological Laboratory, Sapporo College, Hokkaido University of Education, Sapporo, Hokkaido, Japan

1. INTRODUCTION

According to Smith (personal communication), the chromosome survey of bisexual curculionid weevils has been extended to about 340 species. In addition, 51 parthenogenetic species and races are known in five allied subfamilies of the Curculionidae, i.e., Otiorrhynchinae, Brachyderinae, Eremninae, Leptopinae, and Cylindrorrhyninae. In weevils parthenogenesis is usally associated with polyploidy. Of the 51 taxa known cytologically 49 are polyploids: 29 triploids, 13 tetraploids, 5 pentaploids, and 2 hexaploids; the remaining two are diploids ($2x = 2n = 22$) (Suomalainen, 1940*a,b*, 1947, 1954, 1955, 1966; Mikulska, 1960; Seiler, 1947; Takenouchi, 1964, 1965, 1970*b,c,d*, 1972*a,b,c*). Hexaploidy, the highest degree of polyploidy so far encountered, was found for the first time in the Japanese *Blosurus japonicus* Sharp by Takenouchi (1970*b*), and again in the Japanese *Callirhopalus (= Pseudocneorhinus) obesus* Roelofs (Takenouchi, 1972*c*). The latter also has a tetraploid race (Takenouchi, 1972*c*). No hexaploid species have been found in other countries.

I have recently examined two additional polyploid parthenogenetic weevil species collected from several localities in Japan (fig. 1): one has two allopatric races with different degrees of ploidy; the other is tetraploid. This paper reports the details.

2. MATERIALS AND METHODS

Two species, *minimus* Roelofs and *setosus* Roelofs, belonging to the genus *Callirhopalus (= Pseudocneorhinus)* in the tribe Callirhopalini, subfamily Eremninae, have been examined which were not previously known to be parthenogenetic. Both are wingless or vestigial-winged, as are most other parthenogenetic weevils (Takenouchi, 1970*b*; Suomalainen, 1969), and so uncommon that more than 20 years were spent collecting them. This is the first record of either occurring in Hokkaido, though another tetraploid parthenogenetic species *C. (= P.) bifasciatus* Roelofs is distributed over most of Honshu. A total of 52 adult *minimus* were collected at several localities in Hokkaido as well as at Morioka and Honshu, and 30 *setosus* specimens in three parts of Abashiri District, Hakodate, Kitami, and Hidaka District. Mature eggs were fixed in Allen-Bouin's solution modified by Momma (1954) and sectioned to obtain first meiotic metaphase chromosomes. The slides were stained with Heidenhain's iron-haematoxylin. To study oogonial metaphases, young females were fed colchicine, and their ovarioles were squashed according to Smith's (1943) method. They were stained in basic fuchsin-methyl green (Smith and Takenouchi, 1969).

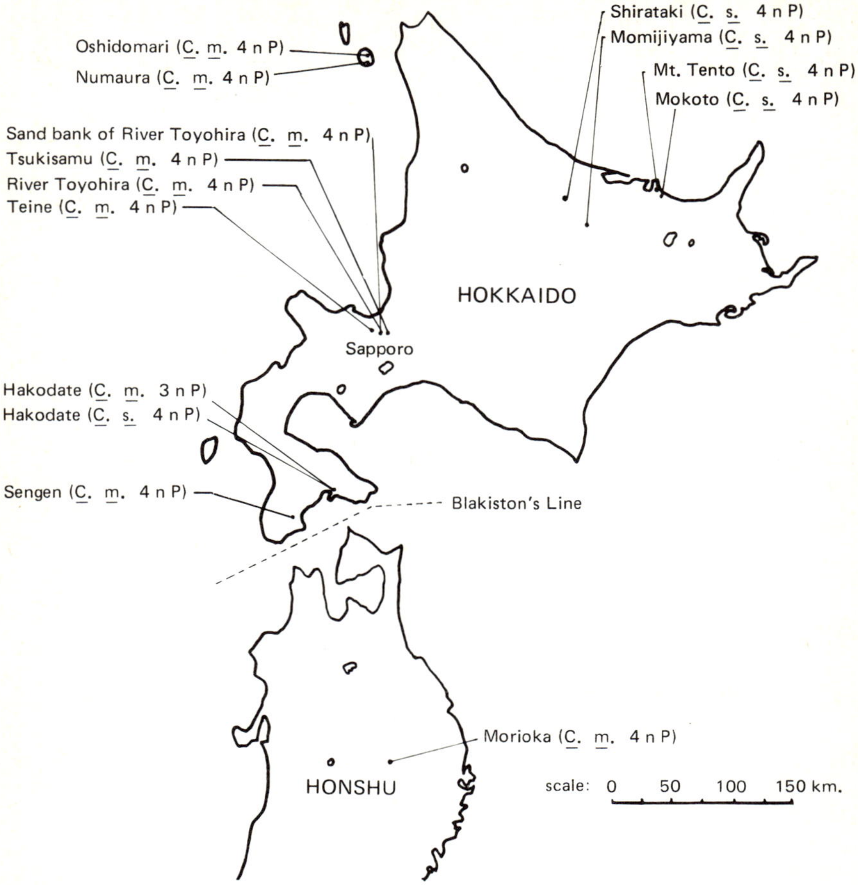

FIG. 1.—Map of northern Japan showing collecting localities of *Callirhopalus minimus (C. m.)* and *Callirhopalus setosus (C. s.)* examined in this study.

3. OBSERVATIONS

(a) C. minimus *Roelofs (figs. 2–11)*

Since 1964, 52 adults have been collected from several localities: a grassy area of the foot of Mt. Moiwa, Teinemachi, around the Toyohira River, the sand bank of the Toyohira River, Kawazoimachi, and a grassy site in the Government Agricultural Experimental Station at Tsukisamu, Sapporo; a bushy area of Hakodate; Sengen near Hakodate; Kamuiwaki, Okushiri Island; Numaura and Oshidomari, Rishiri Island; Bôdaira, Yamagata Prefecture; and the suburbs of Morioka. Dissection proves that all were females of which 15 were suitable for chromosome study in either oogonial cells or meiotic metaphases.

Triploid race (fig. 2): A single female from Hakodate provided eggs showing a first meiotic metaphase plate with 33 unpaired chromosomes (fig. 2).

Tetraploid race (figs. 3–8): Hokkaido specimens (figs. 3–7).

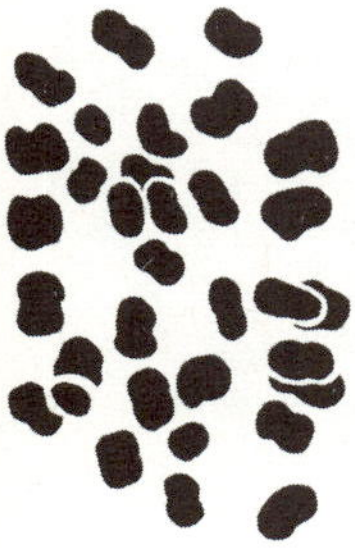

2

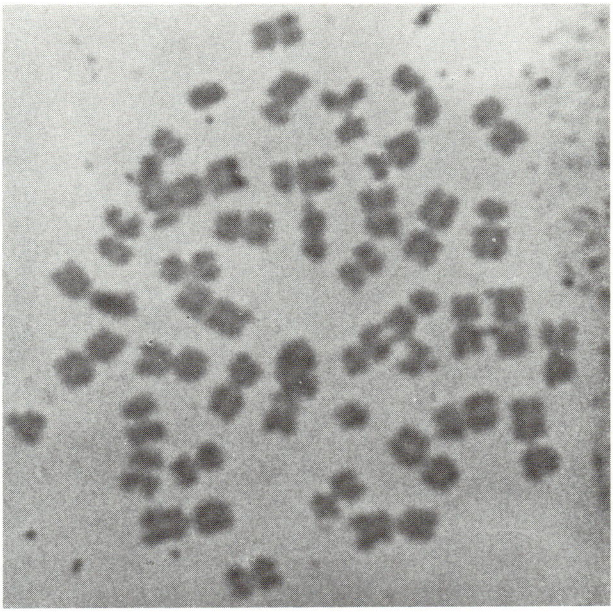

3

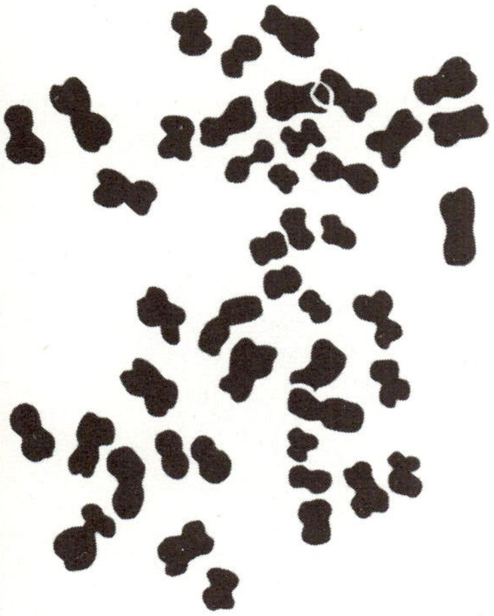

4

5

FIGS. 2–5.—Chromosomes of two races of *Callirhopalus minimus*. FIG. 2.—First metaphase (Hakodate) showing 33 univalent chromosomes; FIG. 3.—Oogonial metaphase (Toyohira River) showing 45 chromosomes (ca. × 3,140); FIG. 4.—Oogonial metaphase (Government Agricultural Experimental Station, Tsukisamu) showing 44 chromosomes; FIG. 5.—Oogonial metaphase (Sengen) showing 44 chromosomes. Drawings × 3,140.

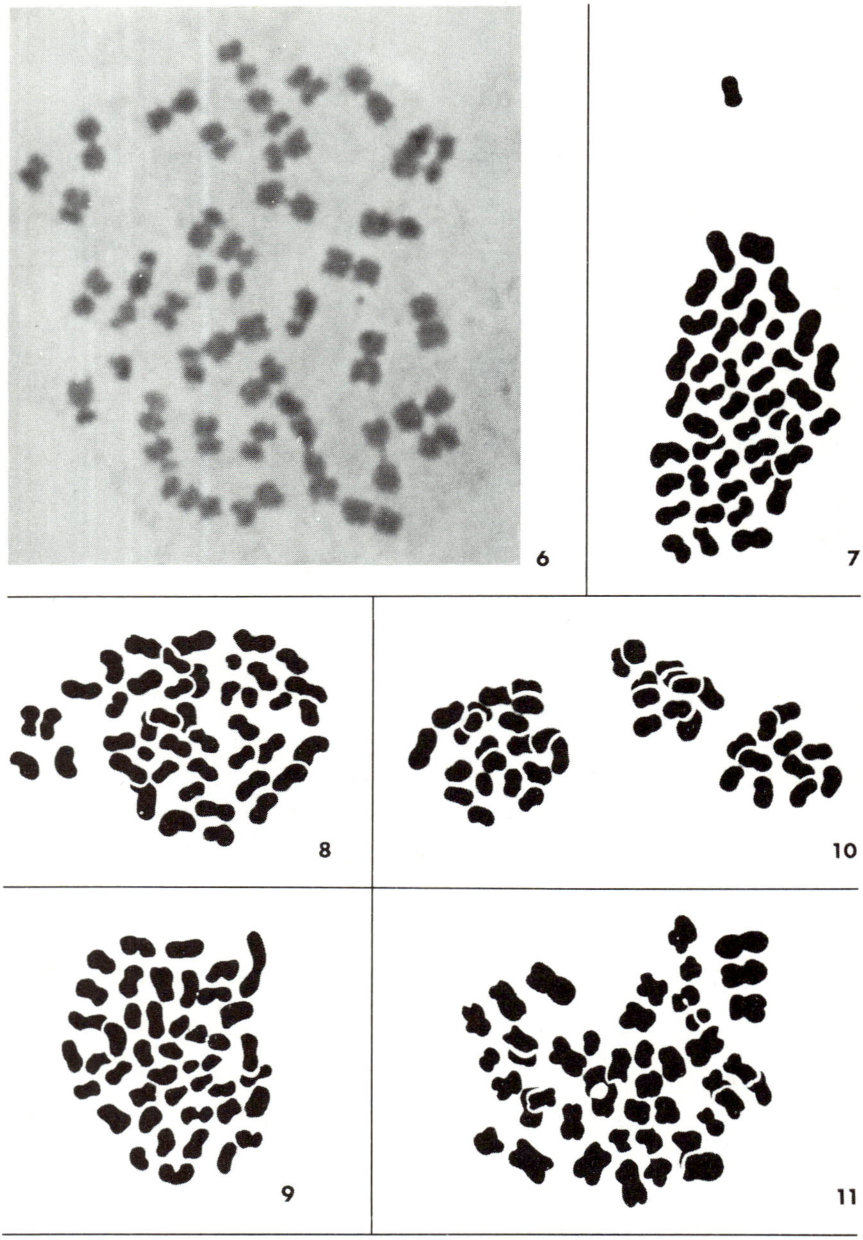

FIGS. 6–11.—Chromosomes of *Callirhopalus minimus*. FIG. 6.—Oogonial metaphase (Tsukisamu) showing 44 chromosomes (ca. × 3,140); FIGS. 7 and 8.—First metaphase of *C. minimus* from Oshidomari: figure 7 shows 43 chromosomes and figure 8 shows 44 chromosomes; FIG. 9.—First metaphase (sand bank of the Toyohira River) showing 44 chromosomes; FIG. 10.—First metaphase (Teine) showing three plates with 43 chromosomes; FIG. 11.—Oogonial metaphase (Morioka City) showing 44 chromosomes. Drawings × 3,140.

Hokkaido specimens (figs. 3–7): Thirteen females collected from Sengen near Hakodate, around the Toyohira River and the sand bank of the Toyohira River, Sapporo, the grounds of the Government Agricultural Experimental Station at Tsukisamu and at Teine, Sapporo, and Oshidomari, Rishiri Island at the north end of Hokkaido, provided oogonial or meiotic metaphase plates. Oogonial metaphase plates consist of meta- or submeta-centric chromosomes of various sizes (figs. 3–6). In most cases the chromosome number is exactly 44; however, one Toyohira River specimen clearly showed 45 chromosomes (fig. 3) and another ca. 42. Meiotic metaphase chromosomes were observed in three Oshidomari specimens, and one specimen from the sand bank of the Toyohira River. Two Oshidomari specimens showed first maturation metaphases, one with 43 (fig. 7) and the other with 44 chromosomes (fig. 8). However, one egg from an Oshidomari specimen showed only 40 chromosomes. The single specimen from the sand bank of the Toyohira River had 44 chromosomes (fig. 9). One egg from a Teine specimen had 43 chromosomes at first metaphase. It consisted of three plates: two with 11 and one with 21 chromosomes (fig. 10). The first metaphase of a specimen from Numaura (Rishiri Island) was also tripartite.

Morioka specimens (Japan-Hondo) (fig. 11): Two specimens obtained in the suburbs of Morioka City were both females. Oogonial metaphase observed in one showed exactly 44 chromosomes, mostly metacentric and of various sizes (fig. 11). This specimen is therefore a member of a tetraploid race. The other had no divisions.

(b) C. setosus *Roelofs (12–16)*

Since 1964, 30 adults have been collected from Hakodate; several localities of Abashiri District; Sekihoku Pass of Kitami District; and Honbetsu, Hidaka District, Hokkaido. Dissection proved that all were females and six were satisfactory for chromosome study. Oogonial and follicular metaphases had exactly 44 chromosomes without exception (figs. 12–14). The specimens were from Mokoto, Mt. Tento (ca. 500 m), and the hill named Momijiyama, Rubeshibe, in Abashri District. A Shirataki individual near Sekihoku Pass, Kitami District, showed ca. 40 chromosomes. A first metaphase in an egg from a Mt. Tento specimen showed exactly 44 (fig. 16) and a Hakodate specimen ca. 44 chromosomes. No specimens have so far been obtained from Honshu.

4. DISCUSSION

Among the 82 specimens of *C. minimus* and *C. setosus* that were collected over a period of 10 years no males were found in either species. According to the literature, all weevils with 33 or 44 chromosomes propagate by thelytokous, or apomictic, parthenogenesis. *C. minimus* has two races; one is triploid with 33 chromosomes and the other tetraploid with mostly 44. These chromosomecounts were carried out in either or both gonial and meiotic divisions, showing that no reduction division occurs. The triploid race was found only in Hakodate; in other localities, including Morioka, Iwate Prefecture, Honshu, they were all tetraploid.

Some variation in chromosome number in both oogonial and first meiotic metaphases within a specimen or a species is commonly found in parthenogenetic curculionids (Suomalainen, 1969; Mikulska, 1960; Takenouchi, 1969*a,b*, 1970*b*). The

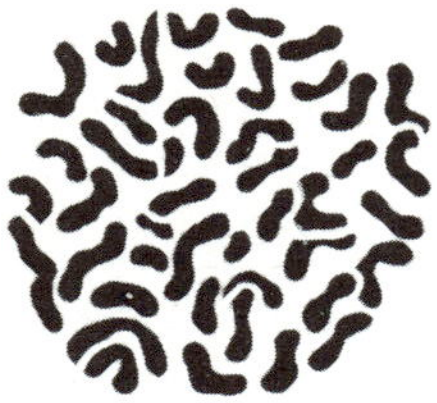

12

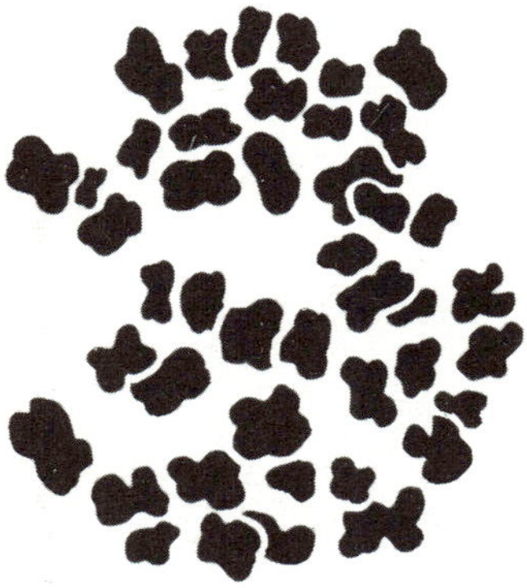

13

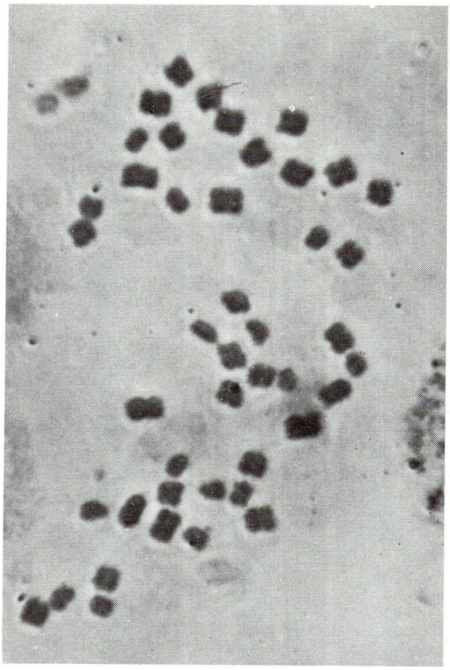

14

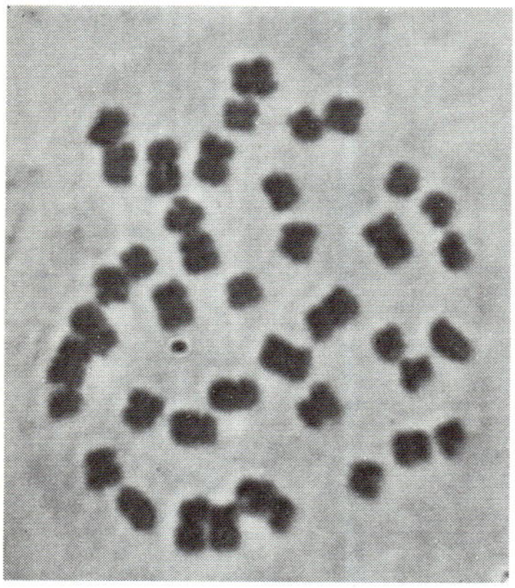

15

16

FIGS. 12–16.—Chromosomes of *Callirhopalus setosus*. FIG. 12.—Follicular metaphase (Mokoto) showing 44 chromosomes (sectioned slide); FIG. 13.—Oogonial metaphase (Mt. Tento) showing 44 chromosomes; FIGS. 14 and 15.—Oogonial metaphases from the single Momijiyama specimen: figure 14 shows 44 and figure 15, 41 chromosomes (magnification ca. × 1,080); FIG. 16.—First metaphase (Mt. Tento) showing 44 chromosomes. Drawings × 3,140.

same situation was found in both species studied here. The tetraploid race of *C. minimus* has 40, ca. 42, 43, 44, and 45 chromosomes, but the most frequent number was 44. Similarly, *C. setosus* had 40, 41, and 44 chromosomes, the commonest number again being 44. Clearly both are tetraploid races.

In general, in bisexual and parthenogenetic curculionids and scolytids, the first meiotic metaphase plates can be obtained from newly laid eggs and also the mature eggs in calyies of the mother insects. The first cleavage occurs soon after oviposition. However, the author found cleavage occurrring in two eggs extracted from a *C. minimus* specimen (Takenouchi, 1970*a*). The chromosome count of this specimen was impossible but it might be tetraploid.

Meiotic metaphases of polyploid parthenogenetic weevil species occasionally have two-, three-, or four-partite plates (Suomalainen, 1940*b*; Seiler, 1947; Takenouchi, 1969*b*). The same situation was observed in an egg examined from a *minimus* female from Teine. In the egg the meiotic spindle was tripartite: two subplates contained 11 chromosomes, the third 21.

Hokkaido is separated from Honshu by Blakiston's line (fig. 1). Certain native Japanese curculionid species have races with different degrees of polyploidy. For instance, *Catapionus gracilicornis* Roelofs is known to have three different races: a diploid bisexual one (2x = 22), a tetraploid (2x = 44), and a pentaploid (2x = 55). The tetraploid race is distributed throughout Hokkaido and coexists with the pentaploid race in Aomori, Akita, and Iwate Prefectures. The diploid bisexual race is found in Niigata Prefecture, Honshu (Takenouchi, 1970*b*,*c*,*d*). *Scepticus insularis* Roelofs has four races, i.e., a diploid bisexual (2x = 22) and diploid (2x = 22), triploid (2x = 33), and pentaploid (2x = 55) parthenogenetic races. The triploid race has been found only on Mikuni Pass in Niigata Prefecture, the others occur in Hokkaido (Takenouchi, 1968). On the other hand, *Blosurus japonicus* Sharp has four races within Hokkaido, namely, a diploid bisexual (2x = 22), tetraploid (2x = 44), pentaploid (2x = 55), and hexaploid (2x = 66) parthenogenetic races. *Callirhoparus setosus* is tetraploid from all localities of Hokkaido, but nothing can be said about it in Honshu, because no insects were collected from there.

5. SUMMARY

1. The chromosomes of two weevil species, *Callirhopalus (= Pseudocneorhinus) minimus* Roelofs and *C. (= P.) setosus* Roelofs, were studied in germ-line cells using sections and squash preparations.

2. The former has two parthenogenetic races, 3x and a more common 4x, with distinct geographical distributions.

3. In *C. setosus* only tetraploids were found, within Abashiri and Kitami Districts and at Hakodate in Hokkaido.

Acknowledgments. The author expresses his sincere gratitude to Dr. S. G. Smith, Insect Pathology Research Institute, Sault Ste. Marie, Canada, for checking the manuscript, and to Dr. K. Morimoto, Kyûshu Branch, Government Forest Experimental Station, Kurokami, Kumamoto, for identification of species. Mr. M. Muramoto, La Salle High School, Hakodate, Mr. K. Ando, Entomological Laboratory, Department of Agriculture, Iwate University, Mr. T. Shiitsu and the author's students helped collect the material.

6. REFERENCES

MIKULSKA, I. 1960. New data to the cytology of the parthenogenetic weevils of the genus *Otiorrhynchus* Germ. (Curculionidae, Coleoptera) from Poland. *Cytologia (Tokyo), 25,* 322–333.

MOMMA, E. 1954. *Drosophila* survey of Hokkaido. II. Chromosomes of seven species. *J. Fac. Sci. Hokkaido Univ. Ser. VI Zool., 12,* 200–208.

SEILER, J. 1947. Die Zytologie eines parthenogenetischen Rüsselkäfers, *Otiorrhynchus sulcatus* F. *Chromosoma (Berl.), 3,* 88–109.

SMITH, S. G. 1943. Techniques for the study of insect chromosomes. *Can. Entomol., 75,* 21–34.

SMITH, S. G., and TAKENOUCHI, Y. 1969. Chromosomal polymorphism in *Pissodes* weevils: Further on incompatibility in *Pissodes terminalis. Can. J. Genet. Cytol., 11,* 761–782.

SUOMALAINEN, E. 1940*a*. Polyploidy in parthenogenetic Curculionidae. *Hereditas, 26,* 21–34.

SUOMALAINEN, E. 1940*b*. Beiträge zur Zytologie der parthenogenetischen Insecten. *Ann. Acad. Sci. Fenn., 53,* 1–145.

SUOMALAINEN, E. 1947. Parthenogenese und Polyploidie bei Rüsselkäfern (Curculionidae). *Hereditas, 26,* 425–456.

SUOMALAINEN, E. 1954. Zur Zytologie der parthenogenetischen Curculioniden der Schweiz. *Chromosoma (Berl.), 6,* 627–655.

SUOMALAINEN, E. 1955. A further instance of geographical parthenogenesis and polyploidy in the weevils, Curculionidae. *Arch. Soc. Zool.—Bot. Fenn. 'Vanamo'* (Suppl.), *9,* 350–354.

SUOMALAINEN, E. 1966. The first known case of polyploidy in a parthenogenetic curculionid native of America. *Hereditas, 56,* 213–216.

SUOMALAINEN, E. 1969. Evolution in parthenogenetic Curculionidae. In *Evolutionary Biology, 3* (TH. DOBZHANSKY, M. K. HECT, and W. C. STEERE, eds.), pp. 251–296. North-Holland Publ. Co., Amsterdam.

TAKENOUCHI, Y. 1964. A preliminary note on the chromosomes of 4 parthenogenetic weevils (Brachyrininae) in Canada. *Jap. J. Genet., 39,* 74–79.

TAKENOUCHI, Y. 1965. Chromosome survey in thirty-four species of bisexual and parthenogenetic weevils of Canada. *Can. J. Genet. Cytol., 7,* 663–687.

TAKENOUCHI, Y. 1968. A chromosome study on bisexual and parthenogenetic races of *Scepticus insularis* Roelofs (Curculionidae, Coleoptera). *Can. J. Genet. Cytol., 10,* 845–950.

TAKENOUCHI, Y. 1969*a*. A further study on the chromosomes of the parthenogenetic weevil, *Listroderes costirostris* Schönherr, from Japan. *Cytologia (Tokyo), 34,* 360–368.

TAKENOUCHI, Y. 1969*b*. On the chromosomes of the parthenogenetic weevil, *Listroderes costirostris* Schönherr, from Nagasaki Prefecture. *Chrom. Inform. Serv., 10,* 3–4.

TAKENOUCHI, Y. 1970*a*. The cleavage nuclei found in the eggs in a female of the parthenogenetic weevil, *Callirhopalus minimus* Roelofs (Curculionidae, Coleoptera). *J. Hokkaido Univ. Educ. II B, 20,* 39–41.

TAKENOUCHI, Y. 1970*b*. Three further studies of the chromosomes of Japanese weevils (Coleoptera: Curculionidae). *Can. J. Genet. Cytol., 12,* 273–277.

TAKENOUCHI, Y. 1970*c*. A further chromosome study in bisexual and parthenogenetic races of the weevil, *Catapionus gracilicornis* Roelofs (Curculionidae: Coleoptera). *Jap. J. Genet., 45,* 457–466.

TAKENOUCHI, Y. 1970*d*. A bisexual race of the reportedly parthenogenetic Japanese weevil *Catapionus gracilicornis* Roelofs (Coleoptera: Curculionidae). *J. Hokkaido Univ. Educ. II B, 22,* 1–17.

TAKENOUCHI, Y. 1972*a*. A chromosome study on two new Japanese parthenogenetic weevils (Coleoptera: Curculionidae). *Jap. J. Genet., 47,* 19–22.

TAKENOUCHI, Y. 1972*b*. A chromosome study of a new polyploid parthenogenetic weevil, *Myllocerus nipponicus* Zumpt (Coleoptera: Curculionidae). *Kontyû, 40,* 121–123.

TAKENOUCHI, Y. 1972*c*. A chromosome study on two hexaploid parthenogenetic weevils (Coleoptera: Curculionidae). IVth Intern. Chrom. Conf. at Jerusalem. *Chromosomes Today, 4* (J. WAHRMAN and K. R. LEWIS, eds.), p. 432. Israel Universities Press, Jerusalem, and John Wiley & Sons, New York.

SCREENING HUMAN-MOUSE CELL HYBRIDS FOR HUMAN CHROMOSOMES

M. BOBROW and JANE E. CROSS

Genetics Laboratory, Department of Biochemistry, South Parks Road, Oxford, England

1. INTRODUCTION

Interspecific cell hybrids, produced by viral-mediated fusion of somatic cells (Harris and Watkins, 1965), provide one of the most useful systems in biological research. For many purposes, characterization of the chromosome complement of the cell hybrid is highly relevant, enabling the loss or retention of specific functions to be related to defined parts of the genome. We have been particularly concerned with the application of somatic cell fusion to human gene mapping, a subject of much recent research (Rotterdam Conference, 1975).

Such work usually involves fusing diploid human cells with a permanent cell line derived from some other species. These hybrids characteristically lose most of their human chromosomes in a more or less random fashion. Several hybrid clones can then be characterized biochemically and cytologically, enabling the presence of particular human gene products to be correlated with one another (gene linkage) and with individual chromosomes (gene assignment). Because its biochemistry and immunology have been widely studied, the mouse has obvious advantages as donor of the permanent cell line in these studies.

Cytologically however, human-mouse hybrid cells are far from ideal. Chromosome numbers tend to be high, with large numbers of acrocentrics. The chromosome complements of some permanent cell lines show considerable heterogeneity from cell to cell (e.g., Allderdice et al., 1973*a*). Since many hybrid clones must usually be scored to resolve a particular problem, full karyotyping by standard methods is laborious. Similarities in morphology make some human chromosomes, particularly the acrocentrics, difficult to distinguish from mouse chromosomes except in preparations of exceptional quality.

We have tried to minimize these difficulties by applying a variety of chromosome banding procedures to human-mouse cell hybrids with the aim of "screening" the cells fairly rapidly to determine the number of human chromosomes present, and their gross morphology. It was hoped that this information would greatly expedite the formal karyotyping of G- or Q-banded preparations, which would be the final step in the cytological characterization of each hybrid.

2. METHODS

(a) *Chromosome preparation*

About 20 hybrid lines between mouse cells (1R, A9 and Clone 1D) and diploid human cells (fibroblasts and lymphocytes) have been studied (detailed in Van Heyningen et al., 1974). Many of the 1R hybrids give overly contracted chromo-

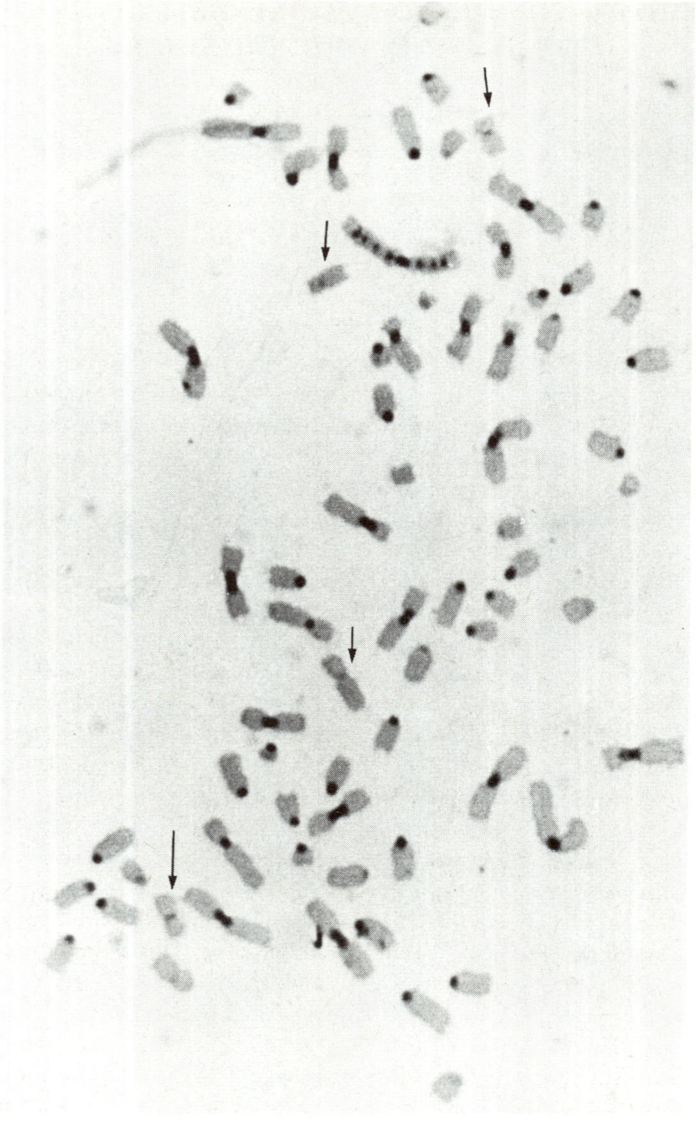

FIG. 1.—C-banding of human-mouse hybrid. Human chromosomes (some indicated by arrows) have smaller C-bands than mouse chromosomes.

somes after even short exposures to Colcemid. For these, dividing cells were dislodged into the medium by tapping the flask. The medium was then decanted into tubes containing Colcemid (0.25 mg/ml final conc.), incubated at 37°C for 5–30 minutes, and then processed. This procedure also has the advantages of preserving the growing culture intact, and giving a relatively high yield of metaphases. The cells were exposed to either 0.075 M KCl, or whole medium diluted 1:3 with distilled water; fixed in methanol-acetic acid, and air-dried. Igniting the fixative to promote cell spreading, which was sometimes found to be necessary, did not appear to have a consistently detrimental effect on subsequent chromosome banding.

(b) *Differential staining procedures*

1. *C. banding* (fig. 1): Constitutive heterochromatin was demonstrated by the method of Sumner (1972). Mouse chromosomes have much larger centromeric heterochromatin regions than do human chromosomes, and have been distinguished in hybrids on this basis (e.g. Allderdice et al., 1973*b*). Both human and mouse C-bands are, however, heteromorphic, and the parent cell lines should therefore be carefully characterized before such analysis of cell hybrids is attempted. The distinction between species is a quantitative one, and rather subject to variability in the quality of differential staining.

The definitive procedure for demonstrating the species of origin of a particular centromere region would be *in-situ* hybridization, using, for example, RNA complementary to mouse satellite DNA (Pardue and Gall, 1970; Jones, 1970). Although practicable, the procedure appears too time-consuming for routine cytological use.

2. *Hoechst 33258* (fig. 2): This fluorescent compound has been shown to stain

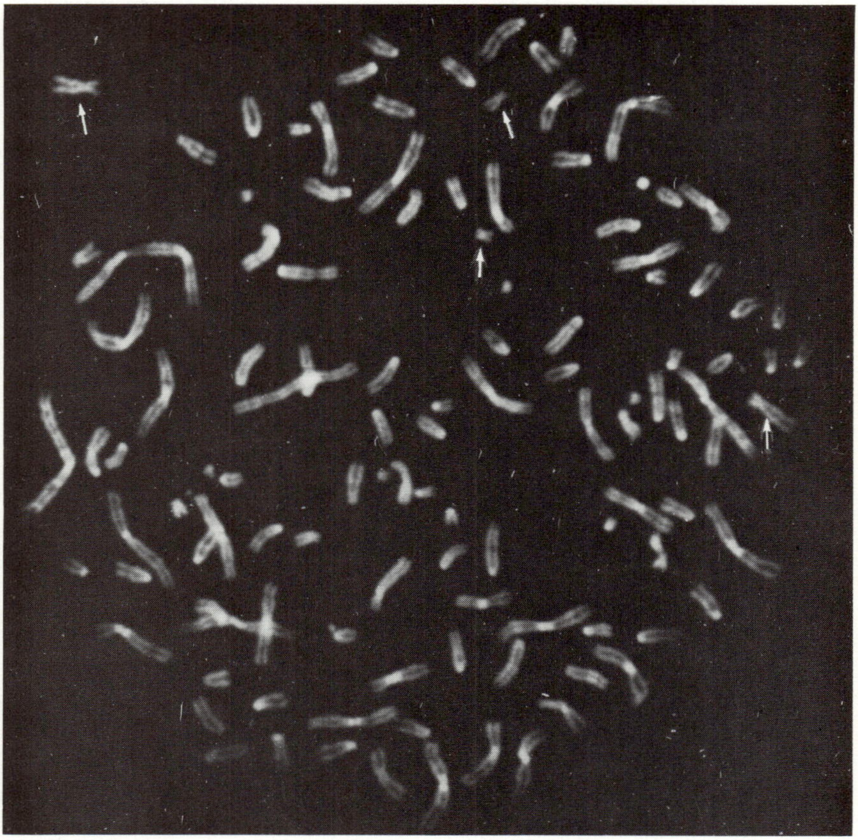

FIG. 2.—Human-mouse hybrid metaphase, staining with Hoechst 33258. Human chromosomes (arrowed) do not exhibit bright centromeric fluorescence.

mouse constitutive heterochromatin (Hillwig and Gropp, 1972). Some human centromere regions, particularly Nos. 1, 9, and 16 which have large paracentric secondary constrictions, also stain positively (Raposa and Natarajan, 1974). The level of staining is, however, much less intense than that of mouse chromosomes, enabling the human contribution to a hybrid metaphase to be picked out visually (fig. 2). The result is similar to that obtained with C-banding, but is simpler as no pretreatment is required. Further, faint Q-banding patterns are often revealed by 33258, allowing positive identification of the human chromosomes. Our staining and microscopic procedures are essentially as described by Latt (1973).

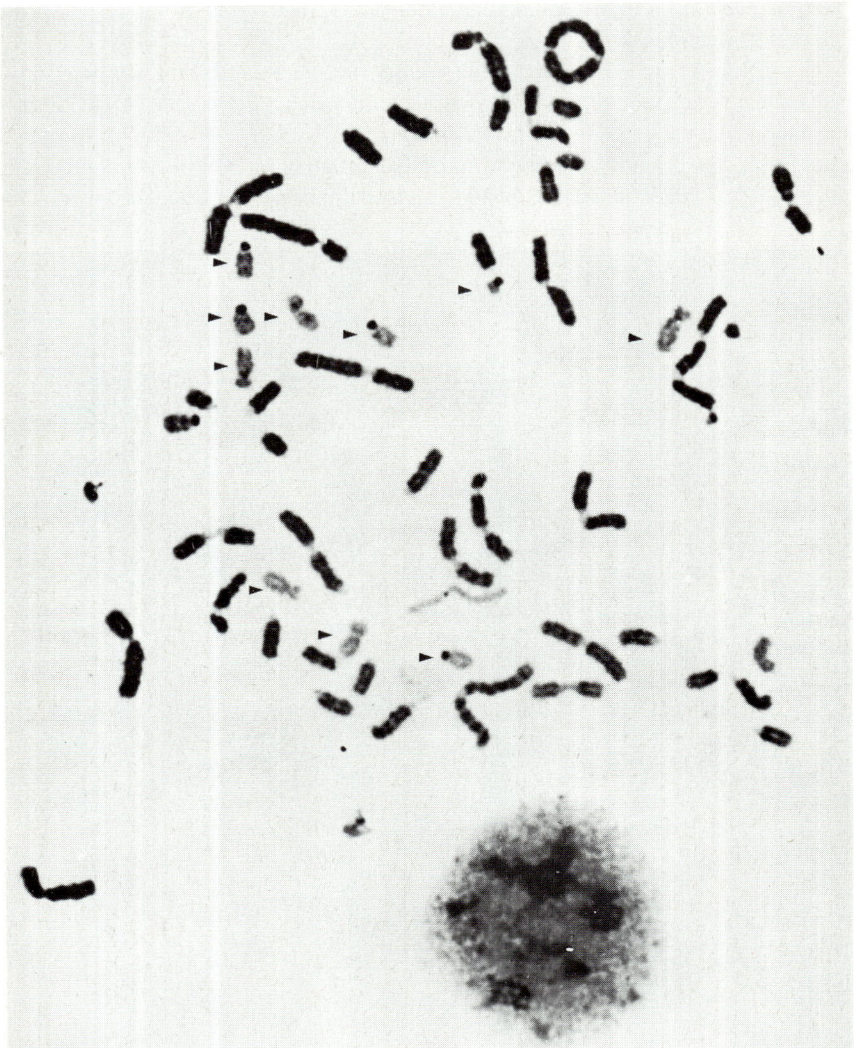

FIG. 3.—Hybrid metaphase stained by the Giemsa-11 technique. Human chromosomes are of lighter colour than mouse, and some have darkly stained paracentric heterochromatic segments.

Staining with 33258 provides more information than standard C-banding, and we now apply the method routinely for the analysis of human-mouse hybrids. It has proved particularly valuable for the rapid inspection of early outgrowths after fusion experiments, to determine whether the cells contain both human and murine chromosomes.

3. *Giemsa-11* (fig. 3): Staining human chromosomes with Giemsa at pH 11.0–11.5 gives differential staining of specific regions of paracentric constitutive heterochromatin (Bobrow et al., 1972). The heterochromatic regions are a definite red against the blue colour of the euchromatic chromosome arms. Mouse chromosomes stained by this procedure show a reciprocal pattern, the centromeric heterochromatin being pale blue while the chromosome arms are dark red. These staining properties are retained in interspecific cell hybrids (Bobrow and Cross, 1975) enabling the species of origin of individual chromosomes within a metaphase to be readily determined.

One to two weeks after air drying, slides are stained for 12–15 minutes in a 1/50 dilution of Giemsa (Harleco) made up in 0.007 N NaOH. Staining time, pH, and concentration of dye need to be varied for different batches of slides. The procedure is temperamental, but we have almost always eventually succeeded in getting differential staining, and the quality of information obtained compensates for the trouble in obtaining it.

After G-11 staining, slides can be destained in alcohol or acetic-alcohol and restained with quinacrine (fig. 4), or G-banded using trypsin (Seabright, 1972).

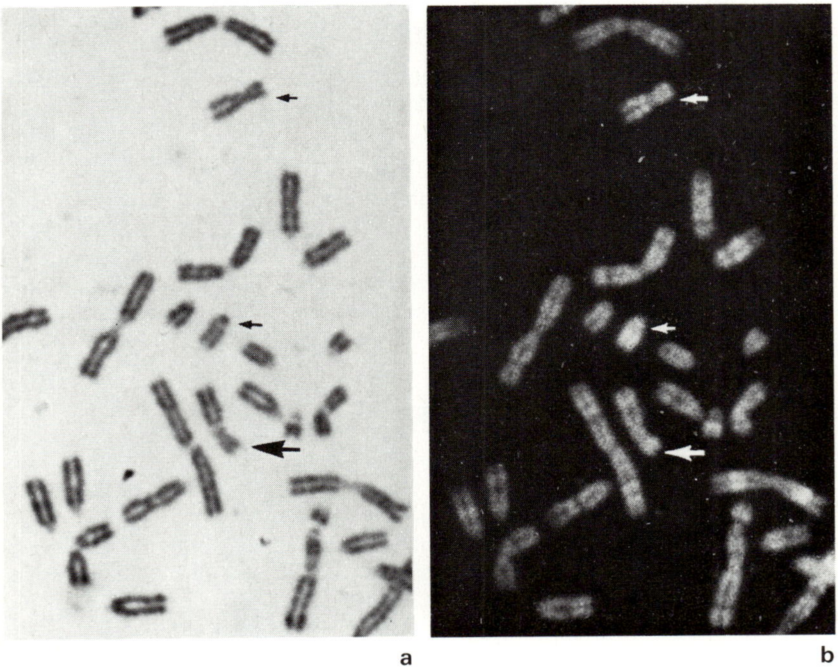

FIG. 4.—Partial metaphase of line 2W1-R70, which contains a possible translocation between a mouse chromosome and the short arm of the human X, stained with Giemsa-11 (a) and restained with quinacrine (b). Small arrows indicate human chromosomes 7 and 13; large arrow shows possible mouse-human translocation.

Staining with quinacrine also identifies any human chromosomes which carry intensely fluorescent markers. The double staining process enables a firm identification to be made of the human chromosomes in a human-mouse hybrid cell and we now use this procedure regularly for the karyotyping of hybrid cells.

After staining with the 33258 and G-11 techniques, we conclude the analysis of interspecific hybrids by confirming the chromosome identifications on slides G-banded by a modification of the method of Seabright (1972).

3. CONCLUSIONS

We believe that the techniques described here greatly increase the precision of cytological work with human-mouse hybrids. It is likely that the relative usefulness of individual staining techniques will vary depending on the particular cell lines under consideration. It is of course essential to characterize the parental cell lines as thoroughly as possible before studying their hybrid derivatives.

The specific application to human gene mapping will become less relevant with time. Once a sufficient number of well characterized clones are available, new biochemical markers would be mapped by simply screening for them in appropriate clones. However, finer mapping using rearranged chromosomes, and the development of many totally different projects are likely to provide a prolonged interest in the cytological characterization of interspecific cell hybrids.

4. SUMMARY

1. A variety of different staining techniques are described which aid the identification of human chromosomes in human/mouse cell hybrids.

3. Three principal techniques are used, namely, Q-banding, C-banding, and Giemsa-11 staining.

3. The last technique has the advantage that it can be used to detect small fragments of human chromosomes.

Acknowledgements. Hoechst 33258 was a gift from Dr. H. Loewe, Farbwerke Hoechst. The hybrid cells were provided by various people working with Professor W. F. Bodmer, particularly Dr. V. van Heyningen, Mrs. E. Jones, and Mr. D. Buck.

5. REFERENCES

Allderdice, P. W., Miller, O. J., Miller, D. A., Warburton, D., Pearson, P. L., Klein, G., and Harris, H. 1973*a*. Chromosome analysis of two related heteroploid mouse cell lines by quinacrine fluorescence. *J. Cell Sci., 12,* 263–274.

Allderdice, P. W., Miller, O. J., Pearson, P. L., Klein, G., and Harris, H. 1973*b*. Human chromosomes in 18 man-mouse somatic hybrid cell lines analysed by quinacrine fluorescence. *J. Cell Sci., 12,* 809–830.

Bobrow, M., and Cross, J. 1975. Differential staining of human and mouse chromosomes in interspecific cell hybrids. *Nature (Lond.), 251,* 77–79.

Bobrow, M., Madan, K., and Pearson, P. L. 1972. Staining of some specific regions of human chromosomes, particularly the secondary constriction of no. 9. *Nat. New Biol., 238,* 122–124.

Harris, H., and Watkins, J. F. 1965. Hybrid cells from mouse and man: artificial heterokaryons of mammalian cells from different species. *Nature (Lond.), 205,* 640–646.

HILLWIG, I., and GROPP, A. 1972. Staining of constitutive heterochromatin in mammalian chromosomes with a new fluorochrome. *Cell. Res., 75,* 122–136.

JONES, K. W. 1970. Chromosomal and nuclear location of mouse satellite DNA in individual cells. *Nature (Lond.), 225,* 912–915.

LATT, S. A. 1973. Micro-fluorometric detection of deoxyribonucleic acid replication in human metaphase chromosomes. *Proc. Natl. Acad. Sci. U.S.A., 70,* 3395–3399.

PARDUE, M. L., and GALL, J. G. 1970. Chromosomal localization of mouse satellite DNA. *Science (Wash. D.C.), 168,* 1356–1358.

RAPOSA, T., and NATARAJAN, A. T. 1974. Fluorescence banding pattern of human and mouse chromosomes with a benzimidazol derivative. (Hoechst 33258). *Humangenetik, 21,* 221–226.

ROTTERDAM CONFERENCE. *Second International Workshop on Human Gene Mapping,* Birth Defects, Original Article Series XI, *3,* 1975, The National Foundation, New York.

SEABRIGHT, M. 1972. The use of proteolytic enzymes for the mapping of structural rearrangements in the chromosomes of man. *Chromosoma (Berl.), 36,* 204–210.

SUMNER, A. T. 1972. A simple technique for demonstrating centromeric heterochromatin. *Exp. Cell Res., 75,* 304–306.

VAN HEYNINGEN, B., BOBROW, M., BODMER, W. F., GARDINER, S. E., POVEY, S., and HOPKINSON, D. A. 1974. Chromosome assignment of some human enzyme loci: mitochondrial malate dehydrogenase to 7, mannosephosphate isomerase and pyruvate kinase to 15 and, probably, esterase D to 13. *Ann. Hum. Genet. (Lond.), 38,* 395–403.

R-BANDING IN CELL HYBRIDS

C. PANGALOS, D. WEIL, and J. FREZAL

Clinique et Unité de Recherches (I.N.S.E.R.M.U.12) de Génétique Médicale Hôpital des Enfants-Malades, 149, rue de Sévres—73730 PARIS CEDEX 15.

1. INTRODUCTION

In this communication we present preliminary data obtained from using an adaptation of the Dutrillaux and Lejeune (1971) procedure of controlled heating denaturation for the identification of chromosomes in man-hamster somatic cell hybrids. The R-banding technique has permitted us to identify human chromosomes in several hybrids examined.

2. MATERIALS AND METHODS

Chromosomal analysis was performed upon the hamster parental lines V 79-4 and CH. and upon interspecific human-hamster hybrids obtained by fusion of the preceding lines with human diploid fibroblasts. The cultures were kept under a stable temperature of 37°C for 48 hours. Two and a half hours before the starting of the chromosomal examination we added 2 ml of an isotonic colchicin solution to the cell medium in the final concentration of 0.04% per ml. of medium. Cells were removed from the growth vessel by trypsinization and collected by centrifugal treatment of 5 min. at 800 revolutions/min.. The culture medium was removed, and the cells resuspended in hypotonic medium of the following composition: 12.5% animal serum and 87.5% of a 0.3 M aqueous solution of $MgCl_2$.

The most favorable duration of the hypotonic treatment is 30–35 min. at room temperature. It is useful to proceed with a prefixing of cells at the end of the hypotonic shock by adding 2 ml of Carnoy I fixative, drop by drop, and at the same time putting the cells delicately in suspension. After that the hypotonic solution and fixative are separated from the cells by centrifugation and replaced by Carnoy II fixative for 30 min. After that time the cells are again centrifuged and the supernatant replaced by the Carnoy I fixative for at least 30 min. more. The composition of the two Carnoy fixatives is as follows:—

1) *Carnoy I*

Absolute ethyl alcohol	75%
acetic acid	25%

2) *Carnoy II*

absolute ethyl alcohol	60%
chloroform	30%
acetic acid	10%

The spreading should be carried out on very clean slides covered by a very thin layer of iced, bi-distilled water.

Slides prepared a week or more before are dipped for 10 to 30 min. into a modified Earle solution buffered to pH 5.8 with a phosphate buffer and a temperature of 85°C. The time must be varied for different preparations to produce suitable banding patterns. After the 85°C treatment the slides are rapidly taken away from the container, rinsed for some seconds in running water, and stained for 10 min. in Giemsa buffered to pH 8.3.

3. RESULTS

Hamster and human chromosomes show definite R-banding patterns which permit the specific identity and hence origin of individual chromosomes to be ascertained (figs. 1–3).

We started our study by an examination of the parental strains of hamster cells used in our laboratory. The analysis of numerous mitoses showed a great difference from one cell to another both as regards the number and the structure of the chromosomes. The existence of many rearrangements did not allow the identification of chromosomes in homologous pairs, and the classification was therefore done by arranging the chromosomes in order of diminishing height. The same applies to the karyotypes of cells from human-hamster hybrids where the human chromosomes were arranged separately.

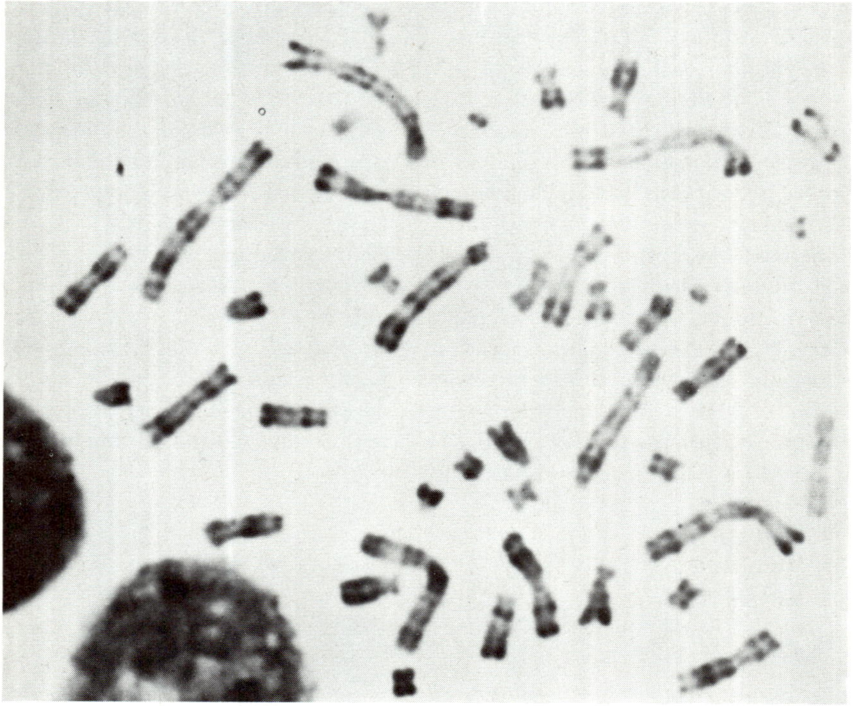

FIG. 1.—Metaphase spread from a man-hamster hybrid after treatment with the R-banding technique described in the text.

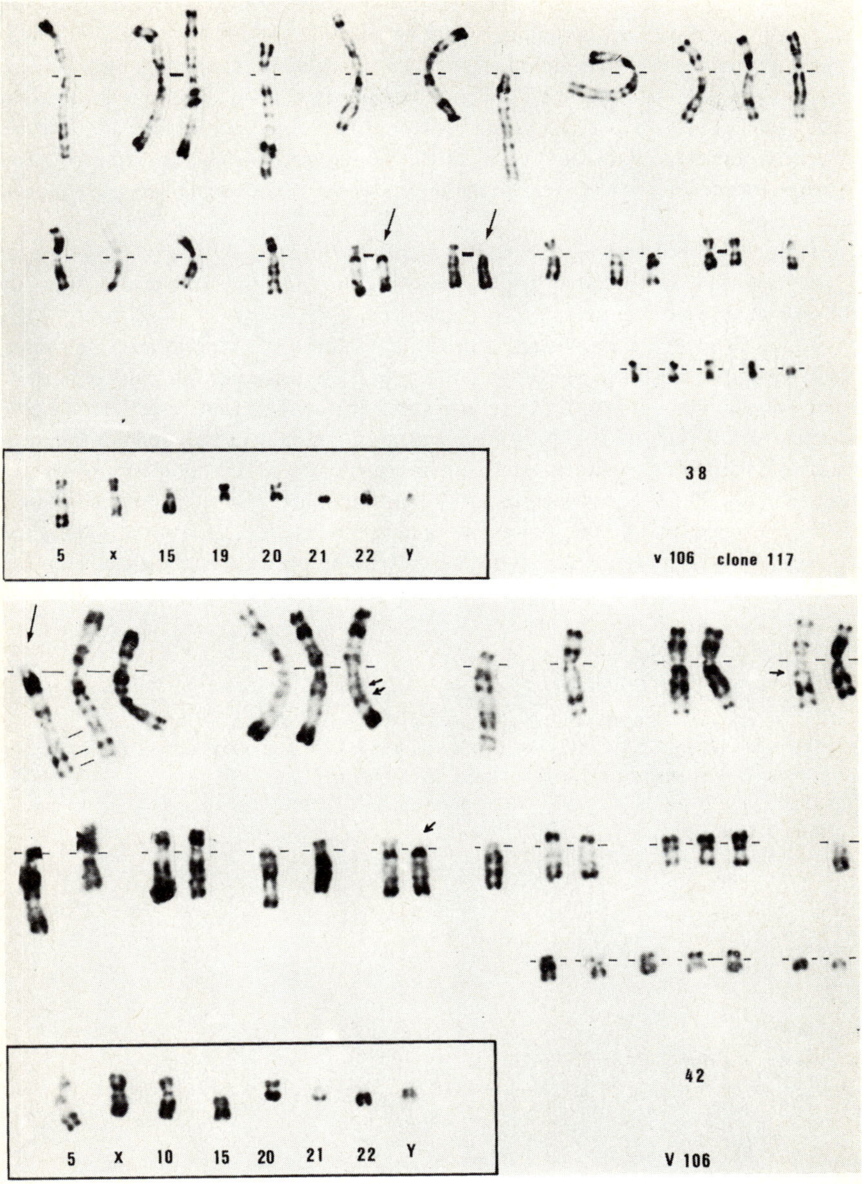

FIGS. 2 and 3.—Two karyotypes from a man-hamster hybrid clone showing the large diversity in the hamster chromosomes. The human chromosomes have been set out below in each karyotype.

4. DISCUSSION

The parent strains of hamster used are heteroploid strains of tumoral origin. Their origin and the longevity of these strains in laboratory can explain the evolution toward heteroploidy and the constant rearrangement of the chromosomes. Comparison of the chromosomes in the parental strain and in the hybrid lines shows that the chromosomal evolution continues after hybridization. Chromosomal rearrangement in the hybrids appears to be a common event since they involve practically all the chromosomes. This fact may be explained by the cell hybridization technique applied. In fact, cell fusion is favored by Sendai virus which also has the property of provoking breakage and chromosomal rearrangements. The frequency of rearrangement is certainly related to the Sendai virus doses used for the production of hybrids.

Human chromosomes in hybrid cells have been identified so far by Q-, C-, and G-banding. Our work demonstrates that R-banding is also a safe and convenient way for such identification.

Several precautions are necessary to obtain satisfactory preparations (Dutrillaux and Covic, 1974). According to our experience on hybrid cells the most important ones are the temperature of the solution and the heating time. Overheating at a temperature higher than 87°C leads to weak staining with no definite banding patterns. The duration of the treatment is also related to the temperature on the one hand and to the age of the preparation on the other. The older the preparation is, the shorter should be the treatment. As a rule, it is better to treat the slides after storage of a few days in order to get the clearest appearance of the chromosomes. Finally, in order to obtain the best results it is necessary to proceed via trials of several times of heating for each series of slides.

5. REFERENCES

DUTRILLAUX, B., and COVIC, M. 1974. Etude de facteurs influencant la denaturation thermique ménagée des chromosomes. *Exp. Cell Res., 85,* 143–153.

DUTTRILLAUX, B., and LEJEUNE, J. 1971. Sur une nouvelle technique d'analyse du caryotype human. *C. R. Acad. Sci. (Paris), 272,* 2638.

THE STRUCTURE OF THE PARACENTRIC REGION IN MOUSE CHROMOSOMES

KARL-HEINZ GRZESCHIK and MY. ALBERT KIM

Institut für Humangenetik der Universität Münster, D-44 Münster, Vesaliusweg 12–14, Germany

1. INTRODUCTION

Hilwig and Gropp (1973) described a decondensation effect in the pericentric area of mouse metaphase chromosomes induced by the benzimidazole compound "33258 Hoechst." We have examined whether the compound acts also on human chromosomes, or whether this reaction is characteristic only for mouse chromosomes so that it can be used for specifically marking the murine chromosomes in man-mouse cell hybrids.

As the centromeric area is stretched to a considerable length, examination of suitable metaphases, even by conventional light microscopy, offers an opportunity to obtain information on its structure in "acrocentric" and metacentric mouse chromosomes.

2. MATERIALS AND METHODS

Cells of the established mouse cell line Rag, diploid mouse embryo cells, the established human cell line D98-AH, one normal diploid human cell strain, and several clones of a man-mouse somatic cell hybrid line were maintained in MEM as described elsewhere (Grzeschik, 1973).

The benzimidazole compound "33258 Hoechst" (kindly supplied by Drs. H. Loewe and I. Hilwig, Farbwerke Hoechst) was added to the culture medium at a concentration of 40 μg/ml for 24, 48, or 73 hr before chromosome preparation, which was performed as previously described (Grzeschik, 1973).

The chromosomes were stained by the standard orcein technique or the Q- and G-banding methods of Caspersson et al. (1970) and Seabright (1971), respectively.

3. RESULTS

After the growth in the presence of "33258 Hoechst" all chromosomes of the Rag karyotype—except mouse chromosomes 1 and 7—showed a decondensation effect in the pericentric region after 24 hr (fig. 1). A mouse Y chromosome could not be detected. In the diploid mouse cells there was only a slight effect to be seen in some chromosomes.

At a prolonged growth in the presence of the drug, viability of the cells was greatly reduced. Human chromosomes did not show any effect under any of the conditions used. This species difference could also be found in the cell hybrids: in hybrid metaphases human chromosomes could easily be discriminated by their lack of the decondensation effect. Chromosome identification by banding techniques confirmed

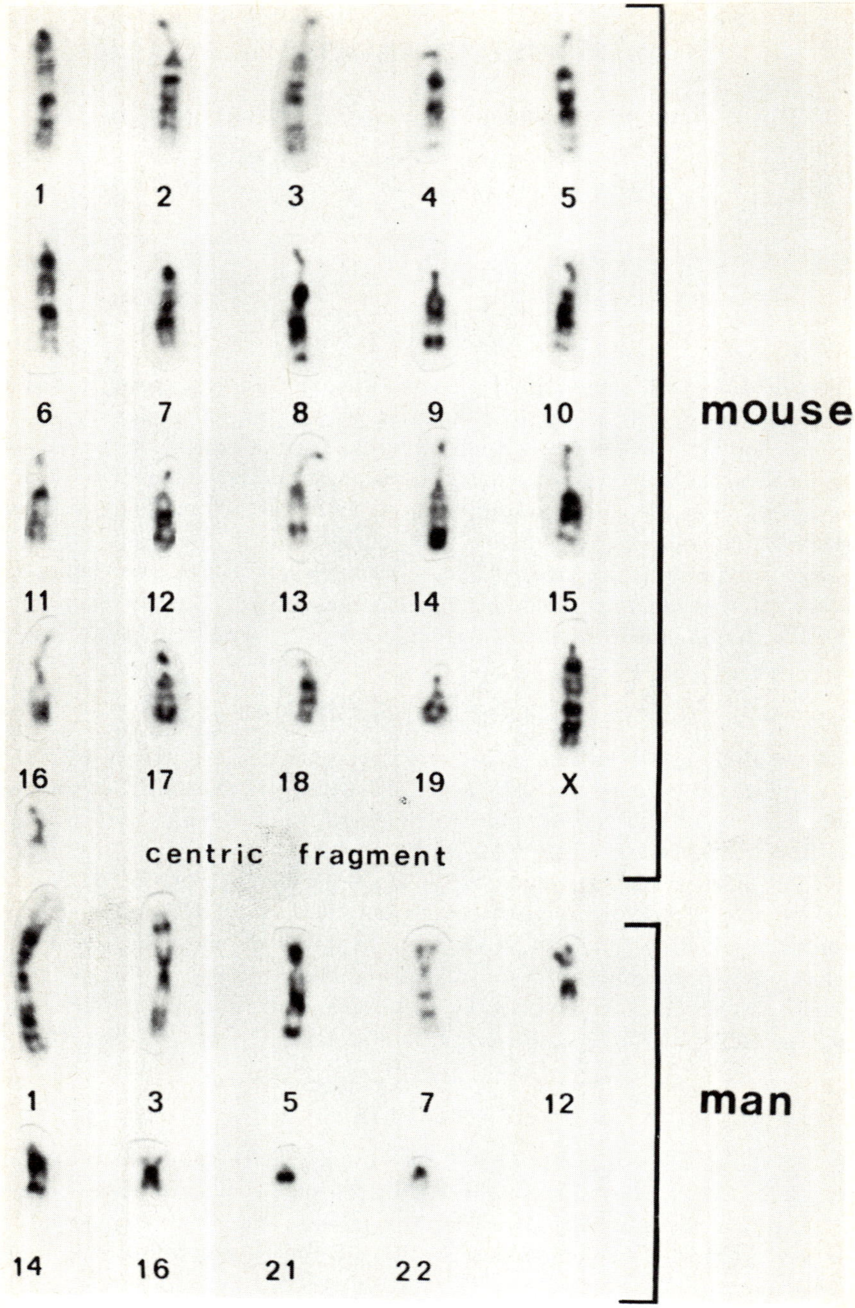

FIG. 1.—One mouse chromosome set, a centric fragment of murine origin, and several human chromosomes selected from a man-mouse hybrid karyotype stained with the G-banding technique after pretreatment with "33258 Hoechst" (from Kim and Grzeschik, 1974).

this result (fig. 1). Mouse chromosomes 1 and 7, which did not show the effect, differed in size from human D- and G-group chromosomes. It was particularly easy to allocate small centric fragments to either man or mouse chromosomes.

In suitable metaphases the decondensation effect was very pronounced. The extended structures could be as long as the rest of the chromatids. They mostly formed a threadlike structure with two condensed areas, one situated within the extended region and the other at the end. In order to obtain further information on the structure of these regions, rare metaphases had to be searched for, in which the individual chromatids could be distinguished within the decondensed areas. From these cells, two types of pericentric areas could be basically distinguished (fig. 2).

A few chromosomes, presumably 1 and 7, showed only very short decondensed structures.

In the second type the site connecting the chromatids (the centromere) was within the decondensed region. The structures above this site (fig. 2) can be considered as short arms. The metacentric chromosomes in the Rag karyotype, formed by Robertsonian fusion, did not show any visible loss of chromosome material. The ends of the short arms were connected with each other by threads which were thinner than most of the decondensed material (fig. 3). From the presence of two chromatid connecting sites, it appears that these metacentric chromosomes were in fact dicentric.

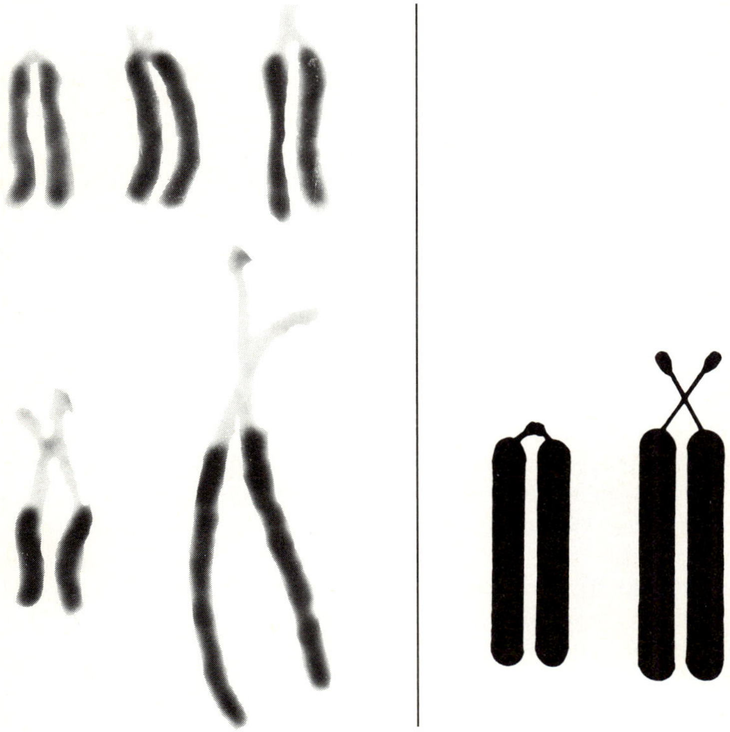

FIG. 2.—Various types of acrocentric mouse metaphase chromosomes from Rag cells after pretreatment for 24 hours with 40 μg/ml "33258 Hoechst" in the culture medium. The length of the decondensated area varies with the metaphases but is a stable characteristic of each chromosome.

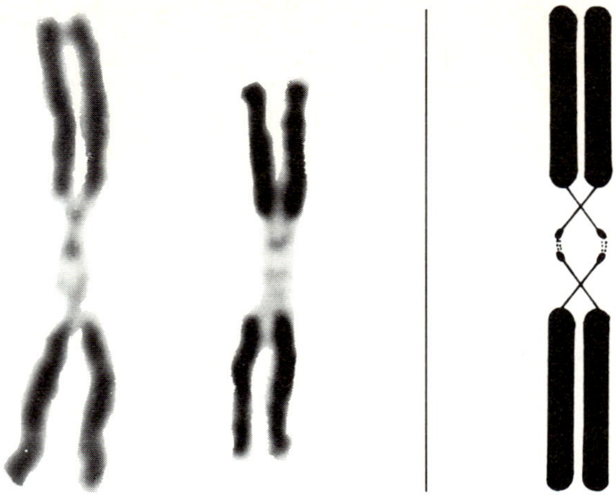

FIG. 3.—Metacentric mouse chromosomes from Rag cells grown in the presence of "33258 Hoechst." This type of metacentric mouse chromosomes is generated in the animals as well as in cell culture by "Robertsonian translocation." The centric fusion happens without visible loss of chromosome material giving rise to dicentric chromosomes.

4. DISCUSSION

The data presented indicate that a combination of pretreatment with "33258 Hoechst" and banding techniques is a very useful tool for chromosome identification in somatic cell hybrids.

It is the only known procedure which permits chromosome identification and discrimination of mouse and human chromosomes in one step.

It is evident from the rather unexpected decondensation phenomenon that the structure of eukaryote chromosomes can be hidden by condensation to such an extent that it does not even show up clearly in electron microscopy (Comings and Okada, 1970).

The incorporation of chemicals into the DNA or the proteins establishing the structure of metaphase chromosomes is found to be one of the procedures for inhibiting complete condensation and thus provides some insight into chromosome structure. In the mouse chromosomes shown here (fig. 2), we consider the point where the chromatids are connected as the centromere (centromeric chromomere of Lima de Faria, 1956). In most mouse chromosomes, it is imbedded in the centric heterochromatin.

If one includes this chromatin in the term centromere, as was done by Lima de Faria (1956) and Marks (1957), then telocentric chromosomes occur in the mouse by definition. If, on the other hand, one considers the piece of chromatin above the centromere as short arm material (White, 1954), telocentric chromosomes do not occur. We prefer the second version and speak of acrocentric, instead of telocentric, chromosomes.

The events leading to the Robertsonian fusion of mouse chromosomes apparently do not involve the centromeres per se but the centric chromatin around this site. As already found by chemical observation, little chromosome material is lost during this fusion (Comings and Avelino, 1972). However, a translocation occurring close to the telomers would result in the loss of only a few thousand base pairs and would be very hard to detect biochemically.

The mechanism of the connection of the DNA-strands of both chromosomes remains to be elucidated.

5. SUMMARY

1. Growth of established mouse cells in the presence of the benzimidazole compound "33258 Hoechst" causes an elongation of the paracentric area in metaphase chromosomes. The length of this enlargement is a stable characteristic of each chromosome.

2. Identification of the individual chromosomes by the use of banding techniques revealed that most mouse chromosomes, except Nos. 1 and 7, do have short arms and are therefore acrocentric.

3. Metacentric chromosomes frequently generated by Robertsonian translocation in cell cultures as well as in animals are dicentric.

4. The decondensation phenomenon does not appear in pretreated human chromosomes. Therefore, a combination of pretreatment of the cells with "33258 Hoechst" followed by banding pattern analysis of the metaphase chromosomes is a very useful method for the discrimination of murine from human chromosomes in man-mouse somatic cell hybrids.

Acknowledgement. This study was supported by the Deutsche Forschungsgemeinschaft.

6. REFERENCES

CASPERSSON, T., ZECH, L., and JOHANSSON, C. 1970. Differential binding of alkylating fluorochromes in human chromosomes. *Exp. Cell. Res., 60,* 315–319.

COMINGS, D. E., and AVELINO, E. 1972. DNA loss during Robertsonian fusion of the tobacco mouse. *Nat. New Biol., 237,* 199.

COMINGS, D. E., and OKADA, T. A. 1970. Whole mount electron microscopy of the centromere region of metacentric and telocentric mammalian chromosomes. *Cytogenetics (Basel), 9,* 436–449.

GRZESCHIK, K.-H. 1973. Syrian hamster-human somatic cell hybrids: isolation and characterization. *Humangenetik, 20,* 211–218.

HILWIG, I., and GROPP, A. 1973. Decondensation of constitutive heterochromatin in L cell chromosomes by a benzimidazole compound ("33258 Hoechst"). *Exp. Cell Res., 81,* 474–477.

KIM, MY. A., and GRZESCHIK, K.-H. 1974. A method for discriminating murine and human chromosomes in somatic cell hybrids. *Exp. Cell Res., 88,* 406–410.

LIMA de FARIA, A. 1956. The role of the kinetochore in chromosome organization. *Hereditas, 42,* 85–160.

MARKS, G. E. 1957. Telocentric chromosomes. *Am. Nat., 91,* 223–232.

ROBERTSON, W. R. B. 1916. Chromosome studies: taxonomic relationships shown in the chromosomes of tettigidae and acrididae: V-shaped chromosomes and their significance in acrididae, locustidae, and gryllidae: chromosomes and variation. *J. Morphol., 27,* 179–331.

SEABRIGHT, M. 1971. A rapid banding-technique for human chromosomes. *Lancet, ii,* 971–972.

WHITE, M. J. D. 1954. *Animal cytology and evolution.* 2nd Edition. Cambridge Univers. Press, Cambridge.

LONGITUDINAL AND LATERAL DIFFERENTIATION OF METAPHASE CHROMOSOMES BASED ON THE DETECTION OF DNA SYNTHESIS BY FLUORESCENCE MICROSCOPY

SAMUEL A. LATT

Clinical Genetics Division, Children's Hospital Medical Center, and Department of Pediatrics and Center for Human Genetics, Harvard Medical School

1. INTRODUCTION

Fluorescent staining techniques, using the dyes quinacrine and quinacrine mustard, have greatly advanced cytogenetics, allowing unambiguous identification of metaphase chromosomes and revealing the existence of a banded organization along these chromosomes (Caspersson et al., 1968; Zech, 1969; Caspersson et al., 1972*a*). The generality of this organization is underscored by the observation of similar staining patterns with a variety of modified Giemsa techniques (O. J. Miller et al., 1973; Hsu, 1973). While the precise chemical basis for these results is still under investigation (Ellison and Barr, 1972; Weisblum and De Haseth, 1972; Pachmann and Rigler, 1972; Weisblum, 1973; Gottesfeld et al., 1974; Sumner and Evans, 1973), the staining patterns thus far obtained can serve as a reference system (Paris Conference, 1971) relative to which regional variations in chromosome replication, stability, and repair can be described.

Cytological studies of chromosome replication have previously suggested that chromosome banding patterns correlate with the distribution of regions late to complete DNA synthesis (Miller et al., 1971; Ganner and Evans, 1971; Breg et al., 1972; Calderon and Schnedl, 1973). However, the autoradiographic techniques employed do not possess an effective resolution comparable to that of chromosome staining methods. A direct optical method for analyzing DNA synthesis, employing a DNA base analogue with suitable biological and absorptive or fluorescent characteristics, is not yet available. However, an indirect technique, allowing detection of DNA synthesis by fluorescence microscopy, has recently been developed (Latt, 1973).

Heavy polarizable atoms are known to affect the fluorescence and phosphorescence of a number of organic dyes (Hercules, 1966; Orgel, 1954; Galley and Purkey, 1972). Fluorescence of the bisbenzimidazole dye 33258 Hoechst (Hilwig and Gropp, 1972; Loewe and Urbanietz, 1974) was found to be less when bound to poly (dA-dBrU) than when bound to poly (dA-dT) (Latt, 1973). 33258 Hoechst fluorescence is also quenched by BrdU incorporated biosynthetically into chromosomes. The fluorescence of chromosome regions containing DNA replicating either early or late in the DNA synthesis period can be suppressed by the appropriate schedule of cell growth in medium containing BrdU (Latt, 1974*a*; Latt, 1974*b*). These regions correlate with standard banding patterns, and within this set of regions, further discrimination according to replication time is possible. In a few chromosome regions, sister chromatids can be differentiated after one cycle of replication in BrdU, presumably signaling regions containing DNA with an uneven distribution of thymine between complementary polynucleotide chains (Lin et al., 1974; Latt et al., 1974). After two cycles of BrdU incorporation, chromosomes stained with 33258 Hoechst exhibit one brightly and one dully fluorescing chromatid, relecting incorporation of BrdU into one or two DNA polynucleotide chains, respectively. Sister chromatid exchanges are evident as sharply demarcated reciprocal alterations in fluorescence along chromosomes and can be located relative to quinacrine banding patterns (Latt, 1974*c*). These exchanges, which may reflect differential stability of chromosome regions, are also very sensitive indicators of chromosome damage by chemicals such as mitomycin C (Kato, 1974*a*; Latt, 1974*d*).

2. MATERIALS AND METHODS

Human peripheral leukocytes were cultured at 37°C in Eagle's MEM supplemented with 20% fetal bovine serum, 2 mM L-glutamine, and a saline extract of kidney beans containing phytohemagglutinin. Four types of protocols were followed for different applications of the method.

(1) *Analysis of sister chromatid exchanges.* BrdU (0.006–0.09 mM) was added to the cultures at the start of growth, and cells were harvested 70–74 hours later. FdU (0.4 μM) was added to suppress endogenous thymidine synthesis during growth in BrdU, and U (6 μM) was added to reduce toxic effects of FdU (Priest et al., 1967*b*; Knight and Luzzatti, 1973). After two replication cycles in BrdU-containing medium, sister chromatids contain either one or two chains substituted with BrdU and thus exhibit markedly different 33258 Hoechst fluorescence (Latt, 1973; Latt, 1974*c*). A similar difference in sister chromatid fluorescence, with a greater overall total fluorescence intensity, is observed if the cells incorporate thymidine rather than BrdU during the second replication cycle. In this case, only one polynucleotide chain, located in the dully fluorescent chromatid, is appreciably substituted with BrdU.

(2) *Analysis of late-replicating regions.* Cells were grown nearly one division (40–45 hours) in medium containing 0.09 mM BrdU. The medium was then replaced with Ham's F-10 supplemented with 20% fetal bovine serum and 6 μM [^{3}H] dT (2 μCi/ml) and the cells were grown an additional 5–7 hr before harvest (Latt, 1973; Latt, 1974*a* and *b*). Late-replicating regions of chromosomes from cells grown according to this protocol exhibit bright 33258 Hoechst fluorescence against a BrdU-suppressed background.

(3) *Analysis of early-replicating regions.* After 65–69 hr of growth in medium without BrdU, 0.09 mM BrdU, 0.4 μM FdU, and 6 μM U were added to the cultures. [^{3}H] BrdU, when used, was at a final specific activity of 11 μCi/μmole. Cells were harvested 5–7 hr after BrdU addition. Early-replicating regions of chromosomes from these cells exhibit bright 33258 Hoechst fluorescence, while fluorescence is suppressed in late-replicating regions which have incorporated BrdU.

(4) *Analysis of asymmetry in the distribution of thymine between polynucleotide chains.* Cells were grown one replication cycle in medium containing 0.09 mM BrdU. Certain regions, presumably those containing DNA with an uneven distribution of thymine between polynucleotide chains, exhibit unequal sister chromatid

fluorescence after one round of replication in BrdU when stained with 33258 Hoechst (Lin et al., 1974; Latt el al., 1974).

(a) *Slide preparation*
Cells were harvested by centrifugation 2 hr after the addition of colcemid (Ciba) to a final concentration of 0.1 μg/ml.; suspended in 0.075 M KCl for 12 min; fixed in at least two changes of 3:1 methanol:acetic acid; air-dried on glass microscope slides.

(b) *Staining and photography*
Slides were stained for 10 min in 0.5 μg/ml. 33258 Hoechst in 0.14 M NaCl, 0.004 M KCl, 0.01 M phosphate, pH 7. 33258 Hoechst and related bisbenzimidazole dyes (Hilwig and Gropp, 1972; Loewe and Urbanietz, 1974) were the generous gift of Dr. H. Loewe, Hoechst A/G, Frankfurt am Main, Germany. For observation of the effect of BrdU on 33258 Hoechst fluorescence, slides were mounted in 0.16 M sodium phosphate, 0.04 M sodium citrate, pH 7. If slides are mounted in a 10% solution of pH 4.1 citrate-phosphate buffer in glycerol, the quenching due to BrdU is not observed (Latt, 1974*e*). Chromosome fluorescence was observed in a Leitz Orthoplan microscope equipped with incident illumination using a 200 W mercury light source, a UG-1 filter and TK 400 dichroic mirror for excitation and K400 and K460 filters for emission. Photographs were taken on Tri-X film through a 100 X achromat objective with an Orthomat II automatic camera. These combinations are appropriate for the excitation and emission spectra of 33258 Hoechst-DNA complexes, peaking near 360 and 475 nm, respectively. The quinacrine and quinacrine mustard staining procedures followed established methodology (Caspersson et al., 1972*a*; O. J. Miller et al., 1973; Lubs et al., 1973). Removal of quinacrine was accomplished in 3:1 methanol:acetic acid prior to staining with 33258 Hoechst. Slides for autoradiography were dipped in Kodak NTB-2 emulsion (diluted 1:1 with water), exposed at 5°C, and then developed with Dektol. Photography of these slides employed high contrast copy film.

BrdU and thymidine were obtained from Sigma and their tritiated derivatives from New England Nuclear. Quinacrine and uridine were obtained from Sigma, ethidium bromide and FdU from Calbiochem, and acridine orange from G. Gurr. Daunomycin was a gift of Dr. Norman Jaffe. Calf thymus DNA was purchased from Worthington Biochemicals, while synthetic polynucleotides were purchased from Miles or P. L. Biochemicals.

Fluorescence intensities of 33258 Hoechst-polynucleotide complexes were determined with a Hitachi MPF3 spectrofluorometer. Emission spectra were corrected for wavelength variation of instrument response (Chen, 1967). Quantum yields are calculated relative to a value of 0.51 for quinine sulfate in 0.1N H_2SO_4 (Chen, 1973). Fluorescence lifetimes were obtained with a nanosecond fluorometer (Yguerabide, 1972) kindly made available by Professor Lubert Stryer, Yale University. Values reported were obtained by a least squares fit of the fluorescence decay data to that of a single exponential.

3. RESULTS

The fluorescence of 33258 Hoechst at pH 7 is weak (quantum yield slightly greater than 0.01) but increases about forty-fold upon binding to calf thymus DNA (quantum yield about 0.5). A similar enhancement of dye fluorescence occurs upon binding to the synthetic polynucleotide poly(dA-dT). However, relative to this the fluorescence of the complex with poly(dA-BrdU) in a low ionic strength solution is only about one-fourth as intense (Latt, 1973). The fluorescence of 33258 Hoechst is also quenched by BrdU incorporated into interphase chromatin isolated from cells or into chromosomes examined in cytological preparations.

33258 Hoechst can be used to study DNA replication in cells which incorporate BrdU for only a fraction of one DNA synthesis period. If cells undergo an entire replication cycle in medium containing BrdU, each chromatid will contain one polynucleotide chain substituted with BrdU, resulting in suppressed 33258 Hoechst fluorescence. However, if cells which have replicated nearly once in BrdU are given a pulse of thymidine 5–7 hr before harvest, the regions last to complete replication incorporate thymidine rather than BrdU. They exhibit bright 33258 Hoechst fluorescence against a BrdU-suppressed background (Latt, 1974*a*) (fig. 1). For example, the late-replicating female X chromosome incorporates more of a terminal [^{3}H]dT pulse than does its homologue (Latt, 1973, 1974*b*). This is manifest both as greater fluorescence intensity (fig. 2A) and increased autoradiographic grain density

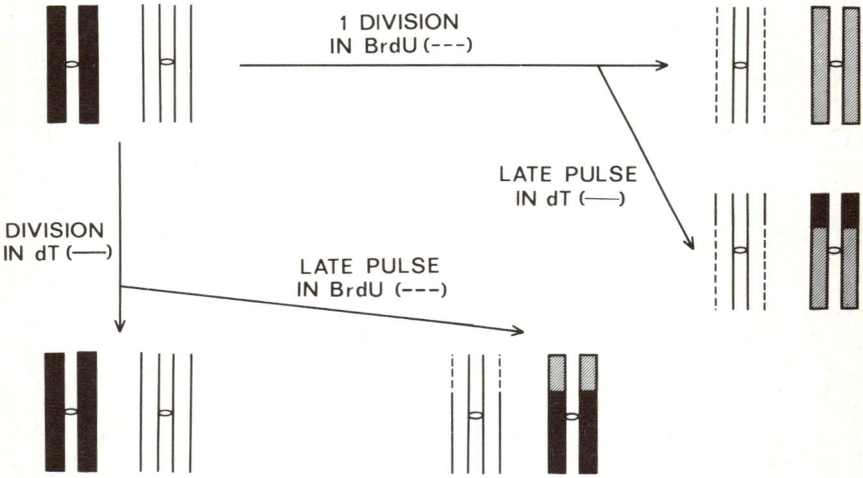

FIG. 1.—Diagram of the use of terminal pulses of BrdU (------) or dT (——) to study early- or late-replicating chromosome regions. DNA unsubstituted with BrdU is represented as two solid parallel lines. The 33258 Hoechst fluorescence of chromatids containing such DNA (drawn as black rectangles) is very bright. DNA containing BrdU in one chain is represented by parallel solid and dashed lines. The fluorescence of chromatids containing this DNA and stained with 33258 Hoechst (drawn as partially shaded rectangles) is less bright. Growth of cells for one complete replication cycle in BrdU medium results in reduced 33258 Hoechst fluorescence along both chromatids of a chromosome (upper right). Substitution of dT for BrdU a few hours before harvest results in bright 33258 Hoechst fluorescence over late-replicating regions which are relatively devoid of BrdU. Conversely, administration of a terminal pulse of BrdU to cells otherwise grown in control medium (lower left) selectively suppresses 33258 Hoechst fluorescence in late-replicating regions which now have incorporated BrdU. Changes in chromosome condensation association with BrdU incorporation might further alter dye fluorescence (Latt, 1974*a*).

(fig. 2B). Other regions of the genome, such as the secondary constrictions of chromosomes 1, 9 and 16, the long arm of chromosome 13, and much of chromosome 4 also exhibit corresponding bright fluorescence and autoradiographic grains.

The procedure of highlighting the fluorescence of late replicating regions with a terminal pulse of thymidine allows detection of these regions throughout an individual karyotype (fig. 3). With the exception of previously mentioned secondary

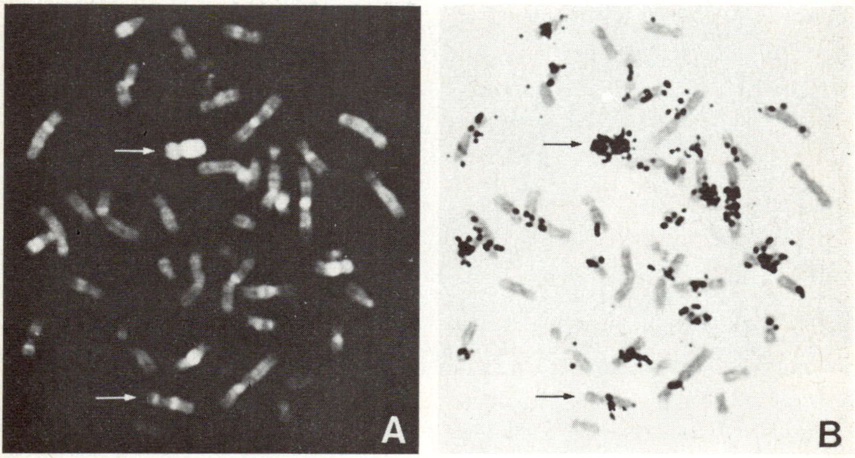

FIG. 2.—Late replication in human X chromosomes detected by fluorescence microscopy and autoradiography. Slides were stained with 33258 Hoechst (A), exposed for autoradiography, and rephotographed (B). The upper and lower arrows indicate the late and early replicating X chromosomes, respectively (Latt, 1973).

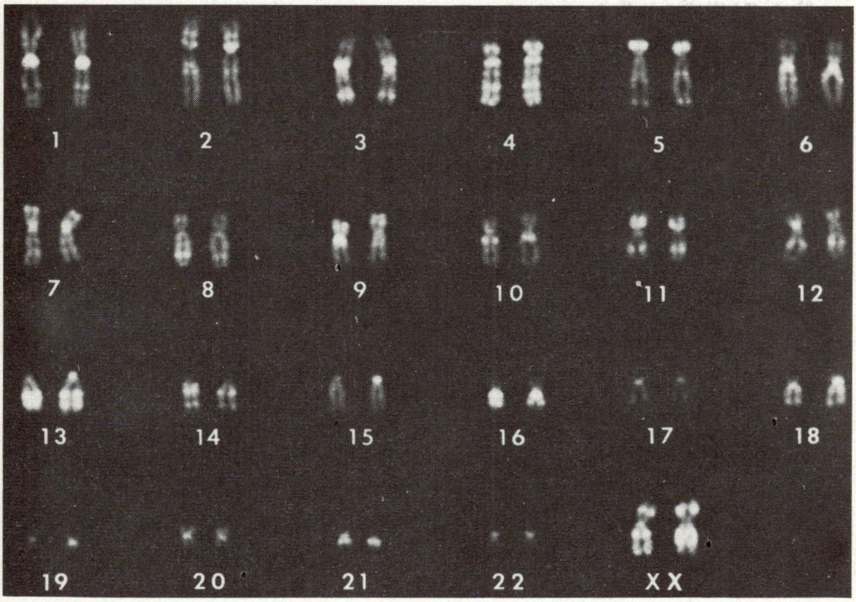

FIG. 3.—Regions of late DNA replication in human female chromosomes. Cells and slides were treated as described in the text (Latt, 1974*a*).

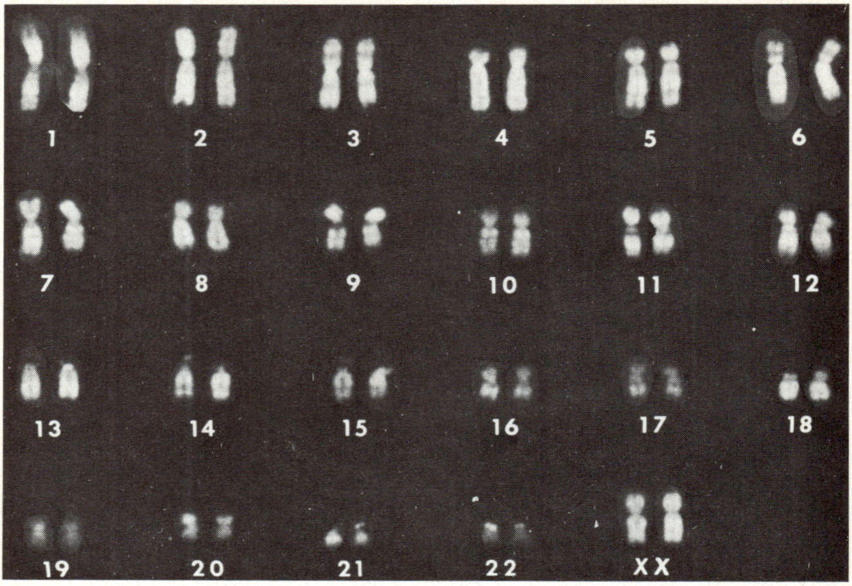

FIG. 4.—Fluorescence of human female chromosomes stained with quinacrine. Chromosomes from lymphocytes of the same individual as in figure 3 grown in medium without BrdU and stained with quinacrine.

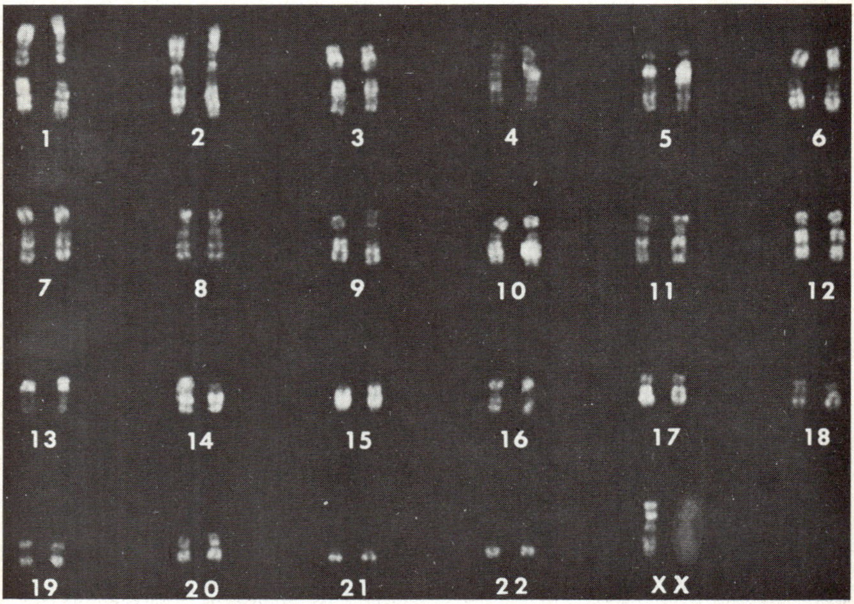

FIG. 5.—Regions of early DNA replication in human female chromosomes. Chromosomes from the same individual as in figure 3 were treated as described in the text.

constrictions, the regions exhibiting bright 33258 Hoechst fluorescence correspond to those which also fluoresce brightly with quinacrine (fig. 4). However, not all of the quinacrine bands are equally late labeling. Furthermore, in some chromosome regions, such as the secondary constriction of No. 9, there is a homologue difference in fluorescence.

If cells are administered BrdU at the end of the DNA synthesis period rather than at its beginning, then early replicating regions will exhibit bright 33258 Hoechst fluorescence (fig. 1). This pattern (fig. 5) is largely the converse of that in figure 3 obtained with a terminal thymidine pulse. Dull fluorescence of the late replicating X chromosome is especially striking with this protocol. This may reflect the observation that DNA synthesis in the late replicating X is delayed in its initiation to an even greater extent than in its completion (Petersen, 1964; Priest et al., 1967*a*; Takagi and Sandberg, 1968). Incorporation of a terminal pusle of BrdU might also influence dye fluorescence by altering chromosome condensation (Kaback et al., 1963; Palmer, 1970; Zakharov and Egolina, 1972; Baranovskaya et al., 1972; Zakharov et al., 1974).

Suppression of 33258 Hoechst fluorescence by a terminal pulse of BrdU is especially marked in the short arm of chromosome 5. This facilitates the differentiation between chromosomes 4 and 5 (fig. 6). Differences in the fluorescence of the long arms of these chromosomes are also apparent. Band resolution may in part be accentuated by chromosome decondensation in regions of terminal BrdU incorporation. A number of other chromosome assignments may be facilitated by suppressing the fluorescence of late replicating regions.

33258 Hoechst fluorescence can also be used to differentiate between sister chromatids. This is possible because of the semiconservative distribution of newly replicated DNA between sister chromatids, an event first observed by J. H. Taylor et al. (1957), using autoradiography. After two cycles of semiconservative replication in medium containing BrdU, each metaphase chromosome will contain one chromatid containing BrdU (bifilarly) in both polynucleotide chains, while the other contains BrdU (unifilarly) in only one polynucleotide (Latt, 1973, 1974*c*) (fig. 7).

Differentiation of sister chromatids by fluorescence microscopy reveals sister

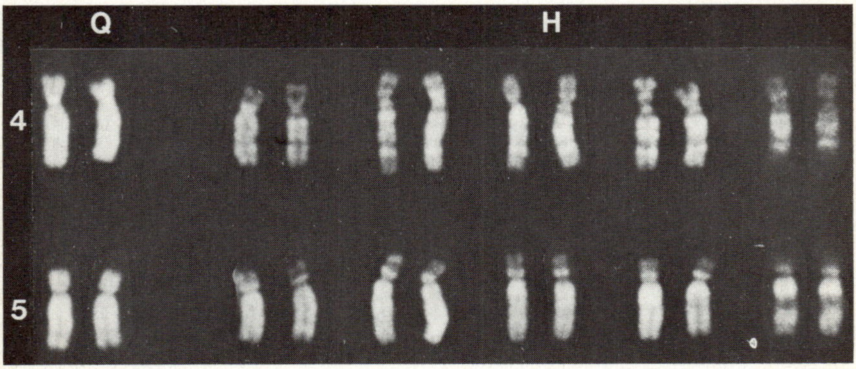

FIG. 6.—Effect of a terminal pulse of BrdU on the fluorescence of human chromosomes 4 and 5. Chromosomes were first identified with quinacrine (extreme left side), destained and then restained with 33258 Hoechst (right side).

chromatid exchanges as sharply demarcated reciprocal alterations in fluorescence intensity along chromosomes (fig. 8). The number of such exchanges in human lymphocytes depends somewhat on the BrdU concentration during the two replication cycles. The average exchange frequency increases from about 11 per cell at 0.006 mM BrdU to approximately 17 per cell at 0.09 mM BrdU (Latt, 1974*d*).

In a small fraction of cells undergoing two replications in culture, sister chromatid separation does not take place after the first replication. The resulting endoreduplicated chromosomes (Herreros and Giannelli, 1967; Schwarzacher and Schnedl, 1966) consist of pairs of laterally apposed metaphase chromosomes containing the products of two replication cycles. If these replications occur in a medium containing BrdU, then the sister chromatids of each component metaphase chromosome exhibit unequal 33258 Hoechst fluorescence as expected (fig. 9). Interestingly, within each endoreduplicated chromosome, the two dully fluorescing chromatids are on the outside with the brightly fluorescing chromatids inside. This confirms by fluorescence microscopy the previous observations based on autoradiography which suggested that the template and daughter polynucleotide chains of DNA in metaphase chromosomes are asymmetrically oriented relative to the centromere

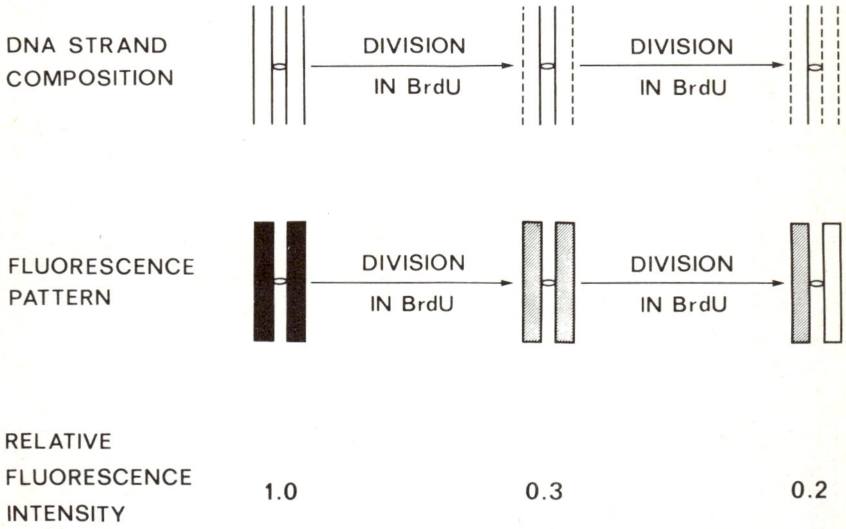

FIG. 7.—Diagrammatic interpretation of the correlation between BrdU incorporation into chromosomal DNA and the fluorescence of chromatids stained with 33258 Hoechst. Unsubstituted DNA chains are represented by solid lines and those incorporating BrdU for one replication cycle as dashed lines. Fluorescence of unsubstituted DNA (represented as solid rectangles) is very bright. Incorporation of BrdU into one chain of the DNA reduces chromatid fluorescence by about two thirds (partially shaded rectangles). Another cycle of replication in BrdU results in one chromatid substituted with BrdU in one DNA chain and one chromatid containing BrdU in both DNA chains. The latter (open rectangle) exhibits fluorescence with about one-third the intensity of that of the partially substituted sister chromatid, and the overall chromosome fluorescence is reduced about one-third by this second division in BrdU. Fluorescence intensity was measured on slides of chromosomes mounted in pH 7.0 McIlbraine's buffer.

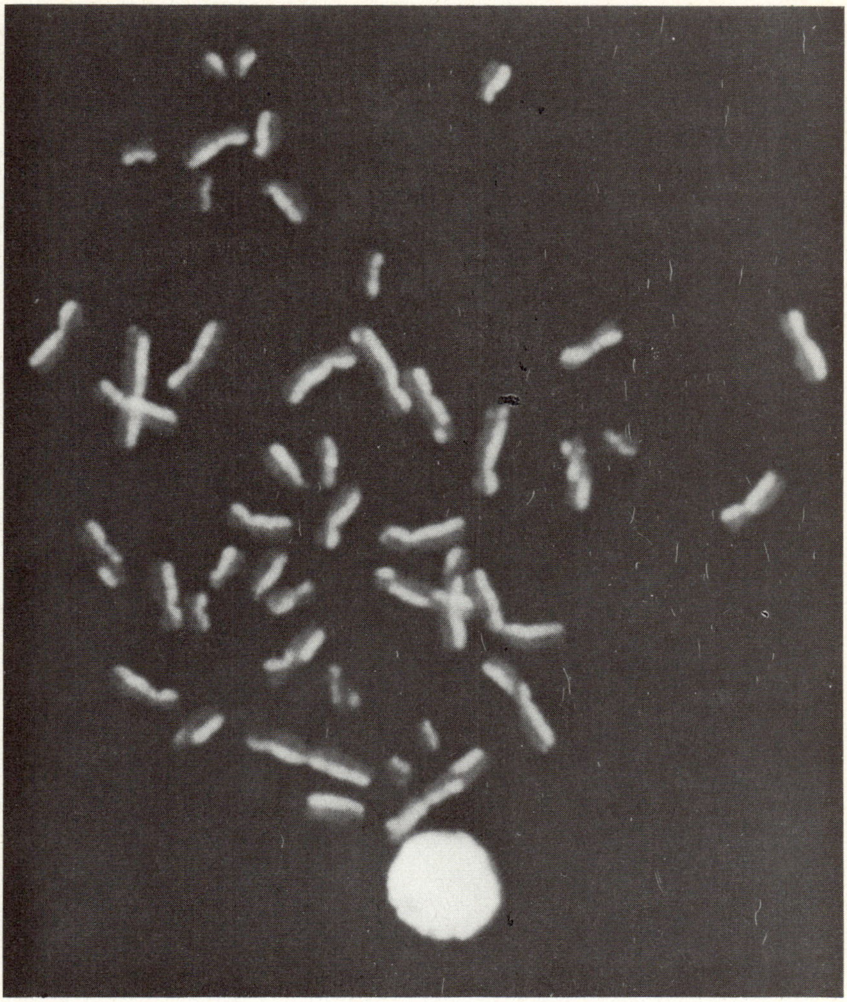

FIG. 8.—33258 Hoechst fluorescence of human chromosomes from lymphocytes after two cycles of BrdU incorporation.

(fig. 10). Sister chromatid exchanges which occurred during the first replication cycle are found in both components of an endoreduplicated chromosome, while those which occurred during the second cycle are present in only one component.

If cells are grown three replication cycles in BrdU, then an average of only one-fourth of the chromatids fluoresce brightly. Sister chromatid exchanges which occurred prior to the final replication are apparent as non-reciprocal segmental variations in fluorescence intensity (fig. 11A). Further information about the timing of the exchanges can be obtained if replication takes place in relatively low BrdU concentrations, apparently because of changes in BrdU concentration in the DNA precursor pool during this culture interval. A gradation of chromatid fluorescence intensities is observed which differentiates the two expected classes of chromatids

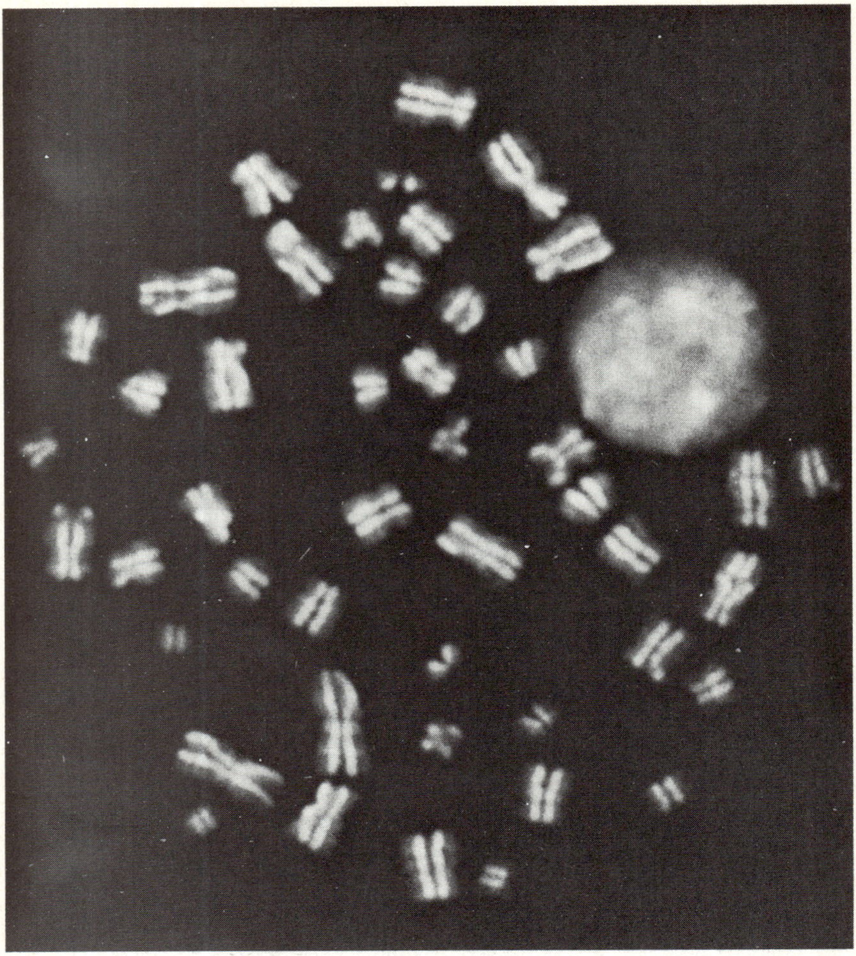

FIG. 9.—33258 Hoechst fluorescence of endoreduplication. The metaphase chromosomes shown are from a human lymphocyte which exhibited endoreduplication after 96 hr of growth in medium containing 0.01 mM BrdU.

containing BrdU in both polynucleotide chains (fig. 11B). If cells incorporate BrdU for one cycle followed by one cycle of growth in its absence, unequal sister chromatid fluorescence again is found (fig. 11C). In this case, dully fluorescing chromatids contain appreciable amounts of BrdU in only one polynucleotide chain, while the other chromatids contain very little BrdU. After a second cycle of growth in the absence of BrdU, the fluorescence observed (fig. 11D) is essentially the converse of that after three cycles of BrdU incorporation (fig. 11A).

Sister chromatid exchanges in cells such as those incorporating BrdU for two replication cycles can be localized relative to the quinacrine banding patterns if the chromosomes are first stained with quinacrine, destained, and then stained with 33258 Hoechst (fig. 12). The distribution of sister chromatid exchanges in these cells generally correlates with metaphase chromosome length (fig. 13), although in

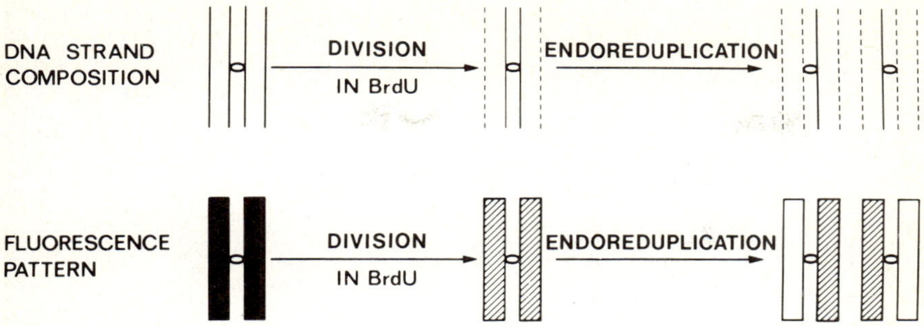

FIG. 10.—Diagrammatic representation of DNA composition (top row) and 33258 Hoechst fluorescence (bottom row) in endoreduplicated chromosomes. Unsubstituted DNA chains are drawn as solid lines and substituted chains as dashed lines. Brightly fluorescing chro-chromatids are drawn as black rectangles, chromatids with intermediate fluorescence are drawn as shaded rectangles, and chromatids with dull fluorescence are drawn as open rectangles. Sister chromatid separation is shown to occur after the first, but not after the second division.

a few chromosome size groups there is considerable variation in the exchange frequency. However, within individual chromosomes the majority of exchanges appear to be located either in between bands, as defined by quinacrine fluorescence, or very near band-interband junctions (Latt, 1974*a,c*). This is especially clear in chromosomes such as No. 1, 7, and 11 in which the banding patterns are pronounced (fig. 14). Certain regions, such as some extensive pale areas adjacent to very bright bands (e.g., 1q32, 3p21, 4q31, Xq22), are involved in exchanges with an unusually high frequency.

In addition to their use in signaling the location of "exchange-labile" areas, sister chromatid exchanges are very sensitive indicators of certain types of chromosome damage. At 0.01–0.02 mM BrdU, chromatid exchanges outnumber chromosome breaks by more than 200:1. If these exchanges reflect discontinuities in chromosome DNA that are healed with interchange of replication products, then it can be concluded that most of these discontinuities are repaired, with only a small fraction surviving as breaks. The bifunctional alkylating agent mitomycin C (Iyer and Szybalski, 1963; Lipsett and Weissbach, 1968), at low concentrations, dramatically increases the sister chromatid exchange frequency while producing relatively few breaks (fig. 15). Multiple exchanges often occur sufficiently close together that they would probably appear as "isochromatid labeling" (Prescott, 1970) were autoradiography used for their detection. A similar analysis of other chemical and physical agents that affect chromosomes may provide an insight into both chromosome damage and repair.

Further use of 33258 Hoechst fluorescence to study chromosomes would benefit from an increased understanding of the factors influencing this fluorescence. At high polynucleotide concentrations, 33258 Hoechst fluorescence shows very little base composition dependence (table 1). Replacement of one or both polynucleotide chains of poly(dA)-poly(dT) with ribopolymers slightly reduces the fluorescence of bound dye. BrdU was used as a fluorescence quenching agent because of its heavy, polarizable bromine atom (Hercules, 1966; Orgel, 1954; Galley and Purkey, 1972).

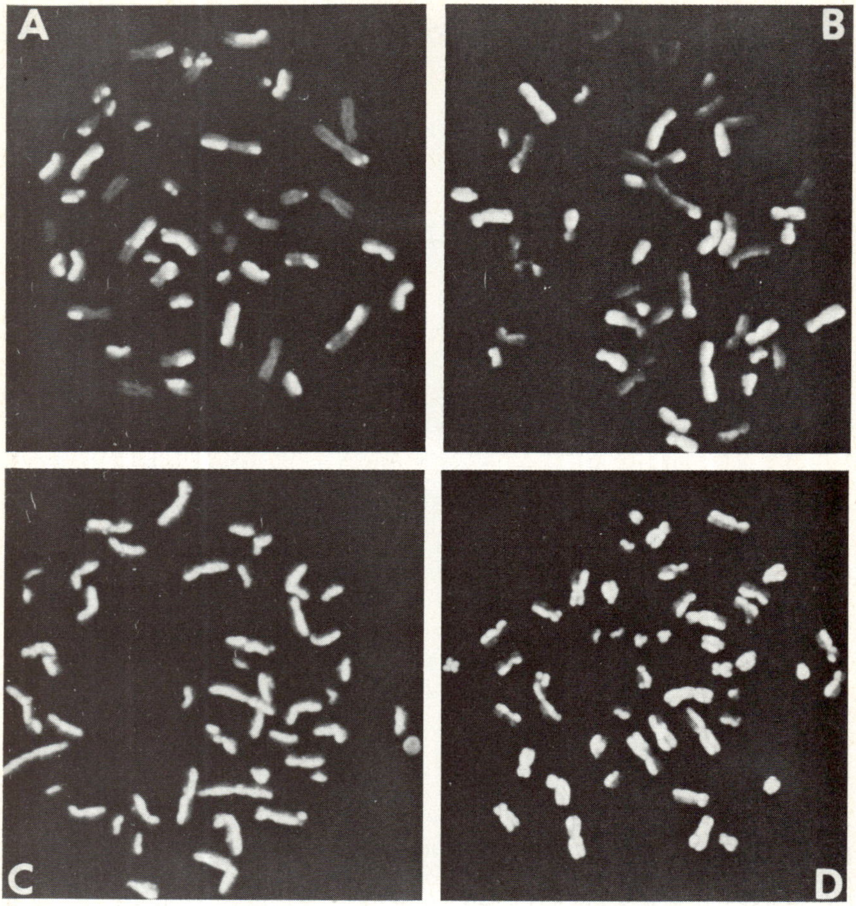

FIG. 11.—Alternate protocols for visualizing semiconservative DNA segregation and sister chromatid exchanges in human lymphocyte chromosomes. Chromosomes are from a normal 46, XX human female (A) or 46, XY male (B, C, D). The cell in (A) was grown 74 hr in medium containing 0.09 mM BrdU before harvest. The cell in (B) was grown 74 hr in medium containing 0.02 mM BrdU. The cells in (C) and (D) were grown 45 hr in medium containing 0.02 mM BrdU, and then for an additional 26 hr in normal medium. The timing of the medium change in (C) evidently overlapped the end of the first DNA synthesis period since the fluorescence of a number of characteristically late replicating regions is highlighted in both chromatids.

Another heavy atom-containing thymidine analogue, IdU, incorporated into poly(dA-IdU), also quenches 33258 Hoechst fluorescence (table 1).

The fluorescence decay kinetics of complexes of 33258 Hoechst with DNA and synthetic polynucleotides were measured to further characterize quenching mechanisms. The fluorescence lifetime of 33258 Hoechst at pH 7 increases upon binding to DNA but appears insensitive to DNA base composition. The decay times of the poly(dAdT) and poly(dA-dBrU) complexes with 33258 Hoechst are both 4.0 nsec, under conditions (pH 7, low ionic strength) such that the fluorescence intensities

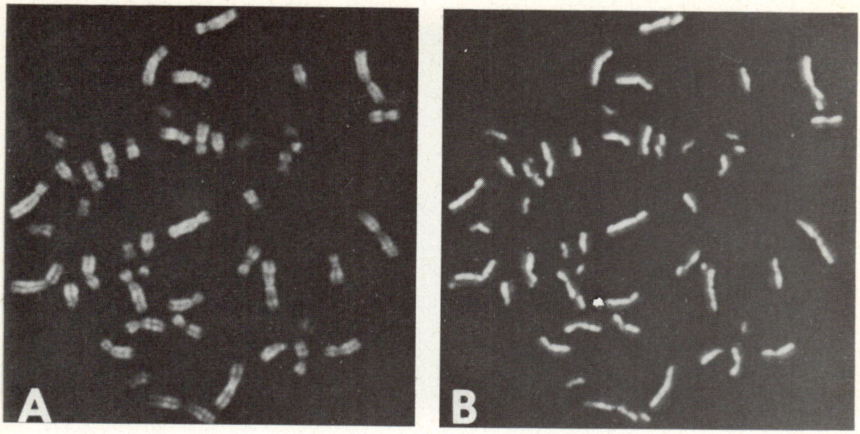

FIG. 12.—Quinacrine and 33258 Hoechst fluorescence of the same human cell grown two divisions in medium containing BrdU. The metaphase was stained first with quinacrine, photographed (A), destained, and then stained with 33258 Hoechst and rephotographed (B).

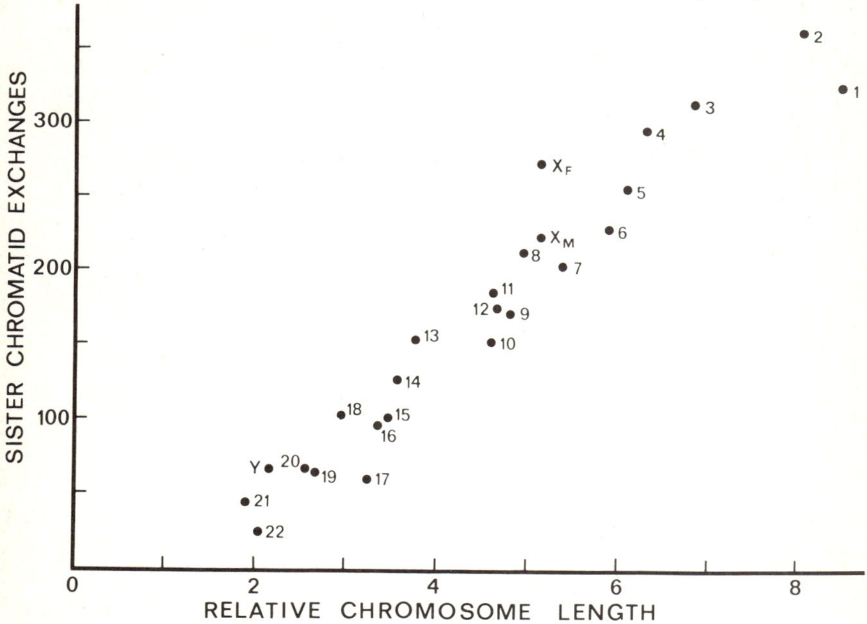

FIG. 13.—The dependence of sister chromatid exchange frequency on metaphase chromosome length. A total of 296 human lymphocyte metaphases (146 from three females, 150 from three males) were examined after the following treatment. Prior to harvesting the cells were grown two replication cycles in medium containing 0.01 or 0.02 mM BrdU, 6 μM U, and 0.4 μM FdU. Chromosomes were first identified by their quinacrine fluorescence patterns, and then the sister chromatid exchanges detected using 33258 Hoechst fluorescence. The total number of sister chromatid exchanges detected for each chromosome is plotted against the relative metaphase chromosome (Paris Conference, 1971). The chromosome identification number is given beside each point. The points for X and Y chromosome were normalized relative to the autosomes for the number of chromosomes examined. Data for male and female X chromosomes (X_M and X_F) are shown separately.

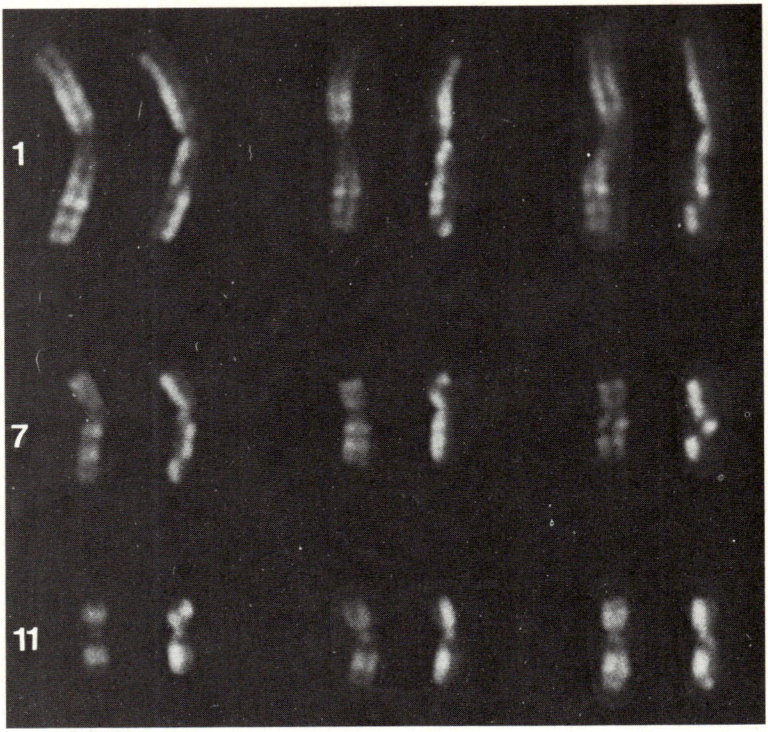

FIG. 14.—Sister chromatid exchanges in human chromosomes 1 (top row), 7 (middle row), and 11 (bottom row). Chromosomes were treated as described in caption to figure 13. The left picture of each chromosome shows quinacrine fluorescence and the right displays the 33258 Hoechst fluorescence (Latt, 1974*a*).

TABLE 1

*Relative fluorescence of complexes of 33258 Hoechst with different polynucleotides**

Polynucleotide	Fluorescence
Poly(dA-BrdU)	0.25
Poly(dA-IdU)	0.37
Poly(dA-dT)	1.00
Poly(dA)-poly(dT)	0.97
Calf thymus DNA	0.88
Poly(rA-dT)	0.71
Poly(rA-rU)	0.51

* Measurements were made with 5×10^{-7} M dye and 6×10^{-5} M polynucleotide in 0.01 M NaCl, 0.005 M Hepes, pH 7.0. Excitation was at 350 nm. Emission spectra were corrected for variation in instrument response with wavelength. The ratios listed are proportional to the relative areas of curves of fluorescence emission versus wavelength.

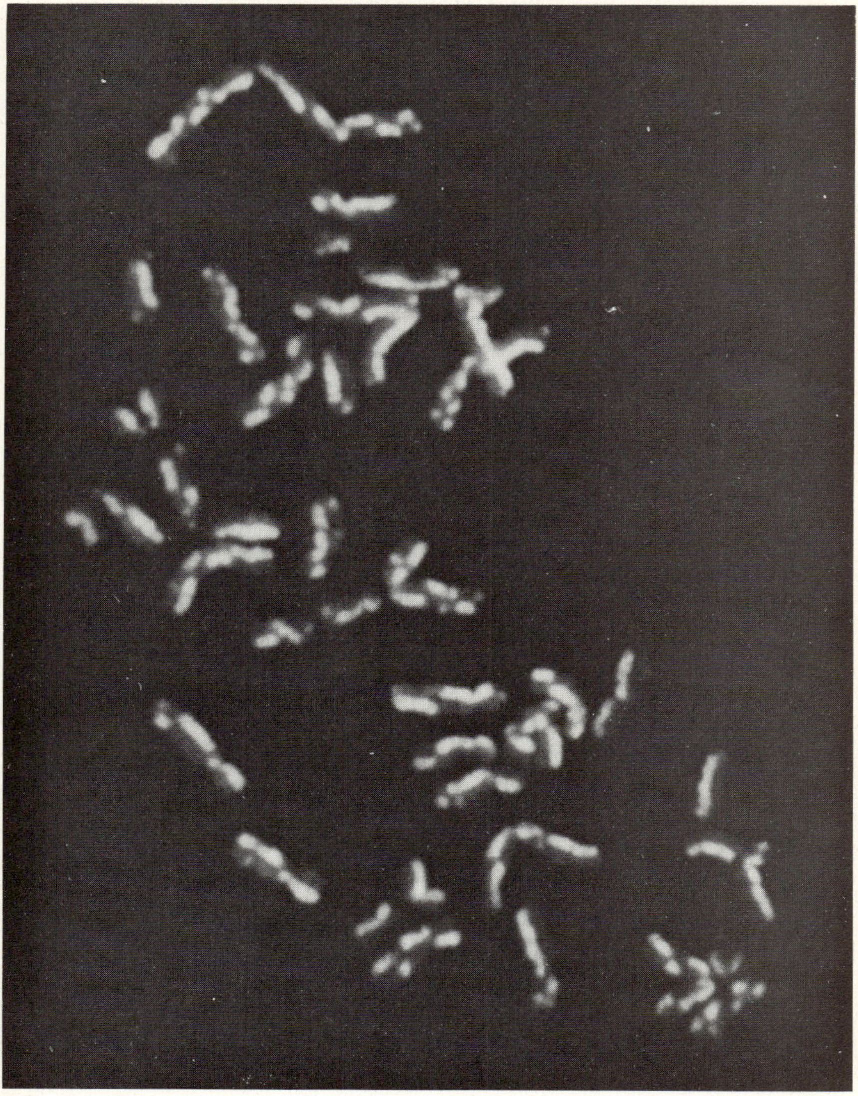

FIG. 15.—Induction of sister chromatid exchanges in human lymphocyte chromosomes by mitomycin C. Lymphocytes from the same individual as in figure 8 were cultured under the same conditions except for the addition of 0.03 μg/ml mitomycin C. An increase in the number of sister chromatid exchanges is apparent.

of these complexes differ by a factor of four. This result could occur if the quenching of dye fluorescence were heterogeneous, with the residual emission originating from totally unquenched molecules. Reduction in fluorescence efficiency without a comparable decrease in fluorescence lifetime could also occur if the quenching interaction were sufficiently strong to compete with dye excited state relaxation.

The fluorescence of two other bisbenzimidazole dyes, 33242 and 32021 Hoechst, is quenched by BrdU to a similar extent as that of 33258 Hoechst. Fluorescence of another bisbenzimidazole, 32030 Hoechst, under the same conditions, is quenched to a lesser degree. The fluorescence of all of these dyes is also suppressed by BrdU incorporation into cytological chromosome preparations, although these dyes offer no apparent advantage over 33258 Hoechst for this purpose. As might be expected from published phosphorescence measurements (Galley and Purkey, 1972), the fluorescence of both proflavine and acridine orange is quenched by BrdU, although to a lesser extent than that of 33258 Hoechst (table 2). Dutrillaux (1973) has used acridine orange to study the effects of terminal pulses of BrdU on chromosome fluorescence, obtaining patterns similar to those observed with 33258 Hoechst (fig. 5).

The fluorescence of 33258 Hoechst is also dependent on pH and solvent. At pH 4.1, in contrast to pH 7.0, there is relatively little difference in the fluorescence of complexes of 33258 Hoechst with poly(dA-BrdU) and poly(dA-dT). Similarly, glycerol, even at pH 7, decreases the quenching effect of BrdU in chromosome preparations and increases the apparent dye photostability. Thus, if slides are mounted in pH 4.1 buffer containing glycerol, fluorescence intensity is little affected by BrdU (Latt, 1974*e*). Upon changing the mounting medium to pH 7 buffer, BrdU quenching is now apparent (fig. 16). This effect is especially striking in chromo-

TABLE 2

*Effect of BrdU on dye fluorescence**

Dye	Fluorescence ratio poly(dA-BrdU)/ poly(dA-dT) complexes
33258 Hoechst	0.25
33342 Hoechst	0.27
32021 Hoechst	0.28
Proflavine	0.36
Acridine orange	0.44
Quinacrine	0.88
Daunomycin	1.00
Ethidium bromide	1.02

* Measurements were made in 0.01 M NaCl, 0.005 M Hepes, pH 7 at a polynucleotide concentration of approximately 6×10^{-5} M. Fluorescence ratios were determined from areas of corrected emission spectra except for the daunomycin and ethidium bromide complexes (for which relative fluorescence amplitudes were used). Phosphate/dye ratios were about 40 for the quinacrine and daunomycin complexes, 80 for the ethidium bromide and proflavine complexes, and more than 100 for the other complexes. Excitation wavelengths employed were 350 nm (33258, 32021, 33342 Hoechst), 440 nm (proflavine), 470 nm (acridine orange), 458 nm (quinacrine), 500 nm (daunomycin), and 520 nm (ethidium bromide).

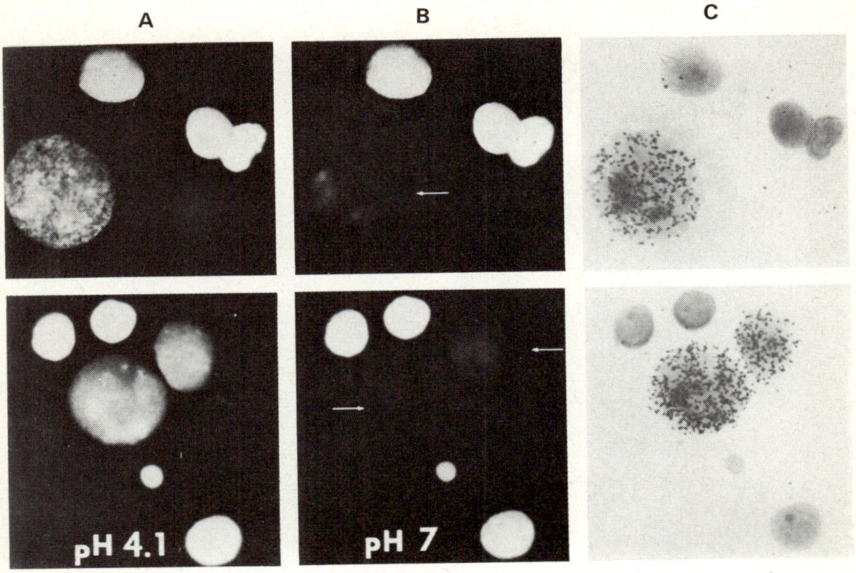

FIG. 16.—Detection of DNA synthesis in interphase nuclei using fluorescence microscopy. Slides were prepared from peripheral leukocytes grown 48 hr in medium containing BrdU as described. Photographs in each row are of the same field, but taken under different conditions. (A) Cells were stained with 33258 Hoechst and mounted in pH 4.1 McIlvaine's buffer and 90% glycerol for photography. (B) The slides were washed and mounted in pH 7 McIlvaine's buffer and the same field rephotographed. Nuclei with relatively decreased fluorescence at pH 7 are indicated by arrows. (C) The slides were then dipped in Kodak NTB-2 emulsion for autoradiography, developed after 14 days exposure, and stained with Giemsa. Nuclei which have incorporated [^{3}H) BrdU and exhibit numerous grains correspond to those indicated by arrows in (B) (Latt, 1974*e*).

somes from cells which had replicated twice in medium containing BrdU (fig. 17). The dependence of the quenching of 33258 Hoechst fluorescence on pH and mounting medium can be used to test other instances in which variations in 33258 Hoechst fluorescence are thought to be due to BrdU incorporation.

The distal part of the long arms of Y chromosome from cells which have replicated once in BrdU-containing medium exhibits unequal sister chromatid fluorescence when stained with 33258 Hoechst (fig. 18). This difference, which seems localized to the region of very bright quinacrine fluorescence, has been hypothesized to reflect an asymmetrical distribution of thymine between polynucleotide chains in this presumably adenine-thymine rich region (Latt et al., 1974). Such an observation in the centromeric regions of mouse chromosomes has been similarly interpreted in terms of the known difference in thymine content between the two chains of mouse satellite DNA (Flamm et al., 1967). The interchromatid fluorescence differences in human Y chromosomes are smaller than those in mouse centromere regions. However, in a chromosome consisting of two fused Y long arms, the bright regions are located contralaterally, as expected if the supposed basis for this effect were correct and if chromatid DNA were continuous through the centromere (fig. 19). Such fluorescence asymmetry is not observed if slides are mounted in pH 4.1 buffer containing glycerol, consistent with the interpretation described previously.

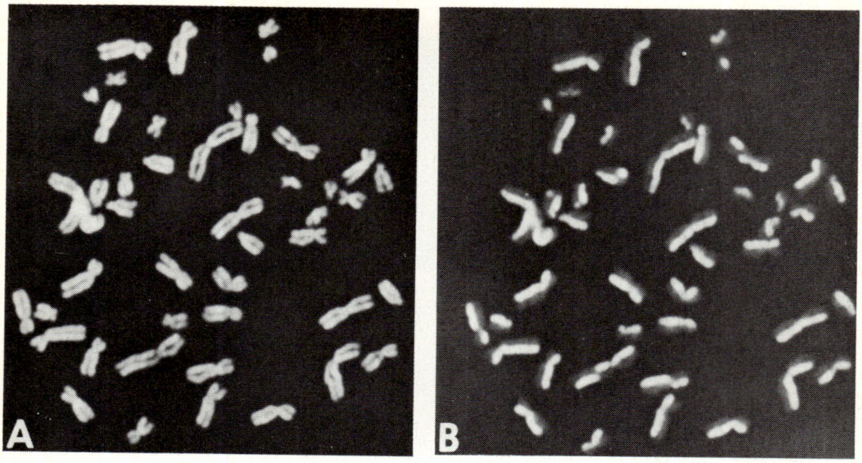

FIG. 17.—pH dependence of the suppression of 33258 Hoechst fluorescence of chromosomes after two cycles of BrdU incorporation. Lymphocytes from a normal female were grown for 73 hr in medium containing 0.02 mM BrdU. Slides were stained with 33258 Hoechst and first mounted in pH 4.1 McIlvaine's buffer and 90% glycerol, photographed (A), rinsed with water, remounted in pH 7.0 buffer, and rephotographed (B).

4. DISCUSSION

Detection of DNA synthesis by fluorescence microscopy should in many instances constitute a convenient alternative or adjunct to autoradiography. A single fluorescent photograph can often convey a visual impression of results apparent by autoradiography only after extensive statistical analysis. The fluorescent method in addition allows analysis of chromosome replication and sister chromatid exchanges at an effective resolution level comparable to that of the banding stains used to characterize chromosome structure. The early and late replication patterns themselves constitute an extremely useful means of chromosome identification. In addition, use of fluorescence to monitor DNA synthesis makes it possible to simultaneously employ tritium autoradiography for another purpose, e.g., to study chromosomal proteins in relation to DNA synthesis. However, absolute microfluorometric quantitation of DNA synthesis may in many instances be less convenient or precise than autoradiography. Finally, the present fluorescent method requires incorporation into chromosomal DNA of the base analogue BrdU, an agent known to have a toxic effect on cells (D. A. Miller et al., 1973; Djordjevic and Szybalski, 1960; Puck and Kao, 1967; Hsu and Somers, 1961; Chu, 1965; Rommelaere et al., 1974).

Analysis of replication kinetics provides a longitudinal differentiation of chromosomes based on selective incorporation of BrdU into a limited number of regions along a DNA polynucleotide chain. Regions fluorescing brightly with quinacrine often complete replication relatively late in the DNA synthesis period. In addition, the secondary constriction regions of chromosomes 1, 9 and 16 are late replicating, and the two X chromosomes, which exhibit essentially indistinguishable standard banding patterns, differ in their replication kinetics. Terminal thymidine or BrdU pulses of different durations alter the fluorescence of different late replicating

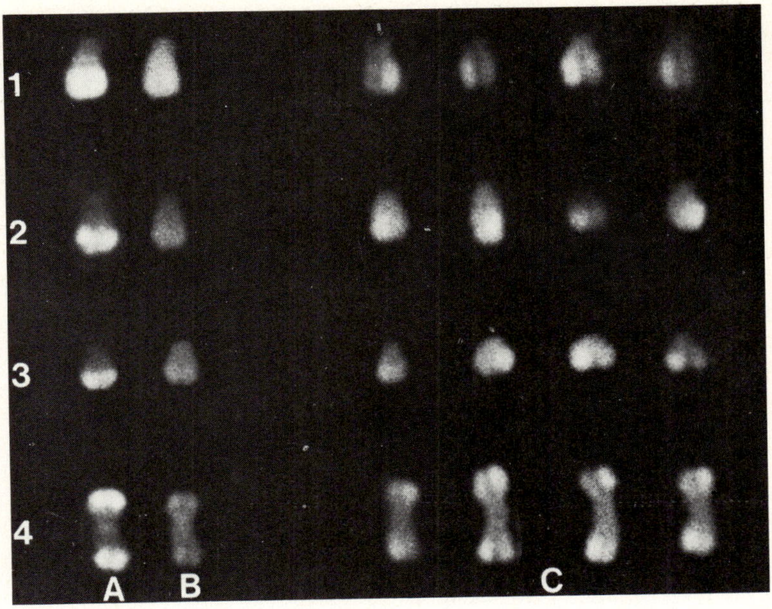

FIG. 18.—Quinacrine mustard and 33258 Hoechst fluorescence of human Y chromosomes. The Y chromosome in each row is from the same individual. The first three rows are from three normal males, but contain bright regions of different lengths. The chromosomes in the fourth row were obtained from a phenotypic female with Turner's syndrome possessing leukocytes with either a 45,XO or 46,X,Abn.Y chromosome complement. The abnormal Y chromosome shown may be a dicentric Y, an isochromosome for the long arm of Y, or a translocation between two Y chromosome long arms. Chromosomes in columns A and B were from cells grown in the absence of BrdU. Each pair of pictures was obtained on the same chromosome (stained with quinacrine mustard (column A)) or stained with 33258 Hoechst (column B) as detailed in the Methods section. The chromosomes in each row of column C are from four different cells of the same individual grown one replication cycle in medium containing BrdU and stained with 33258 Hoechst (Latt et al., 1974).

bands. This behavior provides a temporal coordinate for further discrimination of chromosome regions. Differentiation of homologous chromosomes by kinetic polymorphisms may be possible (Latt, 1974*a*). It is also conceivable that a pathological process might be reflected as a deviation in replication order. Precise determination of the extent to which fluorescent and autoradiographic methods for detecting DNA synthesis correlate will assist such applications.

Individual bands are sharply defined. Fluorescence contrast in this case is largely determined by replication kinetics, which vary sharply between regions, rather than by chemical composition, which appears to exhibit a more gradual variation. The path by which replication spreads throughout a given band has not previously been determined because of optical resolution limitations. However, results now obtained give the impression that the fluorescence of any particular band changes over a fairly narrow time interval. This suggests that there might exist regional factors that exert coordinate control over the timing of replication, perhaps at multiple sites in the vicinity of a band.

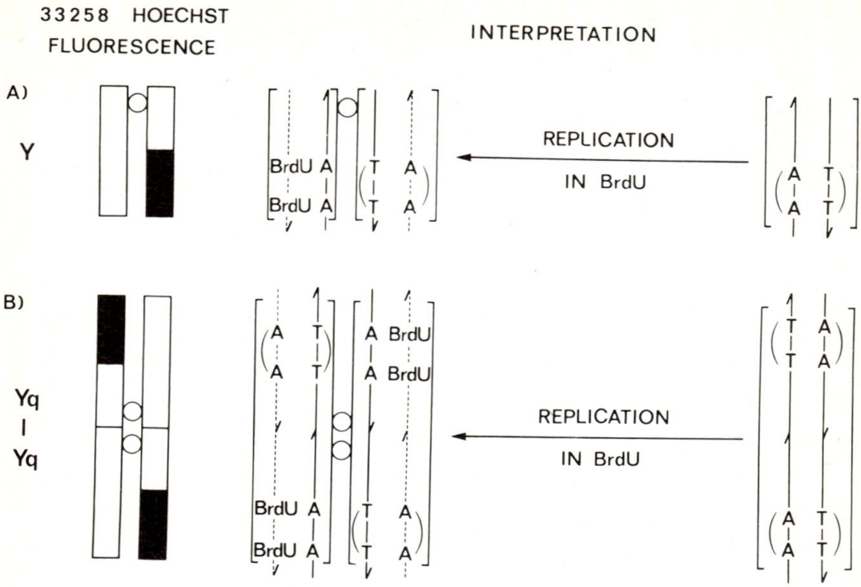

FIG. 19.—Diagrammatic representation of chromatid composition and 33258 Hoechst fluorescence in the polymorphic regions of the long arm of the human Y chromosome after one replication in medium containing BrdU. Fluorescence patterns are shown on the left. Areas of bright fluorescence are indicated in black. On the right is shown the interpretation in terms of BrdU incorporation. Diagrams are drawn for a normal Y chromosome (top row) and an abnormal Y chromosome containing two long arms (bottom row).

It should now be possible to examine the kinetics of replication of "active" and "inactive" (Lyon, 1972) human X chromosomes at high resolution. Since replication kinetics of X chromosomes have been correlated with genetic activity, analysis of these kinetics may provide a means of exploring the basis of X chromosome inactivation. Results thus far obtained show differences between the fluorescence of the two female X chromosomes after a terminal pulse of thymidine (fig. 2). As expected, the early replicating female X chromosome exhibits a pattern virtually indistinguishable from that of the single male X chromosome. A particularly useful application of the BudR fluorochrome techniques should be the study of X chromosome abnormalities, particularly X-autosome translocations. Any localized alterations in replication kinetics near translocation points (essentially "position effects") will be of special interest. Experiments of Dutrillaux (this volume), using acridine orange and a terminal pulse of BrdU, have already indicated that such alterations might exist. Comparison of these fluorescence patterns with those employing a terminal thymidine pulse might prove especially enlightening. As indicated by Dutrillaux, any discrepancies between fluorescent and autoradiographic patterns might also provide an indication of the effect of BrdU on protein-DNA interactions in chromosomes.

Lateral differentiation of metaphase chromosomes can be based on the number of DNA chains substituted with BrdU in sister chromatids. This is accomplished by one cycle of BrdU incorporation followed by a second replication during which the present of the base analogue is optional. Determination of the replication cycle at which sister chromatid exchanges occurred can be accomplished either in endoreduplicated chromosomes (fig. 9) or in chromosomes from cells which had replicated three cycles in medium containing a marginal BrdU concentration (fig. 11B).

Sister chromatid exchanges are unevenly distributed along individual chromosomes, although the average number of exchanges per chromosome generally correlates with chromosome length (fig. 13). The majority of exchanges occur in interband regions or very near band-interband junctions. "Hot spots" which are sites of especially high exchange frequencies exist. These show a remarkable correlation with zones of pale Feulgen staining following treatment of cytological chromosome preparations with high pH solutions (Rodman and Tahiliani, 1973; Rodman, 1974). Nonuniformity in the sister chromatid exchange distribution may reflect underlying variations in chromosome structure.

It is especially intriguing to consider the implication of the distribution of sister chromatid exchanges regarding other processes involving breakage and repair of DNA. The distribution of radiation or mitomycin-C induced chromosome breaks resembles that of the exchanges in its band-interband orientation (Caspersson et al., 1972*b*; Seabright, 1973; Holmberg and Honassum, 1973). Many reciprocal translocations reported in the literature occur in interband regions or near band-interband junctions (Francke, 1972; Jacobs et al., 1974), often at sites that are "hot spots" for sister chromatid exchanges. However, translocations are subject to additional selective pressures, and many exceptions to this correlation exist. In particular, the high frequency of Robertsonian translocations is not accompanied by a comparable concentration of sister chromatid exchanges in the centromeric regions of acrocentric chromosomes.

Genetic recombination, at least superficially, would appear to involve breakage and rejoining steps similar to those of sister chromatid exchange. It will be interesting if the distribution of sister chromatid exchanges is paralleled by the susceptibility of chromosome regions to recombination. Recombination "hot spots" would distort the colinearity between recombination and physical genetic maps. The preferential localization of exchanges outside of the bands themselves is reminiscent of the preferential occurrence of recombination outside of heterochromatin in some species (Brown, 1966), since quinacrine positive bands have been postulated to correlate with heterochromatin (Comings, 1972; Caspersson et al. 1970). Chemical features such as the distribution of repeated DNA sequences and histones might similarly affect the distribution of sister chromatid exchanges.

The influence of BrdU on replication kinetics and sister chromatid exchanges (see, for example, D. A. Miller et al., 1973) is unavoidable, but it does not appear to induce unacceptable distortion in these processes. High concentrations of BrdU are toxic to cells, retarding replication. However, at least in one system, the relative order of replication kinetics was not altered by BrdU (Taylor et al., 1973). Moreover, replication sequences obtained using a terminal pulse of thymidine are generally consistent with those obtained with a terminal pulse of BrdU. The frequency of sister chromatid exchanges increases with BrdU incorporation, but the detailed dependence is most consistent with a small BrdU-induced increase superimposed upon a baseline frequency (Latt, 1974*d*). The requirements for approximately 0.006 mM or more BrdU in order to accurately detect exchanges precludes resolving the possibility that this baseline frequency is also due to BrdU, acting in a second mode with a very low concentration threshold.

Whatever the influence of BrdU on sister chromatid exchanges, these exchanges are very sensitive indicators of the repair of chromosome damage by a number of agents (Kato, 1974*a*). Under "baseline" conditions, sister chromatid exchanges are more than 200 times as frequent as chromosome or chromatid breaks. If sister chromatid exchanges are viewed as healed breaks, this suggests that most of the background damage to human chromosomes is repaired. Analyses of chromosome damage solely in terms of breaks or gross rearrangements might thus detect only the "tip of the iceberg" of actual damage. The average number of exchanges per cell appears to vary with the type of cell, perhaps reflecting differences in either the induction of breaks or in the ability to repair chromosomes. Addition of *nanogram* per ml concentrations of bifunctional alkylating agents to lymphocyte cultures produces a marked increase in the sister chromatid exchange frequency under conditions causing very few breaks (Latt, 1974*d*). Previous studies of chromosome breakage with these agents have employed much higher mitomycin C concentrations (Cohen and Shaw, 1964; Nowell, 1964; German and LaRock, 1969). A similar increase in sister chromatid exchanges in cells exposed to mitomycin C and related agents has been observed using autoradiography (Kato, 1974*a*). This latter technique, however, is not able to resolve closely spaced exchanges which appear to be characteristic in mitomycin C treated cells.

Current experimentation is directed at investigating the influence of other agents on the sister chromatid exchange frequency. Such an examination may constitute a very sensitive biological test system for agents thought to induce genetic damage. Differences in the relative number of exchanges and breaks induced by various agents should provide insight into the processes by which different types of damage are repaired. For example, the results with mitomycin C are consistent with a previously hypothesized recombinational repair mechanism for damage due to bifunctional agents (Howard-Flanders and Lin, 1973; Cole, 1973).

Following the demonstration of sister chromatid exchanges with 33258 Hoechst, two new methods employing BrdU have been developed, both of which offer advantages regarding photomicrography. Acridine orange staining can also differentiate sister chromatids after two replication cycles in BrdU (see p. 395). The fluorescence of these chromosomes exhibits greater photostability than obtained with 33258 Hoechst, and differences in fluorescence color as well as intensity have been observed. Perry and Wolf (1974) have exposed chromosomes to light after two rounds of BrdU incorporation and staining with 33258 Hoechst. The slides are subsequently incubated in warm saline solution and then stained with Giemsa, resulting in a permanent preparation in which darkly staining chromatids correspond to those fluorescing brightly with 33258 Hoechst. This method has already been used (German, this volume) to demonstrate an increase of sister chromatid exchanges in Bloom's syndrome, a condition associated with chromosome instability. It will be useful if conditions are also found which allow Giemsa to be used for replication kinetics studies.

A special case of lateral differentiation of chromosomes using 33258 Hoechst fluorescence appears to involve regions containing DNA with an uneven distribution of thymine between complementary polynucleotide chains. This was first demonstrated in the centromeric regions of mouse chromosomes (Lin et al., 1974), which in a sense constitute a "model system" since the difference in thymine content between the two chains of mouse satellite DNA contained in these regions has been documented chemically (Flamm et al., 1967). One would thus infer a similar situation in the polymorphic quinacrine bright region of the long arm of the human Y chromosome (fig. 18). It is interesting that an A-T rich species of satellite DNA, which hybridizes *in situ* to the Y chromosome, appears to possess a small difference in thymine content between polynucleotide chains (K. Jones, personal communication). In addition to providing a possible means of identifying DNA chains containing thymine-rich regions, the ability to follow a particular polynucleotide chain has yielded cytological evidence supporting the continuity of DNA through the centromeres of mouse and human chromosomes (Lin et al., 1974; Latt et al., 1974). Evidence for such continuity has previously been obtained from viscoelastic relaxation measurements in *Drosophila* (Kavenoff and Zimm, 1973).

While the present technique was developed after a search for heavy atom-dependent fluorescence quenching, the means by which BrdU incorporation suppresses the fluorescence of nearby 33258 Hoechst molecules is still under investigation. The suppressed fluorescence of the dye when complexed with poly(dA-IdU) is consistent with a heavy atom effect. Similarly, the additive nature of BrdU on fluorescence quenching, whether it is incorporated into one or two polynucleotide chains (Latt, 1974*d*), supports a short range interaction such as might be expected from a heavy atom. The absence of quenching of ethidium bromide or quinacrine fluorescence is most simply explained in terms of dye binding away from the major groove of the DNA helix into which the bromine atom projects. Alternatively, this insensitivity to BrdU might reflect differences in dye electronic structure. Proflavine and acridine orange, dyes previously shown to undergo phosphorescence changes when bound to poly(dA-BrdU) (Galley and Purkey, 1972) compatible with a heavy atom effect, also experience a reduction in fluorescence intensity when bound to this polymer. An influence of proteins on chromosome fluorescence must also be considered, especially since BrdU may alter DNA-protein interactions (Palmer, 1970; Zakharov and Egolina, 1972; Baranovskaya et al., 1972).

33258 Hoechst fluorescence exhibits little sensitivity to BrdU at low pH or in glycerol. Independent of its basis, this observation is of practical use for estimating baseline variations in 33258 Hoechst fluorescence which are not due to BrdU. The results with chromosomes from cells which have replicated twice in medium containing BrdU (fig. 17) rule against chromosomal proteins as being the major determinants of 33258 Hoechst fluorescence patterns.

Finally, it should be emphasized that use of BrdU and 33258 Hoechst fluorescence to follow DNA synthesis is not restricted to microscopical investigations. The rapidity of fluorescence measurement compared with methods employing radioactivity should be useful in following DNA synthesis kinetics in *in-vitro* systems. A further wide area of potential use is flow fluorometry (Hulett et al, 1969; van Dilla et al., 1969), in which fluorescence changes associated with DNA synthesis might be used as the basis for sorting cells or chromosomes. Combination of present methodology with spectroscopic probes sensitive to other aspects of DNA or protein components may similarly serve to investigate different features of chromosome structure and function.

5. SUMMARY

1. Fluorescence of the bis-benzimidazole dye 33258 Hoechst, when complexed with DNA, is partially quenched by substitution of 5-bromodeoxyuridine for thymidine. DNA synthesis in cytological chromosome preparations can thereby be detected by fluorescence microscopy.

2. The fluorescence of regions synthesizing DNA during a particular interval can be highlighted by the appropriate administration of 5-bromodeoxyuridine to cultured cells. For example, segments partitioned by the longitudinal banding patterns of metaphase chromosomes can be further differentiated according to their replication kinetics.

3. Incorporation of 5-bromodeoxyuridine for one replication cycle permits detection of chromosome regions containing DNA with an asymmetric distribution of thymine between polynucleotide chains.

4. Replication of cells for two cycles in BrdU reveals lateral differentiation between sister chromatids, permitting identification of sister chromatid exchanges. The distribution of exchanges relative to quinacrine banding patterns is uneven, resembling that of radiation-induced breaks in being preferentially located either in interband regions or very near band-interband junctions. Sister chromatid exchanges, analyzed by fluorescence microscopy, are much more frequent than breaks and appear to be very sensitive indicators of chromosome damage by exogenous agents.

5. The suppression of 33258 Hoechst fluorescence by 5-bromodeoxyuridine should also be useful for *in vitro* experimentation with isolated cells and subcellular components.

Acknowledgements. The expert technical assistance of Miss Lois Juergens and the skillful photography of Mr. Dixon Yun and Mr. Gary Gladstein are greatly appreciated. Portions of this research were supported by N.I.H. Grants HD 06276 and GM 21121, and grants from the National Foundation March of Dimes (1–353) and the American Cancer Society (National (VC-144) and Massachusetts Divisions).

6. REFERENCES

Baranovskaya, L. T., Zakharov, A. F., Dutrillaux, B., Carpentier, S., Prieur, M., and Lejeune, J. 1972. Differentiation des chromosomes X par les methodes de despiralisation au 5 bromodeuxyuridine et de denaturation thermiaue menagée. *Ann. Génét., 15,* 271–274.

Breg, W. R., Allderdice, P. N., Miller, D. A., and Miller, O. J. 1972. Quinacrine fluorescence patterns and terminal DNA labelling of human C group chromosomes. *Nat. New Biol., 236,* 76–78.

Brown, S. W. 1966. Heterochromatin. *Science (Wash. D.C.), 151,* 417–425.

Calderon, D., and Schnedl, W. 1973. A comparison between quinacrine fluorescence banding and 3H-thymidine incorporation patterns in human chromosomes. *Humangenetik, 18,* 63–70.

Caspersson, T., Farber, S. Foley, G. E., Kudynowski, J., Modest, E. J., Simonsson, E., Wagh, U., and Zech, L. 1968. Chemical differentiation along metaphase chromosomes. *Exp. Cell Res., 49,* 219–222.

Caspersson, T., Zech, L., Johansson, C., Lindsten, J., and Hulten, M. 1970. Fluorescent staining of heteropycnotic chromosome regions in human interphase nuclei. *Exp. Cell. Res., 61,* 472–474.

CASPERSSON, T., LINDSTEN, J., LOMAKKA, G., MOLLER, A., and ZECH, L. 1972*a*. The use of fluorescence techniques for the recognition of mammalian chromosomes and chromosome regions. *Int. Rev. Exp. Pathol., 11,* 1–72.

CASPERSSON, T., HAGLUND, O., LINDELL, B., and ZECH, L. 1972*b*. Radiation-induced non-random chromosome breakage. *Exp. Cell Res., 75,* 541–543.

CHEN, R. 1967. Practical aspects of the calibration and use of the Aminco-Bowman spectrophotofluorometer. *Anal. Biochem., 20,* 339–357.

CHEN, R. 1973. Measurements of absolute values in biochemical fluorescence spectroscopy. *U.S. Natl. Bur. Stand.* (Special Publ.), *378,* 183–196.

CHU, E. H. Y. 1965. Effects of ultraviolet radiation on mammalian cells. I. Induction of chromosome aberrations. *Mutat. Res., 2,* 75–94.

COHEN, M. M., and SHAW, M. W. 1964. Effects of mitomycin C on human chromosomes. *J. Cell Biol., 23,* 386–395.

COLE, R. S. 1973. Repair of DNA containing interstrand crosslines in Escherichia coli: sequential excision and recombination. *Proc. Natl. Acad. Sci. U.S.A., 70,* 1064–1068.

COMINGS, D. E. 1972. The structure and function of chromatin. *Adv. Hum. Genet., 3,* 237–431.

DJORDJEVIC, B., and SZYBALSKI, W. 1960. Genetics of human cell lines. III. Incorporation of 5-bromo and 5-iododeoxyuridine into the deoxyribonucleic acid of human cells and its effect on radiation sensitivity. *J. Exp. Med., 112,* 509–531.

DUTRILLAUX, B. 1973. New techniques in the study of human chromosomes. *Birth Defects International Congress Series No. 310* (ISBN 90 219 0211 7) (A. G. MOTULSKY and W. LENTZ, eds.). Exerpta Medica, Amsterdam.

ELLISON, J. R., and BARR, H. J. 1972. Quinacrine fluorescence of specific chromosome regions. *Chromosoma (Berl.), 36,* 375–390.

FLAMM, W. G., MCCALLUM, M., and WALKER, P. M. B. 1967. The isolation of complementary strands from a mouse DNA fraction. *Proc. Natl. Acad. Sci. U.S.A., 57,* 1729–1734.

FRANCKE, U. 1972. Characterization of unusual translocations. *Am. J. Hum. Genet., 24,* 189–213.

GALLEY, W. C., and PURKEY, R. M. 1972. Spin-orbital probes of bimolecular structure. A model DNA-acridine system. *Proc. Natl. Acad. Sci. U.S.A., 69,* 2198–2202.

GANNER, E., and EVANS, H. J. 1971. The relationships between patterns of DNA replication and of quinacrine fluorescence in the human chromosome complement. *Chromosoma (Berl.), 35,* 326–341.

GERMAN, J., and LA ROCK, J. 1969. Chromosomal effects of mitomycin; a potential recombinogen in mammalian cell genetics. *Tex. Rep. Biol. Med., 27,* 409–418.

GOTTESFELD, J. M., BONNER, J., RADDA, G. K., and WALKER, I. O. 1974. Biophysical studies on the mechanism of quinacrine staining of chromosomes. *Biochemistry, 13,* 2937–2945.

HERCULES, D. M. (Ed.). 1966. *Fluorescence and Phosphorescence Analysis,* pp. 2–40. Interscience, New York.

HERREROS, B., and GIANNELLI, F. 1967. Spatial distribution of old and new chromatid subunits and frequency of chromatid exchanges in induced human lymphocyte endoreduplication. *Nature (Lond.), 216,* 286–288.

HILWIG, I., and GROPP, A. 1972. Staining of constitutive heterochromatin in mammalian chromosomes with a new fluorochrome. *Exp. Cell Res., 75,* 122–126.

HOLMBERG, M., and JONASSON, J. 1973. Preferential location of X-ray induced chromosome breakage in the R-bands of human chromosomes. *Hereditas,74,* 57–68.

HOWARD-FLANDERS, P., and LIN, P. F. 1973. Genetic recombination induced by DNA cross-links in repressed phage. *Genetics (Suppl.), 73,* 85–90.

HSU, T. C. 1973. Longitudinal differentiation of chromosomes. *Ann. Rev. Genet., 7,* 153–176.

HSU, T. C., and SOMERS, C. E. 1961. Effect of 5-bromodeoxyuridine on mammalian chromosomes. *Proc. Natl. Acad. Sci. U.S.A., 47,* 396–403.

HULETT, H. R., BONNER, N. A., BARRETT, J., and HERZENBERG, L. A. 1969. Cell sorting: automated separation of mammalian cells as a function of intracellular fluorescence. *Science (Wash. D.C.), 166*, 747–749.

IYER, V. N., and SZYBALSKI, N. 1963. A molecular mechanism of mitomycin C action: linking of complementary DNA strands. *Proc. Natl. Acad. Sci. U.S.A., 50*, 355–362.

JACOBS, P. A., BUCKTON, K. E., CUNNINGHAM, C., and NEWTON, M. 1974. An analysis of the break points of structural rearrangements in Man. *J. Med. Genet., 11*, 50–64.

KABACK, M. M., SAKSELA, E., and MELLMAN, W. S. 1963. The effect of 5-bromodeoxyuridine on human chromosomes. *Exp. Cell. Res., 34*, 182–186.

KATO, H. 1974*a*. Induction of sister chromatid exchanges by chemical mutagens and its possible relevance to DNA repair. *Exp. Cell Res., 85*, 239–247.

KATO, H. 1974*b*. Spontaneous sister chromatid exchanges detected by a BudR-labelling method. *Nature, 251*, 70–72.

KAVENOFF, R., and ZIMM, B. 1973. Chromosome sized DNA molecules from *Drosophila*. *Chromosoma (Berl.), 41*, 1–27.

KNIGHT, L. A., and LUZZATTI, L. 1973. Replication pattern of the X and Y chromosomes in partially synchronized human lymphocyte cultures. *Chromosoma (Berl.), 40*, 153–166.

LATT, S. A. 1973. Microfluorometric detection of deoxyribonucleic acid replication in human metaphase chromosomes. *Proc. Natl. Acad. Sci. U.S.A., 70*, 3395–3399.

LATT, S. A. 1974*a*. Microfluorometric analysis of DNA replication and sister chromatid exchanges in human chromosomes. *J. Histochem. Cytochem., 22*, 478–491.

LATT, S. A. 1974*b*. Microfluorometric analysis of DNA replication in human X chromosomes. *Exp. Cell Res., 86*, 412–415.

LATT, S. A. 1974*c*. Localization of sister chromatid exchanges in human chromosomes. *Science (Wash. D.C.), 185*, 74–76.

LATT, S. A. 1974*d*. Sister chromatid exchanges, indices of human chromosome damage and repair: detection by fluorescence and induction by mitomycin C. *Proc. Natl. Acad. Sci. U.S.A., 71*, 3162–3166.

LATT, S. A. 1974*e*. Detection of DNA synthesis in interphase nuclei by fluorescence microscopy. *J. Cell. Biol., 62*, 546–550.

LATT, S. A., DAVIDSON, R. L., LIN, M. S., and GERALD, P. S. Lateral asymmetry in the fluorescence of human Y chromosomes stained with 33258 Hoechst. *Exp. Cell. Res.* (in press).

LIN, M. S., LATT, S. A., and DAVIDSON, R. L. 1974. Microfluorometric detection of asymmetry in the centromeric region of mouse chromosomes. *Exp. Cell Res., 86*, 392–395.

LIPSETT, M. N., and WEISSBACH, H. 1968. The site of alkylation of nucleic acids by mitomycin C. *Biochemistry, 4*, 206–211.

LOEWE, H., and URBANIETZ, J. 1974. Basisch substitutiente 2,6-Bis-Benzimidazol-derivate, eine neue chemotherapeutisch aktive Körperklasse. *Arzneim.-Forsch., 24*, 1927–1933.

LUBS, H. A., MCKENZIE, J., PATIL, S. R., and MERRICK, S. 1973. New staining methods for chromosomes. In *Methods in Cell Biology* (D. M. PRESCOTT, ed.), Vol. VI, pp. 345–380. Academic Press, New York.

LYON, M. F. 1972. X chromosome inactivation and developmental patterns in mammals. *Biol. Rev. (Camb.), 47*, 1–35.

MILLER, D. A., ALLDERDICE, P. W., MILLER, O. J., and BREG, W. R. 1971. Quinacrine fluorescence patterns of human D group chromosomes. *Nature (Lond.), 232*, 24–27.

MILLER, D. A., DEWEY, W. C., and MILLER, H. H. 1973. X-ray induced delay in the Chinese-hamster cell-cycle: Dependence on phase BrdU damage irratiated under different culturing conditions, BudR incorporation, and hypertonic treatment. *Int. J. Radiat. Biol., 23*, 591–602.

MILLER, O. J., MILLER, D. A., and WARBURTON, D. 1973. Application of new staining techniques to the study of human chromosomes. *Prog. Med. Genet., 9*, 1–47.

NOWELL, P. C. 1964. Mitotic inhibition and chromosome damage by mitomycin in human leukocyte cultures. *Exp. Cell Res., 33*, 445–449.

Orgel, L. E. 1954. Chargetransfer spectra and some related phenomena, *Q. Rev. Chem. Soc. Lond., 8,* 422–450.

Pachmann, U., and Rigler, R. 1972. Quantum yield of acridines interacting with DNA of defined base sequences. *Exp. Cell Res., 72,* 602–608.

Palmer, C. G. 1970. 5-Bromodeoxyuridine-induced constrictions in human chromosomes *Can. J. Genet. Cytol., 12,* 816–830.

Pardue, M. L., and Gall, J. G. 1970. Chromosomal localization of mouse satellite DNA. *Science (Wash. D.C.), 168,* 1356–1358.

Paris Conference. 1971. *Standardization in Human Cytogenetics.* Birth Defects, Original Article Series, 8:7 (1972). The National Foundation, New York.

Perry, P., and Wolf, S. 1974. *Nature (Lond.), 251,* 156–158.

Petersen, A. J. 1964. DNA synthesis and chromosomal asynchrony. *J. Cell Biol., 23,* 651–654.

Prescott, D. M. 1970. The structure and replication of eukaryotic chromosomes. *Adv. Cell Biol., 1,* 57–117.

Priest, J. H., Heady, J. E., and Priest, R. E. 1967*a*. Delayed onset of replication of human X chromosome. *J. Cell. Biol., 35,* 483–487.

Priest, J. H., Heady, J. E., and Priest, R. E. 1967*b*. Synchronization of human diploid cells by fluorodeoxyuridine. The first ten minutes of synthesis in female cells. *J. Natl. Cancer Inst., 38,* 61–67.

Puck, T. T., and Kao, F. T. 1967. Genetics of somatic mammalian cells. V. Treatment with 5-bromodeoxyuridine and visible light for isolation of nutritionally deficient mutants. *Proc. Natl. Acad. Sci. U.S.A., 58,* 1227–1234.

Rodman, T. C. 1974. Human chromosome banding by Feulgen stain aids in localizing classes of chromatin. *Science (Wash. D.C.), 184,* 171–173.

Rodman, T. C., and Tahiliani, S. 1973. The Feulgen banded karyotype of the mouse: analysis of the mechanism of banding. *Chromosoma (Berl.), 42,* 37–56.

Rommelaere, J., Cornelis, J. J., Miller-Faures, A., and Erreva, M. 1974. The influence of 5-bromodeoxyuridine on DNA repair in Chinese hamster cells exposed to ultraviolet radiation. *Biochim. Biophys. Acta, 340,* 388–399.

Schwarzacher, H. G., and Schnedl, W. 1966. Position of labelled chromatids in diplochromosomes of endo-reduplicated cells after uptake of tritiated thymidine. *Nature (Lond.), 209,* 107–108.

Seabright, M. 1973. High resolution studies on the pattern of induced exchanges in the human karyotype. *Chromosoma (Berl.), 40,* 333–346.

Sumner, A. T., and Evans, H. J. 1973. Mechanisms involved in the banding of chromosomes with quinacrine and Giemsa. II. The interation of dyes with chromosomal components. *Exp. Cell Res., 81,* 223–236.

Takagi, N., and Sandberg, A. A. 1968. Chronology and pattern of human chromosomes replication. VIII. Behavior of the X and Y in early S sphase. *Cytogenetics (Basel), 7,* 135–143.

Taylor, J. H., Woods, R. S., and Hughes, W. L. 1957. The organization and duplication of chromosomes as revealed by autoradiographic studies using tritium-labelled thymidine. *Proc. Natl. Acad. Sci. U.S.A., 43,* 122–127.

Taylor, J. H., Adams, A. G., and Kurek, M. P. 1973. Replication of DNA in mammalian chromosomes. II. Kinetics of H^3-thymidine incorporation and the isolation and partial characterization of labelled subunits at the growing point. *Chromosoma (Berl.), 41,* 361–384.

Van Dilla, M. A., Trujillo, T. T., Mullaney, P. F., and Coulter, J. R. 1969. Cell microfluorométry: a method for rapid fluorescence measurement. *Science (Wash. D.C.), 163,* 1213–1214.

Weisblum, B. 1973. Why centric regions of quinacrine-treated mouse chromosomes show diminished fluorescence. *Nature (Lond.), 246,* 150–151.

WEISBLUM, B., and DE HASETH, P. L. 1972. Quinacrine, a chromosome stain specific for deoxyadenylate-deoxythymidylate-rich regions in DNA. *Proc. Natl. Acad. Sci. U.S.A.*, *69*, 629–632.

YGUERABIDE, J. 1972. *Meth. Enz.*, *26*, (Part C) (C. H. W. HIRS and S. N. TIMASHEFF, eds.), pp. 498–578. Academic Press, New York.

YUNIS, J. J., and YASMINEH, W. G. 1971. Heterochromatin satellite DNA and cell function. *Science (Wash. D. C.)*, *174*, 1200–1209.

ZAKHAROV, A. F., and EGOLINA, N. A. 1972. Differential spiralization along mammalian mitotic chromosomes. I. BUdr-revealed differentiation in Chinese hamster chromosomes. *Chromosoma (Berl.)*, *38*, 341–365.

ZAKHAROV, A. F., BARONOVSKAYA, L. I., IBRAIMOV, A. I., BENJUSCH, U. A., DEMINTESEVA, V. S., and OBLAPENKO, N. G. 1974. Differential spiralization along mammalian mitotic chromosomes. *Chromosoma (Berl.)*, *44*, 343–359.

ZECH, L. 1969. Investigation of metaphase chromosomes with DNA binding fluorochromes. *Exp. Cell Res.*, *58*, 463.

STUDY OF HUMAN X CHROMOSOMES WITH THE 5-BrdU-ACRIDINE ORANGE TECHNIQUE. APPLICATION TO X CHROMOSOME PATHOLOGY

BERNARD DUTRILLAUX*

Institut de Progenèse (Pr. J. Lejeune), 15 rue de l'Ecole de Médicine, 75006 Paris, France

1. INTRODUCTION

The major application of autoradiography to human cytogenetics has been the recognition of the late replicating X chromosome. Although the results were generally clear they did not permit a detailed analysis of the inactivation pattern in cases of complex structural rearrangements.

Zakharov et al. (1971) showed that treatment of cultured cells with 5-BrdU (5-bromodeoxyuridine) induces segmentation of some chromosomes, and especially of the X chromosome. A study of abnormal cases (Baranovskaya et al., 1972), indicated that this technique was a very reliable method of analysis when abnormalities were present.

In 1973, we improved the technique by adding acridine orange staining (Dutrillaux et al., 1973) and began a systematic analysis of X anomalies.

Up until the present ime, we have examined:

3 cases of isochromosome X
1 case of deletion of the long arm
1 case of deletion of the short arm
6 cases of X-autosome translocations
5 cases of X-X translocation.

These data, although still inadequate, enable us to try to partially answer the following questions:

Is there a topologic correlation between the late labeling segments after autoradiography and the segmentation induced by the 5-BrdU treatment?

For the X chromosomes, is there a correlation between inactivation, Barr body formation and 5-BrdU induced uncoiling?

Is there a regular pattern of segmentation induced by the 5-BrdU treatment, in late and early replicating X-chromosomes?

Is the segmentation, which is presumably associated with late DNA replication, modified in structurally abnormal X chromosomes?

Is the replication of the X chromosome modified in cases of X-autosome translocation and of X-X translocation?

---

* Technical collaboration: Martine Lombard and Anne Marie Fosse.

2. MATERIALS AND METHODS

1) *BrdU treatment*

The incorporation of 5-BrdU is carried out during the last hours before harvesting. For recognition of the late replicating X, the correct duration of treatment is between 4 and 8 hours. The final concentration of 5-BrdU is 200 μg/ml (Zakharov et al., 1971).

2) *Acridine orange staining*

Stock solution: 100 mg of acridine orange in 100 ml of distilled water. This solution remains stable for several months.

Staining solution: 2.5 ml of stock solution in approximately 50 ml of Sorensen's buffer, pH 6.7. This solution must be replaced every week.

Old slides must be hydrated in alcohol baths of decreasing concentration (90, 70, 50 %) before staining. Good results can be obtained with one-year-old slides. Fresh slides may be directly stained for a period of 20 min. Proper rinsing is a very important part of the procedure. If insufficiently rinsed, the slides will be too orange, whereas if excessively rinsed, the slides will be too green. A short rinsing of 4–5 sec in tap water, followed by another rinse of 4–5 sec in Sorensen's buffer should give good staining. Two or three drops of the same buffer are dropped onto the slides and a coverslip gently applied.

The wet preparations are examined with a U.V. light microscope fitted with a Zeiss B.G. 38 excitor filter or an overvolted ordinary white light microscope fitted with a Schoit filter K.P. 500 and dark field illumination (Couturier et al., 1973, Dutrillaux et al., 1973).

The same staining procedure may be used in fibroblast cultures, to demonstrate the presence of the Barr body (intense green fluorescence) and its relation to the nucleolus (orange fluorescence). For this kind of study, the A.O. staining is preferable to the conventional methods.

3. RESULTS AND DISCUSSION

(a) *Topologic correlations between tritiated thymidine labeling and 5-BrdU-induced segmentation*

There are several direct and indirect demonstrations of these correlations.

After incorporation of tritiated 5-BrdU and tritiated thymidine, Zakharov and Egolina (1972) have demonstrated, in Chinese hamster cell lines, that the segmentation of the chromosomes corresponds to the late replicating regions.

In human chromosomes after 5-BrdU treatment (fig. 1), condensed segments correspond to R-bands and elongated ones to Q-bands (Dutrillaux et al., 1973, Zakharov et al., 1974). Using a very brief incorporation time of 5-BrdU, we have found that the segments modified in the very late S period seem identical to those showing very late labeling after autoradiography (Dutrillaux and Fosse, 1974). This correlation is not valid for the early S period treatment in that it does not induce reciprocal segmentation to late S treatment (Dutrillaux and Fosse, 1974), while tritiated thymidine does (Cave, 1966).

When 5-BrdU treatment induces segmentation, it has always the same localization as late S labeling with tritiated thymidine. This does not necessarily indicate that

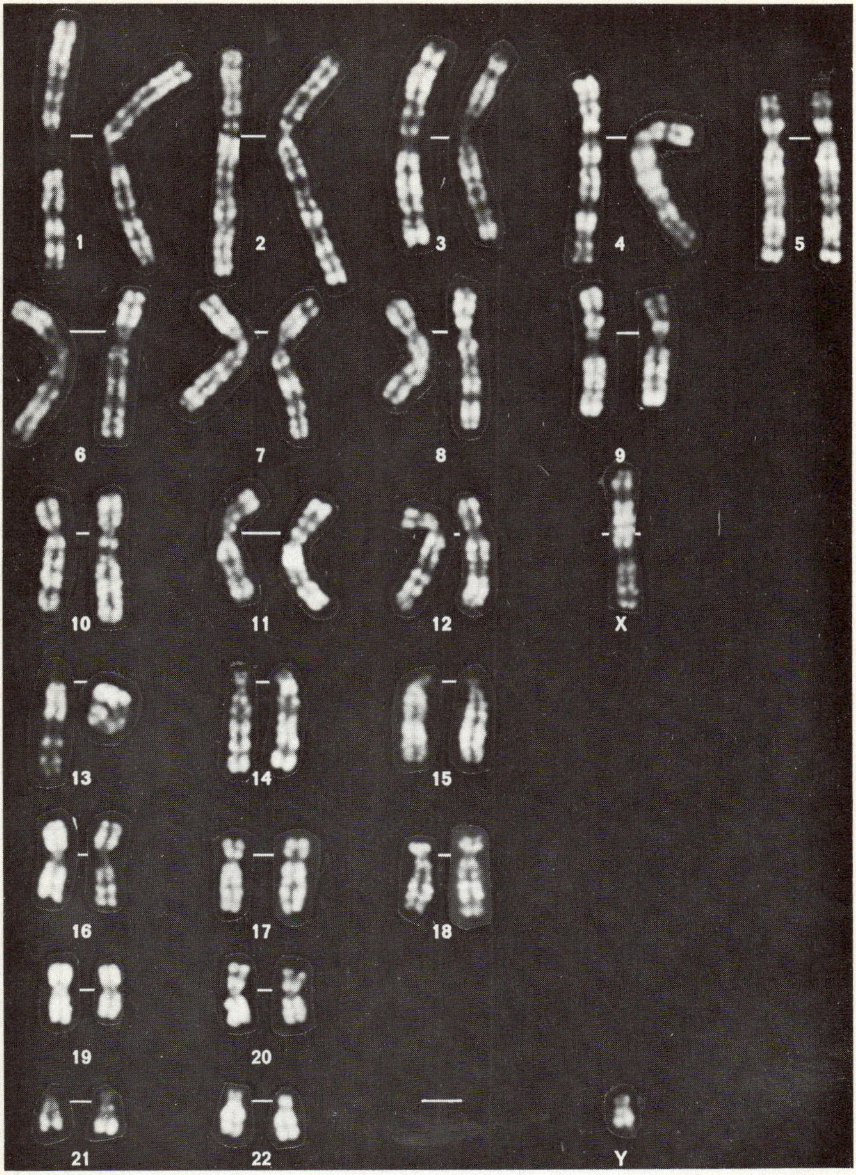

FIG. 1.—Karyotype of a patient showing a ring chromosome 13. The 5-BrdU treatment followed by acridine orange staining reveals segmentation and banding corresponding mostly to R-bands.

both methods play a role at the level of DNA replication. Segmentation of the chromosomes, and especially elongation of the late replicating X chromosomes, could result from a 5-BrdU-induced modification of the association of DNA and proteins.

Treatment of 5-BrdU over 24 hr does not produce further segmentation and the chromosomes appear nearly normal. After 40 hr treatment, an asymmetry of staining of the chromatids appears without segmentation (fig. 2). These differing results indicate that mechanisms other than incorporation of 5-BrdU in DNA are probably also involved.

(b) *Correlations with X inactivation and Barr body formation*

In the normal human male, the appearence of the X chromosome, after 5-BrdU treatment, is the same as the rest of the mitosis (fig. 1).

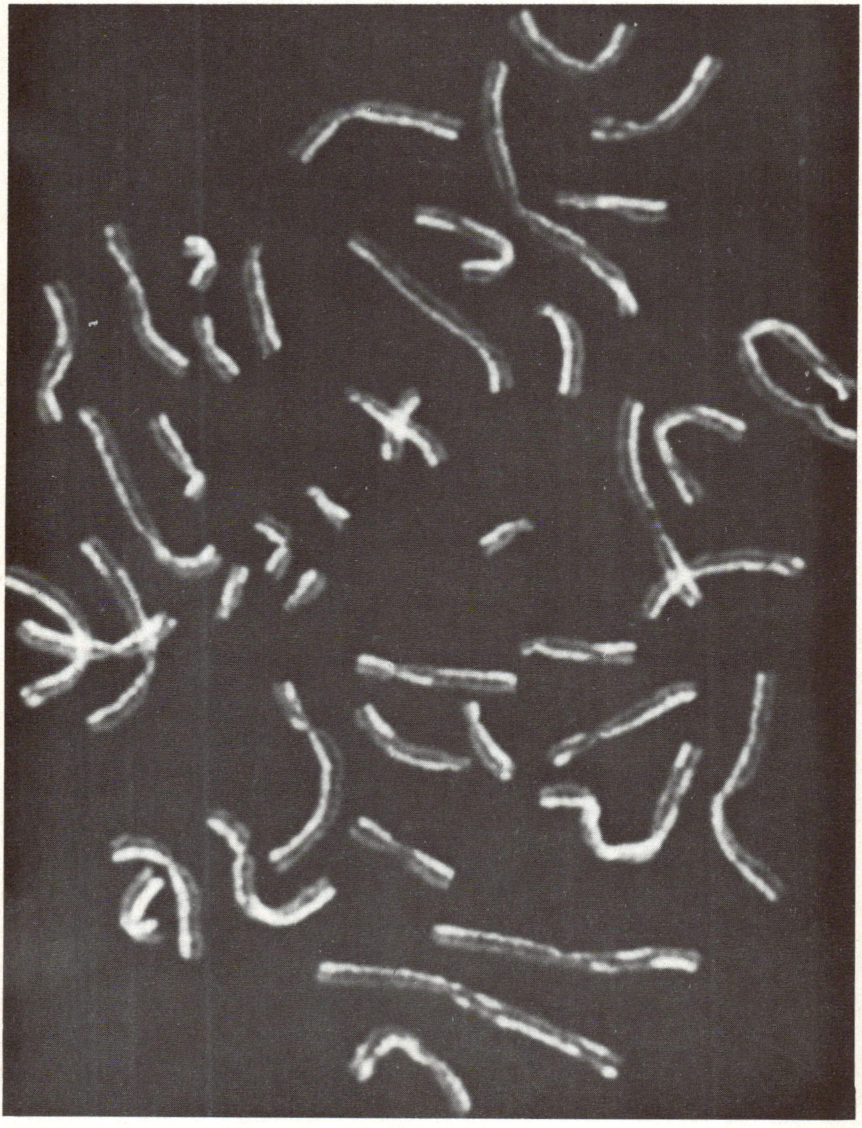

FIG. 2.—Asymmetry of the chromatids appearing after two days of treatment with 5-BrdU. The sister chromatid exchanges are very distinct.

In the normal female, one X chromosome has the same appearence as in the male, whereas the other is generally very elongated (Baranovskaya et al., 1972). After acridine orange staining, it has a reddish appearance and low fluorescence (fig. 3).

In people with three, four, or five X chromosomes, there are two, three, or four elongated X chromosomes (fig. 4). This obviously corresponds to the results obtained by autoradiography, showing an increase in the total number of late replicating X chromosomes, depending on the number of X chromosomes per cell. We also regularly observed that the number of elongated X chromosomes corresponds to the maximum number of Barr bodies in all the tissues examined.

Finally, in two people with anomalies of the X-chromosome, the abnormal late labeling X defined by autoradiography was also the elongated one after 5-BrdU treatment (Dutrillaux et al., 1974).

In conclusion, the recognition of the late replicating (inactivated) X chromosome is very precise with the 5-BrdU treatment.

(c) *Pattern of segmentation induced by 5-BrdU in late and early replicating X chromosomes*

The appearence of chromosomes after 5-BrdU treatment is rather difficult to interpret because the segmentation of the chromosomes, and particularly of the X chromosomes, depends at least on two different and changing parameters: contraction of the chromosomes and the reaction of the cells to the treatment. The latter may depend on the length of time that the cells are in contact with 5-BrdU.

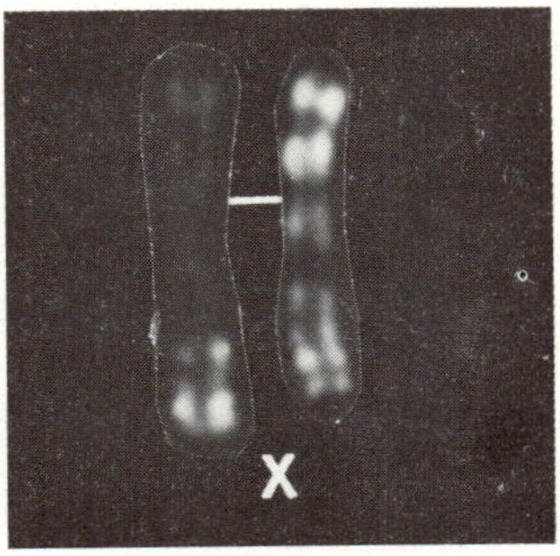

FIG. 3.—X chromosomes from a normal female showing early (condensed) and late replication (elongated and pale).

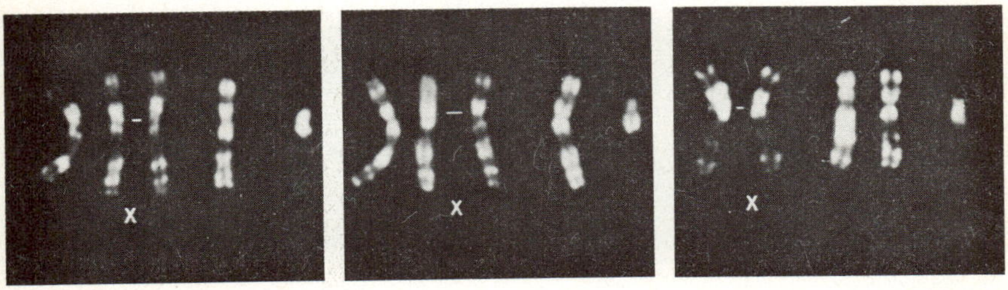

FIG. 4.—Sex chromosomes of 3 cells of a patient with an XXXXY constitution. There are generally 3 elongated X chromosomes, their segmentation is variable from cell to cell and from chromosome to chromosome.

From our preliminary observations it appears that (fig. 5):

The usual banding pattern of the early replicating X chromosome corresponds to R-bands;

The early replicating X of the female has the same banding pattern as the X chromosome of the normal male;

The appearence of the early replicating X depends directly on the stage of the condensation of the whole mitosis. There are many small bands in prometaphase, and fewer larger bands in metaphase;

The late replicating X is much more variable in appearance. Its condensation does not depend so strictly on the stage of the mitosis. For instance, it may be very elongated when the rest of the chromosomes are at metaphase. However, the segmentation of the late replicating X chromosome in metaphase cells often corresponds to that of the early replicating X in prometaphase cells. The segmentation pattern of the late replicating X is variable. In some cells, nearly all the bands corresponding to the Q- and R-bands have disappeared. In others, almost all or all of the R-bands

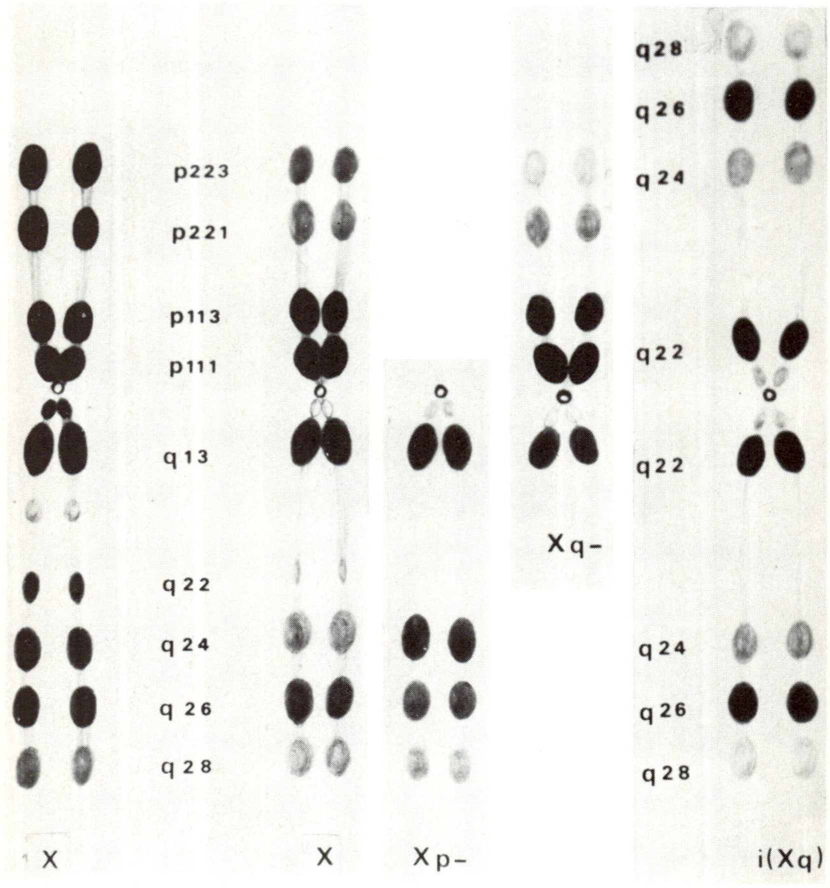

FIG. 5.—Comparative diagrams of early (left) and late (right) replicating normal X chromosomes, and of Xp-, Xq-, and i(Xq). (Drawings by Dr. Gamboa.)

are still present and separated by elongated segments in the same positions as the Q-bands. In addition, all the intermediate situations seem to exist. Among the observable R-bands, there are in order of decreasing frequency p11, q13, p22, q26, q24, q28, and q22. Figure 5 represents a "standardized" late replicating X chromosome, and some of the various appearances can be seen in figures 1, 3, and 4.

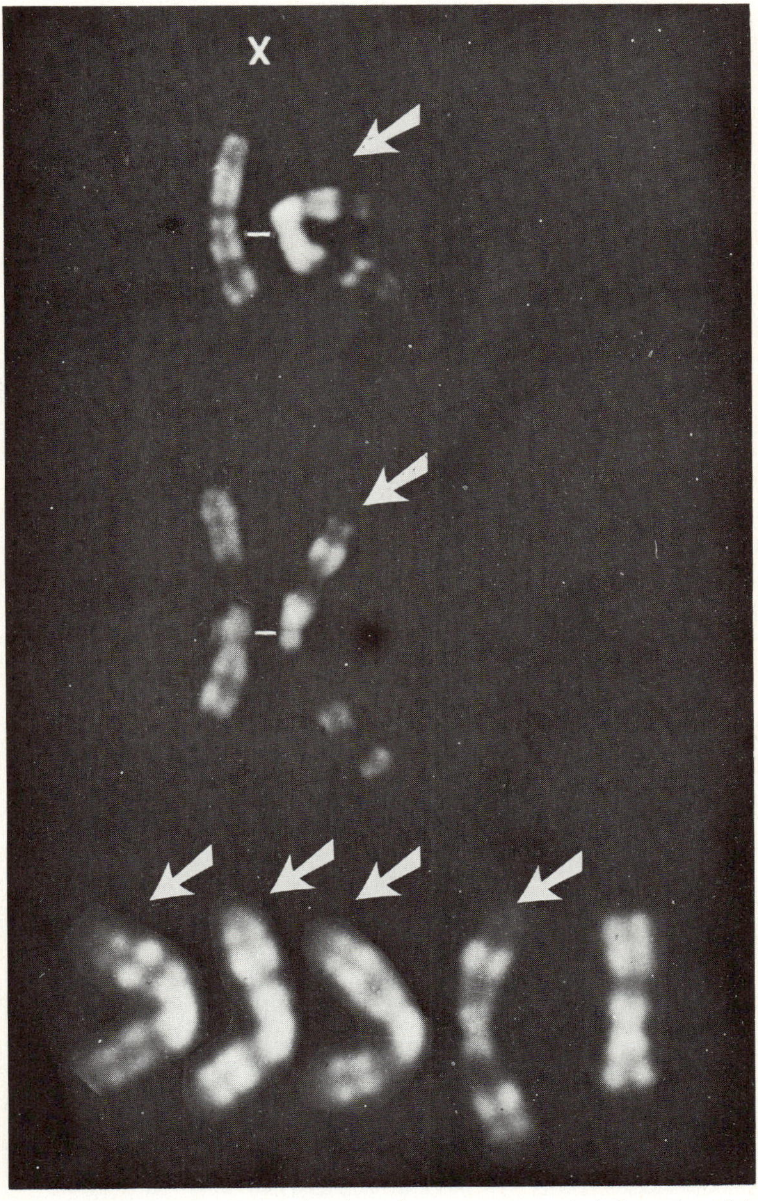

FIG. 6.—Different aspects of i(Xq), showing a frequent asymmetrical elongation of the two arms (with normal banding techniques, the two arms are symmetrical).

In conclusion, although the appearance of the X chromosomes varies from cell to cell, it is generally easy to distinguish between late and early replicating X chromosomes. In the late replicating X chromosome, there is a disappearence of some of the R-bands, which is more frequent for some bands than for others.

(d) *Segmentation pattern of structurally abnormal X chromosomes*

Isochromosome for the long arm—i(Xq). Three cases of i(Xq) have been investigated. In all cases, the isochromosome was late replicating. The segmentation pattern was rather characteristic, as shown in figure 5. In particular, in the long arm of the very elongated chromosomes, only the band q26 remains strongly condensed and fluorescent. Conversely, in rather condensed i(Xq), the band q24 is predominant. In the majority of the cells, there is frequently an asymmetry between the two arms (fig. 6). It must be stressed that in normal late replicating X's, the band q24 is very rarely predominant.

Deletion of the short arm—Xp –. The segmentation and the fluorescent pattern are very similar to that of i(Xq): disappearance of band q24, attenuation of band q28 in very elongated X's, and a frequent predominance of band q24 in rather condensed ones (fig. 5).

Deletion of the long arm—Xq –. In the one patient examined, the Xq-chromosome was always late replicating. Compared with the short arms of the normal late replicating X chromosome, it seems likely that the band p22 is more frequently and extensively uncoiled in the Xq-situation (fig. 5).

In conclusion, the structurally abnormal X chromosomes (i(Xq), Xq –, Xp –) are always late replicating. In addition, the segmentation and fluorescent patterns seem to be statistically somewhat different from the equivalent seqments of normal late replicating X chromosomes. This may indicate a modified function of the segments of abnormal X chromosomes.

(e) *Replication of X-autosome translocations*

Balanced translocations. Four cases have been investigated in our laboratory. In three of them, the normal X was always late replicating: one t(2;X) in a woman with primary amenorrhea; one t(8;X) in a woman with secondary amenorrhea; one t(15; X) in a phenotypically and mentally retarded girl (fig. 7).

In the case of a slightly abnormal girl involving a t(1;X), the normal X was generally, but not always, late replicating (in about 90% of the cells) (fig. 8).

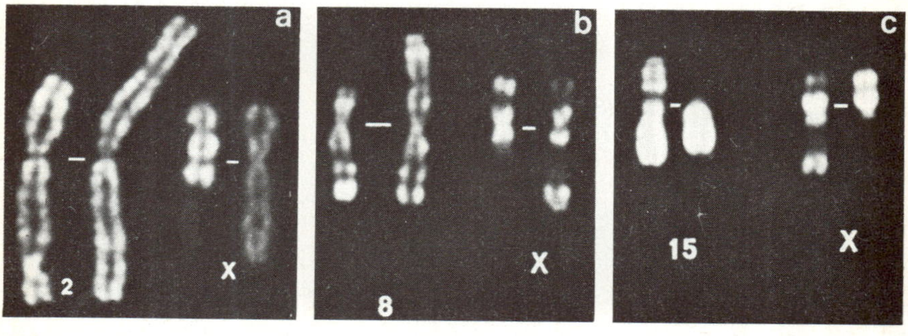

FIG. 7.—Partial karyotypes of balanced X-autosome translocations showing elongation (late replication) of the normal X. (a) t(2;X); (b) t(8;X); (c) t(15;X).

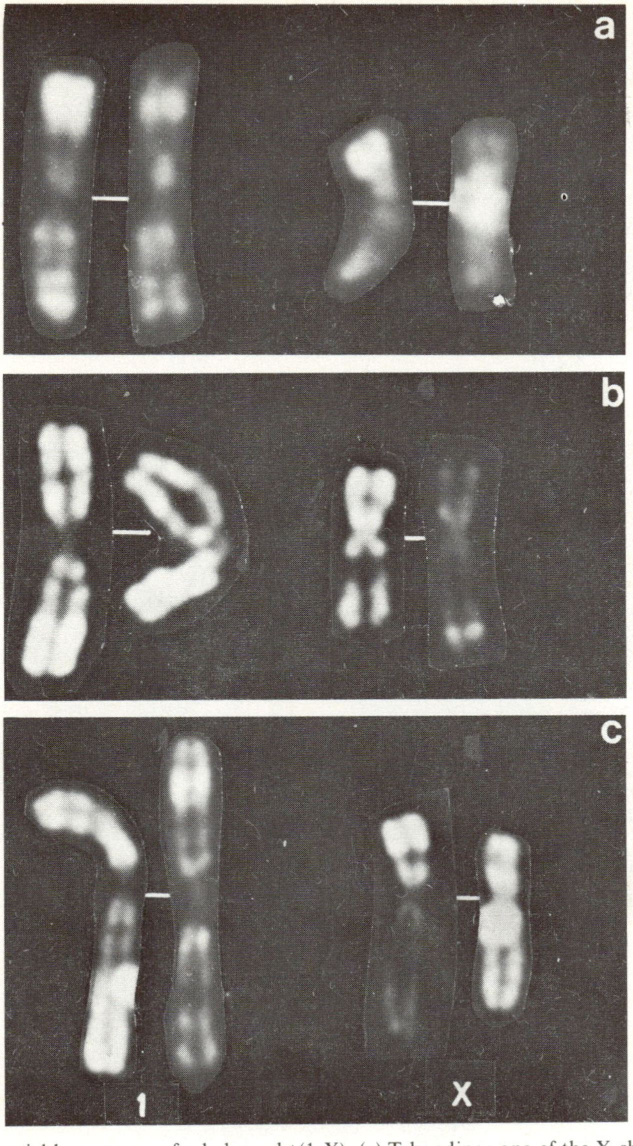

FIG. 8.—Partial karyotypes of a balanced t(1;X): (a) T-banding: one of the X chromosomes has a T-band in the short arm translocated from one chromosome 1; (b) 5-BrdU acridine orange banding of a cell with late replication of the normal X (90% of the examined cells); (c) 5-BrdU acridine orange banding of a cell with late replication of the derivative X (10% of the examined cells).

Unbalanced translocations. In both cases examined, the small autosomal segment translocated onto the X could not be identified with precision.

Case I was a girl who was Turner like, but without dysmorphia. The abnormal X was deleted of segment q22 → q*ter* and carried a short autosomal segment, equivalent in length to half a chromosome 21. It had a brilliant T-band. This derivative chromosome was always late replicating, and the intense fluorescence of the segment of autosome disappeared in most of the cells after 5-BrdU treatment (fig. 9). At this place, the chromosome was pale and elongated.

Normally after 5-BrdU treatment, all the T-bands remain condensed and brilliant, and we must conclude that the translocation has modified the response of the autosomal segment to the treatment.

Case II was a woman with a slightly abnormal phenotype, who had had two spontaneous abortions. The abnormal X was deleted of segment p21→p22 which was substituted by a slightly longer segment of autosome carrying a T-band. In all the cells, the derivative chromosome was late replicating and the segment of autosome uncoiled with weak fluorescence (fig. 10).

Both cases are partially trisomic and the inactivation of the autosomal segment could explain the phenotype of the patients being nearly normal.

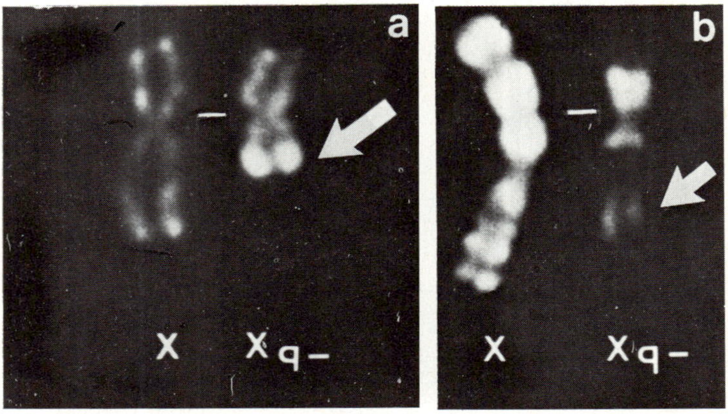

FIG. 9.—Partial karyotype of an unbalanced t(X;autosome). (a) T-banding showing an extra T-band in the derivative X chromosome (arrowed); (b) 5-BrdU acridine orange banding showing elongation and extinction of fluorescence of the segment corresponding to the T-band (arrowed).

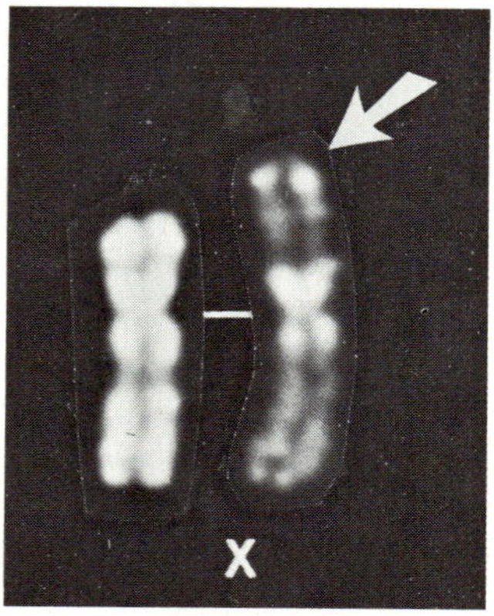

FIG. 10.—Partial karyotype of an unbalanced t(X;autosome). The 5-BrdU acridine orange banding also shows the disappearance and elongation of the translocated autosomal segment (arrowed).

In conclusion the principle of random inactivation in X-autosome translocations is not valid. If the translocation is balanced, the normal X is generally inactivated and if the translocation is unbalanced, the abnormal X is generally inactivated. It also appears that excess autosomal material, when translocated onto the X, is inactivated as well. This mechanism would tend to give the patient a more favorable genetic constitution.

However, the apparent necessity for one of the two X chromosomes to be systematically inactivated may induce deleterious effects in some cases. In particular, the reproductive function is often affected.

(f) *X-X translocations*

We have examined five cases with X-X translocation, two of them being mother and son. In all the patients, there was one normal and one abnormal X chromosome, the latter being formed by the fusion of two X chromosomes. All the adults had reproductive difficulties including amenorrhea and oligomenorrhea.

In each case, the abnormal X was late replicating. The segmentation of the long arms corresponded very closely to that of the isochromosomes described earlier (fig. 11).

Two cases resulting from a telomeric fusion are very informative. One of them has been previously described by Disteche et al. (1972). The other is presently being investigated by Doctors Fraisse and Laurent. In both cases, the telomeric fusion has induced inactivation of one of the centromeres, so that the chromosomes appear monocentric (Dutrillaux et al., 1975). This situation is probably the same as occurred during evolution of man from the common ancestor of man and the chimpanzee, leading to the formation of the chromosome 2 of man from two submetacentrics still existing in the chimpanzee (Lejeune et al., 1973; Dutrillaux, 1975). In these abnormal X chromosomes, the segment between the two centromeres, consisting of the two short arms, is very elongated (fig. 12). This may indicate intense inactivation of these regions and explain why two women are Turner like, although they possess three copies of the X chromosome.

In conclusion, in cases of X-X translocation, the abnormal chromosome is inactivated and the regulation of the abnormal X may depend upon the type of structural rearrangement.

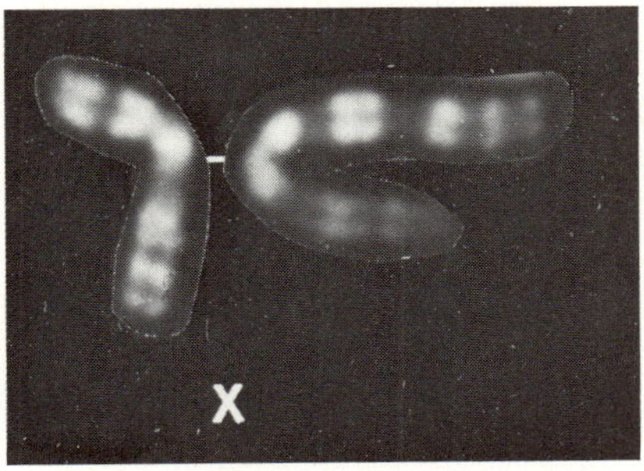

FIG. 11.—Partial karyotype of a t(X:X), after 5-BrdU treatment and acridine orange staining. The abnormal X (arrowed), results from translocation of the long arm of an X onto the short arm of another. This derivative chromosome is late replicating.

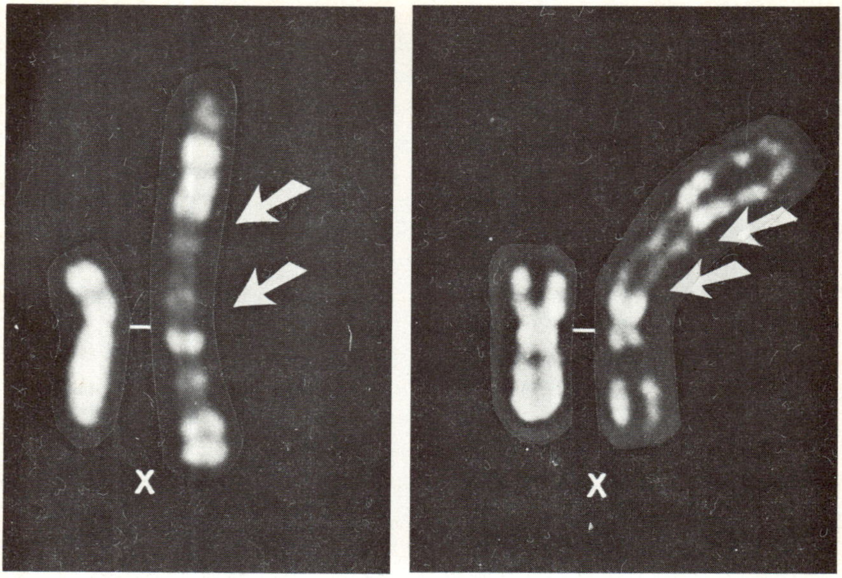

FIG. 12.—Partial karyotypes of two cases of short arm telomeric fusion of two X chromosomes. 5-BrdU-acridine orange banding reveals elongation of the segment corresponding to the short arms (arrows).

4. GENERAL CONCLUSIONS

1. 5-BrdU treatment followed by acridine orange staining is an excellent method for the analysis of the replication of the X's.

2. The mechanism of the segmentation induced may not depend directly on the characteristics of DNA replication. However, the topologic correlations with the labeling produced by tritiated thymidine are very good.

3. The comparative analysis of several patients with different clinical problems, and carrying various anomalies of the X chromosome, permits us to conclude that it is probably possible to localize active and inactive segments of these chromosomes. This opens up interesting possibilities for the study of the genetic content of this chromosome.

4. It seems very likely that a structural rearrangement of the X chromosome may also modify its regulation. Thus, an analysis of the quantitative variation of chromosomal material is insufficient to explain the correlation between the karyotype and the phenotype.

5. The analysis with 5-BrdU treatment will probably help explain some apparent inconsistencies of X chromosome pathology.

Acknowledgements. I am grateful to my colleagues who kindly referred many interesting cases, especially Doctors Colette Laurent, Simone Gilgenkrants, Claude Turc, Jaqueline Fraisse, Yves Rumpler, and J. Frederic, and to my colleagues from the Institut de Progenése.

5. REFERENCES

BARANOVSKAYA, L. T., ZAKHAROV, A. F., DUTRILLAUX, B., CARPENTIER, S., PRIEUR, M., and LEJEUNE J. 1972. Différentiation des chromosomes X par les méthodes de despiralisation au 5 bromodéoxyuridine (B.U.D.R.) et de dénaturation thermique ménagée. *Ann. Genet.*, *15*, 271–274.

CALDERON, D., and SCHNEDL, W. 1973. A comparison between quinacrine fluorescence banding and H3-thymidine incorporation patterns in human chromosomes. *Humangenetik*, *18*, 63–70.

CAVE, M. 1966. Reverse pattern of thymidine-H3 incorporation in human chromosomes. *Hereditas*, *54*, 338.

COUTURIER, J., DUTRILLAUX, B., and LEJEUNE, J. 1973. Etude des fluorescences spécifiques des bandes R et des bandes Q des chromosomes humains. *C. R. Acad. Sc. (Paris)*, *276*, 339.

DISTECHE, C., HAGEMEIJER, A., FREDERIC, J., and PROGNEAUX D. 1972. An abnormal large human chromosome identified as an end-to-end fusion of two X's by combined results of the new banding techniques and microdensitometry. *Clin. Genet.*, *3*, 388.

DUTRILLAUX, B. 1975. Histoire naturelle des chromosomes humains. Monographie des Annales de Génétique. Ed. l'Expansion Scientifique Francaise.

DUTRILLAUX, B., and FOSSE, A. M. 1974. Sur la segmentation chromosomique induite par le B.U.D.R. (5-bromodéoxyuridine). *Ann. Génét.*, *17*, 106.

DUTRILLAUX, B., LAURENT, C., COUTURIER, J., and LEJEUNE, J. 1973. Coloration par l'acridine orange de chromosomes préalablement traités par le 5 bromodéoxyuridine (B.U.D.R.) *C. R. Acad. Sc. (Paris)*, *276*, 3179.

DUTRILLAUX, B., LAURENT, C., GILGENKRANTZ, S., FREDERIC, J., CARPENTIER, S., COUTURIER, J. and, LEJEUNE, J. 1974. Les translocations du chromosome X. Etude aprés traitement par le B.U.D.R. et coloration par l'acridine orange. *Acta Paed. Helvet.* (Suppl.), *34*, 19.

GANNER, E. and, EVANS H. J. 1971. The relationship between patterns of DNA replication and of quinacrine fluorescence in the human chromosome complement. *Chromosoma (Berl.)*, *35*, 326.

LEJEUNE, J. DUTRILLAUX, B., RETHORÉ, M. O., and PRIEUR, M. 1973. Comparaison de la structure fine des chromatides d'Homo sapiens et de Pan troglodytes. *Chromosoma (Berl.)*, *43*, 423.

ZAKHAROV, A. F., and EGOLINA, N. A. 1972. Differential spiralization along mammalian chromosomes. I BudR-revealed differentiation in chinese Hamster chromosomes. *Chromosoma (Berl.)*, *38*, 341.

ZAKHAROV, A. F., SELEZNEV, J. V., BENJUSCH, V. A., BARANOVSKAYA, L. I., and DEMINTSEVA, V. S. 1971. Differentiation along human chromosomes in relation to their identification. *Excerpta Med. Int. Congr. Ser.*, *233*, 193.

ZAKHAROV, A. F., BARANOVSKAYA, L. I., BENJUSCH, V. A., DEMINTSEVA, V. S., and OBLAPENKO, N. G. 1974. Differential spiralization along mammalian mitotic chromosomes. II 5-bromodeoxyuridine and 5-bromodeoxycitidine revealed differentiation in human chromosomes. *Chromosoma (Berl.)*, *44*, 343.

IDENTIFICATION OF ACTIVE AND INACTIVE X CHROMOSOMES BY BrdU INCORPORATION AND FLUOROCHROME STAINING

MARGARETA MIKKELSEN*

John F. Kennedy Institute, Glostrup, Denmark

1. INTRODUCTION

Although females possess two X chromosomes, only one of these homologues is active, providing a dose compensation which ensures that females and males both display the same number of active X linked genes, as first suggested by Lyon (1961). Moreover, individuals with additional X chromosomes have only one of them active while the others are inactive.

Autoradiography with ^{3}H-thymidine incorporation was the method used to distinguish the inactive X chromosome(s) by their labeling patterns from other chromosomes in the C group, including the active X chromosome (German, 1964; Mukherjee et al., 1964). Banding procedures such as those giving Q-, G-, and R-bands (Paris Conference, 1971) have made it possible to distinguish the X chromosomes from the other C group chromosomes. But banding methods do not enable the active X chromosomes to be distinguished from the inactive ones. As shown by Palmer (1970) and Baranovskaya (1973), 5-BrdU incorporation in the late S phase alters the structure of genetically inactive X chromosomes. Certain areas of the inactive X chromosomes appear more stretched than in the active X. When 5-BrdU incorporation is combined with acridine orange staining, the chromosomes show an R banding pattern and the inactive X chromosome appears more stretched and less intensively stained then the active X (Dutrillaux et al., 1973).

The aim of this investigation was to determine if the 5-BrdU-acridine-orange-technique could render autoradiography superfluous in the study of X chromosome aberrations in man.

2. MATERIALS AND METHODS

Two individuals with a 49, XXXXY karyotype, one female with a 48,XXXX karyotype, one male with a 48,XXXY and one with a 48,XXYY karyotype, and a girl with an X/autosomal translocation were studied. In all patients the chromosome abnormality had been diagnosed previously; all cases, except the one with the 48, XXXY karyotype, were studied autoradiographically.

In the two XXXXY patients and in the case of X/autosomal translocation combined fluorescence and autoradiographical studies were carried out with the method described by Mikkelsen and Dahl (1973).

* With assistance of Birthe Jespersen and Hanne Poulsen.

For the 5-BrdU technique lymphocytes were cultured in the usual way with addition of phytohaemagglutinin for 48 hr. Five hours prior to harvesting 100 to 200 μg/ml of 5-BrdU were added to the cell suspension. The cells were harvested as usual and air-dried slides were prepared without heating. The slides were passed through an alcohol series to distilled water and then stained in a 0.005% solution of acridine orange in Sørensen's phosphate buffer, pH 6.7. The slides were rinsed twice in distilled water and mounted in buffer. For microscopy a Leitz Orthoplan

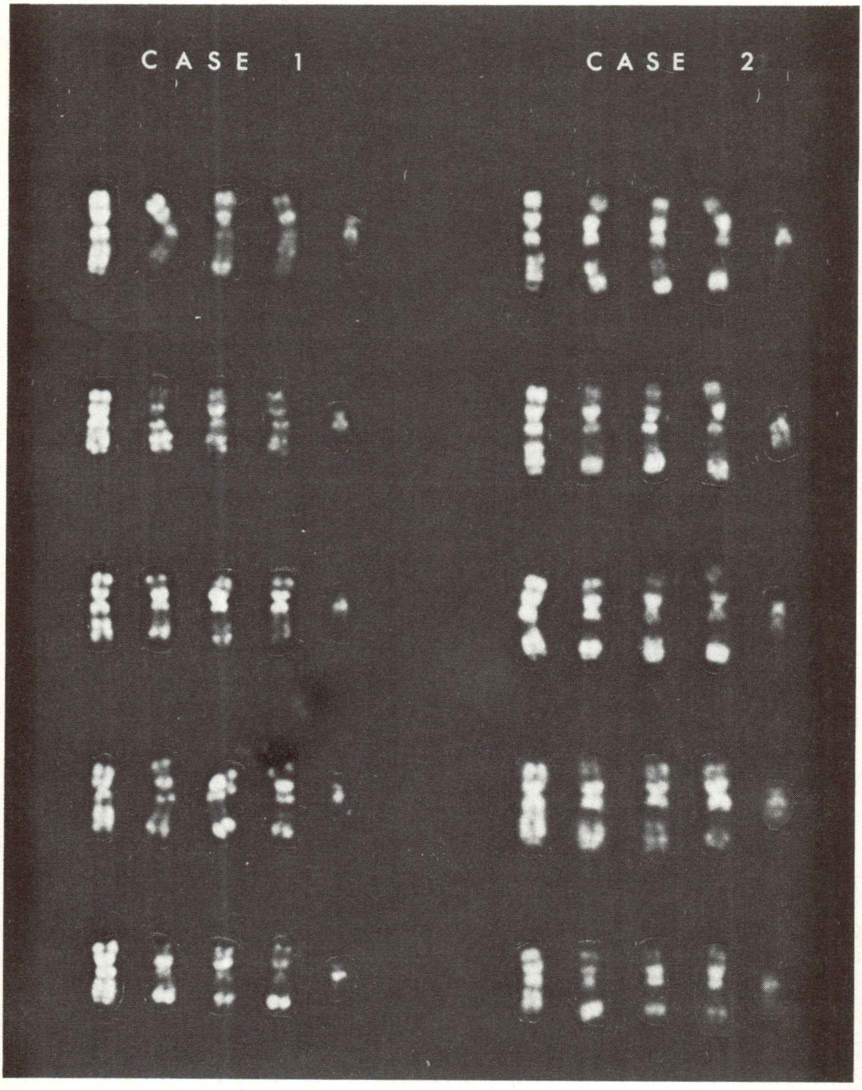

FIG. 1.—The X and Y chromosomes from 5 different cells from 2 patients with 49,XXXXY karyotype examined with the 5-BrdU-acridine-orange-technique. Note that one X is more condensed and more intensively stained in all cells. The other X chromosomes show different degrees of elongation.

fluorescence microscope fitted with a vertical illuminator and HBO 200 lamp was used. Suitable cells were photographed on Ilford Pan F film (18 Din) with an exposure time of about 2 sec.

3. RESULTS

(a) *5-BrdU-acridine-orange studies*

The banding patterns observed were in all cases R-bands (Paris Conference, 1971). All chromosomes could be identified without difficulty. In all cases with multi X syndromes one X chromosome showed the same banding intensity as the autosomes. The other X chromosome(s) were more stretched and less intensively stained. The elongation was especially prominent at bands p21, q23, and q25 (figs. 1 and 3). The degree of stretching varied in different cells and among the different additional X chromosomes. Often in cells with more than two X chromosomes the condensation of the additional X chromosomes was uneven, some being more extended than others.

The centromeric region of the elongated X chromosomes was almost invariably more intensely stained than the rest of the short and long arms (fig. 1).

In the X/autosomal translocation, the normal X showed the stretching phenomenon (fig. 3d).

(b) *Fluorescence and autoradiographic studies*

In suitable cells in the two XXXXY cases one of the X chromosomes was either slightly labeled or unlabeled. The other X chromosomes were more or less labeled and showed a variation in the number of silver-grains. Generally two X chromosomes were "hotter" than the third and one was either nearly or completely unlabeled (fig. 2). The centromeric part of the late labeling X chromosomes labeled earlier than the rest of the chromosome. Even in heavily labeled X chromosomes a gap was observed in the silver-grains around the centromeric region. In the X/autosomal translocation the normal X labeled late (Mikkelsen and Dahl, 1973).

4. DISCUSSION

The finding of one X with the same staining intensity and lack of stretching as the autosomes and the elongated and weakly stained additional X chromosomes in multi X syndromes was interpreted as a 5-BrdU incorporation late in the S phase of the genetically inactive X chromosomes.

In the cases examined with both 5-BrdU-acridine-orange and autoradiography the same inactivation pattern was obtained. The 5-BrdU method is simpler and much less time consuming. In addition, one step in the autoradiographic procedure—the fluorescence with quinacrine—is omitted, as the chromosomes can be identified individually by their A.O. banding patterns. Thus, it seems likely that the 5-BrdU-acridine-orange-technique will replace autoradiography for identification of X chromosome abnormalities.

The variation in the degree of differential condensation or elongation, when more than one inactivated X chromosome was found, was also observed as a different degree of labeling in autoradiographic preparations. These differences have been observed by us for many years, but were interpreted as artefacts. As both methods

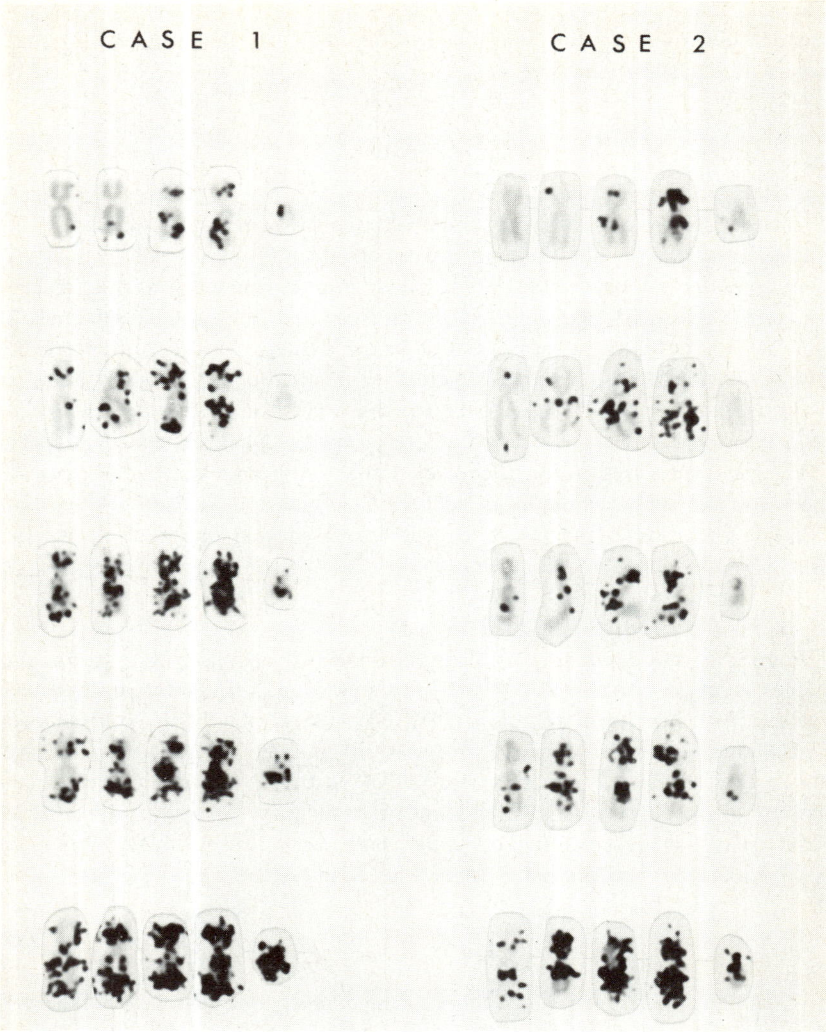

FIG. 2.—The ^{3}H-thymidine labeled X and Y chromosomes from the same cases as in figure 1. All chromosomes have been identified by quinacrine staining before autoradiographic study.

show this variation it may reflect the replication patterns of additional X chromosomes. Similar differences between extra X chromosomes were also observed by Baranovskaya and Zakharov (1974) in patients with multi X syndromes, examined with a combination of 5-BrdU incorporation and ^{3}H-deoxycytidine incorporation.

Frøland (1967) showed that the centromeric part of the X chromosome replicates earlier than the rest of the late labeling X. In addition, the staining intensity of the centromeric region of the inactivated X chromosomes resembles the intensity of the same region in the active one. Similarly, the stretching phenomenon seems much less marked in the centromeric region. This part of the X may carry genes which are not normally inactivated, e.g., the Xg blood group system.

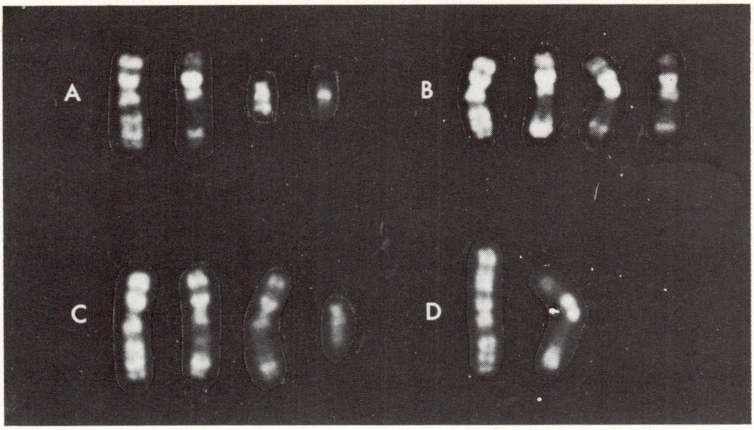

FIG. 3.—5-BrdU-acridine-orange method. Sex chromosomes from: (A) a male with 48,XXYY karyotype; (B) a female with 48,XXXX karyotype; (C) a male with 48,XXXY karyotype (note only 1 condensed X in the multi X syndromes); (D) a female with a translocation (X;8) (note the inactive elongated weakly stained normal X chromosome).

5. SUMMARY

1. In patients with X chromosome abnormalities, the active X chromosome could be distinguished from the inactive ones by 5-BrdU incorporation and acridine-orange staining.

2. The method revealed R bands and showed an elongation and weak staining of inactivated X chromosomes. Compared with autoradiography, this method was much faster and very reliable.

3. In multi X syndromes a variation in the degree of condensation of inactive X chromosomes was observed and may reflect the replication pattern of X chromosomes.

Acknowledgements. Thanks are due to Dr. Petrea Jacobsen and Dr. Gudrun Dahl for permission to study their patients and for sending us blood samples. The work has been supported in part by grants from the Danish Medical Research Council.

6. REFERENCES

Baranovskaya, L. I. 1973. Differentiation of X-chromosomes by the length in cases of X-polysomy in man. *Byull. Eksp. Biol. Med.*, *75*, 94–99. (Russian)

Baranovskaya, L. I., and Zakharov, A. F. 1974. H^3-Deoxycytidine incorporation into X-chromosomes differentially condensed under 5-bromodeoxyuridine treatment in cases of 49,XXXXY, 48,XXXX, 47,XXX, 46,X,i(Xq), and 45,X/46,X,1(Xq). *Humangenetik*, *23*, 131–136.

Dutrillaux, M. B., Laurent, C., Couturier, J., and Lejeune, J. 1973. Coloration des chromosomes humains par l'acridine orange apres traitement par le 5 bromodéoxyuridine. *C. R. Acad. Sc. Paris*, *276*, 3179–3181.

Frøland, A. 1967. Internal asynchrony in late replicating X chromosomes. *Nature (Lond.)*, *213*, 512–513.

German, J. 1964. The pattern of DNA synthesis in the chromosomes of human blood cells. *J. Cell Biol.*, *20*, 37–55.

LYON, M. F. 1961. Gene action in the X-chromosome of the mouse (*Mus musculus* L.). *Nature (Lond.), 190,* 372–373.

MIKKELSEN, M., and DAHL, G. 1973. Unbalanced X/autosomal translocation with inactivation of the normal X chromosome. *Cytogenet. Cell Genet., 12,* 357–366.

MUKHERJEE, B. B., MILLER, O. J., BREG, W. R., and BADER, S. 1964. Chromosome duplication in cultured leucocytes from presumptive XXX and XXXXY human subjects. *Exp. Cell Res., 34,* 333–350.

PALMER, C. G. 1970. 5-Bromodeoxyuridine induced constrictions in human chromosomes. *Can. J. Genet. Cytol., 12,* 816–830.

PARIS CONFERENCE. 1971. *Standardization in Human Cytogenetics.* Birth Defects, Original Article Series, *8:7* (1972). The National Foundation, New York.

SOME BIOPHYSICAL TOOLS FOR CHROMOSOME ANALYSIS

TORBJÖRN CASPERSSON

Institute for Medical Cell Research and Genetics
Medical Nobel Institute, Karolinska Institutet, Stockholm, Sweden

The first observations of faint banding patterns on metaphase chromosomes after fluorochroming with quinacrine mustard led immediately to the development of a high resolution fluorometric procedure for recording the patterns. Obviously, only an objective measuring procedure could give information as to whether the banding patterns were constant and possibly different for different chromosomes.

For the complex human karyotype with its 24 chromosome types, much observational material would be needed for judging the factors mentioned. Thus, a simplified photographic fluorometric system was also built up with semiautomatic recording of the fluorescence profiles of individual chromosomes. In addition a digitizing arrangement was included and, simultaneously with the recording, the profile data were fed into a tape punch. The tape could then be read automatically, which greatly simplified the following computerized statistical analysis.

About 30,000 fluorescence profiles were recorded with this instrument and subjected to computer-assisted statistical analysis. On this basis an identification and numbering system for the human chromosomes was proposed which was internationally accepted at the meeting in Paris, 1971 (Paris Conference, 1971; Caspersson et al., 1972*a*; Caspersson, 1973*a*).

For details regarding techniques and methods used in the above work the reader is referred to the last two references.

The methods for recording the fluorescence profiles were primarily developed to provide the statistical background of the degree of constancy and reproducibility of the patterns or profiles and they are generally not needed in present-day routine chromosome identification work. In the detailed analysis of complex chromosome aberrations they are, however, a useful complement to the photographic work.

In the machine analysis of karyotypes, profile measurements play a fundamental role. The statistical work referred to above also involved the development of a computerized program for machine recognition of the 24 different profile types (Möller et al., 1972). A related program was developed and used in a collaborative effort with a group at the Jet Propulsion Laboratory, working on automated microscopy and recognition systems, which led to the first successful machine sorting of a complete human karyotype (Caspersson et al., 1971).

Several groups are at present working on wholly automated chromosome analysis. Mere chromosome sorting and identification could hardly justify large investments in apparatus nowadays, when so many easily manageable banding techniques are available. Machine sorting and analysis of chromosome aberrations could, however, be a very great help in many fields, especially those where large series of metaphases have to be studied. This is the case, for instance, in the studies of the effects of chromosome breakage through external mutagens and carcinogens (which is important for many medical problems). The technical problems here are very difficult. Most or possibly all present techniques operate with considerable operator interaction and none of them has reached a state of making application to practical routine work possible.

The main limitations of the conventional application of the banding techniques, of which a whole little arsenal is at present available, are imposed by the slowness and the tedious character of the work.

Two factors dominate here. One is the investment of time and labor needed to find enough suitably spread metaphase plates in the preparation. The second is the laboriousness of the photographic work, which is as yet unavoidable for practically all types of application of banding procedures.

In connection with the work on machine analysis, several laboratories have developed arrangements for automated searching for metaphases. These are as yet quite complex and expensive but it is to be hoped that as a spin-off from that work a simpler system suitable for use in routine laboratories will be developed.

Much can be gained, however, by partial or complete elimination of the photography. For most detailed aberration analysis, photography will probably always be indispensable, possibly in combination with pattern records. Most applications of the banding techniques do not require such penetrating analysis, and photography can here be dispensed with more or less completely. An additional reason for photography is the need for a system to mark the chromosomes already analyzed, as the work proceeds.

In fluorescence procedures, the major part of the photographic work concerns the preparation of the series of differently exposed prints which is necessary for the detailed study of bands lying in regions of different overall fluorescence intensity. This can be eliminated by replacing this procedure by an adjustable image contrast enhancement device incorporated in a TV system in which the photographic negative is observed by a TV camera.

Figure 1 shows such an arrangement (Caspersson et al., 1970; Caspersson, 1973*b*; Caspersson et al., 1972*b*). The TV camera, focused on the photographic negative, is equipped with a zoom lens for a magnification range from that of a survey picture of a whole metaphase plate to the picture of an individual chromosome projected onto the monitor screen.

The image contrast enhancement system is a crucial part of the instrument (Caspersson et al., 1972*b*). In principle it can be said to increase the steepness of the intensity response curve of the TV system so that the whole gray scale realm of the monitor can be brought to reproduce an arbitrarily selected small part of the gray scale in the object.

Figure 2 illustrates the mode of application. If a chromosome has a fluorescence profile like the left-hand curve with fine banding details in the faintly fluorescing region, as well as in the highly fluorescent regions, these details can be brought out very clearly on the monitor after each other with different settings of the contrast enhancement regulator—as indicated by the right-hand curve. Figure 3 exemplifies the use of the procedure on chromosomes.

The instrument in figure 1 is equipped with two TV cameras, the pictures of which

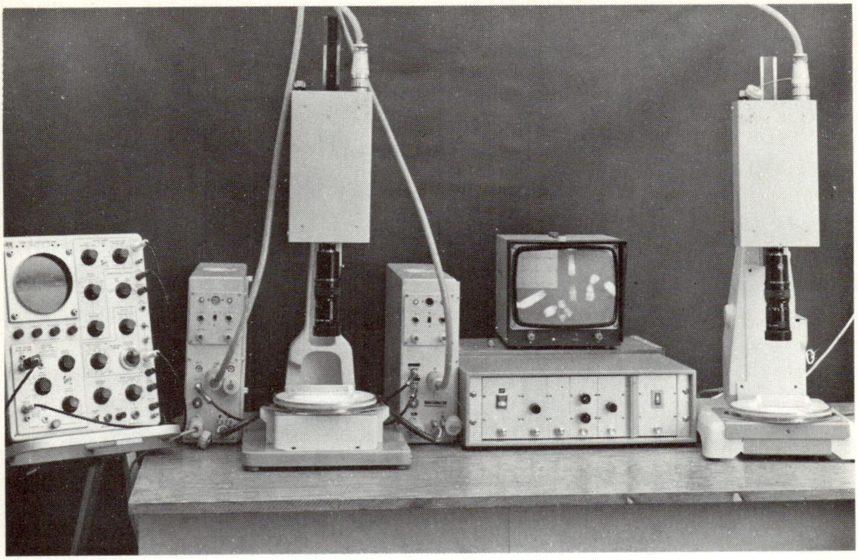

FIG. 1.—TV system for analysis of fluorescence photographs.

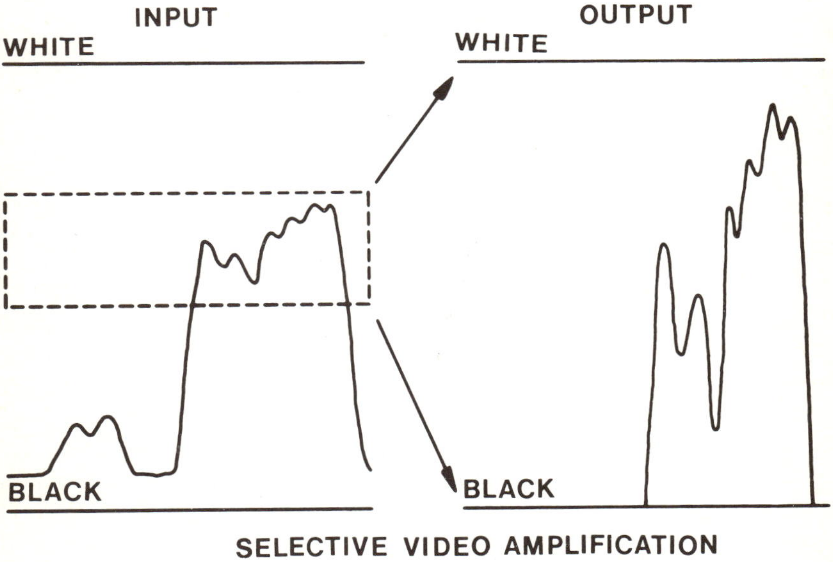

FIG. 2—Diagram illustrating the mode of function for the image contrast enhancement system.

can be displayed side by side on the same monitor in order to facilitate comparisons between chromosomes taken from different metaphase plates or stained by different procedures. It has proved practical to use TV monitors with prolonged response time as the flickering of the screen is somewhat tiring in protracted work.

The necessary marking of the chromosomes already analyzed during the progress of the work can be made on a transparent sheet in contact with the negative.

FIG. 3.—Chromosomes 5, 3 and 19 photographed so as to emphasize different levels of contrast, QM-staining.

The simplification of the work and the relatively convenient mode of work with the TV monitor result in a considerable saving of time. In large-scale routine work the time input can be reduced to about a twentieth.

The promising results of this instrument promoted efforts to try and eliminate photography in Giemsa-based methods, too, and to make the observational work less tiresome.

Figure 4 shows an experimental model of such an instrument. A TV camera looks directly into the microscope and a system for varying the microscope magnification permits changes of the magnification of the picture on the monitor. Also crucial here is an image contrast enhancement system (cf. fig. 5), in principle identical with the one described above. The combination of variable magnification and adjustable contrast enhancement permits a very convenient study of the fine banding details both in the heavily and in the weakly absorbing parts of the chromosomes (fig. 5).

In order to entirely eliminate photography, a video recorder is attached to the instrument. At the beginning of the work a survey picture of the whole metaphase plate to be studied is recorded on an endless loop of tape. This takes only a few seconds. This picture from the recorder is then continuously displayed on a second monitor throughout the detailed analysis of the individual chromosomes, which is made by means of the primary monitor. The analyzed chromosomes are then marked on a transparent sheet in front of the second monitor as the work progresses.

This arrangement can also be used for comparison purposes. In figure 4, as a demonstration, two different metaphase plates are displayed on the two monitors.

Experience with this instrument in routine work is as yet very limited. However,

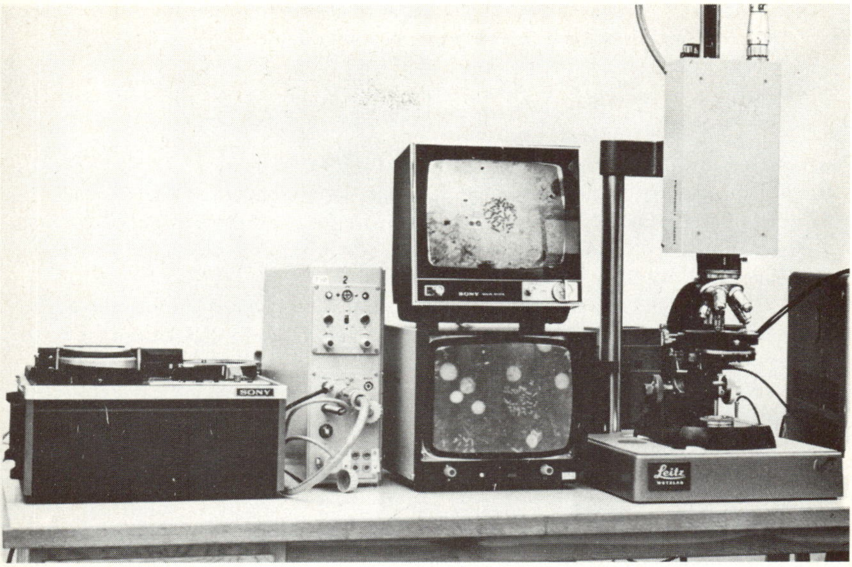

FIG. 4.—The TV microscope system for analysis of stained chromosome preparations.

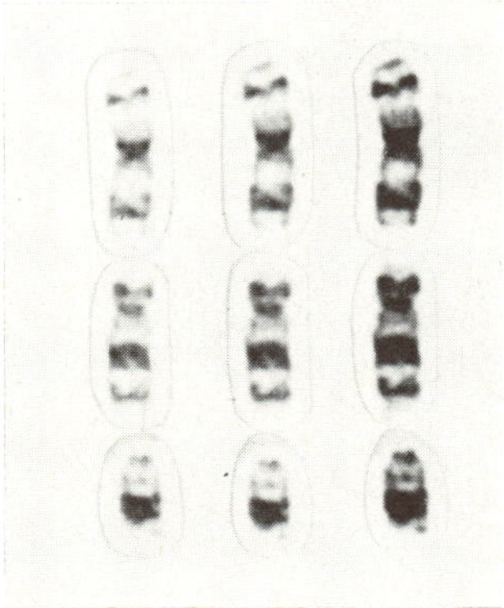

FIG. 5.—Chromosomes 3, 5 and 13, Giemsa stained and photographed so as to emphasize different levels of contrast.

the quality of the picture of the monitor and the amount of details conveniently observable with the aid of the combination of adjustable contrast enhancement and variable magnification are quite impressive. The instrument is unlikely to give any essential information beyond that which photography could provide, but the ease of the work and the elimination of all photography must lead to a considerable gain in time, especially in work involving large series of metaphases.

It appears probable that techniques of this general type will in the future improve the efficiency and speed of different applications of banding techniques. It should be pointed out that for the main part of the TV arrangement, commercially available equipment can be used and, thus, the overall costs of the TV parts in the equipment described above are approximately of the same order as the cost of the microscope.

Acknowledgements. This project was supported by research grants from the Swedish Cancer Society and the Swedish Natural Science Research Council.

REFERENCES

CASPERSSON, T. 1973*a*. Procedures for the study of the reproducibility of normal mammalian banding patterns and for analyses of aberrant chromosome patterns. Chromosome identification-techniques and applications in biology and medicine. *Nobel Symp. 23,* Stockholm, September 25–27, 1972 (T. CASPERSSON and L. ZECH, eds)., p. 50. Nobel Foundation, Stockholm, and Academic Press, New York.

CASPERSSON, T. 1973*b*. Fluorometric recognition of chromosomes and chromosome regions. In *Fluorescence Techniques in Cell Biology* (A. A. THAER and M. SERNETZ, eds.), p. 107. Springer-Verlag.

CASPERSSON, T., LINDSTEN, J., LOMAKKA, G., WALLMAN, H., and ZECH, L. 1970. Rapid identification of human chromosomes by TV-techniques. *Exp. Cell Res., 63,* 477.

CASPERSSON, T., CASTLEMAN, K. R., LOMAKKA, G., MODEST, E. J., MÖLLER, A., NATHAN, R., WALL, R. J., and ZECH, L. 1971. Automatic karyotyping of quinacrine mustard stained human chromosomes. *Exp. Cell Res., 67,* 233.

CASPERSSON, T., LINDSTEN, J., LOMAKKA, G., MÖLLER, A., and ZECH, L. 1972*a*. The use of fluorescence techniques for the classification of mammalian chromosomes. *Int. Rev. Exp. Pathol.* (G. W. RICHTER and M. A. EPSTEIN, eds.), p. 1. Academic Press, New York.

CASPERSSON, T., ISSLER, P., and LOMAKKA, G. 1972*b*. A TV-based technique for optical analysis of chromosome regions. *Exp. Cell Res., 75,* 543.

MÖLLER, A., NILSSON, H., CASPERSSON, T., and LOMAKKA, G. 1972. Identification of human chromosome regions by aid of computerized pattern analysis. *Exp. Cell Res., 70,* 475.

PARIS CONFERENCE. 1971. *Standardisation in Human Cytogenetics*. Birth Defects, Original Article Series, *8:7* (1972). The National Foundation, New York.

IMAGE ANALYSIS AIDS IN CYTOGENETICS

DENIS RUTOVITZ

Medical Research Council, Clinical and Population Cytogenetics Unit, Western General Hospital, Edinburgh, U.K.

1. INTRODUCTION

This paper describes the approach to the automation of some aspects of image analysis work developed in the MRC Clinical and Population Cytogenetics Unit in Edinburgh. References are given only to indicate where a fuller account of our work can be found. Papers by many of the other groups in the field will be found in *Comput. Biol. Med.*, Vol. 2 (1972).

There are broadly speaking three main areas in which modern image analysis techniques can be usefully applied in the cytogenetic laboratory. The first of these is karyotyping: this has been for some years one of the "glamour" targets of pattern recognition specialists, and, while a number of systems are now either entering service or on the point of doing so, it still remains to be seen whether substantial benefits will accrue from their use. The main objective of this work (see table 1) is the replacement of the human operator. In laboratories such as ours, in which karyotyping is done directly down the microscope the operator/machine combination has to compete with timings for screening purposes (on conventional preparations) of 2 to 3

TABLE 1

Possible applications of image analysis aids in cytogenetics

	Screening (for karyotypically abnormal individuals)	Highspeed counting (e.g., aberration scoring)	Accurate measurement
Objective	replace operator		scientific results unobtainable by other methods
Most suitable scanners	T.V., mech./C.R.T.	T.V.	mechanical
Automatic microscope	desirable	essential	not essential
Metaphase finding	desirable	essential	not essential
Speed important	yes	fundamental	no
Error tolerance	false negatives inadmissible in clinical studies	considerable cell-to-cell variation permissible if overall statistical results are correct	recognition errors avoidable by extensive use of operator
Interaction	seemingly essential	possibly avoidable	desirable

minutes per cell achieved by the skilled cytogenetic technician. Since the equipment involved (table 2) will probably cost more than 20 times an operator's yearly salary in the U.K., to be competitive it will have to do the work of four or five technicians, taking interest, depreciation, and running costs into account. This implies an analysis rate of less than half a minute per cell; and one would have to have the same degree of confidence in the machine as in operator-analysed cells for this comparison to be valid. No system so far deployed meets these requirements.

Another type of work frequently performed in cytogenetic laboratories is counting of various sorts: examples are radioactive spotting on stripping film, percentages of dividing cells in relation to all cells, and especially aberration scoring. The requirements for effective performance of the first two of these three tasks are simpler and in many respects different from those for karyotyping (see table 1). Aberration scoring is of a complexity about equal to that of karyotyping, but one can probably obtain statistically adequate results even if a considerably larger number of errors is made in the scoring of individual cells. Consequently it may be possible to use scanning and computing equipment of lesser cost and precision than is required for full karyotyping, especially if this includes analysis of banding patterns. The third application of importance is the use of precision scanning equipment, backed up by small computers for convenience in evaluating numeric parameters, to obtain scientific results which cannot be obtained by the qualitative judgement of the human human technician. In this type of work a pattern recognition capability is not always essential, as rapid operation is in any case often incompatible with extreme accuracy of measurement (e.g., long photometric integration times, individual item focussing)· so that there may be no significant loss in using an operator to direct the measurements and do all the pattern recognition.

TABLE 2

Probable cost of a chromosome analysis system (in units of £1000)

Computer controlled microscope	7
Metaphase search	
diode array, logic, and interface	3
Precision digitiser	
mechanical scanner and interface	4
Computer	
16 bit, less than 1 μsec. cycle time	
64 K store	
discs	
hard copy peripherals	
2 processors	50*
Interaction facilities	
graphics unit	5
manual controls, joystick, etc.	1
	70

* Depends on throughput required.

2. KARYOTYPING

We have gone to considerable lengths to try to speed up the process of machine karyotyping. Investigation some years ago indicated that the time bottleneck lay principally in the actual computer analysis of images by conventional sequentially working computers. We therefore set up a multi-processor machine configuration which makes it possible either for different parts of an image to be analyzed simultaneously, or for different processes to be carried out in parallel on the same image segment. However, it is still not clear whether this will in fact yield a significant time advantage, as one of the great difficulties in an undertaking of this type is the effective scheduling of different operations. We estimate that the use of two processors reduces the total analysis time by perhaps 30%. However, a law of diminishing returns seems to apply, and further worthwhile gains will probably not be obtainable without substantially increasing the total amount of computing equipment used. Our own experience indicates that the processing time per picture point by general purpose computer, in even the most trivial image analysis undertaking, is measured in hundreds of microseconds and more usually in milliseconds. In chromosome analysis this tends to be an order of magnitude higher still, and since at reasonable resolution one will always be dealing with about 10^4 points per spread, the central processor time alone for karyotyping will be of the order of minutes rather than seconds. Really fast karyotyping is therefore not likely to be achieved without specialised array processing equipment or other purpose-built hardware.

In our current chromosome analysis system (Rutovitz et al., 1970; Hilditch, 1970) the process commences with the automatic retrieval of a cell previously logged by the metaphase finding equipment. The pattern of bright and dark regions of the microscope field due to the light transmitted through the cell is now scanned by an "image dissector" tube, under the control of a PDP9 computer, in a two-stage process. Initially a coarse ($\frac{1}{2}$-micron interval) scan of a region containing the cell is carried out. The computer now performs the following operations:

1. corrects for variations in intensity of field illumination and sensitivity of the scanning instrument,
2. determines a threshold value separating the chromosome from the background (Mason et al., 1975).
3. segments the picture into discreet above-background regions, and, for each of the regions found:
4. expands by $\frac{1}{2}$ micron all round,
5. re-scans at $\frac{1}{8}$ micron spacing,
6. corrects for shading,
7. re-determines the threshold value,
8. re-segments.

As each component is located on the second scan it is transmitted to a Modular 1 computer which then carries out the analysis. This consists of a sequence of procedures for mensuration and geometric feature extraction. At many points alternative paths must be chosen, depending on the relation of measurements so far retrieved to statistics previously compiled. Whenever such a decision is taken or a geometric feature extracted, statistics are again used to measure the probability of the decision or feature identification being correct (for example, a procedure to find the centromere line of a chromosome will always locate a line: it is important to know the probability of its being the right one!). If at any stage the confidence in a step is too low, the calculation is repeated using a more complex (and usually more time-consuming) procedure, if one is available, or the question is referred back to the PDP9 and the operator for decision.

The main steps in the analysis are:

1. The area, optical density, first and second moments, and perimeter of each object are calculated. Using these measurements it is then classified as a single chromosome, part of a chromosome, noise, a composite group of chromosomes, undivided nucleus, or an artefact (if in doubt it is referred to an operator). Composites are split and pieces are retained awaiting other pieces to which they can be joined.

2. (For single chromosomes): the centromere line is located by looking for a minimum or shoulder in the density profile along the principal axis. A number of variants of this procedure are available for more difficult cases, including a method which finds density profiles with respect to an axis of arbitrary shape found by skeletonisation (Hilditch, 1968). Operator assistance is sought if required.

3. When all chromosomes have been dealt with, the area of each chromosome is re-expressed as a percentage of the sum of areas for the whole cell; it is then classified, using Bayesian statistics of size and centromeric index measurements of chromosomes for each of the ten groups recognised (Hilditch and Rutovitz, 1972; Paton, 1969).

One can choose to have the findings presented for individual chromosomes or individual cells; normally, however, the results from a number of cells from the the same slide are collated to give a "composite karyotype", in which i) the number of chromosomes in each group is the modal one; ii) chromosomes are only acknowledged as abnormal if there is a cluster in the size/centromeric index plane not fitting into one of the standard groupings.

The time taken for the coarse/fine scan is about 2 minutes, and for the karyotype analysis about 5 minutes. This will be improved substantially by program optimisation; the scan and analysis run substantially in parallel and the latter can be parcelled out amongst different units of our multi-processor computer complex. Whilst we feel therefore that we are in sight of an acceptable elapsed time for individual analyses, we are not yet economically competitive with a trained technician carrying out the same task.

3. COUNTING

As remarked above, the design considerations and constraints involved in high-speed counting differ in several important respects from requirements for karyotyping work. Although we have, from time to time, investigated numbers of different projects of this sort, for example radiographic hot-spot counting, our main effort here has been directed towards metaphase cell location and mitotic indexing. In most projects of this type the standards of densitometry may be considerably relaxed without unduly prejudicing the reliability of the results. Nevertheless we have found that we get significantly better performance from a precision Plumbicon camera than from a cheap CCTV device. Television cameras of one sort or another have excellent properties for this type of work as their charge-integrating architecture enables high signal-to-noise ratios to be achieved with relatively low light levels and very high point-scanning rates. Linear diode arrays are an inexpensive alternative to television systems if mechanical movement of the slide can be used to provide the second scan axis, but evidently it can be much more difficult to meet signal-to-noise requirements when integrating over a single line rather than a whole frame. Diode arrays, however, have two advantages over TV systems in this connection.

1. A special erase scan is not necessary as the diodes are automatically zeroed as they are read. Without special arrangements one can only use every third or fourth Vidicon or Plumbicon frame if the field is changing between scans, because the charge pattern due to a previously scanned image persists for some time. Even with optimal arrangements, alternate scans must be erase passes.

2. To work with continuous stage movement with a frame TV system, the image must be strobed onto the photocathode to staticise it. Powerful strobed light sources add substantially to the costs of a scanning system; this problem does not arise in the case of diode arrays.

3. Diodes can be individually shading corrected.

Another point is that if a conventional computer is used for any part of the analysis, high speeds can only be achieved if there is very substantial data compression (Farrow, 1974). An example of this is furnished by our metaphase finding procedure (Green and Cameron, 1972; Green, 1974).

A dividing cell may be characterized as an agglomeration, over an area of about 70 microns diameter, of either a discrete set of connected regions darker than the background or of a set of above background scan intervals of length less than 4 microns, separated from each other by not more than 20 microns. It is easy to detect suitable intervals and ends of connected two-dimensional objects (a delay line and comparator suffice), and the mean data rate of either phenomenon is not unmanageable (10^4/sq. cm. for regions, 10^5/sq. cm. for intervals). On the other hand, the peak rate within a metaphase cell is far too high for direct output to a computer. Both the data rate and the total to be handled are drastically reduced by notionally dividing each field into 256 small squares of about 20 micron side and accumulating counts of whichever feature is wanted, for each square. As a single scan line passes through only 16 such squares, 16 counters are enough; and after each strip amounting to 1/12 of the picture has been scanned the entire non-zero count pattern is transmitted to our PDP9 computer. From this information a program is able to work out the location of metaphase cells, and an index of quality which takes into account the uniformity of count distribution in the cell, symmetry and so forth. While occasionally the scan will have to be held up to empty the computer storage buffers, normally the machine is able to operate at the maximum scan speed, i.e., alternate frames of the 44 frames per second Plumbican to give an over-all search rate of roughly 1 sq. cm. minute.

The same equipment can be used for mitotic indexing and measuring percentages of polyploid cells. If the image is defocussed, metaphase cells, which are an agglomerate of small image features, disappear, whereas the larger cells do not. It is thus possible to obtain estimates of the total cell population and therefore also the mitotic index.

4. ACCURATE MEASUREMENT

All measurements of objects in a visual field are ultimately dependent on accurate densitometry. This may not seem to be the case if we are measuring, say lengths of chromosomes, but it is instructive to view a thresholded chromosome on an interactive display of some kind: as the threshold is increased from the background level the chromosome will vary from a large, ill-defined, rather fuzzy object to a set of isolated bright regions on the arms and eventually disappear. By varying the threshold one will usually be able to obtain lengths differing by 20% or more before disjunction occurs (this is not necessarily the case when working from film, for then the thresholding has in effect occurred earlier). Thresholds are set using various algorithms for detecting edges and so forth, but in the end one is always limited by the quality of the data at one's disposal.

Densitometry is affected by geometric aberrations if these alter the area of field sampled according to the position in it; by chromatic operations as the receptor will have different sensitivities at different wavelengths; by glare, scatter, and halo; by non-uniform illumination; by variable sensitivity of the photoreceptor which may be a multiplicative or (as with television) exponential effect; by low energy levels giving rise to photon noise; by dark current and other sources of noise in the electronics; by thermal drift affecting both focus and electronics. Some types of variation are quite readily compensated for; in particular, photocathode shading and time-constant variations in illumination level can be compensated by the use of a shading map of one kind or another. We have found, for example, that variations over the whole field of an image dissector can be compensated by interpolating mean compensation figures from approximately 1,000 sample points (some commercial systems use a similar procedure). This does not, however, deal with high frequency sensitivity variations or "blemishes", though partial compensation can be achieved by detecting and smoothing over any very sudden variations in intensity in digitised pictures.

One is considerably better off with a flying spot device, as in this case it can be arranged for a reference beam to follow an optical path equivalent to that of the transmitted beam, the effective signal being the difference between the two. In many systems of this type a simpler approach is used, in which the reference is simply a measure of the spot intensity. In this case it may still be necessary to use a shading map to compensate for variations in transmission and spot size which are geometry dependent.

For best high resolution densitometry, it is necessary to use conjugate apertures in an optical system which is symmetric on both sides of the object: this ensures that the light measured is only that transmitted through the point one is attempting to sample and not scattered through surrounding areas. The only practical way of doing this is to move the object rather than the spot, but the commercial systems available for this type of measurement are as yet limited in resolution and speed. We are currently attempting to produce a 100μ deflection mechanical table with optical position feedback and servo-hold for accurate positioning along scan lines, in the hope that this will result in an instrument capable of maximal densitometric accuracy and resolution, which should nevertheless work as fast as the available light energy permits.

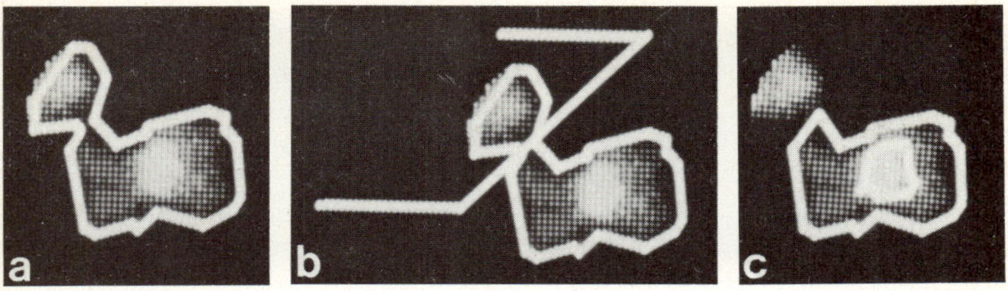

FIG. 1.—A trimmer, steered by the operator, can be used to correct outlines of chromosome or C-band as found by the machine.

In many applications in which the goal is accurate measurement rather than rapid screening or counting the operator's speed of selection and identification of patterns is adequate but considerable instrumentation is required for obtaining and logging the data. A good example of this is offered by the problem of measuring differences in C-bands of homologous chromosomes (Mason et al., 1975). Once a suitable metaphase cell has been found an operator can select the chromosomes of interest (Nos. 9 and 16, for example) quickly enough by, for example, positioning a steerable disc on a displayed image of the cell. The program then takes over, segments the picture within the disc, and displays to the operator what it has found (fig. 1). At each "inspection window" the technician pushes the space bar of the teletype to indicate "proceed"; alternatively, correcting action may be taken. The successive steps are:

1. determine initial threshold level,
2. segment the picture within the disc, eliminating all but the largest connected region,
3. show to operator,
4. border the region,
5. optimise focus,
6. find chromosome and band threshold,
7. display boundaries for operator approval,
8. carry out the measurements.

This approach uses the pattern recognition capability of the human operator and the precision and arithmetic competence of the machine to carry out far more complex measurements than would otherwise be feasible.

5. REFERENCES

FARROW, A. S. J. 1974. TV scanner to computer in real time. In *Oxford Conference on Computer Scanning, 2* (P. G. DAVEY and B. M. HAWES, eds.), pp. 407–422.

GREEN, D.K. 1974. Machine to find metaphase cells. *Exp. Cell Res., 86,* 170–174.

GREEN, D. K., and CAMERON, J. 1972. Metaphase cell finding by machine. *Cytogenetics (Basel), 11,* 475–487.

HILDITCH, C. J. 1968. Linear skeletons from square cupboards. In *Machine Intelligence 4* (B. MELTZER and D. MICHIE, eds.), pp. 403–420. Edinburgh University Press.

HILDITCH, C. J. 1970. The principles of a software system for karyotype analysis. In *Human Population Cytogenetics* (P. A. JACOBS, W. H. PRICE and P. LAW, eds.), pp. 297–325. Pfizer Med. Monographs 5, Edinburgh University Press.

HILDITCH, C. J., and RUTOVITZ, D. 1972. Normalization of chromosome measurements. In *Comput. Biol. Med., 2,* pp. 167–179. Pergamon Press.

MASON, D., LAUDER, I., RUTOVITZ, D., and SPOWART, G. 1975. Measurement of C-bands in human chromosomes. *Comput. Biol. Med., 5,* pp. 179–201, Pergamon Press.

PATON, K. 1969. Automatic chromosome identification by the maximum-likelihood method. *Ann. Hum. Genet., 33,* 177.

RUTOVITZ, D., CAMERON, J., FARROW, A. S. J., GREEN, D. K., and HILDITCH, C. J. 1970. Instrumentation and organisation for chromosome measurement and karyotype analysis. In *Human Population Cytogenetics* (P. A. JACOBS, W. H. PRICE, and P. LAW, eds.), pp. 282–296. Pfizer Med. Monographs 5, Edinburgh University Press.

AUTOMATED ANALYSIS OF R BANDED CELLS: EARLY RESULTS AND FUTURE PROSPECTS

H. A. LUBS,[1] R. S. VERMA,[1] and R. S. LEDLEY[2]

[1] *Department of Pediatrics, University of Colorado Medical Center, 4200 East Ninth Avenue, Denver, Colorado, U.S.A.*

[2] *National Biomedical Research Foundation, Georgetown University Medical Center, 3900 Reservoir Road, N.W., Washington, D.C., U.S.A.*

1. INTRODUCTION

R banding is currently an undervalued and underutilized technique. The principle exception is in the laboratory of Dutrillaux and Lejeune where R banding has been utilized as the primary clinical technique. Their results, moreover, have been quite impressive (Lejeune, 1973; Dutrillaux, 1973*a*). In other laboratories it has occasionally been used as a confirming or supplementary technique. Our preliminary results indicate that R banding is not only an excellent technique for routine use but that the prospects for automated analysis of R banded cells are probably better than with any of the other currently available banding techniques. The purpose of this report is to present both the reasons for considering R banding as a primary technique and the preliminary results of automatically determined R banded curves.

2. METHODOLOGY

(a) *R banding*

The method of R banding employed in these studies was a simple modification of the technique originally described by Dutrillaux and Lejuene (1971) and Laurent et al. (1972). It differs primarily in using a simple phosphate buffer throughout, without any of the more complex solutions described by Dutrillaux and Lejeune, and in the use of acridine orange staining (Verma and Lubs, 1975). The combination of irregular staining with Giemsa and the advantage of somewhat better discrimination of bands provided by the fluorescence colors lead to the latter change. The various methods were reviewed in the above publication. The cells were prepared as previously described (Lubs et al., 1973) using hypotonic KCl (0.075 M) for 16–18 min and air-dried. Heat drying on a hot plate was not used, however, since slightly better delineation of bands was obtained when cells were air-dried on wet slides without heating. A single slide was incubated in a coplin jar in fresh phosphate buffer* at pH 6.5 for 20–25 min in a water bath maintained at 85°C. If the incubation time was too long the chromosomes became fuzzy and orange in fluorescence. Generally, slides were stained 7–14 days after culture. A shorter incubation time was required for older slides. Slides were stained for 4–6 min with 0.01 % acridine orange prepared in the same phosphate buffer, rinsed in phosphate buffer at pH 6.5 for

* Phosphate buffer: 32 cc of 0.07 M disodium hydrogen phosphate dodecahydrate (Na_2H $PO4.12H_2O$) + 68cc of 0.07 M potassium dihydrogen phosphate (KH_2PO4). The pH was adjusted by adding 0.07 M $Na_2HPO4.12H_2O$ to the solution.

1.5–3 min, and mounted in the same buffer without sealing the cover slip. Over staining produced an orange-red fluorescence which could be corrected by additional rinsing. The orange-red fluorescence due to overheating, however, is not generally corrected by additional rinsing. Understaining was indicated by green fluorescence without banding; this could be corrected by reintroducing the slide into the staining solution for a short time and rinsing again. An understanding of these variables is extremely important in producing the desired results. The same photographic system was used as with Q banding but optimal results were obtained from color transparency film with subsequent printing from the color positive transparency in black and white. The black and white karyotypes can then be compared with the projected color transparency. With this system, the green fluorescence regions print as dark regions and orange-red regions as gray. Additional photographic details are given in the previous publication (Verma and Lubs, 1975). Most importantly, the technique is simple, repeatable, adjustable and produces a high proportion of well banded metaphases. Black and white photography can also be carried out directly but this results in prints with a black background and white chromosomes, which are both more difficult to read and less aesthetically pleasing. The presentation of results in laboratory reports and publication is also less satisfactory with a black background.

(b) *Automation*

The details of the system currently in use at National Biomedical Research Foundation have been presented in considerable detail (Ledley et al., 1972; Lubs and Ledley, 1973). The system consists of a 360-44 computer, FIDAC scanner, an operator interaction device with a display screen (which permits separating adjacent chromosomes, relocating centromeres, interchanging chromosomes in a karyotype display, etc.), a Leitz microscope equipped with a video scanner and TV monitor for observing the metaphase finding aspect of the operation, an automatic stage control unit, and a silicon video memory system. All work reported here was carried out directly from 35mm negatives derived from fluorescence microscopy. As with Q banding, where there is also a light background with dark chromosomes in the negatives, the recorded gray levels were reversed around an appropriate middle level, thereby enabling the G banding analysis programs to be employed. Hence, the same program has been found to be satisfactory for G, C, Q, and R banding. As previously reported, all curves were derived after first fitting the best parabolic axis to each chromosome, then determining the mean gray levels aross both chromatids at right axis to this parabolic line. The curves were displayed after smoothing as squared mean levels, normalized to a standard length and height, or as unnormalized curves. The present illustrations were prepared from Calcomp plots in which the density curves were darkened by drawing over the original Calcomp plot to enhance the visibility of the curves. Although visual output in the form of banded karyotypes can be obtained, the principle means of working with the system at the present time is with the displayed density curves and karyotypes.

Although the metaphase finding system was not used in this work, the system currently permits the detection of excellent metaphases at the rate of one per minute in a good preparation. In a recent trial, for example, an average of five potential metaphases/minute could be evaluated by the operator and accepted or rejected for analysis. On the average, one of the five fields proved to be a metaphase of sufficient quality to permit a good analysis (no overlaps, clear centromeres, 46 chromosomes, etc.), three of five were metaphases of less good quality, and one was artifact.

3. RESULTS AND DISCUSSION

Various R banded karyotypes with this technique are shown in figs. 1–3. The ends of arms and major regions are especially well delineated. The banding pattern of each of the 24 types is sufficiently clear so that it is not generally necessary to make comparisons with similar chromosomes. All chromosomes can be quickly identified from a 5 × 7 print. The system is especially well adapted for the detection of small differences in length between homologs and for accurate localization of structural alterations. Chromosomes that are often similar in many G or Q banding cells, such as 14 and 15 or 4 and 5, are particularly well distinguished. The relative merits of R and other banding techniques are given in the table. The clear demarcation of major regions and the sharply demarcated paracentric regions are particularly useful aspects of the technique. The major limitation of the technique is the fact that somewhat fewer bands are generally seen than with trypsin G banding in metaphases of average length. It is extremely unlikely, however, that a structural change would result in a detectable banding difference without a change in arm length or ratio and this, therefore, does not constitute a significant limitation in its routine use. The ability to compare arm lengths with considerable accuracy remains a powerful tool in screening clinical specimens either by eye or automated techniques. This limitation can also be overcome by ascertaining several prometaphase cells in each clinical study, since the number of bands seen in these cells is comparable to that seen with excellent Q and G banding. Pericentric inversions should be especially well detected

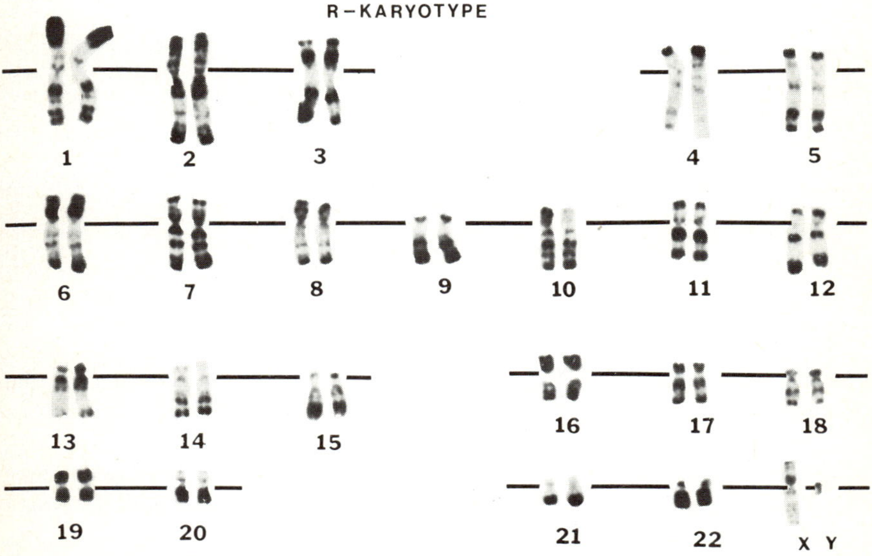

FIG. 1.—R band karyotype obtained by printing in black and white from a color transparency (Kodachrome-X).

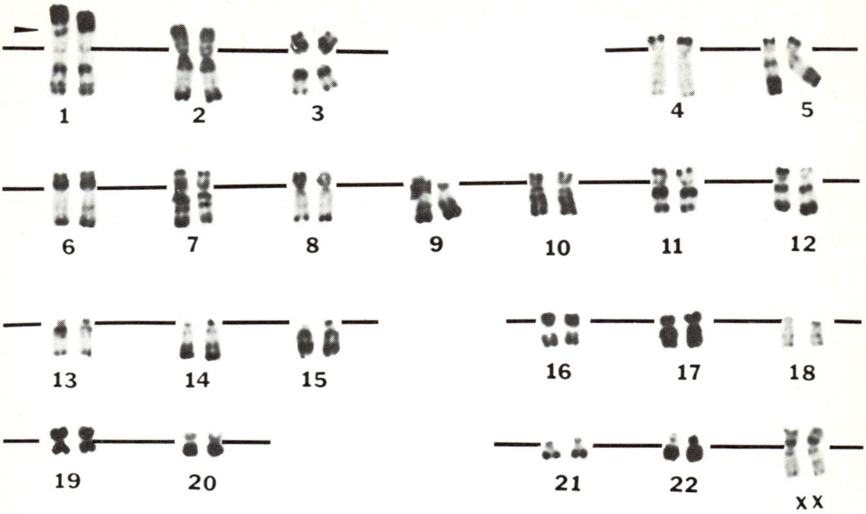

FIG. 2.—Two extra bands in 1q were present in all cells of this child. See text.

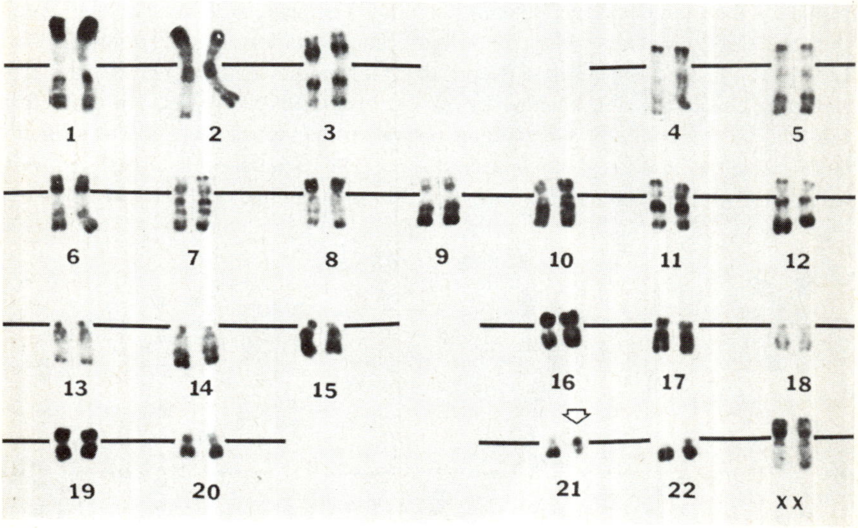

FIG. 3.—The ring chromosome probably includes the centromere and 2/3 of 21q. The color projection was especially helpful in determining the composition of the ring.

by this system in the X and many other chromosomes. The dark pericentric band in the short arm of X, for example, is always larger than the comparable region in the long arm. In figs. 2 and 3, two structural abnormalities are shown. In the first, a partial trisomy is present in 1p. It is most likely that this represents a duplication of bands p22–p31 in this arm although an insertion from another chromosome cannot be ruled out. In the karyotype shown in fig. 3 a 21 is replaced by a ring chromosome. The ring probably includes at least the centromere and most of 21q (except the distal part of band q22). In both these children the use of the color projections materially

TABLE

Comparison of R banding with G and Q banding

	Q and G	R
1. Identification of each chromosome	May be uncertain (4, 5, 14–15, and X)	*Rapid and certain
2. End of arms (telomeres)	Often dim	*Sharply demarcated
3. Proportion of banded cells	Variable	*> 95%
4. Density curves	Some curves similar, especially in Group C	Curves for each of the 24 types are unique
5. Number of bands/ chromosome	Greater number of bands with G and Q banding in average length metaphase	In prometaphase cells the number of bands is equal in G, Q, and R bands
6. Special advantage in identifying abnormalities	See 5	*Color difference helpful
7. Use of sequential banding techniques	*Up to 6 months	Only if used as final technique
8. Frequency of variants	*Q > R	R > G
9. Presentation of results	Often difficult	*Clear and easy to reproduce

* Major advantage

assisted in the identification of the abnormality. The ring chromosome, for example, included a bright yellow portion similar in color to the initial part of band q22 in the normal homolog. Similarly, in fig. 2 a duplication was strongly suggested by the similarity of the colors in the abnormal region and adjacent bands p22–p31. Although the numbers of patients involved is still small, excellent results have been obtained in using this technique for routine work in clinical cytogenetics.

Ten cells have been run in the automated analysis system from black and white negatives. The cytogeneticist's identification of each chromosome was entered into the display system using the sequential identification number on the Calcomp plot of the cell. In fig. 4 a "curve karyotype" of an R banded cell is presented and in fig. 5 unnormalized but smoothed curves are presented together with a photographic representation of the chromosome from which the curve data were derived. The consistency of the curves for each chromosome is shown by the results obtained in the first five cells (fig. 6). Even for smaller chromosomes, such as 21, the consistency of the curves is quite striking. Most of the variation, as discussed, is due to factors inherent in the preparation of metaphases and not to the computer analysis. Concomitantly, the greater consistency of the curves with R banding is due to the consistency of the banding patterns in the metaphases themselves and not to improved computer analysis, since the analytic program has been the same with all banding techniques. The R curves (fig. 7) on the top row show a much greater vertical variation, steeper slopes, and more characteristic curve profiles than the Q curves below. It would appear very likely that these will permit a higher rate of correct automated identification, and such studies are now in progress using a set of 50 cells from which Fourier coefficients and other parameters will be extracted and tested against a second set of 50 cells from the same individuals.

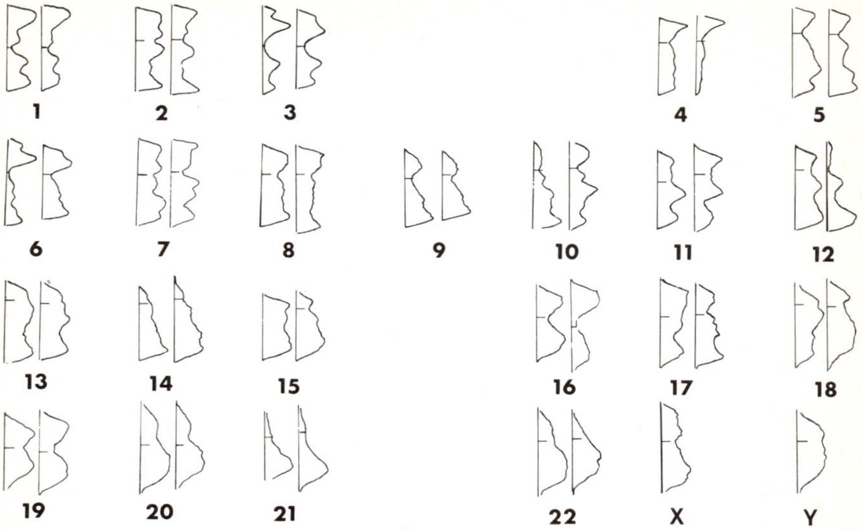

FIG. 4.—Curves are normalized to a standard length and height. Note the similarity of homologous curves in nearly all instances. Variations between homologs in the height of certain parts of the curves (chromosomes 4, 6 and 12) are due to the peripheral location of these chromosomes on the metaphase and the accompanying stretching that often occurs; the computer program has given a reasonable presentation of the actual appearance in these chromosomes. Note that in most chromosomes the curves rise sharply in the telomeric regions.

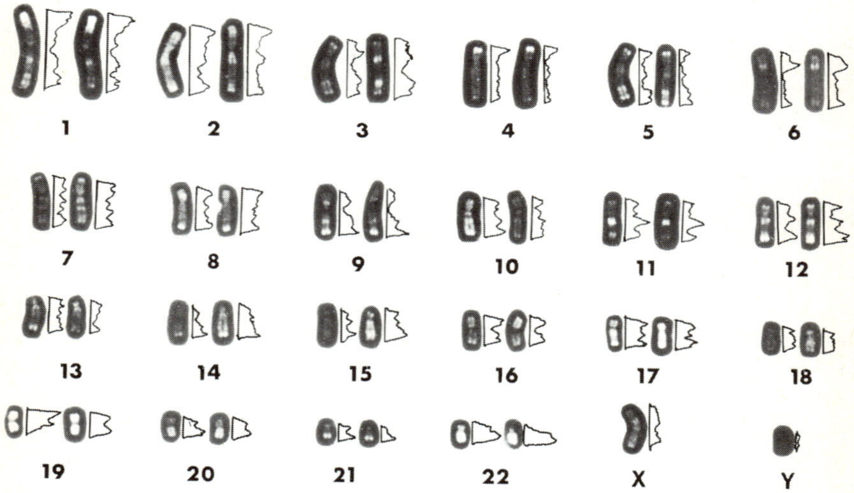

FIG. 5.—Unnormalized, smoothed curves. The chromosomes from which the curves were derived were placed adjacent to the appropriate curves on the printout to permit visual comparison of the original chromosome and derived curves; lengths and heights in this instance give a better representation of the overall karyotype. Routine work would be carried out with this type of curve karyotype. Note particularly the "headlights" in the 4's compared with the two "tail-lights" in 5q. Such characteristic features permit both a ready visual representation and very likely an accurate identification using curve information.

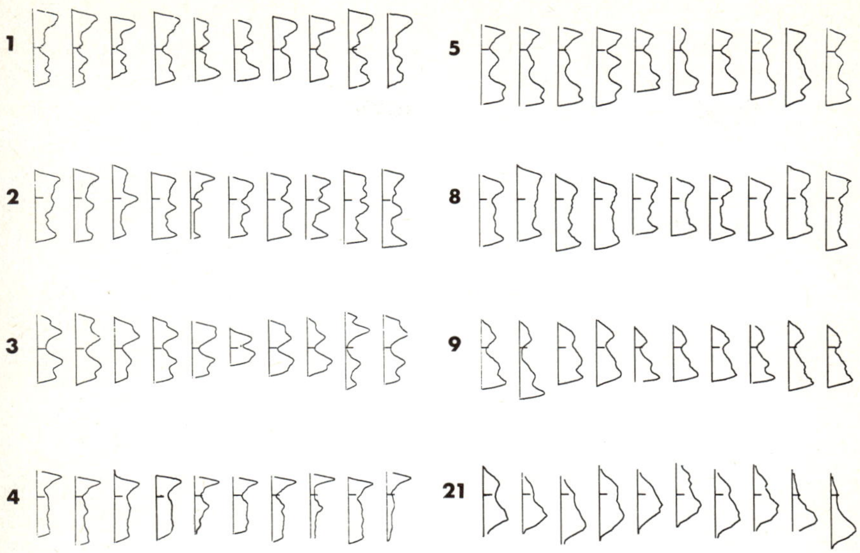

FIG. 6.—The results are shown for selected chromosomes in the first five cells studied. The first two curves of chromosome 1 represent homologs from the first cell, the second two from the second cell, etc. The similarity of the curves between cells is considerably greater than that obtained with Q and G banded cells in our experience.

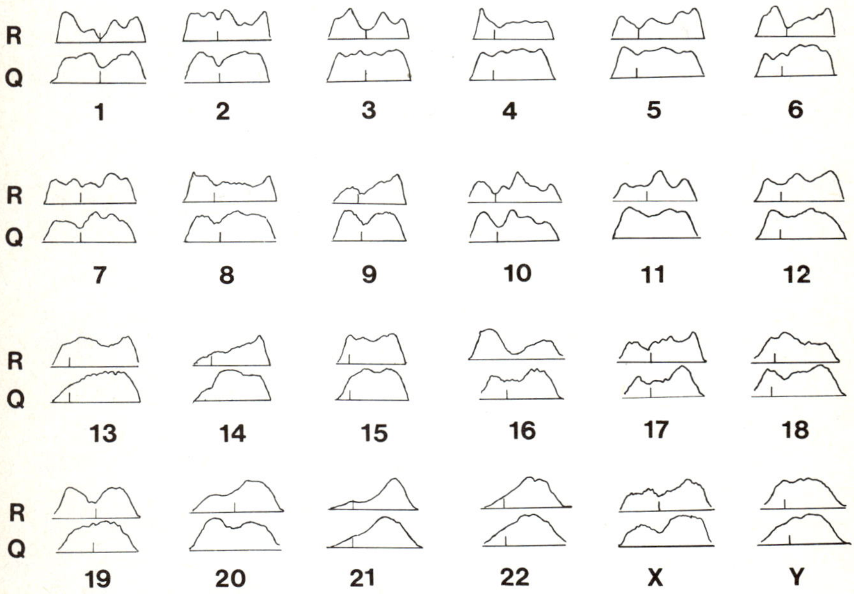

FIG. 7.—Comparison of R and Q curves in the same cell. Only the better homolog is presented. The results, however, demonstrate the difference between Q and R curves in the same chromosome sequentially stained for Q and R banding.

It is of some interest to compare the details of the Q and R curves of the same chromosome and to determine exactly what is meant by "reverse" banding. Is it indeed reverse? In certain instances, as can be seen best in 3p and q and 7q, the major landmarks indeed show reversal in the direction of the Q and R curves (figs. 7 and 8). In other regions, such as the telomeric regions in 4p and 5p, "reverseness" is represented in the curves by a steeper slope in portions of the R curves. In still other instances, such as 9p, "reverseness" is shown by a relatively lower height of the curve with R banding than with Q banding although the direction of the curves is the same. Thus, although the designation R banding is appropriate to describe the visual appearance in these cells, it is not a completely appropriate term from the standpoint of the density curves. R banding, however, remains a very useful descriptive term for the appearance of chromosomes in a karyotype, and it is not suggested in any way that it be changed.

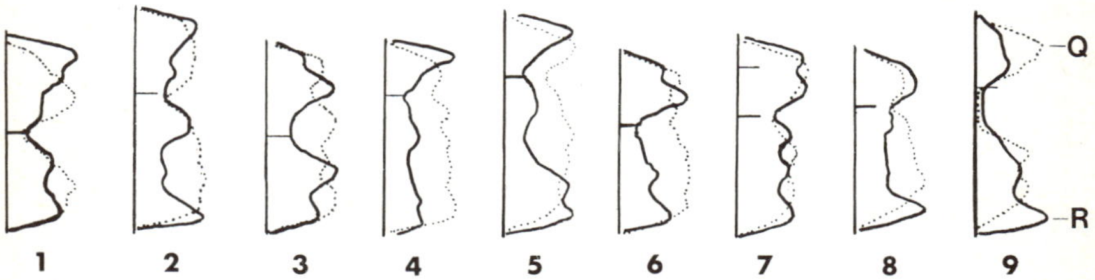

FIG. 8.—The Calcomp plots for the same chromosomes were superimposed and the Q and R curves traced by hand; the Q curve is shown in dotted lines and the R in a solid line for chromosomes 1–9. Chromosomes are from different cells in this case and were selected because they give the best comparison of the Q and R curves.

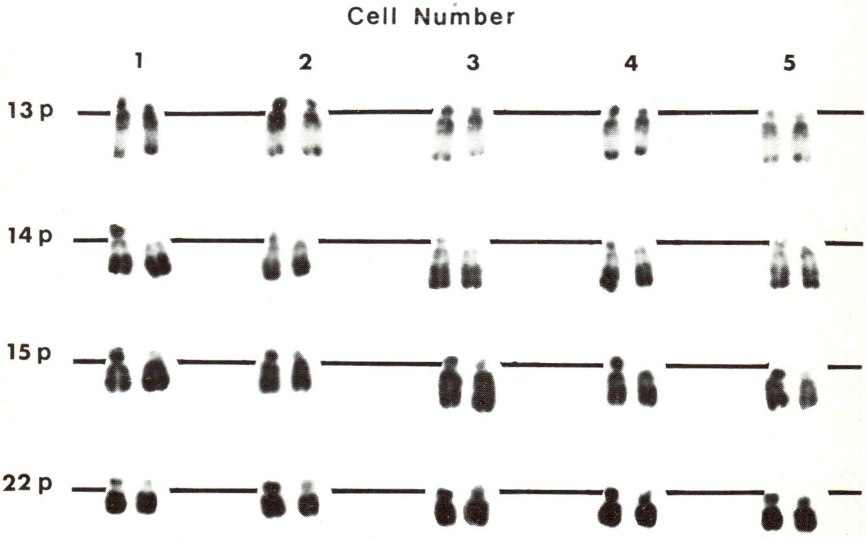

FIG. 9.—Examples of R variants in D and G groups. Detailed criteria are being developed for each chromosome but preliminary evidence suggests that the size and density of 18p serves as useful point of reference for determining variations in D and G short arms.

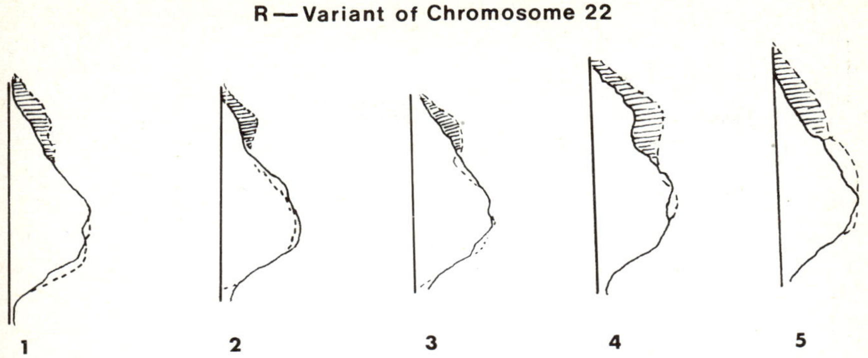

FIG. 10.—Curves of both homologs superimposed; chromosome 22 as shown in figure 9.

4. SUMMARY AND CONCLUSIONS

Although optimal cytogenetic information is obtained from sequential banding techniques in the same cell, R banding provides adequate information for the detection of abnormalities on a routine basis and is probably the method of choice because of its excellent delineation of arm lengths and clear banding patterns. A further evaluation of R banding for routine use by additional laboratories appears warranted. Our preliminary results suggest that the automated analysis of R banded cells will probably yield a higher rate of correct identification than with Q and G banded cells. Studies to determine whether this is correct are in progress. Moreover, current results with the automated system and R banding indicate that there is minimal between cell and between person variation in the major bands and that small length and density variants in the D and G groups can be detected and displayed by the automated system.

Acknowledgements. Research supported by N.I.H. Grant No. HD 05361-10.

5. REFERENCES

DUTRILLAUX, B. 1793 *a*. Application to the normal karyotype of R band and G band techniques involving proteolytic digestion. In *Nobel Symposia XXIII, Medicine and Natural Sciences, Chromosome Identification Technique and Application in Biology and Medicine* (T. CASPERSSON and L. ZECH, eds.), pp. 38–42. Academic, New York.

DUTRILLAUX, B. 1973*b*. Chromosomal aspects of human male sterility. *Ibid,* 205–208.

DUTRILLAUX, B., and LEJEUNE, J. 1971. Sur une nouvelle technique d'analyse du caryotype humain. *C. R. Acad. Sci. (Paris), 272,* 2638–2640.

LAURENT, C., DUTRILLAUX, B., and BINDER, P. 1972. Application de la methode de denaturation menagee: Denaturation de preparation colorees anterieurement. *Ann.Génét., 15,* 201–202.

LEDLEY, R. S., LUBS, H. A., and RUDDLE, R. H. 1972. Introduction to chromosome analysis. *J. Computers Biol. Med., 2,* 107–128.

LEJEUNE, J. 1973. Scientific impact of the study of fine structure of chromatids. In *Nobel Symposia XXIII, Medicine and Natural Sciences, Chromosome Identification Technique and Application in Biology and Medicine* (T. CASPERSSON a d L. ZECH, eds), pp. 16–24. Academic, New York.

LUBS, H. A., and LEDLEY, R. S. 1973. Automated analysis of differentially stained human chromosomes—a review of goals, problems and progress. In *Nobel Symposia XXIII, Medicine and Natural Sciences, Chromosome Identification Technique and Application in Biology and Medicine* (T. CASPERSSON and L. ZECH, eds.), pp. 61–76. Academic, New York.

LUBS, H. A., MCKENZIE, W. H., PATIL, S. R., and MERRICK, S. 1973. New staining methods for chromosomes. In *Methods in Cell Biology* (D. M. PRESCOTT, ed.), pp. 345–380. Academic, New York.

VERMA, R. S., and LUBS, H. A. 1975. A simple R banding technique. *Am. J. Hum. Genet., 27,* 110–117.

MECHANICAL PREPARATION OF CELLS FOR CHROMOSOME STUDIES

HANS CHRISTIAN WULF

The Finsen Institute, Department of Dermatology, Copenhagen, Denmark

In order to standardize, speed up, and simplify chromosome preparation, a machine for the hypotonic treatment and fixation of cell cultures has been developed together with an apparatus for carrying out the decanting procedure.

1. WORKING PRINCIPLE OF THE PREPARATION APPARATUS

The centrifuge tubes with the specimens are shaken in a movable, detachable test-tube rack (1, fig. 1) at a frequency of approx. 2800/min in a way which keeps the contents in rotary motion against the walls of the tubes.

The liquid distribution chamber (4) functions as follows: a groove (2) at the top of the chamber is filled with about 100 ml liquid, sufficient for 12 tubes. The liquid runs from the groove (2) to the distribution chamber (4) through a hole (3, fig. 2) of sufficiently small diameter that a brief excess of pressure can be established by firm pressure on a bulb (5, figs. 1 and 2). The chamber is connected to the air by a series of inverted J-tubes (6, figs. 2 and 3) opening above each centrifuge tube.

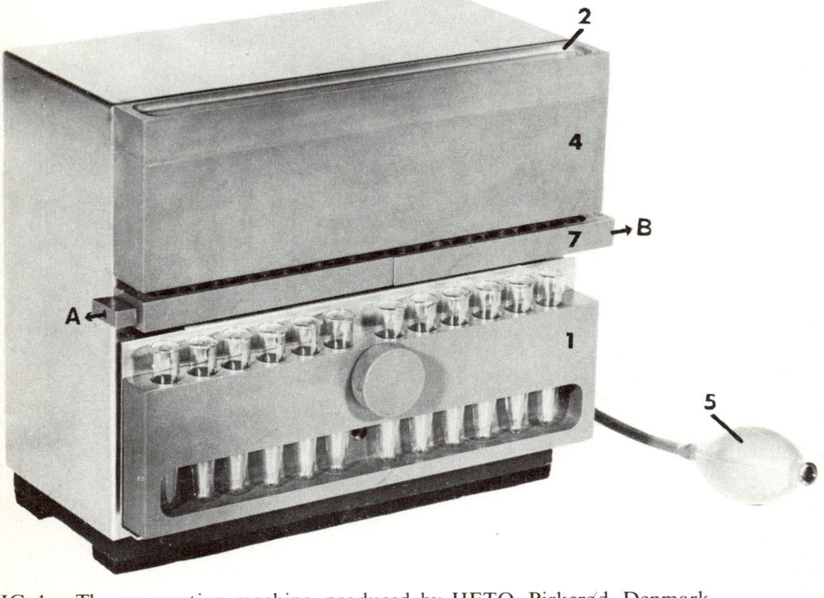

FIG. 1.—The preparation machine, produced by HETO, Birkerød, Denmark.

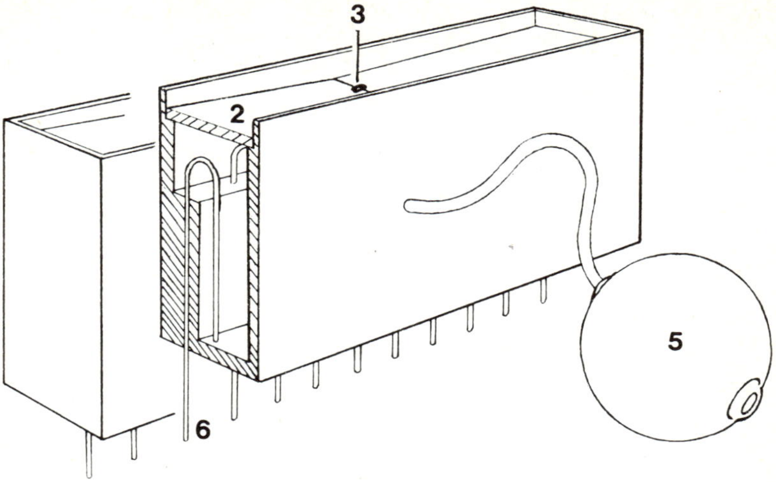

FIG. 2.—Principle of fluid distribution chamber (4). For explanation see text.

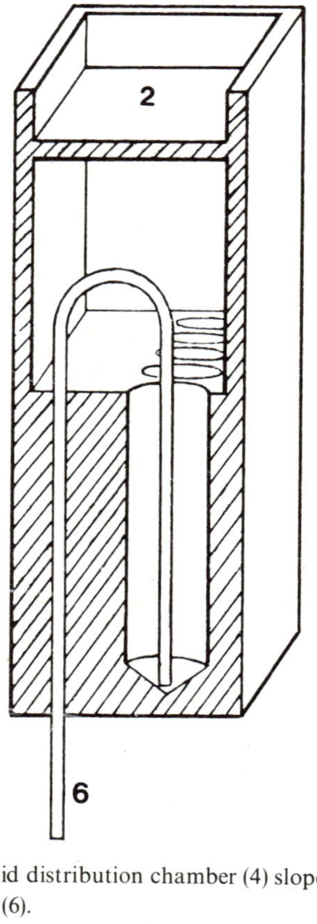

FIG. 3.—The bottom of the fluid distribution chamber (4) slopes down toward the opening in the short limb of the J tubes (6).

When the liquid has run into the chamber (4), a brief excess of pressure is produced. The liquid is pressed through the J-tubes (6) into the centrifuge tubes when the gutter (7, fig. 1) is in position A, but runs out of the apparatus when the gutter is pressed in the opposite direction B.

As the external opening of the J-tube (6) is lower than its internal opening, the system empties itself automatically (siphon effect). The quantity of liquid in each centrifuge tube, and the inlet speed to the centrifuge tubes depend, amongst other things, on the bore of the J-tubes.

With a narrower bore the system would start automatically because of capillary action, and with a wider bore the outlet speed would become so high as to involve a risk of clotting in the tubes.

2. PROCEDURE

With the bore selected the inlet speed into the centrifuge tubes is 30 sec for the hypotonic liquid, and the fixation time is 20 sec.

During this time about 5 ml liquid are added to each of 12 or 6 tubes, as required.

There is no need to rinse the machine on changing from hypotonic fluid to fixative. On the other hand, rinsing with water is necessary on changing from fixative to hypotonic liquid, even though the bottom of the distribution chamber slopes down (fig. 3) toward the opening of the short limb of each J-tube and the chamber is emptied completely.

3. RESULTS

This machine, and others operating on the same principle, have prepared about 9,000 cultures. A maximum of 90 cultures a day has been handled by one machine and one technician (Philip et al., in press).

The number of samples is not limited by the capacity of the machine which was evaluated by an independent investigator as 576 per day (Radiometer, 1973). Further, the unpleasant manual shaking and inhalation of the methanol-glacial acetic acid are avoided. The time used for adding the solutions during shaking and the intervals have thus been standardized, except for differences in decanting time.

Another apparatus for simultaneous decanting has been developed.

4. WORKING PRINCIPLE OF THE DECANTING APPARATUS

The detachable rack (1, figs. 1 and 4) with the centrifuge tubes is placed in the apparatus and raised until the lower part of the J-tubes (8, figs. 4 and 5) projects down to the level at which the decanting is desirable.

The 12 inverted J-tubes (8) enter by their longer limb into a common chamber (9, fig. 5) from which the outlet (10) is so small that a brief vacuum can be established by pressing a bulb (11). This starts the decanting process which will be completed in all tubes despite different quantities of liquid, as there will be a siphon effect in each centrifuge tube into which the short limb of the J-tube has been passed.

FIG. 4.—Decanting apparatus.

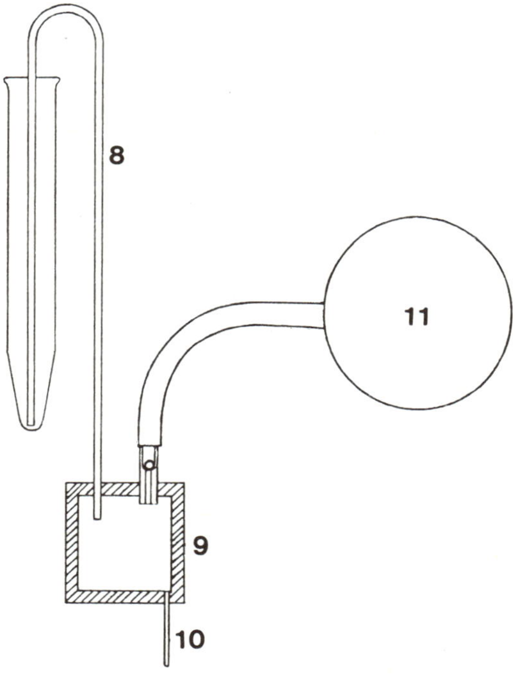

FIG. 5.—Principle of decanting apparatus.

5. RESULTS

After centrifugation of the centrifuge tubes, the supernatant is decanted simultaneously from 12 tubes within 4–5 sec, and the entire rack is then transferred to the preparation apparatus.

During decanting, the J-tubes of the apparatus come into contact with preparation liquids, and a small drop may collect at the end of each J-tube.

This might be imagined to give rise to false mosaics by admixture of foreign cells to new cultures, if the technician did not rinse the tubes between the decanting procedures. But when the cells from uncleaned tubes were collected between each step of the preparation, total scanning of 6 slides showed only 20 leucocytes and no mitoses. Even this very slight risk can be eliminated by mounting, between the decanting procedures, a special rack which automatically rinses the tubes with tap water.

By these aids the method of preparation is now standardized, quick and convenient; and the quality of machine-made chromosome preparations, banded and not banded, has reached the standard of the best manually handled ones.

6. SUMMARY

1. A machine performing hypotonic treatment and fixation of blood samples for chromosome analysis under standard conditions is described. The machine has now handled about 9,000 cultures.

2. Twelve tubes are shaken at a rate of approximately 2800/min, and simultaneously solutions for a hypotonic treatment and fixation are added during a period of 20–30 sec from a distribution chamber.

3. A decanting apparatus has also been developed which removes simultaneously the supernatant from twelve tubes within five seconds.

4. The whole system has standardized the preparation method and produces long slender chromosomes suitable for staining by modern techniques which yield banded chromosomes.

7. REFERENCES

PHILIP, J., LUNDSTEEN, C., OWEN, D., and HIRSCHHORN, K. The frequency of chromosome aberrations in tall men with special regard to 47,XYY and 47,XXY. *Amer. J. Hum. Genet.* (in press).

RADIOMETER. 1973. Report 1500–120–17 (personal communication).

ABSTRACTS OF ADDITIONAL PAPERS

CHROMOSOMES, SEX CHROMATIN AND PHYLOGENY OF THE ASIAN PANGOLIN, *MANIS PENTADACTYLA*

N.V. ASWATHANARAYANA and K. L. S PRAKASH
University of Mysore, India

Chromosomes of the Asian pangolin, *Manis pentadactyla* Linn. (Pholidota: Mammalia) are described. Two female specimens investigated revealed a diploid number of 36 with 7 pairs of metacentric, 6 pairs of submetacentric, 3 pairs of subtelocentric, and one pair of minute telocentric chromosomes. The X chromosomes are medium sized and metacentric.

Makino and Tateishi (1951) reported 42 chromosomes while Raychaudhuri et al. (1969) used current cytological techniques and reported 36 chromosomes. Both groups performed studies on the male sex alone. The results of the present investigation confirm the findings of Raychaudhuri et al. However, the achromatic gap described in one of the subtelocentric chromosomes in the male is not observed in the subtelocentric chromosomes of the female.

Sex chromatin was analyzed using spleen, kidney, intestinal epithelial cells, stromal cells of the ovary, and epithelial cells from the vagina. Early interphase nuclei showed a clear nuclear matrix, while late interphase nuclei showed 2–4 dense chromatin bodies (autosomal heterochromatin). Thus a characteristic sex chromatin body was not discerned in any case.

The affinities of Pholidota are discussed on the basis of chromosome number and palaeontological evidence.

A NEW CHROMOSOME NUMBER FOR THE ASIAN HOUSE SHREW, *SUNCUS MURINUS*

N. V. ASWATHANARAYANA and K. L. S. PRAKASH
University of Mysore, India

A novel chromosome number for the Asian house shrew, *Suncus murinus* is presented. The modal diploid chromosome number of the Asian house shrew, *S. murinus* has been reported to be 40. Recently, the Malayan taxon was found to be polymorphic and specimens examined exhibited diploid numbers of 40, 39, 38 and 37, the least being 36. This variation was attributed to Robertsonian fusions of 4 pairs of acrocentric autosomes in different combinations resulting in 9 karyotypic classes. The present communication describes yet another lower diploid number. Ten specimens collected from Mysore and Madras in southern India exhibited a uniform karyotype with $2n = 32$. The X and Y chromosomes are large submeta- and small metacentric elements, respectively, and simulate those of the Malayan taxon. This low diploid number thus emphasizes a new "karyotypic class" for *Suncus murinus*. The identification of the translocation acrocentric chromosomes is difficult from both somatic and meiotic ivestigations. Meiotic investigations revealed 16 distinct bivalents with the X and Y being held by a terminal chiasma. Further, the X and Y chromosomes become conspicuous in pachytene showing their terminal association. The interphase nuclei reveal prominent chromocentres in both sexes, however, the characteristic sex chromatin is clear in the female.

The stability of the karyotype in different geographic populations and its relationship with the other taxa are considered and discussed.

1 Q + CHROMOSOME IN TWO FAMILIES WITH A SMITH–LEMLI–OPITZ AND SECKEL'S SYNDROME

F. BALLESTA, A. FERRER, and M. SERRA
Hospital Clinico, Spain

Morphological variants of chromosome 1 have been reported in individuals with a variety of syndromes as well as in normal individuals.

We have studied two families with a variant chromosome. In family I the propositus had the Smith–Lemli–Opitz syndrome and in family II Seckel's syndrome. Other members of the families with the same variant chromosome were phenotypically normal.

The banding patterns in all cases with the variant chromosome demonstrated a partial duplication of the paracentromeric region by duplication of the q1 band.

Since the same anomaly was present in two unrelated families and in two different syndromes, it is possible to conclude that variations in this region are not the cause of psychic and phenotypic abnormalities.

THE APPLICATION OF MICRODENSITOMETRIC DNA MEASUREMENTS TO CELL CYCLE ANALYSIS IN CULTURED PLANT CELLS

M. W. BAYLISS and A. R. GOULD
Leicester University, U.K.

Analysis of the cell cycle in exponentially growing suspension cultures of *Acer pseudoplatanus* and *Daucus carota* has been performed following fixation of single samples labelled with tritiated thymidine. DNA measurements, by scanning microdensitometer, of unlabelled, non-dividing nuclei on autoradiographs give directly the proportion of cells in the G1 and G2 phases of the cell cycle. The labelling and mitotic indices similarly give the relative durations of mitosis and S phase. With suitable correction for exponential growth, these proportions are converted to absolute durations using the specific growth rate (mean doubling time for cell number) of the culture as a measure of the total cell cycle time. The results of this analysis performed under a variety of cultural conditions will be presented together with the conclusions these data allow on the control of the cell cycle in cultured plant cells.

USE OF IMAGE ANALYSING COMPUTERS

C. P. BOND
Image Analysing Computers, U.K.

Image analysing computers using video imaging and digital logic techniques are now being increasingly used for biological applications. Although these hardwired systems lack some of the flexibility of the general purpose software approach, their actual versatility is frequently underestimated.

Consideration of an image analyser's optical requirements and its different modes of operation often yields very powerful results. Recent applications include the direct presentation of chromosome banding patterns, the analysis of nuclear chromatin distribution, and the use of fluorescence techniques.

Potential extension of the use of hardwired image analysis will be discussed, with particular reference to the life sciences.

A CATALOGUE OF CHROMOSOME CHANGES IN MAN

S. BORGAONKAR
Johns Hopkins University, Baltimore, U.S.A.

A method has been developed to encode and catalog chromosome changes in man. Each entry in the first two columns refers to chromosome number, e.g., 01 to 22, OX, and OY; in the third column to the chromosome arms, p and q; and in the fourth and fifth columns to the major and minor bands, respectively. The first autosome item encoded will be 01p11 and the last, 22q13. All the breakpoints reported in aberrations such as deletions, inversions, translocations, etc. can thus be entered. Another catalog lists all the monosomies and trisomies, in a similar fashion, e.g., +08 and −21. Reports on polyploids are recorded in a third listing. The catalog has been put on computer tape, hence is convenient to update.

Each entry will consist of appropriate reference citation(s), complete nomenclature of the chromosome abnormality as per the Paris Conference (1971) report.

The catalog will list the identification numbers of the Human Genetic Mutant Cell Repository, Institute for Medical Research, Camden, New Jersey.

The catalog should serve, among others, particularly those who want to report new chromosome changes and those interested in regional localization of gene loci by utilizing abnormal cell lines in somatic cell hybridizations.

PERMANENT INTERCHANGE HYBRIDITY IN *HALWORTHIA REINWARDTII* VAR. *CHALUMNENSIS*

P. E. BRANDHAM
Royal Botanic Gardens, Kew, U.K.

The basic karyotype in the *Aloineae* is very stable, four long and three acrocentrics, and occurs in every member of the tribe. Interchange heterozygotes are normally very rare, and homozygotes do not occur. In tetraploid *Haworthia reinwardtii* var. *chalumnensis* natural selection has been reversed and every individual is heterozygous for at least one interchange, sometimes two or three. Twelve interchanges have been found in 145 plants. The taxon also includes triploids of hybrid origin, some of which are interchange heterozygotes.

SEQUENCES OF HIGHLY REPEATED DNA IN *DROSOPHILA MELANOGASTER*

D. L. BRUTLAG and W. J. PEACOCK
Canberra, Australia

Most of the highly repeated DNA of *Drosophila melanogaster* is composed of four homogeneous species with buoyant densities 1.672, 1.686, 1.688, and 1.705 g/cc in CsCl. The 1.672 species has the 12 nucleotide repeating unit 5′ AATATAATATAT3′ as determined by partial and complete pancreatic ribonuclease digests of complementary RNA synthesized *in vitro*. The basic repeating units of the 1.686 and 1.705 DNA species are longer but both appear to be related to the 1.672 sequence by simple nucleotide substitutions.

The absence of G and C nucleotides within the 1.672 unit repeat and the low amount of GC nucleotides detected in purified 1.672 DNA ($<0.1\%$) indicate that the 12 nucleotide sequence is unaltered over long regions within the chromosomes. The homogeneity of the 1.672 DNA argues that this DNA must be of recent origin or that it has an extreme evolutionary stability.

Sequence analysis of similar AT-rich satellites from closely related species may resolve these possibilities. This homogeneity also contrasts with the large amount of sequence alteration detected in repeated DNA of several other organisms.

USE OF RADIATION INDUCED BREAKS IN CHROMOSOME 1 FOR REGIONAL MAPPING IN INTERSPECIFIC CELL HYBRIDS

W. G. BURGERHOUT
Rotterdam, The Netherlands

The application of enzyme electrophoresis and differential chromosome staining methods in genetic analysis of human-rodent hybrid cell lines has led to the assignment of seven enzyme loci to the human chromosome 1. Mapping of these genes relative to the chromosome banding pattern was attempted by the study of hybrid cell lines in which a broken chromosome 1 was present. Suitable hybrid cell lines were obtained in the following ways:

1. X-irradiation of a human-Chinese hamster hybrid cell line, in which an intact human chromosome 1 was present, followed by cloning of the irradiated population.
2. X-irradiation of a human fibroblast line, which was subsequently cloned. Cells from a clone, in which a translocation involving chromosome 1 was detected, were fused with Chinese hamster cells.

The results of the analyses suggest the following positions of the loci: phosphogluconate dehydrogenase and phosphopyruvate hydratase to band p 35 (Paris Conference, 1971); phosphoglucomutase 1 either distal to p 35 or within p 33; peptidase c, fumarate hydratase, guanylate kinase, and uridylyldiphosphoglucose prophosphorylase distal to q 12.

This work was carried out in collaboration with H. van Someren and H. Beyersbergen van Henegouwen (Medical Biological Laboratory TNO, Rijswijk) and P. Meera Khan (Department of Human Genetics, State University, Leiden).

INTERACTION OF QUINACRINE MUSTARD WITH REPETITIOUS DNA IN SOLUTION

A. DE LA CHAPELLE, R.-K. SELANDER, and K. SIMOLA
Folkhälsan Institute of Genetics, Helsinki, Finland

The fluorescence of quinacrine mustard (QM) in the presence of DNA in solution was assayed by fluorimetry. Artificial mixtures of microbial DNAs having 31-71% GC displayed a linear and inverse proportionality between GC content and intensity of fluorescence with QM. When microbial DNAs were fractionated by heat denaturation into fractions containing different proportions of GC, similar results were obtained. In contrast, mammalian DNA did not show a similar clear-cut relationship between base content and quenching of QM fluorescence. In repetitious DNA from calf thymus ($C_0t \leqq 10$) fractionated by heat denaturation several GC-rich fractions showed stronger fluorescence with QM than several AT-rich fractions. The degree of base repetition *per se* did not have any consistent influence on the intensity of QM fluorescence as shown by testing DNA fractions having different degrees of repetition. It is likely that the pattern rather than the degree of repetition is an important factor determining the effect of DNAs on the fluorescence of QM *in vitro*.

BANDS OF CHROMOMERES: A FUNCTIONAL INTERPRETATION OF BANDING AND SPECULATION ABOUT A MODEL OF NUCLEUS AND CHROMOSOME ORGANIZATION IN THE EUCARYOTES

B. CHIARELLI
University of Turin, Italy

An attempt is made here to synthesize a model of chromosome organization which presumes to explain the structure of the interphase nucleus and the process of chromosome organization from interphase to metaphase for eucaryote systems.

The model is arranged into 11 sequential points most of which presently are only partially supported by experimental evidence.

In the paper supporting evidence from the literature and experimental observation will be provided to substantiate each of these points.

1. Each metaphase chromosome is the result of the condensation of a single chromatin filament of about 200 Å which is composed of the double helix of DNA compactly organized within a proteinous matrix.

2. The filament does not only form a single chromosome but the whole haploid cellular set of chromosomes (genome) which is ring-shaped.

3. Thus in each eucaryote nucleus would exist two chromosomal structures which are formed by only two circular chromatin filaments, one of maternal origin and the other of paternal origin.

4. These filaments are not free in the nucleoplasm but are attached at several points associated with the annuli of the nuclear envelope.

5. The two filaments (maternal and paternal) would have attachments in homologous regions to the inner annuli of the same pore or of near ones.

6. The starting signal for reduplication is mediated by the nuclear envelope and could originate from the centriole.

7. The reduplication of the chromatin filament would start therefore at these several attachment points near the pores of the nuclear envelope and continue along the filament which extends into the nuclear sap.

8. As reduplication goes on the newly formed filament would develop a folded structure and produce entangled aggregations in the single filament. These aggregations would grow progressively larger as more of the filament is condensed together. When reduplication is over each section of the chromatin filament which is included between joined. Under the optical and electron microscope these chromatin aggregations could be identified as chromomeres.

9. Not all the attachment points with the nuclear envelope would have the same significance. Most of them would be relatively weak and would detach as soon as reduplication is over; in contrast a few others would be stronger and would last till the disappearance of the nuclear envelope. In the metaphasic chromosomal structure these latter attachment points could be assigned to centromeric and telomeric regions of each chromosome.

10. At metaphase a number of dense masses of each haploid filament appear as chromosomes.

11. The meiotic process is reductive. Therefore the processes described for points 7 and 8 could take place in reverse order.

If the model is verified the interpretation of the organization of the genome such as chromosome behavior and function, structural mutation and meiotic process would be significantly affected.

CYTOCHEMISTRY OF CHROMOSOME STRUCTURE

D. E. COMINGS

City of Hope Medical Center, Duarte, U.S.A.

A series of biochemical studies have been undertaken to further elucidate the mechanisms of chromosome banding.

1. Good G-, C- and Q-banding can be obtained even after treatment of slides with 0.2 N HCl for 4 hr. Gel electrophoresis of fixed chromatin so treated demonstrates that all the histones have been completely removed, indicating histones do not play a role in chromosome banding.

2. Methylene blue and azure A, B and C all give good chromosome banding, indicating eosin is not an essential component.

3. Studies of quinacrine-DNA complexes by optical hypochromism DNA-Tm, viscosity, and equilibrium dialysis indicated the majority of quinacrine is intercalated with little side binding.

4. When DNA is complexed with polylysine, polyarginine or spermine, all of which bind in the small groove, its ability to bind and quench quinacrine is inhibited. Histones, which probably bind in the large groove, do not inhibit binding or quenching. Circular dichroism studies indicating changes in the B–C conformation of DNA are not involved.

5. GC-rich mid-band, AT-rich, and satellite DNA of the mouse, isolated by CsCl or Cs_2SO_4-Ag^+ centrifugation, show no detectable differences in their ability to quench quinacrine fluorescence, indicating that when the DNA's are derived from the same organism the base composition (except for highly AT-rich satellites) playes little role in Q-banding.

6. Studies of mouse chromatin subfractions indicated there were fewer binding sites for quinacrine on a heterochromatin-rich 400 g pellet, and a finely dispersed euchromatin supernatant fraction. These two fractions possessed significantly more non-histone proteins than the other fractions.

These results are interpreted to indicate that in Q-banding, negative or pale staining regions are due to the presence of non-histone proteins binding in the small groove of DNA and preventing the intercalative binding of quinacrine. A similar mechanism is probably involved in G-banding.

THE DISTRIBUTION OF BREAKS, INDUCED BY X-RAYS, BETWEEN LIGHT AND DARK REGIONS OF SPECIFIC HUMAN CHROMOSOMES

P. COOKE, M. SEABRIGHT and M. WHEELER

University of Southampton, U.K.

From trypsin-banded preparations of human karyotypes, the widths of each light and dark band region in all 23 pairs of human chromosomes have been calculated at different stages of contraction.

The number of breaks occurring in each light band region has been studied in relation to the hypothesis that the number of breaks in each region is related to its size.

HUMAN RAPIDLY RENATURING MAIN BAND DNA

G. CORNEO

University of Milan, Italy

Human DNA contains two components of rapidly renaturing main band (r.r.m.b.) DNA displaying densities of 1.703 g/ml and 1.707 g/ml in CsCl in the renatured form.

The 1.703 component is obtained from high molecular weight DNA, while the 1.707 component is obtained only from low molecular weight sonicated DNA. Therefore while the first appears to be clustered, the second is more finely distributed along the genome. These two components differ from simple sequence satellite DNA's.

The 1.703 r.r.m.b. DNA is eluted early from a methylated albumin kieselguhr column, while the 1.707 r.r.m.b. DNA, although more widespread, is enriched mainly in the fractions eluted late and corresponding to the portion of DNA which is more homogeneous in density in an analytical CsCl gradient.

ULTRASTRUCTURAL CYTOGENETICS, A NEW LEVEL IN CELL BIOLOGY RESEARCH

R. F. DONOSO, R. WETTSTEIN and Y. J. R. SOTELO
Montevideo, Uruguay

Standard electron microscopy complemented by cytochemical analysis did not provide satisfactory answers to one of the most important problems of meiosis: organization of chromosomes and distribution of specific molecules during the different phases of the meiotic cycle. However, previous research based on EM tridimensional reconstruction of nuclei proved that this could be the best method of obtaining information on chromosome relationship and behavior.

The results obtained up to now concern the construction of pachytene idiograms based on the length and other characteristics of synaptonemal complexes (pachytene karyotype), and are presented with the structural patterns of sex chromosomes in vertebrate and invertebrate species.

The nature of this technical approach, as well as the type of information it provides, permits the introduction of ultrastructural cytogenetics as a new developing branch of cell biology.

NUCLEAR CHANGES DURING THE VEGETATIVE AND SPORULATING CYCLE OF *SACCHAROMYCES CEREVISIAE*

P. FISHER, U. WINTERSBERGER and M. BINDER
Krebsforschungs-Institut, Vienna, Austria

Photographs of nuclear changes in protoplasts of *Saccharomyces cerevisiae* during both vegetative and sporulating phases of the cycle will be presented, and details of a technique for the visualization of yeast chromosomes in the light and electron microscopes will be described.

SOMATIC ASSOCIATION IN *LOCUSTA MIGRATORIA*

D. P. FOX, T. MELLO-SAMPAYO and K. C. CARTER
University of Aberdeen, U.K.

At metaphase in embryonic cells of *Locusta migratoria* all the chromosomes are arranged on a "hollow" spindle. Neuroblast cells, which are particularly large, have longer chromosomes and at least six pairs of autosomes, and the sex chromosomes can be recognized on the basis of secondary constrictions.

An analysis of the unambiguous circular order of chromosomes in these cells indicates that the two members of a homologous pair are placed at random. In contrast to this finding, colchicine-metaphases in neuroblasts show clear evidence for somatic pairing. It is suggested that spindle formation disrupts the somatic pairing that exists during the interphase and that this association of homologues is re-established in each cell generation.

WHOLE MOUNT HUMAN CHROMOSOMES IN ELECTRON MICROSCOPY

A. GENEIZ and J. Y. JAFFRAY
Beaumont, France

The authors present some chromosome electron microscopic pictures, obtained from a peripheral human lymphocyte culture.

The preparation of the grids is according to the author's new technique, avoiding the water spreading on a Langmuir Trough.

Compact metaphasic plates and isolated chromosomes emphasize other observations on interchromatid and interchromosomal fibers. Banded chromosomes (without enzymatic digestion) are also presented.

Longitudinal and looping fibers (diameters in agreement with the classical data) appear along the chromatids.

CHROMATID INTERCHANGES AT HOMOLOGOUS CHROMOSOME REGIONS: A CHARACTERISTIC FINDING IN BLOOM'S SYNDROME

J. GERMAN
New York Blood Center, U.S.A.

Bloom's syndrome, a rare autosomal recessively transmitted disorder of man, is characterized clinically by growth retardation, a sun-sensitive telangiectatic eruption of the face, an immunopathy, and a strong disposition to cancer. Cells dividing *in vitro* display increased numbers of chromatid gaps, breaks, and rearrangements (chromatid interchanges, polycentrics, and abnormal monocentrics). One particular aberration, a symmetrical quadriradial configuration (Qr) with centromeres in opposite rays of the four-armed figure and with the opposite rays of equal length, is found in 0.5 to 14.0% of lymphocytes (usually 1.0–2.0%). Such symmetrical Qr's are only very rarely observed in cells from normal persons. Their great frequency in Bloom's syndrome has not been observed in other of the "chromosome breakage syndromes."

The first 101 Qr's detected in Bloom's syndrome in this laboratory have been analyzed and show a strikingly non-random distribution of affected sites. In addition to the preferential involvement of homologous (or apparently homologous) chromosome segments in these interchanges, the centromeric regions were found affected in most cells, and certain chromosome pairs clearly are affected more often than others. The observations show that points of exchange of partners are in C-band regions preferentially and that such regions may associate during interphase.

DNA CONTENT AND MORPHOLOGY OF ANEUPLOID SPERM CELLS

A. GROPP, U. LANGENBECK and R. STOLLA
University of Lübeck, West Germany

The tobacco mouse × laboratory mouse F_1-hybrids produce high rates of aneuploid secondary spermatocytes. This is due to meiotic malsegregation of trivalents in a multiple Robertsonian system. The significantly higher variation of the DNA content (determined by UV-photometry) in morphologically normal spermatozoa of F_1-males, compared with the parental strains, was attributed to the presence of a considerable fraction of chromosomally hypo- and hypermodel spermatozoa. While a majority of aneuploid precursor cells develop to morphologically normal through chromosomally unbalanced spermatozoa, a minority may give rise to malformed sperm cells. Also near-diploid spermatozoa occur at an increased rate.

Feulgen-photometry of spermatozoa washed out from the female genital tract after time-controlled mating of F_1-males provided evidence that abnormal sperm cells do not pass the utero-tubal junction and fail to take part in the fertilization process. By the same studies it can be assumed that an incomplete loss of extremely unbalanced but morphologically normal spermatozoa takes place before they penetrate the uterus.

TRISOMY SYNDROME IN THE FETAL MOUSE

A. GROPP and G. NOACK
University of Lübeck, West Germany

In the mouse, double metacentric heterozygotes with monobrachial homology may produce specific trisomic conditions among the fetal progeny in backcross matings with homozygous animals. The particular nature of the trisomy may be predetermined by the choice of the double heterozygote combination. Actually, the phenotypes and the developmental profiles of trisomy Nos. 1, 8, 9, 10, 11, 12, 13, 15, 16, and 17 are under study. All trisomic conditions cause early or later fetal death and become eliminated at least before term.

Trisomy No. 1 exhibits slight developmental retardation and moderate general hypoplasia until the affected embryos die at about day 14. No gross malformations are observed. Similar features may be found in trisomy Nos. 10, 13, and 16.

Severe developmental retardation characterizes trisomy Nos. 8, 11, 15, and 17. In contrast, embryos with trisomy No. 12 display exencephaly, mostly without developmental retardation. They may survive until day 17/18. As a rule, hypoplasia of the placenta can be found in the trisomic conditions. So far, the causal factors of fetal death in trisomy syndromes remain obscure. It is improbable that malformation per se is a major responsible factor.

EVOLUTION OF THE KARYOTYPE IN POPULATIONS OF ESTABLISHED CELLS OF *D. MELANOGASTER*

C. HALFER, S. FACCIO DOLFINI and C. BARIGOZZI
University of Milan, Italy

Previous chromosomal analysis on three continuous cell lines derived from wild-type embryos of *Drosophila melanogaster* showed a karyotypic situation, different in each line, close to diploidy. The chromosomes involved in the variations were only the first and fourth pairs. Recently, however, some lines obtained from embryos carriers of a translocation between the Y and one II chromosome were found to be exclusively polyploid.

The karyotypes of these different lines are described and a possible interpretation of their origin from the embryonic cells is given. Comparing the situation in the lines derived from the wild-type stock and from the stock with translocation, the significance of the polyploidy is discussed.

ORIGIN OF POLYMORPHIC Y CHROMOSOME IN A MOLE RAT, *NESOKIA INDICA*

S. C. JHANWAR and S. R. V. RAO
University of Delhi, India

The Y chromosome in *Nesokia* is polymorphic (Jhanwar and Rao, 1973) We have attempted on the basis of banding pattern, the homology of autosomes in males differing in Y chromosome morphology and the mode of origin of different Y chromosomes occurring in a single population. The results and possible interpretation will be presented.

RECOGNITION OF MEIOTIC EXCHANGE IN A PERICENTRIC INVERSION IN MAN

A. G. J. M. VAN DER LINDEN and P. L. PEARSON
University of Leiden, The Netherlands

Meiotic preparations from a man, carrying a pericentric inversion in chromosome 4, were stained with a C-banding technique. The C-bands in the heterozygous bivalent occupy different positions along the longitudinal axis of the bivalent during diakinesis, dependent upon whether there has been exchange within or outside the inversion loop. Moreover it is possible to recognize whether there have been 0, 1 and 2 exchanges within the inversion segment.

This technique allows, for the first time, a direct assessment in man of the percentage of gametes carrying an aberrant chromosome resulting from crossing-over within a pericentric inversion.

CHROMOSOME BEHAVIOUR IN THE *TRADESCANTIA CRASSIFOLIA* COMPLEX

A. MARTINEZ
Royal Botanic Gardens, Kew, U.K.

The *Tradescantia crassifolia* complex is divided approximately into the following species: *T. crassifolia* 2n = 12, 24 and 36; *T. iridescens* 2n = 12 and 24; *T. sillamontana* 2n = 24; *T. burchii* 2n = 24; *T. tepoxtlana* 2n = 12; and *Tradescantia* sp. 2n = 12, 24 and 36. These species occur in Mexico and *T. crassifolia* is distributed throughout the central plateau more widely than the rest, but sometimes overlaps them. In *T. crassifolia* it was found that the diploids have a mean chiasma frequency per paired arm of 1.10 ± 0.029 and the tetraploids 0.84 ± 0.014. The tetraploids show two different levels of quadrivalent formation per plant, one with a mean of 4 per cell and the other with 2. Interchange heterozygosity was found, particularly tetraploids, but also in 2 diploids.

BEHAVIOR AND TRANSMISSION OF SUPERNUMERARY CHROMOSOMES IN *AEGILOPS SPELTOIDES*

D. MENDELSON and D. ZOHARY
The Hebrew University, Jerusalem, Israel

1. The somatic stability of supernumerary chromosomes was studied in plants containing 1–6 B's: Carriers were found to maintain constant number of B's in their various tillers and spikes. In contrast, B chromosomes were universally absent in roots.

2. Partial loss of supernumeraries (due to lagging) was noted in microsporocytes at the anaphase I stage of meiosis (particularly in plants containing a single B). Also occasional unipolar distribution of B's was detected at this stage.

3. Cytological examinations of pollen grains revealed accumulation of B's in the generative nucleus of the male gametophyte. This is brought about by directed non-disjunction of supernumeraries at the first pollen mitosis.

4. Crosses were made between plants containing 1–3 B's and plants free of accessory chromosomes. The progeny tests showed that on the male side the accumulated B chromosomes are effectively transmitted to progeny. Reciprocal crosses revealed that no parallel accumulation occurs on the female side.

5. Stunted growth and progressive increase of pollen abortion was found in plants carrying numerous (3–6) supernumeraries.

CHROMOSOME POLYMORPHISM IN PRIMATES

D. A. MILLER
Columbia University, New York, U.S.A.

Three types of variation between homologous chromosomes have been observed in primates. The gorilla is most striking, having polymorphisms of at least half the chromosomes.

Very bright quinacrine-stained regions are found in man, the gorilla, and the chimpanzee, but not the orangutan.

The location of this material differs markedly among the three species. Variation in the size of these regions is seen both between individuals and between homologous chromosomes.

A second type of variation is the presence of bright quinacrine bands at the distal end of some chromosomes in gorilla and chimpanzee, but not in man or the orangutan. These bands show polymorphic variation and may be absent without phenotypic effect. In the chimpanzee they sometimes stain darkly with a C-banding technique and are probably composed of heterochromatin.

Finally, variation between homologues in the amount of heterochromatic (C-band) material has been found in some chromosomes of all four species.

In man three, and in gorilla two, biarmed chromosomes can have particularly large blocks of heterochromatin.

CHROMOSOMAL LOCATION OF 5-METHYLCYTOSINE

O. J. MILLER, W. SCHNEDL, and B. F. ERLANGER
Columbia University, New York, U.S.A.

Antibodies specific for 5-methylcytosine which react with this base in single stranded DNA have been used to study the chromosomal locations of this minor base in various mammals.

Large concentrations of 5-methylcytosine have been found in many but not all regions of constitutive heterochromatin.

These include the C-banding regions of mouse, cow, sheep, and goat and of human chromosomes 1, 9 and 16, in addition to the distal part of the Y chromosome and the short arm of chromosome 15 in the human. Large concentrations of 5-methylcytosine are seen on several chromosomes in the gorilla but none are seen on chimpanzee chromosomes. Kangaroo rat chromosomes contain at least two classes of repetitive DNA rich in 5-methylcytosine.

These can be distinguished by using different methods for denaturing DNA, perhaps reflecting differences in the sequence of nucleotides.

CHROMOSOME BANDING PATTERNS AND THE ORIGIN OF THE B GENOME IN WHEAT

A. T. NATARAJAN and N. P. SARMA
University of Stockholm, Sweden

Cultivated wheat, *Triticum aestivum* (2n = 6x = 42), is a hexaploid containing three different genomes, viz., AA, BB, DD, and is assumed to have arisen as an amphiploid during the course of evolution. Of these three genomes, it is fairly certain that the A and D genomes have been contributed by *Triticum boeoticum* (or its derivative *T. monococcum*) and *Aegilopes squarrosa*, respectively. The source of the B genome is still uncertain. Originally, this genome was attributed to *Agropyron triticeum* but later on to *Aegilops speltoides*. There is evidence both for and against the contribution of *Ae. speltoides* toward the B genome of wheat. We have studied the distribution of the heterochromatic regions in the chromosomes of diploid, tetraploid, and hexaploid wheats, using the C-band technique. A and D genome chromosomes were found to possess only small blocks of heterochromatin around the centromere, whereas the B genome chromosomes had very large blocks of heterochromatin, near the intercalary and terminal regions. An analysis of probable B genome donors such as *Ae. speltoides*, *Ae. bicornis*, *Ae. longissima*, and *Ae. sharonensis* revealed that *Ae. speltoides* has a pattern of distribution of heterochromatin, i.e., large blocks near the centromeres similar to those of the B genome chromosomes. Additional characteristics such as diffuse dot-like distribution of heterochromatin, which is very characteristic of *Ae. sharonensis*, indicates that a polyphyletic origin of tetraploid wheat seems more plausible.

IDENTIFICATION OF CHINESE HAMSTER CHROMOSOME BIVALENTS BY QM FLUORESCENCE

J. L. OUD
Utrecht, The Netherlands

The Chinese hamster has 22 chromosomes (10 pairs of autosomes and XY or XX). In both sexes 11 bivalents are formed in meiosis. On account of their morphology—i.e., relative length and centromere position—at best 9 out of the 11 bivalents can be identified. Since each bivalent shows a characteristic fluorescence pattern, staining with QM makes identification of all bivalents possible.

The most suitable stage to identify bivalents is diakinesis. The X and Y chromosomes are partly homologous and in the prophase of the first meiotic division in male animals a chiasma is formed. At least three different opinions exist about the homology between X and Y. Comparison of the fluorescence pattern of the sex bivalent with that of the sex chromosomes in mitosis or second meiotic division is informative about the homology. According to these fluorescence patterns the homologous parts are probably the distal part of the short arm of X and the distal part or whole short arm of Y.

An essential part of the work described here was performed at the Department of Human Genetics, University of Amsterdam. The lymphocyte cultures were made at the Department of Pharmacology, Institute of National Health, Bilthoven, The Netherlands.

CHROMOSOME-SPECIFIC CONTROL OF CHIASMA FORMATION

J. S. PARKER
University of London, U.K.

A desynaptic mutant of *Hypochoeris radicata* (Compositae) has been isolated from a natural population in France. This mutant appears to be unique in that only one of the four pairs of chromosomes (pair IV) exhibits desynapsis.

Over 90% of PMC's are affected. Trisomic-IV offspring of the mutant as egg parent show that the PMC's have the same abnormality. The course of meiosis in this mutant will be demonstrated and the implications for the control of chiasma formation will be discussed.

A NEW GIEMSA METHOD FOR THE DIFFERENTIAL STAINING OF SISTER CHROMATIDS AND DIRECTION OF SISTER CHROMATID EXCHANGES

P. E. PERRY and S. WOLFF
M.R.C. Unit, Edinburgh, U.K.

If cells are grown for two rounds of replication in the presence of the base analogue BrdUrd and then stained with the fluorescence dye Hoechst 33258 (Latt, 1973. *Proc. Natl. Acad. Sci.*, *70*, 3395) or acridine orange, the sister chromatids fluoresce differentially. The unifilarly substituted chromatids fluoresce more intensely than their bifilarly substituted sister chromatids. Sister chromatid exchanges can be readily detected. The preparations made with Hoechst 33258, however, show extreme photoinstability which limits their usefulness. A new technique has now been developed in which staining with the Hoechst compound is combined with Giemsa staining to produce preparations that show sister chromatid exchanges with even greater resolution. The preparations are permanent and can be observed leisurely without resorting to fluorescence microscopy and photography.

Exponentially dividing Chinese hamster ovary cells were cultured in medium containing 10M BrdUrd for 24 hr, during which time two rounds of replication occurred. The cells were harvested and preparations made by the usual method for cultured mammalian cells. These slides were stained in Hoechst 33258 for 12 min, rinsed, mounted in deionised water, and left to age with the cover slip on for 24 hr, after which time the cover slip was removed and the slides incubated in 2 × SSC or H_2O for 2 hr, followed by 30 min staining in 3% Giemsa solution. The chromatid that incorporated BrdUrd into both strands of the DNA double helix stains weakly with Giemsa, whereas the chromatid that incorporated BrdUrd into only one strand stains deeply. Photographs and slides showing CHO cells with differentially stained sister chromatids are demonstrated.

FACTS AND FANCIES IN INSTRUMENTATION

J. S. PLOEM
University of Leiden, The Netherlands

Development of automated instrumentation for chromosome studies is necessitated by the extreme information density present in a metaphase spread, but hampered by the small size of chromosomes. For some differential staining techniques, developed in the last years, new instrumentation has been developed for the extraction of detailed cytochemical information.

In this context a new type of vertical fluorescence illuminator for two-wavelengths excitation methods and a new type of microspectrofluorograph will be described.

For quantitative and qualitative computer-operated densitometry results of high-resolution techniques will be discussed. In particular some results will be presented of photomicrograph scanning, specimen scanning, and image scanning (vibration mirror). Against the background of these techniques, the practical and theoretical possibilities and limitations of quantitative television methods will be extrapolated.

^{3}H-THYMIDINE LABELLING OF A MAMMALIAN X CHROMOSOME THROUGH TWO CONSECUTIVE MITOSES

S. R. V. RAO and S. C. JHANWAR
University of Delhi India

^{3}H-thymidine labelling of a mammalian X chromosome twice in the two consecutive divisions is attempted, in order to verify whether it is the same X chromosome always replicating late (forms the sex chromatin). In the majority of instances the facultative portion of the X chromosome (Lyonised) synthesizes its DNA in the late S segment of both the divisions. Some unexpected observations have been recorded. In a minor percent of cases (about 13 %) the Lyonised segment of the first cycle (late replicating) seems to have completed its DNA synthesis by the time it enters the late S phase of the second cycle (early replicating). It may not be an unreasonable interpretation that an X could be heteropycnotic in one cell cycle and euchromatic in the next although it seems inconsistent with the genetic data.

USE OF THE FLUOROCHROME BIS-BENZIMIDAZOL DERIVATIVE HOECHST 33258 IN THE STUDY OF HUMAN CHROMOSOME BANDING PATTERN, MECHANISM OF ACTION, AND PRACTICAL APPLICATIONS

T. RAPOSA
University of Budapest, Hungary

The staining of the human chromosomes with Hoechst 33258 results in a distinct banding pattern on the chromosome arms and reveals the localization of the constitutive heterochromatin at the same time. Thus the technique combines the characteristics of the Q and C bandings without requiring any pretreatment altering the chromosomal organization.

Experiments show that the dye binds to the DNA, and has a greater affinity to the chromosomal areas being more resistant to the DNase digestion and denaturation-reassociation procedures.

The experimental details to clarify the mechanism of action of this fluorochrome and its use to study the denaturation-reassociation kinetics of various classes of human chromosomal DNA will also be discussed.

Some examples such as mitomycin-C induced aberrations in mouse and human cells, chromosomal changes in gastric cancer, identification of the Philadelphia chromosome, and associated translocation in chronic myelogenous leukemia are presented to illustrate the practical utility of this fluorochrome.

DEVELOPMENT OF CHROMOSOMAL ABERRATIONS IN HUMAN DIPLOID CELLS FOLLOWING INFECTION WITH PARAMYXOVIRUSES

D. J. ROTHE, P. B. BALDRIDGE and L. B. SENTERFIT
Cornell University, New York, U.S.A.

Infection of WI-38 cells with Paramyxoviruses results in the development of significant numbers of hyperdiploid cells in the cell culture. These hyperdiploid cells show increased numbers of A, B, C, E and G groups, as well as unclassifiable "marker" chromosomes and chromosomal fragments. The observed effects on the cell are dependent on the relative virus–cell concentration used in the virus inoculum. If excess amounts of virus are used the cytopathic effects are so marked that few if any cells in metaphase could be found. As these experiments are acute in nature the stability of the chromosomal alterations observed is not known.

CT BANDING OF HUMAN CHROMOSOMES

J. M. J. C. SCHERES, TH. W. J. HUSTINX and F. J. RUTTEN
University of Nijmegen, The Netherlands

Heat treatment of human chromosomes in $Ba(OH)_2$ solution at 60°C followed by incubation in 2SSC and subsequent staining with "Stains-all" results in typical banding patterns. In addition to reverse and terminal bands some chromosomes—especially chromosomes 1, 9 and 16—show staining of the paracentromeric regions. With slight modifications this method can also be applied to chromosomes which have previously been banded with the trypsin-Giemsa technique. However, in that case the C-band characteristics predominate and the reverse bands are only faintly visible. In interphase nuclei this treatment results in prominently stained chromocentra varying in size and number.

The method has already proved useful in the interpretation of an abnormal extra chromosome 9.

ELECTRON MICROSCOPY OF METAPHASE AND PRECOCIOUS CONDENSED CHROMOSOMES TREATED BY DIFFERENT BANDING TECHNIQUES

H. G. SCHWARZACHER and F. RUZICKA
University of Vienna, Austria

Total preparations of mitotic chromosomes treated and stained as for G-banding (using both NaOH-buffer and trypsin techniques) show that they are composed of irregularly folded fibrils of at least 400 Å thickness. In the G-band regions the chromatids are as a whole thicker and the fibrils are darker stained than in the interband regions. Chromosomes treated by the Giemsa-11 method show a very strong contrast of the fibrils in the regions stained red in light microscopic preparations.

Precociously condensed chromosomes obtained by fusion of cells in interphase and metaphase (using Sendai virus) show a very fine banding pattern.

G1-chromosomes are presumably built up of only one fibril laid in irregular foldings and loops, G2-chromosomes of two fibrils. In S-chromosomes no constant structure could be observed between the non-replicating fragments.

RNA SYNTHESIS IN CHROMOCENTRES FORMED BY LARGE BLOCKS OF AUTOSOMAL CONSTITUTIVE HETEROCHROMATIN OF THE FLYING SQUIRREL *HYLOPETES A. ALBONIGER*

T. SHARMA and G. S. GARG
University of Buenos Aires, Argentina

The flying squirrel *Hylopetes a. alboniger* (Hodgson) has large blocks of heterochromatin in 7 pairs of autosomes, 3 large and 4 small. Each of the three large pairs has a secondary constriction at the heterochromatic regions. At interphase the heterochromatic blocks form prominent chromocentres.

The autosomal constitutive heterochromatin replicates late and it terminates its DNA synthesis later than the facultative heterochromatin. The large blocks of autosomal constitutive heterochromatin are C-band negative, and when stained for G-band they show neither dark nor light G-banding pattern and instead they appear rather diffuse.

The prominent chromocentres incorporate uridine. On *in situ* hybridization with hot *Xenopus* ribosomal RNA the constitutive heterochromatic regions of metaphase chromosomes do not show grains.

A few nuclei, however, have fairly heavy grain concentrations spread all over the nuclei. The significance of the findings will be discussed in the light of transcriptional activity of the constitutive heterochromatin.

THREE DIMENSIONAL PATTERN OF CHROMOSOMAL AXES DURING MEIOTIC PROPHASE

A. J. SOLARI
University of Buenos Aires, Argentina

The chromosomal axes of the XY pairs and of some autosomal pairs from five mammalian species (including man) were spatially reconstructed with electron microscope techniques, and these results were correlated with the light microscopical picture of these chromosomes. These results include:

1. The demonstration of partial synapsis between the X and Y chromosomes in these five species.
2. The demonstration of the length and shape constancy of each chromosomal axis.
3. The tetravalent configuration of the four involved axes in Searle's X-autosome translocation in the mouse.
4. The characteristic structure developed in chiasmatic regions of mouse autosomes and the XY pair of the Armenian hamster.
5. The evolving pattern of the axes during synaptic and post-synaptic stages.

It is concluded that the axial pattern accurately shows the synaptic, and in some cases the post-synaptic behavior of the chromosomes. Spreading and extraction-digestion techniques show that the bulk material of the axes is protein which differs from other protein involved in the formation of the central element of the synaptonemal complex.

STABILIZATION OF THE HIGHLY COMPACT CHROMATIN ORGANIZATION OF HUMAN SPERMATOZOA. I. NUCLEAR OXIDATIVE PHOSPHORYLATION

A. SOSA, L. CALZADA, Q. HERNANDEZ-JUAREGUI and A. ROSADO
Department for Scientific Investigation, I.M.S.S., Mexico

Recent developments in spermatozoa fractionation have permitted us to take advantage of the special morphology of this cell to obtain completely pure isolated human spermatozoa nuclei as judged from electron microscopy studies and the activities of marker enzymes.

These sperm organelles showed a detectable basal oxygen uptake of 2.4 nAtoms/min/mg DNA that was modified by the addition of exogenous substrates, particularly succinate and malate (4.6 and 4.2 nAtoms/min/mg DNA, respectively). This oxygen consumption is able to induce a significant increase in the ATP content of the sperm nuclei (0.12 μmoles/hr/mg DNA) with a P/O ratio of 0.83. Respiratory metabolism of isolated sperm nuclei was not modified by DNase treatment, although it was susceptible to several biological reagents such as testosterone which induce a significant increase in ATP synthesis and in the P/O ratio.

The existence of this process makes it possible to postulate that in human spermatozoa nuclear oxidative phosphorylation might be involved in the stabilization of the complex genome organization of this cell and/or in the membrane processess which accompany egg penetration by spermatozoa.

CHROMOSOME POLYMORPHISM OF TEOSINTE

Y. C. TING
Boston College, Chestnuthill, Mass, U.S.A.

During the last few years studies on the chromosome polymorphism of teosinte (*Zea mexicana*) from four geographic areas were carried out. These teosintes were named Florida teosinte from Honduras, Monajil teosinte and Huixta teosinte from northern Guatemala, and Guanajuato from Mexico. Of these teosintes chromosome polymorphism was revealed in their F_1 hybrids with an inbred maize (*Zea mays*). Polymorphism was due to: (1) the presence or absence of heterochromatic knobs (repetitive DNA); (2) with or without In8; and (3) including or excluding B-chromosomes.

At the meiotic prophase of these hybrids, chromosomes of teosintes manifested about the same degree of homology to maize, except for certain inversions. However, phenotypically neither teosintes nor maize exerted any dominant role over the other. Hence the classical theory that maize has originated from teosinte through mutation should be discarded. An alternative theory that maize evolved from interspecific hybridization between a diploid 10-chromosome pod-pop maize and a diploid 10-chromosome teosinte-like grass is proposed. Following hybridization the chromosome number was spontaneously doubled and thus it transformed a 10-chromosome maize progenitor into a 20-chromosome modern maize.

HUMAN CHROMOSOME BANDING REVEALED BY NN-DIETHYL-PSEUDOISOCYANINCHLORIDE AFTER HEAT DENATURATION IN LIGHT AND FLUORESCENCE MICROSCOPY

A. M. VAGNER-CAPODANO and A. STAHL
University of Marseille, France

N N′-diethyl-pseudoisocyaninchloride is a metachromatic dye which fluoresces strongly under ultraviolet light.

Fixed chromosome preparations have been denatured at 87°C and stained with N N′-diethyl-pseudoisocyaninchloride at a concentration of 25 mg/100 ml in water during 12 hr at 5°C, either directly, or after oxidation in acid permanganate (2.5% $KMnO_4$ + 5% H_2SO_4 + H_2O, 1/1/8, v/v).

Stained preparations can be observed in light microscopy. Chromosomes appear purple. The use of monochromatic light (570 μM) gives the best results, specially for microphotography. Under these conditions a banding pattern similar to the R-bands described by Dutrillaux and Lejeune is observed. Phase contrast optics are not necessary.

The same preparation, when examined under ultra-violet light (excitation filter Zeiss 530), shows the same pattern of strongly fluorescent yellow-orange bands. The emission is remarkably stable.

DISJUNCTION AND ULTRASTRUCTURE OF A SEX-CHROMOSOME COMPLEX

J. WAHRMAN and R. NEZER
The Hebrew University, Jerusalem, Israel

In males of *Blaps cribrosa* (Coleoptera, Tenebrionidae) 18 out of 36 chromosomes are involved in sex determination (Guenin, 1953. *Rev. Suisse Zool.*, *60*, 462). During first meiotic prophase and metaphase six Y's are each end-to-end attached to six X's and, in addition, there are six univalent X's. All 12 X's are associated with a "segregation body" (Wahrman, Nezer and Freund, 1973, *Chromosomes Today*, *4*, 434).

The organization and fine structure of the sex complex have been followed throughout most of the first meiotic division. At early prophase the complex, devoid of synaptons, is already formed in close association with the nuclear membrane. It consists of a hollow spherical segregation body, the interior of which is filled with nucleoplasm-like material, surrounded by all sex chromosomes; the X's are inserted at its periphery. This configuration is preserved until the beginning of anaphase when the orientation of the six univalent X's to one pole and the six Y's to the opposite pole results in their as well as the other X's regular segregation.

The segregation body is pulled along with the X's until eventually lost in the cytoplasm.

SEX CHROMOSOME SEGREGATION

J. WAHRMAN
The Hebrew University, Jerusalem, Israel

The meiotic apparatus probably originated as a device for assuring proper disjunction of homologous chromosomes.

Sex chromosome evolution involved partial or complete loss of homology and therefore necessitated modifications in the original mechanism.

Based on light- and electron microscope studies, chromosome segregation will be described in mammalian species which differ in the extent of homology between their sex chromosomes, or in which the sexes have different numbers of sex chromosomes.

Also, chromosome disjunction in insects with several X's or Y's, or both, will be discussed.

AUTOMATIC CHROMOSOME ANALYSIS: SYSTEM REVIEW AND FUTURE PROSPECTS

R. J. WALL and K. R. CASTLEMAN
Jet Propulsion Laboratory, Pasadena, U.S.A.

This paper describes a system for computer analysis of homogeneously stained and differentially stained (banded) human chromosomes. The system accepts input from microscope slides or photomicrograph negatives, and produces statistical data (size measurements, centromere measurements, and band pattern curves) and a high resolution karyotype picture.

We discuss the special problems that face computer analysis of conventionally stained and banded chromosomes.

We present recent results in the quantitative representation of the chromosome band structure. This process detects each chromosome band and represents it by three parameters: band position, band width and band intensity. Using this representation, we present statistics of individual bands for 24 human chromosome types.

In conclusion we discuss the present and near future expectations for automated chromosome analysis. In particular, we discuss what type of help the cytogeneticist can and cannot expect from the system.

SOME ASPECTS OF A RARE Y/AUTOSOME CHROMOSOME TRANSLOCATION IN CERTAIN AFRICAN MAMMALS

C. WALLACE
University of Witwatersrand, Johannesburg, South Africa

During the course of a chromosome survey of free-roaming wild mammals, the author reported on the presence of a Y/autosome fusion in all three Kudu males studied. This fusion was confirmed by studies of meiotic configurations in one of the Kudu males.

Studies by other workers have since shown that all the African members of the Tragelaphini Tribe show a characteristic Y/autosome fusion.

African animals studied up to date include Nyala, Eland, Sitatunga, Bongo and Kudu. No other African species in the order Artiodactyla so far studied have been shown to possess a Y/autosome fusion.

It is postulated that all the species studied have originated from a common ancestral species and that the event that led to each of the above-mentioned species possessing a Y/autosome fusion took place in a single cell of a single specific male ancestor.

The author was able to attend the Conference owing to the generosity of the S. L. Sive Memorial Travelling Fellowship.

SISTER CHROMATID EXCHANGES INDUCED IN CHINESE HAMSTER CELLS AT DIFFERENT STAGES OF THE CELL CYCLE. THE NECESSITY OF CELLS TO PASS THROUGH S

S. WOLFF

University of San Francisco, U.S.A.

Experiments on the induction of sister chromatid exchanges by ultraviolet light have shown that in Chinese hamster cells such exchanges can be induced in any stage of the cell cycle.

The effect is caused by the formation of persistent lesions that lead to exchanges only if the lesions bearing chromosomes pass through the S period of the cell cycle.

UV light can induce exchanges in cell lines that carry out DNA repair replication efficiently as well as on a cell line in which no or very little repair can be found.

The induction of sister chromatid exchanges by UV light thus seems to be independent of DNA repair replication.

Postreplication repair might be responsible for the formation of the exchanges, but they encompass longer switches of label than has been observed for this type of repair.

TRANSFER OF GENETIC INFORMATION BY MEANS OF ISOLATED MAMMALIAN CHROMOSOMES

G. WULLEMS

Erasmus University, Rotterdam, The Netherlands

The addition of isolated chromosomes from cultured human cells to HGPRT deficient Chinese hamster cells (Wg3-h) resulted in cells which were able to grow in medium containing hypoxanthine, aminopterine and thymidine (HAT).

When the acceptor cells were in mitosis during the addition of the chromosomes, 1 in 8×10^4 cells was able to grow in HAT medium. The frequency was 1 in 3×10^5 cells when the acceptor cells were in interphase.

Twenty-four hours after the addition of the chromosomes, the HGPRT positive cells were recognizable via the incorporation of ^{3}H-hypoxanthine. The proportion of labelled cells was 0.3%.

Chromosomes, labeled with ^{3}H-TdR, were added to the Wg3-h cells and were found 24 hr later in the metaphase plates of the acceptor cells. Several cells contained a chromosome with label in only one chromatid. This probably means that the incorporated chromosomes took part in the DNA replication of the Wg3-h cell.

HGPRT positive cell lines were isolated after incubating HGPRT negative Chinese hamster cells with isolated human chromosomes. The HGPRT activity in these lines was 20–40% of the activity of the wild type Chinese hamster cells.

Electrophoresis followed by autoradiography has shown that 8 isolated cell lines contained *Human* HGPRT.

Similar experiments were carried out using the Thymidine-kinase deficient Chinese hamster line A3 as acceptor line. 5 TK positive cell lines were isolated after addition of human chromosomes.

DNA AND CELL SIZE IN SALAMANDERS

E. OLMO and A. MORESCALCHI
Institute of Histology and Embryology, Naples, Italy

There is no general agreement on the roles played by the interspecific variability in the nuclear DNA content, which reaches its highest levels (among vertebrates) in the Urodele amphibians (from 30 to about 190 pg/nucleus of DNA).

We have approached this kind of problem by examining the possible relations between the nuclear DNA amount (cells in G_1) and the main morphometric cell parameters on a fairly large sample of salamanders: 39 species belonging to all the eight families of the order. The following are the main conclusions from our study:

1. The nuclear DNA amount is directly (and significantly) correlated to the nuclear and cell volume, the cell surface, and the nucleo/cytoplasmic ratio
2. The DNA concentration (pg/μ^3) and the relative cell surface (cell surface/cell volume) rapidly decrease as the total DNA amount increases; however, both tend to be stabilized as the nuclear DNA exceeds the value of about 80 pg/N.
3. Enormous DNA values are reached by a few metamorphosing Plethodontids and by all the members of the paedogenetic families of Urodeles. Since the relative cell surface is generally related to the metabolic rate, we concluded that the exceedingly high DNA amounts (and large cell sizes) achieved by paedogenetic salamanders in their evolution has not necessarily been paralleled by drastic changes in the cell metabolism.

CONTRIBUTORS INDEX

SPECIES INDEX